INTRODUCING. . .

PowerWeb

The McGraw-Hill solution for getting course-specific current events into your classroom.

What *is* PowerWeb?

PowerWeb is a dynamic supplement to your course materials. Course-specific rather than book-specific, PowerWeb engages your students in three levels of resource materials: refereed, carefully selected articles available in the last year in journals and magazines; weekly updates providing a comprehensive discussion of relevant and current issues that occurred in the prior week; and links to course-specific, current news of the day. A series of study aids such as quizzes, web links, and interactive exercises including a glossary, makes PowerWeb a true avenue to extending learning about a subject and gives the instructor many options in incorporating PowerWeb into the course.

To see what PowerWeb is all about, go to the website at **www.dushkin.com/powerweb** and click on the link entitled, "Professors, to learn more, click here" or ask your local McGraw-Hill sales representative.

Basic Business Communication
SKILLS FOR EMPOWERING THE INTERNET GENERATION

BUSINESS COMMUNICATION TITLES

INTRODUCTION TO BUSINESS COMMUNICATION

Business Communication Design: Creativity, Strategies, Solutions with PowerWeb and BComm Skill Booster, 1/e
Pamela Angell, Hudson Valley Community College
Teeanna Rizkallah, California State University—Long Beach
ISBN: 0072859857
© 2004

Business Communication: Building Critical Skills, 2/e
Kitty O. Locker, Ohio State University
Steven Kyo Kaczmarek, Columbus State Community College
ISBN: 0072865717
© 2004

College English and Communication, Student Edition, 8/e
Sue C. Camp, Gardner-Webb University
Marilyn Satterwhite, Danville Area Community College
ISBN: 007825860X
© 2003

Business and Administrative Communication, 6/e
Kitty O. Locker, Ohio State University
ISBN: 0072551348
© 2003

Business Communication at Work Student Text/Workbook 2003, 2/e
Marilyn Satterwhite, Danville Area Community College
Judith Olson-Sutton, Madison Area Technical College
ISBN: 00728290805
© 2003

The Gregg Reference Manual, 9/e
William A. Sabin
ISBN: (Spiral Bound) 0028040465
(Spiral Bound with Flap) 0028040473
(Hardcover) 0028040481

Basic Business Communication: Skills for Empowering the Internet Generation, 10/e
Raymond Lesikar, Emeritus, Louisiana State University
Marie Flatley, San Diego State University
ISBN: 0072880023
© 2005

Professional Business Writing, 7/e
Elizabeth Kerbey, San Jacinto College Central
Marilyn Satterwhite, Danville Area Community College
ISBN: 0078211654
© 2002

BUSINESS ENGLISH

Business English at Work, 2/e
Susan Jaderstrom, Santa Rosa Junior College
Joanne Miller
ISBN: 0078290821
© 2003

The English Workshop: A Programmed Approach, Text/Workbook, 5/e
Keith Slocum, Montclair State University
ISBN: 0078262879
© 2003

English Made Easy, 4/e
Mary Margaret Hosler, University of Wisconsin–Whitewater
Bernadine Branchaw
ISBN: 002801961X
© 1999

TECHNICAL/REPORT WRITING

Developing Proofreading and Editing Skills, 4/e
Sue C. Camp, Gardner-Webb University
ISBN: 0028050029
© 2001

Technical Communication, 2/e
Mary M. Lay, University of Minnesota
Billie J. Wahlstrom
Carolyn D. Rude, Texas Tech University
Cynthia L. Selfe, Michigan Technological University
Jack Selzer, Penn State University
ISBN: 0256220581
© 2000

Report Writing for Business, 10/e
Raymond Lesikar, Emeritus, Louisiana State University
John Pettit, Jr.
ISBN: 0256236917
© 1998

MANAGERIAL COMMUNICATIONS

Corporate Communication, 3/e
Paul Argenti, Dartmouth College
ISBN: 0072314028
© 2003

Managerial Communication: Strategies and Applications, 2/e
Larry R. Smeltzer, Arizona State University
Donald J. Leonard, Arizona State University
Geraldine E. Hynes, Sam Houston State University
ISBN: 0256170819
© 2002

Interpersonal Skills in Organizations with Management Skill Booster Passcard
Suzanne de Janasz, James Madison University
Karen O. Dowd, James Madison University
Beth Schneider, James Madison University
ISBN: 0072874260
© 2002

Management Communication: Principles and Practice, 1/e
Michael Hattersley,
Linda McJannet, Bentley College
ISBN: 0070270414
© 1997

INTERNATIONAL BUSINESS COMMUNICATION

Intercultural Communication in the Global Workplace, 2/e
Linda Beamer, California State University—Los Angeles
Iris Varner, Illinois State University
ISBN: 0072396903
© 2001

Basic Business Communication

SKILLS FOR EMPOWERING THE INTERNET GENERATION

TENTH EDITION

Raymond V. Lesikar, Ph.D.
EMERITUS, LOUISIANA STATE UNIVERSITY

Marie E. Flatley, Ph.D.
SAN DIEGO STATE UNIVERSITY

Boston   Burr Ridge, IL   Dubuque, IA   Madison, WI   New York   San Francisco   St. Louis
Bangkok   Bogotá   Caracas   Kuala Lumpur   Lisbon   London   Madrid   Mexico City
Milan   Montreal   New Delhi   Santiago   Seoul   Singapore   Sydney   Taipei   Toronto

The McGraw·Hill Companies

McGraw-Hill
Irwin

BASIC BUSINESS COMMUNICATION:
SKILLS FOR EMPOWERING THE INTERNET GENERATION

Published by McGraw-Hill/Irwin, a business unit of The McGraw-Hill Companies, Inc., 1221 Avenue of the Americas, New York, NY, 10020. Copyright © 2005, 2002, 1999, 1996, 1993, 1991, 1988, 1985, 1982, 1979 by The McGraw-Hill Companies, Inc. All rights reserved. No part of this publication may be reproduced or distributed in any form or by any means, or stored in a database or retrieval system, without the prior written consent of The McGraw-Hill Companies, Inc., including, but not limited to, in any network or other electronic storage or transmission, or broadcast for distance learning. Some ancillaries, including electronic and print components, may not be available to customers outside the United States.

This book is printed on acid-free paper.

2 3 4 5 6 7 8 9 0 VNH/VNH 0 9 8 7 6 5 4

ISBN 0-07-288002-3

Vice president and editor-in-chief: *Robin J. Zwettler*
Editorial director: *John E. Biernat*
Executive editor: *Linda Schreiber*
Development editor I: *Anna M. Chan*
Marketing manager: *Keari Bedford*
Producer, Media technology: *Damian Moshak*
Senior project manager: *Lori Koetters*
Senior production supervisor: *Rose Hepburn*
Freelance design coordinator: *Kami Carter*
Photo research coordinator: *Judy Kausal*
Photo researcher: *PoYee Oster*
Supplement producer: *Betty Hadala*
Senior digital content specialist: *Brian Nacik*
Cover and interior design: *Kiera Pohl*
Typeface: *10.5/12 Times Roman*
Compositor: *ElectraGraphics, Inc.*
Printer: *Von Hoffmann Corporation*

Library of Congress Cataloging-in-Publication Data

Lesikar, Raymond Vincent.
    Basic business communication : skills for empowering the internet generation / Raymond
V. Lesikar, Marie E. Flatley.—10th ed.
        p, cm.
    Includes bibliographical references and index.
    ISBN 0-07-288002-3 (alk. paper) — ISBN 0-07-111152-2 (international : alk. paper)
    1. Commercial correspondence. 2. English language—Business English. 3. Business
communication. I. Flatley, Marie Elizabeth. II. Title.
HF5271.L37 2005
651.7'4—dc22

                                                                                        2003068612

www.mhhe.com

To those dear ones, both here and departed, whose love, patience, and encouragement are a part of this book. —R.V.L.

To my family, friends, and colleagues who helped make working on this text possible and enjoyable. —M.E.F.

Raymond V. Lesikar

Dr. Raymond V. Lesikar has served on the faculties of the University of North Texas, Louisiana State University at Baton Rouge, The University of Texas at Austin, and Texas Christian University. He served also as a visiting professor at the University of International Business and Economics, Beijing, China. His contributions to the literature include six books and numerous articles.

Dr. Lesikar has been active in consulting, serving over 80 companies and organizations. He is a Fellow, Distinguished Member, and former president of the Association for Business Communication. In addition, he has served ABC in many capacities over the years. He also holds membership in the Federation of Administrative Disciplines and is a former president of the Southwest Social Science Association. His distinguished teaching career was highlighted by his service as major professor for 23 recipients of the doctoral degree.

Marie E. Flatley

Dr. Marie E. Flatley is a Professor of Information and Decision Systems at San Diego State University, where she teaches various courses in business communication. Additionally, she has served as a Fellow at the university's Center for Teaching and Learning. Dr. Flatley received her B. B. A., M. A., and Ph.D. from the University of Iowa. In addition, she has done postgraduate study in AACSB-sponsored programs at the University of Minnesota and Indiana University.

Dr. Flatley is active in numerous professional organizations, including the Association for Business Communication, the California Business Education Association, Delta Pi Epsilon, and the National Business Education Association. She has served as president of the Association for Business Communication and is a distinguished member of the Association. Additionally, she has served as associate editor for the *Journal of Business Communication* and editor the *NABTE Review.* Currently, she is a member of the editorial board for the *Delta Pi Epsilon Journal.*

Her current research interests involve using technology to assist with the communication process. Her current research spans the investigation of the effectiveness of video email to wireless communication technologies.

Our overall objective in this revision was to produce the most technologically current and pedagogically effective book in the field. We modestly believe we have succeeded. Because in a sense business communication is technology in today's business world, to thoroughly emphasize technology wherever it applies was a logical first goal in our efforts. In working to produce the most pedagogically effective book possible, we continued to pursue the goals that enabled preceding editions to enjoy wide acceptance. These goals were to produce the most authoritative, thorough, learnable, and teachable book possible. Our specific efforts in pursuing all these goals are summarized as follows.

TECHNOLOGICALLY CURRENT

Because the computer and the Internet have affected business communication in so many ways, we worked this subject into the book wherever applicable. Where technology is integral to the way business communicates today, we integrated it into the text discussion. In those cases where technology helps students perform special tasks, we presented it in boxes. Additionally, both the textbook cases and the web cases use technology in ways typical of today's businesspeople. We believe these efforts will enable students to leverage the power of the computer to save time and improve work quality.

AUTHORITATIVE

Our efforts to present the subject matter authoritatively involved a thorough review of the field. The information presented and procedures recommended are not just our ideas and preferences, though we support them. They represent the mainstream of business communication thought developed by researchers, teachers, and practitioners over the years.

THOROUGH

We worked diligently to cover the subject thoroughly. The content of the earlier editions was based on the results of two extensive surveys of business communication teachers. In this edition we supplemented the results of those surveys with suggestions from the highly competent professionals who reviewed the book. And we implemented the research findings and suggestions we heard from colleagues at professional meetings. The result is a book whose content has been developed and approved by experts in the field. As well as we can determine, this edition covers every topic that today's business communication leaders say it should have.

LEARNABLE

As in earlier editions, we worked hard to make the book serve the student in every practical way. Our goal was to make the learning experience easy and interesting. Our efforts led us to implement the following features, all of which have proved to be highly successful in preceding editions:

Readable writing. The writing is in plain, everyday English—the kind the book instructs the students to use.

Chapter objectives. Placed at the beginning of all chapters, clearly worded objectives emphasize the learning goals and are tied in to the chapter summaries.

Introductory situations. A realistic description of a business scenario introduces the student to each topic, providing context for discussion and examples.

Outlines of messages. To simplify and clarify the instructions for writing the basic message types, outlines of message plans follow the discussions.

Margin notes. Summaries of content appear in the margins to help students emphasize main points and to review text highlights.

Specialized report topics. List of research topics by major business discipline is available for teachers who prefer to assign reports in the students' area of specialization.

Communications in brief. Boxes containing anecdotal and authoritative communication messages add interest and make points throughout the book.

Abundant real business illustrations. Both good and bad examples with explanatory criticisms show the student how to apply the text instructions.

Cartoons. Carefully selected cartoons emphasize key points and add interest.

Photographs. Full-color photographs throughout the text emphasize key points and add interest to content. Teaching captions enhance the textual material.

Computer and Internet applications. Computer and Internet applications have been integrated throughout the book wherever appropriate—into topics such as readability analysis, graphics, research methods, and formatting.

Computer use suggestions. For students who want to know more about how useful computers can be in business communication, pertinent suggestions appear in boxes and on the text website.

Chapter summaries by chapter objectives. Ending summaries in fast reading outline form and by chapter objectives enable students to recall text highlights.

Critical thinking problems. Fresh, contemporary, in-depth business cases are included for all message and report types—more than in any competing text.

Critical thinking exercises. Challenging exercises test the student's understanding of text content.

Critical thinking questions. End-of-chapter questions emphasize text concepts and provide material for classroom discussion.

New cases. As in past editions, the realistic and thorough case problems are new.

With this edition, we have up-to-date learning tools:

CD-ROM. (Free with every new text) This supplement is designed to reinforce the text instruction in the student's mind by providing interactive exercises and grammar exercises. It includes a free *one-year* subscription to Merriam-Webster Collegiate website <www.merriam-webstercollegiate.com> and the Bullfighter jargon fighter software tool.

Student Resource portion of the Online Learning Center <www.mhhe.com/lesikar05>. Additional resources are provided on a comprehensive, up-to-date website. Included are online quizzes, PowerPoint slides, web cases, video cases, an extensive collection of annotated links to relevant websites organized by topic, and more.

TEACHABLE

Perhaps more than anything we can do to help the teacher teach is to help the student learn. The features designed to provide such help are listed above. But there are additional things we can do to help the teacher teach. We worked very hard to develop these teaching tools; and we think we were successful. We sincerely believe the following list of features created for this edition are the most useful and effective ever assembled for a business communication textbook.

Instructor's Resource Manual. The following support material is available for easy use with each lecture:

Sample syllabi and grading systems.

Summary teaching notes.

Teaching suggestions with notes for each kind of message.

Illustrated discussion guides for the slides/transparencies.

Answers to end-of-chapter critical thought questions.

Answers to end-of-chapter critical thinking exercises.

Sample solutions to cases.

Case problems from the previous edition (online).

Transparency package. Available on demand.

PowerPoint slides. Complete full-chapter slide shows are available for the entire text. These colorful slides provide summaries of key points, additional examples, and examples to critique. Several new ones are presented as voiceover slides.

Grading checklists and software. (Part of the Online Learning Center) Lists of likely errors keyed to marking symbols are available for messages and reports. Similarly, symbols for marking errors of grammatical and punctuation correctness are available. They help the teacher in the grading process and provide the students with explanations of their errors. Similarly, a software tool coordinated with the text grading symbols is available. It's particularly helpful with students documents received digitally.

The McGraw-Hill/Irwin Business Communication Video Series. This series consists of self-contained, informative segments covering such topics as writing correctly and the power of listening. Presented in a clear and engaging style, every segment holds students' interest while presenting the techniques for sharpening their communication skills. (Contact your McGraw-Hill/Irwin representative for more information.)

Test bank. This comprehensive collection of objective questions covers all chapters.

Computerized testing software. This advanced test generator enables the teacher to build and restructure tests to meet specific preferences.

Instructor Resources portion of the Online Learning Center. <www.mhhe.com/lesikar05>. A new website fully supports the text. It includes a database of cases, new web cases that entail using web resources to write solutions, an author-selected collection on annotated links to relevant websites organized by topic, enhanced links for technology chapter, and other active learning material.

Blackboard/WebCT plug-ins for testing and review.

ORGANIZATION OF THE BOOK

Because the reviewers and adopters generally approve of the organization of the book we made no major organization changes. Thus the plan of presentation that has characterized this book through nine successful editions remains as follows:

Part I begins with an introductory summary of the role of communication in the organization, including a description of the process of human communication.

Part II is a review of the basic techniques of writing and an introduction to messages and the writing process. Here the emphasis is on clear writing, the effect of words, and applications to messages, especially to email.

Part III covers the patterns of business messages—the most common direct and indirect ones.

Part IV concentrates on report writing. Although the emphasis is on the shorter report forms, the long, analytical reports also receive complete coverage.

Part V reviews the other forms of business communication. Included here are communication activities such as participating in meetings, telephoning, dictating, and listening as well as giving presentations.

Part VI comprises a four-chapter group of special communication topics—cross-cultural communication, correctness, technology-assisted communication, and business-research methods. Because teachers use these topics in different ways and in different sequences, they are placed in this final part so that they can be used in the sequence and way that best fit each teacher's needs.

ADDITIONS TO CONTENT

As with previous editions, we thoroughly updated this edition. We expanded coverage wherever we and our reviewers thought it would improve content. Although not an addition in the true sense, we continued to use the word *message* in place of *letter* in most places. Our purpose was to use a word more consistent with the additional means of communication (fax, email, text messaging) brought about by technology. Our most significant additions or expansions are the following:

As a result of the recent scandals concerning corporate behavior, ethics was emphasized in this revision wherever appropriate. For added effect, a special icon appears at each discussion involving this topic.

The related ethics problem of plagiarism has been thoroughly addressed with all its ramifications and moral implications.

Email writing has been expanded and made current.

The Communication in Brief boxes have been expanded to include supporting words from leading scholars in business communication.

Text messaging has been added to content.

Coverage of research has been expanded to

emphasize web-based information gathering and evaluation of websites.

The job-search chapter has been updated with new résumé models and portfolios.

The number of challenging and proven problems for student assignment has been increased.

DOI (digital object identification) has been added to the documentation coverage.

Finally, the website has updated online quizzes and new web-based and video cases. The web-based cases include ones for PDA devices, where students can sync using Avantgo.com to get the cases from a simulated in-box. The all-new video cases are delivered by real businesspeople presenting real business problems.

ACKNOWLEDGMENTS

Any comprehensive work such as this must owe credit to a multitude of people. Certainly, we should acknowledge the contributions of the pioneers in the business communication field, especially those whose teachings have become a part of our thinking. We are especially indebted to those business communication scholars who served as reviewers for this edition. They truly deserve much of the credit for improvements in this book. It is with a sincere expression of gratitude that we recognize them:

Melinda Knight, *University of Rochester*

Diana Green, *Weber State University*

Kathryn Rentz, *University of Cincinnati*

Robert Insley, *University of North Texas*

Lecia Barker, *University of Colorado*

Karen Schneiter Williams, *San Diego Mesa College*

Zane Quible, *Oklahoma State University*

Without exception, their work was good and helpful. Because this tenth edition has evolved from all the previous editions, we also acknowledge those who contributed to those editions. These reviewers and the schools with which they were affiliated at the time of the reviews are as follows:

Bertee Adkins, *Eastern Kentucky University*

Barbara Alpern, *Walsh College*

Frank Andera, *Central Michigan University*

J. Douglas Andrews, *University of Southern California*

Dan Armstrong, *Oregon State University*

Joan Beam, *Ferris State University*

James Bell, *Southwest Texas State University*

Don Berinson, *California State University–Fresno*

Mary Kay Boyd, *Florida Atlantic University*

Peter Bracher, *Wright State University*

Stuart Brown, *New Mexico State University*

John J. Brugaletta, *California State University–Fullerton*

Dwight Bullard, *Middle Tennessee State University*

Connie Jo Clark, *Lane Community College*

Nancy Cooper, *Edison Community College*

Andrea Corbett, *University of Lowell*

Ben Crane, *Temple University*

Joan Feague, *Baker College*

Gay Gibley, *University of Hawaii at Manoa*

Barbara Hagler, *Southern Illinois University*

Larry Honl, *University of Wisconsin–Eau Claire*

Phyllis Howren, *University of North Carolina*

Carol L. Huber, *Skagit Valley College*

Edna Jellesed, *Lane Community College*

Pamela Johnson, *California State University–Chico*

Edwina Jordan, *Illinois Central College*

Shelby Kipplen, *Michael Owens Technical College*

Richard Lacey, *California State University–Fresno*

Suzanne Lambert, *Broward Community College*

Jon N. Loff, *Allegheny Community College*

Charles Marsh, *University of Kansas*

Ethel A. Martin, *Glendale Community College*

Judy F. McCain, *Indiana University*

Mary Miller, *Ashland University*

Evelyn Morris, *Mesa Community College*

Frank E. Nelson, *Eastern Washington State College*

Julia Newcomer, *Texas Woman's University*

Rita Thomas Noel, *Western Carolina University*

Delores Osborn, *Central Washington University*

Doris Phillips, *University of Mississippi*

Marilyn Price, *Kirkwood Community College*

Carolyn Rainey, *Southeast Missouri State University*

David Ramsey, *Southeastern Louisiana University*

Diana Reep, *University of Akron*

Elizabeth Regimbal, *Cardinal Stritch College*

Deborah Roebuck, *Kennesaw State College*

Jim Rucker, *Fort Hays State University*

Tim Sabin, *Portland Community College*

Donna Sarchet, *Wayland Baptist University–Plainview*

Betty Schroeder, *Northern Illinois University*

Jean Shaneyfelt, *Edison Community College*

Barbara Shaw, *University of Mississippi*

Cheryl Shearer, *Oxnard College*

Douglas H. Shepherd, *State University of New York*

C. Douglas Spitler, *University of Nebraska–Lincoln*

Lila B. Stair, *Florida State University*

Jerry Sullivan, *University of Washington*

Phyllis Taufen, *Gonzaga University*

Sandy Thomas, *Kansas City Kansas Community College*

Ruth Walsh, *University of South Florida*

George Walters, *Emporia State University*

Kathy Wessel, *South Suburban College*

James J. Weston, *California State University–Sacramento*

Michael Wunsch, *Northern Arizona University*

In addition, over the life of this book many of our professional colleagues have made a variety of inputs. Most of these were made orally at professional meetings. Our memories will not permit us to acknowledge these colleagues individually. Nevertheless, we are grateful to all of them. Finally, on our respective home fronts, we acknowledge the support of our loved ones. Marie acknowledges husband Len Deftos and her immediate family. Ray acknowledges all his family members, both present and departed, who have provided love and inspiration over the years. Without the support of all these dear people this book would not exist.

Raymond V. Lesikar
Marie E. Flatley

A Quick Look

BASIC BUSINESS COMMUNICATION by Raymond Lesikar and Marie Flatley attends to the dynamic, fast-paced, and ever-changing means by which business communication occurs by being the most technologically current and pedagogically effective book in the field. The 10th edition continues to set the standard by incorporating a multitude of real business examples and a thorough treatment of technology-driven business communication.

NEW PART OPENERS

Each section in the book begins with part-openers featuring quotes from distinguished business leaders from recognized companies such as Disney and Dell Computer. This illustrates for students the importance of business communication skills in the real-world.

PART ONE

Introduction

1   Communication in the Workplace

Michael Eisner is credited with leading the Walt Disney Corporation out of financial decline to become the media empire it is today. As an English major, he has always loved to write; but he believes that today email requires a new set of skills, skills that today's students are equipped to elevate in the 21st century. In his commencement address at USC, he reminded the graduates that the biggest threat to a business these days is careless and misunderstood email. And he advised them to take care that their email messages are clear and cordial. Additionally, he told them that it was equally important to know when to use email and when to pick up a phone, get in a car, or board a plane. He charged them with realizing email's "bright potential for productive and enlightened communication in a new century and a new millennium."

Michael Eisner, CEO and Chairman of the Board,
Walt Disney Corporation

PART FOUR

Fundamentals of Report Writing

10   Basics of Report Writing

11   Report Structure: The Shorter Forms

12   Long, Formal Reports

13   Graphics

Jerry Yang's success stems from knowing what information is needed and packaging it in a user-friendly way.

"The ability for people to obtain information down the line is going to be the critical way for people to communicate with each other, the critical way for people to influence thought and opinion, and it is going to change the way we think about issues and the way we think about our lives."

Jerry Yang, Co-Founder and "Chief Yahoo,"
Yahoo

at the New Edition

FIGURE 9–2 Incompleteness and Bad Arrangement in a Traditional Print Résumé. This résumé presents Jason Andrews ineffectively (see "Introductory Situation to Résumés and Applications"). It is scant and poorly arranged.

RÉSUMÉ

JASON L. ANDREWS

3177 North Hawthorne Boulevard
Olympia, New York 12407

Telephone?
Email?

*Bad form—
Type heavily
weighted to
left*

Personal

Age: 27
Married
One child, age 1
5 ft. 11 in. tall
Interests: tennis, fishing, reading
Active in sports
Weight: 165 lbs.
Memberships: Delta Sigma Pi, Sigma Iota Epsilon, Methodist Church, Olympia
    Community League

*Not
parallel
and some
extraneous
information*

Experience

2001–2005 Pollster, Olympia State University, Olympia, NY
1999–2001 Sales Associate, The GAP, Inc., New York, NY
1997–1999 Host and Food Server, Grimaldi's, Brooklyn, NY

*Scant
information
on work done*

Education

2001–2005 Olympia State University, Bachelor of Business Administration
    degree, major in marketing, 24 semester hours in marketing and
    psychology courses, a 3.7 grade-point average, 3.9 in major field.
Not needed — 1998–2001 C.H. Aldridge High School, New York, NY

References

Ms. June Rojas
Davidson Electric
Olympia, N.Y. 12509

Prof. Helen K. Robbins
Olympia State University
Olympia, NY 12507

Mr. Todd Frankle
Wayland Trucking Co.
47723 Beecher
New York, NY 10029

Prof. Carl Cueno
Olympia State University
Olympia, NY 12507

*Incomplete
addresses —
No job titles
Missing school
addresses*

GOOD AND BAD EXAMPLES

Numerous good and bad examples of various business documents—from messages to memos to reports—are featured throughout the text. These writing samples allow students to learn by example and are highlighted with a stoplight icon for easy referencing.

get a negative reaction. In addition, the comments about how much to give tend to lecture rather than suggest. Some explanation follows, but it is weak and scant. In general, the message is poorly written. It has little of the you-viewpoint writing that is effective in persuasion. Perhaps its greatest fault is that the persuasion comes too late.

Dear Mr. Williams:

Will you please donate to the local Junior Achievement program? We have set $50 as a fair minimum for businesses to give. But larger amounts would be appreciated.

The organization badly needs your support. Currently, about 900 young people will not get to participate in Junior Achievement activities unless more money is raised. Junior Achievement is a most worthwhile organization. As a business leader, you should be willing to support it.

If you do not already know about Junior Achievement, let me explain. Junior Achievement is an organization for high school youngsters. They work with local business executives to form small businesses. They operate the businesses. In the process, they learn about our economic system. This is a good thing, and it deserves our help.

Hoping to receive your generous donation, I am,

Sincerely,

This bad message has no persuasion strategy.

The old-style close is a weak reminder of the action requested.

Skillful Persuasion in an Indirect Order. The next message shows good imagination. It follows the indirect pattern described above. Its opening has strong interest appeal and sets up the persuasion strategy. Notice the effective use of you-viewpoint throughout. Not until the reader has been sold on the merits of the request does the

Dear Mr. Williams:

Right now—right here in our city—620 teenage youngsters are running 37 corporations. The kids run the whole show, their only adult help being advice from some of your business associates who work with them. Last September they applied for charters and elected officers. They created plans for business operations. For example, one group planned to build websites for local businesses. Another elected to conduct a rock concert. Yet another planned to publish newsletters for area corporations. After determining their plans, the kids issued stock—and sold it, too. With the proceeds from stock sales, they began their operations. Now they are operating. This May they will liquidate their companies and account to their stockholders for their profits or losses.

You, as a public-spirited citizen, will quickly see the merits of the Junior Achievement program. You know the value of such realistic experience to the kids—how it teaches them the operations of business and how it sells them on the merits of our American system of free enterprise. You can see, also, that it's an exciting and wholesome program, the kind we need more of to combat economic illiteracy. After you have considered these points and others you will find at http://www.ja.org/, I know you will see that Junior Achievement is a good thing.

Like all good things, Junior Achievement needs all of us behind it. During the 13 years the program has been in our city, it has had enthusiastic support from local business leaders. But with over 900 students on the waiting list, our plans for next year call for expansion. That's why I ask that you help make the program available to more youngsters by contributing $50 (it's deductible). Please make your donation now by completing our *online contribution* form. You will be doing a good service for the kids in our town.

Sincerely,

This better message uses good persuasion strategy.

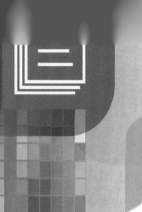

THEMATIC BOXES

Each chapter features thematic boxes to highlight and reinforce important topics.

INTRODUCTORY SITUATION

The Nature of Business Messages

Introduce yourself to this chapter by shifting to the role of Max Schwartz (your subordinate in the preceding chapters). As Max, you are grateful to your boss for deftly instructing you in readable and sensitive writing. You have been convinced of the importance of good communication to the success of a struggling small business. You are especially grateful because most of the work you do involves communicating with fellow employees, customers, and suppliers. Every day you process dozens of internal email messages. Occasionally you write and receive memorandums. Then there are the more formal communications you exchange with people outside the company—both email and hard copy. This chapter introduces you to these messages and begins the process of writing them.

Our study of the types of written business communication begins with messages. As we shall view them, messages are the shorter written presentations of information that occur in business. They are the everyday exchanges between people—the communications that enable the business to conduct its affairs, both internally and externally. Messages fall into three basic types: text messages, email, and traditional letters and memorandums.

- We begin with written messages—the shorter communications of business.

INTRODUCTORY SITUATION

Each box shows a realistic description of a business scenario and provides students with a context for the topics discussed in the text.

TECHNOLOGY IN BRIEF

Web Page Profiles Can Work for You

Since employers often search university web pages for prospective employees, posting a web page profile is a good idea. Not only can you add much more detail than on a print résumé, but you can also use colorful photos, videos, and sounds. You can show examples of real projects, documents, and presentations you have created as well as showcase your skills and creativity. A web page profile can range from a simple résumé as shown in Figure 9–6 to a sophisticated, interactive profile such as the Flash page you see here. In this section of the web profile, the author provides an overview of experience (Track Record). The reader can view the job candidate's résumé for more details and even link to examples of some

continuity in use of color help the reader find needed information easily and quickly. On the textbook website, you will find a link to this web page where you can explore its links.

Today, creating a simple web page profile is pretty easy, even for the beginner. In addition to full-featured website authoring tools such as FrontPage, Dreamweaver, and others, you already may have tools such as FrontPage Express or Netscape Composer. And websites such as GeoCities, Tripod, Homestead, Zy, and others offer inexpensive hosting as well as online web builder tools. You can link to some of these sites on your textbook website. Once you have posted your page profile, you will

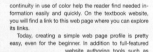

TECHNOLOGY IN BRIEF

These boxes reflect how current technologies are associated with business communication, covering topics such as text messaging, email etiquette, and other software tools and technologies that students will encounter in the workplace.

COMMUNICATION IN BRIEF

Professorial Words of Wisdom

We can see, then, that using the Internet to recruit for managerial and non-managerial jobs offers many benefits. For example, turnaround times are considerably shorter than they are for traditional recruiting techniques. Also, the recruiters are sometimes able to recruit passive job candidates. Those who are not looking for another position are often more highly qualified than those who are. Furthermore, using Websites has turned out to be less expensive than other forms of job advertising . . .

C. Glenn Pearce, Virginia Commonwealth University
Tracy L. Tuten, Longwood College

C. Glenn Pearce and Tracy L. Tuten, "Internet Recruiting in the Banking Industry," *Business Communication Quarterly*, 64, no. 1 (March 2001): 17.

- Gain attention and set up the information review in the opening.

- Gaining attention in the opening makes the letter stand out.

correspondence).

Gaining Attention in the Opening. As in sales writing, the opening of the cover message has two requirements: It must gain attention and it must set up the review of information that follows.

Gaining attention is especially important in prospecting messages (cover messages that are not invited). Such letters are likely to reach busy executives who have many things to do other than read cover messages. Unless the writing gains favorable attention right away, the executives probably will not read them. Even invited

COMMUNICATION IN BRIEF

These boxes contain anecdotal and authoritative communications messages to emphasize concepts from each chapter.

Some reports written in business are produced in collaboration with others. Although you will do some work individually, you can expect to plan, organize, and revise the report as a group.

Derive the Factors. The group next determines what is needed to achieve the purpose. This step involves determining the factors of the problem, as described earlier in the chapter. An advantage of collaboration is that several minds are available for the critical thinking that is so necessary for identifying the factors of the problem.

- Next, derive the factors involved.

Gather the Information Needed. Before the group can begin work on the report, it must get the information needed. This activity could involve conducting any of the research designs mentioned earlier in this chapter and in Chapter 19. In some cases, group work begins after the information has been assembled, thus eliminating this step.

- If necessary, make a plan for gathering the information needed.

Interpret the Information. Determining the meaning of the information gathered is the next logical step for the group. In this step, the participants apply the findings to the problem, thereby selecting the information to be used in the report. In applying the findings to the problem, they also give meaning to the facts collected. The facts do not speak for themselves. Rather, group participants must think through the facts, apply the facts to the problem, and derive logical meaning from the facts. Interpretations are no better than the thinking of the people in the group.

- The members interpret the information, applying it to the problem.

Organize the Material. Just as in any other report-writing project, the group next organizes the material selected for presentation. They will apply time, place, quantity, factor (or combinations) relationships to the data collected in steps as shown in Figure 10–1.

- They organize the information for presentation in the report.

Plan the Writing. A next logical step is that of planning the makeup of the report. In this step the formality of the situation and the audience involved determine the

- They plan the writing of the report.

MARGIN NOTES

Extensive, running margin notes highlight important key concepts for student review and study.

REAL BUSINESS CASE ILLUSTRATIONS

Numerous examples feature real business companies with explanatory criticisms to show students how to apply the concepts discussed in the text.

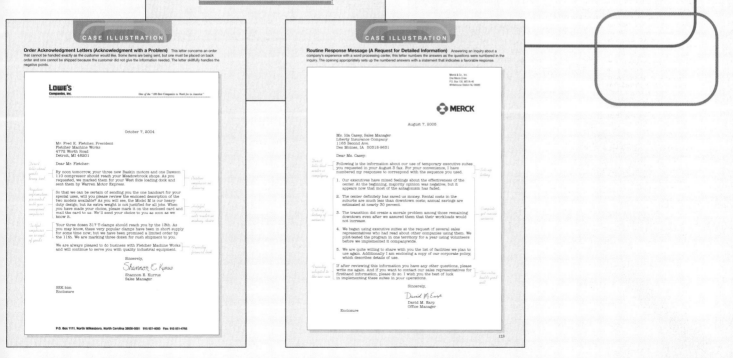

A Wealth

NEW STUDENT CD-ROM

The NEW Student CD-ROM featuring the **Basic Business Communication Resource Kit.** This kit consists of a one-year subscription to the **Merriam-Webster Collegiate Website**—this site features a dictionary, a thesaurus, an encyclopedia, a Spanish to English translation function, a style guide, and an abundance of word games. The Resource Kit also includes **Bullfighter**™—software that focuses on minimizing jargon and maximizing readability in documents—and **Endnote,** a program that allows students to search databases of reference material on the Internet and build bibliography lists. Exercises integrating all of these resources are also included on the CD to help students sharpen their business communication skills.

NEW INSTRUCTOR'S RESOURCE CD-ROM

Exclusively packaged with the Lesikar/Flatley IRCD is a grading tool called **Markin** that allows instructors to easily place marks/comments on documents submitted by their students. When marking is complete, the documents can be sent directly back to students, all from within the Markin program. Also included on the IRCD is the Instructor's Manual, the Test Bank, and an annotated PowerPoint presentation, including new slides with voiceovers.

# of Supplements

ONLINE LEARNING CENTER

Numerous resources that are available for both Instructors and Students are online at **www.mhhe.com/lesikar05**. Downloadable supplements for the Instructor include: Instructor's Manual, Test Bank, and PowerPoint slides. Students can access self-grading quizzes, review material, or work through interactive exercises.

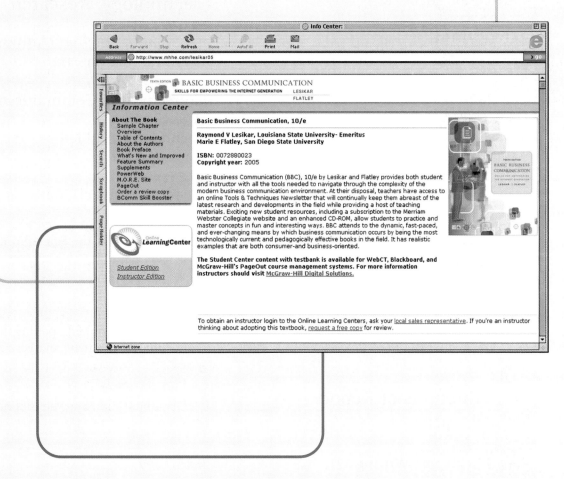

BRIEF CONTENTS

CONTENTS

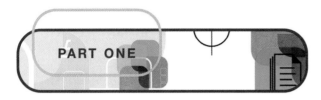

PART ONE

Introduction

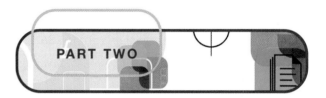

PART TWO

Fundamentals of Business Writing

PART THREE

Basic Patterns of Business Messages

CHAPTER FIVE

Introduction to Messages and the Writing Process 84

CHAPTER SIX

Directness in Good-News and Neutral Messages 105

CHAPTER SEVEN

Indirectness in Bad-News Messages   163

CHAPTER EIGHT

Indirectness in Persuasion and Sales Messages   191

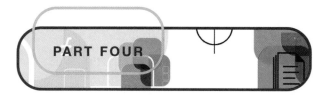

Fundamentals of Report Writing

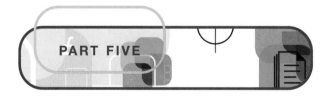

PART FIVE

Other Forms of Business Communication

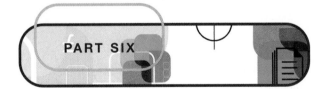

PART SIX

Cross-Cultural, Correctness,
Technology, Research

CHAPTER SIXTEEN

Techniques of Cross-Cultural
Communication 452

CHAPTER SEVENTEEN

Correctness of Communication 469

PART ONE

Introduction

1 Communication in the Workplace

Michael Eisner is credited with leading the Walt Disney Corporation out of financial decline to become the media empire it is today. As an English major, he has always loved to write; but he believes that today email requires a new set of skills, skills that today's students are equipped to elevate in the 21st century. In his commencement address at USC, he reminded the graduates that the biggest threat to a business these days is careless and misunderstood email. And he advised them to take care that their email messages are clear and cordial. Additionally, he told them that it was equally important to know when to use email and when to pick up a phone, get in a car, or board a plane. He charged them with realizing email's "bright potential for productive and enlightened communication in a new century and a new millennium."

Michael Eisner, CEO and Chairman of the Board,
Walt Disney Corporation

CHAPTER ONE

Communication in the Workplace

CHAPTER OBJECTIVES

Upon completing this chapter, you will understand the role of communication in business. To achieve this goal, you should be able to

1 Explain the importance of communication to you and to business.

2 Describe the three main forms of communication in the business organization.

3 Describe the formal and informal communication networks in the business organization.

4 Explain the process of communication among people.

5 Explain three basic truths about communication.

6 Describe the plan of this book.

THE ROLE OF COMMUNICATION IN BUSINESS

Your work in business will involve communication—a lot of it—because communication is a major and essential part of the work of business.

• Communication is important to business

The Importance of Communication Skills to You

Because communication is so important in business, businesses want and need people with good communication skills. Evidence of the importance of communication in business is found in numerous surveys of executives, recruiters, and academicians conducted in recent years. Without exception, these surveys found communication (especially written communication) ranking at or near the top of the business skills needed for success. Typical of these surveys is one by Robert Half International of the 1,000 largest employers in the United States. This study found that 96 percent of the executives reported that today's employees must have good communication skills to get ahead.[1] A recent study of skills and competencies needed by accountants strongly supports the value of writing, speaking, and listening.[2] Similar results were found in an unpublished survey made by the Jones Graduate School of Management, Rice University, in 2000. The deans of the 90 programs surveyed reported that they see communication as one of the greatest teaching priorities of an MBA program. These words to job seekers in *The Wall Street Journal* lend additional support to the importance of communication: "To stand out from the competition, you must demonstrate the unwritten requirements that are now most in demand: leadership and communication skills . . ."[3]

• Business needs good communicators,

Unfortunately, business's need for employees with good communication skills is all too often not fulfilled. Most employees, even the college trained, do not communicate well. But new studies show there is a high correlation between communication skills and income. Even among college graduates, those with higher scores in literacy (use of printed and written information) earn 47 percent more than lower scoring graduates earn.[4] A study by Office Team concluded that such skills as writing and speaking well, displaying proper etiquette, and listening attentively will probably determine career success. This study also reported that technology magnifies the view of one's communications skills, forcing workers to communicate more effectively and articulately because these skills will be showcased more. Email often results in a sender's language skills being placed in front of different people simultaneously, while audio and video will reveal the caliber of one's verbal and diplomacy strengths as well.[5]

• but most people do not communicate well.

The communication shortcomings of employees and the importance of communication in business explain why you should work to improve your communication skills. Whatever position you have in business, your performance will be judged largely by your ability to communicate. If you perform (and communicate) well, you are likely to be rewarded with advancement. And the higher you advance, the more you will need your communication ability. The evidence is clear: Improving your communication skills improves your chances for success in business.

• By improving your communication ability, you improve your chances for success.

Why Business Needs to Communicate

To understand how important communication is to business, note how much communication business requires. Take, for example, a pharmaceutical manufacturer. Throughout the company employees send and receive information. They process

• Communication is vital to every part of business.

---

[1] Ann Fisher, "The High Cost of Living and Not Writing Well," *Fortune,* December 7, 1998, 244.

[2] *Keying In: Newsletter of the National Business Education Association* 10, no. 3 (2000), 4.

[3] D. Perry, "Do You Have the Skills Most in Demand Today?" *Career Journal* from *The Wall Street Journal, 2002* <http://www.careerjournal.com/columnist/perspective/20020520-fmp.html> (June 6, 2003).

[4] Paul T. Decker et al., *Education and the Economy: An Indicators Report* (Washington, DC: Government Printing Office, 1997), 131.

[5] "The Challenges Facing Workers in the Future," *HR Focus,* August 1999, 6ff.

Some Quotes on Communication by Today's Businesspeople

Communication is the most used skill in almost every job. How you communicate your accomplishments to others is a reflection of the quality of your work. Sure, you must know how to do your tasks to accomplish great results but that is only a portion of professional success. Good communication skills are required to report your results to others, persuade colleagues to take action, and (most importantly at review time) sell your successes to management.

> Don Zatyko, Enterprise Program Manager
> Cost and Performance Analytics (Operational Excellence
> Group), Intuit

Communication is essential to building trust and teamwork among employees. To become a successful leader, you must have a great team. Just look at Michelangelo. He didn't paint the Sistine Chapel by himself, but with the help of his team. It is considered one of the best works in history. It's all about the team.

> Mark Federighi, National Manager of Business Development
> E & J Gallo Winery

Your message will get lost if it's not clear, concise and high-impact! Get to the point quickly, let the recipient know exactly what you want, and use attention grabbing techniques whenever possible.

> Amy Betterton, IT Manager
> San Diego Hospice and Palliative Care

Whenever I see a business document that has uncorrected typos and other grammatical mistakes, I wonder whether the author is (a) not very bright or (b) sloppy.

> Glenda K. Moehlenpah, CPA, CFP®
> Financial Bridges

Good communication skills are vital for your success on the job. It makes the difference in how well your writing and spelling are perceived by others (if you can't explain it, maybe you don't know it), in your confidence in speaking to customers or giving presentations (which helps your company bring in revenue), and in your ability to be productive and efficient when working in a team (takes advantage of collective knowledge and shared resources).

> Doris J. Towne, Technical Writer, Development
> Computer Associates

Good communication is necessary in order to continually apply research findings and improve business operations.

> Rosemary Lenaghan, Transportation Policy Analyst, Research
> and Analysis Section
> Illinois Commerce Commission

information with computers, write messages, fill out forms, give and receive orders, and talk over the telephone. More specifically, salespeople receive instructions and information from the home office and send back orders and regular reports of their activities. Executives use written and oral messages to initiate business with customers and other companies and respond to incoming messages. Production supervisors receive work orders, issue instructions, and submit production summaries. Research specialists receive problems to investigate and later communicate their findings to management. Similar activities occur in every niche of the company. Everywhere workers receive and send information as they conduct their work.

- Communication takes many forms: oral, written, and computer.

Oral communication is a major part of this information flow. So, too, are various types of forms and records, as well as the storage and retrieval facilities provided by computers. Yet another major part consists of various forms of written communication—instant messaging, text messaging, email, letters, and reports.

Peter Drucker, on the Importance of Communication in Business

Peter Drucker, recipient of the Presidential Medal of Freedom and one of the most respected management consultants, educators, speakers, and writers of our time, made these observations about communication:

> Colleges teach the one thing that is perhaps most valuable for the future employee to know. But very few students bother to learn it. This one basic skill is the ability to organize and express ideas in writing and speaking.
>
> As soon as you move one step from the bottom, your effectiveness depends on your ability to reach others through the spoken or the written word. And the further away your job is from manual work, the larger the organization of which you are an employee, the more important it will be that you know how to convey your thoughts in writing or speaking. In the very large organization . . . this ability to express oneself is perhaps the most important of all the skills a person can possess.

All of this communicating goes on in business because communication is essential to the organized effort involved in business. Communication enables human beings to work together. In a business, it is the vehicle through which management performs its basic functions. Managers direct through communication, coordinate through communication, and staff, plan, and control through communication.

- All organized effort, including the work of business, requires communication.

Main Forms of Communication in Business

The importance of communication in business becomes even more apparent when we consider the communication activities of an organization from an overall point of view. These activities fall into three broad categories: internal operational, external operational, and personal.

- There are three categories of communication in business:

Internal-Operational Communication. All the communication that occurs in conducting work within a business is classified as internal operational. This is the communication among the business's workers that is done to implement the business's operating plan. By *operating plan* we mean the procedure that the business has developed to do whatever it was formed to do—for example, to manufacture products, provide a service, or sell goods.

- (1) Internal operational—the communicating done in conducting work within a business,

Internal-operational communication takes many forms. It includes the orders and instructions that supervisors give workers, as well as oral exchanges among workers

- such as giving orders, assembling reports, and writing email.

WARPED   **BY MIKE CAVNA**

SOURCE: WARPED by Mike Cavna reprinted by permission of United Feature Syndicate, Inc.

In large businesses, much of the work done involves internal-operational communication.

about work matters. It includes reports that workers prepare concerning sales, production, inventories, finance, maintenance, and so on. It includes the email messages that workers write in carrying out their assignments.

Much of this internal-operational communication is performed on computer networks. Workers send electronic mail and post information on company intranets or portals for others throughout the business, whether located down the hall, across the street, or around the world. As you will learn in Chapter 18, the computer also assists the business writer and speaker in many other aspects of communication.

- (2) External operational— work-related communication with people outside the business,

- such as personal selling, telephoning, advertising, and writing messages.

External-Operational Communication. The work-related communicating that a business does with people and groups outside the business is external-operational communication. This is the business's communication with its publics—suppliers, service companies, customers, and the general public.

External-operational communication includes all of the business's efforts at direct selling: salespeople's "spiels," descriptive brochures, telephone callbacks, follow-up service calls, and the like. It also includes the advertising the business does, for what is advertising but communication with potential customers? Radio and television messages, newspaper and magazine advertising, website advertising, and point-of-purchase display material obviously play a role in the business's plan to achieve its work objective. Also in this category is all that a business does to improve its public relations, including its planned publicity, the community service of its employees, the courtesy of its employees, and the environmental friendliness of its products and facilities. And of very special importance to our study of communication, this category includes all the messages that workers write in carrying out their assignments.

- Messages display a company's etiquette.

This public relations category includes a topic very important to us in our study of business communication: business messages. As we shall see, business messages do more than communicate information. They take the place of human contact. Thus they have the effect of human contact. The clarity, warmth, and understanding they display also send a message. The positiveness of this message is what we refer to as good business etiquette. And good business etiquette contributes greatly to a company's good image.

- Both internal and external communications are vital to business success.

The importance of external-operational communication to a business hardly requires supporting comment. Every business is dependent on outside people and groups for its success. And because the success of a business depends on its ability to satisfy customers' needs, it must communicate effectively with its customers. In today's complex business society, businesses depend on each other in the production and distribution of goods and services. This interdependence requires communication. Like internal communication, external communication is vital to business success.

Personal Communication. Not all the communication that occurs in business is operational. In fact, much of it is without purpose as far as the operating plan of the business is concerned. Such communication is called personal.

Personal communication is the exchange of information and feelings in which we human beings engage whenever we come together. We are social animals. We have a need to communicate, and we will communicate even when we have little or nothing to say.

We spend much of our time with friends in communication. Even total strangers are likely to communicate when they are placed together, as on an airplane flight, in a waiting room, or at a ball game. Such personal communication also occurs in the workplace, and it is a part of the communication activity of any business. Although not a part of the business's plan of operation, personal communication can have a significant effect on the success of that plan. This effect is a result of the influence that personal communication can have on the attitudes of the employees.

The employees' attitudes toward the business, each other, and their assignments directly affect their productivity. And the nature of conversation in a work situation affects attitudes. In a work situation where heated words and flaming tempers are often present, the employees are not likely to make their usual productive efforts. However, a rollicking, jovial work situation is likely to have an equally bad effect on productivity. Somewhere between these extremes lies the ideal productive attitude.

Also affecting the employee's attitudes is the extent of personal communication permitted. Absolute denial of personal communication could lead to emotional upset, for most of us hold dear our right to communicate. On the other hand, excessive personal communication could interfere with the work done. Again, the middle ground is probably the best.

- (3) Personal communication—non-business-related exchanges of information and feelings among people.

- Personal communication affects employee attitudes.

- And attitudes affect employee performance.

- The extent of personal communication permitted affects employee attitudes.

Communication Network of the Organization

Looking over all of a business's communication (internal, external, and personal), we see an extremely complex network of information flow. We see an organization feeding on a continuous supply of information. More specifically, we see dozens, hundreds, or even thousands of individuals engaging in untold numbers of communication events throughout each workday.

Most of the information flow of operational communication is downward and follows the formal lines of organization (from the top executives down to the workers). This is so because most of the information, instructions, orders, and such needed to achieve the business's objectives originate at the top and must be communicated downward. However, most good companies recognize the value of open upward communication. Their executives use open channels of communication to be better informed of the status of things on the front line. They also have found that information from the lower levels can be important in achieving company work goals.

- Information flow in a business forms a complex network.

- The flow is mainly downward, but upward communication is also important.

The Formal Network. In simplified form, information flow in a modern business is much like the network of arteries and veins in the body. Just as the body has arteries, the business has major, well-established channels of information flow. These are the formal channels—the main lines of operational communication. Through these channels flows the bulk of the communication that the business needs to operate. Specifically, the flow includes the upward, lateral, and downward movements of information by report, email, records, and such within the organization: of orders, instructions, and messages down the authority structure; of working information through the organization's email, intranet, or portal; and of externally directed messages, sales presentations, advertising, and publicity. These main channels should not just happen; they should be carefully thought out and changed as the needs of the business change.

- The main (formal) lines of flow are like the network of arteries in the body.

FIGURE 1–1

Formal and Informal
Communication Networks
in a Division of a Small
Business

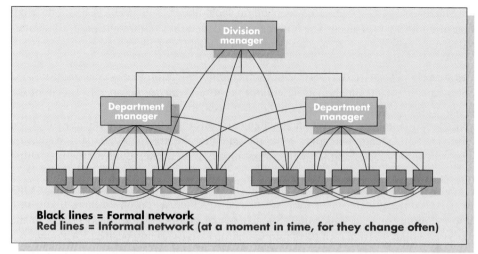

Black lines = Formal network
Red lines = Informal network (at a moment in time, for they change often)

- The secondary (informal) network is like the veins.

The Informal Network. Parallel to the formal network lies the informal network, a secondary network consisting primarily of personal communication (see Figure 1–1). It consists of that part of personal communication that relates to the operations of the organization. Just as the formal network is like the arteries, the informal one is like the veins. It comprises the thousands upon thousands of personal communications that support the formal communication network of a business. Such communications follow no set pattern; they form an ever-changing and infinitely complex structure linking all the members of the organization.

- This secondary network is highly complex and continually changing.

The complexity of this informal network, especially in larger organizations, cannot be overemphasized. Typically, it is really not a single network but a complex relationship of smaller networks consisting of groups of people. The relationship is made even more complex by the fact that these people may belong to more than one group and that group memberships and the links between and among groups are continually changing. Truly, the informal network in a large organization is so complex as to defy description.

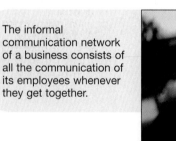

The informal communication network of a business consists of all the communication of its employees whenever they get together.

Known as the *grapevine* in management literature, this communication network is far more effective than a first impression might indicate. Certainly, it carries much gossip and rumor, for this is the nature of human conversation. And it is as fickle and inaccurate as the human beings who are a part of it. Even so, the grapevine usually carries far more information than the formal communication system; and on many matters it is more effective in determining the course of an organization. Wise managers recognize the presence of the grapevine. They give the talk leaders the information that will do the most good for the organization. That is, they keep in touch with the grapevine and turn it into a constructive tool.

- Managers can use this network (the grapevine) effectively.

Variation in Communication Activity by Business

Just how much communicating a business does depends on several factors. The nature of the business is one. For example, insurance companies have a great need to communicate with their customers, especially through letters and mailing pieces, whereas housecleaning service companies have little such need. The business's operating plan affects the amount of internal communication. Relatively simple businesses, such as repair services, require far less communication than complex businesses, such as automobile manufacturers. Yet another factor is the geographic dispersion of the operations of a business. Obviously, internal communication in a business with multiple locations differs from that of a one-location business. Also, the people who make up a business affect its volume of communication. Every human being is unique. Each has unique communication needs and abilities. Thus, varying combinations of people will produce varying needs for communication.

- The extent of a business's communication depends on the nature of the business, its operating plan, its geographic dispersion, and the people involved.

THE PROCESS OF HUMAN COMMUNICATION

Although we may view the communication of a business as a network of information flow, we must keep in mind that a business organization consists of people and that the communication in the organization occurs among people. Thus, it is important to our basic understanding of business communication to know how communication among people occurs. The following review of the human communication process will give you that knowledge.

- The following review describes how communication among people works.

FIGURE 1–2   A Model of the Communication Process

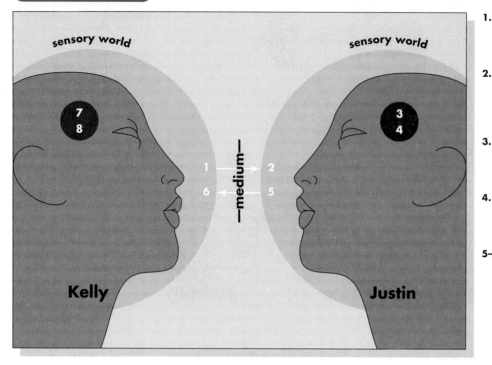

1. Kelly sends a message to Justin through a carefully selected medium or channel.

2. Justin's senses pick up the message, but also pick up competing information from his sensory world.

3. Kelly's message is filtered through Justin's unique mind and is given meaning.

4. The meaning given may trigger a response (feedback), which Justin's unique mind forms.

5–8. Justin sends the message to Kelly. It enters her sensory world, and a second cycle begins that is the same as the first cycle.

The Beginning: A Message Sent

- The process begins when Kelly sends a message to Justin.

To describe the communication process, we will use a situation involving two people—Kelly and Justin (see Figure 1–2). Although the steps described may suggest that Justin and Kelly are communicating in separate actions, the actions occur simultaneously. As one is sending, the other is receiving. Our description begins with Kelly, the sender, communicating (or encoding) a message through a carefully selected medium to Justin, the receiver. Her message could be in any of a number of forms—gestures, facial expressions, drawings, or, more likely, written or spoken words. Whatever the medium, Kelly sends the message to Justin.

Entry in the Sensory World

- The message enters Justin's sensory world,

Kelly's message then enters Justin's sensory world. By *sensory world* we mean all the noise that surrounds a person that the senses (sight, hearing, smell, taste, touch) can detect. As we will see, Justin's sensory world contains more than Kelly's message.

Detection by the Senses

- where his senses may detect it.

From his sensory world Justin picks up stimuli (messages) through his senses. We must note, however, that Justin's senses cannot detect *all* that exists in the world around him. Just how much they can detect depends on a number of factors. One is the ability of his senses. As you know, not all eyes see equally well and not all ears hear equally well. And so it is with the other senses. Another factor is Justin's mental alertness. There are times when he is keenly alert to all that his senses can detect, and there are times when he is dull—in a stupor, a daydream, or the like. Then there are the distractions ("noises") that occur around Justin at the moment. They can weaken, perhaps even eliminate, the stimuli sent. Furthermore, Justin's cultural background has sensitized him more to some stimuli than to others. Yet another limiting factor is Justin's will. In varying degrees, the mind is able to tune in or tune out events in the sensory world. In a noisy room full of people, for example, the conversation of a single person can be selected and the other voices ignored.

When Justin's senses pick up Kelly's message, they relay it to his brain—that is, as much or as little of the message as they detect. But Kelly's message may not be all that Justin's senses pick up. In addition to Kelly's message, his sensory world may contain outside sounds, movements of objects, facial expressions, and the like. In fact, his senses are continually picking up messages from the world around him. Kelly's message is just the primary one at the moment. The others are there, and they might interfere with Kelly's message.

- What Justin's senses detect, they send to his brain,

The Filtering Process

When Kelly's message gets to Justin's brain, it goes through a sort of filtering (or decoding) process. Through that process Justin's brain gives meaning to Kelly's message. In other words, the message is filtered through the contents of Justin's mind. Those contents are made up of all Justin knows, all he thinks, and all he thinks he knows. It includes his entire emotional makeup and all his opinions, attitudes, and beliefs. It includes all the cultural influences of his family, his organization memberships, his social groups, and such. In fact, it includes all Justin has learned, experienced, and thought throughout his life. Obviously, no two people have precisely identical filters, for no two people have minds with precisely the same contents.

- where it goes through a filtering process.

Because people's filters differ, the meanings they give to comparable messages may differ. Thus, the meaning Justin gives Kelly's message may not be precisely the same as the one that someone else would give it. And it may not be the meaning Kelly intended. For example, assume that Kelly used the word *liberal* in her message. Now assume that Kelly and Justin have had sharply differing experiences with the word. To Kelly the word is negative, for her experience has made her dislike things liberal. To Justin the word is positive. Thus, the message Justin receives from the word would not be precisely the message Kelly sent. And so it could be with other words in Kelly's message. Moreover, even the meanings they give to the same messages may differ under different circumstances.

- Because minds differ, message meanings differ.

Formation and Sending of the Response

After his mind has given meaning to Kelly's message, Justin may react to the message. If the meaning he received is sufficiently strong, he may react by communicating some form of response (called feedback). This response may be through words, gestures, physical actions, or some other means.

- Justin's mind reacts to the meaning, and he may respond.

- Through his mind and its contents, Justin determines the meaning of the response.

When Justin elects to communicate a response, through his mind he determines the general meaning (encoding) that the response will take. This process involves the most complex workings of the mind, and we know little about it. There is evidence, however, that ability, here and throughout this stage, is related to one's intelligence and the extent that one permits the mind to react. Justin's ability to evaluate filtered information and formulate meaning also is related to his ability with language. Ability with language equips one with a variety of symbols (words and other ways of expressing meaning). And the greater the number of symbols one possesses, the better one can be at selecting and using them.

- Justin forms a message and sends it.

Justin ends this stage of the communication process by forming a message. That is, he converts meanings into symbols (decodes mainly into words), and then he sends these symbols to Kelly. He may send them in a number of ways: as spoken words, written words, gestures, movements, facial expressions, diagrams on paper, and so on.

The Cycle Repeated

- Then the cycle is repeated.

When Justin sends his message to Kelly, one cycle of the communication process ends. Now a second cycle begins. This one involves Kelly rather than Justin, but the process is the same. Justin's message enters Kelly's sensory world. Her senses pick it up and send it through her nervous system to her brain. There her unique mental filter influences the meaning she gives Justin's message. This filtered meaning also may bring about a response. If it does, Kelly, through her mind, selects the symbols for her response. Then she sends them to Justin, and another cycle of communication begins. The process may continue, cycle after cycle, as long as Kelly and Justin want to communicate.

The Communication Process and Written Communication

Although our description of the communication process illustrates face-to-face, oral communication, it also fits written communication. But there are some differences. Perhaps the most significant difference is that written communication is more likely to involve creative effort. It is more likely to be thought out, and it may even begin in the mind rather than as a reaction to a message received.

- Written communication differs from oral communication in that it (1) is more likely to involve creative effort,

- (2) has longer cycles, and

A second difference is the time between cycles. In face-to-face communication, cycles occur fast, often in rapid succession. In written communication, some delay occurs. How long the delay will be varies. While instant and text messaging may be read within a few seconds of sending, fax or email messages may be read a few minutes after they are transmitted, letters in a few days, reports perhaps in days, weeks, or months. Because they provide a record, written messages may communicate over extremely long time periods.

- (3) usually has fewer cycles.

A third difference is that written communication usually involves a limited number of cycles and oral communication usually involves many. In fact, some written communication is one-cycle communication. That is, a message is sent and received, but none is returned.

Some Basic Truths about Communication

- The communication process reveals some basic truths.

Analysis of the communication process brings out three underlying truths that will help us understand its complexity.

- Because our mental filters differ, meanings sent may differ from meanings received.

Meanings Sent Are Not Always Received. The first underlying truth is that the meanings transmitted are not necessarily the meanings received. No two minds have identical filters. No two minds have identical storehouses of words, gestures, facial expressions, or any of the other symbol forms. And no two minds attach exactly the same meanings to all the symbols they have in common. Because of these differences in minds, errors in communication are bound to occur. Skilled communicators work hard to minimize these errors.

Meaning Is in the Mind. A second underlying truth is that meaning is in the mind—not in the words or other symbols used. How accurately a sender conveys meaning in symbols depends on how skillful one is in choosing symbols with the receiver in mind and on how skillful the receiver is in interpreting the meaning intended. Thus, you should look beyond the symbols used. You should consider both the communication abilities and sensory world of those with whom you want to communicate. When they receive your messages, they do not look at the symbols alone. They also look for the meanings they think you intended.

- Meanings are in the mind—not in symbols.

The Symbols of Communication Are Imperfect. The third underlying truth is that the symbols used in communication are imperfect. One reason for this is that the symbols we use, especially words, are at best crude substitutes for the real thing. For example, the word *man* can refer to billions of human beings of whom no two are precisely alike. The word *dog* stands for any one of countless animals that vary sharply in size, shape, color, and every other visible aspect. The word *house* can refer equally well to structures ranging from shanties to palatial mansions. The verb *run* conveys only the most general part of an action; it ignores countless variations in speed, grace, and style. These illustrations are not exceptions; they are the rule. Although words help us classify similar things, their meanings can vary widely because of context and usage.

- Because symbols are imperfect and people differ in their ability to communicate, communication is far from perfect.

Communication is also imperfect because communicators vary in their ability to convey thoughts. Some find it very difficult to select symbols that express their simplest thoughts. Variations in ability to communicate obviously lead to variations in the precision with which thoughts are expressed.

Communication across cultures is especially imperfect, for often there are no equivalent words in the cultures. For example, usually there is no precise translation for our jargon in other cultures. Words such as *condo, computer virus,* and *geek* are not likely to have equivalents in every other culture. Similarly, other cultures have specialized words unique and necessary to them that we do not have. For instance, the Eskimo have many words for *snow,* each describing a unique type. Obviously, such distinctions are vital to their existence. We can get along very well with the one word. As you will see in Chapter 16, this subject is so vital to today's business communication that an entire chapter is devoted to it.

- Communication across cultures is especially difficult.

Although these basic truths bring to light the difficulties, complexities, and limitations of communication, they also help us understand where our efforts are needed to improve communication. On the whole we human beings do a fairly good job of communicating, but miscommunication still occurs. In business, miscommunication can be costly in terms of lost profits as well as damaged personal relationships. We rely on our communication skills to help us run our business effectively and to serve our customers efficiently.

- Even so, we communicate reasonably well.

Resulting Stress on Adaptation

Understanding the communication process can help you become a better communicator. The process shows that communication is a unique event—that every mind is different from every other mind. No two of us know the same words; and no two of us know equal amounts about all subjects. Obviously, such differences make communication difficult. Unless the words (or other symbols) used in a message have the same meanings in the minds of both the sender and the receiver, communication suffers. Communication scholars have tried to solve this problem by stressing the adaptation of messages to the minds of their receivers. By *adaptation* we mean fitting the message to the receivers—using words and other symbols that they understand. As you will see, adaptation is the foundation for our review of communication principles in

- The communication process shows the need for adaptation—an underlying principle in our study of communication.

the pages ahead. Continuing to develop these skills by learning and practicing them will serve you well personally and professionally.

THE GOAL, PLAN, AND PHILOSOPHY OF THIS BOOK

- The goal of this book is to help you improve your communication skills.

The preceding discussion shows that communication is important to business, that it is performed in various and complex ways, and that it is imprecise. These observations suggest that communicating in business is not to be taken lightly. If you want to excel at it, you must develop your communication skills. Helping you do this is the goal of this book.

The Plan: Situations, Solutions, Summaries

- The book introduces topics by situations—then it shows solutions. Summaries help your study.

To achieve this goal, the book introduces each major topic through a business communication situation that realistically places you in the business world. Each situation describes a possible communication problem. Then the following material instructs you on how to solve the problem. For your study convenience, summaries of the text material appear in the margins. A general summary by chapter objectives appears at the end of each chapter.

The Philosophy: Communicate to Communicate

- Successful communication is the purpose of communicating.
- Some writers have other goals (to impress, to entertain). Business communicators should seek only to communicate.

In presenting this subject matter, the book takes a practical, realistic approach. That is, it views business communication as having one primary goal—to communicate.

Although this statement may appear elementary, it has significant meaning. All too often other goals creep in. For example, communicators sometimes seek to impress—perhaps by using big words and involved sentences. Or they seek to entertain with a clever choice of words. Good business communicators rarely have these goals. They primarily seek to communicate. They use words and sentences that communicate clearly and quickly. If the message has any difficulty, the reason is that the subject matter is difficult. In no way should the words and the sentence structures add to the difficulty.

An Underlying Rule: Ethical Communication

- We stress only ethical communication.

In the pages ahead, you will see how to achieve business goals through communication. In all cases, our emphasis will be only on achieving legitimate business goals. We emphasize this point because of the recent wave of corporate dishonesty that has swept the American business scene. All too often this dishonesty was performed through deceitful communication. Through skillfully used words, dishonest messages were communicated to the financial world and to the public. In the pages ahead you will learn how words can be selected and organized to achieve desired goals. These goals can range from the extreme good to the extreme bad. Without exception, our emphasis will be on achieving effects consistent with honorable goals.

SUMMARY BY CHAPTER OBJECTIVES

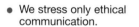
Explain the importance of communication to you and to business.

1. Business needs and rewards people who can communicate, for communication is vital to business operations.
   - But good communicators are scarce.
   - So, if you can improve your communication skills, you increase your value to business and business will reward you.

2. Communicating in business falls into three categories:
   - The communicating a business does to implement its operating plan (its procedure for doing what it was formed to do) is called *internal-operational* communication.
   - The communicating a business does with outsiders (suppliers, other businesses, customers, and such) is called *external-operational* communication.
   - Informal exchanges of information not related to operations are called *personal* communication.

Describe the three main forms of communication in the business organization.

3. The flow of communication in a business organization forms a complex and ever-changing network. Information continually flows from person to person—upward, downward, and laterally.
   - The communicating that follows the formal structure of the business forms the *formal* network. Primarily, operational information flows through this network.
   - The flow of personal communication forms the *informal* network.

Describe the formal and informal communication networks in the business organization.

4. The human communication process is as follows:
   - A message arrives in a receiver's sensory world (all that one can detect with the senses).
   - The senses pick up the message and relay it to the brain.
   - The brain filters the message through all its contents (knowledge, emotions, biases, and such) and gives it a unique meaning (decodes).
   - This meaning may trigger a response, which the mind then forms (encodes).
   - The person then sends by some medium this message into the sensory world of another person.
   - Within this person the process described above is repeated (another cycle begins).
   - The process continues, cycle after cycle, as long as the people involved care to communicate.

Explain the process of communication among people.

5. The communication process reveals these truths:
   - Meanings sent are not always received (our mental filters differ).
   - Meaning is in the mind—not in the symbols (mainly words) used.
   - The symbols we use are imperfect, primarily because the reality they describe is so complex.

Explain three basic truths about communication.

6. The plan of this book is to introduce you to the primary types of business communication strategies through realistic situations.
   - You are placed in a business communication situation.
   - Then you are shown how to handle it.
   - And always the emphasis is on ethics.

Describe the plan of this book.

CRITICAL THINKING QUESTIONS

1. Is the ability to communicate more important to the successful performance of a supervisor than to the successful performance of a company president? Defend your answer.

2. Make a list of types of companies requiring extensive communication. Then make a list of types of companies requiring little communication. What explains the difference in these two groups?

3. List the types of external-operational and internal-operational communication that occur in an organization with which you are familiar (school, fraternity, church, or such).

4. Identify the types of technology used primarily in internal- and external-operational communication to transmit messages. Explain what you think might account for the differences.

5. Discuss the question of how much personal communication should be permitted in a business organization. Defend your view.

6. Describe the network of communication in an organization with which you are familiar (preferably a simple one). Discuss and explain.

7. Describe what is in your sensory world at this moment. Contrast the parts that are usually in your awareness with the parts that are usually not in your awareness.

8. Using the model for the communication process as a base, explain how people reading or hearing the same message can disagree on its meaning.

9. Give an example of a simple statement that could be misunderstood. Explain why. Then revise the statement for more precise understanding.

CRITICAL THINKING EXERCISES

1. Megan Cabot is one of 12 workers in Department X. She has strong leadership qualities, and all her co-workers look up to her. She dominates conversations with them and expresses strong viewpoints on most matters. Although she is a good worker, her dominating personality has caused problems for you, the new manager of Department X. Today you directed your subordinates to change a certain work procedure. The change is one that has proven superior wherever it has been tried. Soon after giving the directive, you noticed the workers talking in a group, with Megan the obvious leader. In a few minutes she appeared in your office. "We've thought it over," she said. "Your production change won't work." Explain what is happening. How will you handle the situation?

2. After noticing that some workers were starting work late and finishing early, a department head wrote this message to subordinates: It is apparent that many of you are not giving the company a full day's work. Thus, the following procedures are implemented immediately:

   a. After you clock in, you will proceed to your workstations and will be ready to begin work promptly at the start of the work period.

   b. You will not take a coffee break or consume coffee on the job at the beginning of the work period. You will wait until your designated break times.

   c. You will not participate in social gatherings at any time during the workday except during designated break periods.

   d. You will terminate work activities no earlier than 10 minutes prior to the end of the work period. You will

   use the 10 minutes to put up equipment, clean equipment, and police the work area.

   e. You will not queue up at the exit prior to the end of the work period.

   The message was not well received by the workers. In fact, it led to considerable anger, misunderstanding, and confusion. Using the model of communication as a base, analyze the message and explain the probable causes of the difficulties.

3. After being introduced to a candidate for the presidency of their company, two workers had the following discussion. One worker is Scott, a college-age man who is holding a full-time job while going to school part-time. The other is Will, an old-timer—a self-made man and master craftsman.

   Scott: I like the candidate. He appears young, energetic, and bright.

   Will: He's young all right. Too young! Too bright! That fancy Harvard degree won't help him here. Why, I'll bet he hasn't spent one day in a working-man's shoes.

   Scott: Now that's not fair. He was trained to be an administrator, and he has had experience as an administrator—high-level experience. You don't need experience as a soldier to be a general.

   Will: Don't tell me what this company needs. I've spent 40 years here. I know. I was here when old J.P. (the company founder) was president. He started as a machinist and worked to the top. Best president any company could have. We loved the man. He knew the business and he knew the work we do.

Scott: But that doesn't happen today. Administrators have to be trained for administration. They have to know administration, finance, marketing—the whole business field. You don't get that in the shop.

Will: All you kids think that knowledge only comes from books. You can't substitute book sense for experience and common sense. I've been here 40 years, son. I know.

The dialogue continued to accelerate and soon led to angry words. Neither Scott nor Will changed positions. Analyze the dialogue using the model of communication as the base.

Carlos Dominguez is responsible for one of networking giant Cisco Systems' fastest growing markets. In spite of his annual revenue responsibility of $2 billion, he takes time for mentoring employees and students about skill development.

"The ability to write and communicate your thoughts clearly in a presentation are the most essential skills you need to achieve any success in business. If you have a great mind and great thoughts, but you're not able to express them, it's very hard to be successful."

Carlos Dominguez, Vice President,
U.S. Service Provider Organization,
Cisco Systems, Inc.

CHAPTER TWO

Adaptation and the Selection of Words

CHAPTER OBJECTIVES

Upon completing this chapter, you will be able to adapt your language to specific readers and to select the most effective words for use in business communication. To reach this goal, you should be able to

1 Explain the role of adaptation in selecting words that communicate.

2 Simplify writing by selecting short and familiar words.

3 Use technical words and acronyms appropriately.

4 Discuss the differences in the strength of words and select the words that communicate your message best.

5 Write concretely and use active voice.

6 Write with clarity and precision by avoiding camouflaged verbs, by selecting the right words, and by using idioms correctly.

7 Use words that do not discriminate.

THE BASIC NEED FOR ADAPTATION

The study of clear writing logically begins with adaptation. By *adaptation* we mean fitting the message to the specific reader. Obviously, readers do not all have the same ability to understand a message. They do not all have the same vocabulary, the same knowledge of the subject, or the same mentality. Thus, to communicate clearly you first should know the person with whom you wish to communicate. You should form your message to fit that person's mind. This approach not only helps you communicate but also is the basis of good business etiquette. Making your message easy to understand is simply good business manners.

- For writing to be clear, it must be adapted to the reader.

Visualizing the Reader

In adapting your message, you begin by visualizing your reader. That is, you form a mental picture of what he or she is like. You imagine what the reader knows about the subject, what his or her educational level is, and how he or she thinks. In general, you consider whatever you believe could have some effect on your reader's understanding of your message. With this in mind, you form the message.

- Adaptation begins with visualizing the reader—imagining what he or she knows, feels, thinks, and such.

Technique of Adapting

In many business situations, adapting to your reader means writing on a level lower than the one you would normally use. For example, you will sometimes need to communicate with people whose educational level is below your own. Or you may need to communicate with people of your educational level who simply do not know much about the subject of your message.

- Often you will need to write at levels lower than your own.

To illustrate, assume that you need to write a message to a group of less-educated workers. You know that their vocabularies are limited. If you are to reach them, you will have to use simple words. If you do not, you will not communicate. On the other hand, if you had to write the same message to a group of highly educated people, you would have a wider choice of words. These people have larger vocabularies than the

- In writing to less-educated workers, for example, you may need to simplify. You may write differently for highly educated people.

A Classic Case of Adaptation

There is a story told around Washington about a not-too-bright inventor who wrote the Bureau of Standards that he had made a great discovery: Hydrochloric acid is good for cleaning clogged drains.

He got this response: "The efficacy of hydrochloric acid is indisputable, but the corrosive residue is incompatible with metallic permanence."

Believing that these big words indicated agreement, this not-so-bright inventor wrote back telling how pleased he was that the bureau liked his discovery.

The bureaucrat tried again: "We cannot assume responsibility for the production of toxic residue with hydrochloric acid and suggest alternative procedure."

The inventor was even more gratified. He again expressed his appreciation to the bureau for agreeing with him.

This time the bureaucrat got the message. He replied in words any inventor would be certain to understand: "Don't use hydrochloric acid. It'll eat hell out of pipes."

first group. In either case, however, you would select words that the intended readers understand.

Adaptation Illustrated

The following paragraphs from two company annual reports illustrate the basic principle of adaptation. The writer of the first report apparently viewed the readers as people who were not well informed in finance.

> Last year your company's total sales were $117,400,000, which was slightly higher than the $109,800,000 total for the year before. After deducting for all expenses, we had $4,593,000 left over for profits, compared with $2,830,000 for 2003. Because of these increased profits, we were able to increase your annual dividend payments per share from the 50 cents paid over the last 10 years.

The writer of the second report saw the readers as being well informed in finance. Perhaps this writer believed the typical reader would come from the ranks of stockbrokers, financial managers, financial analysts, and bankers. So this writer adapted the annual report to these readers with language like this:

> The corporation's investments and advances in three unconsolidated subsidiaries (all in the development stage) and in 50 percent–owned companies was $42,200,000 on December 31, 2000, and the excess of the investments in certain companies over net asset value at dates of acquisition was $1,760,000. The corporation's equity in the net assets as of December 31, 2003, was $41,800,000 and in the results of operations for the years ended December 31, 2000 and 2001, was $1,350,000 and $887,500, respectively. Dividend income was $750,000 and $388,000 for the years 2003 and 2000, respectively.

Which writer was right? Perhaps both. Perhaps neither. The answer depends on what the stockholders of each company were really like. Both examples illustrate the technique of adaptation. They use different words for different audiences, which is what you should try to do.

Adapting to Multiple Readers

- If you write for one person in a group, you may miss the others.

Adapting your message to one reader is easy. But how do you adapt when you are communicating with two or more readers? What if your intended readers vary widely

In talking to a child, we naturally adapt the language to the child. Similarly, in business communication we need to adapt the language to the reader.

in education, knowledge of the subject, and so on? Writing to the level of the best-educated and best-informed persons would miss those at lower levels. Adapting your message to the lowest level runs the risk of insulting the intelligence of those at higher levels.

The answer is obvious. You have to adapt to the lowest level you need to reach. Not doing so would result in not communicating with that level. Of course, by writing for readers at the lowest level, you run the risk of offending those at higher levels. You can minimize this risk by taking care not to talk down. For example, you can carefully work in "as you know" and similar expressions to imply that you know the reader knows what you are writing about.

- To communicate with all of them, write for the lowest member of the group.

Governing Role of Adaptation

The preceding discussion shows that adaptation is basic to communication. In fact, it is so basic that you will need to apply it to all the writing and speaking instructions in the pages ahead. For example, much of what will be said about writing techniques will stress simplicity—using simple words, short sentences, and short paragraphs. You will need to think of simplicity in terms of adaptation. Specifically, you will need to keep in mind that what is simple for one person may not be simple for another. Only if you keep in mind the logical use of adaptation will you fully understand the intended meaning of the writing instructions.

- Adaptation underlies all that will be said about writing. Apply it to the other writing instructions.

SUGGESTIONS FOR SELECTING WORDS

A major part of adaptation is selecting the right words. These are the words that communicate best—that have correct and clear meanings *in the reader's mind.*

Selecting the right words depends on your ability to use language, your knowledge of the reader, and your good judgment. Few hard-and-fast rules apply. Still, you should keep in mind the suggestions presented in the following paragraphs. As you review them, remember that you must use them with good judgment. You must consider them in light of the need to adapt the message to your reader or readers.

As you will see, most of the suggestions support simplicity in writing. This approach is justified by three good reasons. The first is that many of us tend to write at

- Selecting the right words is a part of adaptation. Following are some suggestions to help you select such words.

- These suggestions stress simplicity for three reasons: (1) many people tend to write at a difficult level;

too difficult a level. Instead of being ourselves, we change character when we write. Rather than being friendly, normal people, we become cold and stiff. We work to use big words and complex structures. Winston Churchill referred to this tendency when he made his classic remark: "Little men use big words; big men use little words." We would do well to follow the example of this big man.

(2) the writer usually knows the subject better than the reader; and

The second reason for simplicity is that the writer usually knows the subject of the message better than the reader. Thus, the two are not equally equipped to communicate on the matter. If the writer does not work at reducing the message to the reader's level, communication will be difficult.

(3) the results of research support simplicity.

The third reason for simplicity is that convincing research supports it. According to the readability research of such experts as Gunning, Dale, Chall, and Flesch, writing slightly below the reader's level of understanding communicates best.

Use Familiar Words

The foremost suggestion for word selection is to use familiar words. These are the everyday words—the words with sharp and clear meanings in the mind. Because words that are familiar to some people may be unfamiliar to others, you will need to select familiar words with care. You have no choice but to rely on your judgment.

Familiar words communicate. Use them. Use your judgment in determining what words are familiar.

Specifically, using familiar words means using the language that most of us use in everyday conversation. We should avoid the stiff, more difficult words that do not communicate so precisely or quickly. For example, instead of using the more unfamiliar word *endeavor,* use *try.* Instead of using *terminate,* use *end.* Prefer *use* to *utilize, do* to *perform, begin* to *initiate, find out* to *ascertain, stop* to *discontinue,* and *show* to *demonstrate.*

Difficult words are not all bad. Use them when they fit your needs and are understood.

The suggestion to use familiar words does not rule out some use of more difficult words. You should use them whenever their meanings fit your purpose best and your readers understand them clearly. The mistake that many of us make is to overwork the more difficult words. We use them so much that they interfere with our communication. A good suggestion is to use the simplest words that carry the meaning without offending the readers' intelligence. Perhaps the best suggestion is to write the words you would use in face-to-face communication with your readers.

The following contrasting examples illustrate the communication advantages of familiar words over less familiar ones.[1] As you read the examples, consider the effect on communication of an entire message or report written in the styles illustrated.

Unfamiliar Words	Familiar Words
This machine has a tendency to develop excessive and unpleasant audio symptoms when operating at elevated temperatures.	This machine tends to get noisy when it runs hot.
Ms. Smith's idiosyncrasies supply adequate justification for terminating her employment status.	Ms. Smith's peculiar ways justify firing her.
This antiquated mechanism is ineffectual for an accelerated assembly-line operation.	This old robot will not work on a fast assembly line.
The most operative assembly-line configuration is a unidirectional flow.	The most efficient assembly-line design is a one-way flow.
The conclusion ascertained from a perusal of pertinent data is that a lucrative market exists for the product.	The data studied show that the product is in good demand.
Company operations for the preceding accounting period terminated with a substantial deficit.	The company lost much money last year.

---

[1] For some of these examples, we are indebted to students and friends who gave them to us over the years.

An example supporting the use of familiar words came from Cape Kennedy while scientists were conducting research in preparation for long spaceflights. In one experiment, a monkey was placed in a simulated spaceship with enough food to last many days. With an unlimited supply of food available, the monkey simply ate too much and died. A scientist used these words to record the incident: "One monkey succumbed unexpectedly apparently as a result of an untoward response to a change in feeding regimen." Most readers of the report missed the message. Why didn't the scientist report in everyday language, "One monkey died because it ate too much"?

Another real-life example involved President Franklin D. Roosevelt. Across his desk came a memorandum advising federal workers to do the following in the event of an air raid:

> Such preparations shall be made as will completely obscure all federal buildings and nonfederal buildings occupied by the federal government during an air raid for any period of time from visibility by reason of internal or external illumination. Such obscuration may be obtained either by blackout construction or by termination of the illumination.

Irked by the heavy wording, FDR sent this memorandum to the author:

> Tell them that in buildings where they have to keep the work going to put something over the windows; and, in buildings where they can let the work stop for a while, turn out the lights.

In this and the preceding examples, the familiar words are clearly better. Readers understand them.

Use Slang and Popular Clichés with Caution

At any given time in any society some slang words and clichés are in vogue. As this book goes to press, "yada, yada, yada," "master of your domain" (*Seinfeld*), "voted off the island" (*Survivor*), and "Is that your final answer?" (*Who Wants to Be a Millionaire*) are widely used. Such expressions may convey a desired effect in a communication. But they are likely to be meaningful only for the moment. They may be out of vogue tomorrow along with "Where's the beef?" "$64,000 question," "to beat sixty," and the countless others from past generations. Thus, you should use such expressions sparingly and always only in informal communication with people who know and appreciate them.

- Use popular slang and clichés when meaningful.

Choose Short Words

According to studies of readability, short words generally communicate better than long words. Of course, part of the explanation is that short words tend to be familiar words. But there is another explanation: A heavy use of long words—even long words that are understood—leaves an impression of difficulty that hinders communication.

- Generally, short words communicate better.

The suggestion that short words be chosen does not mean that all short words are easy and all long words are hard. Many exceptions exist. Few people know such one-syllable words as *gybe, verd,* and *id.* Even children know such long words as *hippopotamus, automobile,* and *bicycle.* On the whole, however, word length and word difficulty are related. Thus, you should concentrate on short words and use long words with caution. Use a long word only when you think your readers know it.

- Some exceptions exist.

This point is illustrated by many of the examples presented to support the use of familiar words. But the following illustrations give it additional support. In some of them, the long-word versions are likely to be understood by more highly educated readers. Even so, the heavy proportion of hard words clouds the message. Without question, the short-word versions communicate better. Note that the long words and their short replacements are in italics.

Long Words	Short Words
The decision was *predicated* on the *assumption* that an abundance of *monetary* funds was *forthcoming*.	The decision was *based* on the *belief* that there *would be more money*.
They *acceded* to the *proposition* to *terminate* business.	They *agreed to quit* business.
During the *preceding* year the company *operated* at a *financial deficit*.	*Last year* the company *lost money*.
Prior to *accelerating productive operation,* the supervisor inspected the machinery.	Before *speeding up* production, the supervisor inspected the machinery.
Definitive action was *effected subsequent* to the reporting date.	*Final* action was *taken after* the reporting date.
The *unanimity* of current forecasts is not *incontrovertible evidence* of an *impending* business acceleration.	*Agreement* of the forecasts is not *proof* that business *will get better*.
This *antiquated merchandising* strategy is *ineffectual* in *contemporary* business *operations*.	This *old sales* strategy *will not work* in *today's* business.

Mark Twain understood the value of using short words when he made this often-quoted statement: "I never use a word like *metropolis* when I can get the same price for *city.*" One bureaucrat who did not understand the principle created a position to improve communication and gave it the title of Coordinator for the Obliteration of Proliferation of Obfuscation!

Use Technical Words and Acronyms with Caution

- All fields have technical words.

Every field of business—accounting, information systems, finance—has its technical language. This language can be so complex that in some cases specialized dictionaries are compiled. Such dictionaries exist for computers, law, finance, and other business specialties. There are even dictionaries for subareas such as databases, e-commerce, and real estate.

- These words are useful when you communicate with people in your field. But they do not communicate with outsiders. Use them with caution.

As you work in your chosen field, you will learn its technical words and acronyms. In time you will use these terms freely in communicating with people in your field. This is as it should be, for such terms are useful. Frequently, one such word will communicate a concept that would otherwise take dozens of words to describe.

A problem comes about, however, when you use technical terms with people outside your field. Because these words are everyday words to you, you tend to forget that not everyone knows them. The result is miscommunication. You can avoid such miscommunication by using technical words with extreme caution. Use them only when your readers know them.

- Some examples are *covered employment, cerebral vascular accident, annuity, bobtail.* These words are well known to people in special fields, but not to most outsiders.

Examples of misuse of technical writing are easy to find. To a worker in the Social Security Administration, the words *covered employment* commonly mean employment covered by social security. To some outsiders, however, they could mean working under a roof. When a physician uses the words *cerebral vascular accident* with other physicians, they understand. Most people would get little meaning from these words, but they could understand a *little stroke*. *Annuity* has a clear meaning to someone in insurance. A *contract that guarantees an income for a specified period* would have more meaning to uninformed outsiders. Computer specialists know C# and Java to be popular programming languages, but these words may have different meanings for others. To a trucker *bobtail* means a tractor cab without trailer. Nontruckers might get other meanings from that word—or perhaps no meaning at all.

- Use initials cautiously. Spell out and define as needed.

Initials (including acronyms) should be used with caution, too. While some initials, such as IBM, are widely recognized, others, such as XML (extensible markup language), are not. Not only might your readers not know certain initials, they might confuse them with others. For example, if you saw SARS, you might think of the virus,

Technical Language?

When an ordinary person wants to give someone an orange, he or she would merely say, "I give you this orange." But when a lawyer does it, the words are something like this: "Know all persons by these present that I hereby give, grant, bargain, sell, release, convey, transfer, and quitclaim all my right, title, interest, benefit, and use whatever in, of, and concerning this chattel, otherwise known as an orange, or Citrus orantium, together with all the appurtenances thereto of skin, pulp, pip, rind, seeds, and juice, to have and to hold the said orange together with its skin, pulp, pip, rind, seeds, and juice for his own use and behoof, to himself and his heirs, in fee simple forever, free from all liens, encumbrances, easements, limitations, restraints, or conditions whatsoever, any and all prior deeds, transfers, or other documents whatsoever, now or anywhere made, to the contrary notwithstanding, with full power to bite, cut, suck, or otherwise eat the said orange or to give away the same, with or without its skin, pulp, pip, rind, seeds, or juice."

severe acute respiratory syndrome, and someone else might think of segmentation and reassembly sublayer. And a South African might think of South African Revenue Service. If you have any question as to whether your reader is familiar with the initials, the best practice is to spell out the words the first time you use them and follow them with the initials. Also, if you are writing a long document with several pages between where you defined initials originally and where you use them again, it is courteous to your reader to spell out again.

Probably the most troublesome technical language is that of the legal profession. Legal terms too often have worked their way into business communication. The result has been to add unnecessary words as well as words not understood by many business readers. Such words also produce a dull and formal effect.

- Legal language has worked its way into business writing.

Among the legal words that may add little real meaning are *thereto, therein, whereas, herewith,* and *herein.* For example, "the land adjacent thereto" can be written "the adjacent land" without loss in meaning. In addition, legal wordings such as *cease and desist* and *bequeath and devise* contain needless repetition.

- Words like *thereto, herewith,* and *ipso facto* are examples.

Some legal words can be replaced with plain words. *Despite* can replace *notwithstanding. Ipso facto, sub judice,* and other such Latin phrases can be replaced by plain language with the same meaning.

- Replace legal language with plain words.

Your technical language may not be any of the ones illustrated here, but you will have one. You will need to be careful not to use it when you write to people who do not understand it.

Select Words with the Right Strength and Vigor

In a way, words are like people; they have personalities. Some words are strong and vigorous. Some are weak and dull. And some fall between these extremes. Good writers know these differences, and they consider them carefully. They use the words that do the best job of carrying the intended meaning. As a rule, they make the stronger words stand out.

- Words have personalities. Select the stronger ones.

Selecting words with just the right personalities requires that you learn language well—that you learn to distinguish shades of difference in the meanings of words. For example, you should recognize that *tycoon* is stronger than *eminently successful businessperson,* that *bear market* is stronger than *generally declining market,* that *boom* is stronger than *a period of business prosperity,* and that *mother* is stronger than *female parent.*

- To select words wisely, you should consider shades of difference in meanings.

You will not always want the strongest and most vigorous words. Sometimes, for good reason, you will choose weaker ones. The word *bill* is strong. Because it has a harsh meaning in some minds, you may prefer *statement* in some instances. The same

- Sometimes weaker words serve your purpose best.

Grammar and Style Checkers Help Writers with Word Selection

Grammar Settings

Writing style:
Grammar & Style

Grammar and style options:

Require
Comma required before last list item: don't check
Punctuation required with quotes: don't check
Spaces required between sentences: don't check

Grammar:
- Capitalization
- Fragments and Run-ons
- Misused words
- Negation
- Noun phrases
- Possessives and plurals
- Punctuation
- Questions

Reset All   OK   Cancel

Grammar Settings

Writing style:
Grammar & Style

Grammar and style options:

- Subject-verb agreement
- Verb phrases

Style:
- Clichés, Colloquialisms, and Jargon
- Contractions
- Fragment - stylistic suggestions
- Gender-specific words
- Hyphenated and compound words
- Misused words - stylistic suggestions
- Numbers
- Passive sentences
- Possessives and plurals - stylistic suggestions
- Punctuation - stylistic suggestions

Reset All   OK   Cancel

Document1 - Microsoft Office Word 2003

File Edit View Insert Format Tools Table Window Help   Type a question for help

Times New Roman 12 B I U 83% Read

following the occurrence. All employees will follow these guidelines of the security policy or they will be suspended from the job until their supervisor is notified. This will be determined by the head of your department.

If you have any questions

The head of your department will determine this

Ignore Once

Grammar...

About This Sentence

Look Up...

Cut

Copy

Paste

Page 1   Sec 1   1/1   At 1.5"   Ln 4   Col 34   REC TRK EXT OVR

Today, word processors will help writers with grammar and style as well as with spelling. By default Word checks spelling and grammar automatically, using red and green underlines to distinguish between them. But as you see in the grammar settings screen shots here, writers can spec-ify whether or not they want help and even which rules are applied to their documents. And they can choose to correct as they go along or to correct on demand. Although grammar and style checkers are not as accurate as spelling checkers, they will identify words, phrases, and sentences that could be improved. In fact, they often suggest a way to fix problems.

In the example shown here, the checker found the use of passive voice and suggested a change to active voice. However, the writer decides whether to accept the suggestion, revise, or ignore the suggestion. The writer needs to determine whether this passive voice was used intentionally for one of the reasons discussed in this chapter or whether it was used by accident and should be changed.

- Verbs are the strongest words. Nouns are second.

- Adjectives and adverbs are weak words. They involve judgment. Use them sparingly.

goes for *debt* and *obligation, die* and *passed on, spit* and *saliva, labor boss* and *union official,* and *fired* and *dismissed.*

In selecting the stronger words, you should keep in mind that the verb is the strongest part of speech. Second is the noun. Verbs are action words, and action carries interest. Nouns are the doers of action—the heroes of the sentence. Thus, they also attract attention.

Adjectives and adverbs are weak words. They add length and distract from the key words, the nouns and the verbs. As Voltaire wrote, "The adjective is the enemy of the noun." In addition, adjectives and adverbs are judgment words. As we will see, objectivity—which is opposed to judgment—is a requirement of much business communication. But you should know that adjectives and adverbs are among the weaker words, and you should use them sparingly.

Use Concrete Language

Good business communication is marked by words that form sharp and clear meanings in the mind. These are the concrete words. You should prefer them in your writing.

Concrete is the opposite of abstract. Abstract words are vague. In contrast, concrete words stand for things the reader can see, feel, taste, or smell. Concrete words hold interest, for they refer to the reader's experience.

Among the concrete words are those that stand for things that exist in the real world. Included are such nouns as *chair, desk, computer, road, automobile,* and *flowers.* Also included are words that stand for creatures and things: *Carla Fiori, Tiger Woods, Mickey Mouse, Barney,* the *Empire State Building,* and *Rodeo Drive.*

Abstract nouns, on the other hand, cover broad meanings—concepts, ideas, and the like. Their meanings are general, as in these examples: *administration, negotiation, wealth, inconsistency, loyalty, compatibility, conservation, discrimination, incompetence,* and *communication.* Note how difficult it is to visualize what these words stand for.

Concreteness also involves how we put words together. Exact or specific wordings are concrete; vague and general wordings are abstract. For example, take the case of a researcher who must report the odor of a newly developed cleaning agent. The researcher could use such general words as "It has an offensive, nauseating odor." Now note how much more concrete language communicates: "It has the odor of decaying fish." The second example is concrete because it recalls an exact odor from memory. Notice the difference in communication effect in these contrasting pairs of wordings:

Abstract	Concrete
A significant loss	A 53 percent loss
Good attendance record	100 percent attendance record
The leading company	First among 3,212 competitors
The majority	62 percent
In the near future	By noon Thursday
A labor-saving robot	Does the work of seven workers
Light in weight	Featherlight
Substantial amount	$3,517,000

Now let us see the difference concreteness makes in the clarity of longer passages. Here is an example of abstract wording:

> It is imperative that the firm practice extreme conservatism in operating expenditures during the coming biennium. The firm's past operating performance has been ineffectual for the reason that a preponderance of administrative assignments have been delegated to personnel who were ill-equipped to perform in these capacities. Recently instituted administrative changes stressing experience in operating economies have rectified this condition.

Written for concreteness, this message might read as follows:

> We must reduce operating expenses at least $2 million during 2003–04. Our $1,350,000 deficit for 2001–02 was caused by the inexperience of our two chief administrators, Mr. Sartan and Mr. Ross. We have replaced them with Ms. Pharr and Mr. Kunz, who have had 13 and 17 years, respectively, of successful experience in operations management.

Another illustration of concreteness is the story of the foreign nation that competed strenuously with the United States in an international automobile show. In one category, only automobiles from these two countries were entered. One would surely win first place, the other second. The U.S. automobile won. The government-controlled press of the losing country gave this report to its people: "In worldwide competition, our excellent entry was judged to be second. The entry from the United States was

Marginal notes

- Use concrete words.
- Concrete words are specific words.
- They stand for things that exist in the real world: *deck, chair, road.*
- Abstract nouns have general meanings: *administration, negotiation.*
- Concreteness also means exactness: *a 53 percent loss, the odor of decaying fish.*

rated next to last." The words sound concrete—*second, next to last.* But they omitted one fact needed for ethical concreteness—that only two automobiles were entered.

Use the Active Voice

- Prefer the active voice to the passive voice.

- In active voice, the subject does the action. In passive voice, it receives the action.

- Active voice is stronger and shorter.

You should prefer the active voice to the passive voice. Active voice produces stronger, livelier writing. It emphasizes the action, and it usually saves words.

In active voice, as you will recall, the subject does the action. In passive voice, the subject receives the action. For example, the sentence "The auditor inspected the books" is in active voice. In passive voice, the sentence would read: "The books were inspected by the auditor."

These two sentences show the advantages of active voice. Clearly, the active-voice sentence is stronger. In it the doer of action acts, and the verb is short and clear. In the passive-voice sentence, the extra helping word *were* dulls the action. In addition, placing the doer of the action (*auditor*) in a prepositional phrase presents the information indirectly rather than directly. Note also that the active-voice sentence is shorter.

For further proof of the advantages of active over passive voice, compare the following sentences:

Passive	Active
The results were reported in our July 9 letter.	We reported the results in our July 9 letter.
This policy has been supported by our union.	Our union supported this policy.
The new process is believed to be superior by the investigators.	The investigators believe that the new process is superior.
The policy was enforced by the committee.	The committee enforced the policy.
The office will be inspected by Mr. Hall.	Mr. Hall will inspect the office.
A gain of 30.1 percent was reported for hardware sales.	Hardware sales gained 30.1 percent.
It is desired by the director that this problem be brought before the board.	The director desires that the secretary bring this problem before the board.
A complete reorganization of the administration was effected by the president.	The president completely reorganized the administration.

- Passive voice has a place. It is not incorrect.

- Passive is better when the doer of the action is not important.

The suggestion that active voice be preferred does not mean passive voice is incorrect or you should never use it. Passive voice is correct, and it has a place. The problem is that many writers tend to overuse it, especially in report writing. Writing is more interesting and communicates better when it uses active voice.

Your decision on whether to use active or passive voice is not simply a matter of choice. Sometimes passive voice is preferable. For example, when identifying the doer of the action is unimportant to the message, passive voice properly de-emphasizes the doer.

Advertising is often criticized for its effect on price.

Petroleum is refined in Texas.

- Passive helps avoid accusing the reader.

Passive voice may enable you to avoid accusing your reader of an action:

The damage was caused by exposing the material to sunlight.

The color desired was not specified in your order.

- Passive is better when the performer is not known.

Passive voice also may be preferable when the performer is unknown, as in these examples:

During the past year, the equipment has been sabotaged seven times.

Anonymous complaints have been received.

Yet another situation in which passive voice may be preferable is one in which the writer does not want to name the performer:

The interviews were conducted on weekdays between noon and 6 pm.

Two complaints have been made about you.

In other instances, passive voice is preferable for reasons of style.

● It is also better when the writer prefers not to name the performer.

Avoid Overuse of Camouflaged Verbs

An awkward construction that should be avoided is the camouflaged verb. When a verb is camouflaged, the verb describing the action in a sentence is changed into a noun. Then action words have to be added. For example, suppose you want to write a sentence in which *eliminate* is the action to be expressed. If you change *eliminate* into its noun form, *elimination,* you must add action words—perhaps *was effected*—to have a sentence. Your sentence might then be: "Elimination of the surplus was effected by the staff." The sentence is indirect and passive. You could have avoided the camouflaged construction with a sentence using the verb *eliminate:* "The staff eliminated the surplus."

● Avoid camouflaged verbs. You camouflage a verb by changing it to a noun form and then adding action words.

Here are two more examples. If we take the good action word *cancel* and make it into a noun, *cancellation,* we would have to say something like "to effect a cancellation" to communicate the action. If we change *consider* to *consideration,* we would have to say "give consideration to." So it would be with the following examples:

● For example, if *cancel* becomes *cancellation,* you must add "to effect a" to have action.

Action Verb	Noun Form	Wording of Camouflaged Verb
acquire	acquisition	make an acquisition
appear	appearance	make an appearance
apply	application	make an application
appraise	appraisal	make an appraisal
assist	assistance	give assistance to
cancel	cancellation	make a cancellation
commit	commitment	make a commitment
discuss	discussion	have a discussion
investigate	investigation	make an investigation
judge	judgment	make a judgment
liquidate	liquidation	effect a liquidation
reconcile	reconciliation	make a reconciliation
record	recording	make a recording

Note the differences in overall effect in these contrasting sentences:

Camouflaged Verb	Clear Verb Form
An *arrangement was made* to meet for breakfast.	We *arranged* to meet for breakfast.
Amortization of the account *was effected* by the staff.	The staff *amortized* the account.
Control of the water *was not possible.*	They *could not control* the water.
The new policy *involved the standardization of* the procedures.	The new policy *standardized* the procedures.
Application of the mixture *was accomplished.*	They *applied* the mixture.
We must *bring about a reconciliation of* our differences.	We must *reconcile* our differences.
The *establishment* of a rehabilitation center *has been accomplished* by the company.	The company *has established* a rehabilitation center.

Professorial Words of Wisdom

The plain language movement crosses many continents. The European Union (EU) has written a booklet entitled, "How to Write Clearly, Fight the Fog." It is designed for all writers of English at the European Commission. The first section is about the readers of Commission documents—EU insiders, outside specialists, and the general public. The public is to be considered the most important audience.

Paula J. Pomerenke, Illinois State University

Paula J. Pomerenke, "Challenges for ABC Members in 2,000," *The Journal of Business Communication* 38, no. 1 (January 2001): 6.

- Avoid camouflaged verbs by (1) writing concretely and (2) preferring active voice.

- To comply with these suggestions, (1) make subjects persons or things and (2) write sentences in normal order.

From these illustrations you can see that our suggestion on camouflaged verbs overlaps our two preceding suggestions. First, camouflaged verbs are abstract nouns. We suggested that you prefer concrete words over abstract words. Second, camouflaged verbs frequently require passive voice. We suggested that you prefer active voice.

You can comply with these related suggestions by following two helpful writing hints. The first is to make the subjects of most sentences either persons or things. For example, rather than write "consideration was given to . . . ," you should write "we considered . . . ." The second is to write most sentences in normal order (subject, verb, object), with the doer of the action as the subject. Involved, strained, passive structures often result from attempts at other orders.

Select Words for Precise Meanings

- Writing requires a knowledge of language.

Obviously, writing requires some knowledge of language. In fact, the greater your knowledge of language, the better you are likely to write. Unfortunately, all too many of us treat language routinely. We use the first words that come to mind. We use words without thinking of the meanings they convey. We use words we are not sure of. The result is vague writing.

- You should study language and learn the shades of difference in the meanings of similar words.

If you want to be a good writer, you will need to study words carefully. You will need to learn their precise meanings, especially the shades of difference in the meanings of similar words. For example, *weary, tired, pooped, fagged out,* and *exhausted* all refer to the same thing. Yet in most minds there are differences in the meaning of these words. In a rather formal message, *weary* would certainly be more acceptable than *pooped* or *fagged out.* Similarly, *fired, dismissed, canned, separated, terminated,* and *discharged* refer to the same action but have different shades of meaning. So it is with each of the following groups of words:

die, decease, pass on, croak, kick the bucket, check out, expire, go to one's reward

money, funds, cash, dough, bread, finances

boy, youth, young man, lad, shaver, stripling

fight, brawl, fracas, battle royal, donnybrook

thin, slender, skinny, slight, wispy, lean, willowy, rangy, spindly, lanky, wiry

ill, sick, poorly, weak, delicate, cachectic, unwell, peaked, indisposed, out of sorts

- You should learn the specific meanings of other words.

Knowledge of language also enables you to use words that carry the meanings you want to communicate. For example, *fewer* and *less* mean the same to some people. But careful users select *fewer* to mean "smaller numbers of items" and *less* to mean "reduced value, degree, or quantity." The verbs *affect* and *effect* are often used as synonyms. But those who know language select *affect* when they mean "to influence" and *effect* when they mean "to bring to pass." They use *feel* to express physical contact, perception, or such—not as a substitute for *believe* or *think*. Similarly, careful writers use *continual* to mean "repeated but broken succession" and *continuous* to mean "unbroken succession." They write *farther* to express geographic distance and *further* to indicate "more, in addition." They know that *learn* means "to acquire knowledge" and *teach* means "to impart knowledge."

In your effort to be a precise writer, you should use correct idiom. By *idiom* we mean the way things are said in a language. Much of our idiom has little rhyme or reason, but if we want to be understood, we should follow it. For example, what is the logic in the word *up* in the sentence "Look up her name in the directory"? There really is none. This is just the wording we have developed to cover this meaning. "Independent of" is good idiomatic usage; "independent from" is not. What is the justification? Similarly, you "agree to" a proposal, but you "agree with" a person. You are "careful about" an affair, but you are "careful with" your money. Here are some additional illustrations:

- Use correct idiom. *Idiom* is the way ideas are expressed in a language.

Faulty Idiom	Correct Idiom
authority about	authority on
comply to	comply with
different than	different from
enamored with	enamored of
equally as bad	equally bad
in accordance to	in accordance with
in search for	in search of
listen at	listen to
possessed with ability	possessed of ability
seldom or ever	seldom if ever
superior than	superior to

- There is little reason to some idioms, but violations offend the reader.

SUGGESTIONS FOR NONDISCRIMINATORY WRITING

Although discriminatory words are not directly related to writing clarity, our review of word selection would not be complete without some mention of them. By discriminatory words we mean words that do not treat all people equally and with respect. More specifically, they are words that refer negatively to groups of people, such as by sex, race, nationality, sexual orientation, age, or disability. Such words run contrary to acceptable views of fair play and human decency. They do not promote good business ethics, and thus have no place in business communication.

Many discriminatory words are a part of the vocabularies we have acquired from our environments. We often use them innocently, not realizing how they affect others. We can eliminate discriminatory words from our vocabularies by examining them carefully and placing ourselves in the shoes of those to whom they refer. The following review of the major forms of discriminatory words should help you achieve this goal.

- Avoid words that discriminate against sex, race, nationality, age, sexual orientation, or disability.

- We often use discriminatory words without bad intent.

Use Gender-Neutral Words

All too prevalent in today's business communication are words that discriminate by gender ("sexist" words). Although this form of discrimination can be directed against men, most instances involve discrimination against women because many of our words suggest male superiority. This condition is easily explained. Our language developed in a society in which it was customary for women to work in the home and for men to be the breadwinners and decision makers. As a result, our language reflects this male dominance. For reasons of fair play and to be in step with today's society in

Pepper . . . and Salt

"Believe me, if there was any sexism in this office,
my girl Friday here would know about it."

SOURCE: From *The Wall Street Journal*—Permission, Cartoon Features Syndicate.

which gender equality is the goal, you would do well to use gender-neutral words. Suggestions for doing this follow.

Masculine Pronouns for Both Sexes. Perhaps the most troublesome sexist words are the masculine pronouns (*he, his, him*) when they are used to refer to both sexes, as in this example: "The typical State University student eats *his* lunch at the student center." Assuming that State is coeducational, the use of *his* suggests male supremacy. Historically, of course, the word *his* has been classified as generic—that is, it can refer to both sexes. But many modern-day businesspeople do not agree and are offended by the use of the masculine pronoun in this way.

You can avoid the use of masculine pronouns in such cases in three ways. First, you can reword the sentence to eliminate the offending word. Thus, the illustration above could be reworded as follows: "The typical State University student eats lunch at the student center." Here are other examples:

Sexist	Gender-Neutral
If a customer pays promptly, *he* is placed on our preferred list.	A customer who pays promptly is placed on our preferred list.
When an unauthorized employee enters the security area, *he* is subject to dismissal.	An employee who enters the security area is subject to dismissal.
A supervisor is not responsible for such losses if *he* is not negligent.	A supervisor who is not negligent is not responsible for such losses.
When a customer needs service, it is *his* right to ask for it.	A customer who needs service has the right to ask for it.

A second way to avoid sexist use of the masculine pronoun is to make the reference plural. Fortunately, the English language has plural pronouns (*their, them, they*) that refer to both sexes. Making the references plural in the examples given above, we have these nonsexist revisions:

If customers pay promptly, *they* are placed on our preferred list.

When unauthorized employees enter the security area, *they* are subject to dismissal.

Supervisors are not responsible for such losses if *they* are not negligent.

When customers need service, *they* have the right to ask for it.

- Avoid using the masculine pronouns (he, him, his) for both sexes.

- You can do this (1) by rewording the sentence;

- (2) by making the reference plural,

- as illustrated here;

In business today, men and women, the young and the old, and people of all races work side by side in roles of mutual respect. It would be unfair to use words that discriminate against any of them.

A third way to avoid sexist use of *he, his,* or *him* is to substitute any of a number of neutral expressions. The most common are *he or she, he/she, s/he, you, one,* and *person.* Using neutral expressions in the problem sentences, we have these revisions:

If a customer pays promptly, *he or she* is placed on our preferred list.

When an unauthorized employee enters the security area, *he/she* is subject to dismissal.

A supervisor is not responsible for such losses if *s/he* is not negligent.

When *one* needs service, *one* has the right to ask for it.

You should use such expressions with caution, however. They tend to be somewhat awkward, particularly if they are used often. For this reason, many skilled writers do not use some of them. If you use them, you should pay attention to their effect on the flow of your words. Certainly, you should avoid sentences like this one: "To make an employee feel he/she is doing well by complimenting her/him insincerely confuses her/him later when he/she sees his/her co-workers promoted ahead of him/her."

Words Derived from Masculine Words. As we have noted, our culture was male dominated when our language developed. Because of this, many of our words are masculine even though they do not refer exclusively to men. Take *chairman,* for example. This word can refer to both sexes, yet it does not sound that way. More

- or (3) by substituting neutral expressions,

- as in these examples.

- Neutral expressions can be awkward; so use them with caution.

- Avoid words suggesting male dominance,

Meaning and the Appearance of a Word

A real-life illustration of how words don't always mean what they may appear to mean is the case of the ombudsman to the mayor of Washington, D.C. The ombudsman, who is white, used these words in commenting on his budget: "I will have to be 'niggardly' with these funds . . ."

The word "niggardly" means "miserly." It is derived from a Scandinavian word and has no racial origin or meaning. Even so, the mayor's office was deluged with protest calls from the black community. So intense were the objections that the ombudsman resigned, and his resignation was accepted.

The appropriateness of the resignation was intensely argued. Those favoring the resignation generally argued that the ombudsman should have been more sensitive in his choice of words—that he should have known that the word's sound would offend. Those opposing generally argued that the man should not be criticized because of the ignorance of others. After considerable argument was heard, the mayor appointed the man to another position.

What is to be learned from this incident? Does the sound of a word affect its meaning?

---

appropriate and less offensive substitutes are *chair, presiding officer, moderator,* and *chairperson.* Similarly, *salesman* suggests a man, but many women work in sales. *Salesperson, salesclerk,* or *sales representative* would be better. Other sexist words and gender-neutral substitutes are as follows:

● such as these examples.

Sexist	Gender-Neutral
man-made	manufactured, of human origin
manpower	personnel, workers
congressman	representative, member of Congress
businessman	business executive, businessperson
mailman	letter carrier, mail carrier
policeman	police officer
fireman	fire fighter
repairman	repair technician
cameraman	camera operator

● But not all man-sounding words are sexist.

Many words with *man, his,* and the like in them have nonsexist origins. Among such words are *manufacture, management, history,* and *manipulate.* Also, some clearly sexist words are hard to avoid. *Freshperson,* for example, would not serve as a substitute for *freshman.* And *personhole* is an illogical substitute for *manhole.*

● Do not use words that lower one's status.

Words that Lower Status by Gender. Thoughtless writers and speakers use expressions belittling the status of women. You should avoid such expressions. To illustrate, male executives sometimes refer to their female secretaries as *my girl,* as in this sentence: "I'll have my girl take care of this matter." Of course, *secretary* would be a better choice. Then there are the many female forms for words that refer to work roles. In this group are *lady lawyer, authoress, sculptress,* and *poetess.* You should refer to women in these work roles by the same words that you would use for men: *lawyer, author, sculptor, poet.* Using words such as *male nurse* or *male teacher* can be demeaning as well.

Examples of sexist words could go on and on. But not all of them would be as clear as those given above for the issue is somewhat complex and confusing. In deciding which words to avoid and which to use, you will have to rely on your best judgment. Remember that your goal should be to use words that are fair and that do not offend.

Avoid Words That Stereotype by Race, Nationality, or Sexual Orientation

Words that stereotype all members of a group by race, nationality, or sexual orientation are especially unfair and frequently they reinforce stereotypical beliefs about this group. Members of any minority vary widely in all characteristics. Thus, it is unfair to suggest that Jews are miserly, that Italians are Mafia members, that Hispanics are lazy, that African Americans can do only menial jobs, that gays are perfectionists, and so on. Unfair references to minorities are sometimes subtle and not intended, as in this example: "We conducted the first marketing tests in the low-income areas of the city. Using a sample of 200 African-American families, we . . . " These words unfairly suggest that only African Americans live in low-income areas.

Also unfair are words suggesting that a minority member has struggled to achieve something that is taken for granted in the majority group. Usually well intended, words of this kind can carry subtle discriminatory messages. For example, a reference to a "neatly dressed Hispanic man" may suggest that he is an exception to the rule—that most Hispanics are not neatly dressed, but here is one who is. So can references to "a generous Jew," "an energetic Puerto Rican," "a hardworking African American," and "a Chinese manager."

Eliminating unfair references to minority groups from your communication requires two basic steps. First, you must consciously treat all people equally, without regard to their minority status. You should refer to minority membership only in those rare cases in which it is a vital part of the message to be communicated. Second, you must be sensitive to the effects of your words. Specifically, you should ask yourself how those words would affect you if you were a member of the minorities to which they are addressed. You should evaluate your word choices from the viewpoints of others.

- Words depicting minorities in a stereotyped way are unfair and untrue.

- Words that present members of minorities as exceptions to stereotypes are also unfair.

- Eliminate such references to minorities by treating all people equally and by being sensitive to the effects of your words.

Avoid Words That Stereotype by Age

Your sensitivity in not discriminating by sex also should be extended to include discriminating by age—against both the old and the young. While those over 55 might be retired from their first jobs, many lead lives that are far from the sedentary roles in which they are sometimes depicted. They also are not necessarily feeble, forgetful, or forsaken. While some do not mind being called *senior citizens*, others do. Be sensitive with terms such as *mature*, *elderly*, and *golden ager*, also. Some even abhor *oldster* as much as the young detest *youngster*. The young are often called *teenagers* or *adolescents* although *young person*, *young man*, and *young woman* are much fairer. Some slang terms show lack of sensitivity, too—words such as *brat*, *retard*, and *dummy*. Even harsher are *juvenile delinquent*, *truant*, and *runaway*, for these labels often are put on the young based on one behavior over a short time period. Presenting both the old and the young objectively is only fair.

As we have suggested, use labels only when relevant, and use positive terms when possible. In describing the old, be sensitive to terms such as *spry*, which on the surface might be well intended but also can imply a negative connotation. Present both groups fairly and objectively when you write about them.

- Words that label people as old or young can arouse negative reactions.

Avoid Words That Typecast Those with Disabilities

People with disabilities are likely to be sensitive to discriminatory words. Television shows those with disabilities competing in the Special Olympics, often exceeding the performance of an average person, and common sense tells us not to stereotype these people. However, sometimes we do anyway. Just as with age, we need to avoid derogatory labels and apologetic or patronizing behavior. For example, instead of describing one as *deaf and dumb*, use *deaf*. Avoid slang terms such as *fits, spells, attacks;* use *seizures, epilepsy,* or other objective terms. Terms such as *crippled* and *retarded* should be avoided because they degrade in most cases. Work to develop a nonbiased attitude, and show it through carefully chosen words.

- Disabled people are sensitive to words that describe their disabilities.

In Conclusion about Words

- More about words appears in the following pages.

- The preceding suggestions are realistic ways to improve your writing. Use them.

The preceding review of suggestions for selecting words is not complete. You will find more—much more—in the pages ahead. But you now have in mind the basics of word selection. The remaining are refinements of these basics.

As you move along, you should view these basics as work tools. Unfortunately, the tendency is to view them as rules to memorize and give back to the instructor on an examination. Although a good examination grade is a commendable goal, the long-run value of these tools is their use in your writing. So do yourself a favor. Resolve to keep these basics in mind every time you write. Consciously use them. The results will make you glad you did.

SUMMARY BY CHAPTER OBJECTIVES

1 Explain the role of adaptation in selecting words that communicate.

2 Simplify writing by selecting short and familiar words.

3 Use technical words and acronyms appropriately.

4 Discuss the differences in the strength of words and select the words that communicate your message best.

5 Write concretely and use active voice.

6 Write with clarity and precision by avoiding camouflaged verbs, by selecting the right words, and by using idioms correctly.

7 Use words that do not discriminate.

1. To communicate clearly, you must adapt to your reader.
   - Adapting means using words the reader understands.
   - It also involves following the suggestions.

2. Select words that your reader understands.
   - These are the familiar words (words like *old* instead of *antiquated*).
   - They are also the short words (*agreed to quit* rather than *acceded to the proposition to terminate*).

3. Use technical words and acronyms with caution.
   - For example, use *a little stroke* rather than *a cerebral vascular accident.*
   - Spell out and define acronyms as needed.
   - However, technical words are appropriate among technical people.

4. Select words with adequate strength and vigor.
   - Develop a feeling for the personalities of words.
   - Understand that words like *bear market* are stronger than *generally declining market.*

5. Prefer the concrete words and active voice.
   - Concrete words are the specific ones. For example, *57 percent majority* is more concrete than *majority.*
   - In active voice, the subject acts; in passive voice, it receives the action. For example, use *we reported the results* rather than *the results were reported by us.*
   - Active voice is stronger, more vigorous, and more interesting. But passive voice is correct and has a place in writing.

6. Write more clearly and precisely by following these suggestions:
   - Avoid overuse of camouflaged verbs—making a noun of the logical verb and then having to add a verb (*appear* rather than *make an appearance*).
   - Select words for their precise meanings (involves studying words to detect shades of difference in meaning—for example, differences in *fight, brawl, fracas, donnybrook, battle royal*).
   - Also, learn the specific ways that words are used in our culture (called *idiom*).

7. Avoid discriminatory words.
   - Do not use words that discriminate against women. (For example, using *he, him,* or *his* to refer to both sexes and words such as *fireman, postman, lady lawyer,* and *authoress.*)
   - Do not use words that suggest stereotyped roles of race, nationality, or sexual orientation (African Americans and menial jobs, Italians and the Mafia, gays and perfectionists), for such words are unfair and untrue.
   - Do not use words that discriminate against age or disability.

1. A fellow student says, "So I'm not a good writer. But I have other places to put my study time. I'm a management major. I'll have secretaries to handle my writing for me." Give this student your best advice, including the reasoning behind it.

2. Evaluate this comment: "Simplifying writing so that stupid readers can understand it is for the birds! Why not challenge readers? Why not give them new words to learn—expand their minds?"

3. Explain how you would apply the basic principle of adaptation to each of the following writing assignments:

    a. An editorial in a company newsletter.

    b. A message to Joan Branch, a supervisor of an information systems department, concerning a change in determining project priorities.

    c. A report to the chief engineer on a technical topic in the engineer's field.

    d. A message to employees explaining a change in pension benefits.

    e. A letter to company stockholders explaining a change in company reporting dates.

4. "Some short words are hard, and some long words are easy. Thus, the suggestion to prefer short words doesn't make sense." Discuss.

5. "As technical language typically consists of acronyms and long, hard words, it contributes to miscommunication. Thus, it should be avoided in all business communication." Discuss.

6. Using examples other than those in the book, discuss differences in word strength. Be sure to comment on strength differences in the parts of speech (nouns, verbs, adjectives, adverbs).

7. Define and give examples of active and passive voice. Explain when each should be used.

8. Discuss this statement: "When I use *he, him,* or *his* as a generic, I am not discriminating against women. For many years these words have been accepted as generic. They refer to both sexes, and that's the meaning I have in mind when I use them."

9. List synonyms (words with similar meanings) for each of the following words. Then explain the differences in shades of meaning as you see them.

    a. fat   g. dog

    b. skinny   h. misfortune

    c. old   i. inquire

    d. tell   j. stop

    e. happiness   k. lie

    f. understand   l. mistake

10. Discuss this statement: "The boss scolded Susan in a grandfatherly manner."

Using Familiar Words

Instructions, Sentences 1–20: Assume that your readers are at about the 10th-grade level in education. Revise these sentences for easy communication to this audience.

1. We must terminate all deficit financing.

2. We must endeavor to correct this problem by expediting delivery.

3. A proportionate tax consumes a determinate apportionment of one's monetary flow.

4. Business has an inordinate influence on governmental operations.

5. It is imperative that consumers be unrestrained in determining their preferences.

6. Mr. Sanchez terminated Kevin's employment as a consequence of his ineffectual performance.

7. Our expectations are that there will be increments in commodity value.

8. Can we ascertain the types of customers that have a predisposition to utilize our instant-credit offer?

9. The preponderance of the businesspeople we consulted envision signs of improvement from the current siege of economic stagnation.

10. If liquidation becomes mandatory, we shall dispose of these assets first.

11. Recent stock acquisitions have accentuated the company's current financial crisis.

12. Mr. Coward will serve as intermediary in the pending labor–management parley.

13. Ms. Smith's idiosyncrasies supply adequate justification for terminating her employment.

14. Requisites for employment by this company have been enhanced.

15. The unanimity of current forecasts is not incontrovertible evidence of an impending business acceleration.

16. People's propensity to consume is insatiable.

17. The company must desist from its deficit financing immediately.

18. This antiquated merchandising strategy is ineffectual in contemporary business operations.

19. Percentage return on common stockholders' equity averaged 23.1 for the year.

20. The company's retained earnings last year exceeded $2,500,000.

Instructions: Exercise 21 concerns adaptation and technical language. As you must find your own sentences for it, this exercise differs from the others.

21. From a scholarly business journal, select a paragraph (at least 150 words long) that would be difficult for a student less advanced in the subject than you. Rewrite the paragraph so that this student can understand it easily.

Instructions, Sentences 22–58: Revise these sentences to make them conform to the writing suggestions discussed in the book. They are grouped by the suggestion they illustrate.

Using Strong, Vigorous Words

22. I have an idea in mind of how we can enhance our savings.

23. Ms. Jordan possesses qualities that are characteristic of an autocratic executive.

24. Many people came into the store during the period of the promotion.

25. We are obligated to protect the well-being of the hired employees.

26. Companies promoting their products in the medium of the newspaper are advised to produce verbal messages in accord with the audience level of the general consuming public.

Selecting Concrete Words

27. We have found that young men are best for this work.

28. She makes good grades.

29. John lost a fortune in Las Vegas.

30. If we don't receive the goods soon, we will cancel.

31. Profits last year were exorbitant.

32. Some years ago she made good money.

33. His grade on the aptitude test was not high.

34. Here is a product with very little markup.

35. The cost of the online subscription was reasonable.

36. We will need some new equipment soon.

Limiting Use of Passive Voice

37. Our action is based on the assumption that the competition will be taken by surprise.

38. It is believed by the typical union member that his or her welfare is not considered to be important by management.

39. We are serviced by the Bratton Company.

40. Our safety is the responsibility of management.

41. You were directed by your supervisor to complete this assignment by noon.

42. It is believed by the writer that this company policy is wrong.

43. The union was represented by Cecil Chambers.

44. These reports are prepared by the salespeople every Friday.

45. Success of this project is the responsibility of the research department.

46. Our decision is based on the belief that the national economy will be improved.

Avoiding Camouflaged Verbs

47. It was my duty to make a determination of the damages.

48. Harold made a recommendation that we fire Mr. Schultz.

49. We will make her give an accounting of her activities.

50. We will ask him to bring about a change in his work routine.

51. This new equipment will result in a saving in maintenance.

52. Will you please make an adjustment for this defect?

53. Implementation of the plan was effected by the crew.

54. Acceptance of all orders must be made by the chief.

55. A committee performs the function of determining the award.

56. Adaptation to the new conditions was performed easily by all new personnel.

57. Verification of the amount is made daily by the auditor.

58. The president tried to effect a reconciliation of the two groups.

Selecting Precise Words

Instructions, Sentences 59–70: Following is an exercise in word precision. Explain the differences in meaning for the word choices shown. Point out any words that are wrongly used.

59. Performance during the fourth quarter was (average) (mediocre).

60. This merchandise is (old) (antique) (secondhand) (preowned) (used).

61. The machine ran (continually) (continuously).

62. The mechanic is a (woman) (lady) (female person).

63. His action (implies) (infers) that he accepts the criticism.

64. Her performance on the job was (good) (topnotch) (excellent) (superior).

65. On July 1 the company will (become bankrupt) (close its door) (go under) (fail).

66. The staff members (think) (understand) (know) the results were satisfactory.

67. Before buying any material, we (compare) (contrast) it with competing products.
68. I cannot (resist) (oppose) her appointment.
69. Did you (verify) (confirm) these figures?
70. This is an (effective) (effectual) (efficient) plan.

Using Proper Idiom

Instructions, Sentences 71–80: These sentences use faulty and correct idioms. Make any changes you think are necessary.

71. The purchasing officer has gone in search for a substitute product.
72. Our office has become independent from the Dallas office.
73. This strike was different than the one in 2000.
74. This letter is equally as bad.
75. She is an authority about mutual funds.
76. When the sale is over with, we will restock.
77. Our truck collided against the wall.
78. We have been in search for a qualified supervisor since August.
79. Murphy was equal to the task.
80. Apparently, the clock fell off the shelf.

Avoiding Discriminatory Language

Instructions, Sentences 81–90: Change these sentences to avoid discriminatory language.

81. Any worker who ignores this rule will have his salary reduced.
82. The typical postman rarely makes mistakes in delivering his mail.
83. A good executive plans his daily activities.
84. The committee consisted of a businessman, a lawyer, and a lady doctor.
85. A good secretary screens all telephone calls for her boss and arranges his schedule.
86. An efficient salesman organizes his calls and manages his time.
87. Our company was represented by two sales representatives, one Hispanic engineer, and one senior citizen.
88. Three people applied for the job, including two well-groomed black women.
89. Handicap parking spaces are strictly for use by the crippled.
90. He didn't act like a gay.

CHAPTER THREE

Construction of Clear Sentences and Paragraphs

CHAPTER OBJECTIVES

Upon completing this chapter, you will be able to construct clear sentences and paragraphs by emphasizing adaptation, short sentences, and effective paragraph design. To reach this goal, you should be able to

1 Explain the role of adaptation in writing clear sentences.

2 Write short, clear sentences by limiting sentence content and economizing on words.

3 Design sentences that give the right emphasis to content.

4 Employ unity and clarity in writing effective sentences.

5 Compose paragraphs that are short and unified, use topic sentences effectively, show movement, and communicate clearly.

Writing Sentences and Paragraphs That Communicate

Introduce yourself to this chapter by continuing in the role of small business manager and immediate superior to Max Schwartz (preceding chapter). Max's writing problem would be of concern in any business, but it is especially important in small businesses such as yours. Your company is struggling to survive with its competition. It must be more efficient in every aspect of its operations if it is to survive. Communication is one of these aspects. This is why you are concerned about what you see in Max's writing.

As you continue your review of Max's writing, you detect more than problems with word choice. Something else is wrong. His sentences just do not convey sharp, clear meanings. Although grammatically correct, they appear to be needlessly complex and heavy. His long and involved paragraphs also cause you concern.

What you have seen in Max's writing are problems concerning two other determinants of readability: the sentence and the paragraph. As you will learn in the pages ahead, these two writing units play major roles in communicating. This chapter will show you (and Max) how to construct sentences and paragraphs that produce readable writing.

FOUNDATION OF ADAPTATION

As you have seen, choosing the right words is basic to clear communication. Equally basic is the task of arranging those words into clear sentences. Like choosing words, constructing clear sentences involves adaptation to the minds of the intended readers.

- Sentences should be adapted to readers.

Fitting sentences to the minds of readers requires the reader analysis we discussed in the preceding chapter. You should simply study your readers to find out what they are like—what they know, how they think, and such. Then construct sentences that will communicate with them.

In general, this procedure involves using the simpler sentence structures to reach people with lower communication abilities and people not knowledgeable about the subject. It involves using the more complex sentence structures only when they are appropriate, usually when communicating with knowledgeable people. As we will see, even with knowledgeable people, simplicity is sometimes needed for the best communication effect.

- Use the simpler sentence structures for those less able to understand; use the more complex structures when appropriate.

In adapting sentences, you should aim a little below the level of your reader. Readability research tells us that writing communicates best when it does not tax the mind. Thus, some simplification is best for all readers. Keep this point in mind as you read through the rest of this chapter.

EMPHASIS ON SHORT SENTENCES

Writing simpler sentences largely means writing shorter sentences. Readability research tells us that the more words and the more relationships there are in a sentence, the greater is the possibility for misunderstanding. Apparently, the mind can hold only so much information at one time. Thus, to give it too much information is to risk miscommunication.

- Short sentences communicate better because of mind limitations.

What constitutes a short, readable sentence is related to the reader's ability. Readability studies show that writing intended to communicate with the middle-level adult reader should average about 16 to 18 words per sentence. For more advanced readers, the average may be higher. For less advanced readers, it should be lower.

- Short means about 16–18 words for middle-level readers.

Our emphasis on short sentences does not mean that you should use all short sentences. In fact, you should avoid overusing them. The overuse of short sentences results in a choppy effect and suggests primer simplicity. You should use moderately long sentences occasionally. They are sometimes useful in subordinating information

- But the excessive use of short sentences is also bad.

Readability Statistics Help Writers Evaluate Document Length and Difficulty

Readability Statistics ☒

Counts

Words	1431
Characters	7781
Paragraphs	164
Sentences	52

Averages

Sentences per Paragraph	3.4
Words per Sentence	20.7
Characters per Word	5.2

Readability

Passive Sentences	0%
Flesch Reading Ease	26.8
Flesch-Kincaid Grade Level	12.0

[OK]

Grammar and style checkers give writers the option of reporting readability statistics. These statistics report the number of words, characters, paragraphs, and sentences in a document along with averages of characters per word, words per sentence, and sentences per paragraph.

The report you see here was generated for a scholarly manuscript. It reports an average of 20.7 words per sentence, a bit high for a business document but probably at an acceptable level for a scholarly document's readers. The Flesch-Kincaid score confirms that the reading grade level is 12.0, too high for business documents but likely appropriate for a scholarly audience. However, the Flesch Reading Ease score should give the writer cause to review the document for accessibility, even for its targeted audience. The 26.8 score is well below the 60–70 range Microsoft recommends.

and in increasing interest by adding variety. And sometimes the information needed to convey a thought requires a long sentence. Even so, you should take care to not make the long sentences excessively long. Always you should make certain that they are clear.

The following sentence from an employee handbook illustrates the effect of long sentences on communication:

> When an employee has changed from one job to another job, the new corresponding coverages will be effective as of the date the change occurs, provided, however, if due to a physical disability or infirmity as a result of advanced age, an employee is changed from one job to another job and such change results in the employee's new job rate coming within a lower hourly job-rate bracket in the table, the employee may, at the discretion of the company, continue the amount of group term life insurance and the amount of accidental death and dismemberment insurance that the employee had prior to such change.

The chances are that you did not get a clear message from this sentence when you first read it. The explanation is not in the words used; you probably know them all.

A Marathon Sentence (308 Words) from U.S. Government Regulations

That no person in the classified civil service of the United States shall be removed therefrom except for such cause as will promote the efficiency of said service and for reasons given in writing, and the person whose removal is sought shall have notice of the same and of any charges preferred against him, and be furnished with a copy thereof, and also be allowed a reasonable time for personally answering the same in writing; and affidavits in support thereof; but no examination of witnesses nor any trial or hearing shall be required except in the discretion of the officer making the removal; and copies of charges, notice of hearing, answer, reasons for removal, and of the order of removal shall be made a part of the records of the proper department or office, as shall also the reasons for reduction in rank or compensation; and the copies of the same shall be furnished to the person affected upon request, and the Civil Service Commission also shall, upon request, be furnished copies of the same: *Provided, however,* that membership in any society, association, club, or other form of organization of postal employees not affiliated with any outside organization imposing an obligation or duty upon them to engage in any strike, or proposing to assist them in any strike, against the United States, having for its objects, among other things, improvements in the condition of labor of its members, including hours of labor and compensation therefore and leave of absence, by any person or groups of persons in said postal service, or the presenting by any such person or groups of persons of any grievance or grievances to the Congress or any Member thereof shall not constitute or be cause for reduction in rank or compensation or removal of such person or groups of persons from said service.

Neither is it in the ideas presented; they are relatively simple. The obvious explanation is the length of the sentence. So many words and relationships are in the sentence that they cause confusion. The result is vague communication at best—complete miscommunication at worst. Now look at the message written in all short sentences. The meanings may be clear, but the choppy effect is distracting and irritating. Imagine reading a long document written in this style.

> An employee may change jobs. The change may result in a lower pay bracket. The new coverage is effective when this happens. The job change must be because of physical disability. It can also be because of infirmity. Old age may be another cause. The company has some discretion in the matter. It can permit continuing the accidental death insurance. It can permit continuing the dismemberment insurance.

The following paragraph takes a course between these two extremes. Clearly, it is an improvement. Generally, it emphasizes short sentences, but it combines content items where appropriate.

> The new insurance coverage becomes effective when because of disability, infirmity, or age an employee's job change results in lower pay. But at its discretion, the company may permit the old insurance coverage to continue.

You can write short, simple sentences in two basic ways: (1) by limiting sentence content and (2) by using words economically. The following pages contain specific suggestions for doing this.

- Short sentences are achieved in two ways.

Limiting Sentence Content

Limiting sentence content is largely a matter of mentally selecting thought units and making separate sentences of most of them. Sometimes, of course, you should combine thoughts into one sentence, but only when you have good reason. You have good reason, for example, when thoughts are closely related or when you want to de-emphasize content. The advantage of limiting sentence content is evident from the following contrasting examples:

- Limiting content is one way to make short sentences.

Long and Hard to Understand

This letter is being distributed with enrollment confirmation sheets, which are to serve as a final check on the correctness of the registration of students and are to be used later when obtaining semester grades from the regline system, which are to be available two weeks after the term officially ends.

Some authorities in human resources object to expanding normal salary ranges to include a trainee rate because they fear that through oversight or prejudice probationers may be kept at the minimum rate longer than is warranted and because they fear that it would encourage the spread from the minimum to maximum rate range.

Regardless of their seniority or union affiliation, all employees who hope to be promoted are expected to continue their education either by enrolling in the special courses to be offered by the company, which are scheduled to be given after working hours beginning next Wednesday, or by taking approved online courses selected from a list, which may be seen on the company portal.

Short and Clear

This letter is being distributed with enrollment confirmation sheets. This sheet will serve now as a final check on student registration. Later, the codes on it will be used to access course grades through the regline system; the grades will be available two weeks after the term officially ends.

Some authorities in human resources object to expanding the normal salary range to include a trainee rate for two reasons. First, they fear that through oversight or prejudice probationers may be kept at the minimum rate longer than is warranted. Second, they fear that expansion would increase the spread between the minimum and the maximum rate range.

Regardless of their seniority or union affiliation, all employees who hope to be promoted are expected to continue their education in either of two ways. (1) They may enroll in special courses to be given by the company. (2) They may take approved online courses selected from the list on the company portal.

Without question, the long sentences in the examples are hard to understand, and the shorter versions are easy to understand. In each case, the difference is primarily in sentence length. Clearly, the shorter sentences communicate better. They give more emphasis to content and to organization of the subject matter.

However, you can overdo the writing of short sentences. As we noted previously, a succession of short sentences can give the impression of elementary writing and draw attention from the content of the sentences to their choppiness. You should avoid these effects by varying the length and order of your sentences. But you should keep the length of your sentences within the grasp of your readers.

Economizing on Words

A second basic technique of shortening sentences is to use words economically. Anything you write can be expressed in many ways, some shorter than others. In general, the shorter wordings save the reader time and are clearer and more interesting.

Economizing on words generally means seeking shorter ways of saying things. Once you try to economize, you will probably find that your present writing is wasteful and that you use uneconomical wordings.

To help you recognize these uneconomical wordings, a brief review of them follows. This review does not cover all the possibilities for wasteful writing, but it does cover many troublesome problems.

Cluttering Phrases. An often used uneconomical wording is the cluttering phrase. This is a phrase that can be replaced by shorter wording without loss of meaning. The little savings achieved in this way add up.

Here is an example of a cluttering phrase:

In the event that payment is not made by January, operations will cease.

- Avoid overdoing this suggestion. Too many short sentences give a choppy effect.

- Another way to shorten sentences is through word economy.

- Seek shorter ways of saying things.

- Following are some suggestions.

- Avoid cluttering phrases. Substitute shorter expressions.

Hagar the Horrible

SOURCE: Reprinted with Special Permission of King Features Syndicate.

The phrase *in the event that* is uneconomical. The little word *if* can substitute for it without loss of meaning:

If payment is not made by January, operations will cease.

Similarly, the phrase that begins the following sentence adds unnecessary length:

In spite of the fact that they received help, they failed to exceed the quota.

Although makes an economical substitute:

Although they received help, they failed to exceed the quota.

You probably use many cluttering phrases. The following partial list (with suggested substitutions) should help you cut down on them:

Cluttering Phrase	Shorter Substitution
Along the lines of	Like
At the present time	Now
For the purpose of	For
For the reason that	Because, since
In accordance with	By
In the amount of	For
In the meantime	Meanwhile
In the near future	Soon
In the neighborhood of	About
In very few cases	Seldom
In view of the fact that	Since, because
On the basis of	By
On the occasion of	On
With regard to, with reference to	About
With a view to	To

Surplus Words. To write economically, eliminate words that add nothing to sentence meaning. As with cluttering phrases, we often use meaningless extra words as a matter of habit. Eliminating these surplus words sometimes requires recasting a sentence, but sometimes they can just be left out.

- Eliminate surplus words.

With the advent of computers, the way business messages are composed has changed, but the mental process involved remains unchanged. One still must select words and build sentences that form precise meanings in the minds of readers.

The following is an example of surplus wording from a business report:

It will be noted that the records for the past years show a steady increase in special appropriations.

The beginning words add nothing to the meaning of the sentence. Notice how dropping them makes the sentence stronger—and without loss of meaning:

The records for the past years show a steady increase in special appropriations.

Here is a second example:

His performance was good enough *to enable him* to qualify for the promotion.

The words *to enable* add nothing and can be dropped:

His performance was good enough to qualify him for the promotion.

The following sentences further illustrate the use of surplus words. In each case, the surplus words can be eliminated without changing the meaning.

Contains Surplus Words	**Eliminates Surplus Words**
He ordered desks *that are of the* executive type.	He ordered executive-type desks.
There are four rules *that* should be observed.	Four rules should be observed.
In addition to these defects, numerous other defects mar the operating procedure.	Numerous other defects mar the operating procedure.
The machines *that were* damaged by the fire were repaired.	The machines damaged by the fire were repaired.

Contains Surplus Words	Eliminates Surplus Words
By *the* examining *of* production records, they found the error.	By examining production records, they found the error.
In the period between April and June, we detected the problem.	Between April and June we detected the problem.
I am prepared to report *to the effect* that sales increased.	I am prepared to report that sales increased.

Roundabout Constructions. As we have noted, you can write anything in many ways. Some of the ways are direct. Some cover the same ground in a roundabout way. Usually the direct ways are shorter and communicate better.

- Avoid roundabout ways of saying things.

This sentence illustrates roundabout construction:

The department budget *can be observed to be decreasing* each *new* year.

Do the words *can be observed to be decreasing* get to the point? Is the idea of *observing* essential? Is *new* needed? A more direct and better sentence is this one:

The department budget decreases each year.

Here is another roundabout sentence:

The union *is involved in the task of reviewing* the seniority provision of the contract.

Now if the union is *involved in the task of reviewing,* it is really *reviewing.* The sentence should be written in these direct words:

The union *is reviewing* the seniority provision of the contract.

The following sentence pairs further illustrate the advantages of short, direct wording over roundabout wording:

Roundabout	Direct
The president *is of the opinion that* the tax was paid.	The president *believes* the tax was paid.
It is essential that the income be used to retire the debt.	The income *must* be used to retire the debt.
Reference is made to your May 10 report *in which you concluded* that the warranty is worthless.	Your May 10 report *concluded* that the warranty is worthless.
The supervisors *should take appropriate action to determine* whether the absentee reports are being verified.	The supervisors *should determine* whether the absentee reports are being verified.
The price increase *will afford* the company *an opportunity* to retire the debt.	The price *will enable* the company to retire the debt.
During the time she was employed by this company, Ms. Carr was absent once.	*While* employed by this company, Ms. Carr was absent once.
He criticized everyone he *came in contact with.*	He criticized everyone he *met.*

Unnecessary Repetition of Words or Ideas. Repeating words obviously adds to sentence length. Such repetition sometimes serves a purpose, as when it is used for emphasis or special effect. But all too often it is without purpose, as this sentence illustrates:

- Repeat words only for effect and emphasis.

We have not received your payment covering invoices covering June and July purchases.

It would be better to write the sentence like this:

We have not received your payment covering invoices for June and July purchases.

Professorial Words of Wisdom

As Daniel Defoe understood in the eighteenth century, it is not the message as one wishes to send it that matters most but the message as it is received.

If any man was to ask me, what I would suppose to be a perfect stile of language, I would answer that in which a man speaking to five hundred people, of all common and various capacities . . . should be understood by them all, in the same manner with one another, and in the same sense which the speaker intended to be understood, this would certainly be a most perfect stile. (quoted from Daniel Defoe's 1728 publication, *The Complete English Tradesman in Familiar Letters,* 1, p. 26)

Roger D. Lund, Le Moyne College

Roger D. Lund, "Writing the History of Business Communication: The Example of Defoe," *The Journal of Business Communication* 35, no. 4 (October 1998): 511.

Another example is this one:

He stated that he believes that we are responsible.

The following sentence eliminates one of the *thats*:

He stated that he believes we are responsible.

● Avoid repetitions of ideas (redundancies).

Repetitions of ideas through the use of different words that mean the same thing (*free gift, true fact, past history*) also add to sentence length. Known as redundancies, such repetitions are illogical and can rarely be defended. Note the redundancy in this sentence:

The provision of Section 5 provides for a union shop.

The duplication, of course, is in the meaning of *provides.* By definition, a *provision* provides. So the repetition serves no purpose. The following sentence is better:

Section 5 provides for a union shop.

You often hear this expression:

In my opinion, I think the plan is sound.

Do not *in my opinion* and *I think* express the same thought? Could you possibly think in an opinion other than your own? The following sentence makes better sense:

I think the plan is sound.

Here are other examples of redundancies and ways to eliminate them:

Needless Repetition	Repetition Eliminated
Please *endorse your name on the back* of this check.	Please *endorse* this check.
We must *assemble together* at 10:30 AM *in the morning.*	We must *assemble* at 10:30 AM.
Our new model *is longer in length* than the old one.	Our new model is *longer* than the old one.
If you are not satisfied, *return it back* to us.	If you are not satisfied, *return* it to us.
Tod Wilson is the *present incumbent.*	Tod Wilson is the *incumbent.*
One should know the *basic fundamentals* of clear writing.	One should know the *fundamentals* of clear writing.

Needless Repetition	Repetition Eliminated
The *consensus of opinion* is that the tax is unfair.	The *consensus* is that the tax is unfair.
By acting now, we can finish *sooner than if we wait until a later date.*	By acting now, we can finish *sooner.*
At the present time, we *are* conducting two clinics.	We *are* conducting two clinics.
As a matter of interest, I am interested in learning your procedure.	I am *interested* in learning your procedure.
We should *plan in advance for the future.*	We should *plan.*

Determining Emphasis in Sentence Design

The sentences you write should give the right emphasis to content. Any written business communication contains a number of items of information, not all of which are equally important. Some are very important, such as a conclusion in a report or the objective in a message. Others are relatively unimportant. Your task as a writer is to form your sentences to communicate the importance of each item.

- You should give every item its due emphasis.

Sentence length affects emphasis. Short, simple sentences carry more emphasis than long, involved ones. They stand out and call attention to their contents. Thus, they give the reader a single message without the interference of related or supporting information.

- Short sentences emphasize contents.

Longer sentences give less emphasis to their contents. When a sentence contains two or more ideas, the ideas share emphasis. How they share it depends on how the sentence is constructed. If two ideas are presented equally (in independent clauses, for example), they get about equal emphasis. But if they are not presented equally (for example, in an independent and a dependent clause), one gets more emphasis than the other.

- Long sentences de-emphasize contents.

To illustrate the varying emphasis you can give information, consider this example. You have two items of information to write. One is that the company lost money last year. The other is that its sales volume reached a record high. You could present the information in at least three ways. First, you could give both items equal emphasis by placing them in separate short sentences:

The company lost money last year. The loss occurred in spite of record sales.

Second, you could present the two items in the same sentence with emphasis on the lost money.

Although the company enjoyed record sales last year, it lost money.

Third, you could present the two items in one sentence with emphasis on the sales increase:

The company enjoyed record sales last year, although it lost money.

Which way would you choose? The answer depends on how much emphasis each item deserves. You should think the matter through and follow your best judgment. But the point is clear: Your choice makes a difference.

- Determining emphasis is a matter of good judgment.

The following paragraphs illustrate the importance of thinking logically to determine emphasis. In the first, each item of information gets the emphasis of a short sentence and none stands out. However, the items are not equally important and do not deserve equal emphasis. Notice, also, the choppy effect that the succession of short sentences produces.

The main building was inspected on October 1. Mr. George Wills inspected the building. Mr. Wills is a vice president of the company. He found that the building has 6,500 square feet of floor space. He also found that it has 2,400 square feet of storage space. The new store must have a minimum of 6,000 square feet of floor space. It must have 2,000 square feet of storage space. Thus, the main building exceeds

the space requirements for the new store. Therefore, Mr. Wills concluded that the main building is adequate for the company's needs.

In the next paragraph, some of the items are subordinated, but not logically. The really important information does not receive the emphasis it deserves. Logically, these two points should stand out: (1) the building is large enough and (2) storage space exceeds minimum requirements. But they do not stand out in this version:

Mr. George Wills, who inspected the main building on October 1, is a vice president of the company. His inspection, which supports the conclusion that the building is large enough for the proposed store, uncovered these facts. The building has 6,500 square feet of floor space and 2,400 square feet of storage space, which is more than the minimum requirement of 6,000 and 2,000 square feet, respectively, of floor and storage space.

The third paragraph shows good emphasis of the important points. The short beginning sentence emphasizes the conclusion. The supporting facts that the building exceeds the minimum floor and storage space requirements receive main-clause emphasis. The less important facts, such as the reference to George Wills, are treated subordinately. Also, the most important facts are placed at the points of emphasis—the beginning and ending.

The main building is large enough for the new store. This conclusion, reached by Vice President George Wills following his October 1 inspection of the building, is based on these facts. The building's 6,500 square feet of floor space exceed the minimum requirement by 500 square feet. The 2,400 square feet of storage space exceed the minimum requirement by 400 square feet.

The preceding illustrations show how sentence construction can determine emphasis. You can make items stand out, you can treat them equally, or you can de-emphasize them. The choices are yours. But what you do must be the result of good, sound thinking and not simply a matter of chance.

Giving the Sentences Unity

- All parts of a sentence should concern one thought.

Good sentences have unity. For a sentence to have unity, all of its parts must combine to form one clear thought. In other words, all the things put in a sentence should have a good reason for being together.

PART 2   Fundamentals of Business Writing

Violations of unity in sentence construction fall into three categories: (1) unrelated ideas, (2) excessive detail, and (3) illogical constructions.

There are three causes of unity error.

Unrelated Ideas. Placing unrelated ideas in a sentence is the most obvious violation of unity. Putting two or more ideas in a sentence is not grammatically wrong, but the ideas must have a reason for being together. They must combine to complete the single goal of the sentence.

First, placing unrelated ideas in a sentence violates unity.

You can give unity to sentences that contain unrelated ideas in three basic ways: (1) You can put the ideas in separate sentences. (2) You can make one of the ideas subordinate to the other. (3) You can add words that show how the ideas are related. The first two of these techniques are illustrated by the revisions of the following sentence:

You can avoid this error by (1) putting unrelated ideas in separate sentences, (2) subordinating an idea, or (3) adding words that show relationship.

Mr. Jordan is our sales manager, and he has a degree in law.

Perhaps the two ideas are related, but the words do not tell how. A better arrangement is to put each in a separate sentence:

Mr. Jordan is our sales manager. He has a law degree.

Or the two ideas could be kept in one sentence by subordinating one to the other. In this way, the main clause provides the unity of the sentence.

Mr. Jordan, our sales manager, has a law degree.

Adding words to show the relationship of ideas is illustrated in the revision of the following example:

Our production increased in January, and our equipment is wearing out.

The sentence has two ideas that seem unrelated. One way of improving it is to make a separate sentence of each idea. A closer look reveals, however, that the two ideas really are related. The words just do not show how. Thus, the sentence could be revised to show how:

Even though our equipment is wearing out, our production increased in January.

The following contrasting pairs of sentences further illustrate thé technique:

Unrelated	Improved
Our territory is the southern half of the state, and our salespeople cannot cover it thoroughly.	Our territory is the southern half of the state. Our salespeople cannot cover it thoroughly.
Using the cost-of-living calculator is simple, but no tool will work well unless it is explained clearly.	Using the cost-of-living calculator is simple, but, like any tool, it will not work well unless it is explained clearly.
We concentrate on energy-saving products, and 70 percent of our business comes from them.	As a result of our concentration on energy-saving products, 70 percent of our business comes from them.

Excessive Detail. Putting too much detail into one sentence tends to hide the central thought. If the detail is important, you should put it in a separate sentence.

Excessive detail is another cause of lack of unity. If the detail is important, put it in a separate sentence. This means using short sentences.

This suggestion strengthens another given earlier in the chapter—the suggestion that you use short sentences. Obviously, short sentences cannot have much detail. Long sentences—full of detail—definitely lead to lack of unity, as illustrated in these contrasting examples:

Excessive Detail	Improved
Our New York offices, considered plush in the 1990s, but now badly in need of renovation, as is the case with most offices that have not been maintained, have been abandoned.	Considered plush in the 1990s, our New York offices have not been maintained properly. As they badly need repair, we have abandoned them.

Excessive Detail

We have attempted to trace the Plytec insulation you ordered from us October 1, and about which you inquired in your October 10 message, but we have not yet been able to locate it, although we are sending you a rush shipment immediately.

In 2003, when I, a small-town girl from a middle-class family, began my studies at Bradley University, which is widely recognized for its business administration program, I set my goal for a career with a large public company.

Improved

We are sending you a rush shipment of Plytec insulation immediately. Following your October 10 inquiry, we attempted to trace your October 1 order. We were unable to locate it.

A small-town girl from a middle-class family, I entered Bradley University in 2003. I selected Bradley because of its widely recognized business administration program. From the beginning, my goal was a career with a large public company.

- Illogical constructions can rob a sentence of unity.

Illogical Constructions. Illogical constructions destroy sentence unity. These constructions result primarily from illogical thinking. Illogical thinking is too complex for meaningful study here, but a few typical examples should acquaint you with the possibilities. Then, by thinking logically, you should be able to reduce illogical constructions in your writing.

- Active and passive voice in the same sentence can violate unity.

The first example contains two main thoughts in two correct clauses. But one clause is in active voice (*we cut*), and the other is in passive voice (*quality was reduced*).

First we cut prices, and then quality was reduced.

We achieve unity by making both clauses active, as in this example:

First we cut prices, and then we reduced quality.

- So can mixed constructions.

The mixed constructions of the following sentence do not make a clear and logical thought. The technical explanation is that the beginning clause belongs with a complex sentence, while the last part is the predicate of a simple sentence.

Because our salespeople are inexperienced caused us to miss our quota.

Revised for good logic, the sentence might read:

The inexperience of our salespeople caused us to miss our quota.

These sentences further illustrate the point:

Illogical Construction

Job rotation is when you train people by moving them from job to job.

Knowing that she objected to the price was the reason we permitted her to return the goods.

I never knew an executive who was interested in helping workers who had got into problems that caused them to worry.

My education was completed in 2004, and then I began work as a manager for Home Depot.

Improved

Job rotation is a training method in which people are moved from job to job.

Because we knew she objected to the price, we permitted her to return the goods.

I never knew an executive who was interested in helping worried workers with their problems.

I completed my education in 2004 and then began work as a manager for Home Depot.

Arranging Sentences for Clarity

- Clear writing requires that you follow the established rules of grammar.

As you know, various rules of grammar govern the structure of sentences. You know, for example, that modifying words must follow a definite sequence—that altering the sequence changes meaning. "A venetian blind" means one thing. "A blind Venetian" means quite another. Long-established rules of usage determine the meaning.

- These rules are based on custom and logical relationships.

Many such rules exist. Established by centuries of use, these rules are not merely arbitrary requirements. Rather, they are based on custom and on logical relationships between words. In general, they are based on the need for clear communication.

Take the rule concerning dangling modifiers. Dangling modifiers confuse meaning by modifying the wrong words. On the surface, this sentence appears correct: "Believing that the price would drop, our purchasing agents were instructed not to buy." But the sentence is correct only if the purchasing agents did the believing—which is not the case. The modifying phrase dangles, and the intended meaning was probably this: "Believing that the price would drop, we instructed our purchasing agents not to buy."

- For example, dangling modifiers confuse meaning.

Other rules of grammar also help to make writing clear. Unparallel constructions leave wrong impressions. Pronouns that do not clearly refer to a definite preceding word are vague and confusing. Subject–verb disagreements confuse the reader. The list goes on and on. The rules of grammar are useful in writing clear sentences. You should know them and follow them. You will want to study Chapter 17 for a review of these rules and complete the diagnostic exercise at the chapter end for feedback on your understanding of them.

- So do unparallel constructions, pronouns without antecedents, and subject–verb disagreements.

CARE IN PARAGRAPH DESIGN

Paragraphing is also important to clear communication. Paragraphs show the reader where topics begin and end, thus helping organize information in the reader's mind. Paragraphs also help make ideas stand out.

- Paragraphing shows and emphasizes organization.

How one should design paragraphs is hard to explain, for the procedure is largely mental. Designing paragraphs requires the ability to organize and relate information. It involves the use of logic and imagination. But we can say little that would help you in these activities. The best we can do is give the following points on paragraph structure.

- It involves logical thinking.

Giving the Paragraphs Unity

Like sentences, paragraphs should have unity. When applied to paragraph structure, unity means that a paragraph builds around a single topic or idea. Thus, everything you include in a paragraph should develop this topic or idea. When you have finished the paragraph, you should be able to say, "Everything in this paragraph belongs together because every part concerns every other part."

- The contents of a paragraph should concern one topic or idea (unity).

Unity is not always easy to determine. As all of a message or a report may concern a single topic, one could say that the whole message or report has unity. One could say the same about a major division of a report or a long paper. Obviously, paragraph unity concerns smaller units than these. Generally, it concerns the next largest unit of thought above a sentence.

- But unity can vary in breadth. Paragraph unity concerns a narrow topic.

A violation of unity is illustrated in the following paragraph from an application letter. As the goal of the paragraph is to summarize the applicant's coursework, all the sentences should pertain to coursework. By shifting to personal qualities, the third sentence violates paragraph unity. Taking this sentence out would correct the fault.

At the university I studied all the basic accounting courses as well as specialized courses in taxation, international accounting, and computer security. I also took specialized coursework in the behavioral areas, with emphasis on human relations. Realizing the value of human relations in business, I also actively participated in organizations, such as Sigma Nu (social fraternity), Alpha Kappa Psi (professional fraternity), Intramural Soccer, and A cappella. I selected my elective coursework to round out my general business education. Among my electives were courses in investments, advanced business report writing, financial policy, and management information systems. A glance at my résumé will show you the additional courses that round out my training.

Keeping Paragraphs Short

As a general rule, you should keep your paragraphs short. This suggestion overlaps the suggestion about unity, for if your paragraphs have unity, they will be short.

- Generally, paragraphs should be short.

As noted earlier, paragraphs help the reader follow the writer's organization plan. Writing marked by short paragraphs identifies more of the details of that plan. In

- Short paragraphs show organization better than long ones.

Uniqueness and Clarity in a Definition

Written by a fifth grader, the following definition of a nut and bolt is a classic:

A bolt is a thing like a stick of hard metal, such as iron, with a square bunch on one end and a lot of scratches going round and round the other end. A nut is similar to the bolt only just the opposite, being a hole in a little square sawed off short with rings also around the inside of the hole.

addition, such writing is inviting to the eye. People simply prefer to read writing with frequent paragraph breaks.

- Most readers prefer to read short paragraphs.

This last point is easily proved by illustration. Assume you have a choice of reading either of two business reports on the same subject. One report has long paragraphs. Its pages appear solid with type. The second report has short paragraphs and thus provides frequent rest stops. You can see the rest stops at first glance. Now, which would you choose? No doubt, you would prefer the report with short paragraphs. It is more inviting, and it appears less difficult. Perhaps the difference is largely psychological, but it is a very real difference.

- About eight lines is a good average length.

How long a paragraph should be depends on its contents—on what must be included to achieve unity. Readability research has suggested an average length of eight lines for longer papers such as reports. Shorter paragraphs are appropriate for messages.

- But length can and should vary with need.

Keep in mind that these suggestions concern only an average. Some good paragraphs may be quite long—well over the average. Some paragraphs can be very short—as short as one line. One-line paragraphs are an especially appropriate means of emphasizing major points in business messages. A one-line paragraph may be all that is needed for a goodwill closing comment.

- A good practice is to question paragraphs over 12 lines.

A good rule to follow is to question the unity of all long paragraphs—say, those longer than 12 lines. If after looking over such a paragraph you conclude that it has unity, leave it as it is. But you will sometimes find more than one topic. When you do, make each topic into a separate paragraph.

Making Good Use of Topic Sentences

- Topic sentences can help make good paragraphs. But not every paragraph must have a topic sentence.

One good way of organizing paragraphs is to use topic sentences. The topic sentence expresses the main idea of a paragraph, and the remaining sentences build around and support it. In a sense, the topic sentence serves as a headline for the paragraph, and all the other sentences supply the story. Not every paragraph must have a topic sentence. Some paragraphs, for example, introduce ideas, relate succeeding items, or present an assortment of facts that lead to no conclusion. The central thought of such paragraphs is difficult to put into a single sentence. Even so, you should use topic sentences whenever you can. You should use them especially in writing reports that discuss a number of topics and subtopics. Using topic sentences forces you to find the central idea of each paragraph and helps you check paragraph unity.

- Placement of the topic sentence depends on the writer's plan.

How a topic sentence should fit into a paragraph depends primarily on the subject matter and the writer's plan. Some subject matter develops best if details are presented first and then followed by a conclusion or a summary statement (the topic sentence). Other subject matter develops best if it is introduced by the conclusion or the summary statement. Yet other arrangements are possible. You must make the decision, and you should base it on your best judgment. Your judgment should be helped, however, by a knowledge of the paragraph arrangements most commonly used.

Topic Sentence First. The most common paragraph arrangement begins with the topic sentence and continues with the supporting material. As this arrangement fits most units of business information, you should find it useful. In fact, the arrangement is so appropriate for business information that one company's writing manual suggests that it be used for virtually all paragraphs.

• The topic sentence can come first.

To illustrate the writing of a paragraph in which the topic sentence comes first, take a paragraph reporting on economists' replies to a survey question asking their view of business activity for the coming year. The facts to be presented are these: 13 percent of the economists expected an increase; 28 percent expected little or no change; 59 percent expected a downturn; 87 percent of those who expected a downturn thought it would come in the first quarter. The obvious conclusion—and the subject for the topic sentence—is that the majority expected a decline in the first quarter. Following this reasoning, we would develop a paragraph like this:

> *A majority of the economists consulted think that business activity will drop during the first quarter of next year.* Of the 185 economists interviewed, 13 percent looked for continued increases in business activity, and 28 percent anticipated little or no change from the present high level. The remaining 59 percent looked for a recession. Of this group, nearly all (87 percent) believed that the downturn would occur during the first quarter of the year.

Topic Sentence at End. The second most common paragraph arrangement places the topic sentence at the end, usually as a conclusion. Paragraphs of this kind usually present the supporting details first, and from these details they lead readers to the conclusion. Such paragraphs often begin with what may appear to be a topic sentence. But the final sentence covers their real meat, as in this illustration:

• It can come last.

> The significant role of inventories in the economic picture should not be overlooked. At present, inventories represent 3.8 months' supply. Their dollar value is the highest in history. If considered in relation to increased sales, however, they are not excessive. In fact, they are well within the range generally believed to be safe. *Thus, inventories are not likely to cause a downward swing in the economy.*

Topic Sentence within the Paragraph. A third arrangement places the topic sentence somewhere within the paragraph. This arrangement is rarely used, for good reason. It does not emphasize the topic sentence, although the topic sentence usually deserves emphasis. Still, you can sometimes justify using this arrangement for special effect, as in this example:

• Or it can come in the middle.

> Numerous materials have been used in manufacturing this part. And many have shown quite satisfactory results. *Material 329, however, is superior to them all.* When built with material 329, the part is almost twice as strong as when built with the next best material. It is also three ounces lighter. Most important, it is cheaper than any of the other products.

Leaving out Unnecessary Detail

You should include in your paragraphs only the information needed. The chances are that you have more information than the reader needs. Thus, a part of your communication task is to select what you need and discard what you do not need.

• In writing paragraphs, leave out unnecessary information.

What you need, of course, is a matter of judgment. You can judge best by putting yourself in your reader's place. Ask yourself questions such as these: How will the information be used? What information will be used? What will not be used? Then make your decisions. If you follow this procedure, you will probably leave out much that you originally intended to use.

• But deciding what to include is a matter of judgment.

The following paragraph from a message to maintenance workers presents excessive information.

> In reviewing the personnel records in our company database, I found that several items in your file were incomplete. The section titled "work history" has blanks for

three items of information. The first is for dates employed. The second is for company name. And the third is for type of work performed. On your record only company name was entered, leaving two items blank. Years employed or your duties were not indicated. This information is important. It is reviewed by your supervisors every time you are considered for promotion or for a pay increase. Therefore, it must be completed. I request that you sign on the company portal and update your personnel record at your earliest convenience.

The message says much more than the reader needs to know. The goal is to have the reader update the personnel record, and everything else is of questionable value. This revised message is better:

Please sign on the company portal at your earliest convenience to update your personnel record.

Giving the Paragraphs Movement

- Each paragraph should move an additional step toward the goal.

Good writing has movement. Movement is the writing quality that takes the reader toward the goal in definite and logical steps, without side trips and backward shifts.

The progress is steadily forward—step by step. The sentences move step by step to reach the paragraph goal, and the paragraphs move step by step to reach the overall goal.

Perhaps movement is best explained by example:

Three reasons justify moving from the Crowton site. First, the building rock in the Crowton area is questionable. The failure of recent geologic explorations in the area appears to confirm suspicions that the Crowton deposits are nearly exhausted. Second, the distances from the Crowton site to major markets make transportation costs unusually high. Obviously, any savings in transportation costs will add to company profits. Third, the obsolescence of much of the equipment at the Crowton plant makes this an ideal time for relocation. The old equipment at the Crowton plant could be scrapped.

The flow of thought in this paragraph is orderly. The first sentence sets up the paragraph structure and the parts of that structure follow.

SUMMARY BY CHAPTER OBJECTIVES

1
Explain the role of adaptation in writing clear sentences.

1. Writing that communicates uses words that the reader understands and sentence structures that organize the message clearly in the reader's mind. It is writing that is *adapted* to the reader.

2
Write short, clear sentences by limiting sentence content and economizing on words.

2. In general, you should use short sentences, especially when adapting to readers with low reading ability. Do this in two ways:
   - Limit sentence content by breaking up those that are too long.
   - Use words economically by following these specific suggestions:
     — Avoid cluttering phrases (*if* rather than *in the event that*).
     — Eliminate surplus words—words that contribute nothing (*It will be noted that*).
     — Avoid roundabout ways of saying things (*decreases* rather than *can be observed to be decreasing*).
     — Avoid unnecessary repetition (*In my opinion, I think*).

3
Design sentences that give the right emphasis to content.

3. Give every item you communicate the emphasis it deserves by following these suggestions:
   - Use short sentences to emphasize points.
   - Combine points in longer sentences to de-emphasize them.
   - But how you combine points (by equal treatment, by subordination) determines the emphasis given.

4. Achieve unity and clarity in your sentences.
   - Make certain all the information in a sentence belongs together—that it forms a unit. These suggestions help:
     — Eliminate excessive detail.
     — Combine only related thoughts.
     — Avoid illogical constructions.
   - Ensure clarity by following the conventional rules of writing (standards of punctuation, grammar, and such).

5. Design your paragraphs for clear communication by following these standards:
   - Give the paragraphs unity.
   - Keep the paragraphs short.
   - Use topic sentences effectively, usually at the beginning but sometimes within and at the end of the paragraph.
   - Leave out unessential details.
   - Give the paragraphs movement.

4 Employ unity and clarity in writing effective sentences.

5 Compose paragraphs that are short and unified, use topic sentences effectively, show movement, and communicate clearly.

1. How are sentence length and sentence design related to adaptation?
2. Discuss this comment: "Long, involved sentences tend to be difficult to understand. Therefore, the shorter the sentence, the better."
3. What is the effect of sentence length on emphasis?
4. How can unity apply equally well to a sentence, to a paragraph, and to longer units of writing?
5. What are the principal causes of lack of unity in sentences?
6. Discuss this comment: "Words carry the message. They would carry the same meanings with or without paragraphing. Therefore, paragraphing has no effect on communication."
7. Defend the use of short paragraphs in report writing.
8. "Topic sentences merely repeat what the other sentences in the paragraph say. As they serve only to add length, they should be eliminated." Discuss.

CRITICAL THINKING EXERCISES

Instructions, Sentences 1–8: Break up these sentences into shorter, more readable sentences.

1. Records were set by both the New York Stock Exchange Composite Index, which closed at 5,585.50, up 27.08 points, topping its previous high of 5,558.42, set Wednesday, and Standard & Poor's 500 Index, which finished at 990.14, up 3.90, moving up significantly, also set a five-day high.
2. Dealers attributed the rate decline to several factors, including expectations that the U.S. Treasury will choose to pay off rather than refinance some $4 billion of government obligations that fall due next month, an action that would absorb even further the available supplies of short-term government securities, leaving more funds chasing skimpier stocks of the securities.
3. If you report your income on a fiscal-year basis ending in 2004, you may not take credit for any tax withheld on your calendar-year 2004 earnings, inasmuch as your taxable year began in 2003, although you may include, as a part of your withholding tax credits against your fiscal 2005 tax liability, the amount of tax withheld during 2004.
4. The Consumer Education Committee is assigned the duties of keeping informed of the qualities of all consumer goods and services, especially of their strengths and shortcomings, of gathering all pertinent information on dealers' sales practices, with emphasis on practices involving honest and reasonable fairness, and of publicizing any of the information collected that may be helpful in educating the consumer.
5. The upswing in business activity that began in 2004 is expected to continue and possibly accelerate in 2005, and gross domestic product should rise by $664 billion, representing an 8 percent increase over 2004, which is significantly higher than the modest 5 percent increase of 2003.
6. As you will not get this part of Medicare automatically, even if you are covered by Social Security, you must sign up for it and pay $58.70 per month, which the government will match, if you want your physician's bills to be covered.
7. Students with approved excused absences from any of the hour examinations have the option of taking a special makeup examination to be given during dead week or of using their average grade on their examinations in the course as their grade for the work missed.
8. Although we have not definitely determined the causes for the decline in sales volume for the month, we know that during this period construction on the street adjacent to the store severely limited traffic flow and that because of resignations in the advertising department promotion efforts dropped well below normal.

Instructions, Sentences 9–38: Revise the following sentences for more economical wording.

9. In view of the fact that we financed the experiment, we were entitled to some profit.
10. We will deliver the goods in the near future.
11. Mr. Watts outlined his development plans on the occasion of his acceptance of the presidency.
12. I will talk to him with regard to the new policy.
13. The candidates who had the most money won.
14. There are many obligations that we must meet.
15. We purchased coats that are lined with rabbit fur.
16. Mary is of the conviction that service has improved.
17. Sales can be detected to have improved over last year.
18. It is essential that we take the actions that are necessary to correct the problem.
19. The chairperson is engaged in the activities of preparing the program.

20. Martin is engaged in the process of revising the application.

21. You should study all new innovations in your field.

22. In all probability, we are likely to suffer a loss this quarter.

23. The requirements for the job require a minimum of three years of experience.

24. In spite of the fact that the bill remains unpaid, they placed another order.

25. We expect to deliver the goods in the event that we receive the money.

26. In accordance with their plans, company officials sold the machinery.

27. This policy exists for the purpose of preventing dishonesty.

28. The salespeople who were most successful received the best rewards.

29. The reader will note that this area ranks in the top 5 percent in per capita income.

30. Our new coats are made of a fabric that is of the wrinkle-resistant variety.

31. Our office is charged with the task of counting supplies not used in production.

32. Their salespeople are of the conviction that service is obsolete.

33. Losses caused by the strike exceeded the amount of $640,000.

34. This condition can be assumed to be critical.

35. Our goal is to effect a change concerning the overtime pay rate.

36. Mr. Wilson replaced the old antiquated machinery with new machinery.

37. We must keep this information from transpiring to others.

38. The consensus of opinion of this group is that Wellington was wrong.

Instructions, Paragraphs 39–43: Rewrite the following paragraphs in two ways to show different placement of the topic sentence and variations in emphasis of contents. Point out the differences in meaning in each of your paragraphs.

39. Jennifer has a good knowledge of office procedures. She works hard. She has performed her job well. She is pleasant most of the time, but she has a bad temper, which has led to many personal problems with the work group. Although I cannot recommend her for promotion, I approve a 5 percent raise for her.

40. Last year our sales increased 7 percent in California and 9 percent in Arizona. Nevada had the highest increase, with 14 percent. Although all states in the western region enjoyed increases, Oregon recorded only a 2 percent gain. Sales in Washington increased 3 percent.

41. I majored in marketing at Darden University and received a B.S. degree in 2004. Among the marketing courses I took were marketing strategy, promotion, marketing research, marketing management, and consumer behavior. These and other courses prepared me specifically for a career in retailing. Included, also, was a one-semester internship in retailing with Macy's Department Stores.

42. Our records show that Penn motors cost more than Oslo motors. The Penns have less breakdown time. They cost more to repair. I recommend that we buy Penn motors the next time we replace worn-out motors. The longer working life offsets Penn's cost disadvantage. So does its better record for breakdown.

43. Recently China ordered a large quantity of wheat from the United States. Likewise, Germany ordered a large quantity. Other countries continued to order heavily, resulting in a dramatic improvement in the outlook for wheat farming. Increased demand by Eastern European countries also contributed to the improved outlook.

CHAPTER FOUR

Writing for Effect

CHAPTER OBJECTIVES

Upon completing this chapter, you will be able to write business communications that emphasize key points and have a positive effect on human relations. To reach this goal, you should be able to

1 Explain the need for effect in writing business messages.

2 Use a conversational style that eliminates the old language of business and "rubber stamps."

3 Use the you-viewpoint to build goodwill.

4 Employ positive language to achieve goodwill and other desired effects.

5 Explain the techniques of achieving courtesy.

6 Use the four major techniques for emphasis in writing.

7 Write documents that flow smoothly through the use of a logical order helped by the four major transitional devices.

Affecting Human Relations through Writing

To prepare yourself for this chapter, once again play the role of a small business manager and Max Schwartz's superior. As you review Max's writing, you see more evidence of how his communication shortcomings affect your company's effectiveness as it strives to compete. This new evidence appears in the messages Max writes—primarily letters and email. These messages go to the people inside and outside the company. They affect the human relationships that go far to determine the success of the operation. Poorly written, insensitive messages can produce serious negative reactions. Typical of Max's messages is the following letter:

Dear Mr. Morley:

Your December 3d complaint was received and contents noted. After reviewing the facts, I regret to report that I must refuse your claim. If you will read the warranty brochure, you will see that the shelving you bought is designed for light loads—a maximum of 800 pounds. You should have bought the heavy-duty product.

I regret the damage this mistake caused you and trust that you will see our position. Hoping to be of service to you in the future, I remain,

Sincerely yours,

In this message you detect more than just the readability problem you saw in Max's reports. The words are not polite. Instead of showing concern for the reader, they are blunt, tactless, and unfriendly. Overall, they leave a bad impression in the reader's mind—the impression of a writer, and a business, unconcerned about the needs for good human relations. This chapter will show you how to avoid such impressions.

BUSINESS ETIQUETTE AND THE NEED FOR EFFECT

As noted in the preceding chapters, clarity will be your major concern in most of the writing you will do in business—especially your writing within the organization. Most of this writing concerns matters that do not involve the readers personally. Thus you can communicate the information in a matter-of-fact way. Your primary concern will be to communicate, and you will want to do so quickly and accurately. This is the way your fellow workers want and expect you to write. Even so, you will want to maintain the courtesy and friendliness that is so vital to good working relationships.

- Written communication within a business primarily requires clarity.

When you write messages that tend to be more personal, however, you will be concerned about more than just communicating information. Most often this will be the case when you communicate with people outside the organization and a major concern is to gain or maintain favorable relationships. Email messages or letters written for a company to its customers are examples of such communications. The information in these messages will be important, of course. In fact, probably it will be the most important part. But you also will need to communicate certain effects—effects that tend to convey a favorable image of the company.

- Business writing requires clarity and planned effect. The goodwill effect is valuable to business.

One effect you will need to communicate is the goodwill effect. Building goodwill through written messages is good business practice. Wise business leaders know that the success of their business is affected by what people think about the business. They know that what people think about a business is influenced by their human contact with that business: the services they receive, how they are treated, the manners (etiquette) displayed, and such. The written word is a major form of human contact.

The goodwill effect in messages is not desirable for business reasons alone. It is, quite simply, the effect most of us want in our relations with people. The things we do and say to create goodwill are the things we enjoy doing and saying. They are friendly, courteous things that make relations between people enjoyable. Most of us would

- Most people enjoy building goodwill.

. . . you-attitude requires writers first to view a real-world situation from the reader's perspective and then to show in the text of the document a sensitivity to the reader's perspective. . . . While simply using "you" and "yours" rater than "I" or "mine" will sometimes help to express a you-attitude, it would be both simple-minded and incorrect to equate you-attitude with the dominance of "you" in the text.

Lilita Rodman, University of British Columbia

Lilita Rodman, "You-Attitude: A Linguistic Perspective," *Business Communication Quarterly* 64, no. 4 (December 2001): 11–12.

want to do and say them even if they were not profitable. Clearly, they display the good manners of business practice. They display good business etiquette.

As you read the following chapters, you will see that other effects sometimes ensure the success of written messages. For example, in writing to persuade a reader to accept an unfavorable decision, you can use the techniques of persuasion. In applying for a job, you can use writing techniques that emphasize your qualifications. And in telling bad news, you can use techniques that play down the negative parts. These are but a few of the effects that you may find helpful in writing.

Getting such effects in messages is largely a matter of skillful writing and of understanding how people respond to words. It involves keeping certain attitudes in mind and using certain writing techniques to work them into your documents. The following review of these attitudes and techniques should help you get the effects you need.

- For their success, letters and some email messages often require other effects.

- Getting the desired effects is a matter of writing skill and of understanding people.

CONVERSATIONAL STYLE

- Writing in conversational language has a favorable effect.

One technique that helps build the goodwill effect is to write in conversational language. By conversational language we mean language that resembles conversation. It is warm and natural. Such language leaves an impression that people like. It is also the language we use most and understand best. Because it is easily understood, it is good business etiquette to use it.

Resisting the Tendency to Be Formal

- Writing in conversational language is not easy, for we tend to be stiff and formal.

Writing conversationally is not as easy as you might think, because most of us tend to write formally. When faced with a writing task, we change character. Instead of writing in friendly, conversational language, we write in stiff and stilted words. We seek the big word, the difficult word. The result is a cold and unnatural style—one that doesn't produce the goodwill effect you want your messages to have. The following examples illustrate this problem and how to correct it.

Stiff and Dull	Conversational
Reference is made to your May 7 email, in which you describe the approved procedure for initiating a claim.	Please refer to your May 7 email, in which you tell how to file a claim.
Enclosed herewith is the brochure about which you make inquiry.	Enclosed is the brochure you asked about.
In reply to your July 11 letter, please be informed that your adherence to instructions outlined therein will greatly facilitate attainment of our objective.	By following the procedures you listed in your July 11 letter, you will help us reach our goal.

Grammar and Style Checkers Help Identify Clichés, Colloquialisms, and Jargon

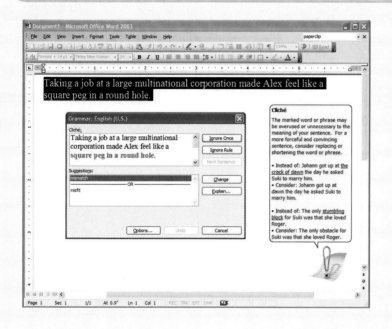

While not perfect, grammar and style checkers can help writers identify some clichés, colloquialisms, and jargon that creep into their writing. The checker here illustrates that it found a cliché and provided two suggestions for correcting it. By clicking on the explain button, the office assistant will tell the writer what it determines is the case here. Although this software can help, writers still need to be able to identify the trite and overused expressions the software misses. Also, writers need to be able to recast the sentences for clarity and sincerity.

Stiff and Dull

This is in reply to your letter of December 1, expressing concern that you do not have a high school diploma and asking if a GED would suffice as prerequisite for the TAA Training Program.

I shall be most pleased to avail myself of your kind suggestion when and if prices decline.

Conversational

The GED you mention in your December 1 letter qualifies you for the TAA Training Program.

I'll gladly follow your suggestion if the price falls.

Cutting Out "Rubber Stamps"

Rubber stamps (also called *clichés*) are expressions used by habit every time a certain type of situation occurs. They are used without thought and do not fit the present situation exclusively. As the term indicates, they are used much as you would use a rubber stamp.

Because they are used routinely, rubber stamps communicate the effect of routine treatment, which is not likely to impress readers favorably. Such treatment tells readers that the writer has no special concern for them—that the present case is being handled in the same way as others. In contrast, words specially selected for this case are likely to impress. They show the writer's concern for and interest in the readers. Clearly, specially selected wording is the better choice for producing a goodwill effect. Some examples of rubber stamps you have no doubt heard before are listed below. These phrases, while once quite appropriate, have become stale with overuse.

- Rubber stamps are expressions used by habit every time a certain type of situation occurs.

- They give the effect of routine treatment. It is better to use words written for the present case.

a blessing in disguise	last but not least
as good as gold	learning the ropes
back against the wall	leave no stone unturned
call the shots	to add insult to injury

Expressions from the old language of business are rubber stamps. Some new ones exist.

Some of the rubber stamps used today are relics from the old language of business—a way of writing that was in vogue over a century ago. In the early days of business writing, a heavily formal, stilted, and unnatural style developed. Messages typically began with expressions such as "your letter of the 7th inst. received . . ." and "your esteemed favor at hand . . ." They ended with dangling closes such as "trusting to be favored by your response . . ." and "thanking you in advance, I remain . . ." Messages were filled with expressions such as "deem it advisable," and "beg to advise," "this is to inform," and "wherein you state." Fortunately, these awkward and unnatural expressions have faded from use. Even so, a few of the old expressions remain with us, some with modern-day changes in wording. One example is the "thank you for your letter" form of opening sentence. Its intent may be sincere, but its roots in the old language of business and its overuse make it a rubber stamp. Another is the "if I can be of any further assistance, do not hesitate to call on me" type of close. Other examples of rubber stamps in this category are the following:

I am happy to be able to answer your message.

I have received your message.

This will acknowledge receipt of . . .

According to our records . . .

This is to inform you that . . .

In accordance with your instructions . . .

You can avoid rubber stamps by writing in your conversational vocabulary.

You do not need to know all the rubber stamps to stop using them. You do not even need to be able to recognize them. You only need to write in the language of good conversation, for these worn-out expressions are not a part of most conversational vocabularies. If you use rubber stamps at all, probably you learned them from reading other people's writings.

Proof through Contrasting Examples

The advantages of conversational writing over writing marked by old business language and rubber stamps are best proved by example. As you read the following contrasting sentences, note the overall effects of the words. The goodwill advantages of conversational writing are obvious.

Dull and Stiff	Friendly and Conversational
This is to advise that we deem it a great pleasure to approve subject of your request as per letter of the 12th inst.	Yes, you certainly may use the equipment you asked about in your letter of August 12.
Pursuant to this matter, I wish to state that the aforementioned provisions are unmistakably clear.	These contract provisions are clear on this point.
This will acknowledge receipt of your May 10th order for four dozen Docker slacks. Please be advised that they will be shipped in accordance with your instructions by UPS on May 16.	Four dozen Docker slacks should reach your store by the 18th. As you instructed, they were shipped today by UPS.
The undersigned wishes to advise that the aforementioned contract is at hand.	I have the contract.
Please be advised that you should sign the form before the 1st.	You should sign the form before the 1st.
Hoping this meets with your approval . . .	I hope you approve.
Submitted herewith is your notification of our compliance with subject standards.	Attached is notification of our compliance with the standards.

Dull and Stiff	Friendly and Conversational
Assuring you of our continued cooperation, we remain . . .	We will continue to cooperate.
Thanking you in advance . . .	I'll sincerely appreciate . . .
Herewith enclosed please find . . .	Enclosed is . . .
I deem it advisable . . .	I suggest . . .
I herewith hand you . . .	Here is . . .
Kindly advise at an early date.	Please let me know soon.

YOU-VIEWPOINT

Writing from the you-viewpoint (also called *you-attitude*) is another technique for building goodwill in written messages. As you will see in following chapters, it focuses interest on the reader. Thus, it is a technique for persuasion and for influencing people favorably. It is fundamental in the practice of business etiquette.

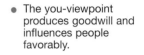

- The you-viewpoint produces goodwill and influences people favorably.

In a broad sense, you-viewpoint writing emphasizes the reader's interests and concerns. It emphasizes *you* and *your* and de-emphasizes *we* and *our*. But it is more than a matter of just using second-person pronouns. *You* and *your* can appear prominently in sentences that emphasize the we-viewpoint, as in this example: "If you do not pay by the 15th, you must pay a penalty." Likewise, *we* and *mine* can appear in sentences that emphasize the you-viewpoint, as in this example: "We will do whatever we can to protect your investment." The point is that the you-viewpoint is an attitude of mind. It is the attitude that places the reader in the center of things. Sometimes it just involves being friendly and treating people the way they like to be treated. Sometimes it involves skillfully handling people with carefully chosen words to make a desired impression. It involves all these things and more.

- The you-viewpoint emphasizes the reader's interests. It is an attitude of mind involving more than the use of *you* and *yours*.

The You-Viewpoint Illustrated

Although the you-viewpoint involves much more than word selection, examples of word selection help explain the technique. First, take the case of a person writing to present good news. This person could write from a self-centered point of view, beginning with such words as "I am happy to report . . ." Or he or she could begin with the

In face-to-face communication, words, voice, facial expressions, gestures, and such combine to determine the effect of the message. In writing, the printed word alone must do the job.

you-viewpoint words "You will be happy to know . . ." The messages are much the same, but the effects are different.

Next, take the case of a writer who must inform the reader that a request for credit has been approved. A we-viewpoint beginning could take this form: "We are pleased to have your new account." Some readers might view these words favorably. But some would sense a self-centered writer concerned primarily with making money. A you-viewpoint beginning would go something like this: "Your new charge account is now open for your convenience."

The third case is that of an advertising copywriter who must describe the merits of a digital camera. Advertising copywriters know the value of the you-viewpoint perhaps better than any other group. So no advertising copywriter would write anything like this: "We make Kodak digital cameras for three levels: beginner, intermediate, and professional." An advertising copywriter would probably bring the reader into the center of things and write about the product in reader-satisfaction language: "So that you can choose the one camera that is just right for you, Kodak makes cameras for you in three models: basic, standard, and full-featured."

The you-viewpoint can even be used in bad-news messages. For example, take the case of an executive who must say no to a professor's request for help on a research project. The bad news is made especially bad when it is presented in we-viewpoint words: "We cannot comply with your request to use our staff on your project, for it would cost us more than we can afford." A skilled writer using the you-viewpoint would look at the situation from this reader's point of view, find an explanation likely to satisfy this reader, and present the explanation in you-viewpoint language. The you-viewpoint response might take this form: "As a business professor well acquainted with the need for economizing in all phases of support, you will understand why we must limit our staff to work in our office."

The following contrasting examples demonstrate the different effects that changes in viewpoint produce. With a bit of imagination, you should be able to supply information on the situations they cover.

- Even a bad-news situation can benefit from you-viewpoint wording.

We-Viewpoint	**You-Viewpoint**
We are happy to have your order for Hewlett-Packard products, which we are sending today by UPS.	Your selection of Hewlett-Packard products should reach you by Saturday, as they were shipped by UPS today.
We sell the Chicago cutlery set for the low price of $24 each and suggest a retail price of $36.50.	You can reap a $12.50 profit on each Chicago Cutlery set you sell at $36.50, for your cost is only $24.00.
Our policy prohibits us from permitting outside groups to use our equipment except on a cash-rental basis.	As your tax dollars pay our office expense, you will appreciate our policy of cutting operating costs by renting our equipment.
We have been quite tolerant of your past-due account and must now demand payment.	If you are to continue to enjoy the benefits of credit buying, you must clear your account now.
We have received your report of May 1.	Thank you for your report of May 1.
So that we may complete our file records on you, we ask that you submit to us your January report.	So that your file records may be completed, please send us your January report.
We have shipped the two dozen Cross desk sets you ordered.	Your two dozen Cross desk sets should reach you with this letter.
We require that you sign the sales slip before we will charge to your account.	For your protection, you are charged only after you have signed the sales slip.

A Point of Controversy

- Some say that the you-viewpoint is insincere and manipulative. It can be insincere, but it need not be. Using the you-viewpoint is just being courteous. Research supports its use.

The you-viewpoint has been a matter of some controversy. Its critics point out two major shortcomings: (1) it is insincere and (2) it is manipulative. In either event, they argue, the technique is dishonest. It is better, they say, to just "tell it as it is."

These arguments have some merit. Without question, the you-viewpoint can be used to the point of being insincere; and it can be obvious flattery. Thus it can be used to pursue unethical goals. But those who favor the technique argue that insincerity, flattery, and unethical manipulation need not—in fact, should not—be the result of you-viewpoint effort. The objective is to treat people courteously—the way they like to be treated. People like to be singled out for attention. They are naturally more interested in themselves than in the writer. Overuse of the technique, the defenders argue, does not justify not using it. Their argument is supported by research comparing readers' responses to a case written to determine the effect of the you-attitude. The study evaluated the readers' perception of the writer's tone, commitment to comply to the message, and satisfaction. It found support for using the you-viewpoint.[1]

- The you-viewpoint can manipulate. But condemn the goal, not the technique.

On the matter of manipulative use of the you-viewpoint, we must again concede a point. It is a technique of persuasion, and persuasion may have bad as well as good goals. Supporters of the you-viewpoint argue that it is bad goals and not the techniques used to reach them that should be condemned. Persuasion techniques used to reach good goals are good.

The correct approach appears to lie somewhere between the extremes. You do not have to use the you-viewpoint exclusively or eliminate it. You can take a middle ground. You can use the you-viewpoint when it is friendly and sincere and when your goals are ethical. In such cases, using the you-viewpoint is "telling it as it is"—or at least as it should be. With this position in mind, we apply the technique in the following chapters.

- A middle-ground approach is best. Use the you-viewpoint when it is the right thing to do.

ACCENT ON POSITIVE LANGUAGE

Whether your written message achieves its goal often will depend on the words you use. As you know, one can say anything in many ways, and each way conveys a different meaning. Much of the difference lies in the meanings of words.

- Of the many ways of saying anything, each has a unique meaning.

Effects of Words

Positive words are usually best for achieving your message goals. This is not to say that negative words have no place in business writing. Such words are strong and give emphasis, and you will sometimes want to use them. But your need will usually be for positive words, for such words are more likely to produce the effects you seek. When your goal is to change someone's position, for example, positive words are most likely to do the job. They tend to put the reader in the right frame of mind, and they emphasize the pleasant aspects of the goal. They also create the goodwill atmosphere we seek in most messages.

- Positive words are usually best for message goals, especially when persuasion and goodwill are needed.

Negative words tend to produce the opposite effects. They may stir up your reader's resistance to your goals, and they are likely to be highly destructive of goodwill. Thus, to reach your writing goals, you will need to study carefully the negativeness and positiveness of your words. You will need to select the words that are most appropriate in each case.

- Negative words stir up resistance and hurt goodwill.

In doing this you should generally be wary of strongly negative words. These words convey unhappy and unpleasant thoughts, and such thoughts usually detract from your goal. They include such words as *mistake, problem, error, damage, loss,* and *failure.* There are also words that deny—words such as *no, do not, refuse,* and *stop.* And there are words whose sounds or meanings have unpleasant effects. Examples would differ from person to person, but many would probably agree on these: *itch, guts, scratch, grime, sloppy, sticky, bloody,* and *nauseous.* Or how about *gummy, slimy, bilious,* and *soggy?* Run these negative words through your mind and think about the meanings they produce. You should find it easy to see that they tend to work against most of the goals you may have in your messages.

- So beware of strongly negative words (*mistake, problem*), words that deny (*no, do not*), and ugly words (*itch, guts*).

[1] Annette N. Shelby and Lamar Reinsch Jr., "Positive Emphasis and You-Attitude: An Empirical Study," *Journal of Business Communication* (October 1995): 319.

"Yes, I've learned from my mistakes. I've learned if you call them 'missed opportunities' you get in less trouble."

SOURCE: Copyright 2003 by Randy Glasbergen. www.glasbergen.com

Examples of Word Choice

To illustrate your positive-to-negative word choices in handling written messages, take the case of a company executive who had to deny a local civic group's request to use the company's meeting facilities. To soften the refusal, the executive could let the group use a conference room, which might be somewhat small for its purpose. The executive came up with this totally negative response:

> We *regret* to inform you that we *cannot* permit you to use our auditorium for your meeting, as the Ladies Investment Club asked for it first. We can, however, let you use our conference room, but it seats *only* 60.

The negative words are italicized. First, the positively intended message "We *regret* to inform you" is an unmistakable sign of coming bad news. "*Cannot* permit" contains an unnecessarily harsh meaning. And notice how the good-news part of the message is handicapped by the limiting word *only*.

Had the executive searched for more positive ways of covering the same situation, he or she might have written:

> Although the Ladies Investment Club has reserved the auditorium for Saturday, we can instead offer you our conference room, which seats 60.

Not a single negative word appears in this version. Both approaches achieve the primary objective of denying a request, but their effects on the reader differ sharply. There is no question as to which approach does the better job of building and holding goodwill.

For a second illustration, take the case of a writer granting the claim of a woman for cosmetics damaged in transit. Granting the claim, of course, is the most positive ending that such a situation can have. Even though this customer has had a somewhat unhappy experience, she is receiving what she wants. The negative language of an unskilled writer, however, can so vividly recall the unhappy aspects of the problem that the happy solution is moved to the background. As this negative version of the message illustrates, the effect is to damage the reader's goodwill:

> We received your claim in which you contend that we were responsible for *damage* to three cases of Estée Lauder lotion. We assure you that we sincerely *regret* the *problems* this has caused you. Even though we feel in all sincerity that your receiv-

ing clerks may have been *negligent,* we will assume the *blame* and replace the *damaged* merchandise.

Obviously, this version grants the claim grudgingly, and the company would profit from such an approach only if there were extenuating circumstances. The phrase "in which you contend" clearly implies some doubt about the legitimacy of the claim. Even the sincerely intended expression of regret only recalls to the reader's mind the event that caused all the trouble. And the negatives *blame* and *damage* only strengthen the recollection. Certainly, this approach is not conducive to goodwill.

In the following version of the same message, the writer refers only to positive aspects of the situation—what can be done to settle the problem. The job is done without using a negative word and without mentioning the situation being corrected or suspicions concerning the honesty of the claim. The goodwill effect of this approach is likely to maintain business relations with the reader:

> Three cases of Estée Lauder lotion are on their way to you by FedEx and should be on your sales floor by Saturday.

For additional illustrations, compare the differing results obtained from these contrasting positive-negative versions of messages (italics mark the negative words):

Negative	Positive
You *failed* to give us the fabric specifications of the chair you ordered.	So that you may have the one chair you want, will you please check your choice of fabric on the enclosed card?
Smoking is *not* permitted anywhere except in the lobby.	Smoking is permitted in the lobby only.
We *cannot* deliver until Friday.	We can deliver the goods on Friday.
Chock-O-Nuts do not have that *gummy, runny* coating that makes some candies *stick* together when they get hot.	The rich chocolate coating of Chock-O-Nuts stays crispy good throughout the summer months.
You were *wrong* in your conclusion, for paragraph 3 of our agreement clearly states	Please read paragraph 3 of our agreement, which explains . . .
We *regret* that we *overlooked* your coverage on this equipment and apologize for the *trouble* and *concern* it must have caused you.	You were quite right in believing that you have coverage on the equipment. We appreciate your calling the matter to our attention.
We *regret* to inform you that we must deny your request for credit.	For the time being, we can serve you on a cash basis only.
You should have known that the camera lens *cannot* be cleaned with tissue, for it is clearly explained in the instructions.	The instructions explain why the camera lens should be cleaned only with a nonscratch cloth.
Your May 7 *complaint* about our remote control is *not* supported by the evidence.	Review of the situation described in your May 7 email explains what happened when you used the remote control.

COURTESY

A major contributor to goodwill in business documents is courtesy. By courtesy we mean treating people with respect and friendly human concern. Used in business messages, courtesy is the foundation of business etiquette. It produces friendly relations between people. The result is a better human climate for solving business problems and doing business.

- Courtesy is a major contributor to goodwill in business documents.

Developing courtesy in a message involves a variety of specific techniques. First, it involves the three discussed previously: writing in conversational language, employing the you-viewpoint, and choosing words for positive effect. It also involves other techniques.

- Courtesy involves the preceding goodwill techniques.

A French General's Justification of Politeness

Once, at a diplomatic function, the great World War I leader Marshal Foch was maneuvered into a position in which he had to defend French politeness.

"There is nothing in it but wind," Foch's critic sneered.

"There is nothing in a tire but wind," the marshal responded politely, "but it makes riding in a car very smooth and pleasant."

Singling Out Your Reader

- It also involves writing directly for the one reader.

- This means writing for the one situation.

One of the other techniques is to single out and write directly to your reader. Messages that appear routine have a cold, impersonal effect. On the other hand, messages that appear to be written for one reader tend to make the reader feel important and appreciated.

To single out your reader in a message, you should write for the one situation. What you say throughout the document should make it clear that the reader is getting individual treatment. For example, a message granting a professor permission to quote company material in the professor's book could end with "We wish you the best of success on the book." This specially adapted comment is better than one that fits any similar case: "If we can be of further assistance, please let us know." Using the reader's name in the message text is another good way to show that the reader is being given special treatment. We can gain the reader's favor by occasionally making such references as "You are correct, Ms. Brock" or "As you know, Helen."

Refraining from Preaching

- The effect of courtesy is helped by not preaching (lecturing).

- Usually preaching is not intended. It often results from efforts to persuade.

- Elementary, flat, and obvious statements often sound preachy.

You can help give your documents a courteous effect by not preaching—that is, by avoiding the tone of a lecture or a sermon. Except in the rare cases in which the reader looks up to the writer, a preaching tone hurts goodwill. We human beings like to be treated as equals. We do not want to be bossed or talked down to. Thus, writing that suggests unequal writer–reader relations is likely to make the reader unhappy.

Preaching is usually not intended. It often occurs when the writer is trying to convince the reader of something, as in this example:

> You must take advantage of savings like this if you are to be successful. The pennies you save pile up. In time you will have dollars.

It is insulting to tell the reader something quite elementary as if it were not known. Such obvious information should be omitted.

Likewise, flat statements of the obvious fall into the preachy category. Statements like "Rapid inventory turnover means greater profits" are obvious to the experienced retailer and would probably produce negative reactions. So would most statements including such phrases as "you need," "you want," "you should," and "you must," for they tend to talk down to the reader.

Another form of preachiness takes this obvious question-and-answer pattern: "Would you like to make a deal that would make you a 38 percent profit? Of course you would!" What intelligent and self-respecting businessperson would not be offended by this approach?

Doing More Than Is Expected

- Doing more than necessary builds goodwill.

One sure way to gain goodwill is to do a little bit more than you have to do for your reader. We are all aware of how helpful little extra acts are in other areas of our per-

The language used in a message communicates more than the message. It tells how friendly, how formal, how careful the writer is—and more.

sonal relationships. Too many of us, however, do not use them in our messages. Perhaps in the mistaken belief that we are being concise, we include only the barest essentials in our messages. The result is brusque, hurried treatment, which is inconsistent with our efforts to build goodwill.

The writer of a message refusing a request for use of company equipment, for example, needs only to say no to accomplish the primary goal. This answer, of course, is blunt and totally without courtesy. A goodwill-conscious writer would explain and justify the refusal, perhaps suggesting alternative steps that the reader might take. A wholesaler's brief extra sentence to wish a retailer good luck on a coming promotion is worth the effort. So are an insurance agent's few words of congratulations in a message to a policyholder who has earned some distinction.

Likewise, a writer uses good judgment in an acknowledgment message that includes helpful suggestions about using the goods ordered. And in messages to customers a writer for a sales organization can justifiably include a few words about new merchandise received, new services provided, price reductions, and so on.

To those who say that these suggestions are inconsistent with the need for conciseness, we must answer that the information we speak of is needed to build goodwill. Conciseness concerns the number of words needed to say what you must say. It never involves leaving out information vital to any of your objectives. On the other hand, nothing we have said should be interpreted to mean that any kind or amount of extra information is justified. You must take care to use only the extra information you need to reach your goal.

- As the extras add length, they appear not to be concise. But conciseness means word economy—not leaving out essentials.

Avoiding Anger

Expressing anger in messages—letting off steam—may sometimes help you emotionally. But anger helps achieve the goal of a message only when that goal is to anger the

- Rarely is anger justified in messages. It destroys goodwill.

reader. The effect of angry words is to make the reader angry. With both writer and reader angry, the two are not likely to get together on whatever the message is about.

To illustrate the effect of anger, take the case of an insurance company employee who must write a message telling a policyholder that the policyholder has made a mistake in interpreting the policy and is not covered on the matter in question. The writer, feeling that any fool should be able to read the policy, might respond in these angry words:

If you had read Section IV of your policy, you would know that you are not covered on accidents that occur on water.

One might argue that these words "tell it as it is"—that what they say is true. Even so, they show anger and lack tact. Their obvious effect is to make the reader angry. A more tactful writer would refer courteously to the point of misunderstanding:

As a review of Section IV of your policy indicates, you are covered on accidents that occur on the grounds of your residence only.

Most of the comments made in anger do not provide needed information but merely serve to let the writer blow off steam. Such comments take many forms: sarcasm, insults, exclamations. You can see from the following examples that you should not use them in your writing:

No doubt, you expect us to hold your hand.

I cannot understand your negligence.

This is the third time you have permitted your account to be delinquent.

We will not tolerate this condition.

Your careless attitude has caused us a loss in sales.

We have had it!

We have no intention of permitting this condition to continue.

Being Sincere

- Efforts to be courteous must be sincere.

Courteous treatment is sincere treatment. If your messages are to be effective, people must believe you. You must convince them that you mean what you say and that your efforts to be courteous and friendly are well intended. That is, your messages must have the quality of sincerity.

- Sincerity results from believing in the techniques of courtesy.

The best way of getting sincerity into your writing is to believe in the techniques you use. If you honestly want to be courteous, if you honestly believe that you-viewpoint treatment leads to harmonious relations, and if you honestly think that tactful treatment spares your reader's sensitive feelings, you are likely to apply these techniques sincerely. Your sincerity will show in your writing.

- The goodwill effort can be overdone. Too much you-viewpoint sounds insincere.

Overdoing the Goodwill Techniques. There are, however, two major areas that you might alertly check. The first is the overdoing of your goodwill techniques. Perhaps through insincerity or as a result of overzealous effort, the goodwill techniques are frequently overdone. For example, you can easily refer too often to your reader by name in your efforts to write to the one person. Also, as shown in the following example, you-viewpoint effort can go beyond the bounds of reason.

So that you may be able to buy Kantrell equipment at an extremely low price and sell it at a tremendous profit, we now offer you the complete line at a 50 percent price reduction.

The following example, included in a form letter from the company president to a new charge customer, has a touch of unbelievability:

I was delighted today to see your name listed among Macy's new charge customers.

Or how about this one, taken from an adjustment message of a large department store?

We are extremely pleased to be able to help you and want you to know that your satisfaction means more than anything to us.

Avoiding Exaggeration. The second area that you should check is exaggerated statements. It is easy to see through most exaggerated statements; thus, they can give a mark of insincerity to your message. Exaggerations are overstatements of facts. Although some puffery is conventional in sales writing, even here bounds of propriety exist. The following examples clearly overstep these bounds:

Already thousands of new customers are beating paths to the doors of Martin dealers.

Never has there been, nor will there be, a fan as smooth running and whispering quiet as the North Wind.

Everywhere coffee drinkers meet, they are talking about the amazing whiteness Rembrandt gives their teeth.

Many exaggerated statements involve the use of superlatives. All of us use them, but only rarely do they fit the reality about which we communicate. Words like *greatest, most amazing, finest, healthiest,* and *strongest* are seldom appropriate. Other strong words may have similar effects—for example, *extraordinary, stupendous, delicious, more than happy, sensational, terrific, revolutionary, colossal,* and *perfection.* Such words cause us to question; we rarely believe them.

- Exaggerated statements are obviously insincere.

- Superlatives (*greatest, finest, strongest*) often suggest exaggeration.

THE ROLE OF EMPHASIS

Getting desired effects in writing often involves giving proper emphasis to the items in the message. Every message contains a number of facts, ideas, and so on that must be presented. Some of these items are more important than others. For example, the main goal of a message is very important. Supporting explanations and incidental facts are less important. A part of your job as a writer is to determine the importance of each item and to give each item the emphasis it deserves.

To give each item in your message proper emphasis, you must use certain techniques. By far the most useful are these four: position, space, structure, and mechanical devices. The following paragraphs explain each.

- Emphasis also determines effect. Every item communicated should get the proper emphasis.

- There are four basic emphasis techniques.

Emphasis by Position

The beginnings and endings of a writing unit carry more emphasis than the center parts. This rule of emphasis applies whether the unit is the message, a paragraph of the message, or a sentence within the paragraph. (See Figure 4–1.) We do not know why this is so. Some authorities think that the reader's fresh mental energy explains beginning emphasis. Some say that the last parts stand out because they are the most recent in the reader's mind. Whatever the explanation, research has suggested that this emphasis technique works.

In the message as a whole, the beginning and the closing are the major emphasis positions. Thus, you must be especially mindful of what you put in these places. The

- Position determines emphasis. Beginnings and endings carry emphasis.

- The first and last sentences of a message, the first and last sentences of a paragraph, and the first and last words of a sentence all carry more emphasis than the middle parts.

FIGURE 4–1

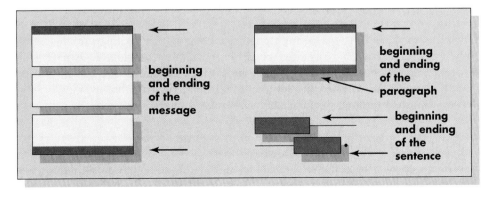

Emphasis by Position

beginnings and endings of the internal paragraphs are secondary emphasis positions. Your design of each paragraph should take this into account. To a lesser extent, the first and last words of each sentence carry more emphasis than the middle ones. Even in your sentence design, you can help determine the emphasis that your reader will give the points in your message. In summary, your organizational plan should place the points you want to stand out in these beginning and ending positions. You should bury the points you do not want to emphasize between these positions.

Space and Emphasis

The more you say about something, the more emphasis you give it; and the less you say about something, the less emphasis you give it. If your message devotes a full paragraph to one point and a scant sentence to another, the first point receives more emphasis. To give the desired effect in your message, you will need to say just enough about each item of information you present.

Sentence Structure and Emphasis

As we noted in Chapter 3, short, simple sentences call attention to their content and long, involved ones do not. In applying this emphasis technique to your writing, carefully consider the possible sentence arrangements of your information. Place the more important information in short, simple sentences so that it will not have to compete with other information for the reader's attention. Combine the less important information, taking care that the relationships are logical. In your combination sentences, place the more important material in independent clauses and the less important information in subordinate structures.

Mechanical Means of Emphasis

Perhaps the most obvious emphasis techniques are those that use mechanical devices. By *mechanical devices* we mean any of the things that we can do physically to give the printed word emphasis. The most common of these devices are the underscore, quotation marks, italics, boldface type, and solid capitals. Lines, arrows, and diagrams also can call attention to certain parts. So can color, special type, and drawings. These techniques are infrequently used in business documents, with the possible exception of sales letters.

COHERENCE

Your documents are composed of independent bits of information. But these bits of information do not communicate the whole message. A part of the message is told in the relationships of the facts presented. Thus, to communicate your message successfully, you must do more than communicate facts. You also must make the relationships clear. Making these relationships clear is the task of giving coherence to your message.

The best thing you can do to give your message coherence is to arrange its information in a logical order—an order appropriate for the strategy of the one case. So important is this matter to message writing that it is the primary topic of discussion in following chapters. Thus, we will postpone discussion of this vital part of coherence. But logical organization is usually not enough. Various techniques are needed to bridge or tie together the information presented. These techniques are known as *transitional devices*. We will discuss the four major ones: tie-in sentences, repetition of key words, use of pronouns, and use of transitional words.

Tie-In Sentences

By structuring your message so that one idea sets up the next, you can skillfully relate the ideas. That is, you can design the sentences to tie in two successive ideas. Notice in the following example how a job applicant tied together the first two sentences of the letter:

> As a result of increasing demand for precision instruments in the Bloomington boom area, won't you soon need another experienced and trained salesperson to call on your technical accounts there?

> With seven successful years of using computer illustration tools and a degree in scientific illustration, I believe I have the qualifications to do this job.

Now substitute the following sentence for the second sentence above and note the abrupt shift it makes.

> I am 32 years of age, married, and interested in exploring the possibilities of employment with you.

For another case, compare the contrasting examples of the sentence that follows the first sentence of a message refusing an adjustment on a trenching machine. As you can see, the strategy of the initial sentence is to set up the introduction of additional information that will clear the company of responsibility.

The Initial Sentence

> Your objective review of the facts concerning the operation of your Atkins Model L trencher is evidence that you are one who wants to consider all the facts in a case.

Abrupt Shift	**Good Tie-In**
We have found some additional information you will want to consider.	In this same spirit of friendly objectivity, we are confident that you will want to consider some additional information we have assembled.

Repetition of Key Words

By repeating key words from one sentence to the next, you can make smooth connections of successive ideas. The following successive sentences illustrate this transitional device (key words in italics). The sentences come from a message refusing a request to present a lecture series for an advertising clinic.

- Repetition of key words connects thoughts.

> Because your advertising clinic is so well planned, I am confident that it can provide a really *valuable* service to practitioners in the community. To be truly *valuable,* I think you will agree, the program must be given the time a thorough preparation requires. As my time for the coming weeks is heavily committed, you will need to find someone who is in a better position to do justice to your program.

Use of Pronouns

Because pronouns refer to words previously used, they make good transitions between ideas. So use them from time to time in forming idea connections. Especially use the demonstrative pronouns (*this, that, these, those*) and their adjective forms, for these words clearly relate ideas. The following examples (demonstrative pronouns in italics) illustrate this technique:

- Pronouns connect with the words they relate to.

> Ever since the introduction of our Model V nine years ago, consumers have suggested only one possible improvement—voice controls. During all *this* time, making *this* improvement has been the objective of Atkins research personnel. Now we proudly report that *these* efforts have been successful.

Transitional Words

When you talk in everyday conversation, you connect many of your thoughts with transitional words. But when you write, more than likely you do not use them enough. So be alert for places that need to be connected or related. Whenever sharp shifts or breaks in thought flow occur, consider using transitional words.

- Use transitional words in your writing.

Among the commonly used transitional words are in *addition, besides, in spite of, in contrast, however, likewise, thus, therefore, for example,* and *also.* A more extensive list appears in Chapter 10, where we review transition in report writing. That these words bridge thoughts is easy to see, for each gives a clue to the nature of the connection between what has been said and what will be said next. *In addition,* for example, tells the reader that what is to be discussed next builds on what has been discussed. *However* clearly shows a contrast in ideas. *Likewise* tells that what has been said resembles what will be said.

A Word of Caution

- Do not use transitional words arbitrarily. Make them appear natural.

The preceding discussion does not suggest that you should use these transitional devices arbitrarily. Much of your subject matter will flow smoothly without them. When you use them, however, use them naturally so that they blend in with your writing.

SUMMARY BY CHAPTER OBJECTIVES

1 Explain the need for effect in writing business messages.

1. Although clarity is a major concern in all business writing, in letters and some email messages you also will be concerned with effect.
   - Specifically, you will need to communicate the effect of goodwill, for it is profitable in business to do so.
   - Sometimes you will need to communicate effects that help you persuade, sell, or the like.
   - To achieve these effects, you will need to heed the following advice.

2 Use a conversational style that eliminates the old language of business and "rubber stamps."

2. Write messages in a conversational style (language that sounds like people talking).
   - Such a style requires that you resist the tendency to be formal.
   - It requires that you avoid words from the old language of business (*thanking you in advance, please be advised*).
   - It requires that you avoid the so-called rubber stamps—words used routinely and without thought (*this is to inform, in accordance with*).

3 Use the you-viewpoint to build goodwill.

3. In your messages, you will need to emphasize the you-viewpoint (*you will be happy to know* . . . rather than *I am happy to report* . . .).
   - But be careful not to be or appear to be insincere.
   - And do not use the you-viewpoint to manipulate the reader.

4 Employ positive language to achieve goodwill and other desired effects.

4. You should understand the negative and positive meanings of words.
   - Negative words have unpleasant meanings (*We cannot deliver until Friday*).
   - Positive words have pleasant meanings (*We can deliver Friday*).
   - Select those negative and positive words that achieve the best effect for your goal.

5 Explain the techniques of achieving courtesy.

5. You should strive for courtesy in your messages by doing the following:
   - Practice the goodwill techniques discussed above.
   - Single out your reader (write for the one person).
   - Avoid preaching or talking down.
   - Avoid displays of anger.
   - Be sincere (avoiding exaggeration and overdoing the goodwill techniques).

6 Use the four major techniques for emphasis in writing.

6. Use the four major techniques for emphasis in writing.
   - Determine the items of information the message will contain.
   - Give each item the emphasis it deserves.
   - Show emphasis in these ways:
     — By position (beginnings and endings receive prime emphasis).
     — By space (the greater the space devoted to a topic, the greater is the emphasis).
     — By sentence structure (short sentences emphasize more than longer ones).
     — By mechanical means (color, underscore, boldface, and such).

7. You should write messages that flow smoothly.
   • Present the information in logical order—so that one thought sets up the next.
   • Help show the relationships of thoughts by using these transitional devices:
      — Tie-in sentences.
      — Word repetitions.
      — Pronouns.
      — Transitional words.

7

Write documents that flow smoothly through the use of a logical order helped by the four major transitional devices.

1. Discuss this comment: "Getting the goodwill effect requires extra effort. It takes extra time, and time costs money."

2. "Our normal conversation is filled with error. Typically, it is crude and awkward. So why make our writing sound conversational?" Discuss.

3. "If a company really wants to impress the readers of its messages, the messages should be formal and should be written in dignified language that displays knowledge." Discuss.

4. After reading a message filled with expressions from the old language of business, a young administrative trainee made this remark: "I'm keeping this one for reference. It sounds so businesslike!" Evaluate this comment.

5. "If you can find words, sentences, or phrases that cover a general situation, why not use them every time that general situation comes about? Using such rubber stamps would save time, and in business time is money." Discuss.

6. Discuss this comment: "The you-viewpoint is insincere and deceitful."

7. Evaluate this comment: "It's hard to argue against courtesy. But businesspeople don't have time to spend extra effort on it. Anyway, they want their documents to go straight to the point—without wasting words and without sugar coating."

8. "I use the words that communicate the message best. I don't care whether they are negative or positive." Discuss.

9. "I like writers who shoot straight. When they are happy, you know it. When they are angry, they let you know." Discuss.

10. A writer wants to include a certain negative point in a message and to give it little emphasis. Discuss each of the four basic emphasis techniques as they relate to what can be done.

11. Using illustrations other than those in the text, discuss and illustrate the four major transitional devices.

Instructions, Rewrite Sentences 1–16 in conversational style.

1. I hereby acknowledge receipt of your July 7 favor.

2. Anticipating your reply by return mail, I remain . . .

3. Attached please find receipt requested in your May 1st inquiry.

4. We take pleasure in advising that subject contract is hereby canceled.

5. You are hereby advised to endorse subject proposal and return same to the undersigned.

6. I shall appreciate the pleasure of your reply.

7. Referring to yours of May 7, I wish to state that this office has no record of a sale.

8. This is to advise that henceforth all invoices will be submitted in duplicate.

9. Agreeable to yours of the 24th, we have consulted our actuarial department to ascertain the status of subject policy.

10. Kindly be advised that permission is hereby granted to delay remittance until the 12th.

11. In conclusion would state that, up to this writing, said account has not been profitable.

12. Replying to your letter of the 3rd would state that we deem it a great pleasure to accept your kind offer to serve on the committee.

13. I beg to advise that, with regard to above invoice, this office finds that partial payment of $312 was submitted on delivery date.

14. In replying to your esteemed favor of the 7th, I submit under separate cover the report you requested.

15. In reply to your letter of May 10, please be informed that this office heretofore has generously supported funding activities of your organization.

16. Kindly advise the undersigned as to your availability for participation in the program.

Instructions, Sentences 17–32: Write you-viewpoint sentences to cover each of the situations described.

17. Company policy requires that you must submit the warranty agreement within two weeks of sale.

18. We will be pleased to deliver your order by the 12th.

19. We have worked for 37 years to build the best lawn mowers for our customers.

20. Today we are shipping the goods you ordered February 3.

21. (From an application letter) I have seven years of successful experience selling office supplies.

22. (From an email to employees) We take pleasure in announcing that, effective today, the Company will give a 20 percent discount on all purchases made by employees.

23. Kraff files are made in three widths—one for every standard size of record.

24. We are happy to report approval of your application for membership.

25. Items desired should be checked on the enclosed order form.

26. Our long experience in the book business has enabled us to provide the best customer service possible.

27. So that we can sell at discount prices, we cannot permit returns of merchandise.

28. We invite you to buy from the enclosed catalog.

29. Tony's Red Beans have an exciting spicy taste.

30. We give a 2 percent discount when payment is made within 10 days.

31. I am pleased to inform you that I can grant your request for payment of travel expenses.

32. We can permit you to attend classes on company time only when the course is related to your work assignment.

Instructions, Sentences 33–48: Underscore all negative words in these sentences. Then rewrite the sentences for positive effect. Use your imagination to supply situation information when necessary.

33. Your misunderstanding of our January 7 email caused you to make this mistake.

34. We hope this delay has not inconvenienced you. If you will be patient, we will get the order to you as soon as our supply is replenished.

35. We regret that we must call your attention to our policy of prohibiting refunds for merchandise bought at discount.

36. Your negligence in this matter caused the damage to the equipment.

37. You cannot visit the plant except on Saturdays.

38. We are disappointed to learn from your July 7 email that you are having trouble with our Model 7 motor.

39. Tuff-Boy work clothing is not made from cloth that shrinks or fades.

40. Our Stone-skin material won't do the job unless it is reinforced.

41. Even though you were late in paying the bill, we did not disallow the discount.

42. We were sorry to learn of the disappointing service you have had from our sales force, but we feel we have corrected all mistakes with recent personnel changes.

43. We have received your complaint of the 7th in which you claim that our product was defective, and have thoroughly investigated the matter.

44. I regret the necessity of calling your attention to our letter of May 1.

45. We have received your undated letter, which you sent to the wrong office.

46. Old New Orleans pralines are not the gummy kind that stick to your teeth.

47. I regret to have to say that I will be unable to speak at your conference, as I have a prior commitment.

48. Do not walk on the grass.

Instructions, Numbers 49 and 50: The answers to these questions should come from message examples to be found in following chapters.

49. Find examples of each of the four major emphasis techniques discussed in this chapter.

50. Find examples of each of the four transitional devices discussed in this chapter.

Basic Patterns of Business Messages

In 1992, Michael Dell was the youngest CEO ever to be listed in the Fortune 500 ranks. His continued success comes from thinking about how Dell products and services can bring value to customers.

"Whenever we're having our discussions with product teams or teams that are focused on unique kinds of customers, we talk about market trends and operating trends—'What are you seeing?' 'What are customers asking for?' 'What are customers buying?' And when I'm out in the field talking to customers, I spend a fair amount of time understanding what our customers are doing, why they're doing it, and where they're going."

Michael Dell, Chairman and CEO, Dell Computer

CHAPTER FIVE

Introduction to Messages and the Writing Process

CHAPTER OBJECTIVES

Upon completing this chapter, you will understand the role of messages in business and the process of writing them. To reach this goal, you should be able to

1 Understand the nature and business uses of text messaging.

2 Understand the phenomenal growth and nature of email.

3 Follow conventional procedures and organize and write clear email messages.

4 Describe the development of the business letter.

5 Explain the variations in the forms of memorandums.

6 Explain the wide range of formality used in memorandums.

7 Describe the process of writing business messages.

The Nature of Business Messages

Introduce yourself to this chapter by shifting to the role of Max Schwartz (your subordinate in the preceding chapters). As Max, you are grateful to your boss for deftly instructing you in readable and sensitive writing. You have been convinced of the importance of good communication to the success of a struggling small business. You are especially grateful because most of the work you do involves communicating with fellow employees, customers, and suppliers. Every day you process dozens of internal email messages. Occasionally you write and receive memorandums. Then there are the more formal communications you exchange with people outside the company—both email and hard copy. This chapter introduces you to these messages and begins the process of writing them.

Our study of the types of written business communication begins with messages. As we shall view them, messages are the shorter written presentations of information that occur in business. They are the everyday exchanges between people—the communications that enable the business to conduct its affairs, both internally and externally. Messages fall into three basic types: text messages, email, and traditional letters and memorandums.

- We begin with written messages—the shorter communications of business.

TEXT MESSAGING

Text messages are the newest type of message. They began as a short message service (SMS), which allowed mobile phone users to send messages, catching on first with teens in Europe and Asia. As U.S. carriers offered interoperability and changed their pricing plans, text-messaging use has begun to pick up in the United States as well. Current forecasts predict that U.S. subscribers will number 75 million by 2007, growing from 21 million in 2002.[1] Mobile phone ownership in the United States for those age 12 and over has already reached 59 percent,[2] and 90 percent of U.S. mobile handsets are digital and nearly all have text messaging capability.[3] So the possibility for immediate adoption is clearly present.

- Text messaging use is posed to grow quickly and dramatically.

A recent study of business students' use of the technology revealed that most use it to send information when a call would inappropriately interrupt the receiver, when important data must be conveyed in a timely fashion, and when the receiver needs exact written facts (names, numbers, places, etc.).[4] Early use by business seems to be for promotional purposes. Using GPS systems to determine your location, some businesses will notify you of sales, special promotions, or events at their businesses when you are nearby. Others are using it to create brand awareness and customer retention. Airlines give their frequent flyers the option to receive up-to-date flight information alerts as text messages. And as the TV show "American Idol" first made many aware, it is being used for polling as well.

- It can be used for a variety of business purposes.

Today in addition to being able to send messages between mobile phones, users can use their email programs on desktop, laptop, or handheld hardware to send text

- Like mobile phones, email and the web can be used to send text messages.

---

[1] "IDC Projects Strong Growth in Wireless SMS and IM with Market Opportunities Varying by Segment," Financial News, PR Newswire, LexisNexis Academic, May 29, 2003.

[2] "US Wireless Text-Messaging Adoption Skyrocketing," February 26, 2003, <http://www.3g.co.uk/PR/Feb2003/4964.htm> (July 5, 2003).

[3] Frank James, "Text Messaging Could Bypass Congested Wireless Networks in Emergency," CentreDaily.com, April 24, 2003, <http://www.centredaily.com/mld/centredaily/news/politics/5705537.htm> (July 4, 2003).

[4] Marie E. Flatley, "For and about Text Messaging," *Business Education Forum* (April 2004), 38.

FIGURE 5–1

An Illustration of a Web-Based Text Messaging Application

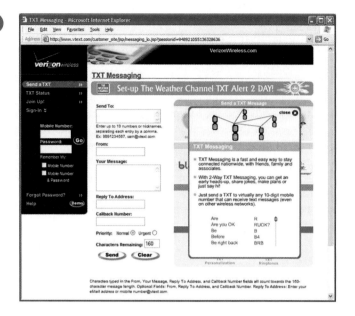

messages. Most carriers provide websites such as the one illustrated in Figure 5–1 where customers can send messages. Today, many carriers limit the number of characters in a message to 160 or fewer; some will allow longer messages but may break them into multiple messages when forwarding them to the receiver. The input screens will count the characters as you enter them, helping you keep your message concise. Others provide common questions or responses users can turn to for shortcuts. Some even allow you to customize your list of shortcuts.

• Shortcuts are accepted if they help meet the objectives and are clear.

When composing text messages, writers should focus primarily on clarity in achieving their objectives. Since keying responses on a mobile phone is slow, users often use abbreviated spelling forms. Some of the common abbreviations are *b4* for *before, u* for *you, gr8* for *great, plz* for *please,* and many others. Other shortcuts include initialisms such as *BTW* for *by the way* and short form spellings such as *nite* for *night.* Because text messaging is less formal than other types of messages, these short-

Pepper . . . and Salt

"Miss Pearson, send me a text message."

SOURCE: From *The Wall Street Journal*—Permission, Cartoon Features Syndicate.

cuts are often used and accepted. However, they still force the reader to stop and interpret the meaning. Users should avoid them if they interfere with clarity.

In composing text messages, the writer's objective should be to convey all critical information the receiver needs and to keep needed responses as short as possible. For example, if you learn that an important visiting customer is a vegetarian and you have reservations for lunch at Ruth's Chris Steakhouse, you might need to let your boss know—before the lunch meeting. However, the boss is leading an important meeting where a phone call would be disruptive and inappropriate. So you decide to send a text message. An immediate thought might be to send something like this: *Marina Smith is a vegetarian. Where should we take her for lunch today? Zeke* Although it does convey the major fact and is only 77 characters counting spaces, it forces the recipient to enter a long response—the name of another place. It might also result in more message exchanges about availability and time. A better version might be this: *Marina Smith is a vegetarian. Shall we go to 1-Fish House, 2-Souplantation, 3-Mandarian House? All are available at noon. Zeke* This version conveys the major fact in 130 characters and allows the recipient to respond simply with a 1, 2, or 3. However, before sending this message, the writer took the initiative to identify appropriate alternatives, perhaps with the help of others, through firsthand knowledge of the boss's preferences, or some basic research. As you will read later in the chapter, gathering needed information is a prerequisite to writing clear, complete messages.

- Text messages should convey ideas completely with minimal need for response.

While text messaging is relatively new for business use, you will find it a valuable tool if your messages are clear, complete, and concise with a pleasant and professional tone.

EMAIL

The rapid growth of email has been the most exciting business communication development in recent years. In just a short time, email has emerged as a mainstream form of business communication. Its volume surpasses that of the U.S. Postal Service. According to one authority, "there are more emails sent every day than telephone calls." It has become widely used in both small and large organizations. The explosive growth of email continues. And it is likely to continue for some time to come.

- Recent growth of email has been phenomenal.

Evaluating Email's Pros and Cons

The reasons for this rapid growth are the advantages email has over other communication forms, especially over its principal competitor, the telephone. Among the reasons, the following are most significant:

- It has grown because it

Internal email forms a significant part of the communication used to coordinate the work in small and large businesses alike.

- eliminates "telephone tag,"

- Email eliminates "telephone tag"—the problem of trying to contact busy people who are not always available for telephone calls. (Messages sent to them can be stored in their electronic mailboxes until they are ready to read them.)

- saves time,

- Conversely, email saves the time of these busy people. They are spared the interruptions of telephone calls.

- facilitates fast decisions, and

- Email can speed up the process of making business decisions, because it permits rapid exchanges from all involved in the decisions.

- is cheap

- Email is cheap. It permits unlimited use at no more than the cost of an Internet connection.

- and provides a written record.
- It has disadvantages, too.
- It is not confidential,

- It provides a written record.

  Email also has its disadvantages. The following stand out:

- Email is not confidential. "It's just about as private as a postcard you drop in the mail box."[5]

- doesn't show emotions, and

- Email doesn't communicate the sender's emotions well. Voice intonations, facial expressions, body movements, and such are not a part of the message. They are in telephone and face-to-face communication.

- may be ignored or delayed.

- Email may be ignored or delayed. The volume of email often makes it difficult for some respondents to read and act on all of their messages.

Including the Prefatory Elements

The mechanical parts of the email message are generally standardized and are a part of the template of the software you use in constructing the message. But the second part of your effort, writing the message, is far from standardized. Although the following review covers both, the writing receives the greater emphasis. It is here that you are likely to need the most help.

- These standard parts precede the message.

Although the various email systems differ somewhat, the elements are standardized (see Figure 5–2). They include the following parts:

- **To:** Here the sender places the email address of the recipients. It must be perfect, for any error will result in failure to reach the recipient.
- **Cc:** If someone other than the prime recipient is to receive a *courtesy copy,* his or her address goes here.
- **Bcc:** This line stands for *blind courtesy copy.* The recipient's message will not show this information; that is, he or she will not know who else is receiving a copy of the message.
- **Subject:** This line describes the message as precisely as the situation permits. The reader should get from it a clear idea of what the message is about.
- **Attachments:** In this area you can enter a file that you desire to send along with the message. As will be emphasized later, you should make certain that what you attach is really needed.
- **The message:** The information you are sending goes here. How to write it is the subject of much of the following discussion.

Beginning the Message

- Begin with the recipient's name or a greeting. Identify yourself if necessary.

Typically, email messages begin with the recipient's name. If writer and reader are acquainted, first name only is the rule. If you would normally address the reader as Ms., Dr., Mr., and such, address him or her this way in an initial email. But you can change the salutation in subsequent messages if the person indicates that informality is desired. A "friendly generic greeting such as Greetings" is appropriate for a group of

---

[5] Monique I. Cuvelier, "Take Control of Your Inbox," *Guide to Email & More* 8, no. 7 (2000): 104.

FIGURE 5–2

Typical Electronic Mail
Clients

people with whom you communicate. Use of the recipient's full name also is acceptable. The salutations commonly used in letters (Dear Mr., Dear Ms.) are rarely used in email. When writing to someone or a group you do not know, it is appropriate to identify yourself early in the message. This identification may include your purpose and your company. Your title and position also may be helpful.

Organizing the Contents

Even though email messages often are written under time pressure, you would do well to organize them carefully. For most short, informative messages, a "top-down" order is appropriate. This plan, used in newspaper writing, involves presenting the most important material first. The remaining information follows in descending order of importance. Such an arrangement permits a busy reader to get the essential facts first, and the reader accessing email on a Web phone or other small screen to get the essential facts more easily. Many writers routinely follow this practice.

• Organize short messages by presenting information in descending order of importance.

Longer, more complex, and formal email messages frequently follow more involved and strategic organization patterns. The most common of these are reviewed in Chapters 6, 7, 8, and 9. As you will see, these patterns vary depending on how the reader will likely perceive the writer's objective. In general, those messages that are likely to be received positively or neutrally are written in a direct pattern. That is, they get to the goal right away and then present their contents systematically and quickly. Those messages that are likely to be received negatively are appropriately written in an indirect pattern. Their negative content is preceded by conditioning and explanation words that prepare the reader to receive the bad news.

• Longer messages usually follow more complex patterns.

- Some resemble business reports.

Some long email messages may resemble business reports. With these messages, you well may follow the organization and writing instructions for business reports (Chapters 10–12). You should use your knowledge of report presentation in writing them. In fact, business reports can be communicated by email just as business letters can. As you will see shortly, some memorandums are communicated by email. The variety of email messages covers the entire spectrum of written business communication.

Writing the Message: Formality Considerations

- Email messages range from highly informal to formal.

A review of email writing is complicated by the fact that email messages are extremely diverse. They run the range from highly informal to formal. The informal messages often resemble face-to-face oral communication; some even sound like chitchat that occurs between acquaintances and friends. Email messages are often written in a fast-paced environment with little time for deliberation.

- The language may be casual, informal, or formal.

Because of this diversity, discussing the formality of email writing is difficult. One approach is to view the language used from three general classifications: casual, informal, and formal.[6]

- Casual language uses slang, colloquialisms, contractions, short sentences.

Casual. By casual language we mean the language we use in talking with close friends in everyday situations. It includes slang and colloquialisms. It uses contractions and personal pronouns freely. Its sentences are short—sometimes incomplete. It uses mechanical emphasis devices and initialisms (to be discussed later). Although in actual practice it may be subject to grammatical incorrectness, as we stress elsewhere this practice is not helpful to the communication and should be avoided. Casual language is best limited to your communications with close friends. Following is an example of casual language:

Hi Cindy:

High-five me! Just back from confab with pinheads. They're high on our marketing plan. But as you crystal balled it, they want a special for the jumbos. ASAP, they said. Let's meet, my cell, 10 A.M., Wed.?

TTFN

Brandon

- Use casual language when writing to friends.

Most of your personal email (messages to friends) are likely to be casually written. This is the way friends talk and their email should be no different. Probably some of the email you will write in business also will fall in this category. Much of it will be with your fellow employees and friends in business. But here some words of caution should be expressed. You would be wise to use casual language only when you know your readers well—when you know they expect and prefer casual communication. Never should you use words, initialisms, emphasis devices, or such that are not certain to communicate clearly and quickly.

- Informal language resembles proper conversation.

Informal. Informal language retains some of the qualities of casual writing. It makes some use of personal pronouns and contractions. Its sentences are relatively short. It occasionally may use colloquialisms, but more selectively than in casual writing. It has the effect of conversation, but it is proper conversation—not chitchat. Its sentences are short, but they are well structured and organized. They have varied patterns that produce an interesting literary style. In general, it is the writing that you will find in most of the illustrations in Chapters 6–9. It is the language that appears in the text of this book. You should use it in most of your business email messages, especially when writing to people you know only on a business basis. An example of an email message in informal language is the following:

---

[6] Heidi Schultz, *The Elements of Electronic Communication* (Boston: Allyn and Bacon, 2000), 43–47.

Cindy:

The management team has heartily approved our marketing plan. They were most complimentary. But as you predicted, they want a special plan for the large accounts. As they want it as soon as possible, let's get together to work on it. Can we meet Wednesday, 10 A.M., my office?

Brandon

Formal. A formal style of writing maintains a greater distance between writer and reader than informal style. It avoids personal references and contractions. Its sentences are well structured and organized. Although there is a tendency to create longer sentences in formal writing, this tendency should be resisted. Formal style is well illustrated in the examples of formal reports in Chapters 11 and 12. It is appropriate to use in email messages resembling formal reports, in messages to people of higher status, and to people not known to the writer.

- Formal language keeps a distance between writer and reader.

Writing the Message: General Considerations

Instructions for writing email messages are much the same as those given in Chapters 2, 3, and 4 for other types of messages. For the purpose of email writing, we may group the more important of these instructions under three heads: conciseness, clarity, and etiquette. A fourth, correctness (covered in Chapter 17), is equally vital. Each of these important qualities for email writing are briefly reviewed in the following paragraphs.

- Follow the writing instructions in preceding chapters.

Conciseness. As we have mentioned, email often is written by busy people for busy people. In the best interests of all concerned, email messages should be as short as complete coverage of the subject matter will permit. This means culling the information available and using only that which is essential. It means also that the information remaining should be worded concisely. In the words of one email authority, "Keep it short. If your email message is more than two paragraphs, maybe you should use the telephone."[7]

- Cut nonessentials and write concisely.

Frequently in email communication, a need exists to refer to previous email messages. The easiest way, of course, is to tell your mailer to include the entire message. Unless the entire message is needed, however, this practice adds length. It is better either to paraphrase the essentials from the original or to quote the selected parts that cover the essentials. All quoted material should be distinguished from your own words by the sign > at the beginning and the sign < at the end of the quoted part. Another technique is to place three of these signs (>>>) at the beginning of all parts you write and three of these signs (<<<) at the beginning of all parts you are quoting from previous messages.

- Minimize references to previous communications.

Clarity. Especially important in email writing is clarity of wording. As suggested in Chapters 2 and 3, you should know and practice the techniques of readable writing. You should select words that quickly create clear meanings. Typically, these are the short, familiar ones. You should strive for concreteness, vigor, and precision. Your sentences should be short, and so should your paragraphs. In fact, all of the advice given in Chapters 2 and 3 is applicable to the writing of clear email messages.

- Use the techniques of clear writing.

Etiquette. It goes without saying that good business etiquette should be practiced in all business relations. We all want to receive courteous and fair treatment. In fact, this is the way we human beings prefer to act. Even so, the current literature has much to say about anger among email participants. "Flaming," as the practice of sending abusive or offensive language is called, has no place in business. Good business etiquette

- Be courteous, as suggested in preceding chapters.

---

[7] Kim Komando, "8 Email Mistakes That Make You Look Bad," April 27, 2003, <http://bcentral.com/articles/komando/115.asp> (April 29, 2003).

Using Good Email Etiquette Helps Writers Convey Intended Message

Using proper email etiquette is as easy as applying a bit of empathy to your messages: send only what you would want to receive. The following additional etiquette guides will help you consider a variety of issues when using email.

- Is your message really needed by the recipient(s)?
- Is your message for routine rather than sensitive messages?
- Are you sure your message is not spam (an annoying message sent repeatedly) or a chain letter?
- Have you carefully checked that your message is going where you want it to go?
- Has your wording avoided defamatory or libelous language?
- Have you complied with copyright laws and attributed sources accurately?
- Have you avoided humor and sarcasm your reader may not understand as intended?
- Have you proofread your message carefully?
- Is this a message you would not mind having distributed widely?
- Does your signature avoid offensive quotes or illustrations, especially those that are religious, political, or sexual?
- Are attached files a size that your recipient's system can handle?
- Are the files you are attaching virus free?

should prevail. Throughout the preceding chapters, especially in Chapter 4, we have emphasized the techniques of showing good business etiquette. As you will recall, Chapter 4 emphasized the effect of your words. The skillful use of positive language and you-viewpoint also can be effective in email. So can the use of conversational language. Nondiscriminatory language also helps, as can emphasis on sincerity. In fact, virtually all the instructions given on goodwill building apply here. Also in the interest of good business etiquette, you will want to let your reader know when no response is required to your email message.

- Write correctly. Some critics disagree.

Correctness. One would think that the need for correctness in email writing would be universally accepted. Unfortunately, such is not the case. Because of the fast pace of email communication, some practitioners argue that "getting the message out there" is the important goal—that style need not be a matter of concern. In the view of one in this group, "You should not add stylistic and grammatical refinements to your email messages because they'll slow you down."[8]

- Correctness is a part of the message.

We cannot accept this view. *How* one communicates is very much a part of the message. As expressed by one authority, "People still judge you on how well you communicate. . . . Commercial email represents your company and your brand. There's no room for excuses."[9] Bad spelling, illogical punctuation, awkward wording, and such stand out like sore thumbs. Such errors reflect on the writer. And they can reflect on the credibility of the message. If one knows correctness, it is easy enough to get it right the first time. What is the logic of doing something wrong when you know better? Clearly, an error-filled message strongly suggests the writer's ignorance.

To avoid any such suggestion of ignorance, you should follow the grammatical and punctuation instructions presented in Chapter 17. And you should follow the basic instructions for using words, constructing sentences, and designing paragraphs pre-

---

[8] Guy Kawasaki, as quoted in David Angell and Brent Heslop, *Elements of Email Style* (Reading, MA: Addison-Wesley, 1994), 3.

[9] Jim Sterne and Anthony Priore, *Email Marketing* (New York: John Wiley & Sons, 2000), 41.

Professorial Words of Wisdom

Although e-mail is an essential communication medium in business today, many businesspeople and business students take it casually and fail to realize its full potential. It's easy to assume that since e-mail can be produced quickly and easily, readers can comprehend e-mail messages quickly and easily too. Yet overly speedy e-mail writing can result in much slower e-mail reading and even miscommunication.

Mary Munter, Dartmouth College
Priscilla S. Rogers, University of Michigan
Jane Rymer, Wayne State University

Mary Munter, Priscilla S. Rogers, Jone Rymer, "Business E-mail: Guidelines for Users," *Business Communication Quarterly* 66, no. 1 (March 2003): 26.

sented in the writing chapters. Before pressing the Send button, proofread your message carefully.

Closing the Message

Most email messages end with just the writer's name—the first name alone if the recipient knows the writer well. But in some messages, especially the more formal ones, a closing statement may be appropriate. "Thanks" and "Regards" are popular. In casual messages, acronyms such as THX (thanks) and TTFN (ta-ta for now) are often used. The conventional complimentary closes used in traditional letters (sincerely, cordially) are not widely used, but they are appropriate in messages that involve formal business relationships. In messages to other businesses, it is important that you include your company and position.

- End with your name and perhaps a closing statement.

Today most email software has a signature feature that will automatically attach a signature file to a message. Most programs even allow the writer to set up an alternative signature, giving users the flexibility to choose between a standard, one alternate, and none attached at all. Writers sometimes set up a formal full signature in one file and an informal signature in another. The important point to remember is to close with a signature that gives the reader the information he or she needs to know.

Using Emphasis Devices

When you write email messages, you may find that certain elements of style are missing either on your system or on your readers' systems. While most of the current versions of Windows and Macintosh email programs support mechanical devices such as underscoring, font variations, italics, bold, color, and even graphics, some older or mainframe-based systems do not. Email writers have attempted to overcome the limitations of these older systems by developing alternative means of showing emphasis. To show underscoring, they use the sign _ at the beginning of the words needing underscoring. They use asterisks (*) before and after words to show boldface. Solid capital letters are another means of emphasis, although some critics believe this practice is greatly overused. In the words of one critic "Don't use solid capital letters. People will think you're shouting."[10] A sign they use to emphasize items in a list is the bullet. Since there is no standardized bullet character that will display on all computers, many writers of email use substitute characters. One is the asterisk (*) followed by a tab

- Email has limited use of emphasis devices. These substitutes have been developed.

---

[10] Mark Kakkurik, "E-mail FAQs," *Guide to E-Mail & More* 8, no. 7 (2000): 14.

space. Another is the dash (—) followed by a tab space. Probably these devices are used best in the email messages written in casual language.

Using Initialisms Cautiously

● Initialisms have been developed to save time. But use them cautiously.

Probably as a result of the early informal development of email, a somewhat standardized system of initialisms has developed. Their purpose has been to cut message length and to save the writer's time. In spite of these apparent advantages, you would be wise to use them cautiously. They have meaning only if readers know them. Even so, you should be acquainted with the more widely used ones, such as those below.[11] You are likely to find others created by your email correspondents.

ASAP	as soon as possible
BTW	by the way
FAQ	frequently asked question
FWIW	for what it's worth
FYI	for your information
IMHO	in my humble opinion
LOL	laughing out loud
TIA	thanks in advance
TTFN	ta-ta for now

As noted previously, initialisms are appropriate primarily in casual messages.

It is important to keep in mind that these practices and some of the other pointers given in this review apply only to current usage. Computers and their use are changing almost daily. The techniques of email writing also are likely to change over time.

Avoiding Inappropriate Use of Email

● Don't use email when

● the message involves these aspects.

In spite of its popularity and ease of use, email is not always a good medium for your communications. As summarized by two authorities, "it should not be used when:

- The message is long, complicated, or requires negotiation.
- Questions or information need clarification and discussion.
- The information is confidential, sensitive, requires security, or could be misinterpreted.
- The message is emotionally charged and really requires tone of voice or conversational feedback to soften the words or negotiate meaning.
- The message is sent to *avoid* direct contact with a person, especially if the message is unpleasant and uncomfortable or seems too difficult to say face-to-face.
- The message contains sensitive issues, relays feelings, or attempts to resolve conflict. Email can make conflict worse."[12]

TRADITIONAL LETTERS

● Letters are the oldest form. The early civilizations used them.

Letters are the traditional form of business messages. They are the oldest form. In fact, they have existed since the early days of civilization. The use of letters has been documented in virtually all the great early civilizations. The ancient Chinese wrote letters. So did the early Egyptians, Romans, and Greeks. Although many of these early letters pertained to military and personal matters, some clearly concerned business.

---

[11] Linda Lamb and Jerry Peek, *Using Email Effectively* (Sebastopol, CA: O'Reilly and Associates, Inc., 1995), 107.

[12] Vera Terminello and Marcia G. Reed, *Email: Communicate Effectively* (Upper Saddle River, NJ: Pearson Education, 2003), 13.

From these early days letters have continued to be used in business. Although the history of their development would be interesting, we need only be concerned with the end product—with the business letter as it has evolved to date. Specifically, we need to view two aspects: its format and its composition.

The format of the business letter probably already is known to you. Although some variations in format are generally acceptable, typically these information items are included: date, inside address, salutation (Dear Ms. Smith), body, and complimentary close (Sincerely yours). Other items sometimes needed are attention line, subject line, return address (when letterhead paper is not used), and enclosure information. Placement of these items as well as guidelines for processing the text of the letter are presented in Appendix B.

Current techniques of composing business letters have been developed by various business scholars and leaders over time, but especially in the past century. In the early days (a century ago) emphasis was on word choice, especially on use of a stiff and stilted manner of expressing courtesy. We referred to this manner of expression in Chapter 4 as "the old language of business."

In more recent times emphasis shifted to structure and strategy of content and humanness of wording. Highlights of the humanness of wording comprise much of the content of the preceding chapter. The current techniques of organizing and presenting business letters are the subjects of the following chapters. As you would expect, this material has been adapted to the needs of today's technological business world. It forms the basis for writing all of the more formal business messages: letters, email messages, and memorandums. It involves much of the content of Chapters 6 through 9.

- We should know about letter format and composition.

- Letter format is described in Appendix B.

- In the early days, techniques emphasized a stilted manner of expressing courtesy.

- Current emphasis is on strategy and humanness, which are covered in detail in this book.

MEMORANDUMS

Defining Memorandums

Memorandums (memos) are a form of letter written inside the business. In rare cases, they may be used in communicating outside the business. They are written messages exchanged by employees in the conduct of their work. They may be distinguished from other messages primarily by their form. Originally, they were used only in hard copy, but with the advent of computers they are now often processed electronically as

- Memos are internal letters. Email is taking over their function.

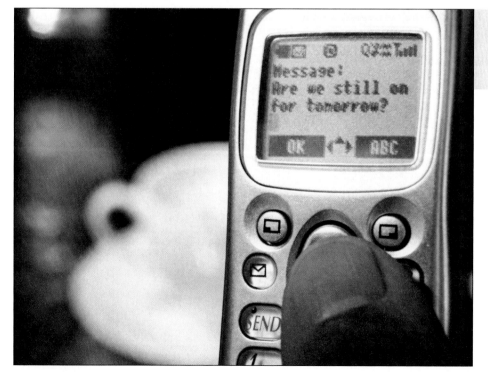

Businesses with multiple locations send many of their documents by fax, email, or text messages.

faxes. In fact, their function of communicating within the business has been taken over somewhat by email. Even so, they still are a part of most company communication. They are especially useful in communicating with employees who do not use computers in their work.

As we shall see in Chapter 11, some memorandums communicate factual, problem-related information and are classified as reports. Those not classified as reports are the memorandums that concern us now. Even so, much of the following discussion applies to both types.

Determining Memorandum Form

As we have noted, memorandums are distinguished from other messages primarily by their form. Some companies have stationery printed especially for memorandums, while many used standard or customized templates in word processors. Sometimes the word *memorandum* appears at the top in large, heavy type. But some companies prefer other titles, such as *Interoffice Memorandum* or *Interoffice Communication.* Below this main heading come the specific headings common to all memorandums: *Date, To, From, Subject* (though not necessarily in this order). This simple arrangement is displayed in Figure 5–3. Because memorandums are often short, some companies use 5 × 8½-inch stationery for them as well as the conventional 8½ × 11-inch size. Hardcopy memorandums are usually initialed by the writer rather than signed.

Large organizations, especially those with a number of locations and departments, often include additional information on their memorandum stationery. *Department, Plant, Location, Territory, Store Number,* and *Copies to* are examples (see Figure 5–4).

- Some memos may be classified as reports.

- Most large companies use standard memo templates or printed memorandum stationery with *Date, To, From,* and *Subject* headings.

- Some larger companies have additional headings (*Department, Plant, Territory, Store Number,* and such).

Illustration of Good Form for the Memorandum Using the MS Word Professional Template

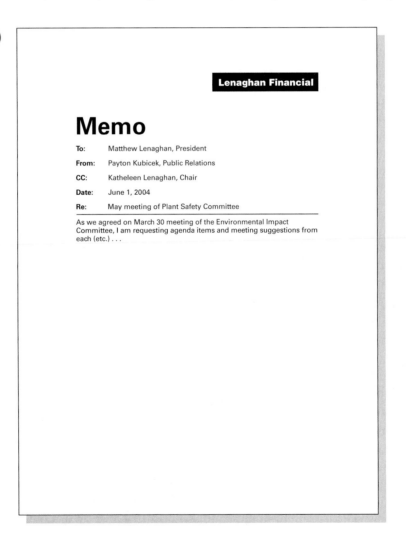

Lenaghan Financial

Memo

To: Matthew Lenaghan, President

From: Payton Kubicek, Public Relations

CC: Katheleen Lenaghan, Chair

Date: June 1, 2004

Re: May meeting of Plant Safety Committee

As we agreed on March 30 meeting of the Environmental Impact Committee, I am requesting agenda items and meeting suggestions from each (etc.) . . .

FIGURE 5–4

Memorandum Stationery with Special Headings Adapted to the Needs of an Organization with Multiple Locations.

PENNY-WISE STORES, INC.

MEMORANDUM

To: **Date:**

                                          From:

Store: **Store:**

At: **At:**

Territory: **Territory:**

Copies to:

Subject: Form for in-house letters (memos)

This is an illustration of our memorandum stationery. It should be used for written communications within the organization.

Notice that the memorandum uses no form of salutation. Neither does it have any form of complimentary close. The writer does not need to sign the message. He or she needs only to initial after the typed name in the heading.

Notice also that the message is single-spaced with double spacing between paragraphs.

Since in some companies memorandums are often addressed to more than one reader, the heading *To* may be followed by enough space to list a number of names.

Viewing Memorandum Formality

Because memorandums usually are messages sent and received by people who work with and know one another, they tend to use casual or informal language. Even so, their degree of formality ranges from one extreme to the other. At one end are the casual notes that workers exchange. At the other are the formal messages written by lower-ranking workers to their top administrators. The typical memorandum falls somewhere between these extremes.

- Memorandums vary widely in formality.

Writing Memorandums

The techniques for writing memorandums (memos) are much like those for writing the other business messages (letters and email). Short, simple memos are often written in casual or informal language, much like short, simple email messages. Longer, more formal memorandums are appropriately organized in the patterns appropriate for longer, more formal messages discussed in Chapters 6–8. Like most of the other business messages, most memorandums are appropriately written in a direct pattern, usually beginning with the most important point and working down. And memorandums conveying sensitive or negative information appropriately are written in an indirect order. Direct and indirect patterns are discussed in detail in following chapters.

- Because the situations involved are similar, the techniques for writing memos and email are similar.

The following example illustrates a memorandum. Obviously, it is one that could be sent in hard copy or by email. It follows the direct order appropriate for most memorandums, beginning with the objective and then systematically and clearly covering the vital bits of information. Its wording is conversational. It is straightforward yet courteous.

DATE: April 1, 2004

TO: Remigo Ruiz

FROM: Becky Pharr

SUBJECT: Request for cost information concerning meeting at Timber Creek Lodge

- The memorandum begins directly—with the objective. The necessary explanation follows.

As we discussed in my office today, please get the necessary cost information for conducting our annual sales meeting at the Timber Creek Lodge, Timber Creek Village, Colorado. Our meeting will begin on the morning of Monday, June 5; we should arrange to arrive on the 4th. We will leave after a brief morning session on June 9.

Specifically, I want the following information:

- Then the specific information needed is listed in logical order.

- Travel costs for all 43 participants, including air travel to Denver and ground travel between the airport and the lodge. I have listed the names and home stations of the 43 participants on the attached sheet.

- Room and board costs for the five-day period, including cost with and without dinner at the lodge. As you know, we are considering the possibility of allowing participants to purchase dinners at nearby restaurants.

- Costs for recreational facilities at the lodge.

- Costs for meeting rooms and meeting equipment (projectors, lecterns, and such). We will need a room large enough to accommodate our 43 participants.

- The memorandum ends with courteous words.

I'd like to have the information by April 15. If you need additional information, please contact me at x3715 or Pharr@yahoo.com.

- Memorandums differ from letters in two major ways: (1) They are more likely to be direct.

Although memorandums are internal letters, they differ from letters in two major ways. First, as we have noted, memorandums are more likely to be written in the direct order. Most letters also are direct, but an even greater percentage of memorandums are direct. Most memorandums are direct because they concern work information, and such information rarely requires preliminary explanation, justification, or persuasion strategies.

- (2) They are less likely to involve concern about word effect.

The second major difference is that usually the writers of memorandums have less need to be concerned about the effect of their words. That is, tactfulness, negativeness–positiveness, you-viewpoint, and such usually are not major concerns. This is not to say that rudeness and harshness are acceptable—that the practice of good business etiquette does not apply to relations between employees. It simply means that people working together in business situations typically want and expect clear, straightforward communication.

Policy Memorandums and Directives

- Company policies and directives may be written in memo form.

A type of memorandum deserving special mention is one that conveys company policies or directives. *Policy* or *directive* memorandums typically are written for all employees. They convey company rules or procedures for operating. They are written by administrators (usually high level) for subordinates and are more important than most internal communications. Typically they are made in hard copy and often are compiled in policy manuals—perhaps kept in loose-leaf form and updated as new policies and directives are issued.

- They should be somewhat formal, direct, clearly written, and well organized.

Policy memorandums and directives are more formally written than most internal communications because of their official nature. Usually they are written in the direct order. They begin with a topic (thesis) statement that repeats the subject-line information and includes the additional information needed to identify the specific situation. The remainder of the message consists of a logical, orderly arrangement of the rules and procedures covered. To ensure that they stand out, the rules and procedures often are numbered or arranged in outline form as in the following example:

DATE: June 10, 2004

TO: All Employees

FROM: Terry Boedeker, President

SUBJECT: Energy conservation

To help us keep costs low, the following conservation measures are effective immediately:

- Thermostats will be set to maintain temperatures of 78 degrees Fahrenheit throughout the air-conditioning season.

- Air conditioners will be shut off in all buildings at 4 PM Monday through Friday.

- Air conditioners will be started as late as possible each morning so as to have the buildings at the appropriate temperature within 30 minutes after the start of the workday.

- Lighting levels will be reduced to approximately 50 to 60 foot-candles in all work areas. Corridor lighting will be reduced to 5 to 10 foot-candles.

- Outside lighting levels will be reduced as much as possible without compromising safety and security.

In addition, will each of you help in conservation areas under your control? Specifically, I ask that you do the following:

Turn off lights not required in performing work.

Keep windows closed when the cooling system is operating.

Turn off all computer monitors and printers at the end of the day.

I am confident that these measures will reduce our energy use significantly. Your efforts to follow them will be greatly appreciated.

- The beginning is direct and immediately identifies the situation.

- Clear writing and listing result in good readability.

- Separate listing of other measures gives order and enhances understanding.

- Closing personal remarks add to effectiveness.

THE PROCESS OF WRITING

With the next chapter you will begin writing business messages. Originally, these message types were letters. But, because today's technology permits other communication forms (fax, email), throughout this part of the book we use the term *message.* Wherever it appears more precise to do so, however, we use the more specific word *letter.*

As you write business messages, you should know what is involved in the process of writing. Although the process may vary somewhat from writer to writer, the following general guidelines as shown in Figure 5–5 and explained here should serve you in your writing efforts.

- We now take up business messages.

- Following is a review of the process of writing.

Planning the Message

A logical first step in writing a business message involves planning. This is the prewriting stage—the stage in which you think through your writing project and develop a plan for doing it.

Then you determine the objective of the message—what the message must do. Must it report information, acknowledge an order, ask for something, request payment of a bill, evaluate an applicant, or what?

Next you predict the reader's likely reaction to your objective. Will that reaction be positive, negative, or somewhere in between? Of course, you cannot be certain of how the reader will react. You can only apply your knowledge of the reader to the situation and use your best judgment. Your prediction will determine the plan of the message you write.

- Begin by planning.

- Determine the objective of the message.

- Predict how the reader will react.

FIGURE 5–5

A Model of the Writing
Process

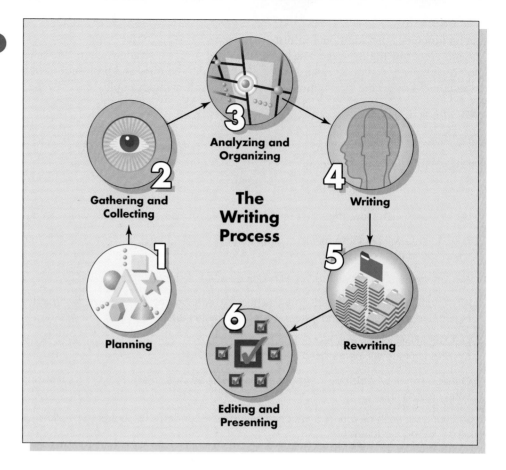

Gathering and Collecting the Facts

- Get the information
  (facts) you need.

With your plan in mind, it is logical for you to get all the information you will need in writing the message. In a business situation, this means finding past correspondence; consulting with other employees; getting sales records, warranties, product descriptions, and inventory records—in fact, doing whatever is necessary to inform yourself fully of the situation. Without all the information you need, you may make costly mistakes. Moreover, if you do not have all the information you need, you will have to look for it in the midst of your writing. This can break your train of thought and cause you to lose time.

In a classroom situation, the write-up of the problem is likely to contain the information you need. So you will need to study the problem carefully, making certain that you understand all the information.

Analyzing and Organizing Information

- Select the message plan.
  Use direct order for
  favorable reactions.

If you predict the reader will react to your message positively, or even neutrally, you will usually organize the message in a direct plan. That is, you will get to your objective right away—at the beginning. In positive situations, you are likely to have no need for opening explanations or introductory remarks, for these would only delay achieving your objective. You simply start with the objective. This plan, commonly called the *direct order,* is easy to use. Fortunately, it is appropriate for most business messages.

- Use indirect order for
  unfavorable reactions.

If you predict that your message will produce a negative reaction, you should usually write it in indirect order. *Indirect order* is the opposite of direct order. This plan gets to the objective after preparing the reader to receive it. As you will see in Chapter 7, such a message typically requires a more skillful use of strategy and word choice than does one written in direct order.

Writing the Message

With your plan in mind, you write the message. You should write it in the clear and effective manner discussed in the preceding chapters—choosing words the reader understands, constructing sentences that present their contents clearly, using words that create just the right effect. You should carefully follow the text instruction for the message you are writing. In addition, you should present it in good format (as described in Appendix B). The product of this effort is a first draft. As you will see, the process does not end here.

- Then write the message, striving for clarity and effect.

Rewriting Your Work

In actual business practice, your first draft may well be the final draft, for often time will not permit additional work on the document. But now you are in a learning situation. You are preparing for the time when you will not have time. Your efforts now should be directed toward improving your writing skills—toward learning writing techniques that can become reflexive in the years ahead when you will write under time pressures. Even so, when you reach the stage of your career when you must write under time pressures, you would be wise to employ as many of these suggestions as time will permit.

- When time permits, review your work.

After completing your first draft, you should review it carefully. Look at each word. Is it the right one? Would another one be more precise? Are there better, more concise ways of structuring your sentence? Did you say what you mean? Could someone read other meanings into your words? Is your organization the best for the situation? What we are suggesting is that you be your own critic. Challenge what you have done. Look for alternatives. Then, after you have conducted a thorough and critical review, make any changes that you think will improve your work.

- Then revise it.

Input from others can also help you refine your writing. As you know, it is often difficult to find errors or weaknesses in your own work; yet others seem to find them easily. Thus, if your instructor permits or encourages any input from associates, consider it. Receive criticisms with an open mind, objectively evaluating them and using that which meets your review. Unfortunately, most of us are thin-skinned about such criticisms, and we tend to be defensive when they are made. You should resist this tendency.

- Get input from others,

The most valuable input may be the written comments your instructor makes about the work submitted. Perhaps this input comes too late to benefit your grades. But it does not come too late to benefit your learning. You would be wise to take these comments and revise a final time, ending with your best possible product.

- including your instructor.

Editing and Presenting the Final Document

After you have made all the changes you think are needed, you should construct the final draft. Here you become a proofreader, looking for errors of spelling, punctuation, and grammar. Probably you will use software analyzers to help you with this task. Then you determine that the format is appropriate. In general, you make certain the final document represents your very best standards—that it will reflect favorably on you and (in later years) your company. Then you present the message. This final message is the best you are capable of writing, and you have learned in the process of writing it.

- Then process, edit, and proof the final draft.

PLAN OF THE PRESENTATION

In the following chapters of this part of the book we cover the basic patterns of formal messages. As we have noted, they were originally developed for business letters. But they apply equally well to the more formal email messages and memorandums.

First, we cover those messages that are appropriately handled in direct order. These are the good-news or neutral messages—those that will be received favorably. In the next chapter come the bad-news messages. As you will see, these messages usually require the more tactful handling that indirect treatment permits. Persuasive messages come next. While these have similarities to indirect messages, you will see that they have their own unique requirements. The final chapter of this part of the book is devoted to job-seeking messages. Their importance to you and their uniqueness justify a special chapter for them.

SUMMARY BY CHAPTER OBJECTIVES

1 Understand the nature and business uses of text messaging.

1. Text messaging is the newest type of business message.
   - Forecasters predict dramatic growth in its use.
   - Individuals and businesses are using it for a wide variety of purposes.
   - Although text messages are received on mobile phones, they can be sent from phones, email, or the web.
   - Since text messages are usually limited to 160 or fewer characters, shortcuts are often used—but never at the expense of clarity.

2 Understand the phenomenal growth and nature of email.

2. Today, email is a mainstream form of business communication.
   - It has grown because it
     — Eliminates "telephone tag."
     — Saves time.
     — Speeds up decision making.
     — Is cheap.
     — Provides a written record.
   - But it has disadvantages:
     — It is not confidential.
     — It doesn't show emotions.
     — It may be ignored or delayed.
   - Email should be avoided when
     — The message is long, complicated, or needs negotiating.
     — Content needs discussion.
     — Content needs softening in tone, voice, or words.
     — The message is used to avoid unpleasant and uncomfortable personal contact.
     — The message contains sensitive issues.

3 Follow conventional procedures and organize and write clear email messages.

3. The way to write good email messages is as follows:
   - Use standardized prefatory parts.
   - Begin with recipient's name or a greeting.
   - Organize logically.
     — For short messages, present the information in descending order of importance.
     — For long messages, use the organization that best presents the information.
   - Make the message short.
   - Write correctly.
   - Close with your name or a closing statement.
   - Use asterisks, dashes, solid caps, and such, as needed, to show emphasis.
   - Sometimes initialisms are useful, but use them cautiously.

4 Describe the development of the business letter.

4. These are the highlights of the development of business letters:
   - The early civilizations (Chinese, Greek, Roman, Egyptian) used them.
   - Letter formats are standardized (see Appendix B).
   - Early business letters used a stilted language.
   - Strategic organization and humanized language mark recent developments.

5 Explain the variations in the forms of memorandums.

5. The conventional memorandum with its variations are as follows:
   - Hard-copy memorandums (letters written inside a company) usually are processed on special stationery (*Memorandum* at the top; *Date, To, From,* and *Subject* follow)

- Large organizations often include more information (*Department, Plant, Location, Copies to, Store Number,* etc.)
- Email memorandums generally follow these forms.
6. Memorandum formality ranges from the very casual to the highly formal.
   - Many are casual or informal exchanges between workers.
   - Some are formal messages to higher authority.
7. The process of writing business messages begins with planning.
   - First, determine the objective of the message (what it must do).
   - Next, predict the reader's probable reaction to the objective.
   - Then assemble all the information you will need.
   - Select the message plan (direct order if positive or neutral reaction; indirect order if negative reaction).
   - Write the message, applying your knowledge of conciseness, readable writing, and effect of words.
   - Review your work critically, seeking ways of improving it.
   - Get input from others.
   - Evaluate all inputs.
   - Revise, using your best judgment. This end product is an improved message, and you have had a profitable learning experience.

6

Explain the wide range of formality used in memorandums.

7

Describe the process of writing business messages.

1. Will hard-copy letters diminish in importance as email continues to grow? Become obsolete? Vanish?

2. a. Discuss the reasons for email's phenomenal growth.

   b. Is this growth likely to continue?

3. Some authorities say that concerns about correctness inhibit a person's email communication. Does this stand have merit? Discuss.

4. Some authorities say that shortcuts in text messaging will lead to users' inability to spell properly in more formal contexts. Discuss.

5. Memorandums and email messages differ more than letters in their physical makeup. Explain and discuss.

6. Explain the logic of using negative words in email and memorandums to fellow employees that you would not use in letters carrying similar messages.

7. Discuss and justify the wide range of formality used in memorandums and email messages.

8. Identify and explain the steps in the writing process.

Instructions: Write a text message in less than 160 characters for each of the cases below. Be sure your message is both clear and complete.

1. You own three coffee shops around your area. Although you have a loyal base of regular customers, you realize that there is both room to grow this base and a real need to compete with the growing presence of Starbucks and other competitors. Your coffee is good and reasonably priced, but your emphasis on seasonal fruit has long been your specialty. You serve fruit fresh, in muffins, and as toppings for pancakes, French toast, and waffles. In fact, since the local television station included your shop in a healthy eating segment, your low-fat muffins are selling out every day even though you have been increasing production. When some of your loyal customers started grumbling about not always being able to get them, you knew you wanted to serve them better.

   Because most of them have mobile phones, text messaging seemed like an obvious solution. You decided to offer an opt-in polling service that would ask their preference for a particular low-fat muffin or fresh fruit. Your customers could select the days of the week they would be interested in getting the poll. Although they would not be placing an order, they would be helping you plan. You'd also be spending well-targeted promotion dollars while creating goodwill with your loyal customers. Now you need to write this poll question.

2. You are on your way to the airport for a trip to a week-long conference when you remember a file you were supposed to send to a customer. So many last-minute details came up that you really don't remember if you sent it. Unfortunately, you cannot access your work computer from outside the company firewall, but you have a colleague, Chris VanLerBerghe, who would be able to check your email outbox to confirm whether or not you sent it. Chris could also send the file, if necessary. However, you cannot reach her by phone now because she is in an important planning meeting, so you decide to send a text message with the exact names and data she will need. Be sure your message is both clear and complete.

3. As you are in the morning sales meeting, your mobile phone vibrates, indicating you have an incoming call. You recognize the source—Yesaya Chan, the high school student you are mentoring/tutoring in math. When you are finally able to listen to the call, you learn that Yesaya needs your help tonight because his teacher moved a test up a couple of days. He wants to know if you can meet him at the local library at 5 PM, noting that it will be open late tonight. You will say yes, but the earliest you can be there on such short notice is 6 PM. Suggest that he still go to the library at 5 PM and work as many of the review problems on his own that he can. You will help him with the others when you get there. Because he is probably in class now, you will send your response as a text message so it won't interrupt his class.

CHAPTER SIX

Directness in Good-News and Neutral Messages

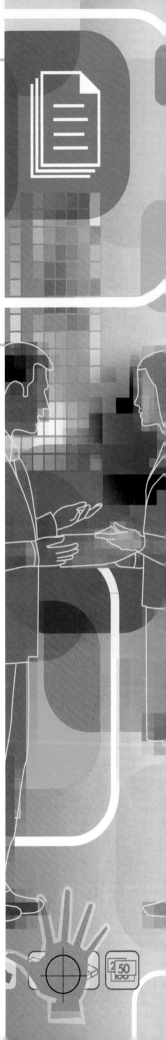

CHAPTER OBJECTIVES

Upon completing this chapter, you will be able to write direct-order messages effectively. To reach this goal, you should be able to

1 Properly assess the reader's reaction to your message.

2 Describe the general plan for direct-order messages.

3 Write clear, well-structured routine requests for information.

4 Compose orderly and thorough inquiries about prospective employees that show respect for human rights.

5 Write direct, orderly, and friendly answers to inquiries.

6 Phrase personnel evaluations that fairly present the essential facts.

7 Compose adjustment grants that regain any lost confidence.

8 Write order acknowledgments that cover problems and build goodwill.

9 Write claims that objectively and courteously explain the facts.

As we noted in Chapter 5, most short business messages appropriately are written in a direct order. In general, this means beginning with the most important point and working downward. These simple messages require little additional instruction.

- Most short messages are in direct order.

Longer, more involved written messages, however, are a different matter for often they involve unique problems and considerations. This chapter is about longer, more involved messages that also are appropriately written in direct order. These are the more formal direct-order messages—those typically written as letters, formal email messages, or formal memorandums. As you will see, because of their uniqueness they require special handling.

- Long, involved messages may be direct or indirect.

Our procedure in covering these messages is first to describe a general plan for writing all messages of this type. Then we will adapt this general plan to some of the more common business situations that generally can be organized by it. We will show why each of these situations requires special treatment and how to handle each. Although our coverage is not complete, we believe that by noting these special requirements, you will be able to adapt to any related situation not covered.

- A general direct plan is presented and then adapted to specific situations.

PRELIMINARY ASSESSMENT

When you write any of the more involved business messages, a good beginning is to assess your reader's probable reaction to what you have to say. If the reaction is likely to be negative, a strategic organization plan is in order. These plans are discussed in following chapters. But if the reaction is likely to be positive, or even neutral, your best approach is likely to be a direct one—that is, one that gets to the objective right away without delaying explanation or conditioning words. The general plan for this direct approach is the following.

- Begin by assessing the reader's probable reaction. A positive or neutral reaction calls for directness; a negative reaction, indirectness.

THE GENERAL DIRECT PLAN

Beginning with the Objective

Begin with your objective. If you are seeking information, start asking for it. If you are giving information, start giving it. Whatever is your objective, lead with it.

- Start with the objective.

To some, this beginning may appear abrupt. They may be tempted to begin with explanation or other delaying talk, as did most business writers a century ago. For example, old-style, indirect beginnings such as "Your April 7 inquiry has been received," do little to further the objective. Directly getting to the objective is efficient. The reader gets the message without delay. And you save words and time.

- Directness saves time for writer and reader.

Presenting Any Necessary Explanation

In most message situations, some explanation is necessary for your reader to know what is going on. Presenting these explanatory facts right after getting the message off to a good start is appropriate. If the explanation is obvious or understood, skip this part.

- If an explanation helps, give it.

Covering the Remaining Part of the Objective

Whatever else must be covered to complete the objective makes up the bulk of the remainder of the message. If you cover all of your objective in the beginning (as in an inquiry in which a single question is asked), nothing else is needed. But if additional questions, answers, or such are needed, you cover them. And you cover them systematically—perhaps listing them or arranging them by paragraphs. If these parts have their own explanations or commentary, you include them. In short, you cover everything else that needs to be covered.

- Complete the objective systematically—perhaps by listing or paragraphing.

Ending with Adapted Goodwill

Because it is the natural thing for friendly people to do, you end this message with some appropriate friendly comment. This is how you would end a face-to-face communication with the reader. There is no reason to do otherwise in writing.

- End with a goodwill comment

These final goodwill words will receive the best reader reaction if they are selected to fit the one case. Such general closes as "A prompt reply will be appreciated" and "Thank you in advance for your response" are positive, for they express a friendly thank-you. And there is nothing wrong with a thank-you sincerely expressed here or elsewhere. The problem is in the routine, rubber-stamp nature of many expressions including it. A more positive reaction results from an individually tailored expression that fits the one case. For example: "If you will answer these questions about Ms. Hill right away, she and I will be most grateful."

- specifically adapted.

Now let us see how you can adapt this general plan to fit the more common direct message situations.

ROUTINE INQUIRIES

INTRODUCTORY SITUATION

Routine Inquiries

Introduce yourself to routine inquiries by assuming you are the assistant to the vice president for administration of Pinnacle Manufacturing Company. Pinnacle is the manufacturer and distributor of an assortment of high-quality products. Your duties involve helping your boss cover a wide assortment of activities. Many of these activities involve writing messages.

At the moment, your boss is working with a group of Pinnacle executives to select offices for a new regional headquarters. They have chosen the city. Now they must find the best possible offices in this city. As chair of this committee, your boss has accepted responsibility for finding office locations from which to choose. Of course, your boss has delegated much of the work to you.

Already you have found three possible office suites in the chosen city. Now you must get the pertinent information about each so that the executives can make their selection. The first of these you found in the classified advertisements of the local newspaper. It is a 3,200-square-foot office suite, but the ad tells little more. So now you must write the advertiser a routine inquiry seeking the information the management team needs.

Choosing from Two Types of Beginnings

The routine inquiry appropriately begins with the objective, just as described in the general plan. Since your objective is to ask for information, this means beginning by asking a question. But here a variation unique to the routine-inquiry message is appropriate. This opening question can be either of two types.

- Routine inquiries appropriately begin asking either of two types of questions.

First, it can be one of the specific questions to be asked (assuming more than one question needs to be asked). Preferably it should be a question that sets up the other questions. For example, if your objective is to get answers to specific questions about test results of a company's product, you might begin with these words:

- (1) a specific question that sets up the information wanted or

Will you please send me test results showing how Duro-Press withstands high temperatures and exposure to sunlight?

In the body of the message you would include the more specific questions concerning temperatures and exposure to sunlight.

Second, the opening question could be a general request for information. The specific questions come later. This beginning sentence illustrates a general request:

- (2) a general request for information.

Will you please answer the following questions about Duro-Press fabric?

The "will you" here and in the preceding example may appear to be unnecessary. The basic message would not change if the words were eliminated. In the minds of some authorities, however, including them softens the request and is worth the additional length.

Answering inquiries that do not include adequate explanation can be frustrating.

Informing and Explaining Adequately

- Somewhere in the message, explain enough to enable the reader to answer.

To help your reader answer your questions, you may need to include explanation or information. If you do not explain enough or if you misjudge the reader's knowledge, you make the reader's task difficult. For example, answers to questions about a computer often depend on the specific needs or characteristics of the company that will use it. The best-informed computer expert cannot answer such questions without knowing the facts of the company concerned.

- Place the explanation anywhere it fits logically.

Where and how you include the necessary explanatory information depend on the nature of your message. Usually, a good place for general explanatory material that fits the entire message is following the direct opening sentence. Here it helps reduce any startling effect that a direct opening question might have. It often fits logically into this place, serving as a qualifying or justifying sentence for the message. In messages that ask more than one question, you will sometimes need to include explanatory material with the questions. If this is the case, the explanation fits best with the questions to which it pertains. Such messages may alternate questions and explanations.

Structuring the Questions

- If the inquiry involves just one question, begin with it.

If your inquiry involves just one question, you can achieve your primary objective with the first sentence. After any necessary explanation and a few words of friendly closing comment, your message is done. If you must ask a number of questions, however, you will need to consider their organization.

- If it involves more than one, make each stand out. Do this by (1) placing each question in a separate sentence,

Whatever you do, you will need to make your questions stand out. You can do this in a number of ways. First, you can make each question a separate sentence with a bullet, a symbol (for example, ●, ○, ■) used to call attention to a particular item. Combining two or more questions in a sentence de-emphasizes each and invites the reader's mind to overlook some.

- (2) structuring the questions in separate paragraphs,

Second, you can give each question a separate paragraph, whenever this practice is logical. It is logical when your explanation and other comments about each question justify a paragraph.

- (3) ordering or ranking the questions, and

Third, you can order or rank your questions with numbers. By using words (*first, second, third,* etc.), numerals (1, 2, 3, etc.), or letters (*a, b, c,* etc.), you make the questions stand out. Also, you provide the reader with a convenient check and reference guide to answering.

How One Might Write a Routine Inquiry

Suppose one wants to write a routine inquiry, say, to find out about a merger. Here is how the message might read when written by a

12-year-old public school student: "What gives on this merger?"

21-year-old college graduate: "Kindly inform me on current general economic and specific pertinent industrial factors relating to the scheduled amalgamated proposals."

40-year-old junior executive: "J.P.—Please contact me and put me in the picture regarding the mooted merger. I have nothing in my portfolio on it. Sincerely, W.J."

55-year-old member of the board, with private secretary: "Without prejudice to our position vis-à-vis future developments either planned or in the stage of actual activating, the undersigned would appreciate any generally informative matter together with any pertinent program-planning data specific to any merger plans that may or may not have been advanced in quarters not necessarily germane to the assigned field of the undersigned."

65-year-old executive, now boss of the company and very busy: "What gives on this merger?"

Fourth, you can structure your questions in question form. True questions stand out. Sentences that merely hint at a need for information do not attract much attention. The "It would be nice if you would tell me . . ." and "I would like to know . . ." types are really not questions. They do not ask—they merely suggest. The questions that stand out are those written in question form: "Will you please tell me . . . ?" "How much would one be able to save . . . ?" "How many contract problems have you had . . . ?"

● (4) using the question form of sentence.

You may want to avoid questions that can be answered with a simple *yes* or *no*. An obvious exception, of course, would be when you really want a simple *yes* or *no* answer. For example, the question "Is the chair available in blue?" may not be what you really want to know. A better wording probably is "In what colors is the chair available?" Often you'll find that you can combine a yes/no question and its explanation to get a better, more concise question. To illustrate, the wording "Does the program run with Windows? We use Windows 2000." could be improved with "What operating system does the program run on?" or "Does the program run with Windows 2000?"

● But take caution in asking questions that produce yes or no answers.

Ending with Goodwill

The goodwill ending described in the general plan is appropriate here, just as it is in most business messages. And we must emphasize again that the closing words do the most toward creating goodwill when they fit the one case.

● End with a friendly comment that fits the one case.

Reviewing the Order

In summary, the plan recommended for the routine inquiry message is as follows:

* Begin directly with the objective—either a specific question that sets up the entire message or a general request for information.

* Include necessary explanation—wherever it fits.

* If a number of questions are involved, ask them.

* Make the questions stand out (using bullets, numbering, paragraphing, question form).

* End with goodwill words adapted to the individual case.

Picture Bullets Allow Writers to List Equal Items with a Bit of Flair

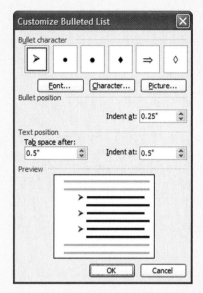
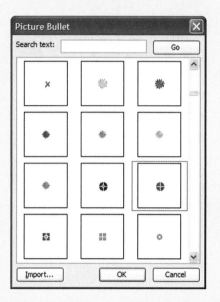
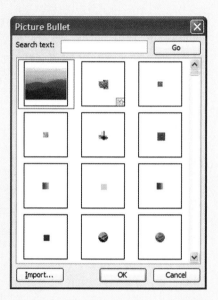

Word processing software allows writers to list items easily with bullets or numbers. Writers generally use numbers to show ordering or ranking and bullets to list unranked or equal items. One way to add interest to lists is to use picture bullets, an easy task today. Rather than selecting one of the six standard bullets, writers can easily customize them with pictures. Microsoft Word includes a nice selection of picture bullets in various colors and styles, some that you see above. However, writers can also select other images to import for use as a bullet. By simply pointing and clicking on the image to import, a writer instantly creates a bullet and resizes it automatically for bullet use.

In a message to its members meeting in Albuquerque, the executive director of the Association for Business Communication might use one picture bullet to list items members should bring with them for a side trip to nearby Sandia Peak. The writer might suggest that members bring these items:

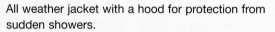 Binoculars for taking in spectacular views.

All weather jacket with a hood for protection from sudden showers.

Cameras with wide lenses for panoramic photos.

The same message might use a different picture bullet for a list of items for a side trip to Santa Fe. Clearly, these bullets could add interest through color and convey differentiation of the lists as well. Through careful use, picture bullets can help writers present lists that get attention.

Contrasting Examples

 Following are good and bad examples. They could be email, fax, or letter.

Illustrating bad and good techniques are the following two routine inquiry messages about office space for a new Pinnacle regional headquarters (recall the introductory situation). The first example follows the indirect pattern that was popular in days gone by. The second is direct. Here they are presented as letters, as indicated by the "Dear" in the salutation and the "Sincerely" closing. In following parts of this book, similar illustrations are presented in email format. As you know, email format uses the conventional subject beginning, name-only salutation, and no complimentary close. The format we use is of little consequence. Our emphasis is on the message, which could be letter, fax, or email. We make this distinction in format only as a matter of clarification.

In addition, the two Case Illustrations show good handling of inquiries. The hand-written comments in the margins of these examples should be especially useful.

As you read the first example below, note that it is marked by a "red light" icon in the side panel. We use this icon throughout the book wherever we show bad examples. Take care not to confuse the bad with the good examples, which are marked by a "green light" icon.

The Old-Style Indirect Message. The less effective message begins slowly and gives obvious information. Even if one thinks that this information needs to be communicated, it does not deserve the emphasis of the opening sentence. The writer gets to the point of the message in the second paragraph. But there are no questions here—just hints for information. The items of information wanted do not stand out but are listed in rapid succession in one sentence. The close is friendly but old style.

Dear Mr. Piper:

We have seen your advertisement for 3,200 square feet of office space in the *Daily Journal*. As we are interested, we would like additional information.

Specifically, we would like to know the interior layout, annual cost, availability of transportation, length of lease agreement, escalation provisions, and any other information you think pertinent.

If the information you give us is favorable, we will inspect the property. Hoping to hear from you by return mail, we are

Sincerely

First is the bad example. Its indirect beginning makes it slow.

The Direct and Effective Message. The second example begins directly by asking for information. The explanation is brief but complete. The questions, with explanation worked in where needed, are made to stand out; thus, they help to make answering easy. The message closes with a courteous and appropriate request for quick action.

Dear Mr. Piper:

Will you please answer the following questions about the 3,200-square-foot office suite advertised in the June 28 issue of the *Daily Journal*? It appears that this space may be suitable for the new regional headquarters we are opening in your city in August.

This direct and orderly letter is better.

- Is the layout of these offices suitable for a workforce of two administrators, a receptionist, and seven office employees? (If possible, please send us a diagram of the space.)

- What is the annual rental charge?

- Are housekeeping, maintenance, and utilities included?

- What is the nature of the walls and flooring?

- Does the location provide easy access to mass transportation and the airport?

- What are your requirements for length of lease agreement?

- Would escalation provisions be included in the lease agreement?

If your answers meet our needs, we will want to physically tour and inspect the offices before requesting a proposal. Since we must move quickly, please respond right away.

Sincerely,

INQUIRIES ABOUT PEOPLE

INTRODUCTORY SITUATION

Inquiries about People

From time to time, your work at Pinnacle involves investigating applicants for employment. Of course, in your position you do no hiring. The Human Resources Department conducts initial interviews, administers aptitude tests, and performs all the other screening tasks. Then it refers the best applicants to the executives in charge of the jobs to be filled. The executives, including your boss, make the final decisions.

This morning Human Resources sent your boss a Mr. Rowe W. Hart, who is applying for the vacant position of office manager. Mr. Hart appears to be well qualified—good test scores and employment record. After talking with Hart, your boss thinks that he is bright and personable. Because your boss believes that he cannot judge ability from a single interview, he has asked you to follow your usual practice of writing the applicant's references for their evaluations. In Hart's case, the best possibility appears to be Ms. Alice Borders, who was his immediate supervisor for three years.

Your task now is to write Ms. Borders a message that will get the information you need. The following discussion and illustrations show you how.

Messages asking for information about people are a special form of routine inquiry. The recommended plan for writing them is virtually the same. But writing them involves two special considerations, which is why we review them separately.

Respecting the Rights of People

- 1. Respect human rights, both legal and moral.

First is the need to respect the rights of the people involved. These rights are both legal and moral. In fact, because of the legal aspects, some companies do not permit their employees to correspond about personnel. Those companies that do permit such exchanges of information should try to protect the rights of the people involved.

- Ask only for information related to the job.

When you write these messages, for legal as well as ethical reasons, you should ask only questions related to the job. Specifically, you should avoid questions about the applicant's race, religion, sex, age, pregnancy, and marital situation.[1] Even questions about the applicant's citizenship status and arrest and conviction record are better not asked. So are questions about mental and physical disabilities and organization (especially union) memberships.

- Stress fact, write for business use and when authorized, and treat confidentially.

In protecting these rights, you must seek truth and act in good faith. You should ask only for information you need for business purposes. You should ask only when the subject has authorized the inquiry. You should hold any information received in confidence. And you would do well to include these points in your message, either in words or by implication.

Structuring around the One Job

- 2. Structure the questions around the job.

A second concern in writing this message is the need to structure the questions around the job involved. Specifically, the information you seek should be determined by your needs. What you need is information that will tell you whether the subject is qualified

---

[1] As required by the following acts and court cases relating to them: Wagner Act of 1935, Immigration and Nationality Act of 1952, Civil Rights Act of 1964, Vocational Rehabilitation Act of 1973, Age Discrimination Act of 1975, and Pregnancy Discrimination Act of 1978.

Routine Inquiries (Getting Information about a Training Program) This email message is from a company training director to the director of a management-training program. The company training director has received literature on the program but needs additional information. The message seeks this information.

Direct—a general request sets up the specific question

Reference to website tells what writer knows—helps reader in responding

Numbered questions stand out—helps reader in responding

Explanations worked into questions where needed

Favorable forward look makes goodwill close

To... sgarbett@sedonagroup.com

Cc...

Subject: Questions on Management Courses

Ms. Garbett

Please send me the additional information we need in determining whether to enroll some of our executives in your online management courses. We have the general information and the schedule posted on your website. Specifically, we need answers to these questions:

1. What are your quantity discount rates? We could enroll about six executives for each course.

2. At what background level is your program geared? We have engineers, accountants, scientists, and business executives. Most have college degrees. Some do not.

3. What arrangements need to be made for them to receive college credit for the course? Some of our executives are working on degrees and want credit.

4. What are the names and email addresses of training directors of companies that have enrolled their executives in your management courses?

We will appreciate having your answers for our October 3 staff meeting. We look forward to the possibility of sending our executives to you in the years ahead.

Ronald Dupree
Director of Training
Sorbet Inc.
Phone: 619.594.6942
Fax: 801.309.2411
www.sorbet.com

Routine Inquiries (An Inquiry about Hotel Accommodations) This fax message to a hotel inquires about meeting accommodations for a professional association. In selecting a hotel, the company's managers need answers to specific questions. The message covers these questions.

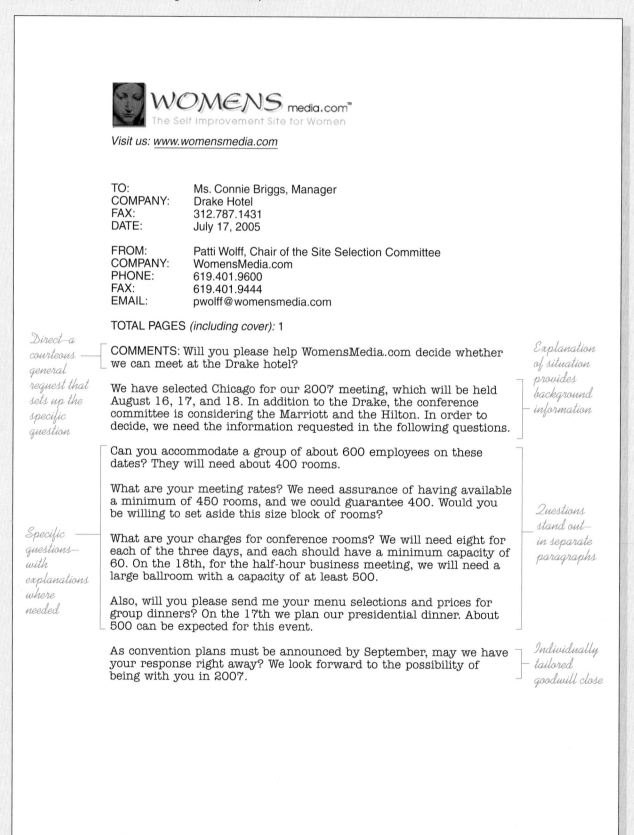

WOMENS media.com™
The Self Improvement Site for Women

Visit us: www.womensmedia.com

TO:	Ms. Connie Briggs, Manager
COMPANY:	Drake Hotel
FAX:	312.787.1431
DATE:	July 17, 2005

FROM:	Patti Wolff, Chair of the Site Selection Committee
COMPANY:	WomensMedia.com
PHONE:	619.401.9600
FAX:	619.401.9444
EMAIL:	pwolff@womensmedia.com

TOTAL PAGES *(including cover):* 1

Direct—a courteous general request that sets up the specific question

COMMENTS: Will you please help WomensMedia.com decide whether we can meet at the Drake hotel?

Explanation of situation provides background information

We have selected Chicago for our 2007 meeting, which will be held August 16, 17, and 18. In addition to the Drake, the conference committee is considering the Marriott and the Hilton. In order to decide, we need the information requested in the following questions.

Specific questions— with explanations where needed

Can you accommodate a group of about 600 employees on these dates? They will need about 400 rooms.

What are your meeting rates? We need assurance of having available a minimum of 450 rooms, and we could guarantee 400. Would you be willing to set aside this size block of rooms?

Questions stand out— in separate paragraphs

What are your charges for conference rooms? We will need eight for each of the three days, and each should have a minimum capacity of 60. On the 18th, for the half-hour business meeting, we will need a large ballroom with a capacity of at least 500.

Also, will you please send me your menu selections and prices for group dinners? On the 17th we plan our presidential dinner. About 500 can be expected for this event.

Individually tailored goodwill close

As convention plans must be announced by September, may we have your response right away? We look forward to the possibility of being with you in 2007.

Some Words of Advice on Letter Writing from the Old Masters

A letter is a deliberate and written conversation.

Gracian

Remember this: write only as you would speak; then your letter will be good.

Goethe

There is one golden rule to bear in mind always: that we should try to put ourselves in the position of our correspondent, to imagine his feelings as he writes his letters, and to gauge his reaction as he receives ours. If we put ourselves in the other man's shoes we shall speedily detect how unconvincing our letters can seem, or how much we may be taking for granted.

Sir Ernest Gowers

Do not answer a letter in the midst of great anger.

Chinese proverb

Seeking an epistle hath chieflie this definition hereof, in that it is termed the familiar and mutual task of one friend to another: it seemeth the character thereof should according thereunto be simple, plain and of the lowest and neatest stile utterly devoid of any shadow of lie and lofty speeches.

Angel Day, *The English Secretorie,* 1586
(early book on letter writing)

And to describe the true definition of an Epistle or letter, it is nothing but an Oration written, containing the mynd of the Orator, or wryter, thereby to give to him or them absent, the same that should be declared if they were present.

William Fulwood, *The Enemie of Idlenesse,* 1568
(earliest known book on letter writing in English)

for the one job involved. Thus, you should analyze the job to determine the information you should have in selecting a person to do it. The questions you would ask about an applicant for a sales job, for example, would be quite different from those you would ask about an applicant for an accounting position.

Summarizing the Plan

When these two requirements are considered, the general plan for inquiries about personnel becomes the following:

• Messages asking questions about people should follow this general plan.

- Begin directly, with a general question seeking information or a specific question that sets up the entire message.
- Explain the situation.
- Cover the additional questions systematically, making certain they cover the work involved and protect the subject's rights.
- End with adapted goodwill talk.

Contrasting Examples

In applying the preceding instructions to Rowe Hart's application for the position of office manager at Pinnacle, assume that analysis of the applicant and the job tells you that you should ask four questions. First, is Hart capable of handling the responsibilities involved? Second, does he know the work? Third, how hard a worker is he?

• Following are good and bad examples of a personnel inquiry.

Answering inquiries about people requires the most careful thought, for the lives and rights of human beings are affected.

Fourth, is he morally responsible? Now, how would you arrange these questions and the necessary explanation in a message?

A Scant and Hurried Example. The first email message shows a not-so-good effort. The opening is indirect. The explanation in the opening is important, but does it deserve the emphasis that the beginning position gives it? Although the question part gives the appearance of conciseness, it is actually scant. It includes no explanation. It does not even mention for what kind of position Hart is being considered. The items of information wanted do not stand out. In fact, they are not even worded as questions but are run together in a single declarative sentence. Though courteous, the closing words are old style.

An Orderly and Thorough Example. The good example gives evidence of good analysis of the job and the applicant. The message begins directly with an opening

This bad one is slow and scant.

Subject: Rowe W. Hart

Ms. Borders

Mr. Rowe W. Hart has applied to us for employment and has given your name as a reference. He indicates that he worked under your supervision during the period 1998–2003.

We would be most appreciative if you would give us your evaluation of Mr. Hart. We are especially interested in his ability to handle responsibility, knowledge of office procedures, work habits, and morals.

Thanking you in advance for your courtesy, I remain,

Susan T. Chambers

Shortcut Tools Help Writers Improve Productivity and Quality

AutoCorrect: English (U.S.)

| AutoText | AutoFormat | Smart Tags |
| AutoCorrect | AutoFormat As You Type | |

☑ Show AutoCorrect Options buttons

☑ Correct TWo INitial CApitals   [Exceptions...]
☑ Capitalize first letter of sentences
☑ Capitalize first letter of table cells
☑ Capitalize names of days
☑ Correct accidental usage of cAPS LOCK key
☑ Replace text as you type

Replace: With: ⦿ Plain text   ○ Formatted text

| ABC | Association for Business Communication |

abbout	about
abotu	about
abouta	about a
aboutit	about it

[Add] [Delete]

☑ Automatically use suggestions from the spelling checker

[OK] [Cancel]

Shortcuts help writers save time and improve quality. One of the easiest to use is the AutoCorrect tool in Word (shown here) or the similar QuickCorrect tool in WordPerfect. This tool will automatically replace a word entered with another word set up to replace that particular word. The default setting is generally set up to correct common misspellings and typos. However, it also can be used to expand acronyms or phrases used repeatedly.

If you worked frequently with the Association for Business Communication, you might set up the AutoCorrect tool to replace the acronym ABC with the full name, as you see at the left. Not only will this shortcut enable you to save time, but it also will improve the quality by inserting a correctly spelled and typed replacement every time.

question that serves as a topic sentence. The beginning also includes helpful explanation. But this part is not given unnecessary emphasis, as it was in the preceding example. Then the message presents the specific questions. Worded separately and in question form, each stands out and is easy to answer. Worked in with each question is explanation that will help the reader understand the work for which Hart is being considered. The close is courteous and tailored for the one case. Note also, throughout the message, the concern for the rights of the people involved. Clearly, the inquiry is authorized, is for business purposes only, and will be treated confidentially.

"First the good news—if I cure you, I'll become world famous."

SOURCE: From *The Wall Street Journal*—Permission Cartoon Features Syndicate.

Inquiries about People (An Inquiry about a Prospective Branch Manager) This is the case of a freight-line executive who is looking for a manager for one of the company's branches. The top applicant is a shipping clerk for a furniture company. With the applicant's permission, the executive has written this letter to the applicant's employer.

✷ ARROW FREIGHT

7171 INDIGO LAKE RD.
AUSTIN, TX 78710
512-212-8908
Fax: 512-212-8904

May 10, 2004

Mr. Amos T. Dodgson, Manager
Easterbrook Furniture, Inc.
3970 Burnham Avenue
Seattle, WA 98125

Dear Mr. Dodgson:

Direct interest-gaining question tells reader what is needed

Will you do George Adams and me the favor of providing an evaluative report on him? He is an assistant shipping clerk with you who wants to manage a branch office for us. He has authorized this inquiry.

Explanation softens possible startling effect of opening

Human rights respected

- How well does he know packing and hauling techniques?

Bullets make questions stand out—questions cover work

- How do you judge his administrative ability to run an office of one administrative assistant and a staff of six?

- What is your appraisal of his ability to meet customers and generally build goodwill with the community?

Explanation as needed

- What do you know about his honesty and integrity? Our managers are solely responsible for their branch's assets—equipment as well as all receipts.

- As a final question, is there anything else you can tell me that might indicate whether Mr. Adams is the right person for our job?

I will be grateful for your answers. Of course, what you report will be held in strict confidence.

Friendly close and respect for human rights

Sincerely,

Mary E. Brooking

Mary E. Brooking
Manager

det

Subject: Your evaluation of Rowe W. Hart

Ms. Borders

Will you help me evaluate Mr. Rowe W. Hart for the position of office manager? In authorizing this inquiry, Mr. Hart indicated that he worked for you from 1998 to 2003. Your candid answers to the following questions will help me determine whether Mr. Hart is the right person for this job.

What is your evaluation of Mr. Hart's leadership ability, including interpersonal skills? Our office has a staff of 11.

How well can Mr. Hart manage a rapidly expanding office system? Ours is a growing company. The person who manages our office not only will need to have good computer skills but also will need to know how to adapt them to changing conditions.

What is your evaluation of Mr. Hart's stamina and drive? The position he seeks often involves working in a fast-paced environment under time pressures.

What is your evaluation of Mr. Hart's moral reliability? Our office manager is responsible for much of our company equipment as well as some company funds.

We will, of course, hold your answers in strict confidence. And we will appreciate whatever help you are able to give Mr. Hart and us.

Susan T. Chambers

This good example shows careful study of the job and the applicant.

GENERAL FAVORABLE RESPONSES

INTRODUCTORY SITUATION

General Favorable Responses

Continue in your role as assistant to the vice president for operations of Pinnacle Manufacturing Company and answer some of the messages sent to you.

Most of the incoming messages you answer favorably. That is, you tell the reader what he or she wants to know. In today's inbox, for example, you have a typical problem of this type. It is a message from a prospective customer for Pinnacle's Chem-Treat paint. In response to an advertisement, this prospective customer asks a number of specific questions about Chem-Treat. Foremost, she wants to know whether the paint is really mildewproof. Do you have evidence of results? Do you guarantee results? Is the paint safe? How much does a gallon cost? Will one coat do the job?

You can answer all but one of the questions positively. Of course, you will report this one negative point (that two coats are needed to do most jobs), but you will take care to give it only the emphasis it deserves. The response will be primarily a good-news message. Because the reader is a good prospect, you will work for the best good-will effect.

When you answer inquiries favorably, your primary goal is to tell your readers what they want to know. Because their reactions to your goal will be favorable, directness is in order.

Beginning with the Answer

As you can deduce from the preceding examples, directness here means giving the readers what they want at the beginning. Thus you begin by answering. When a response involves answering a single question, you begin by answering that question.

- Begin by answering. If there is one question, answer it; if there are more than one, answer the most important.

How Routine Responses Were Written in the Late 1800s

The following model letter for answering routine inquiries appears on page 75 of O. R. Palmer's *Type-Writing and Business Correspondence.* Published in 1896, the book was a leader in its field.

Dear Sirs:

Your favor of Dec. 18th, enclosing blue prints for tank, received. In reply thereto we beg to submit the following:

[*Here was a listing of materials for the tank.*]

Trusting that our price may be satisfactory to you, and that we shall be favored with your order, we beg to remain,

Very truly yours,

When it involves answering two or more questions, one good plan is to begin by answering one of them—preferably the most important. In the Chem-Treat case, this opening would get the response off to a fast start:

Yes, you can use Chem-Treat to prevent mildew.

- Or begin by saying that you are complying with the request.

An alternative possibility is to begin by stating that you are giving the reader what he or she wants—that you are complying with the request. Actually, this approach is really not direct, for it delays giving the information requested. But it is a favorable beginning, and it does not run the risk of sounding abrupt, which is a criticism of direct beginnings. These examples illustrate this type of beginning:

The following information should tell you what you need to know about Chem-Treat.

Here are the answers to your questions about Chem-Treat.

Identifying the Message Being Answered

Because this message is a response to another message, you should identify the message you are answering. Such identification helps the reader recall or find the message being answered. If you are writing an email response, the original message is appended to your message. Hard-copy messages may use a subject line (Subject: Your April 2nd inquiry about Chem-Treat), as illustrated in Appendix B. Or you can refer to the message incidentally in the text ("as requested in your April 2 inquiry"). Preferably you should make this identification early in your message.

Logically Arranging the Answers

- If one answer is involved, give it directly and completely.

If you are answering just one question, you have little to do after handling that question in the opening. You answer it as completely as the situation requires, and you present whatever explanation or other information is needed. Then you are ready to close the message.

- If more that one answer is involved, arrange the answers so that each stands out.

If, on the other hand, you are answering two or more questions, the body of your message becomes a series of answers. As in all clear writing, you should work for a logical order, perhaps answering the questions in the order your reader used in asking them. You may even number your answers, especially if your reader numbered the

Skillful (?) Handling of a Complaint

A traveling man once spent a sleepless night in a hotel room, tormented by the sight of cockroaches walking over the ceiling, walls, and floor. Upon returning home, he indignantly protested the condition in a letter to the hotel management. Some days later, to his delight, he received a masterfully written response. It complimented him for reporting the condition, and it assured him that the matter would be corrected—that such a thing would never happen again. The man was satisfied, and his confidence in the hotel was restored. His satisfaction vanished, however, when he discovered an interoffice memo that had been accidentally inserted into the envelope. The memo said, "Send this nut the cockroach letter."

questions. Or you may decide to arrange your answers by paragraphs so that each stands out clearly.

Skillfully Handling the Negatives

When your response concerns some bad news along with the good news, you may need to handle the bad news with care. Bad news stands out. Unless you are careful, it is likely to receive more emphasis than it deserves. Sometimes you will need to subordinate the bad news and emphasize the good news.

> • Emphasize favorable responses; subordinate unfavorable responses.

In giving proper emphasis to the good- and bad-news parts, you should use the techniques discussed in Chapter 4, especially position. That is, you should place the good news in positions of high emphasis—at paragraph beginnings and endings and at the beginning and ending of the message as a whole. You should place the bad news in secondary positions. In addition, you should use space emphasis to your advantage. This means giving less space to bad-news parts and more space to good-news parts. You also should select words and build sentences that communicate the effect you want. Generally, this means using happy and pleasant words and avoiding unpleasant and sad words. Your overall goal should be to present the information in your response so that your readers get just the right effect.

> • Place favorable responses at beginnings and ends. Give them more space. Use words skillfully to emphasize them.

Considering Extras

For the best in goodwill effect and for reasons of etiquette, you should consider including extras with your answers. These are the things you say and do that are not actually required. Examples are a comment or question showing an interest in the reader's problem, some additional information that may prove valuable, and a suggestion for use of the information supplied. In fact, extras can be anything that does more than skim the surface with hurried, routine answers. Such extras frequently make the difference between success and failure in the goodwill effort.

> • The little extra things you do for the reader will build goodwill.

Illustrations of how extras can be used to strengthen the goodwill effects of a message are as broad as the imagination. A business executive answering a college professor's request for information on company operations could supplement the requested information with suggestions of other sources. A technical writer could amplify highly technical answers with simpler explanations. In the Chem-Treat problem, additional information (say, how much surface area a gallon covers) would be helpful. Such extras genuinely serve readers and serve as evidence of good etiquette.

Routine Response Message (Favorable Response to a Professor's Request) This email message responds to a professor's request for production records that will be used in a research project. The writer is giving the information wanted but must restrict its use.

Direct reports a favorable response

Goodwill adapted to one cause

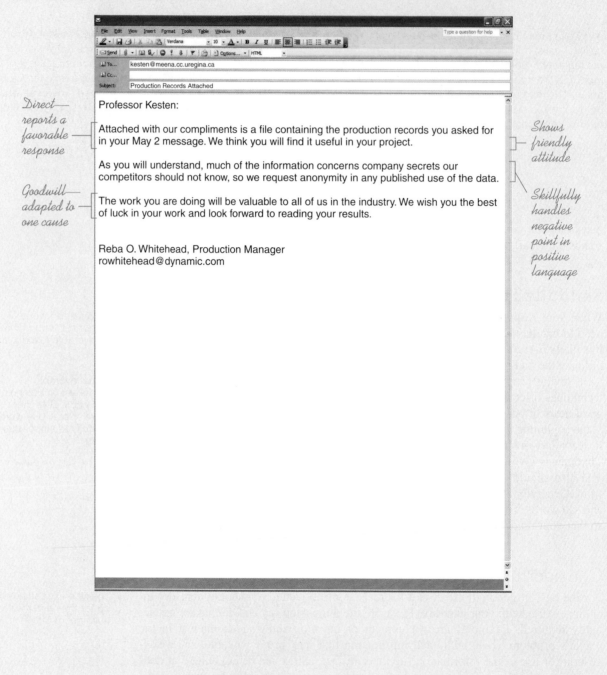

Shows friendly attitude

Skillfully handles negative point in positive language

To... kesten@meena.cc.uregina.ca

Cc...

Subject: Production Records Attached

Professor Kesten:

Attached with our compliments is a file containing the production records you asked for in your May 2 message. We think you will find it useful in your project.

As you will understand, much of the information concerns company secrets our competitors should not know, so we request anonymity in any published use of the data.

The work you are doing will be valuable to all of us in the industry. We wish you the best of luck in your work and look forward to reading your results.

Reba O. Whitehead, Production Manager
rowhitehead@dynamic.com

Routine Response Message (A Request for Detailed Information) Answering an inquiry about a company's experience with a word processing center, this letter numbers the answers as the questions were numbered in the inquiry. The opening appropriately sets up the numbered answers with a statement that indicates a favorable response.

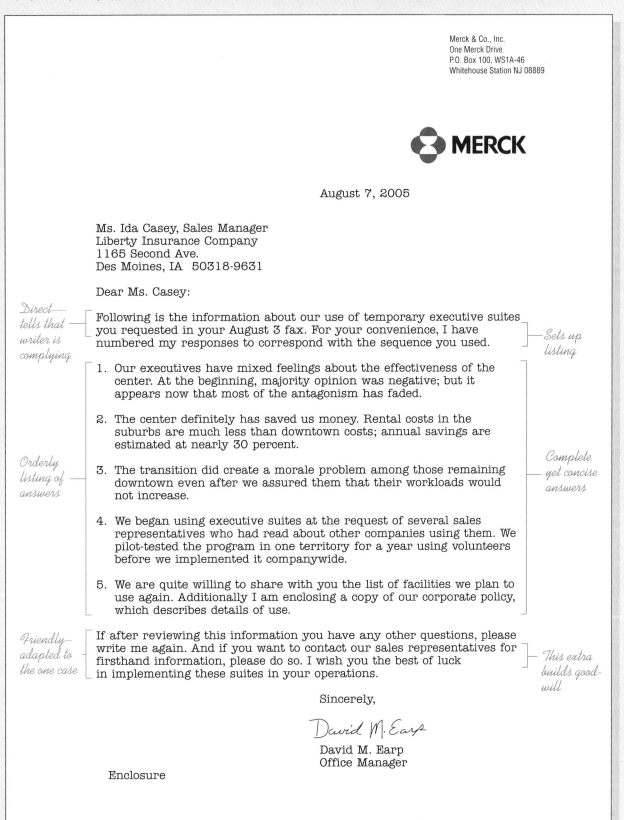

Merck & Co., Inc.
One Merck Drive
P.O. Box 100, WS1A-46
Whitehouse Station NJ 08889

MERCK

August 7, 2005

Ms. Ida Casey, Sales Manager
Liberty Insurance Company
1165 Second Ave.
Des Moines, IA 50318-9631

Dear Ms. Casey:

Direct tells that writer is complying

Following is the information about our use of temporary executive suites you requested in your August 3 fax. For your convenience, I have numbered my responses to correspond with the sequence you used.

Sets up listing

1. Our executives have mixed feelings about the effectiveness of the center. At the beginning, majority opinion was negative; but it appears now that most of the antagonism has faded.

2. The center definitely has saved us money. Rental costs in the suburbs are much less than downtown costs; annual savings are estimated at nearly 30 percent.

Orderly listing of answers

3. The transition did create a morale problem among those remaining downtown even after we assured them that their workloads would not increase.

Complete yet concise answers

4. We began using executive suites at the request of several sales representatives who had read about other companies using them. We pilot-tested the program in one territory for a year using volunteers before we implemented it companywide.

5. We are quite willing to share with you the list of facilities we plan to use again. Additionally I am enclosing a copy of our corporate policy, which describes details of use.

Friendly adapted to the one case

If after reviewing this information you have any other questions, please write me again. And if you want to contact our sales representatives for firsthand information, please do so. I wish you the best of luck in implementing these suites in your operations.

This extra builds goodwill

Sincerely,

David M. Earp

David M. Earp
Office Manager

Enclosure

Truthful (?) Reporting in Recommendation Letters

Some choice double entendres (two-meaning sentences) to be used in letters of recommendation when you don't want to lie or to hurt the person involved:

To describe a lazy person: "In my opinion, you will be very fortunate to get this person to work for you."

To describe an inept person: "I most enthusiastically recommend this candidate with no qualifications whatsoever."

To describe an ex-employee who had problems getting along with fellow workers: "I am pleased to say that this candidate is a former colleague of mine."

To describe a job applicant who is not worth further consideration: "I would urge you to waste no time in making this candidate an offer of employment."

To describe a person with lackluster credentials: "All in all, I cannot say enough good things about this candidate or recommend him too highly."

Robert Thornton

Closing Cordially

As in the other direct messages, your ending should be cordial, friendly words that fit the one case. For example, you might close the Chem-Treat message with these words:

> If I can help you further in deciding whether Chem-Treat will meet your needs, please write me again.

Reviewing the Plan

When we review the preceding special considerations, we produce the following plan for the general favorable response message:

- Begin with the answer, or state that you are complying with the request.
- Identify the message being answered either incidentally or in a subject line.
- Continue to give what is wanted in orderly arrangement.
- If negative information is involved, give it proper emphasis.
- Consider including extras.
- End with a friendly, adapted comment.

Contrasting Illustrations

- Following are bad and good examples of response letters.

Contrasting email messages in answer to the Chem-Treat inquiry illustrate the techniques of answering routine inquiries. The first message violates many of the standards set in this and earlier chapters. The second meets the requirements of a good business message. Its cordiality gives evidence of good business etiquette.

An Indirect and Hurried Response. The not-so-good message begins indirectly with an obvious statement referring to receipt of the inquiry. Though well intended, the second sentence continues to delay the answers. The second paragraph begins to give the information sought, but it emphasizes the most negative answer by position and by wording. This answer is followed by hurried and routine answers to the other questions asked. Only the barest information is presented. The close belongs to the language of business in great-grandfather's day.

Subject: Your inquiry of April 3

Dear Ms. Motley:

I have received your April 3 message, in which you inquire about our Chem-Treat paint. I want you to know that we appreciate your interest and will welcome your business.

In response to your question about how many coats are needed to cover new surfaces, I regret to report that two are usually required. The paint is mildewproof. We do guarantee it. It has been well tested in our laboratories. It is safe to use as directed.

Hoping to hear from you again, I remain

George Moxley

The poor one is indirect and ineffective.

Effectiveness in Direct Response. The better message begins directly, with the most favorable answer. Then it presents the other answers, giving each the emphasis and positive language it deserves. It subordinates the one negative answer, by position, volume of treatment, and structure. More pleasant information follows the negative answer. The close is goodwill talk, with some subtle selling strategy thrown in. "We know that you'll enjoy the long-lasting beauty of this mildewproof paint" points positively to purchase and successful use of the product.

Subject: Your April 3 inquiry about Chem-Treat

Ms. Motley:

Yes, Chem-Treat paint will prevent mildew or we will give you back your money. We know it works, because we have tested it under all common conditions. In every case, it proved successful.

When you carefully follow the directions on each can, Chem-Treat paint is guaranteed safe. As the directions state, you should use Chem-Treat only in a well-ventilated room—never in a closed, unvented area.

One gallon of Chem-Treat is usually enough for one-coat coverage of 500 square feet of previously painted surface. For the best results on new surfaces, you will want to apply two coats. For such surfaces, you should figure about 200 square feet per gallon for a good heavy coating that will give you five years or more of beautiful protection.

We sincerely appreciate your interest in Chem-Treat, Ms. Motley. We know that you'll enjoy the long-lasting beauty of this mildewproof paint.

George Moxley

This direct letter does a better job.

PERSONNEL EVALUATIONS

Personnel Evaluations

A request for an evaluation of a Pinnacle employee is the next item you take from your incoming messages. The writer, Ms. Mary Brooking, president, Red Arrow Transport, Inc., wants information about George Adams, Pinnacle's assistant shipping clerk. Ms. Brooking is considering Adams for the position of manager of a Red Arrow branch office. In her message she asks some specific questions about him and about his ability to do the job. Because Adams works under the supervision of your office, he listed you as a reference.

You are well acquainted with Adams and his work. Just last week he came by your office to tell you that he was looking at an employment opportunity that offered advancement—something that Pinnacle, unfortunately, could not offer soon. Everything you have observed in his work supports your opinion that he is industrious and capable. He knows the shipping business, and he is an able supervisor. He tends to stick to his own ideas too strongly, and this has caused some friction with his superiors—you included. But you feel that this tendency reflects his independence and self-reliance, qualities that may be desirable in a branch manager with no immediate supervisors on the grounds.

Because you believe that Adams has earned the position he seeks, you want to write an evaluation that will help him. But because you are an honest person, you will report truthfully. Thus, you will be fair to all concerned—to Adams, to Ms. Brooking, and to you.

- Because they satisfy the reader, personnel evaluations justifiably use the direct order.

When you receive a request to evaluate a former employee, company policy may prohibit you from answering. For legal reasons, many companies do not permit such messages. But if you do write such messages, you should organize them in the direct order. The justification for direct order is that the message is favorable. You are doing what the reader requested. It is favorable regardless of whether it contains positive or negative information about the employee because the reader is getting the information requested.

Using Typical Direct Order

- Use the typical direct plan and emphasize fairness.

The personnel evaluation message is a special type of response to a routine request. You begin with either an answer to a question asked or with a statement indicating that you are complying with the request. You identify the message you are answering. You give the information requested in an orderly and logical way, usually organized around the questions asked. And you end with adapted, friendly words.

Making the Report Fair and Accurate

- You must report fairly and accurately.

The one unique concern in writing this message is the need to report fairly. Presenting it too negatively would be unfair to the applicant. Presenting it too positively would be unfair to the reader. And, of course, your fair presentation must be accurate.

- Prefer facts to opinions.

In conveying an accurate picture, you should carefully distinguish between facts and opinions. For the most part, you should report facts. But sometimes a reader wants your opinions. If you present opinions, you should clearly label them as such. You should support all opinions with facts.

- Proper emphasis may require subordination.

Conveying an accurate picture of the subject also involves giving the facts proper emphasis. Even if every fact you present is true, the report could be unfair. The reason is that negative points stand out. They overshadow positive points. Thus, sometimes you may need to subordinate the negative points. Not to do so would be to give them more emphasis than they deserve.

- But subordination does not mean altering truth.

This suggestion for subordinating negative points does not mean you should hide shortcomings or communicate wrong information. Quite the contrary. If the subject has a bad work record, you should report this. Purely and simply, your task is to communicate an accurate picture.

For legal reasons, sometimes you will need to leave out certain information. In the United States, laws and court decisions have affected the exchange of information about job applicants. Reports about an applicant's age, race, religion, sex, marital status, and pregnancy are generally prohibited. So are reports about an applicant's criminal record, sexual preference, citizenship, organization memberships, and mental and physical disabilities. Exceptions may be made in the rare cases in which such information is clearly related to the job.

- Abide by legal requirements regarding information that may be reported.

Structuring the Plan for Personnel Evaluations

When applied to the general plan, the preceding considerations produce the following sequence for personnel evaluations:

- These considerations produce this plan.

- Begin by (1) answering a question or (2) saying that you are complying with the request.
- Refer to the inquiry incidentally or in a subject line.
- Report fairly and accurately, arranging the information systematically, giving each item proper emphasis, and stressing fact rather than opinion.
- End with an adapted goodwill comment.

Contrasting Examples

Illustrating good and bad technique in personnel evaluations are the following contrasting email messages about George Adams.

A Slow, Disorganized, and Unfair Report. The weaker message begins indirectly—and with some obvious information. The first words are wasted. The letter shows little concern for proper emphasis. Note that the main negative point (the personality problem) receives a major position of emphasis (at a paragraph beginning). Even the information about the applicant's future at Pinnacle (which does not reflect on his abilities) gets negative treatment. The organization is jumbled. Information about personal qualities and about job performance, for example, appears in two different paragraphs. The close is an attempt at goodwill, but the words are timeworn rubber stamps.

Subject: Your May 10 inquiry

Ms. Brooking:

I have received your May 10 message in which you ask for my evaluation of Mr. George Adams. In reply I wish to say that I am pleased to be able to help you in this instance.

Probably Mr. Adams's greatest weakness is his inability to get along with his superiors. He has his own ideas, and he sticks to them tenaciously. Even so, he has a good work record with us. He has been with us since 1991.

Mr. Adams is a first assistant in our shipping department. He is thoroughly familiar with rate scales and general routing procedure. He gets along well with his co-workers and is a very personable young man. In his work he has some supervisory responsibilities, which he has performed well. He is probably seeking other work because there is little likelihood that we will promote him.

Mr. Adams's main assignment with us has placed him in charge of our car and truck loadings. He has done a good job here, resulting in significant savings in shipping damages. We have found him a very honest, straightforward, and dependable person.

Trusting that you will hold this report in confidence, I remain

Amos T. Dodgson, Manager

This bad example violates the techniques emphasized.

Personnel Evaluation Message (Evaluation of a Good Worker)   Evaluating a well-qualified office worker with no significant deficiencies, this message presents its information systematically. The opening comment is general; but by informing the reader of a favorable response, it has the effect of directness.

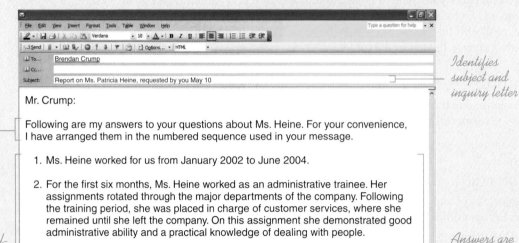

Identifies subject and inquiry letter

Direct—tells that writer is complying

Numbering systematically arranges the answers for the reader's convenience

Answers are complete, yet concise

Summary of evaluation in a recommendation

Goodwill ending

Mr. Crump:

Following are my answers to your questions about Ms. Heine. For your convenience, I have arranged them in the numbered sequence used in your message.

1. Ms. Heine worked for us from January 2002 to June 2004.

2. For the first six months, Ms. Heine worked as an administrative trainee. Her assignments rotated through the major departments of the company. Following the training period, she was placed in charge of customer services, where she remained until she left the company. On this assignment she demonstrated good administrative ability and a practical knowledge of dealing with people.

3. In all her assignments I found Ms. Heine a very capable worker. She worked hard, and she demonstrated good administrative potential. In fact, I had selected her to be groomed for a position with administrative responsibility.

4. I found Ms. Heine a most personable young woman. She got along with all her associates. I believe she is a person of integrity and high ethics.

5. Ms. Heine left us for a higher paying job—one she felt offered her faster advancement and more learning opportunities. We wanted her to stay with us.

I have a high regard for Ms. Heine. I recommend her to you for any work for which her experience has prepared her.

I am pleased to give you this confidential report on Ms. Heine.

Mary L. Lame, Office Manager
The Container Store
mlame@containerstore.com

Good Organization and Fairness in a Direct Report. The better message begins directly, reporting a significant point in the first sentence. The text presents the information in logical order, with like things being placed together. The words present the information fairly. The major negative point is presented almost positively, which is how it should be viewed in regard to the job concerned. The message closes with an appropriate goodwill comment.

Subject: Your May 10 inquiry about George Adams

Ms. Brooking:

Mr. Adams has been our assistant shipping clerk since March 1993 and has steadily improved in usefulness to our company. We want to keep him with us as long as he wants to stay. But with things as they are, it will apparently be some time before we can offer him a promotion that would match the branch managership for which you are considering him.

Of course, I am glad to give you in confidence a report on his service with us. As first assistant, he has substituted at the head clerk's desk and is thus familiar with problems of rate scales and routing. His main assignment, however, is to supervise the car and truck loadings. By making a careful study of this work, he has reduced our shipping damages noticeably within the last year. This job also places him in direct charge of the labor force, which varies from 6 to 10 workers. He has proved to be a good boss.

We have always found Mr. Adams honest, straightforward, and dependable. He is a man of strong convictions. He has his own ideas and backs them up. He is resourceful and works well without direction.

I recommend Mr. Adams to you highly. If you need additional information about him, please write me again.

Amos T. Dodgson, Manager

Directness, good organization, and correct emphasis mark this good message.

ADJUSTMENT GRANTS

INTRODUCTORY SITUATION

Adjustment Grants

Continuing in your role with Pinnacle, this time you find on your computer an email message from an unhappy customer. It seems that Ms. Bernice Watson, owner of Tri-Cities Hardware, is upset because some of the 30 Old London lampposts she ordered from Pinnacle arrived in damaged condition. "The glass is broken in 17 of the units," she writes, "obviously because of poor packing." She had ordered the lights for a special sale. In fact, she notes, she had even featured them in her advertising. The sale begins next Friday. She wants a fast adjustment—either the lamps by sale time or her money back.

Of course, you will grant Ms. Watson's request. You will send her an email message saying that the goods are on the way. And because you want to keep this good customer, you will try to regain any lost confidence with an honest explanation of the problem. This message is classified as an adjustment grant.

When you can grant an adjustment, the situation is a happy one for your customer. You are correcting an error. You are doing what you were asked to do. As in other positive situations, a message written in the direct order is appropriate.

• Good news in adjustment grants justifies directness.

Considering Special Needs

- Follow the good-news pattern, but consider two special needs.

The adjustment-grant message has much in common with the message types previously discussed. You begin directly with the good-news answer. You refer to the message you are answering. And you close on a friendly note. But because the situation stems from an unhappy experience, you have two special needs. One is the need to overcome the negative impressions the experience leading to the adjustment has formed in the reader's mind. The other is the need to regain any confidence in your company, its products, or its service the reader may have lost from the experience.

- Negative impressions remain; so overcome them.

Need to Overcome Negative Impressions. To understand the first need, just place yourself in the reader's shoes. As the reader sees it, something bad has happened—goods have been damaged, equipment has failed, or sales have been lost. The experience has not been pleasant. Granting the claim will take care of much of the problem, but some negative thoughts may remain. You need to work to overcome any such thoughts.

- Overcome them through positive writing.

You can attempt to do this using words that produce positive effects. For example, in the opening you can do more than just give the affirmative answer. You can add goodwill, as in this example:

> The enclosed check for $89.77 is our way of proving to you that we value your satisfaction highly.

Throughout the message you should avoid words that recall unnecessarily the bad situation you are correcting. You especially want to avoid the negative words that could be used to describe what went wrong—words such as *mistake, trouble, damage, broken,* and *loss.* Even general words such as *problem, difficulty,* and *misunderstanding* can create unpleasant connotations.

- Even apologies may be negative.

Also negative are the apologies often included in these messages. Even though well intended, the somewhat conventional "we sincerely regret the inconvenience caused you . . ." type of comment is of questionable value. It emphasizes the negative happenings for which the apology is made. If you sincerely believe that you owe an apology, or that one is expected, you can choose to apologize and risk the negative effect. In most instances, however, your efforts to correct the problem show adequate concern for your reader's interests.

- Regain lost confidence through convincing explanation.

Need to Regain Lost Confidence. Except in cases in which the cause of the difficulty is routine or incidental, you also will need to regain the reader's lost confidence.

Just what you must do and how you must do it depend on the facts of the situation. You will need to survey the situation to see what they are. If something can be done to correct a bad procedure or a product defect, you should do it. Then you should tell your reader what has been done as convincingly and positively as you can. If what went wrong was a rare, unavoidable event, you should explain this. Sometimes you will need to explain how a product should be used or cared for. Sometimes you will need to resell the product. Of course, whatever you do must be ethical—supported by truth and integrity.

Reviewing the Plan

Applying these two special needs to the general plan previously reviewed, we come up with this specific plan for the message granting an adjustment:

- Begin directly—with the good news.
- Incidentally identify the correspondence that you are answering.
- Avoid negatives that recall the problem.
- Regain lost confidence through explanation or corrective action.
- End with a friendly, positive comment.

Contrasting Adjustments

The techniques previously discussed are illustrated by the following adjustment messages. The first, with its indirect order and grudging tone, is ineffective. The directness and positiveness of the second clearly make it the better message.

- Following are good and bad adjustment letters.

A Slow and Negative Treatment. The ineffective message begins with an obvious comment about receiving the claim. It recalls vividly what went wrong and then painfully explains what happened. As a result, the good news is delayed for an additional paragraph. Finally, after two delaying paragraphs, the message gets to the good news. Though well intended, the close leaves the reader with a reminder of the trouble.

Subject: Your broken Old London lights

Mrs. Watson

We have received your May 1 claim reporting that our shipment of Old London lamppost lights reached you with 17 broken units. We regret the inconvenience caused you and can understand your unhappiness.

Following our standard practice, we investigated the situation thoroughly. Apparently the fault is the result of an inexperienced temporary employee's negligence. We have taken corrective measures to assure that future shipments will be packed more carefully.

I am pleased to report that we are sending replacements today. They should reach you before your sale begins. Our driver will pick up the broken units when he makes delivery.

Again, we regret all the trouble caused you.

Stephanie King

This one is bad.

The Direct and Positive Technique. The better message uses the subject line to identify the transaction. The opening words tell the reader what she most wants to hear in a positive way that adds to the goodwill tone of the message. With reader-viewpoint explanation, the message then reviews what happened. Without a single negative word, it makes clear what caused the problem and what has been done to prevent its recurrence. After handling the essential matter of picking up the broken lamps, the message closes with positive resale talk far removed from the problem.

Subject: Your May 1 report on invoice 1248

Mrs. Watson

Seventeen carefully packed Old London lamppost lamps should reach your sales floor in time for your Saturday promotion. Our driver left our warehouse today with instructions to special deliver them to you on Friday.

Because your satisfaction with our service and products is important to us, we have thoroughly checked our shipping procedures. It appears that the shipment to you was packed by a temporary employee who was filling in for a hospitalized veteran packer. Even though we now have our veteran packer back at work, we have instituted a control procedure designed to assure safe arrival of all future shipments.

As you know, the Old London lamppost lights have become one of the hottest products in the lighting field. Their authentic Elizabethan design has made them a smashing success. We are confident they will play their part in the success of your sale.

Stephanie King

ORDER ACKNOWLEDGMENTS

INTRODUCTORY SITUATION

Order Acknowledgments

The next work you take from your in-box is an order for paints and painting supplies. It is from Mr. Orville Chapman of the Central City Paint Company, a new customer whom Pinnacle has been trying to attract for months. You usually acknowledge orders with routine messages, but this case is different. You feel the need to welcome this new customer and to cultivate him for future sales.

After checking your current inventory and making certain that the goods will be on the way to Chapman today, you are ready to write him a special acknowledgment.

- Businesses usually acknowledge orders with form notes, but they sometimes use letters.

Acknowledgments are sent to let people who order goods know the status of their orders. Most acknowledgments are routine. They simply tell when the goods are being shipped. Many companies use form or computer-generated messages for such situations. Some use printed, standard notes with check-off or write-in blanks. But individually written acknowledgments are sometimes justified, especially with new accounts or large orders.

- Acknowledgments can serve to build goodwill.

Skillfully composed acknowledgments can do more than acknowledge orders, though this task remains their primary goal. These messages also can build goodwill. Through a warm, personal, human tone, they can reach out and give a hearty handshake. They can make the reader feel good about doing business with a company that cares. They can make the reader want to continue doing business with that company. To maintain this goodwill for repeat customers, you will want to revise your form acknowledgments regularly.

Using Directness and Goodwill Building

- Directness and goodwill mark the message.

Like the other preceding messages, the acknowledgment message appropriately begins with its good news—that the goods are being shipped. And it ends on a goodwill note. Except when some of the goods ordered must be delayed, the remainder of the message is devoted to goodwill building. This goodwill building can begin in the opening by emphasizing receipt of the goods rather than merely sending the goods:

PART 3   Basic Patterns of Business Messages

Adjustment Grant Messages (Explaining a Human Error) This email message grants the action requested in the claim of a customer who received a leather computer case that was monogrammed incorrectly. The writer has no excuse, for human error was to blame. His explanation is positive and convincing.

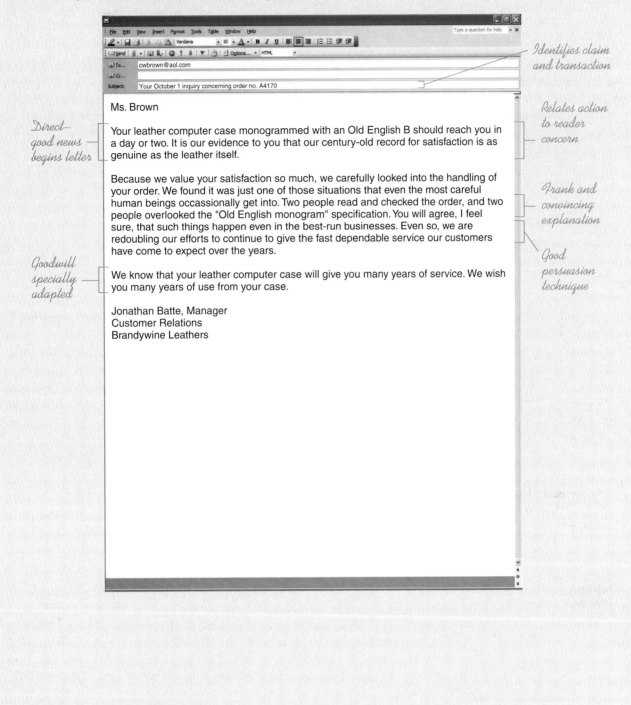

Identifies claim and transaction

Direct good news begins letter

Relates action to reader concern

To... cwbrown@aol.com
Cc...
Subject: Your October 1 inquiry concerning order no. A4170

Ms. Brown

Your leather computer case monogrammed with an Old English B should reach you in a day or two. It is our evidence to you that our century-old record for satisfaction is as genuine as the leather itself.

Because we value your satisfaction so much, we carefully looked into the handling of your order. We found it was just one of those situations that even the most careful human beings occassionally get into. Two people read and checked the order, and two people overlooked the "Old English monogram" specification. You will agree, I feel sure, that such things happen even in the best-run businesses. Even so, we are redoubling our efforts to continue to give the fast dependable service our customers have come to expect over the years.

Frank and convincing explanation

Good persuasion technique

Goodwill specially adapted

We know that your leather computer case will give you many years of service. We wish you many years of use from your case.

Jonathan Batte, Manager
Customer Relations
Brandywine Leathers

Tables Help Writers Organize Data for Easy Reading

Setting up tables within a document is an easy task. The tables feature allows writers to create tables as well as import spreadsheet and database files. In both instances, you can arrange information in columns and rows, inserting detail in the cells. Headings can be formatted and formulas can be entered in the cells. The table you see here could be one the writer created for use in a favorable response to an inquiry about possible locations for a meeting in Chicago.

Organizing information with tables makes it easier for both the writer and the reader. A careful writer will include column and row labels as needed, helping the reader extract information both quickly and accurately.

Hotel Name	Address	Convention Room Rate for Standard Rooms	Rating
Marriott Chicago Downtown	540 North Michigan Avenue, Chicago, IL 60611-3869	$187	☆☆☆
Drake Hotel	140 East Walton Street, Chicago, IL 60611-1545	$229	☆☆☆☆
Palmer House Hilton	17 East Monroe Street, Chicago, IL 60603-5605	$162	☆☆☆☆

The Protect-O paints and supplies you ordered April 4 should reach you by Wednesday. They are leaving our Walden warehouse today by Arrow Freight.

It also can include a warm expression of thanks for the order, especially when a first order is involved. Anything else you can say that will be helpful to the reader is appropriate in this regard—information about new products, services, or such. Specially adapted forward look to continued business relations is appropriate goodwill in the close.

Being Tactful in Shipment Delays

- When goods must be delayed, handle this news tactfully.

Sometimes the task of acknowledging is complicated by your inability to send the goods requested right away. You could be out of them; or perhaps the reader did not give you all the information you need to send the goods. In either case, a delay is involved. In some cases, delays are routine and expected and do not pose a serious problem. In others, they are likely to lead to major disappointments. When this is the case, you will need to use tact.

- In vague orders, request the needed information positively.

Using tact involves minimizing the negative effect of the message. In the case of a vague order, for example, you should handle the information you need without appearing to accuse the reader of giving insufficient information. To illustrate, you gain nothing by writing "You failed to specify the color of phones you want." But you gain goodwill and practice good etiquette by writing "So that we can send you precisely the phones you want, please check your choice of colors on the space below." This sentence handles the matter positively and makes the action easy to take. It shows mannerly etiquette.

- Emphasize receipt of the items in back orders.

Similarly, you can handle back-order information tactfully by emphasizing the positive part of the message. For example, instead of writing "We can't ship the ink jet cartridges until the 9th," you can write "We will rush the ink jet cartridges to you as soon as our stock is replenished by a shipment due May 9." If the back-order period is longer than the customer expects or longer than the 30 days allowed by law, you may choose to give your customer an alternative. You could offer a substitute product or service. Giving the customer a choice builds goodwill. A more complete discussion of how to handle such negative news is provided in Chapter 7.

Summarizing the Structure of Order Acknowledgments

Applying these special considerations to the general plan for direct messages, we arrive at this specific plan for order acknowledgments:

- Give status of order, acknowledging incidentally.
- Include some goodwill—sales talk, reselling, or such.
- Include a thank-you.
- Report frankly or handle tactfully problems with vague or back orders.
- Close with adapted, friendly comment.

Contrasting Acknowledgments

The following two messages show bad and good technique in acknowledging Mr. Chapman's order. As you would expect, the good version follows the plan described in the preceding paragraphs.

- Following are contrasting examples.

Slow Route to a Favorable Message. The bad example begins indirectly, emphasizing receipt of the order. Although intended to produce goodwill, the second sentence further delays telling what the reader wants most to hear. Moreover, the letter is written from the writer's point of view (note the we-emphasis).

Dear Mr. Chapman:

Your April 4 order for $1,743.30 worth of Protect-O paints and supplies has been received. We are pleased to have this nice order and hope that it marks the beginning of a long relationship.

As you instructed, we will bill you for this amount. We are shipping the goods today by Blue Darter Motor Freight.

We look forward to your future orders.

Sincerely,

This one is bad.

Fast-Moving Presentation of the Good News. The better message begins directly, telling Mr. Chapman that he is getting what he wants. The remainder of the message is customer welcome and subtle selling. Notice the good use of reader emphasis and positive language. The message closes with a note of appreciation and a friendly, forward look.

Dear Mr. Chapman:

Your selection of Protect-O paints and supplies should reach you by Wednesday, for the shipment left today by Blue Darter Motor Freight. As you requested, we are sending you an invoice for $1,743.30, including sales tax.

Because this is your first order from us, I welcome you to the Protect-O circle of dealers. Our representative, Ms. Cindy Wooley, will call from time to time to offer whatever assistance she can. She is a highly competent technical adviser on paint and painting.

Here in the home plant we also will do what we can to help you profit from Protect-O products. We'll do our best to give you the most efficient service. And we'll continue to develop the best possible paints—like our new Chem-Treat line. As you will see from the enclosed brochure, Chem-Treat is a real breakthrough in mildew protection.

We genuinely appreciate your order, Mr. Chapman. We are determined to serve you well in the years ahead.

Sincerely,

This message is better.

CLAIMS

Claims

Introduce yourself to claim messages by playing the role of Ms. Bernice Watson, one of Pinnacle's customers and the owner of Tri-Cities Hardware. For the past few days you have been preparing for your annual spring promotion. You have ordered widely, and you have advertised the items to be featured. All has gone well until today when Pinnacle's shipment of Old London lamppost lights arrived. You ordered 30 and the glass coverings on 17 of them are broken. Obviously, the lamps were poorly packed.

Now you must make a fast claim for adjustment. You will send Pinnacle an email message requesting replacement by the sale date or your money back. This message is classified as a claim.

• Claims are written to collect for damages.

When something goes wrong between a business and its customers, usually someone begins an effort to correct the situation. Typically, the offended party calls the matter to the attention of those responsible. This claim can be made in person, by telephone, or by written message (email or letter). Our concern here is how to make it in a written message.

Using Directness for Bad News

• Use directness for this bad news because (1) the reader wants to know and (2) it adds strength.

Claim situations may appear to be bad-news situations. As you know, usually bad-news situations are handled in indirect order. But claims are exceptions—for two good reasons. First, businesspeople want to know when something is wrong with their products or services so they can correct the matter. Thus, there is no reason for delay or gentle treatment. Second, as we have noted, directness lends strength, and strength in a claim enhances the likelihood of success.

Identifying the Problem in a Direct Beginning

• Identify the problem in the direct beginning.

Because of their uniqueness, claim situations involve more special concerns than other direct-order messages. First is the need to identify the transactions involved. This you can do early in the message as a part of the direct beginning that tells what went wrong. One way is to put the identification in the subject head in an email message or in the subject line of a letter, as in this example:

> Subject: Damaged condition of fire extinguishers on arrival, your invoice C13144

Stating the Problem Directly

• State the problem clearly in the opening.

The beginning words appropriately state the problem. They should be courteous yet firm. And they should cover the problem completely, giving enough information to permit the reader to judge the matter. If there are consequences of what happened, you may benefit your case by naming them. This beginning sentence illustrates the point:

> The Model H freezer (Serial No. 713129) that we bought from you September 17 suddenly quit working, ruining $517 of frozen foods in the process.

Giving Choice in Correcting Error

• Handle the claim by either stating what you want or letting the reader decide.

The facts you present should prove your claim. So your next step is to follow logically with the handling of the claim. How you handle the claim, however, is a matter for you

Order Acknowledgments   This routine acknowledgment illustrates good practice in Internet selling. It gives the customer all that is needed to track the status of the order.

To: marie.flatley@sdsu.edu
From: ship-confirm@amazon.com
Subject: Your Amazon.com order has shipped (#002-0212016-9528012)
Date: Sun, 11 May 2004 07:59:16 +0000 (GMT)

Greetings from Amazon.com.

Direct, tells that the goods are on the way.

We thought you'd like to know that we shipped your gift today,
and that this completes your order.

Thanks for shopping at Amazon.com, and we hope to see you again soon.

You can track the status of this order, and all your orders, online by
visiting Your Account at http://www.amazon.com/your-account/

There you can:
    * Track order and shipment status
    * Review estimated delivery dates
    * Cancel unshipped items
    * Return items
    * And do much more

Presents additional ordering information with you-viewpoint.

The following items were included in this shipment:

Qty	Item	Price	Shipped	Subtotal
1	Google Hacks	$17.47	1	$17.47
1	First Look Microsoft Office 20	$13.99	1	$13.99
1	Graphically Speaking: A Visual	$23.09	1	$23.09

                Item Subtotal: $54.55
                Shipping & Handling: $5.97

                Giftwrap: no charge
                Super Saver Discount: −$5.97

                Total: $54.55

Reminds reader of the details of the order and shipping instructions.

This shipment was sent to:

    Marie E. Flatley
    12912 Via Grimaldi
    Del Mar CA 92014

via USPS (5-9 business days).

For your reference, the number you can use to track your package is
9102049390094076192782. You can refer to our Web site's Help page or:

http://www.amazon.com/wheresmystuff

to retrieve current tracking information. Please note that tracking
information may not be available immediately.

Gives helpful information about how to track the order.

If you've explored the links on the Your Account page but still need
to get in touch with us about your order, you can find an e-mail form
in our Help department at http://www.amazon.com/help/

Please note: This e-mail was sent from a notification-only address
that cannot accept incoming e-mail. Please do not reply to this message.

Invites inquiries about the order.

Thank you for shopping with us

Ends with an expression of gratefulness

Amazon.com
Earth's Biggest Selection
http://www.amazon.com/

Order Acknowledgment Letters (Acknowledgment with a Problem) This letter concerns an order that cannot be handled exactly as the customer would like. Some items are being sent, but one must be placed on back order and one cannot be shipped because the customer did not give the information needed. The letter skillfully handles the negative points.

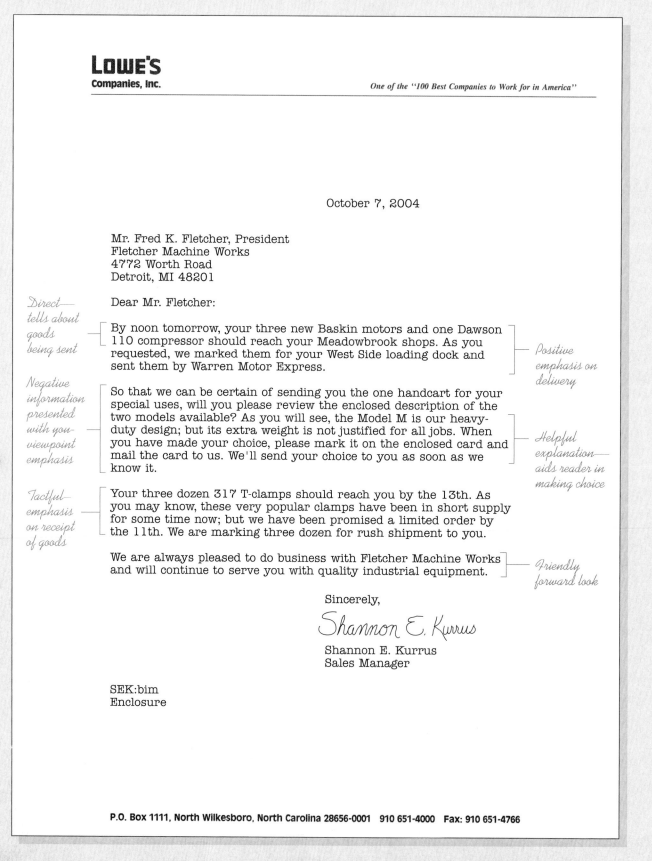

LOWE'S
Companies, Inc.

One of the "100 Best Companies to Work for in America"

October 7, 2004

Mr. Fred K. Fletcher, President
Fletcher Machine Works
4772 Worth Road
Detroit, MI 48201

Dear Mr. Fletcher:

Direct—tells about goods being sent

By noon tomorrow, your three new Baskin motors and one Dawson 110 compressor should reach your Meadowbrook shops. As you requested, we marked them for your West Side loading dock and sent them by Warren Motor Express.

Positive emphasis on delivery

Negative information presented with you-viewpoint emphasis

So that we can be certain of sending you the one handcart for your special uses, will you please review the enclosed description of the two models available? As you will see, the Model M is our heavy-duty design; but its extra weight is not justified for all jobs. When you have made your choice, please mark it on the enclosed card and mail the card to us. We'll send your choice to you as soon as we know it.

Helpful explanation—aids reader in making choice

Tactful emphasis on receipt of goods

Your three dozen 317 T-clamps should reach you by the 13th. As you may know, these very popular clamps have been in short supply for some time now; but we have been promised a limited order by the 11th. We are marking three dozen for rush shipment to you.

We are always pleased to do business with Fletcher Machine Works and will continue to serve you with quality industrial equipment.

Friendly forward look

Sincerely,

Shannon E. Kurrus

Shannon E. Kurrus
Sales Manager

SEK:bim
Enclosure

P.O. Box 1111, North Wilkesboro, North Carolina 28656-0001   910 651-4000   Fax: 910 651-4766

to decide. You have two choices: You can state what you want (money back, replacement) or you can leave the decision to the reader. Because most businesspeople want to do the right thing, often the latter choice is the better one.

Overcoming Negativeness with a Friendly Close

Your final friendly words should remove all doubt about your cordial attitude. For added strength, when strength is needed to support a claim, you could express appreciation for what you seek. This suggestion does not support use of the timeworn "Thanking you in advance." Instead, say something like "I would be grateful if you could get the new merchandise to me in time for my Friday sale." Whatever final words you choose, they should clearly show that yours is a firm yet cordial request in accord with the practice of good business etiquette.

- Your closing words should show your cordial attitude.

Outlining the Claim Message

Summarizing the foregoing points, we arrive at this outline for the claim message:

- Begin directly. Tell what is wrong.
- Identify the situation (invoice number, product information, etc.) in the text or in a subject line.
- Present enough of the facts to permit a decision.
- Seek corrective action.
- End positively—friendly but firm.

Contrasting Examples of Claim Messages

The following two email messages show contrasting ways of handling Tri-Cities Hardware's problem with the Old London lamppost lights. The first is slow and harsh. The second is courteous, yet to the point and firm.

- The following contrasting messages show good and bad handling of a claim.

A Slow and Harsh Message. The first message starts slowly with a long explanation of the situation. Some of the details in the beginning sentence are helpful, but they do not deserve the emphasis that this position gives them. The problem is not described until the second paragraph. The wording here is clear but much too strong. The words are angry and insulting, and they talk down to the reader. Such words are more likely to produce resistance than acceptance. The negative writing continues into the close, leaving a bad final impression.

Subject: Our Order No. 7135

Mr. Goetz

As your records will show, on March 7 we ordered 30 Old London lamppost lights (our Order No. 7135). The units were received by us on March 14 (your Invoice No. 715C).

At the time of delivery, our shipping and receiving supervisor noticed that some of the cartons had broken glass inside. Upon further inspection, he found that the glass on 17 of the lamps was broken. Further inspection showed that your packers had been negligent as there was insufficient packing material in each carton.

It is hard for me to understand a shipping system that permits such errors to take place. We had advertised these lights for our annual spring promotion, which begins next Saturday. We want the lights by then or our money back.

Megan Adami

This bad one is slow and harsh.

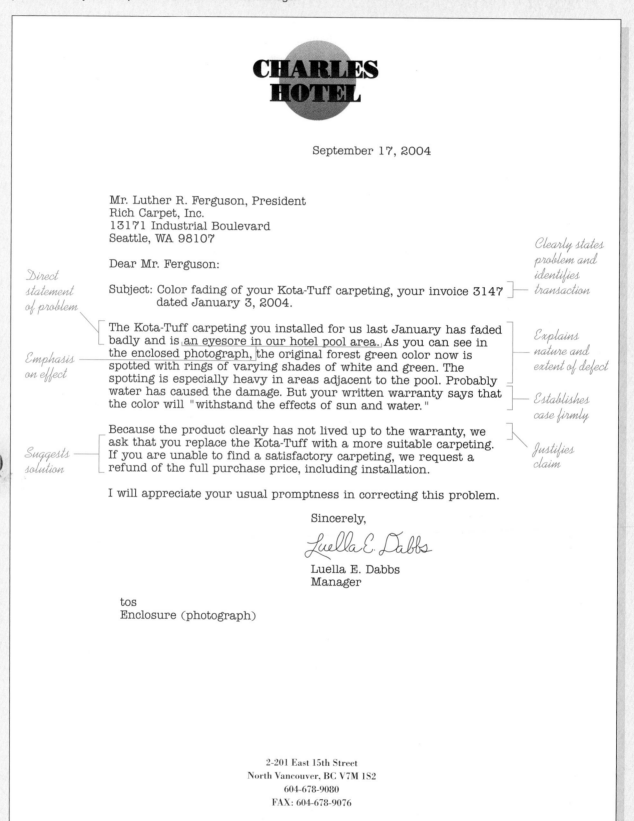

Claim Letters (Polite Firmness in a Claim about Defective Carpeting) In this letter a hotel manager presents a claim about defective carpeting. She makes the claim directly and forcefully—yet politely. She explains the problem clearly and emphasizes the effect of the damage.

CHARLES HOTEL

September 17, 2004

Mr. Luther R. Ferguson, President
Rich Carpet, Inc.
13171 Industrial Boulevard
Seattle, WA 98107

Dear Mr. Ferguson:

Direct statement of problem

Clearly states problem and identifies transaction

Subject: Color fading of your Kota-Tuff carpeting, your invoice 3147 dated January 3, 2004.

Emphasis on effect

Explains nature and extent of defect

The Kota-Tuff carpeting you installed for us last January has faded badly and is an eyesore in our hotel pool area. As you can see in the enclosed photograph, the original forest green color now is spotted with rings of varying shades of white and green. The spotting is especially heavy in areas adjacent to the pool. Probably water has caused the damage. But your written warranty says that the color will "withstand the effects of sun and water."

Establishes case firmly

Suggests solution

Justifies claim

Because the product clearly has not lived up to the warranty, we ask that you replace the Kota-Tuff with a more suitable carpeting. If you are unable to find a satisfactory carpeting, we request a refund of the full purchase price, including installation.

I will appreciate your usual promptness in correcting this problem.

Sincerely,

Luella E. Dabbs

Luella E. Dabbs
Manager

tos
Enclosure (photograph)

2-201 East 15th Street
North Vancouver, BC V7M 1S2
604-678-9080
FAX: 604-678-9076

A Firm Yet Courteous Message. The second message follows the plan suggested in preceding paragraphs. A subject line quickly identifies the situation. The message begins with a clear statement of the problem. Next, in a tone that shows firmness without anger, it tells what went wrong. Then it requests a specific remedy and asks what to do with the damaged goods. The ending uses subtle persuasion by implying confidence in the reader. The words used here leave no doubt about continued friendship.

Subject: Broken glass in 17 Old London lamppost lights received.

Mr. Goetz

Seventeen of the 30 lamppost lights we received today arrived with glass coverings broken.

At the time of delivery, our shipping and receiving manager noticed broken glass in some of the cartons. Upon further inspection, he found that 17 were in this condition. It was apparent to him that insufficient packing material was the cause of the problem.

Because we had advertised these lights for our annual spring promotion, which begins Saturday, please get replacements to us by that date. If delivery is not possible, we request a refund for the broken units. In either event, please instruct me on what to do with the damaged lamps.

I am aware, of course, that situations like this will occur in spite of all precautions. And I am confident that you will replace the units with your usual courtesy.

Megan Adami

This better message follows text recommendations.

OTHER DIRECT MESSAGE SITUATIONS

In the preceding pages, we have covered the most common direct message situations. Others occur, of course. You should be able to handle them with the techniques that have been explained and illustrated.

In handling such situations, remember that whenever possible, you should get to the goal of the message right away. You should cover any other information needed in good logical order. You should carefully choose words that convey just the right meaning. More specifically, you should consider the value of using the you-viewpoint, and you should weigh carefully the differences in meaning conveyed by the positiveness or negativeness of your words. As in all cordial human contacts, you should end your message with appropriate and friendly goodwill words.

- Other direct message situations occur.

- You should be able to handle them by applying the techniques covered in this chapter.

SUMMARY BY CHAPTER OBJECTIVES

1. Properly assess the reader's reaction to your message.
   - If the reaction is negative, indirect order is your likely choice.
   - If it is positive or neutral, you probably will want directness.
2. Describe the general plan for direct-order messages.
   - Begin with the objective.
   - Cover any necessary explanation.
   - Systematically present any remaining parts of the objective.
   - End with adapted goodwill.
3. The routine inquiry is a basic direct-order message.
   - Begin it with a request—either (1) a request for specific information wanted or (2) a general request for information.
   - Somewhere in the message explain enough to enable the reader to answer.

1 Properly assess the reader's reaction to your message.

2 Describe the general plan for direct-order messages.

3 Write clear, well-structured routine requests for information.

- If the inquiry involves more than one question, make each stand out—perhaps as separate sentences or separate paragraphs.
- Consider numbering the questions.
- And word them as questions.
- End with an appropriate friendly comment.

4

Compose orderly and thorough inquiries about prospective employees that show respect for human rights.

4. Inquiries about people follow much the same order as described above.
- But they require special care, since they concern the moral and legal rights of people.
- So seek truth, and act in good faith.
- Also, adapt your questions to the one applicant and the one situation rather than following a routine.

5

Write direct, orderly, and friendly answers to inquiries.

5. When responding to inquiries favorably, you should begin directly.
- If the response contains only one answer, begin with it.
- If it contains more than one answer, begin with a major one or a general statement indicating you are answering.
- Identify the message being answered early, perhaps in a subject line.
- Arrange your answers (if more than one) logically.
- And make them stand out.
- If both good- and bad-news answers are involved, give each answer the emphasis it deserves, perhaps by subordinating the negative.
- For extra goodwill effect, consider doing more than was asked.
- End with appropriate cordiality.

6

Phrase personnel evaluations that fairly present the essential facts.

6. Handle personnel evaluations directly.
- Do so even if they contain negative information, for you are doing what the reader asked.
- You have two logical choices for beginning the message.
  - You can begin by answering a question asked, preferably one deserving the emphasis of the opening position.
  - You can begin with a statement indicating you are complying with the request.
- Refer to the message you are answering early in your message (perhaps in the subject line).
- Present the information in a logical order, making each answer stand out.
  - Numbering the responses is one way of doing this.
  - Arranging answers by paragraphs also helps.
- Report fairly and truthfully.
  - Stress facts and avoid opinions.
  - Give each item the emphasis it deserves.
- End with appropriate friendly comment.

7

Compose adjustment grants that regain any lost confidence.

7. As messages granting adjustments are positive responses, write them in the direct order.
- But they differ from other direct-order messages in that they involve a negative situation.
  - Something has gone wrong.
  - You are correcting that wrong.
  - But you also should overcome the negative image in the reader's mind.
- You do this by first telling the good news—what you are doing to correct the wrong.
- In the opening and throughout, emphasize the positive.
- Avoid the negative—words like *trouble, damage,* and *broken.*
- Try to regain the reader's lost confidence, maybe with explanation or with assurance of corrective measures taken.
- End with a goodwill comment, avoiding words that recall what went wrong.

8

Write order acknowledgments that cover problems and build goodwill.

8. Write order acknowledgments in the form of a favorable response.
- Handle most by form messages or notes.
- But in special cases use individual messages.
- Begin such messages directly, telling the status of the goods ordered.

- In the remainder of the message, build goodwill, perhaps including some selling or reselling.
- Include an expression of appreciation somewhere in the message.
- End with an appropriate, friendly comment.

9. Claims are a special case. Even though they carry bad news, they are best written in the direct order. The reason: the reader usually wants to correct the problem and requires only that the facts be presented; also, directness strengthens the claim. Follow this general plan:

- Somewhere early in the message (in a subject line or incidentally in the first sentence) identify the transaction.
- Then state what went wrong, perhaps with some interpretation of the effects.
- Follow with a clear review of the facts, without showing anger.
- You may want to suggest a remedy.
- End with cordial words.

Write claims that objectively and courteously explain the facts.

1. When is the direct order appropriate in inquiries? When would you use the indirect order? Give examples.

2. "Explanations in inquiries merely add length and should be eliminated." Discuss.

3. What should the writer do to respect the rights of people in inquiries about them?

4. "In writing inquiries about people, I do not ask specific questions. Instead, I ask for 'everything you think I should know' about the person." Discuss this viewpoint.

5. Discuss why just reporting truthfully may not be enough in handling negative information in messages answering inquiries.

6. Defend a policy of doing more than asked in answering routine inquiries. Can the policy be carried too far?

7. What can acknowledgment messages do to build goodwill?

8. Discuss situations where each of the following forms of an order acknowledgment would be preferred: form letter, merged letter, and a special letter.

9. Discuss how problems (vague orders, back orders) should be handled in messages acknowledging orders.

10. Discuss the relationship of positive and negative words to fair treatment in employee evaluation messages.

11. Why is it usually advisable to do more than just grant the claim in an adjustment-grant message?

12. Usually bad-news messages are appropriately written in the indirect order. Why should claims be exceptions?

13. Justify the use of negative words in claims. Can they be overused? Discuss.

1. List your criticisms of this message asking for information about an applicant for a job:

   Dear Ms. Bentley:

   Inez Becker has applied to us for a job as inventory clerk in our parts department. She listed you as a reference and claims that she worked for you as a records clerk in your parts department for the period May 1998 to August 2001. Because I am impressed with Ms. Becker, I would like to have your evaluation of her.

   I am especially interested in her work ethic and how she gets along with other workers. I am curious about why she left the job with you. Also, please tell me whether you would hire her back if you had an opening. In addition, I would like to know about her honesty, character, and attitude.

   Thank you in advance for your prompt response.

   Sincerely yours,

2. Point out the shortcomings in this email response to an inquiry about a short course in business communication taught by a professor for the company's employees. The inquiry included five questions: (1) How did the professor perform? (2) What was the course format (length, meeting structure)? (3) What was the employee evaluation of the instruction? (4) Was the course adapted to the company and its technical employees? (5) Was homework assigned?

   Subject: Course evaluation

   Mr. Braden:

   Your January 17 inquiry addressed to the Training Director has been referred to me for attention since we have no one with that title. I do have some training responsibilities and was the one who organized the in-house course in clear writing. You asked five questions about our course.

   Concerning your question about the instructor, Professor Alonzo Britt, I can report that he did an acceptable job in the classroom. Some of the students, including this writer, felt that the emphasis was too much on grammar and punctuation, however. He did assign homework, but it was not excessive.

   We had class two hours a day from 3:00 to 5:00 PM every Thursday for eight weeks. Usually the professor lectured the first hour. He is a good lecturer but sometimes talks over the heads of the students. This was the main complaint in the evaluations the students made at the end of the course, but they had many good comments to make also. Some did not like the content, which they said was not adapted to the needs of a technical worker. Overall, the professor got a rating of B– on a scale of A to F.

   We think the course was good for our technical people, but it could have been better adapted to our needs and our people. I also think it was too long—about 10 hours (five meetings) would have been enough. Also, we think the professor spent too much time lecturing and not enough on application work in class.

Please be informed that the information about Professor Britt must be held in confidence.

Casey Webster

3. Point out the shortcomings in this message granting a claim for a fax machine received in damaged condition. Inspection of the package revealed that the damage did not occur in transit.

Dear Ms. Orsag:

Your May 3 letter in which you claim that the Rigo FAX391 was received in damaged condition has been carefully considered. We inspect all our machines carefully before packing them, and we pack them carefully in strong boxes with Styrofoam supports that hold them snugly. Thus we cannot understand how the damage could have occurred.

Even so, we stand behind our product and will replace any that are damaged. However, we must ask that first you send us the defective one so we can inspect it. After your claim of damage has been verified, we will send you a new one.

We regret any inconvenience this situation may have caused you and assure you that problems like this rarely occur in our shipping department.

Scott Hilderbran

4. List your criticisms of this email message inquiring about a convenience store advertised for sale:

Subject: Store details needed

Mr. Meeks:

This is in response to your advertisement in the May 17 *Daily Bulletin* in which you describe a convenience store in Clark City that you want to sell. I am very much interested since I would like to relocate in that area. Before I drive down to see the property, I need some preliminary information. Most important is the question of financing. I am wondering whether you would be willing to finance up to $50,000 of the total if I could come up with the rest, and how much interest would you charge and for how long. I also would like to have the figures for your operations for the past two or three years, including gross sales, expenses, and profits. I also need to know the condition of the building, including such information as when built, improvements made, repairs needed, and so on.

Hoping that you can get these answers to me soon so we can do business.

5. Criticize the following email claim.

Subject: Your shipment of candy

Mr. Stanton:

For many years now I have bought your candies and have been pleased with them. However, last June 4 I ordered 48 boxes of your Swiss Decadence chocolates, and it appears you tried to push off some old stock on me. I have sold some of the boxes, and already three customers have returned the candy to me. The candy is rancid—obviously old. Probably the whole lot was bad and I now have a bunch of dissatisfied customers.

I have taken the remaining boxes off the shelves and will send them back to you—after I get my money back.

CRITICAL THINKING PROBLEMS

Routine Inquiries

1. Today you received a sales letter from Anna Cheney, a professional trainer in diversity management, inviting you to purchase her services. It so happens that, as a human resources manager at Custom Engineering (CE), you know of some diversity-related friction in the company caused by several recent hires and promotions. For many years, Custom Engineering, like most engineering firms, employed only white men for the technical, sales, and managerial positions and hired women as support staff only. But the growing company has been increasing its international clientele, and it recently hired a Middle Eastern and two Asian engineers. It also hired a female translator and promoted a female administrative assistant to Project Manager. You know from informal conversations with these minority employees that they're feeling socially isolated and sometimes left out of important information loops, though none of them have filed a formal complaint—yet.

You decide to write to Dr. Cheney to investigate the possibility of her conducting some kind of diversity-appreciation training for CE's employees. You want them to become aware of little ways that newcomers can be made to feel welcome, and you also want the employees to see that it's in the company's best interest to open up to more kinds of co-workers and customers. On the other hand, you don't want the employees to feel preached at or accused of "political incorrectness." This is a delicate situation, and you don't want your efforts to improve it to backfire.

Write to Dr. Cheney to find out if Custom Engineering should hire her. Tell her about your company, including any details that might help her, but without putting the company in too negative a light. Find out what kinds of training she offers and what her fee is (the amount of time and money that you could get approved for this kind of training would probably be limited). You also want a better sense of who she is. What are her credentials? Is she tactful? Is she interesting? It would be great if you could talk to some of her prior clients. Try to get enough information to be able to make a reasonably confident decision on this important issue.

2. On the suggestion of a business friend you checked out the website of Soundview Executive Book Summaries, <http://www.summary.com/>. As your friend explained, this service prepares a monthly publication that summarizes "all the most important business books." The result is a great saving in reading time for managers. Equally important, it enables the managers to keep current on the thinking in their field.

You imagine the service might be good for the 71 members of your management team at Pegasus Technologies. As training director, you like what you see on the website. The books reviewed include all the major ones—popular titles as well as scholarly ones. They are available in electronic, print, and audio formats, fitting all the uses of your managers.

Even so, you need to know more before you order this service. First, you want to see a print copy of the publication. Second, you'd like to know the qualifications of those who make the summaries. Such work requires sophisticated knowledge of management and business. Third, you think an order the size of yours should receive a quantity discount. Does it? You may think of additional questions before you complete the inquiry.

You will send your inquiry by email to the customer service address given in the website.

3. For this assignment, assume the role of merchandise manager for a National Football League team (or other major sports team, as approved by your instructor). Today while traveling home by air you saw an advertisement in the airline magazine that gave you an idea. The Alynn Neckwear Company ad was for ties and scarves with company logos on them. Why not add such ties to the line of products that your department sells to fans as a sideline activity?

In your mind you quickly visualized a specially designed tie and scarf in the team's colors with a large team logo prominently displayed. Your design differs from the one displayed in the ad, which shows a single color field covered with small logos. You'd want a custom tie, if they will do it.

The ad describes only a wool tie and scarf, but you think silk would be more appropriate for your team. And you would want the ties and scarves by August 1 (it is now March). Of course, you'll need to get price information, including quantity discounts. As you

think through the problem other information needs come to mind. Probably you would want 2,000 items, 1,600 ties and 400 scarves on the initial order.

Now back in your office you will prepare an inquiry to the advertiser. The ad only gives the website address, <http://www.alynn.com/contactus.htm/>, where you can enter and submit a message. Write the message that will solicit the information you need in evaluating this possibility.

4. Assume that you are the training director for Alpha-Omega Industries, Inc. Today you received in the mail a brochure from Communication Management, Inc., advertising its three-day, in-plant course in written communication. Alpha-Omega engineers badly need such instruction, you think. As suggested in the brochure, you reviewed the CMI website at <http://www.cmiglobal.com/>. There you learned more. But some questions remain unanswered.

Most important, you'd like to know whether the course is a general one or can be altered to fit the needs of the specific company. Alpha-Omega engineers write mainly technical reports, so you would want a course geared to this form of writing.

You noticed that report format was mentioned in the description of course content. But you don't think this subject matter needs to be covered with your people. Alpha-Omega has its own report format, and the engineers know it. So you'd like to know whether the coverage of format could be excluded. If so, what could be substituted for it?

As stated in the brochure, classes are limited to 20 students. But you have 26 engineers who need to take the course. Does this mean two classes? And two charges?

Then there is the matter of time. Vacations begin in June; so you'd like to schedule the course for March or April (it is now February). If these months won't fit into the Institute's schedule, you'd have to wait until September to offer the course.

Now you will write the message that will get you the information you need. You will send it by email to the address given in the website, TalkToUs@cmiglobal.com.

5. While surfing the Internet you stumbled upon the website of Art Capital Group at <http://www.artcapitalgroup.com/>. As the site explains, this company will lease art pieces (paintings, sculptures, and such) to corporations for a fee. It goes on to say that the art pieces are exchanged every three months to give each office an exciting and cultured appearance. It emphasizes that the atmosphere of your offices is important to your clients as well as to the people who work in them.

Vanguard Financial Services, where you are the manager for administration, generally provides tax, legal, and financial services to high-income clients.

Primarily, your company's financial services involve setting up tax shelters and other income saving strategies. It works hard to maintain a reputation for sophistication and class. Displaying high-quality art in the offices should help maintain this desired image.

Although the website shows a few pieces, it doesn't tell you all you need to know before making a decision. You wonder about other types of art available—modern, portrait, oil, and such. What type of advice does the company receive with its fee? The website is vague concerning the charge for the service, so you will need to get exact figures. What about the artists? Are they well-known and respected? Unknowns? Are the pieces for sale (if a client were to ask)? Who is responsible in case of theft, damage, loss, or such? Then there is the matter of delivery. The company is in New York; you are in Kansas City. Other questions may come to mind as you think through the matter.

Now you will send an email message to Art Capital Group requesting the information that you will need before making a decision. The email address on its website is information@artcapitalgroup.com.

6. Take over the position of vice president for administration for Goliath Insurance. In today's *Wall Street Journal* you read a report on telecommuting (the practice of allowing workers heavily involved with computers to perform much of their duties at home). The article pointed out many benefits of the practice—savings in commuting time, reduced need for office space, greater efficiency, improved morale, and more. You think the practice just might work for some of your people.

While considering the idea, you recall that at last year's meeting of the International Society for Administration you heard a presentation on the subject. It was made by Lorry Badin, who is your counterpart at the Great Southern Insurance Company. You meant to pursue the idea then, but apparently forgot about it. You recall that Lorry reported on a two-month experiment with telecommuting. But you don't remember the particulars. You know Lorry quite well—even had lunch with her at the meeting. Perhaps she can answer the questions that cross your mind.

Specifically, you would like to know the cost savings for her company. Are the savings only related to wages and salaries? Also, you know that your technical workers like one another and have developed a high esprit de corps. What would happen if you permitted them to stay at home, and how could you measure their actual performance there? Much of their work is group oriented; could this group emphasis still be maintained? You wonder also about whether the experience of Great Southern remains as positive today as it was when Lorry made her presentation.

Now you will write Lorry a message asking for the information that will help you in your decision. As you prepare the message, other questions may come to mind. In addition to the specific inquiries, you'll include a warm personal greeting.

7. As the business manager for Dr. Nicole Batla, you are responsible for making all arrangements for this investment adviser's lecture tours. Today you find that a scheduled lecture in Kingston, Ontario, cannot be held at the Ambassador Resort Hotel on the 17th of next month. The hotel's meeting rooms were badly damaged by fire and will be closed for at least two months. You will have to make other arrangements.

Your check of the Kingston Tourist Info website reveals one good possibility—the General Wolfe Hotel, which overlooks the St. Lawrence River and is located on the south side of town. This location appears to be ideal, for Dr. Batla prefers hotels away from the downtown traffic. But the website summary of the hotel gives only scant information. You will write the manager a message to get the information you need.

Specifically, Dr. Batla needs a meeting room that will accommodate a maximum of 80 people who will pay to hear her very popular lecture. The room must be free from outside noise—no loud celebrations, dances, receptions, or such in nearby rooms. Preferably, it should have solid walls and not be a smaller room formed by partitioning a large room with screens. Of course, it must be equipped with the standard lecture equipment—lectern, screen chalkboard, and such. Because the people who attend this evening lecture will come by automobile, the hotel must be able to provide the 80 parking spaces. And since these people pay a handsome fee for the lecture, you'd like to have valet parking available. As you think through the problem, you may find a need for additional information. Send the message by fax to the manager at a number given on the website, 613-385-1038.

8. For the past four months your company, Fun and Games Travel, Inc., has enjoyed good success. You have organized and sold trips to such places as Cancun, Acapulco, Honolulu, Las Vegas, and San Francisco. Now you are working on a seven-day ski vacation to Purple Mountain, a newly developed ski area.

You plan to fly groups of skiers to Ute City and then to take them to nearby Purple Mountain by chartered bus. Each group will arrive in the early afternoon on a Sunday and will depart at noon the following Saturday. Thus, you will need six nights of accommodations for each group. You have already acquired the information you need about air transportation to Ute City and bus transportation to Purple Mountain. Now you must get the information you need about the six nights of lodging, ski rentals, food, lift tickets, and so on.

Your check of the Ute City Tourist Bureau website reveals only one facility that appears to meet your needs. It is the Ute Lodge—a place with 122 rooms, restaurant, ski rental shop, and lounge. The lodge also provides lift discounts for its guests. It should be adequate for housing the 40 people you expect to have in your group. You plan three groups for this ski season (more if demand justifies), beginning in December. (You may select specific dates.)

Now you must ask the manager of the Ute Lodge, Owen Smith, the questions necessary for your planning. The lodge's website provides its standard daily room rates—$125 for single occupancy, $150 double occupancy for most of the season, with higher rates for peak holiday periods. You don't plan to schedule trips during these times. You will want a group discount.

As your group tours usually include breakfasts and dinners, you must inquire about the costs of these meals. The daily schedules of group members will differ, so breakfasts would be eaten individually. Dinners, however, would be a group affair—preferably in a private dining room. A sample menu would make it easier for you to evaluate food costs. Then there is the matter of gratuities for food service workers.

You also have questions about location that must be answered—specifically about distance from lifts and about ski-in, ski-out feasibility. And you have questions about ski rentals and lift tickets—all with discounts, of course. There may be other questions. Think about the possibilities carefully so that one inquiry message will give you all the information you need. You will send the message by email to the manager at osmith@utelodge.com.

9. As Matt Lenaghan, an extremely busy insurance professional, you want to give back to your community. When you were in college and later on your first job, you volunteered through your church to tutor students in math and English. But with the travel your current job requires, along with an irregular work schedule, you have not been able to continue that service. Then you read a story in *BusinessWeek* about icouldbe.org, an online mentoring program.

The article described the program as one that uses email rather than regularly scheduled face-to-face meetings, which you think you could fit into your schedule, even with your travel. Most of the students who sign up at icouldbe.org want career advice. You believe you can share your experiences about getting started on a career, but you are concerned about the privacy issues your employer might raise. Students are probably interested in how much you make. Would your employer want this information revealed? Would you? How do you know it's really a student and not a corporate spy at the other end asking you about your company? You also wonder about the volume of communication expected and the average length of the relationship.

Write an inquiry to the folks at icouldbe.org that gathers this kind of information, along with answers to any other questions you have before volunteering.

10. As Jason Solomon, Vice President of Marketing for PrintSafe, you are always on the lookout for new incentives for your sales representatives. While reading the travel section of your local newspaper recently, you got an idea from an article on America's most scenic railroad trips. Although you normally wouldn't consider travel a good incentive for your sales representatives who travel extensively for their jobs, scenic railroad trips are usually short, focused on nature or history, and unique. Moreover, railroad trips like those mentioned in the article are opportunities for travelers to unwind and relax. You think you'd like to offer a three-day package, including a couple of overnights in nice hotels, evening entertainment, and the scenic railroad trip for two.

After reviewing the websites for the railroads, you've narrowed your choice down to three—the California Western Railroad, <www.skunktrain.com/>, the Boone & Scenic Valley Railroad, <www.scenic-valleyrr.com/>, and the Blue Ridge Scenic Railway, <www.brscenic.com/>. These rides go through the California redwood forests, the Iowa River country, and Georgia's hardwood forests. Riders can sit in open air observation cars, view splendid foliage, and take in miles of stunning scenery—clearly a revitalizing experience for your hardworking sales representatives. In fact, the price is so reasonable that you are thinking about awarding the incentive to any representative who meets or exceeds this year's sales goals. But before you do so, you need answers to a few questions.

A couple of your questions are common to all of your choices, but each choice also involves a unique question not answered on the websites. The general questions include asking for the names of some nice hotels located nearby and specific information about the kind of evening entertainment available during the fall season. Additionally, you would like to know how far in advance reservations should be made for trips during the fall foliage season. Although the websites specify costs, you wonder whether or not the railroads offer any volume discounts. Furthermore, you have a specific question for each railroad regarding its trips or accommodations.

You'll write an email inquiry to the Director of Customer Relations at one of these railroads (you choose one). Because 80 percent of the content can be used in your other messages too, you may want to consider using your word processor's mail merge feature.

11. When Samantha Whisler, returned Peace Corps volunteer and Peace Corps recruiter, spoke on campus last week about her experience in Bulgaria, you were surprised to learn about the opportunity to gain business experience. Furthermore, you learned that in addition to language and cultural training, a living stipend, and $6,000 on completion of their assignments, volunteers' student loans are deferred and they have the opportunity to get MBA credit through the Peace Corps Master's International Program. In addition, participants get a wide variety of networking opportunities that may be useful when they return to the United States.

You were impressed enough to check out the Peace Corps website where you read some stories of business volunteers—one got hands-on experience helping set up ecotourism in Bolivia and another gained leadership experience in the Ukraine, where she directed an international management center and taught business communication.

You are seriously considering applying. Not only can you use your business knowledge and skills but you also get language training and some MBA credit. However, you'd like to know more about the MBA program. Since Samantha encouraged you to send her email if you had any questions, you decide to ask her some specific questions about the MBA. You want to know more about required GMAT scores, the amount and type of credit offered, and whether written papers are required. You also learned on the website which schools now support the MBA program, but you wonder if the credits are transferable should you decide to attend another school. In your inquiry message to Samantha, add any other questions you want to help you make a good decision.

12. Today one of your new employees, Ansley Wolfe, asked for permission to set up her office PC with an Internet-based program that enables her to access it from remote locations. She believes that GoToMyPC.com not only would help her work from home evenings and on other occasions, but it would also help her when she travels out of town to meetings and trade shows. Since most hotels and client sites have Internet connections readily available, she could travel without having to lug a laptop PC with her. She thought the program would cost less than $20 per month. She volunteered to conduct a trial run if the company wants a more in-depth evaluation.

As Scott Hildebrand, Director of Marketing, you are delighted with the enthusiasm Ansley is showing for being a productive, efficient employee. So you decided to learn more about the product by checking out its website at <http://www.gotomypc.com>. There several of your initial questions about pricing, security, and technical support were answered. But you have a few more before you approve Ansley's request.

Your first question relates to the pricing of the corporate plan offered. It appears that you can sign up 10 to 20 PCs on a monthly plan at $22.95/month or prepay a full year at $17.95/month. You wonder if you can start the prepay plan at 10 PCs and add more as needed at the lower annual rate. Would there be any additional fees for making changes to the plan as needs changed? Security also interests you. Although the company reports that the connections are secure, you'd prefer to talk with current users about their experiences. Will they identify some users you can talk to about security? Finally, you know all too well that technical support is both necessary and sometimes costly. You'll ask some specific questions on this concern as well.

Although you are excited about the potential for this product's value for your company, be sure your inquiry does not promise to use it before you get the answers to your questions. You'll send your email inquiry to the address you found on GoToMyPC's website, gotosales@expertcity.com.

13. Yes, your "toner low" message is still reminding you to get another cartridge for your laser printer. It's been on for a week already, but you just haven't had a chance to get one. So today when you read an ad for Hewlett-Packard's new Internet-enabled printer that will not only detect when you are low on toner but will actually order and deliver a new toner cartridge, you were intrigued. At first it seemed like such a good idea, but the more you thought about it the more questions you had.

You realize that Internet-enabled devices are good for manufacturers, letting them manage their inventory better and collect data for marketing and new product development. But do these "smart" devices also collect information on your habits that you don't think they really need? How might they use the information? For example, if they know how often you need cartridges and they know the size of the cartridges you use, they could easily determine how many pages you print. For some businesses this might be a subtle way of gathering competitive intelligence. Will they sell the list of heavy users to paper companies? Will they determine through your usage habits when you are ready for a new printer and time their promotions to reach you then? Will "smart" devices talk to each other, somehow combining data to get even more insight into your habits? Will your camera talk to the printer, telling it to use special photo paper? Will an Internet-enabled device be able to send this kind of information to a paper company?

Still, the idea that this technology will make your life better keeps your interest in this printer. So you decide to send an inquiry message to Sally Short, sales manager, asking these questions and any others you have about price, availability, and other features you need answered before making a purchase.

14. In your position as the official company newsletter editor for the portal your company has been using this past year, you have been collecting many photos. Although you've developed your own system for naming the photos and organizing them, quick retrieval is getting to be a problem. So when you saw Photags mentioned in a brief story in the *New York Times,* you thought it might solve this problem.

    The story reported that not only could you label and date stamp the photos using Photags, you could also annotate them as well as embed watermarks and other hidden text. So you went to the Photags website, <http://www.photags.com>, where you found more information and took the online features tour. The software seems too good to be true. It allows the user to search for any text added through the program or through Windows without having to create an external database. In fact, the price is so low you're a bit suspicious there must be a catch or major flaw. You still have some questions you would like answered before downloading it and devoting your time to learning and testing it.

    The online feature tour pointed out that it works with the user's photo editing software, but it mentioned no names. You use a couple of different programs currently, but one of your favorites is Paint Shop Pro. Its new version is coming out soon with some announced enhancements that already have you convinced you will purchase the upgrade. Not only would you like to know about Photags' compatibility with Paint Shop Pro's new version, but you are also interested in seeing of list of those other photo editors it works with. Another feature that interested you is the slide show capability. Although you realize you can already create running slide shows with PowerPoint, you wonder if Photags' shows are self-running or if they require a program or viewer to view them. You also would like some idea of the increase in file size the tagging adds to photos. And you're curious about the ability to download to Pocket PCs. You would like that explained better, including any capability or plans for downloading to palm devices or cell phones.

    Write an inquiry to the sales manager at sales@photags.com asking these questions and at least one additional one you would like answered before deciding whether to download and run the trial.

Inquiries about People

15. As human resources manager for Custom Engineering, you have been corresponding with Dr. Anna Cheney (see problem 1 under "Routine Inquiries") about the possibility of her conducting diversity-appreciation training for your company. In response to your inquiries, she sent you a detailed description of her qualifications and the range of services that she offers. She also listed her prior clients and invited you to contact any of them as references.

    You think Dr. Cheney looks good on paper, but you want to get more of a sense of the tone and content of her training. You don't want CE's money and time to be wasted, and you don't want the employees to be bored to death. But more importantly, you want to be sure that Dr. Cheney handles delicate situations carefully. You don't want her to make your employees feel criticized or coerced. Finally, does her training actually do any good? Write a letter that you'll send to three of her references to get a better sense of whether or not Dr. Cheney would be likely to help Custom Engineering.

16. Play the role of your professor in this course. You have been appointed chairperson of a committee to find someone to fill a vacant administrative position at your school (dean, department head, or such—as determined by your professor).

    Advertisements of the position have brought in a wide assortment of applicants, which your committee now must evaluate. In order to get the proper information for evaluation, you must write the references furnished by each applicant. So you decide to work up a standard message that will get the information you need. You may use your own logical information to supply the detail you need.

    Write the message, addressing it to Dean Marci Cangeslosi, and ask her about Dr. Tod W. Junco, who is one of the applicants.

17. Assume that you are nearing graduation and are applying for a full-time job in the career field of your choice. You have just completed a long interview with a prospective employer (your choice) about a most interesting and lucrative job (your choice again). As far as you can determine, you made a reasonably good impression in the interview, but you detected certain questions in the interviewer's mind. Apparently, she intends to check out these questions, for at the end of the interview she asked for the names of faculty references—professors who know you and your work.

    Now, switch to the role of the interviewer and write the message that will get the information needed. Of course, the message will cover the one job you seek; and it will ask the appropriate questions that determine your suitability for this work.

18. As an administrative assistant in the human resources department at the home office of Beckman-Tracy Department Stores, Inc., you have the job of completing the application files of a number of prospective management trainees from this year's crop of college graduates. The one you are working on now is Karem Ahmad, a marketing major from Oklahoma

State University (OSU). Mr. Ahmad is being considered for work in sales promotion. The work requires a sound foundation of marketing knowledge—of promotion in particular. Good creative ability and imagination are also important, as is an enthusiasm for work. The work can be exciting, and the people who do it should thrive on excitement.

Your first task in completing the Ahmad file is to write to the references he listed in his application for their evaluation of him. The first of these references is Professor Felicia Couvillion, who was Mr. Ahmad's teacher for two marketing courses and his advisor at OSU.

Your message to Professor Couvillion will ask primarily for information she can report. Obviously, she knows little about Ahmad's work employment experience (11 months part-time employment with an advertising agency). But she can report about things such as his intellectual ability, his knowledge of marketing, and his industriousness. She may also know enough about him personally to report on his character and personality. Study the situation carefully and then write the message that will get the information needed in this case.

19. As Don Zatyko, a product manager for Intuit Inc., <http://www.intuit.com/>, you are always on the lookout for talented employees. Your company is interested in people looking to transform the way people and small businesses manage their finances by delivering innovative, automated financial solutions. Indeed, it gives employees bonuses for referrals that end up being hired.

This month when you attended the regular meeting of the MIT Forum in your area, an energetic and enthusiastic MBA student from your alma mater, Kate Donnelly, approached you about a job at Intuit. The student gave you a résumé—a résumé that made her look like an excellent candidate for an open position as an Interview Interaction Coordinator. In talking casually with Kate, you learned she has a strong educational background in both communications and finance. Additionally, she goes to the MIT Forum meetings to get more exposure to real business problems and solutions. You find her articulate and knowledgeable.

Before you recommend her, though, you check the web profile she listed on her résumé. There you see samples of her writing, as well as a team PowerPoint presentation, showing that she clearly has the skills needed for the position. So you decide to contact the reference she listed from her internship, Erin Williams at Booz Allen and Hamilton, Inc., to verify other work skills. You will ask about Kate's basic skills, including the ability to organize documents and competency in grammar, sentence structure, and punctuation. Furthermore, you want to know if she has experience

writing technical briefs, white papers, case studies, and Internet advertising. And you want to know about her ability to follow directions, take criticism, and work with others. Be specific in your questions to get meaningful responses to help you decide whether you want to recommend her.

20. What a coincidence! Today you were planning on catching a plane to Toronto for an important business meeting with the potential client. Instead, you were stranded at the airport waiting for bad weather to clear when you met Zeke Smith, a potential top-notch recruit. Well, you tried hard to recruit him for an Internet designer position at your firm, Particle Factory, <http://www.particlefactory.com/>. Zeke has had experience with one of your major competitors, but as a new father he is looking for a new position without too much travel.

Although Zeke clearly has the software applications skill sets you require, he is not familiar with the C#, your new Internet programming tool. But he has extensive experience in working with development teams as well as excellent communication skills. And he has all those "plus" skills you seldom see in an applicant: time management skills, database experience, and familiarity with a number of web illustration tools, including Photoshop, JavaScript, and Flash. He has even dabbled in WAP/WML. You feel certain that he would work out, but you decide to check with some of his college professors to see how they would assess his ability to learn quickly. You do need someone to consult with customers on variety of issues related to your customers' use of C#, so it is important he be able to get up to speed quickly.

Write a message you can email to two of Zeke Smith's professors asking about his ability to learn quickly as well as his dedication to doing a job right the first time. In other words, you want to know if he consistently gives his best. Try to elicit this information any way you like: through direct questions, through examples of how he might approach certain tasks, and so on. Also, you know he has presentation experience, but his college professors can probably tell you how well he presents. Ask specific questions about these skills, too. Be sure to remind the professors that Zeke has given you their names and that their responses will be confidential.

21. As regional sales manager for Multi Tech Distributors, Inc., you are looking for an account representative. Thus far, your advertisements in newspapers, trade publications and online have brought you six responses. As you sift through the résumés, you place Megan Morrison's on top because her background facts appear best for the work. After reading her résumé in detail, you decide to write her references before you interview her. Miguel Gutierrez is at the

top of her list. He is her present supervisor at Tioga Sales, where she works as a salesperson calling on retail accounts. She is leaving Tioga because of her husband's transfer. The Tioga people are aware of her search for other employment.

The job of account representative at Multi Tech is a technical one. The representatives sell and service computers and a wide assortment of related hardware and software. This work is somewhat similar to the work she does at Tioga, but it is more applications oriented. Your representatives must be able to assess customers' needs and talk with them about the technical solutions to those needs. Thus, they must know their products and their products' applications thoroughly. Although they are expected to come to the job with some of this knowledge, they all receive additional training before being sent out into the field.

In addition to the technical skills, the account representative must have superior interpersonal skills and be able to relate to a wide variety of customer personalities. Also, the representatives must be self-motivated since they work without direct supervision. And, of course, they must be reliable and conscientious. In summary, you seek an all-around good worker who is has technical skills and exceptional social talents. It is rare to find the right combination in any one person.

But Ms. Morrison appears to have these credentials. Her B.S. degree with honors from Central State in computer science and statistics and her work experience at Tioga appear to give her most of these qualifications. Now you will write Miguel Gutierrez to find out whether she has them all. You have his email address.

Favorable Responses

22. As the manager of a private swim and tennis club, you have just received a letter from the director of your city's Fine Arts Fund, a nonprofit organization that raises money for special concerts, art exhibits, and theatrical performances in the community. The director, Ray Ortiz, asks if it would be possible for the FAF to use the club from 5:00 to 9:00 PM on Saturday, July 29, as the location for its yearly picnic. He expects about 30 people to attend. If the club can host the event, he wonders what the charge would be (a few of the FAF members are club members, but most, including Mr. Ortiz, are not). He also needs to know whether or not the club offers enough grills and tables for a group of this size, what kinds of recreational facilities are available at the club, and what kinds of special rules, if any, the group would need to follow.

You are happy to say yes to Mr. Ortiz's request and to provide the information he seeks. His organization includes members of your club, whom you'd like to accommodate. Furthermore, the picnic can help

generate new members. Also, you appreciate the work of the FAF, which enhances the quality of life in your city.

Tell Mr. Ortiz that, since his organization includes club members, it would be fine for the FAF to use the club for its event. The proposed date would work, except that a swim meet will be going on until 5:30. His event could start no earlier than 6:00, though his people can start setting up for the picnic at 5:00. Your club has three large grills but does not supply charcoal and lighter fluid. There are eight picnic tables that can each seat six comfortably. The lifeguards are on duty only until 9:00, so swimming will have to stop by then, though the club can stay open for Mr. Ortiz's group until 10:00. There are three swimming pools (a recreational pool with two low diving boards and a corkscrew slide, a lap pool, and a baby pool), five lighted tennis courts, two shuffleboard courts, and a large grassy area with a couple of swing sets. Your club provides the shuffleboard equipment, but people have to bring their own tennis equipment, including actual tennis shoes (no other kind of shoes, including gym shoes, or bare feet are allowed on the courts). No flotation devices are allowed except in the baby pool; the club provides kick boards for the lap pool. You usually charge $3 for each guest who is not a member of the club, but, for his organization, you'd just charge a flat fee of $50. Your club does not serve alcoholic beverages or allow them to be carried in. No food or drink is allowed in the swimming area. People need to clean up the picnic area after they've used it.

Show Mr. Ortiz that the Dayton Hills Swim and Tennis Club would be happy to have the Fine Arts Fund members as their guests while also giving him the information he needs in as positive a way as possible.

23. Place yourself in the role of Dr. Olivia Ledbetter, Professor of Business Communication and author of *Effective Business Communication*. Her book has been well received and has justified an early revision.

Today she received an email inquiry from Dr. Sean Kahn, a satisfied user of the first edition. Dr. Kahn is considering continuing use of the book in the second edition. But before he commits, he and his department members want to know what changes you will make. His people are especially concerned about coverage of email writing, an area they think needs improvement. But they like most of the current book's content and would not want to see much overall change.

You think you can satisfy Dr. Kahn and his faculty with your revision plans. Because of the book's wide acceptance, you plan no major changes. And, yes, you will revise the email chapter extensively. You have already reviewed the literature on the topic and plan a thorough and extensive updating.

In addition, you will go through the book carefully,

looking for any topics that need to be changed. Of course, this includes updating the rapidly developing technology topics. You plan some changes in the cross-cultural communication chapter because this area also has seen significant change. In addition, you will include new cases and will provide a grading rubric in the instructors' manual.

Using your logical imagination to supply any additional changes you think appropriate, write the message for Dr. Ledbetter. Keep in mind that you want this department to continue using your book.

24. As president of Soundview, Inc., you must answer the inquiry of Dolores Rodriguez, the training director of Pegasus Technologies (see Problem 2 for background information). The prospect of selling 71 subscriptions to your monthly publication service that summarizes the most significant books on management is indeed good news. You'll work especially hard to cultivate this potential customer. You will answer the woman's questions with the following information.

Her question about the qualifications of those who make the summaries is an easy one to answer. You employ doctoral students from the local university. They are specialists in the areas in which they read, and they have the competency to understand even the most sophisticated literature. To make certain that their work is well done and is presented in easy-to-understand language, their professors review their work periodically. You strongly believe that their excellent work is the primary strength behind the success of your publication.

You can answer her question about discounts positively. Your practice is to grant 10 percent off for orders of 10 or more, 15 percent for orders of 11 through 50, and 20 percent for orders over 50. You will go even further in her case and will grant a 25 percent discount for the order of 71.

Of course, you'll enclose a copy of the most recent issue of *Soundview Executive Book Summaries*. With it you'll send your descriptive brochure. Although the brochure duplicates much of what Ms. Rodriguez probably read on your website, it contains some additional information. Especially significant is its information about the doctoral students who make the summaries and the professors who check their work.

You will respond by email, which is the way Ms. Rodriguez sent her inquiry.

25. As owner–manager of the Alynn Neckwear Company, you are excited about the possibility of manufacturing ties and scarves for an NFL team (see Problem 3 for background information). You are confident you can make just the ones that the marketing manager wants.

For an order of the size suggested in the manager's inquiry, you can produce any desired design. Your artist will work with the customer until the design is precisely what the customer wants. Although you

normally imprint logos on a solid color field, you can design whatever the customer wants. Extremely complex designs may cost a little extra, but the design the manager described doesn't appear to be in this category.

Yes, you can produce the ties and scarves in silk. You have done so many times, but they cost a little more. You can produce the 2,000 items mentioned for $12 each. They should sell for $20. Future costs will depend on the effects of inflation.

Completing the first order by the August deadline is no problem—if the order is placed right away. You'll want to emphasize the "right away," because there is much work to be done. As soon as you receive an order, you will send your artist to the inquirer's office to work out the design. Then you'll start making ties.

You'll send your response by email, which will save precious time.

26. Assume that you are the president of Communication Management, Inc. and have received an inquiry from Michael Foxx, the training director of Alpha-Omega Industries, Inc. (see Problem 4 for background information). In answering this inquiry, you will proceed as follows.

Concerning the question about adapting the course to Alpha-Omega's needs for emphasis on technical reporting, the answer is yes. Dr. Timothy Schwartz, the course instructor, would visit the Alpha-Omega plant a few days before the program begins to determine company needs and requirements. He would adjust the course accordingly.

Foxx's question about deleting coverage of format also can be answered positively. Typically only about 20 minutes is devoted to this topic. This time could be devoted to expanded coverage of the fundamentals of writing clarity—or any other topic the company wants.

Mr. Foxx also inquired about your reference to an enrollment limit of 20 in a class. He has 27 engineers ready for the course. The comment in your brochure is more a suggestion than a requirement. Experience shows that classes 20 and under get best results. But you have had larger classes (34 once). You would do whatever Alpha-Omega wants concerning this matter.

As to the question about scheduling, you must report that you can't run a class for Alpha-Omega before September. You are booked solid until early September. September 4–7 and September 18–21 are open, as are any dates in and after October.

You will answer by email, which is the way the inquiry reached you.

27. For this assignment you are the business manager for the Art Capital Group, a company that leases art pieces (paintings, sculptures, and such) to sophisticated businesses for a fee, exchanging the

pieces every three months. Your website has begun to bring in good business. One of them arrives today in the form of an email message from Betty Baughn, the manager for administration for Vanguard Financial Services (see Problem 5 for background information). Now you must respond to her inquiries, most of which you can handle positively. Your response will convey the following information.

As to the types of art available, you will report that most of the pieces are paintings. But you have a limited number of sculptures, pottery, vases, and tapestries. The paintings are primarily oils, although some acrylics are available. All of your art pieces are the work of successful American artists. You can provide biographies of these artists—their training, awards, exhibitions, and such. In fact, you'll attach biographies of some of these artists to your message.

Yes, you do supply expert advice along with your art pieces. Before assigning the art, Cecil W. Corley, an adjunct professor of art appreciation at the local university, visits each client and personally advises about which types fit in with the business's interests, clientele, and the like. Cecil's goal is both to enhance the appearance and image of the office and to please the client.

Your charge for your service varies with the number and value of the pieces rented. Typically, a suite of four offices and a reception area will run around $200 a month. Mr. Corley will work with each client to meet the client's cost requirements. In other words, the art pieces vary widely in cost.

Clients must provide their own theft and loss insurance. Only in this way can you keep your monthly fee low. But most businesses already have coverage, you have found. It is just a matter of attaching a rider to existing fire and extended coverage contracts.

As to Ms. Baughn's question concerning whether the pieces can be purchased, the answer is yes. All the pieces can be bought. You can provide a list of prices for those desiring it, and you can handle all sales without requiring contact with the artist.

Perhaps there are a few little "extras" you can add to the message for goodwill purposes. Now prepare the message that will get Ms. Baughn's business.

28. As vice president for administration at Great Southern Insurance Company you received a message from Kirk Sutter, your counterpart at Goliath Insurance. Kirk recalls that you presented a paper at last year's meeting of the International Society for Administration on your experiment with telecommuting. He asks some specific questions about your results (see problem 6 for these questions and other background information). You can answer most of his questions with the following information.

Indeed, telecommuting offers cost savings for the organization, but not in the form of wages. You have not determined these savings in dollar amounts. They are in intangibles such as office space, office maintenance, absenteeism, and supervisory time. When technical workers stay home, they don't require an office, so office and related costs are reduced. Also, you have found that when people don't have to be at an office at a certain time every day, their work improves. All supervisors involved are in agreement on this result. There has been no evidence of the workers not putting in a full day's work. Rarely do they fail to log on for the minimum number of hours. Perhaps the reason has to do with their perception of work and their professional ethic.

The supervisors monitor and control the telecommuters' work easily through seeing whether assigned tasks are completed and when. As to Kirk's concern about the effects on esprit de corps, you have noticed nothing negative. It appears that these technical types don't really need a lot of group involvement. You think that they identify more with the task and not the group for morale purposes. Apparently, the group maintains itself through the technical services they provide and not through continuous interpersonal relationships. On the negative side, once every two weeks you require that the telecommuters attend a half-day group meeting at the company. Some have complained, saying that these meetings are a waste of valuable work time.

You want to explain to Kirk that although your experiment was only for two months and involved only 17 people, you remain convinced of its success now, six months later. You intend to permit a few others to work from home within the next month. You want to make it clear, however, that your study was not scientifically controlled and that your results are based more on perceptions than on hard facts. You strongly favor telecommuting for certain areas of work—but not for all. You think that executive jobs, production jobs, and personnel work, for example, are better done in company offices.

Now write the message that gives Kirk what he needs. You may use your logical imagination to supply additional details. Send your message by email or letter, as your instructor directs.

29. Assume the position of manager for the General Wolfe Hotel and answer the inquiry you have received from Dr. Batla's business manager (see Problem 7 for background information). You think you can meet the requirements of Dr. Batla's lecture.

You do have a meeting room that can accommodate 80 people. In fact, well over 100 were packed into it for a meeting last week. It is a separate room—not a partitioned section of a large room. It is your only meeting room, so no other gatherings would compete with Dr. Batla's lecture. You can promise that it will be equipped with all the lecture equipment she may need. She will have only to mention what equipment she needs and you will make certain it is there—even if you have to rent it. The room rents for $750 for the evening.

You can promise that there will be no noisy gatherings near this room. There is a lounge, which features a pianist-singer most nights, but it is on the opposite side of the building. It is too far away to present noise problems, but you'll mention it just to avoid possible objections later.

Your parking lot can easily accommodate the automobiles mentioned in the inquiry. But some of them would have to be parked in an area to the back of the motel. The parking spaces near the motel rooms are reserved for the people renting the rooms. And yes, you can provide valet parking. You have done this before, using students from the local university. The last time you paid $9 an hour for this work. For the 80 cars anticipated, you would need to hire six drivers.

Although the business manager didn't ask about it, you can provide refreshments—coffee, tea, soft drinks, mixed drinks, hors d'oeuvres, and such. You'll mention this service. Since the business manager communicated by fax, you'll respond the same way.

30. For this assignment you are Owen Smith, the manager of the Ute Lodge located just off the ski lifts at Purple Mountain (see Problem 8 for background information) and answer the inquiry from the president of Fun and Games, Inc. As you are trying to recover from last year's disastrous ski season, you welcome inquiries that may lead to business. You will answer the questions as truthfully as you can, and you might even add other helpful information.

Concerning the question about discounts, yes, you can grant them. For a group of 40 or more, you would rent the single rooms (regularly $180) for $160 and the double rooms (regularly $210) for $180. You would offer your breakfast buffet (normally $11) for $9 per person. The buffet is an all-you-can-eat meal offering these items: juices, fruits, eggs, bacon, sausage, biscuits, pancakes, cereal (hot or dry), coffee, tea, and milk. As for dinner, you can handle the group in a private room at prices ranging from $14.50 to $24 per person. These prices reflect a 10 percent discount and include gratuities. You will send your current menu.

As to the location of the lodge, you can present highly favorable information. It is adjacent to the lifts, permitting guests to ski in and ski out. A ski rental shop is located at ground level, and lodge guests get a $4 reduction from the normal $30 per day charge. The price of lift tickets is also reduced for lodge patrons—$38 rather than the usual $45. If you think other information may be needed, you may supply it.

Because you will send full-color, printed enclosures, you will present this information in a letter.

31. Project yourself 15 years down the road in your career. You have been quite successful. The efforts you have expended have been truly well justified given the results.

Today you received a letter congratulating you on being named your college's outstanding alumnus of the year. Among several laudable comments about your success, the letter requests that you attend a special honorary alumni day event May 12. On the evening of May 11 the college faculty will host a reception in your honor. And on the 12th there will be an assembly in Himes Auditorium for the purpose of honoring you. The event organizers would like you to make a short speech (about 30 minutes). As the letter specified, "you may talk on any subject you think appropriate." They ask that you accept this honor and that you provide the title of your presentation in your response. The letter stated that the college would cover all expenses. It also asked for your arrival and departure times and for your preference for a faculty member to introduce you.

Yes, you will accept. You are honored to receive this recognition. After considerable thought, you decide that your presentation will tell how the curriculum you pursued, the instruction you received, and good fortune contributed to making you what you are today. You will give this message the title of "A Good Recipe, Good Cooks, and Good Luck."

If possible, you'd like Dr. Lillian Sanchez to introduce you, as she was one of your favorites. If she can't, you suggest Dr. Lecia Barker.

After checking airline schedules, you book flights on American that will arrive at 3:30 PM on the 11th and depart at 9:35 AM on the 13th. You will not accept reimbursement for travel or for the hotel room you assume they have reserved for you. You'll suggest that they give this money to the college scholarship fund.

Since you received the invitation by mail, you'll respond by mail. Address the letter to the Alumni Day Organization Committee, Tanya Gooden, Chair. Most likely, your response will be posted on the college bulletin board outside the dean's office. As Dr. Sanchez was your business communication teacher, you will try to demonstrate that you learned her lessons well.

32. As Meng Tsai, President of Primrose Schools, you received an email inquiry from Anthony Dullas, a potential franchisee and client, about your plans for a branch near his home in Pearland, TX. When he was visiting relatives in Illinois and California, he learned of Primrose's leadership in providing quality educational childcare and is interested in getting more information about it. He understands that your schools hire teachers, not just baby-sitters. As a biomedical

engineer by training and as a young father, he's interested both in getting the best care for his two children—Payton, 4, and Alex, 2—and in bringing a Primrose franchise to his area.

Although you currently are not located in Texas, you are interested in expanding there. With his educational training and high interest, Dullas would be a perfect candidate for a franchise owner. You'll respond by email, telling him you are interested in locating in Pearland and you wonder if he'd be interested in considering the purchase of a franchise. While the costs are $180,000–$250,000 depending on local construction costs and real estate values, you have connections with financial institutions that will provide up to 90 percent financing to qualified individuals. As an owner, he'd get support in hiring top-notch teaching professionals, developing curriculum, marketing, and much more. You believe that you could have a franchise open within a year, perfect timing for his children.

Respond favorably to his inquiry, giving specific answers to those questions most new business owners ask.

Personnel Evaluations

33. As director of patient information for a children's hospital, you're wondering how to write a letter of evaluation for Margaret Sandburg. She has just completed a 10-week internship with your department as part of the requirements for the writing certificate offered by a local college. Your role, as her supervisor, is to assess her performance for her professors, who will be submitting a grade for her internship hours (she will also receive a copy of the letter as feedback on her work). The internship grade will be based largely on the report that she will write about this learning experience, but you know that your assessment will also be factored in. It is important to make the letter as positive as possible for Ms. Sandburg's sake, but you feel that you also need to address her shortcomings—not just because you want to be honest, but also because it is likely that Ms. Sandburg will want to list you as a reference in the future, and it is only fair that she see how you would represent her abilities to potential employers.

Her duties consisted largely of helping to write information for the hospital's brochures for parents. She had to translate clinical information about childhood medical conditions into language that this audience could understand. She did a good job overall. Her writing was, in general, grammatically correct and easy to understand. You thought she was especially good at getting across the pertinent facts while reducing the scariness of some of the doctors' language. She seemed to be sensitive to the emotional state that the parents would be likely to be in. Oddly,

she wasn't that sensitive to the likely feelings of those around her. She tended to take a high-handed tone with you and the other writer on your staff when you reviewed her work, arguing with you about your suggestions and sometimes criticizing your own writing. She seemed to overestimate her abilities and lack a sense of how to interact with her superiors. Still, she was friendly, conscientious, and hard working, and you did always know where you stood with her—she was honest, to a fault! Her weaknesses are probably due to her lack of experience working in a professional environment; you knew from her résumé that this would be her first real writing job.

Adding supporting details as necessary, write the letter evaluating the work that Ms. Sandburg did for you as an intern.

34. As Professor Felicia Couvillion, you will be evaluating Karem Ahmad for Beckman-Tracy Department Stores (see Problem 18 for background information). You know the man well; in fact, you were his advisor and spent much time talking with him in your office. He has some outstanding qualities, and he has a limitation or two.

In the two courses Ahmad had with you , he made grades of B and C. His course projects were outstanding and demonstrated good imagination, creativity, and talent. You gave him high As on them. But he seldom performed well on examinations—thus his course grades. He appeared to like work that was exciting and to dislike routine work.

As you see Ahmad, he has a very sharp mind. He has a good but not outstanding knowledge of marketing (including promotion), for reasons explained above. He works with great enthusiasm on things that interest him—and you think work in the promotion area would excite him.

Mr. Ahmad appears to be a very personable young man. He has good communication skills (spoken and written), and he makes a very good impression on people. You don't know much about his morals or character, but all that you have observed is good.

In general, you conclude that Mr. Ahmad is well qualified for the work he seeks. You would hire him for such work. Your message will reflect this conclusion.

35. Today you receive a message from Tina Petruy, CEO of Petruy Technologies, Inc., asking for an evaluation of Anita Fogleman. The Petruy people are considering your former head accountant for the position of Chief Financial Officer.

Ms. Fogleman is, in your opinion, one of the best accountants your accounting firm has ever employed. During the seven years she worked with you, she did a remarkably good job. She demonstrated a broad knowledge of all areas of accounting, and her computer skills proved to be exceptional. You know her to be a highly intelligent woman, a very hard worker, and a very nice person. You promoted her as fast as you could, but you knew you could not hold her permanently. So when she came to you saying that she was forming her own firm, you were not surprised. You wished her the best of luck.

For accounting work, you would recommend her to anyone. But you are not so sure how she would perform in work with broad administrative responsibilities, such as the work she is being considered for. She is not aggressive. She has not had broad administrative experience. Unless the work she is to do requires more accounting knowledge than the title suggests, you question whether Ms. Fogleman is suited for it. But the decision is for the Petruy people to make. Your job is to write an evaluation that is fair to all concerned.

36. Assume that you are one of your professors and have received the inquiry discussed in Problem 17. Now you, this professor, must answer the inquiry. In doing so, be as realistic as possible. In other words, your task is to evaluate you for the job of your choice and to present this evaluation in a report that is fair to you and to your prospective employer. For class purposes, attach a brief description of the job you seek and the questions asked in the inquiry to your message.

37. Elise Petan blew into your Pinkerton Advertising Agency offices one day last year much in need of a job, just at a time when you were much in need of a copywriter. You sent her out to dinner, then put her to work. In the eight months she stayed with you, you came to like her. Even her hack-written copy was acceptable; and when inspiration struck her and stayed with her long enough, she wrote masterly, sales-compelling lines that won you some enthusiastic accounts. As she talked engagingly and beguiled you in many a session, you learned much about her future and ideas, little about her past. The brightness of her personality laid the basis for interested friendships with many of your clients as they came to the shop.

One day in April Ms. Petan left as unexpectedly as she had come. You heard no more of her until today when you received a letter from Lisa Kidd, manager of the Great Lakes Advertising Agency in Cleveland, asking about your experience with her. Now you must answer this letter. In seeking to make your answer specific enough to be helpful, fill in plausible details about her successful copywriting. In fairness to the Cleveland agency, you will put them on notice that they may wake up to find her gone with the wind some morning. But because you liked her so much and because she never did you any harm, you will be careful to give this warning no more emphasis than it deserves. In writing your report, cover all points that one hiring a copywriter would want to know.

Adjustment Grants

38. You had thought that the shortage of servers on December 17 might cost you, and, sure enough, you've just received a letter of complaint from Jacqueline Thomas, who held a company party at the Carthage Banquet Center on that evening (see the related problem, number 48, under "Claims"). The letter claims that there were not enough servers available to tend the party, and you know that that's true. On that day, three servers had called in sick at the last minute. You'd tried to make sure that there would be plenty of servers available by hiring extra for the holidays. The thing is, it's hard to keep a supply of reliable temporary help available, and sometimes the temps call in "sick" or simply don't show up. And of course, there's no predicting when employees will actually get sick. You'll probably have to hire even more helpers for the winter holiday next year, especially if business is as good as it is was this year.

But that's not all. The letter also claims that the party room was too warm during the whole event. You figure that this is true, too. That room, the one without any windows, is particularly hard to keep cool, especially when it's full of people. You use that room only when the rest of the party rooms are in use, but that was the case on the evening in question. You could have put a different group in there, but, frankly, all the other groups were important repeat customers. Even though Ms. Thomas got her reservation in ahead of some of these, you gave them the better rooms. Maybe you should just not use that room for so many people. You make a note on Ms. Thomas's customer file to put her party in a better room next time, if there is a next time. She does say that the food was excellent, so maybe you can turn her into a repeat customer with your response. As manager of the center, write a letter that grants Ms. Thomas the reasonable discount that she is requesting (you decide what it is) and repairs her confidence in your services. Add any details that will help your case—and leave out the ones that won't.

39. As manager of Eurotours, Inc., you must answer the claim made by professor Dexter Palmore (see Problem 49 for background information). Professor Palmore does indeed have a valid claim. Luncheons should have been included in the tour of German industrial sites that you organized for him and 16 of his students. You will correct the problem. But you want to go further than just correcting the error. You want to protect the good reputation your company has built over the years. What happened just isn't representative of your operation.

Apparently the new tour guide assigned to Professor Palmore's group confused this group with one scheduled for Jason Munday and his group of industrialists. Luncheons were not included in the Munday group's tour. When Palmore's tour guide called the home office to determine whether lunches were included, apparently the clerk answering the call pulled the Munday records rather than the Palmore records. So no lunches were provided.

Now you will write Professor Palmore. You will send him a check for the $210 owed him personally for the lunches he bought, and you will send that amount to each of his tour members—with an appropriate explanation absolving the professor of any blame. You'll explain what happened as convincingly as you can in an effort to regain any lost confidence in your company. The professor might bring other groups on similar tours, and you want to serve him.

40. You, the sales manager for the Lakeland Cheese Company, Inc., are embarrassed. After receiving the claim message from Technology Supply (see Problem 50 for background information), you checked your records. The claim is correct. You sent the company's 1,244 customers three-pound packages instead of the five-pound packages it ordered. You inspected the original order, and five-pound cheeses are clearly indicated. The price information should have told the shipping clerk the size that was ordered, but apparently the clerk just made an error. You discussed the matter with the clerk and his shipping crew and instituted a procedure to double check all orders in the future. You are confident such errors will not happen again.

Your attention now turns to correcting the damage done to your relations with Technology Supply. You would like to keep this lucrative account, but to do so you'll have to change its thinking about your company's service. So you will do your very best to regain the goodwill lost.

You conclude that you have no choice but to agree to Technology Supply's request to send two-pound packages to each of the 1,244 customers. By doing this, Lakeland will suffer a small loss; but you think that it will profit in the long run. Also, you'll promise to send an explanatory letter with each gift package. (You really don't have to write this second message for this assignment. Just write the message to Eve Stoner, the Technology Supply sales manager and assume the second message is attached.)

41. As the owner-manager of Blue Lake Aquacultural Farms, you were surprised today to receive a claim by email from Wendy Krenek, the vice president for administration at Cutting-Edge Technologies, Inc. It seems that the tropical fish you furnished for the giant aquarium in the lobby of their new building have died or are dying (see Problem 51 for background information). As this transaction was a huge sale for you ($4,258), you remember it well. She states emphatically that she wants the dead fish removed and she wants you to do whatever is necessary to correct the problem. After checking out the situation, you think you know what happened.

Because of a death in your regular driver's family, you entrusted the delivery to your assistant. At the end of the 245-mile trip to the Cutting-Edge plant, your assistant found that the heating equipment had failed. The fish appeared to be OK; so the assistant didn't report it to you. There is no doubt in your mind. The temperature of the water must have dropped as it was very cold that day. Tropical fish can be severely damaged by cold water.

The error is clearly yours, and you will correct it as soon as possible. You will be at the Cutting-Edge plant tomorrow to take care of the dead fish. You will leave early in the morning and should be there by mid morning. Today you will begin assembling the varieties of fish that were in the order. You don't have all the fish types in your tanks now and will have to get some from your competitors. This task should take no more than three or four days. Then you will bring the fish in and make things right. You will follow up with periodic inspections and will promise a tank of healthy, beautiful tropical fish. Of course, you will absorb all expenses involved.

Now write the message that will satisfy Ms. Krenek and regain her confidence. Send it by email.

42. Apparently the buyer for Shelby Laneau and Sons, Inc., made a serious mistake. The material he bought for 500 warm-up suits was not colorfast, as the specifications stated. As a result, the red, green, and blue faded onto the white after washing. To date you have received complaints from five customers—the current one from the Sports Haven manager, Marc Thayer (see Problem 52 for background information).

After checking with the buyer, you, Laneau's sales manager, find that no explanation can justify what happened. Your buyer simply made a mistake. Perhaps he thought that the material was the same as what he had been buying from the supplier. But you think he should have been suspicious when he got it for a much lower price. On the positive side, you can say that Laneau learned from this experience. From now on, it will test all materials before they become garments.

Much as you dislike doing things that reduce profits, you will give money back on every defective garment. You will also make a strong effort to explain (perhaps *confess* is a more precise word) what happened. In addition to making things right, your goal is to regain lost confidence. Now write the message that will take care of the problem. Although you received the claim by regular mail, you will reply to the email address given on Sport Haven's stationery. It will be faster.

Order Acknowledgments (with problems)

43. As one of the office personnel for Silvers Catering, you will be writing to confirm your receipt of an order submitted via your website by Ted McCloud at

Dunleavy & Jackson, a local public relations firm. The order is for your "Barbecue & Turkey" menu, which, as your website says, consists of beef brisket barbecue, home-roasted turkey breast, Swiss, American, and Colby cheeses, sliced tomatoes, pickles, olives, fresh-baked buns and bread, homemade pasta salad, potato salad, and slaw. The PR company ordered enough for 20 people and did not request that any caterers attend the gathering (they just need to set up and leave, and disposable dinnerware means that there's no need for them to return), so the charge will be $10 per person. The requested serving time and date—noon on September 7—are fine, but you'll need to have access to the location by 11:40 to get the buffet set up. You'll need a deposit of $50 by September 1; you'll bill Dunleavy & Jackson for the remainder.

There's one glitch, though. Your supplier of barbecue brisket just went out of business, and you haven't had time to find another one that makes brisket as good as theirs. This was one of your most popular specialty items, so you hate to have to tell Mr. McCloud that it is unavailable. You do have several other nice meats that you could substitute for the brisket. Decide what to do and say about this situation, and then write a letter to fax to Mr. McCloud to acknowledge his order.

44. Place yourself in the position of owner-president of the Classic Uniform Company, Inc. Your sales representative in the western region has just submitted by email an order from one of the big accounts in her area—the Permian Oil Company. The order is for 400 sets of shirts and trousers in a variety of sizes. At $64.50 the set, the order comes to $25,800, not including tax.

The order specifies that the first 100 sets must be delivered in two weeks and the remaining 300 two weeks later. Normally this schedule would pose no problem. But this time the situation is different. The bone-colored fabric specified in the order isn't in stock. A quick check with your suppliers tells you that you can't get the material any earlier than two weeks from today—probably a few days later. Then you'll need four days to make the first 100 sets. The remaining 300 could be ready two weeks later.

Now you will write the Permian purchasing manager (Mr. Justin Fahrendorf) explaining the situation and getting him to wait. You may use your logical imagination to supply any additional information that you think is helpful. Since you have Fahrendorf's email address from previous communications, send this message by email.

45. On your Books Galore website you ran a listing of 100 current books at bargain prices. The response has been great. But as you anticipated, some problems have occurred. One that you are handling now is an order from Mr. Scott Sklar for 11 books. Nine of them you will send right away. But two must wait, each for a different reason.

One book, *A Day without Sunshine,* by Rebecca Stacy Huddleston (hardcover, $22.45), is out of stock due to an inventory error at your distributor. It was by far the most popular book on your list. You have been promised an additional supply within two weeks. The second book, *Napoleons in Grey,* by Gerry S. Sabin, is available in cloth hardback at $24.95 or in the classic edition (gilded pages and cover printing, leather bound) at $36.45. Mr. Sklar specified the classic edition in his order, but the computer mistakenly included the hardback price in the price summary. You have no way of knowing if he wants it at the correct price of $36.45.

Now you'll have to send Mr. Sklar a message by email that will take care of the situation courteously and tactfully.

46. As manager of the email order department of Home and Garden Supply, Inc., you received today a nice order from the Cascade Village Lodge, Bryan O'Connor, owner-manager.

The 48 cartons of 12 by 12-inch self-adhesive tile (stock #512-LT) that O'Connor ordered comes in four colors: chocolate, copper, honey beige, and ultra bone. You need to know which color he wants before you can send the tile. He didn't specify. Also, you are out of the 12-foot width Olefin pile, Turf III indoor-outdoor carpeting he wants, and it will be three weeks before you get another shipment. He ordered 240 feet of it at $14.50 a running foot. You are sending one item he ordered: the six-foot width Olefin pile, Turf II indoor-outdoor carpeting at $8.50 per running foot. It is in stock, and your delivery truck will bring it to his motel Thursday afternoon.

Now you must send Mr. O'Connor an email message covering the status of his order. He is a new customer, so a new customer welcome is in order. As the man apparently is renovating his lodge, he is likely to need additional items. So be sure to cover the situation courteously.

47. A few months ago your importing and jobbing company, Foreign Treasures, Ltd., received its first shipment of jade carvings from the People's Republic of China. A little later you presented these pieces on your website in an attempt to build interest among your customers. The plan worked. It brought in a number of new accounts, and it sold jade carvings. It sold so many, in fact, that your stock of some designs has been exhausted.

Today you received an email order requesting rush shipment from another new customer, Gabriela's House of Gifts, Gabriela Lopez, owner. Ms. Lopez requested shipment of 10 carvings, two each of Serpent Dragon ($430), Gliding Swan ($410),

Running Horse ($460), Guardian Lion ($425), and Sea Serpent ($465). You'll send the first three right away, but Guardian Lion and Sea Serpent are out of stock. You have more on order and have assurances that they will arrive in four weeks. You can promise to send these two items just as soon as they come in.

Now you must email Ms. Lopez a cordial message that combines the function of welcoming a new customer and back-ordering her jade carvings. She didn't say why a rush order was important, but you'll work hard to offset the negative effect of the delay. Perhaps you can help your cause by emphasizing the high quality of the carvings. Your brisk sales, including a number of reorders, suggest that these quality products are in good demand.

Claims

48. You stare at the bill that you've just received from the Carthage Banquet Center for the winter-holiday dinner that your company held there last week. It's for $480.70, which included an elegant three-course dinner, plus drinks, for 16 people. Yes, the center gave you a private party room as you had requested when you made your reservation two months ago, but the room was too warm during the whole event. You repeatedly asked the servers to turn down the temperature, but the small room never did cool off, and since it was the one party room at the center without windows (another thing you weren't thrilled about), you couldn't open any windows to help the situation.

There also weren't enough servers for the party, probably because it was the height of the Christmas season and the center was short on help. Some employees had to wait a long time for their food, while those who had their food either had to start eating before the others or let their food get cold while waiting for all to be served. This ragged timing tended to ruin the dinner, and it also threw off the program, since the speakers didn't quite know when to start.

As owner and president of this company (you name it), you were embarrassed by these problems. The holiday dinner is supposed to be a reflection of how much the company values its employees, and it looked bad that you hadn't managed to arrange things better for them. You'd heard good things about the center, and the food was in fact very good, but you don't feel that you should pay the full amount of the bill. Decide what you do want to pay and write the letter to the center explaining that this is the amount you feel is fair in light of the problems you experienced. You may or may not hold another company function there, depending on the answer.

49. Play the role of Professor Dexter Palmore. Last month you took a group of 16 operations management students on a 15-day tour of German industry. You arranged the tour through Eurotours, Inc., of London.

You bargained for a package costing $3,700, including all travel, housing, and food.

The trip turned out to be excellent in most respects. However, there was one problem. Except for one luncheon sponsored by a host university in Germany, none were covered by the Eurotour guide, and each traveler was required to pay for his or her own lunch. The agreement with Eurotours clearly specified that they would be covered, as a check of the contract confirms. So you will make a claim for reimbursements. You conclude that the out-of-pocket cost for luncheons for each of the participants was about $15 per day, or a total of $210 for the 14 days.

You will insist that Eurotours return this part of the total cost. It can do this individually (to each of the 16 students plus you), or it can send the total amount to you and you will give the students their shares. Write the message that will get this action. You arranged the tour with Eurotours by email, so you will send this message by email.

50. You have just learned that there was a mix-up on the gifts your Technology Supply, Inc., gave to its customers for Christmas last month. You, the Technology Supply sales manager, ordered the five-pound cheese packages from the Lakeland Cheese Company. Your salespeople report they are getting thank-yous for the three-pound packages. After checking your records carefully, you find that you ordered and paid for the five-pound packages—$24.50 each, including mailing. The Lakeland brochure you ordered from shows the three-pound package selling for $15.50.

Obviously, something went wrong. Someone at Lakeland apparently made an error, probably inadvertently. Something has to be done. Besides the difference in money, you are concerned about what your customers think of you. Technology Supply has always been more generous than a three-pound cheese package suggests. So you will write a message to the Lakeland people. You will explain what went wrong and what you want them to do about it. Even though it is well after Christmas, you think they should send every one of your 1,244 customers a two-pound cheese package with an explanation that clears your company of all blame for the error. As you see the matter, Lakeland should bear any losses and inconveniences involved. The brochure gives both the Lakeland plant address and email address.

51. The employees of Cutting-Edge Technologies, Inc., were elated last week when they moved into their new office building. It was truly beautiful. The most beautiful feature was the giant aquarium in the ground floor lobby. It was landscaped with aquatic plants and teeming with colorful tropical fish. Its beauty was short-lived, however; within a day many of the tropical fish were dead or dying.

As vice president for administration for Cutting-Edge, you have to do whatever is necessary to correct the situation. Your first step was to find out who supplied the tropical fish. From the architect you learned that the supplier was Blue Lake Aquacultural Farms, Rich Svenson, manager-owner. The architect also gave you Svenson's email address and the information that Svenson was paid $4,258 for the fish. You will send a claim message to the man.

Your message will tell Mr. Svenson what went wrong and will ask him to correct the situation. Specifically, you want the dead and sick fish removed—immediately—and you want replacements for them. Mr. Svenson's place is over 200 miles from the Cutting-Edge facility, but you don't think this distance should matter. You think he will want to make things right. Your claim will be firm yet courteous.

52. Last month when you ordered 48 women's warm-up suits from Shelby Laneau and Sons using their email order department, you thought you had made an excellent purchase at $48 each. Your Sports Haven store should make a good profit selling them for $79.95, you thought. The red, green, and blue figures on a white background make a beautiful garment. They should sell fast. And they did.

This morning the situation changed abruptly. One of your good customers returned the warm-up suit she purchased, and it was a mess. The snow-white portions of the garment were no longer snow-white but a reddish, muddy color. Obviously, the dye from the colored decorative parts had run. "I hand-washed it just like the instructions said," she told you.

You gave her a refund. And then you tested a warm-up suit from the rack. You washed it, and it faded badly. The product clearly is defective, and you must do something about the situation. After checking your inventory, you find that a total of 27 have been sold. Thus you have 21 remaining—and probably 26 more unhappy customers. You have no choice but to make a claim to the Shelby Laneau people. You will tell them what happened and what you want done. You will want to return all the unsold suits, and you'll want them to reimburse you for any additional returns.

As you have had good relations with the Shelby Laneau organization for some time, you are confident that they will make things right. Your claim message will be both courteous and firm.

53. As owner-manager of your own furniture store, you ordered online 36 Sandman mattresses from the Sleep King Mattress Company. These items were to be offered at bargain prices in your 10th anniversary sale beginning Monday. This morning the Sleep King truck arrived with 36 mattresses—but not Sandman mattresses. Instead, you got their economy product— the Sleepwell. The error wasn't discovered until the delivery truck had departed.

Unfortunately, the flyers advertising your anniversary already have been printed. Some—with your special offer on Sandman mattresses prominently noted in them—have even been distributed. So what must you do? You strongly want the right product in time for the sale opening. The Sleep King company is about 150 miles away and usually delivers to your area on Fridays, but they could make a special delivery in this case. Since they made the error, you think they must.

So you will write a claim message to them. In it you will explain what has happened and its consequences. You may use your logical imagination to bring in any specific information needed (such as prices, dates, invoice number). Make your claim both firm and courteous. Because time is short, send the message by email.

54. When today's credit card bill arrived, you were a bit distressed to see a finance charge for $8 included. On closer inspection, you discovered that the online bookstore (you choose one) where you bought several textbooks this semester had not credited your account for a book returned promptly.

This year you decided to try ordering textbooks online not only to avoid the crowds but also to ensure that you would have copies on the first day of class. Normally you would return to campus about a week before classes start, but this year your family decided to make a special visit to your grandmother the weekend before classes started. So you ordered the books just one week before the start of classes and had them delivered to your campus address. On the first day of classes, one of your instructors changed; the new instructor selected a different book for the class. You remember that you returned the book that day exactly the way the web store specified, via UPS. In fact, you tracked it online to be certain that it got to its appropriate destination. As you recall, it was back in their hands in less than two weeks—far ahead of the 30 days specified in the return policy posted on the website. So when your credit card bill arrived, you deducted the full price of the book.

Since you have all the documentation, you decide to write the textbook website asking that they credit your account immediately for the cost of the textbook plus the $8 finance charge. Not only did they have two weeks to post the credit, but they should also be interested in building a reputation for fairness in their dealings with students.

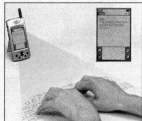

SOURCE: Canesta

55. As Mary Adami, a regional sales manager for Circuit City, you've been asked several times a day about a new laser-

beamed keyboard by Canesta, a company based in San Jose, California. Apparently, tiny components can be integrated in a variety of wireless devices to project a full-sized keyboard onto any flat surface, eliminating the need for stylus tapping and add-on keyboards. From the nature of the questions being asked of you, you think this technology will persuade a lot of people who don't have personal digital assistants (PDAs) or text-enabled mobile devices to buy one and perhaps stimulate those who want to upgrade to do so just to get this feature. You think that if Circuit City can get enough of these products in inventory before the holiday season, sales will soar.

However, before you recommend increasing orders to Circuit City's buyer, you have a couple of questions for the folks at Canesta. First, you would like to know when they expect products to be available, what companies will be including the technology, and in what types of wireless devices. Second, as far as you can determine from the information on the Canesta website, only three additional hardware components are needed. You wonder how much these components would add to the final cost of new products. It seems to you that people might pay as much as $99 extra, but that you would sell considerably more if the added cost were only $49. Finally, you want to know about the safety of the laser beam. If accidentally engaged while directed at someone, will it harm the person?

In writing your inquiry to Mike Willis, mikew@canesta.com, product manager at Canesta, feel free to add any additional questions you need answered in order to obtain good estimates of the number of units you think Circuit City could sell before the end of the year and the projected revenues the sales would bring.

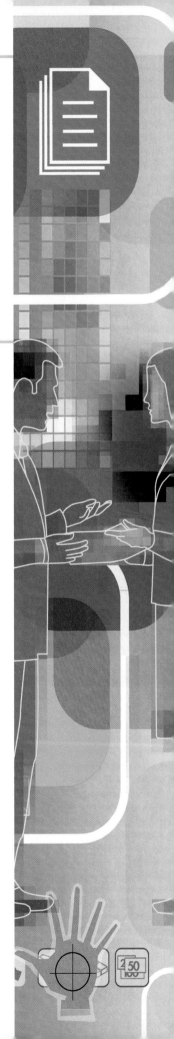

CHAPTER SEVEN

Indirectness in Bad-News Messages

CHAPTER OBJECTIVES

Upon completing this chapter, you will be able to write indirect responses to convey bad news. To reach this goal, you should be able to

1 Determine which situations require using the indirect order for the most effective response.

2 Write indirect-order messages following the general plan.

3 Use tact and courtesy in refusals of requests.

4 Write adjustment refusals that minimize and overcome bad impressions.

5 Compose tactful, yet clear, credit refusals that foster goodwill.

SITUATIONS REQUIRING INDIRECTNESS

- Usually bad-news messages should be in the indirect order.

As explained in Chapter 6, when a message is primarily bad news, you usually should write in the indirect order. The indirect order is especially effective when you must say no or convey other disappointing news. The main reason for this approach is that negative messages are received more positively when an explanation precedes them. An explanation may even convince the reader that the writer's position is correct. In addition, an explanation cushions the shock of bad news. Not cushioning the shock makes the message unnecessarily harsh, and harshness destroys goodwill.

- There are exceptions, as when the bad news is routine or when the reader prefers frankness.

You may want to use directness in some bad-news situations. If, for example, you think that your negative answer will be accepted routinely, you might choose directness. For example, in many buyer–seller relationships in business, both parties expect back-orders and order errors to occur now and then. Thus messages reporting this negative information are considered routine and are written in direct order. You also might choose directness if you know your reader well and feel that he or she will appreciate frankness. And you might choose directness anytime you are not concerned about goodwill. But such instances are not the rule. Usually you would be wise to use indirectness in refusals.

- Following are a general plan for bad-news messages and three applications.

As in the preceding chapter, we first describe a general plan. Then we adapt this plan to specific business situations—three in this case. First is the refusal of a request. We cover it in detail. Next we cover the refusal of a request for adjustment and the refusal of credit. Since these two situations are similar to the first one, we cover them briefly. The focus here is on special considerations involving each type. We work to keep repetition at a minimum.

THE GENERAL INDIRECT PLAN

Using a Strategic Buffer

- Use a buffer in indirect bad-news messages

Indirect messages presenting bad news appropriately begin with a strategic buffer. By buffer we mean a beginning part of the message that is designed to overcome or at least reduce the impact of the negative information that follows. The buffer presents the strategy you select to accomplish this task.

Selecting the Buffer Strategy

- Select a strategy for overcoming the reader's negative reaction.

The strategy you select will depend on the facts of the case. In each case you think through the facts involved, asking yourself what you can say that will change your reader's view of the negative message—or at least influence her or him to accept it as positively as possible. This strategy might be an explanation showing the fairness of a negative action you must take. It might be a review of facts that justify a negative action. It might be the testimonial of a mutually respected authority who supports your view. And there are other such strategies. Whatever you choose, it is what you believe to be the most logical and effective way of preparing the reader to receive the bad news in the most favorable light possible. Examples of how this may be done are better left to the applications that follow.

Setting Up Your Strategy

The beginning words of the message should set up the strategy you have developed. How you do this will depend on the strategy selected. Your goal here is to find words that logically lead into your strategy. For example, if the message objective is to say no to a request to serve on the board of a civic association, the beginning words might compliment the organization's success. This opening sets up the strategy: that such success is clearly the result of much dedicated work, that such work requires time, that time is something the writer cannot give now because of overcommitment to other civic work.

Developing the Strategy

- Then present your strategy convincingly.

After your opening words have set up your strategy, you continue the buffer with the development of the strategy. Ideally you do this without giving away the negative news that follows. Your buffer should be neutral. That is, it doesn't foretell that bad news follows;

neither does it suggest good news. In addition, if the message is a response to one the reader has sent, you need to acknowledge this message. A by-date reference is one way of doing so. Another is simply to use words that clearly indicate that you are responding to this earlier message. Your development of strategy should be as logical and convincing as you can make it, using words and reasoning that emphasize the reader's viewpoint. Again, specific examples of how to do so are better left to the applications that follow.

Presenting the Bad News Positively

Next, you present the bad news. If you have developed your reasoning convincingly, this bad news should appear as a logical outcome. And you should present it as positively as the situation will permit. In doing so, you must make certain that the negative message is clear—that your positive approach has not given the wrong impression.

- Refuse as positively as the situation permits.

One useful technique is to present your reasoning in first and third person, avoiding second person. To illustrate, in a message refusing a request for money back and return of product one could write these negative words: "Since you have broken the seal, state law prohibits us from returning the product to stock." Or one could write these more positive words emphasizing first and third person: "State law prohibits us from returning to stock all such products with broken seals."

Your efforts to present this part of the message positively should stress the positive word emphasis described in Chapter 4. In using positive words, however, you must make certain your words truthfully and accurately convey your message. Your goal is to present truth in a positive way. We are assuming, of course, that in presenting negative news, right and honor are with you—that in no way are your ethics in question.

- Be certain that right and honor are with you.

Ending on a Positive Note

Since even a skillfully handled bad-news presentation is likely to put the reader in an unhappy frame of mind, you should end the message on a happy note. Your goal here is to shift the reader's thoughts to happier things—perhaps what you would say if you were in face-to-face conversation with the person. Preferably your comments should fit the one case, and they should not recall the negative message to the reader's mind.

- End with specially adapted goodwill.

Following are adaptations of this general plan to three of the more common negative business message situations. From these applications you should be able to see how to adapt this general plan to almost any other negative message situation.

REFUSED REQUESTS

INTRODUCTORY SITUATION

Refused Requests

As in Chapter 6, assume again the role of assistant to the Pinnacle vice president. Today your boss assigned you the task of responding to a request from the local chapter of the National Association of Peace Officers. This worthy organization has asked Pinnacle to contribute to a scholarship fund for certain needy children.

The request is persuasive. It points out that the scholarship fund is terribly short. As a result, the association is not able to take care of all the needy children. Many of them are the children of officers who were killed in the line of duty. You have been moved by the persuasion, and you would like to comply, but you cannot.

You cannot contribute now because Pinnacle policy does not permit it. Even though you do not like the effects of the policy in this case, you think the policy is good. Each year Pinnacle earmarks a fixed amount—all it can afford—for contributions. Then it doles out this amount to the causes that a committee of its executives considers the most worthy. Unfortunately, all the money earmarked for this year has already been given away. You will have to say no to the request, at least for now. You can offer to consider the association's cause next year.

Your response must report the bad news, though it can hold out hope for the future. Because you like the association and because you want it to like Pinnacle, you will try to handle the situation delicately. The task will require your best strategy and your best writing skills.

The refusal of a request is definitely bad news. Your reader has asked for something, and you must say no. Your primary goal, of course, is to present this bad news. You could do this easily with a direct refusal. But as a courteous and caring businessperson, you have the secondary goal of maintaining goodwill. To achieve this second goal, you must convince your reader that the refusal is fair and reasonable.

- Refusing a request involves both saying no and maintaining goodwill.

Developing the Strategy

Finding a fair and reasonable explanation involves carefully thinking through the facts of the situation. First, because you should be concerned about good business etiquette, you should consider why you are refusing. Then, assuming that your reasons are just, you should try to find the best way of explaining them to your reader. In doing this, you might well place yourself in your reader's shoes. Try to imagine how the explanation will be received. What comes out of this thinking is the strategy you should use in your message.

- Think through the situation looking for a good explanation.

One often-used explanation is that company policy forbids compliance. This explanation may be valid, but only if this company policy is defensible. Justification of the policy may well be a part of the explanation. Often you must refuse simply because the facts of the case justify a refusal—that is, you are right and the reader is wrong. In such cases, your best course is to review the facts, taking care not to accuse or insult, and to appeal to the reader's sense of fair play. There are other explanations, of course. You select the one that best fits your situation.

Setting Up the Explanation in the Opening

Having determined the explanation, you begin the message with words that set up discussing it. For example, take the case described at the beginning of this discussion—refusing an association's request for a donation. The following opening meets this case's requirements well:

- Begin with words that set up the explanation.

> Your organization is doing a commendable job of educating its needy children. It deserves the help of those who are in a position to give it.

This beginning, on-subject comment clearly marks the message as a response to the inquiry. It implies neither a yes nor a no answer. The statement, "It deserves the help of those who are in a position to give it," sets up the explanation, which will point out that the company is not in a position to give. Also, it puts the reader in an agreeable or open frame of mind—ready to accept the explanation that follows.

Presenting the Explanation Convincingly

As provided in the general plan, you next present your reasoning. To do this you use your best persuasion techniques: positive wording, proper emphasis, convincing logic. In general, you use all your presentation skills in your effort to convince your reader.

- Then present your explanation.

Handling the Refusal Positively

Your handling of the refusal follows logically from your reasoning. If you have built the groundwork of explanation and fact convincingly, the refusal comes as a logical conclusion and as no surprise. If you have done your job well, your reader may even support the refusal. Even so, because the refusal is the most negative part of your message, you should not give it too much emphasis. You should state it quickly, clearly, and positively. You should keep it away from positions of emphasis, such as paragraph endings.

- The refusal should flow logically from the reasoning. Do not emphasize it.

To state the refusal quickly, you should use as few words as possible. Laboring the refusal for three or four sentences when a single clause would do gives it too much emphasis.

- State the refusal quickly,

To state the refusal clearly, you should make certain that the reader has no doubt about your answer. In the effort to be positive, writers sometimes become evasive and unclear. Take, for example, a writer who attempts to show that the facts of the case justify the company policy on which a refusal is based. Such words as "these facts clearly support our policy of . . ." would not communicate a clear refusal to some people. Another example is that of a writer who follows justifying explanation with a compromise offer. In this case, such words as "it would be better if . . ." would make for a vague refusal.

- clearly, and

To state the refusal positively, you should study carefully the effects of your words. Such harsh words as *I refuse, will not,* and *cannot* stand out. So do such timeworn apologies as "I deeply regret to inform you . . ." and "I am sorry to say . . ." You can usually phrase your refusal in terms of a positive statement of policy. For example, instead of writing "your insurance does not cover damage to buildings not connected to the house," write "your insurance covers damage to the house only." Or instead of writing "We must refuse," a wholesaler could deny a discount by writing "We can grant discounts only when . . ." In some cases, your job may be to educate the reader. Not only will this be your explanation for the refusal, but it also will build goodwill.

- positively.

Using a Compromise When Practical

If the situation justifies a compromise, you can use it in making the refusal positive. More specifically, by saying what you can do (the compromise) you can clearly imply what you cannot do. For example, if you write "The best we can do is to (the compromise) . . ." you clearly imply that you cannot do what the reader requested. Such statements contain no negative words and usually are as positive as the situation will permit.

- If a compromise is practical, use it to imply what you cannot do.

Closing with Goodwill

- End with a pleasant off-subject comment.

Even a skillfully handled refusal is the most negative part of your message. Because the news is disappointing, it is likely to put your reader in an unhappy frame of mind. That frame of mind works against your goodwill goal. To reach your goodwill goal, you must shift your reader's thoughts to more pleasant matters.

- Adapt the close to the one case.

The best closing subject matter depends on the facts of the case, but it should be positive talk that fits the one situation. For example, if your refusal involves a counterproposal, you could say more about the counterproposal. Or you could make some friendly remark about the subject of the request as long as it does not remind the reader of the bad news. In fact, your closing subject matter could be almost any friendly remark that would be appropriate if you were handling the case face to face. The major requirement is that your ending words have a goodwill effect.

- Avoid ending with the old, negative apologies.

Ruled out are the timeworn, negative apologies. "Again, may I say that I regret that we must refuse" is typical of these. Also ruled out are the equally timeworn appeals for understanding, such as "I sincerely hope that you understand why we must make this decision." Such words emphasize the bad news.

Fitting the General Plan to Refused Requests

Adapting the preceding analysis to the general plan, we arrive at the following outline for the refused request.

- Begin with words that indicate response to the request, are neutral as to the answer, and set up the strategy.
- Present your justification or explanation, using positive language and you-viewpoint.
- Refuse clearly and positively, including a counterproposal or compromise when appropriate.
- End with an adapted goodwill comment.

Contrasting Refusals

The advantage of the indirect order in refusal messages is evident from the following contrasting examples. Both refuse clearly. But only the one that uses the indirect order gains reader goodwill.

Harshness in the Direct Refusal. The first example states the bad news right away. This blunt treatment puts the reader in a bad frame of mind. The result is that the reader is less likely to accept the explanation that follows. The explanation is clear, but note the unnecessary use of negative words (*exhausted, regret, cannot consider*). Note also how the closing words leave the reader with a strong reminder of the bad news.

This bad letter is harsh because of its directness.

Subject: Your request for donation

Dear Ms. Cangelosi:

We regret to inform you that we cannot grant your request for a donation to the association's scholarship fund.

So many requests for contributions are made of us that we have found it necessary to budget a definite amount each year for this purpose. Our budgeted funds for this year have been exhausted, so we simply cannot consider additional requests. However, we will be able to consider your request next year.

We deeply regret our inability to help you now and trust that you understand our position.

Mark Stephens

Tact and Courtesy in an Indirect Refusal. The second example skillfully handles the negative message. Its opening words are on subject and neutral. They set up the explanation that follows. The clear and logical explanation ties in with the opening. Using no negative words, the explanation leads smoothly to the refusal. Note that the refusal also is handled without negative words and yet is clear. The friendly close fits the one case.

Subject: Your scholarship fund request

Dear Ms. Cangelosi:

Your efforts to build the scholarship fund for the association's needy children are most commendable. We wish you good success in your efforts to further this worthy cause.

We at Pinnacle are always willing to assist worthy causes whenever we can. That is why every January we budget for the year the maximum amount we believe we are able to contribute to such causes. Then we distribute that amount among the various deserving groups as far as it will go. Since our budgeted contributions for this year have already been made, we are placing your organization on our list for consideration next year.

We wish you the best of luck in your efforts to help educate the deserving children of the association's members.

Mark Stephens

This letter using the indirect approach is better.

ADJUSTMENT REFUSALS

INTRODUCTORY SITUATION

Adjustment Refusals

Sometimes your job at Pinnacle involves handling an unhappy person. Today you have to do that, for the morning email has brought a strong claim for adjustment on an order for Pinnacle's Do-Craft fabrics. The claim writer, Ms. Arlene Sanderson, explains that a Do-Craft fabric her upholstering company used on some outdoor furniture has faded badly in less than 10 months. She even includes photographs of the fabric to prove her point. She contends that the product is defective, and she wants her money back—all $2,517 of it.

Inspection of the photographs reveals that the fabric has been subjected to strong sunlight for long periods. Do-Craft fabrics are for inside use only. Both the Pinnacle brochures on the product and the catalog description stress this point. In fact, you have difficulty understanding how Ms. Sanderson missed it when she ordered from the catalog. Anyway, as you see it, Pinnacle is not responsible and does not intend to refund the money. At the same time, it wants to keep Ms. Sanderson as a customer and friend. Now you must write the message that will do just that. The following discussion tells you how.

Adjustment refusals are a special type of refused request. Your reader has made a claim asking for remedy. Usually you grant claims. Most are legitimate, and you want to correct any error for which you are responsible. But such is not the case here. The facts do not justify correction. You must say no.

Determining the Strategy

The primary difference between this and other refusal messages is in the strategy you use for the buffer material. In this case, it is the reason for refusing. The facts support you. The reader is wrong, or perhaps even dishonest. You have good reason to refuse. You use this reason as the strategy of your buffer.

Refused Request Message (Refusing a Request for Examples) Tact and strategy mark this refusal in which an office manager turns down a textbook author's request. The author has asked for model email messages that can be used as examples in a communication guidebook. The office manager reasons that complying with this request would take more time than he is willing or able to give.

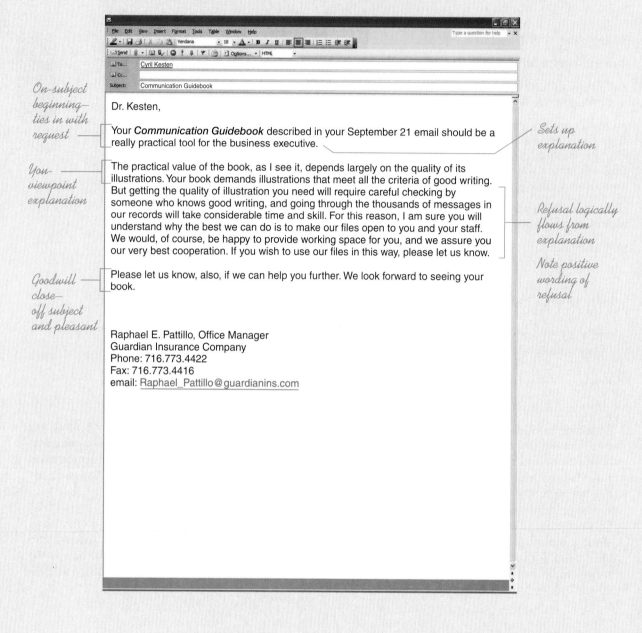

On-subject beginning—ties in with request

You-viewpoint explanation

Goodwill close—off subject and pleasant

Sets up explanation

Refusal logically flows from explanation

Note positive wording of refusal

To... Cyril Kesten
Cc...
Subject: Communication Guidebook

Dr. Kesten,

Your *Communication Guidebook* described in your September 21 email should be a really practical tool for the business executive.

The practical value of the book, as I see it, depends largely on the quality of its illustrations. Your book demands illustrations that meet all the criteria of good writing. But getting the quality of illustration you need will require careful checking by someone who knows good writing, and going through the thousands of messages in our records will take considerable time and skill. For this reason, I am sure you will understand why the best we can do is to make our files open to you and your staff. We would, of course, be happy to provide working space for you, and we assure you our very best cooperation. If you wish to use our files in this way, please let us know.

Please let us know, also, if we can help you further. We look forward to seeing your book.

Raphael E. Pattillo, Office Manager
Guardian Insurance Company
Phone: 716.773.4422
Fax: 716.773.4416
email: Raphael_Pattillo@guardianins.com

Refused Request Message (Turning Down a Speaking Invitation)
This example shows good strategy in turning down a request to speak at a convention.

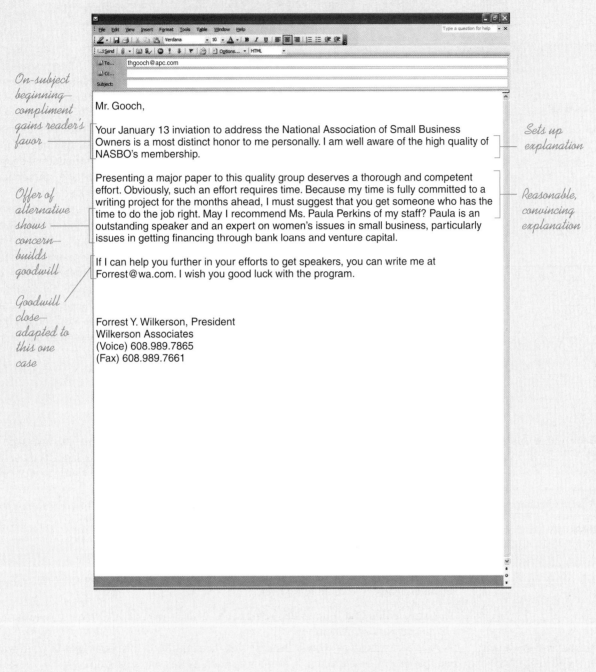

On-subject beginning—compliment gains reader's favor

Offer of alternative shows concern—builds goodwill

Goodwill close—adapted to this one case

Sets up explanation

Reasonable, convincing explanation

To... thgooch@apc.com
Cc...
Subject:

Mr. Gooch,

Your January 13 inviation to address the National Association of Small Business Owners is a most distinct honor to me personally. I am well aware of the high quality of NASBO's membership.

Presenting a major paper to this quality group deserves a thorough and competent effort. Obviously, such an effort requires time. Because my time is fully committed to a writing project for the months ahead, I must suggest that you get someone who has the time to do the job right. May I recommend Ms. Paula Perkins of my staff? Paula is an outstanding speaker and an expert on women's issues in small business, particularly issues in getting financing through bank loans and venture capital.

If I can help you further in your efforts to get speakers, you can write me at Forrest@wa.com. I wish you good luck with the program.

Forrest Y. Wilkerson, President
Wilkerson Associates
(Voice) 608.989.7865
(Fax) 608.989.7661

Email Merge Tool Allows Writers to Customize Frequent Messages

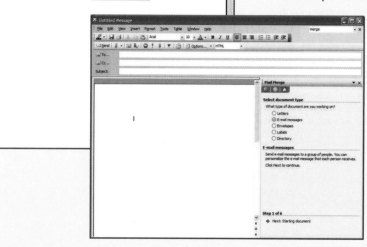

If you use Word as your editor in Outlook, you can use the merge tool to create form documents for those responses you send often. A writer simply creates the message first or uses an existing template or document. Saving it with a descriptive file name is important so that you can identify it easily the next time you need to send the same information. You can insert fields for information you know will be variable and modify other items as needed.

As you see here, once you select Mail Merge from the Tools/Letters and Mailings menus, you will be prompted through a series of steps to create documents that can be customized efficiently. By spending time creating well-written messages to start with, you can let the tool take care of the repetitive use of it.

Beginning by Setting Up Your Reasoning

- Begin with words that set up your reasoning.

With your strategy in mind, you begin with words that set it up. Since this message is a response to one the reader has sent, you also acknowledge this message. You can do this by a date reference early in the message. Or you can do it with words that clearly show you are writing about the specific situation.

- A point of common agreement is one good possibility.

One good way of setting up your strategy is to begin on a point of common agreement and then to explain how the case at hand is an exception. To illustrate, a case involving a claim for adjustment for failure of an air conditioner to perform properly might begin thus:

> You are correct in believing that an 18,000 BTU Whirlpool window unit should cool the ordinary three-room apartment.

The explanation that follows this sentence will show that the apartment in question is not an ordinary apartment.

- Another is to show that the claim goes beyond what is reasonable.

Another strategy is to build the case that the claim for adjustment goes beyond what can reasonably be expected. A beginning such as this one sets it up:

> Assisting families to enjoy beautifully decorated homes at budget prices is one of our most satisfying goals. We do all we reasonably can to reach it.

The explanation that follows this sentence will show that the requested adjustment goes beyond what can be reasonably expected.

Refusing Positively and Closing Courteously

- Refuse positively and end with goodwill.

As in other refusal messages, your refusal derives from your explanation. It is the logical result. You word it clearly, and you make it as positive as the circumstances permit. For example, this one is clear, and it contains no negative words:

For reasons you will understand, we can pay only when our employees pack the goods.

If a compromise is in order, you might present it in positive language like this:

In view of these facts, the best we can do is repair the equipment at cost.

As in all bad-news messages, you should end this one with some appropriate, positive comment not directly related to the situation involved. You could write about new products or services, industry news, or such. Neither negative apologies nor words that recall the problem are appropriate here.

Adapting to the General Plan

When we apply these special considerations to the general plan, we come up with the following specific plan for adjustment refusals.

- Begin with words that are on subject, are neutral as to the decision, and set up your strategy.
- Present the strategy that explains or justifies, being factual and positive.
- Refuse clearly and positively, perhaps including a counterproposal.
- End with off-subject, friendly words.

Contrasting Adjustment Refusal Messages

Bad and good treatment of Pinnacle's refusal to give money back for the faded fabric are illustrated by the following two messages. The bad one, which is blunt and insulting, destroys goodwill. The good one, which uses the techniques described in the preceding paragraphs, stands a fair chance of keeping goodwill.

Bluntness in a Direct Refusal. The bad message begins bluntly with a direct statement of the refusal. The language is negative (*regret, must reject, claim, refuse, damage, inconvenience*). The explanation is equally blunt. In addition, it is insulting ("It is difficult to understand how you failed . . ."). It uses little tact, little you-viewpoint. Even the close is negative, for it recalls the bad news.

Subject: Your May 3 claim for damages

Ms. Sanderson:

I regret to report that we must reject your request for money back on the faded Do-Craft fabric.

We must refuse because Do-Craft fabrics are not made for outside use. It is difficult for me to understand how you failed to notice this limitation. It was clearly stated in the catalog from which you ordered. It was even stamped on the back of every yard of fabric. Since we have been more than reasonable in trying to inform you, we cannot possibly be responsible.

We trust that you will understand our position. We regret very much the damage and inconvenience our product has caused you.

Marilyn Cox, Customer Relations

The bad message shows little concern for the reader's feelings.

Tact and Indirect Order in a Courteous Refusal. The good message begins with friendly talk on a point of agreement that also sets up the explanation. Without accusations, anger, or negative words, it reviews the facts of the case, which free the company of blame. The refusal is clear, even though it is made by implication rather

Adjustment Refusal Letters (Refusing a Refund for a Woman's Dress) An out-of-town customer bought an expensive dress from the writer and mailed it back three weeks later, asking for a refund. The customer explained that the dress was not a good fit and that she really did not like it anymore. But perspiration stains on the dress proved that she had worn it. This letter skillfully presents the refusal.

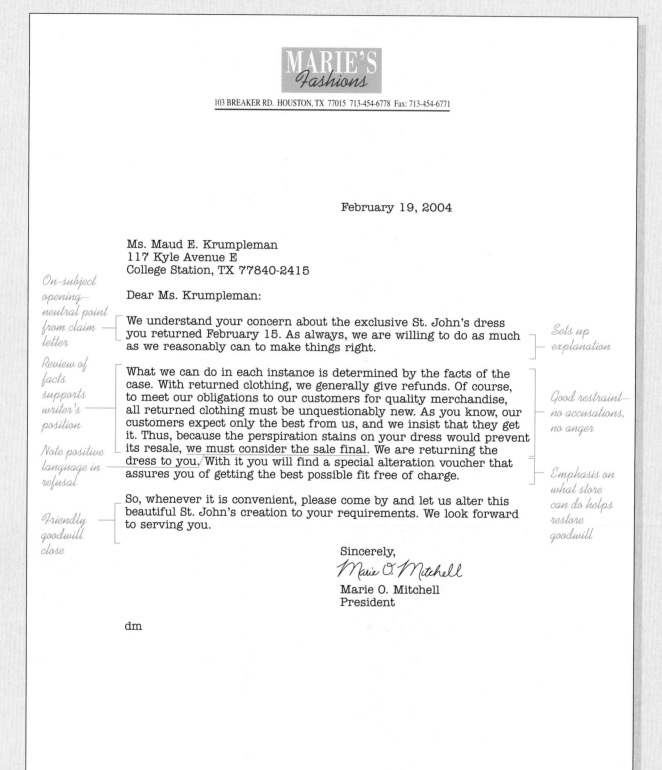

MARIE'S
Fashions

103 BREAKER RD. HOUSTON, TX 77015 713-454-6778 Fax: 713-454-6771

February 19, 2004

Ms. Maud E. Krumpleman
117 Kyle Avenue E
College Station, TX 77840-2415

Dear Ms. Krumpleman:

On-subject opening—neutral point from claim letter

We understand your concern about the exclusive St. John's dress you returned February 15. As always, we are willing to do as much as we reasonably can to make things right.

Sets up explanation

Review of facts supports writer's position

What we can do in each instance is determined by the facts of the case. With returned clothing, we generally give refunds. Of course, to meet our obligations to our customers for quality merchandise, all returned clothing must be unquestionably new. As you know, our customers expect only the best from us, and we insist that they get it. Thus, because the perspiration stains on your dress would prevent its resale, we must consider the sale final. We are returning the dress to you. With it you will find a special alteration voucher that assures you of getting the best possible fit free of charge.

Note positive language in refusal

Good restraint—no accusations, no anger

Emphasis on what store can do helps restore goodwill

Friendly goodwill close

So, whenever it is convenient, please come by and let us alter this beautiful St. John's creation to your requirements. We look forward to serving you.

Sincerely,

Marie O. Mitchell

Marie O. Mitchell
President

dm

than by direct words. It is skillfully handled. It uses no negatives, and it does not receive undue emphasis. The close shifts to helpful suggestions that fit the one case. Friendliness and resale are evident throughout the message, but especially in the close.

Subject: Your May 3 message about Do-Craft fabric

Ms. Sanderson:

Certainly, you have a right to expect the best possible service from Do-Craft fabrics. Every Do-Craft product is the result of years of experimentation. And we manufacture each yard under the most careful controls. We are determined that our products will do for you what we say they will do.

Because we do want our fabrics to please, we carefully inspected the photos of Do-Craft Fabric 103 you sent us through our laboratory. It is apparent that each sample has been subjected to long periods in extreme sunlight. Since we have known from the beginning that Do-Craft fabrics cannot withstand exposure to sunlight, we have clearly noted this in all our advertising, in the catalog from which you ordered, and in a stamped reminder on the back of every yard of the fabric. Under the circumstances, all we can do concerning your request is suggest that you change to one of our outdoor fabrics. As you can see from our catalog, all of the fabrics in the 200 series are recommended for outdoor use.

You probably also will be interested in the new Duck Back cotton fabrics listed in our 500 series. These plastic-coated cotton fabrics are most economical, and they resist sun and rain remarkably well. If we can help you further in your selection, please contact us at service@pinnacle.com.

Marilyn Cox, Consumer Relations

> This better message is indirect and tactful.

CREDIT REFUSALS

INTRODUCTORY SITUATION

Credit Refusals

Although Chester Carter, your boss at Pinnacle, is in charge of the credit department, you do not normally get involved in credit work. But exceptions occur. Today, for example, the credit manager consulted with Chester about a request for credit from Bell Builders Supply Company, one of Pinnacle's longtime cash customers. The financial information Bell submitted with the request does not justify credit. Bell has more debt than it can afford, and still more debt would only make matters worse.

Because a refusal appears to be best for all concerned, Pinnacle will turn down Bell's request. The decision is fair, but it will not be good news to Bell. In fact, it might even end this firm's cash business with Pinnacle. Handling the situation is obviously a delicate task.

The importance of the case prompts Chester to ask you to write the refusal for his signature. A refusal from a top executive, Chester thinks, just might be effective. Now you are faced with the task of writing the message that will refuse the request yet keep the reader as a cash customer.

Messages that refuse credit are more negative than most refusals. The very nature of credit makes them so. Credit is tied to personal things, such as morals, acceptance in society, character, and integrity. So, unless skillfully handled, a credit refusal can be viewed as a personal insult. For the most positive results, such a refusal requires the indirect order and a strategy that demonstrates good business etiquette.

- Because credit is personal, use tact in refusing it.

A Not-So-Successful Refusal

Trusty old Mr. Whiffle bought an umbrella from a mail-order company. When the umbrella did not function to his requirements, Mr. Whiffle wrote the company a letter asking for his money back.

The mail-order company answered with a well-written letter of refusal.

Again Mr. Whiffle wrote, and again the company replied with a nicely written refusal.

Mr. Whiffle wrote a third time. The mail-order company refused a third time.

So angry was Mr. Whiffle that he boarded a bus, traveled to the home office of the mail-order company, and paid a visit to the company's adjustment correspondent. After a quick explanation of his purpose, Mr. Whiffle broke the umbrella over the adjustment correspondent's head. The correspondent then gave Mr. Whiffle his money.

"Now why didn't you do this before?" Mr. Whiffle asked. "You had all the evidence."

Replied the correspondent, "But you never explained it so clearly before."

• Some think tact is not necessary.

• But treating people tactfully pleases us personally.

• It also gains future customers for your business.

Some will argue that you need not be concerned about the reader's reactions in this situation. Since you are turning down the reader's business, why spend time trying to be tactful? Why not just say no quickly and let it go at that? If you will study the situation, the answer becomes obvious.

In the first place, being kind to people is personally pleasing to all of us. At least, it should be. The rewards in business are not all measured in dollars and cents. Other rewards exist, such as the good feelings that come from treating people with courtesy and respect.

In the second place, being kind to people is profitable in the long run. People who are refused credit still have needs. They are likely to satisfy those needs somewhere. They may have to buy for cash. If you are friendly to them, they just might buy from you. In addition, the fact that people are bad credit risks now does not mean that they will never be good credit risks. Many people who are good credit accounts today were bad risks at some time in the past. By not offending bad risks now, you may keep them as friends of your company until they become good risks.

Selecting the Strategy

• Begin by working out the refusal strategy. You can imply the reason with bad moral risks.

As in the other bad-news situations, your first step is to work out your strategy—in this case, your reason for refusing credit. If you are refusing because the applicant is a bad moral risk, you have a very difficult assignment. You cannot just say bluntly that you are refusing because of bad character. Even people with low morals would bristle at this approach. In such cases, you might choose a roundabout approach. For example, you might imply the reason. Since the applicant knows his or her credit reputation, a mere hint should indicate that you also know it.

• But some authorities favor offering an explanation.

Some credit authorities in the United States prefer a more direct approach for bad moral risks, citing the Equal Credit Opportunity Act of 1975 as support. This act states that applicants refused credit are entitled to written explanation of the reasons for the refusal. One way of implementing this approach is to follow the refusal with an invitation to come in (or telephone) to discuss the reasons. This discussion could be followed by a written explanation, if the applicant wants it. Opponents of this approach argue that the applicants already know the facts—that very few of them would pursue the matter further.

• Frank discussion is effective with weak financial risks.

If you are refusing because your applicant's financial condition is weak, your task is easier. Weak finances are not a reflection on character, for instead of being related to personal qualities, they are related to such factors as illness, unemployment, and bad luck. Thus, with applicants whose finances are weak, you can talk about the subject more directly. You also can talk more hopefully about granting credit in the future.

Auto crashes such as this are bitter disappointments to those involved. Messages about the matter should not recall this scene unnecessarily.

In actual practice, cases do not fit neatly into these two groups. But you should be able to adapt the suggestions that follow to the facts of each case.

Adapting to the General Plan

The credit-refusal message clearly follows the general plan for bad-news messages. The opening sets up your strategy, and it is neutral as to the decision. It might well refer to the order or credit application involved, as in this example:

> Your January 22 order for Rock-Ware roofing shows good planning for the rush months ahead. As you will agree, it is good planning that marks the path of business success.

The strategy this opening sets up is to explain that well-managed businesses hold down indebtedness—something the reader needs to do.

A popular and appropriate strategy is to begin with a simple expression of gratefulness for the credit application and then lead into a courteous explanation and refusal. Although it is usually effective, the timeworn "Thank you for your application" variety is better replaced with different wording, such as this:

- A thank-you for the request is an appropriate and popular strategy.

> We are sincerely grateful for your credit application and will do all that we reasonably can to help you get your business started.

The following explanation will show that the facts of this case make granting credit something beyond what the writer can reasonably do.

The explanation set up by the opening can be an additional point of difference. If you are refusing because of the reader's bad credit morals, you need to say little. Bad moral risks know their records. You need only to imply that you also know. For example, this sentence handles such an explanation well, and it also gives the answer.

- Explanations to bad moral risks can be vague.

> Our review of your credit record requires that we serve you only on a cash basis at this time.

"No."

- Explanations to weak financial risks with good morals can be more open.

Your explanation to applicants with good morals but weak finances can be more open financial discussions of the facts of the case. Even so, you should select your words carefully to avoid any unintended negative effect. In some cases, you might want to show concern for the reader's credit problem.

- Refuse clearly and positively.

Whatever explanation you use, your words should lead to a clear but positive refusal. For a good moral risk with bad finances, this one does the job well:

> Thus, for the best interest of both of us, we must postpone extending credit until your current assets-to-liabilities ratio reaches 2 to 1.

- Close with positive, friendly words that fit the one case.

As in the other bad-news messages, you should end the credit refusal with words of goodwill. Preferably, avoid anything routine, and make the words fit the one case. A suggestion for cash buying or comments about merchandise or service can be effective. So can a forward look to whatever future relations appear appropriate. This closing meets these requirements:

> As one of Print Safe's cash customers, you will continue to receive the same courtesy, quality merchandise, and low prices we give to all our customers. We look forward to serving you soon.

Structuring the Credit Refusal

Adapting the preceding comments to the general plan, the following structure for credit-refusal messages emerges:

- Begin with words that set up the strategy (explanation), are neutral as to the decision, and tie in with the application.
- Present the explanation.
- Refuse tactfully—to a bad moral risk, by implication; to a person with weak finances or in a weak economic environment, positively and with a look to the future.
- End with adapted goodwill words.

Contrasting Credit Refusal Illustrations

- The following messages contrast credit refusal techniques.

The following two contrasting messages refusing Bell's credit application clearly show the advantages of tactful indirect treatment. The bad message does little other than refuse. The good one says no clearly, yet it works to build goodwill and cultivate cash sales.

Harshness as a Result of Tactless Treatment. The weaker message does begin indirectly, but the opening subject matter does little to soften the bad news. This obvious subject matter hardly deserves the emphasis that the opening gives it. Next comes the refusal—without any preceding explanation. It uses negative words (*regret,*

CASE ILLUSTRATION

Credit Refusal Messages (A Form Refusal for Bad Moral Risks) As the merge information in the address area indicates, this is a department store's form letter refusing credit to bad moral risks. Such stores ordinarily use form letters because they must handle credit on a mass basis. Because form letters must fit a variety of people and cases, they tend to be general.

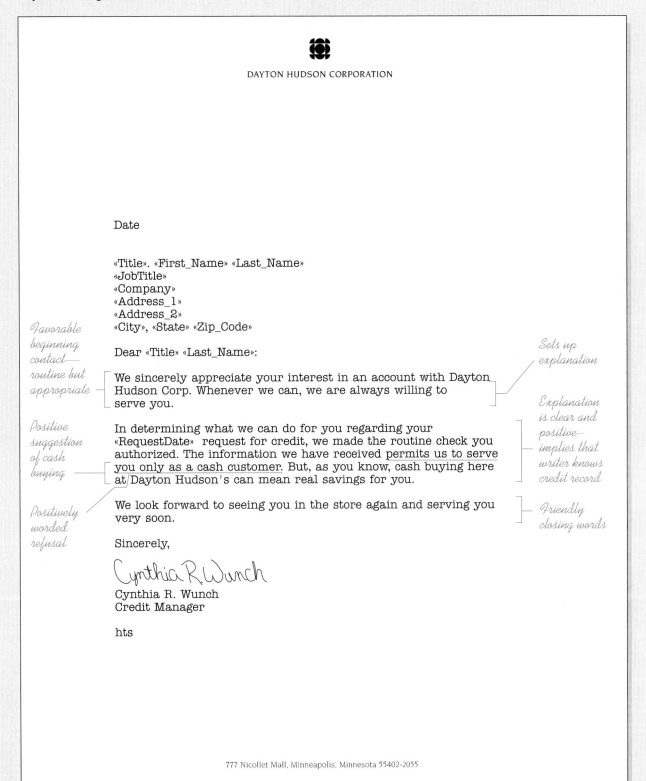

DAYTON HUDSON CORPORATION

Date

«Title». «First_Name» «Last_Name»
«JobTitle»
«Company»
«Address_1»
«Address_2»
«City», «State» «Zip_Code»

Dear «Title» «Last_Name»:

Favorable beginning contact—routine but appropriate

We sincerely appreciate your interest in an account with Dayton Hudson Corp. Whenever we can, we are always willing to serve you.

Sets up explanation

Positive suggestion of cash buying

In determining what we can do for you regarding your «RequestDate» request for credit, we made the routine check you authorized. The information we have received permits us to serve you only as a cash customer. But, as you know, cash buying here at Dayton Hudson's can mean real savings for you.

Explanation is clear and positive—implies that writer knows credit record

Positively worded refusal

We look forward to seeing you in the store again and serving you very soon.

Friendly closing words

Sincerely,

Cynthia R. Wunch

Cynthia R. Wunch
Credit Manager

hts

777 Nicollet Mall, Minneapolis, Minnesota 55402-2055

TARGET   MERVYN'S   DAYTON'S   HUDSON'S   MARSHALL FIELD'S

Some scholars argue that authors delivering a negative message should use an indirect organization, which consists of delaying the main point. Such an approach is believed to secure reader understanding before risking the loss of the reader's attention by delivering bad news. . . . The current results (of the authors' research) appear to support the use of an indirect organization scheme in a negative situation.

Annette Shelby, Georgetown University
N. Lamar Reinsch, Jr., Georgetown University

Annette N. Shelby and N. Lamar Reinsch, Jr., "Positive Emphasis and You-Attitude: An Empirical Study," *Journal of Business Communication* 32, no. 4 (October 1995): 322.

do not meet, weak, deny). Explanation follows, but it is scant. The appeal for a cash sale is weak. The closing words leave a bad picture in the reader's mind.

This one is tactless.

Subject: Credit request

Mr. Bell:

We have received your May 3 order and accompanying request for credit.

After carefully reviewing the financial information you submitted, we regret to report that you do not meet our requirements for credit. It is our considered judgment that firms with your weak assets-to-liabilities ratio would be better off buying with cash. Thus, we encourage you to do so.

We would, of course, be pleased to serve you on a cash basis. In closing, let me assure you that we sincerely regret that we must deny you credit at this time.

Terrence Patrick

Courtesy and Tact in a Clear Refusal. The better message generally follows the plan outlined in preceding pages. Its on-subject, neutral opening sets up the explanation. The explanation is thorough and tactful. Throughout, the impression of genuine concern for the reader is clear. Perhaps the explanation of the values of cash buying would be out of place in some cases. In this case, however, the past relationship between reader and writer justifies it. The message ends with pleasant words that look to the future.

This good letter refuses tactfully.

Subject: Credit request

Mr. Bell:

Your May 3 order for Pinnacle paints and supplies suggests that your company is continuing to make good progress.

To assure yourself of continued progress, we feel certain that you will want to follow the soundest business practices possible. As you may know, most financial experts say that maintaining a reasonable indebtedness is a must for sound growth. About a 2-to-1 ratio of current assets to liabilities is a good minimum, they say. In the belief that this minimum ratio is best for all concerned, we extend credit only when it is met. As soon as you reach this ratio, we would like to review your application again. Meanwhile, we will strive to meet your needs on a cash basis.

We appreciate your interest in Pinnacle paints and look forward to serving you.

Terrence Patrick

OTHER INDIRECT MESSAGES

The types of indirect messages covered in preceding pages are the most common ones. There are others. Some of these (sales, persuasion, and job applications) are rather special types. They are covered in the following chapters. You should be able to handle all the other indirect types that you encounter by adapting the techniques explained and illustrated in this chapter.

- Adapt the techniques of this chapter.

SUMMARY BY CHAPTER OBJECTIVES

1. When the main point of your message is bad news, use the indirect order.
   - But exceptions exist, as when you believe that the news will be received routinely.
   - Make exceptions also when you think the reader will appreciate directness.

   Determine which situations require using the indirect order for the most effective response.

2. In general, bad-news messages follow this general plan.
   - Begin with a buffer that sets up the strategy.
   - Develop the strategy.
   - Present the bad news as a logical result of the strategy.
   - End on a positive note.

   Write indirect-order messages following the general plan.

3. The refusal of a request is one bad-news situation that you will probably choose to treat indirectly.
   - In such situations, strive to achieve two main goals:
     — to refuse and
     — to maintain goodwill.
   - Begin by thinking through the problem, looking for a logical explanation (or reasoning).
   - Write an opening that sets up this explanation.
   - Then present your explanation (reasoning), taking care to use convincing and positive language.
   - Refuse clearly yet positively.
   - Close with appropriate, friendly talk that does not recall the bad news.

   Use tact and courtesy in refusals of requests.

4. Refusals of adjustments follow a similar pattern.
   - First, determine your explanation (reasoning) for refusing.
   - Begin with neutral words that set up your reasoning and do not give away the refusal.
   - Then present your reasoning, building your case convincingly.
   - Refuse clearly and positively.
   - Close with appropriate friendly talk that does not recall the refusal.

   Write adjustment refusals that minimize the negative and overcome bad impressions.

5. Messages refusing credit are more negative than most other types of refusals, for the refusal is tied to personal things.
   - As with other types of refusals, begin by thinking through a strategy.
   - If you are refusing because of the applicant's bad credit character, use a roundabout approach.
   - If you are refusing because of the applicant's weak finances, be more direct.
   - In either case, choose opening words that set up your strategy, are neutral, and tie in with the request being answered.
   - To the bad moral risk, imply the facts rather than stating them bluntly.
   - In refusals because of weak finances, look hopefully to credit in the future.
   - End all credit refusals with appropriate positive words, perhaps suggesting cash buying, customer services, or other appropriate topics.

   Compose tactful, yet clear, credit refusals that foster goodwill.

1. Give examples of when directness is appropriate for responses giving negative (bad-news) information.

2. Writing in the indirect order usually requires more words than does writing in the direct order. Since conciseness is a virtue in writing, how can the indirect order be justified?

3. What strategy is best in a message refusing a request when the reasons for the refusal are strictly in the writer's best interests?

4. Apologies in refusals are negative, for they call attention to what you are refusing. Thus, you should avoid using them. Discuss.

5. An adjustment correspondent explained the refusal of an adjustment request by saying that company policy did not permit granting claims in such cases. Was this explanation adequate? Discuss.

6. Is there justification for positive writing in a message refusing credit? You are not going to sell to the reader, so why try to maintain goodwill?

7. Discuss the difference between refusing credit to a good moral risk with bad finances or in a poor economic environment and refusing credit to a bad moral risk.

1. Point out shortcomings in the following email message from a sports celebrity declining an invitation to speak at the kickoff meeting for workers in a fund-raising campaign for a charity.

Subject: Your request for free lecture

Ms. Chung:

As much as I would like to, I must decline your request that I give your membership a free lecture next month. I receive many requests to give free lectures. I grant some of them, but I simply cannot do them all. Unfortunately, yours is one that I must decline.

I regret that I cannot serve you this time. If I can be of further service in the future, please call on me.

Sincerely yours,

2. Criticize the following message refusing the claim for a defective riding lawn mower. The mower was purchased 15 months earlier. The purchaser has had difficulties with it for some time and submitted with the claim a statement from a local repair service verifying the difficulties. The writer's reason for refusing is evident from the letter.

Subject: Your May 12 claim

Mr. Skinner:

Your May 12 claim of defective workmanship in your Model 227 Dandy Klipper riding mower has been reviewed. After considering the information received, I regret to report that we cannot refund the purchase price.

You have had the mower for 15 months, which is well beyond our one-year guarantee. Even though your repair person says that you had problems earlier, he is not one of our authorized repair people. If you will read the warranty you refer to in your letter, you will see that we honor the warranty only when our authorized repair people find defects. I think you will understand why we must follow this procedure.

If you will take the machine to the authorized service center in your area (La Rue Lawn and Garden Center), I am confident they can correct the defect at a reasonable charge.

If I can be of additional service, please contact me.

Sincerely,

Refused Requests

1. It's a good thing Janet Krendall wasn't around when you received her letter. She would have heard you burst out laughing in response to her request that you reimburse her for the taxi ride that she took from the airport to your company. It's not so funny, though, that you have to figure out now how to refuse this request in a tactful way.

   Ms. Krendall had applied for a training position that your company, Solution Software, recently advertised. Her résumé wasn't as strong as you'd have liked, but you've gotten few applications so far, and you need to fill the position immediately. As customer support manager and the person in charge of the hiring, you invited Ms. Krendall to an on-site interview at Solution's expense. When you were discussing her travel plans, you agreed to pick her up at the airport, which is almost 30 miles away from your company. On the day of her arrival, you were almost at the airport at the designated time when your cell phone rang. It was Ms. Krendall, who said that she had missed her flight and would have to wait for the next one. You kept your anger to yourself and told her that you would try to rearrange her interview schedule. Apologizing for making you drive all that way for nothing, she said that she would just get herself to your company by taxi rather than having you make a second trip.

The interview was so-so. Ms. Krendall did know a lot about training, as her résumé had indicated, and she was lively and personable. But she was a bit too loud and seemed too unprofessional to fit into your company. Worse yet, she didn't seem to pick up on the fact that no one around her was acting as flamboyantly as she was. You can't have someone this clueless interacting with your many different kinds of customers. Overall, you have to admit to yourself, this whole experience was a waste of time and money.

Now you hold in your hands the letter she wrote thanking you for the interview and enclosing her travel receipts for reimbursement. Amazingly, she includes the cost of the airport taxi—$50—in her reimbursement request. You simply will not pay this. Because she missed her first flight, over an hour of your time was wasted and people in your company had to scramble to rearrange their schedules for her. In fairness to her, you should also tell her now that you will not be hiring her for the job, a decision only confirmed by her astonishing request.

Write Ms. Krendall to thank her for her interest in working for your company while also giving her the bad news. Think about reasons why you would want to maintain her goodwill and write the kind of letter that will do so.

2. For this assignment assume that you are the vice president for administration at Data Systems, Inc. You have just selected Lisa Tuttle to head your human resources department. Ms. Tuttle definitely has the credentials for this assignment, you conclude. Her bachelor's degree in human resources from UCLA, her 10 years of related work experience at Ellison Technicraft, and the impressive way she presented herself during the interviews all made her your logical selection. Moreover, she is working on her MBA at night—evidence that she is continuing her career preparation.

Now that you have made your selection, you must inform the other three finalists of your decision. The first one you must inform is the first runner-up, Preston Castaneda, who is the son of Patrick Castenada, one of your good friends from college. You worked in the United Fund drive with Patrick last year, and you know he actively tried to get his son the job. Now you will have to explain and justify your decision to Preston (and his father) in a well-thought-out refusal.

You probably would have selected Patrick if Lisa had not been so outstanding. Patrick is well qualified. He has good experience and education. He is personable. And his references all spoke highly of him. Even so, you concluded that he falls behind Lisa in every category.

You may use your logical imagination to bring in any additional facts you think are needed as long as they are consistent with the information given. Although you have Preston's email address, you will send this message by regular mail.

3. You just got the word via email from President Semantha Polansky. Professor Zachary Broussard's request to conduct his research at your plant site is denied. You, the corporate communications director at Waldon Manufacturing Company, Inc., have been instructed to inform the professor of the decision. You don't agree with the decision, but you have no choice but to follow orders.

Professor Broussard called you a few weeks ago asking permission to use your company as the site for a research project he is undertaking. In the research, he wants to look at the productivity-satisfaction relationship, specifically seeing how communication fits into the picture. More explicitly, he believes that satisfaction with communication produces the environment for productivity, but he needs hard data to prove his idea.

Following the professor's call, you set up a meeting with the company president to discuss the proposal. At the meeting, Professor Broussard presented his proposal in more detail and answered questions. Specifically, he asked to conduct a survey of 500 of your 3,200 employees using three instruments to assess satisfaction, communication, and productivity. In addition, he explained that he would need to collect demographic data on the people he surveyed. This he could do by searching through your personnel files. Because President Semantha Polansky had an extensive travel schedule after the meeting, she ended it by saying that she would have to think about the proposal and let the professor know her decision later.

In this morning's email, President Polansky informed you that the request is denied. As she reasons, "the company has other work to do and a researcher would just get in the way of progress. And besides, we just don't want people having thoughts that we are not doing things right. Those questions he wants to ask are too deep for some of our people. And allowing him to dig into the confidential records probably is illegal."

Although you disagree, you will have to write the refusal message. President Polansky has her reasons, even though they may be selfish. They make good sense to her. Even so, she asks you to use tact. "We want to maintain good relations with the academic community," she states. You will send your message by email to the professor with a copy to the president.

4. For the past few weeks, all your spare time has been spent working on arrangements for the annual meeting of the American Association of Merchandisers. You are the arrangements chairperson.

In today's email comes a message from Penny O'Marley, who is on your committee and has also been working diligently. Penny is vice president for administration at Wimberly Foods, Inc. In her message Penny asks for a special favor. Wimberly will have 13 people at the meeting. All of them will attend the banquet Friday night, and they would like to be seated together "at a long table as near the head table as possible." Penny reasons that the request is appropriate because she is scheduled to become a member of the board of directors at the meeting.

You will have to deny the request. It just is not practical to reserve seats at the banquet. If you did it for one board member, you would have to do it for all; and there are 12 board members. Anyway, the board considered such a request at last year's meeting and concluded that making reservations would be a problem. Thus they adopted a no-reservations policy. As they concluded, over 800 people milling about looking for seats simply would be impractical. Also, the current practice of allowing the members to sit with people they do not know improves the fellowship the association seeks.

With the above information in mind, you will write the message refusing the request. As you will be working with Ms. O'Marley in the years to come, use your most tactful writing skills. You have been communicating with her regarding committee work by email, so you will send this message by email.

5. The invitation to serve on the board of your local United Way organization was most flattering. Apparently you are viewed as a leader in the business community.

Even though you are pleased personally, you cannot accept. For the past year you have been working 12- to 14-hour days getting your insurance agency off the ground. You have made good progress, but you have a way to go. The coming year will be crucial and will require all your available time. United Way deserves more than you would be able to give. But just as soon as your company is well established you will want—even seek—opportunities to do civic work.

Write the message that will convey your decision and keep you in line for similar invitations in the future. Keep in mind that you strongly believe in the good philanthropic work this organization does and would like one day to be able to work hard for it. You may use your logical imagination to bring in supporting factual information, but keep it plausible. You received the invitation by letter from August Giese, who is the local director of United Way. The letterhead gives both the street address and the email address.

6. As the sales manager of Sol-Way, Inc., you must refuse to sell your Sol-Way solar collectors to the Dusek Construction Company. After viewing your website, they sent by email an order worth $64,544. But the prices they used came from the password-protected distributors only section of your website, intended and clearly labeled for your dealers only. You sell exclusively through dealers. You thought you made this clear on the web, but apparently Alfred Dusek, the Dusek president, found a way to obtain these prices. Your dealer in his area is Eli Toms and Son.

Sol-Way management thinks that selling through exclusive dealers is necessary. After all, your technique of collecting and using solar energy is only in its infant stage, and consumers often need technical help. Thus factory-trained technicians are available at every dealership. Experience has shown that they are necessary.

Your task now is to write a message to Mr. Dusek explaining Sol-Way's distribution method and defending it. Probably Mr. Dusek already has learned much about your product from your website—how it uses its exclusive evacuated-glass-tubing technology to convert sunlight into useful heat, how the tubing is vacuum insulated, how it retains heat, how it collects both direct and diffused light, and such. It is a significant improvement over flat-plate collectors. You may want to note some of its points in your response. As Dusek is a good prospective customer, be most tactful in your refusal.

7. As a member of the city council and chairperson of the Police Relations Committee of _____ (your choice of city, or your instructor will name) it is your task today to refuse a request of the local police. In a persuasive letter signed by most of the local police department on the letterhead of the Fraternal Order of Peace Officers, these loyal employees respectfully presented a case for a pay increase (salary and benefits). They brought out convincing facts showing that their pay is well below area and national averages, that the department is losing personnel, and that the families of police officers are suffering hardships.

You and the other committee member were impressed. You carefully studied the city's budget. You tried very hard, but there simply is no money available. The city must have a tax increase before anything can be done for the officers—and the citizens have voted down all increase proposals for the past five years.

Now you must report the bad news to the officers.

You can promise to support a tax increase for improving city employee pay. But you must emphasize the fact that the citizens don't appear to favor any increase.

8. Assume that you are a student member on the traffic control committee at your university. The committee has just concluded a long meeting at which it considered a proposal for open parking on campus. The proposal was submitted by the members of Action, an organization of students interested in enhancing the rights of students. By open parking you mean no parking privileges for anyone. Students, faculty, staff—all would have equal access to parking on a first-come, first-serve basis.

    After considering the pros and cons of the question, the committee voted unanimously to retain the present system, which gives faculty, staff, and handicapped students priorities. This arrangement makes sense, the committee concluded. Open parking would create great problems.

    Since you are the student representative on the committee, the chairperson asks you to write the response to the student organization. "You are a student and know the student side of this question and now you have heard the viewpoints of others; so why don't you write the response to Action," the chairperson said. "It'll give you a chance to put to use the techniques you are learning in that business communication course you said you are taking. After you finish, let me see the message. It can go out under my signature, if you prefer." Needless to say, you accepted the challenge, and you do prefer that Professor Garrett Crenshaw, chair of the committee, sign the message.

    So now you will write the message. You'll think through the question again, reviewing all the pros and cons you heard discussed. Then you'll write the committee's decision and supporting reasoning in a courteous yet clear message. Since you accepted the committee's reasoning, you think you can present it so the Action people will understand its logic. You will send the response to Patti Crowell, the Action president. Probably she will post copies on the Action website and give a copy to the student newspaper.

9. As director of public relations for Electro-Tech Equipment, Inc., manufacturers of medical laser electronic equipment, you must write a special message for the president of your company. The message must inform the mayor and other dignitaries of Atlanta that their efforts to bring Electro-Tech's new plant to their city have failed. The new plant will be built in Houston.

    For the last two years, the leaders of these two cities have appealed vigorously to your company. Each of these groups presented convincing facts and figures supporting its case. You, your president, and other Electro-Tech executives spent long hours at the excellent presentations of the two groups. All of you were impressed with the warmth and enthusiasm of both groups. It wouldn't be easy to turn down either, but you have chosen Houston and must say no to the Atlanta group.

    Both cities appeared to meet all the company's requirements. Atlanta appeared to have a slight edge in tax incentives and community support. But Houston led in the availability of highly trained technical labor. And perhaps even more important, prestigious Rice University, with its internationally known research faculty, is located in Houston.

    In talking to president Theo B. Bruno (you will write the message for his signature), you learned that Mr. Bruno has developed a very warm feeling toward the Atlanta people. "We must handle this matter with utmost delicacy," he instructs you, "especially Mayor Samuel Tedrow. They worked very hard to convince us that Atlanta was the place for us. I think they thought they would win. They will be terribly disappointed."

    You'll soften the blow as skillfully as you can, and you'll emphasize Electro-Tech's sincere appreciation for all the mayor and his associates did to help the president personally and Electro-Tech generally.

10. You recently elected to take an internship in the front office of the athletic department at your school. At first you dismissed the idea of working there because you wanted "real" business experience. However, on reading the job description a little more carefully, you recognized it as an opportunity to gain a broad base of business skills. One task delegated to you is answering some of the email messages the department receives daily, including the request below for a gratis piece of your baseball coach's time.

Dear (Athletic Director):

At its meeting last night, the directors of the St. Patrick's Day Parade Committee unanimously voted to honor your school and department by selecting your baseball coach (you name him or her) as its grand marshal for next year.

Not only will this honor help us get more people to watch the parade, but the coach's marvelous disposition will be showcased through the local media exposure. As you know, such exposure creates goodwill for your school and indirectly may stimulate your alums to donate to the school. And it might even help in recruiting.

Will you please ask the coach to contact us at director@stpatsparade.com to set up a meeting to explain all the activities associated with this honor?

Terry Lenaghan

You know the baseball coach carefully selects gratis appearances, and this isn't one you'd expect him/her to accept. The request doesn't reveal how much time it would involve; it sounds like it might be more than an hour or so on parade day. Moreover, since the parade is during baseball season and likely during championship playoffs, the coach will be very busy then. Additionally, since St. Patrick's Day celebrants often imbibe in a bit too much green beer, you don't believe it would necessarily create the kind of goodwill your school administrators seek. In fact, one of the major campus problems the university is attempting to curb is excessive drinking by students. So you'll refuse this request.

However, recognizing that the organizers believe they are bestowing an honor on the coach and not wanting to insult an ethnic group, you'll refuse while retaining their goodwill toward your school. You might want to suggest someone else, perhaps a well-known alum from your school who could draw a crowd and create some goodwill for your school through his/her association with it.

Adjustment Refusals

11. As conference chairperson for the recent meeting of the Midwest _____ Society (you name it), held this year at the Century Hotel in St. Louis, you've just received a request that you're going to have to refuse. It's from Mark Gomes, a newcomer to your organization. According to his letter, he paid the full registration fee of $120 for the three-day conference, but he'd had to leave on the second day, which meant that he missed not only about half the conference but also the conference banquet, the cost of which had been included in the registration fee. Mr. Gomes wonders if half the registration fee could be refunded, especially since he missed the banquet. He encloses his banquet ticket to show that he didn't use it.

Politely worded as his request is, you have to say no. People come and go all the time at conferences like these—probably only a small percentage of the registrants actually attend the whole conference from beginning to end. It would be a logistical nightmare to try to give everyone refunds for sessions they'd missed. Moreover, since there was one fee for the meeting as a whole, not a fee for each day, Mr. Gomes should have understood when he filled out the registration form that the fee couldn't be broken up or prorated. Experienced conference-goers know that, to be able to plan a meeting like this, you have to have a good idea in advance of how many registrants you will have. You count on that registration money to cover the cost of hotel meeting rooms, presentation equipment, coffee breaks, and other amenities, all of which have to be arranged in advance. You can't give money back that is, in essence, already spent. This is true for the banquet as well. Before the banquet, you'd arranged for the hotel to prepare enough food for a

certain number of guests , and you had paid for that amount. If you were to refund Mr. Gomes's banquet money, you'd be paying twice for his meal.

You need to explain the facts to Mr. Gomes without making him feel angry about your refusal or embarrassed that he didn't understand the situation any better. You want him to feel welcomed into the organization and eager to attend future meetings. Using realistic details that you invent, persuade him that the conference is, in general, a good bargain.

12. In your work in the human resources department of a large, progressive company (you name it), you find that a big part of your job is often helping people understand and interpret correctly the company's policies. Today an email from James Andrews brought such a task.

Human Resources Director,

Today when I checked my personnel record through the company portal, I noticed that the 19 days I missed of work last month had been incorrectly deducted from my accumulated sick leave rather from the organ donor leave.

As required by the policy, I notified the Benefits Office in the Center for Human Resources that I was a match for donating a kidney to my sister and planned to do so as soon as arrangements were set up. Additionally, I completed the form sent to me by your office asking for the dates I anticipated missing. While I estimated it might be as many as 25, everything went well and I was able to return to work earlier than expected. Furthermore, on my return, I submitted copies of the medical records showing the dates and procedures performed.

Since our company now has an organ donor leave program allowing up to 30 days paid leave, please apply these missed days to that program and reinstate the 19 days to my accumulated sick leave total. Your immediate help in clearing up this error would be greatly appreciated.

James Andrews

While you personally think James was extremely charitable in donating a kidney to his sister, you must refuse his adjustment request because his circumstances don't meet the exact guidelines of the new company organ donor policy. This policy allows employees to take up to 30 days paid leave after they have exhausted their sick leave. Since James had accumulated 79 days of sick leave, the missed days were deducted from that total. This same provision applies to bone marrow donors, who may take paid leave for up to five days even if they do not have any sick leave accumulated.

You are proud of your policy because it puts you in the forefront of companies offering humanitarian assistance to employees. You even make it available to all employees—union and nonunion, full-time and part-time, and even student employees. In refusing the adjustment, work to keep James' goodwill toward the company.

13. For this assignment you are the sales manager for the Highlander Hotel. Today you received a claim message from Ms. Tina Hightower, convention chairperson for the National Association of Office Managers. Last week NAOM held its annual convention at your hotel. It was a good meeting for all concerned, you thought. But Ms. Hightower doesn't like the bill for 450 dinners at $22.95 each. "We sold only 396 tickets," she writes, "and didn't consume 450 meals.

Checking through your records concerning the NAOM meeting, you find that she estimated that 450 would attend the president's dinner. You had asked her to give you a final count by noon on the day of the dinner. But she didn't. So you prepared 450 meals but ended up donating 50 of them to the local homeless shelter.

Clearly the fault is not yours. You cannot grant her claim. But you want to make her understand why you must refuse, and you want to keep her happy. You'd like to get the group back for another meeting some day. Now write the message that will accomplish these goals.

14. Play the role of the business manager for the Central Illinois Vocational Institute. Today's mail brings a registered message from Mr. Wilbur I. Grigsby who asks that you refund most of the tuition he paid for his son's 15-week course. Mr. Grigsby, who lives some 150 miles away, states his case in these words: "The course in computer network administration you sold me for my son Dirk is worthless. Dirk attended for two weeks, and at the end of that time he had learned absolutely nothing. I don't like to say this about anybody, but Dirk says the instructor is incompetent and incapable of communicating. After two weeks Dirk quit, and I don't blame him. As I see it, I paid $1,500 for the course and am asking that you refund $1,300. Actually I should get the full amount, but I am willing to pay for the two weeks Dirk attended class."

You found the man's comments hard to believe, so you checked with Phil Knauth, the course instructor. Phil made these comments: "I remember the boy well. He attended class only three of the first nine days. He was always talking and horsing around in class. I had to call him down a number of times. Not once did he come to class prepared. He took the first examination on the ninth day and scored only 17. The class average was 87. I haven't seen him since."

When you told Mr. Knauth about Mr. Grigsby's criticism of the course, he gave you some convincing counterinformation: "The course was completed by all 18 students who enrolled the last time it was offered.

Every student went straight to a good job. The student evaluations of the course were good. I got an average of 9.2 on a 10-point scale—nothing lower than an 8." You conclude that Dirk has a problem, and his dad is making it worse.

You aren't about to give Mr. Grigsby any money back. In addition to Dirk's behavior problem, there is another good reason. Mr. Grigsby contracted for a 15-week course. You limit your classes to 20 students, and you nearly always have a waiting list. Allowing insincere people to enroll and then drop out without full payment would not be fair to the school or the people on the waiting list.

With this information in mind you'll write Mr. Grigsby your decision. And in your usual courteous way, you'll make your decision appear to be the fair one it is.

15. Eight months ago your Red River Valley Kennels established its website displaying its facilities and inventory and offering its American Kennel Club (AKC) registered Doberman pinscher puppies for sale at $900 each. You were delighted when almost immediately your first sale took place. The order was from Ms. Alicia Baumgardner of Modesto, CA, who wanted two. You shipped them by air and assumed that all was well.

Today you received an email message from the lady telling you that "the dogs were not healthy from the beginning. One died yesterday, and the other is also sick and may have to be destroyed. I must ask that you refund the purchase price. I should ask you to pay the veterinarian bills ($540), but I will forget about that."

You cannot accept the blame. You sent Ms. Baumgardner two healthy pups. They had been given all the required shots and were carefully inspected prior to shipment by your veterinarian, Wilfred Capaccio. You have his signed statement supporting the dogs' health. Why didn't Ms. Baumgardner report any health problems before now? You do not believe her story. You do not think you are responsible for what happened. After all, a lot can happen in eight months.

Now you will write Ms. Baumgardner an email message refusing her request. You will be courteous but firm and will try to explain your position, although you suspect she already understands.

16. Assume the role of manager of customer relations for Bartosh Uniforms, Inc, makers of uniforms for various businesses. Recently you began selling online, and with good success. One of your sales was to the Carson Exploration Company, an oil-drilling operation. Carson ordered 24 dozen uniforms in a variety of sizes with the company logo embroidered on the backs. The total cost of the uniforms was $24,488, including delivery.

Today you received a firm and somewhat blunt claim from Jodale Godfrey, Carson's business manager. "You made a serious error on the uniforms that arrived today. You misspelled the company name. The name is *Carson*—not *Catson* as you spelled it. We want the error corrected right away, and at your expense."

This error is serious indeed and it is embarrassing. But Bartosh just doesn't make errors like this. So you check further. After much talk and investigation, Pat Patterson, your superintendent of production, discovered the source of the error. On the original email order in the spot for the name information appears the misspelled *Catson*. Apparently the Carson employee who typed the order made the mistake, striking the *t* rather than the *r*. The keys are near each other.

Because the error is not yours, you do not think you should comply with Ms. Godfrey's request. Correcting the error will be a time-consuming process. But you will offer to do the work at cost, which would be about $5 per uniform. Now you must write the message that will handle this negative incident positively and completely. Probably you should suggest that Ms. Godfrey refer to the original order for verification of the misspelling.

17. The Athlete's Connection, your online sales operation, has been doing great business without a problem— until today. The problem comes by way of this email message from Sean Steagal:

On December 5 I ordered a pair of the Norseman ski boots you listed as being a special buy. I ordered them and charged them to my VISA. The total, in-cluding shipping charges, came to $312. When they arrived I found that they were not what I thought they were. Your picture of them was deceiving. Thus I am returning them and ask that you refund my money. The boots have not been used.

You cannot give Sean his money back. The boots were on sale—discounted 40 percent. The Athlete's Connection policy is that no merchandise bought on sale can be returned. It is a fair policy—fair to your customers and fair to you. If the company had to allow for the cost of returns, it could not offer goods at its low sale prices. The customers would have to pay more.

Now you will inform Mr. Steagal that you will return the boots if you receive them. You hope he hasn't yet sent them. You will explain your decision so that he accepts it as fair, and you will work to keep him as a customer. Perhaps you'll try to convince him that he has a good pair of boots and that he bought them at a very good price.

18. Your online nursery, <http://www.greenthumb.com/>, is having more than its share of problems. One of them is a claim received among today's email messages. It is from Ms. Janet Carpenter of San Marcos, Texas. She wants her money back ($384) for the 24 dozen assorted spring annual bulbs (tulips, daffodils, irises, and such) she ordered from Green Thumb. In her message, Ms. Carpenter wrote that she planted the bulbs right after she received them and that most didn't come up in the spring. She followed your planting instructions and included the recommended fertilizer with each bulb, which she promptly planted in the front of her home.

In checking into the situation, you confirm most of Ms. Carpenter's story. She received the bulbs on September 1. She says she planted them right away. But included in the instruction booklet—in bold type and borders—were these warnings: "Plant bulbs one month before the average freeze date in the fall. Keep refrigerated until planting." It is obvious that the lady didn't follow instructions. She planted much too early to survive the Texas heat. Indeed, September is a hot month in her part of Texas (average daytime highs of 85). November 24 is the average date for the first freezing temperature. It is no wonder the bulbs didn't make it.

Because you printed the instructions clearly and plainly for everyone to see, you are going to refuse the claim. But you don't want to belittle her in the process. You will try to explain why you will not refund her money in such a way that she will keep doing business with you. Of course, you'll send the message the same way she submitted her claim—by email to jcarpenter@yahoo.com.

19. For this assignment you are head of customer relations for your local telephone company. In today's mail comes a claim message from Ms. Shannon Tobias. Ms. Tobias in very strong language insists that $514.45 on her telephone bill is not her debt but represents calls made by Beverly Dopson, who lives in the apartment across the hall. She makes this explanation in her message: "These charges have accumulated over the past few months. I have noted with my past payments that they belong to Beverly Dopson, my neighbor who lives across the hall from me; but you keep billing me for them. I want these charges dropped from my bill and sent to Ms. Dopson." You must refuse this request. And because you get other similar requests, your refusal message will serve as a model for future similar problems.

Your message not only will need to refuse, it will need to educate Ms. Tobias. She signed a contract when she applied for service. The contract specified that she is responsible for all calls made on her telephone. Now she must honor that contract. If someone else has used her telephone, payment for these calls is between that person and Ms. Dopson. The telephone company has no contract with other people who use her telephone.

You may want to suggest that if Ms. Dopson has trouble collecting, she can take her neighbor to small claims court. You may want to give her some other hints for dealing with this situation in the future. But you have no choice but to refuse the claim. Even so, you will work to maintain the goodwill of your customer.

Credit Refusals

20. In addition to running a successful retail store, the bakery for which you are business manager, Les Bonbons, supplies French pastries and other gourmet desserts to several local restaurants. You've received a request from Jan Riga, an entrepreneur who is opening a new café in town, to supply her establishment with your goodies. Ordinarily that would be good news, but unlike your other customers, she doesn't want to have a standing order for which she pays each month. Instead, she asks that you supply her with a range of desserts twice each week, with no money up front from her, and then she'll pay you monthly based on what she has sold.

    Her main reason for proposing this arrangement is that preparing to open the café has stretched her somewhat thin financially, and she doesn't want to obligate herself to pay a monthly amount to your company—at least, not yet. But she feels that she is in an excellent location with excellent prospects of making a go of her business (she includes a positive assessment from her business analyst), and your famous desserts will give her a competitive edge. Her restaurant will be in a neighborhood of well-to-do professionals, and since it will be just a few doors from an arts theater, she anticipates a good bit of dessert business from the movie crowd each evening. She points out that she'll prominently display your name in her ads and menus, thereby giving your pastry shop "free" advertising.

    While you can see her point of view, you cannot supply your desserts with no guarantee in advance of full payment. If you were to accept this proposal, there would be no particular pressure on Ms. Riga to estimate accurately the number of desserts she needs. If she were to order the desserts carelessly, there could be a lot of waste, the cost of which would come out of your company's pockets. True, after a while, your people could help her estimate her needs more accurately, but they're too busy to take on this additional responsibility. Also, how would you keep track of how much Ms. Riga owed you? Send someone from your company back around to pick up the leftover desserts? And what on earth would you do with those?

    Write a letter to Ms. Riga explaining that you cannot deviate from your usual arrangements with restaurants, while helping her figure out a way to feature your desserts at her restaurant anyway.

21. Your credit check on Zelma Kleinschmidt tells you something you didn't detect when she applied to you for credit last week. You saw a vivacious, charming, and beautiful young woman. You thought you would only have to go through the routine of checking references before granting her credit. But it didn't turn out that way.

    Ms. Kleinschmidt is as slow in paying her bills as she is pretty. The three credit references she listed all tell the same story. She is behind in her payments with all three. In fact, she has exceeded her credit limit in two of the three, which might explain why she seeks credit from you. Apparently, she just spends more than she can afford. And although she may have the best of intentions, somebody will be left holding the bag. It won't be you and your Bon Marche, an exclusive shop for ladies who appreciate quality merchandise and the latest fashions.

    So you will write her a message denying her credit. But try not to offend her, for a woman like her is likely to spend a lot of cash in the years ahead. And maybe her fortunes will turn and she will be able to earn credit.

22. Assume that you have just been promoted to credit manager of the local Bedford's Department Store. One of the first things you will do is revise the credit messages used by your predecessor. In your judgment, they are cold and harsh. They do not even closely resemble the messages you learned to write in your college business communication course. The first one you tackle is a credit refusal aimed at middle-income people whose records for payment are not good. It reads like this:

    Dear _____

    Bedford's regrets to inform you that your application for credit cannot be granted. The credit check we ran on you does not show the satisfactory record of payment required of all Bedford credit holders. We appreciate your application. And even though we cannot grant you credit at this time, we invite you to shop with us.

    Sincerely,

    Certainly you can do better—much better. Your message will be unique and original. And it will not borrow plans and wordings from the textbook or from any other such source.

23. For this problem you are the credit manager for Bordelon's Fashions, an exclusive shop for men and women who appreciate high fashion and are willing to pay for it. Most of your customers are from society's upper crust, although you have some who mistakenly think they are in this group. In the past, you have granted credit liberally, on the assumption that people who buy expensive merchandise can and will pay. In

recent months, however, your credit rolls have attracted more and more people who don't qualify. Because your delinquent accounts have increased, now you must handle your credit applications carefully. And you must refuse more often.

Now that you have tightened credit, you will need to compose a credit-refusal message. It will have to be written most diplomatically, for Bordelon's wants no harshly negative messages appearing under its name. Also, the message must not appear to be one that goes to everyone who is refused credit. That is, it must appear to be individually written for the one reader. Bordelon's takes pride in the individual attention it gives all who deal with it. Use your best writing skills and imagination in developing this message.

24. Yesterday Whitney McDermott came into your Co-Ed Fashions and selected merchandise totaling $688.85. Lori Wong, the salesperson who waited on her, thought Whitney was going to pay cash. But after making her selections, Whitney announced that she would like to charge the total to a store credit account. Ms. Wong was startled. But she regained composure and explained that Whitney would have to apply for store credit. She took Whitney to you, and you gave Whitney the credit application form. You asked Ms. Wong to put aside the clothing pending approval of credit.

Now you, the store owner and its credit manager, have the application. Whitney reports on her application that she is a full-time business administration student (a junior) at the local university. Her allowance from home is generous, she says, although she did not indicate its amount. You are skeptical. Not only doesn't she have a credit-rating, but you have also had bad experiences with people not in the work force. Your losses on them have been so high that you just can't grant any more credit to them. Thus, you will refuse this credit request but encourage her to continue shopping at your store for cash purchases.

Now you must write Ms. McDermott a message that will give and explain your decision. Because the woman is a business administration student, perhaps you can make her understand from a businessperson's point of view. The message will be tactful, clear, and courteous, of course.

25. For this assignment assume that you have completed your college studies and are working in the career of your choice. A few days ago while watching television you saw an advertisement for Maxicard, one of the leading credit cards. The ad told how widely accepted Maxicard is and how its holders are an exclusive group, consisting of only established professionals. You thought you qualified. So you went to the website noted in the ad to get more information. In a short time you were sold on this credit card, thinking that you belonged in this exclusive group. You applied for the

card online giving all the information requested. Then you waited.

Today you received the following email message from Maxicard:

Dear _____:

We at Maxicard were pleased to receive your recent application. Based on the information you supplied us, however, we respectfully regret that we must deny your request at this time. We trust that you will understand our position on this matter. We hope you have a successful career and can qualify in the future.

Yours truly,

"That's not the way I was taught to write credit refusals when I was in college," you think to yourself. "The message is blunt and tactless—and poorly worded." Rewrite this form message using a more personalized, courteous, and diplomatic approach. You plan to send your improved version to Maxicard suggesting that they substitute yours for the one they sent you.

26. Play the role of the developer of Blue Lake Resort and Conference Center, a beautiful recreational area with excellent golf, tennis, fishing, and water sports. You are presently working hard to sell your residential lots, which sell for $150,000 and up. You have advertised extensively—on television, in brochures, and online. Today you received the following email:

Dear _____:

Last month I visited my sister in beautiful Blue Lake Resort and I looked over all the amenities you provide. As suggested in your TV ad, I visited your website. After looking over your site map, I have decided to offer to buy Lot 211, which is adjacent to the lot where my sister lives. You list it at $160,000, which is OK with me. I would like to buy it if you will give me credit. I can pay $10,000 down and the rest over 15 years. My banker and three store references are listed below.

Sincerely,

Ms. Calli R. DuBarry

You were elated at first for sales have been slow. While you don't normally finance the lots yourself, you will in some cases. But not in this case. The references Ms. DuBarry gave disappoint you. She appears to have a poor credit record. She is a slow pay and has extended her indebtedness far beyond safe limits. You have no choice but to deny her request.

Even though you must say no, Ms. DuBarry is still a prospect for your lot—if you handle her right. Perhaps she can manage to borrow the money locally, the way most of your buyers do. You will take care to treat her gently and with courtesy, and you will try to convince her that your decision is fair.

CHAPTER EIGHT

Indirectness in Persuasion and Sales Messages

CHAPTER OBJECTIVES

Upon completing this chapter, you will be able to use persuasion effectively in making requests and composing sales messages. To reach this goal, you should be able to

1 Use imagination in writing skillful persuasive requests that begin indirectly, develop convincing reasoning, and close with goodwill and action.

2 Describe the choices available in determining the structure of a direct-sales mailing or email sales message.

3 Describe the preliminary steps of studying the product or service and selecting the appeals to use in a sales message.

4 Discuss the choices of mechanics available to the sales writer.

5 Compose sales messages that gain attention, persuasively present appeals, and effectively drive for action.

- Persuasive messages are appropriately written in indirect order.

Persuasive messages generally are written in the indirect order. While they do not necessarily involve bad news, their goals run contrary to the reader's wishes. The mind-set of the reader must be changed before they can be successful. Achieving this change requires indirectness.

- Following are instructions for two persuasive messages: persuasive requests and sales.

In the following pages we explain how the indirect order is used in two persuasive situations. One is a persuasive request—a situation in which the reader would likely reject the request without convincing explanation. The other is a sales situation. As you will see, this latter situation involves a highly specialized form of writing.

PERSUASIVE REQUESTS

INTRODUCTORY SITUATION

Persuasive Requests

Introduce yourself to the next business message situation by returning to your hypothetical position at Pinnacle. As a potential executive, you spend some time working for the community. Pinnacle wants you to do this for the sake of good public relations. You want to do it because it is personally rewarding.

Currently, as chair of the fund-raising committee of the city's Junior Achievement program, you head all efforts to get financial support for the program from local businesspeople. You have a group of workers who will call on businesspeople. But personal calls take time, and there are many people to call on.

At its meeting today, the Junior Achievement board of directors discussed the problem of contacting businesspeople. One director suggested using a letter to sell them on giving money. The board accepted the idea with enthusiasm. With just as much enthusiasm, it gave you the assignment of writing the letter (for the president's signature).

As you view the assignment, it is not a routine letter-writing problem. Although the local businesspeople are probably generous, they are not likely to part with money without good reason. In fact, their first reaction to a request for money is likely to be negative. So you will need to overcome their resistance in order to persuade them. Your task is indeed challenging.

Requests that are likely to be resisted require a slow, deliberate approach. You must persuade the reader that he or she should grant the request before making the request. More specifically, you must present facts and logical reasoning that support your case. And you must do it convincingly. Such a presentation requires that you begin by developing a plan.

Determining the Persuasion

- Plan the persuasion that will overcome the reader's objections.

Developing this persuasion plan involves using your imagination. You must seek a strategy that will convince your reader. To do this, put yourself in your reader's shoes. Look at the request as the reader is likely to see it. Determine the reader's objections. And then think about what you can say to overcome these objections. From this thinking, your plan should emerge.

- Many persuasive appeals may be used—money rewards, personal benefits, and so on.

The specific plan you develop will depend on the facts of the case. You may be able to show that your reader stands to gain in time, money, or the like. Or you may be able to show that your reader will benefit in goodwill or prestige.

In some cases, you may persuade readers by appealing to their love of beauty, excitement, serenity, or the like. In other cases, you may be able to persuade readers by appealing to the pleasant feeling that comes from doing a good turn. Many other possibilities exist. You select the one that best fits your case.

Persuasive requests and sales messages arrive uninvited. They have goals that are likely to encounter reader resistance. Unless they gain the reader's attention at the beginning, they are likely to end up in a trash-can.

Gaining Attention in the Opening

In the indirect messages previously discussed, the goal of the opening is to set up the explanation. The same goal exists in persuasion messages, but persuasion messages have an additional goal: to gain attention.

- The opening sets the strategy and gains attention.

The need to gain attention in the opening of persuasion messages is obvious. You are writing to a person who has not invited your message and probably does not agree with your goal. So you need to get that person into a receptive mood. An interesting beginning is a good step in this direction.

- Attention is needed to get the reader in a mood to receive the persuasion.

Determining what will gain attention also requires imagination. It might be some statement that arouses mental activity, or it might be a statement offering or implying a reader benefit. Because questions arouse mental activity, they are often effective openings. The following examples indicate the possibilities.

- What you write to gain attention is limited only by your imagination.

From the cover letter of a questionnaire seeking the opinions of medical doctors:

What, in your opinion as a medical doctor, is the future of the private practice of medicine?

From a message requesting contributions for orphaned children:

While you and I dined heartily last night, 31 orphans at San Pablo Mission had only dried beans to eat.

From a message seeking the cooperation of business leaders in promoting a fair:

What would your profits be if 300,000 free-spending visitors came to our town during a single week?

Presenting the Persuasion

- Your persuasion follows.

Following the opening, you should proceed with your goal of persuading. Your task here is a logical and orderly presentation of the reasoning you have selected.

- Present the points convincingly (selecting words for effect, using you-viewpoint, and the like).

As with any argument intended to convince, you should do more than merely list points. You should help convey the points with convincing words. Since you are trying to penetrate a neutral or resistant mind, you need to make good use of the you-viewpoint. You need to pay careful attention to the meanings of your words and the clarity of your expression. Because your reader may become impatient if you delay your objective, you need to make your words travel fast.

Making the Request Clearly and Positively

- Follow the persuasion with the request.

After you have done your persuading, move to the action you seek. You have prepared the reader for what you want. If you have done that well, the reader should be ready to accept your proposal.

- Word the request for best effect.

Like negative points, your request requires care in word choice. You should avoid words that detract from the request. You also should avoid words that bring to mind images and ideas that might work against you. Words that bring to mind reasons for refusing are especially harmful, as in this example:

- Do not use a negative tone.

> I am aware that businesspeople in your position have little free time to give, but will you please consider accepting an assignment to the board of directors of the Children's Fund?

The following positive tie-in with a major point in the persuasion strategy does a much better job:

- Be positive.

> Because your organizing skills are so desperately needed, will you please serve on the board of directors of the Children's Fund?

- The request can end the message or be followed by more persuasion.

Whether your request should end your message will depend on the needs of the case. In some cases, you will profit by following the request with words of explanation. This procedure is especially effective when a long persuasion effort is needed. In such cases, you simply cannot present all your reasoning before stating your goal. On the other hand, you may end less involved presentations with the request. Even in this case, however, you may want to follow the request with a reminder of the appeal. As illustrated in the example message (p. 196), this procedure associates the request with the advantage that saying yes will give the reader.

- Ending with a reminder of the appeal is also good.

Summarizing the General Plan

- Follow this general plan when writing persuasive requests.

From the preceding discussion, the following general plan for the persuasive request message is apparent:

- Open with words that (1) set up the strategy and (2) gain attention.
- Present the strategy (the persuasion) using persuasive language and you-viewpoint.
- Make the request clearly and without negatives (1) either at the end of the message or (2) followed by words that recall the persuasive appeal.

Contrasting Persuasion Messages

- The following messages illustrate good and bad persuasion efforts.

The persuasive request is illustrated by contrasting messages that ask businesspeople to donate to Junior Achievement. The first message is direct and weak in persuasion; the second is indirect and persuasive. The second message, which follows the approach described above, produced better results.

Obvious Failure in Directness. The weaker message begins with the request. Because the request is opposed to the reader's wishes, the direct beginning is likely to get a negative reaction. In addition, the comments about how much to give tend to lecture rather than suggest. Some explanation follows, but it is weak and scant. In general, the message is poorly written. It has little of the you-viewpoint writing that is effective in persuasion. Perhaps its greatest fault is that the persuasion comes too late. The old-style close is a weak reminder of the action requested.

Dear Mr. Williams:

Will you please donate to the local Junior Achievement program? We have set $50 as a fair minimum for businesses to give. But larger amounts would be appreciated.

The organization badly needs your support. Currently, about 900 young people will not get to participate in Junior Achievement activities unless more money is raised. Junior Achievement is a most worthwhile organization. As a business leader, you should be willing to support it.

If you do not already know about Junior Achievement, let me explain. Junior Achievement is an organization for high school youngsters. They work with local business executives to form small businesses. They operate the businesses. In the process, they learn about our economic system. This is a good thing, and it deserves our help.

Hoping to receive your generous donation, I am,

Sincerely,

This bad message has no persuasion strategy.

Skillful Persuasion in an Indirect Order. The next message shows good imagination. It follows the indirect pattern described above. Its opening has strong interest appeal and sets up the persuasion strategy. Notice the effective use of you-viewpoint throughout. Not until the reader has been sold on the merits of the request does the message ask the question. It does this clearly and directly. The final words leave the reader thinking about a major benefit that a yes answer will give.

Dear Mr. Williams:

Right now—right here in our city—620 teenage youngsters are running 37 corporations. The kids run the whole show, their only adult help being advice from some of your business associates who work with them. Last September they applied for charters and elected officers. They created plans for business operations. For example, one group planned to build websites for local businesses. Another elected to conduct a rock concert. Yet another planned to publish newsletters for area corporations. After determining their plans, the kids issued stock—and sold it, too. With the proceeds from stock sales, they began their operations. Now they are operating. This May they will liquidate their companies and account to their stockholders for their profits or losses.

You, as a public-spirited citizen, will quickly see the merits of the Junior Achievement program. You know the value of such realistic experience to the kids—how it teaches them the operations of business and how it sells them on the merits of our American system of free enterprise. You can see, also, that it's an exciting and wholesome program, the kind we need more of to combat economic illiteracy. After you have considered these points and others you will find at http://www.ja.org/, I know you will see that Junior Achievement is a good thing.

Like all good things, Junior Achievement needs all of us behind it. During the 13 years the program has been in our city, it has had enthusiastic support from local business leaders. But with over 900 students on the waiting list, our plans for next year call for expansion. That's why I ask that you help make the program available to more youngsters by contributing $50 (it's deductible). Please make your donation now by completing our *online contribution* form. You will be doing a good service for the kids in our town.

Sincerely,

This better message uses good persuasion strategy.

Persuasive Request Letters (A Request for Information about Employment Applicants)   In this letter a trade publication editor seeks information from an executive for an article on desirable job application procedures. The request involves time and effort for the executive. Thus, persuasion is necessary.

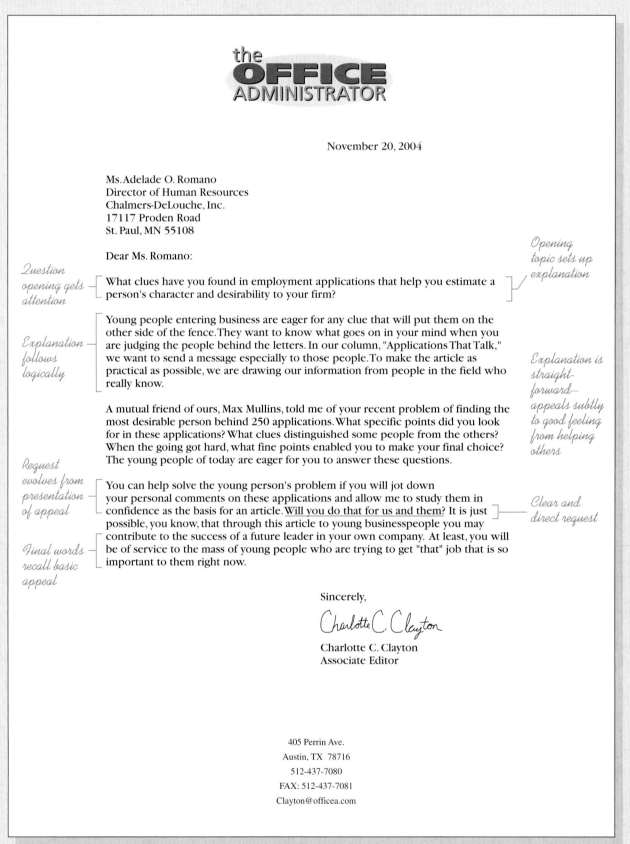

the **OFFICE** ADMINISTRATOR

November 20, 2004

Ms. Adelade O. Romano
Director of Human Resources
Chalmers-DeLouche, Inc.
17117 Proden Road
St. Paul, MN 55108

Dear Ms. Romano:

Opening topic sets up explanation

Question opening gets attention — What clues have you found in employment applications that help you estimate a person's character and desirability to your firm?

Explanation follows logically — Young people entering business are eager for any clue that will put them on the other side of the fence. They want to know what goes on in your mind when you are judging the people behind the letters. In our column, "Applications That Talk," we want to send a message especially to those people. To make the article as practical as possible, we are drawing our information from people in the field who really know.

Explanation is straightforward— appeals subtly to good feeling from helping others

A mutual friend of ours, Max Mullins, told me of your recent problem of finding the most desirable person behind 250 applications. What specific points did you look for in these applications? What clues distinguished some people from the others? When the going got hard, what fine points enabled you to make your final choice? The young people of today are eager for you to answer these questions.

Request evolves from presentation of appeal — You can help solve the young person's problem if you will jot down your personal comments on these applications and allow me to study them in confidence as the basis for an article. Will you do that for us and them? It is just possible, you know, that through this article to young businesspeople you may contribute to the success of a future leader in your own company. At least, you will be of service to the mass of young people who are trying to get "that" job that is so important to them right now.

Clear and direct request

Final words recall basic appeal

Sincerely,

Charlotte C. Clayton

Charlotte C. Clayton
Associate Editor

405 Perrin Ave.
Austin, TX 78716
512-437-7080
FAX: 512-437-7081
Clayton@officea.com

SALES MESSAGES

Questioning the Acceptability of Sales Messages

As we begin our discussion of sales messages, we should note that they are a most controversial area of business communication. Probably you know from your own experience that direct-mail sales literature is not always received happily. Called "junk" mail, these mailings often go into the waste basket without being read. Even so, they must be successful, for the direct-mail business has survived for over a century.

● Direct-mail sales messages are not always well received.

Sales messages sent by email appear to be creating even more hostility among intended customers. Angrily referred to as "spam," unsolicited email sales messages have generated strong resistance among email users. Perhaps it is because these messages clutter up in-boxes. Maybe the rage results from the fact that mass mailings place a heavy burden on Internet providers, driving up costs to the users. Or perhaps the fact that they invade the reader's privacy is to blame. There are the downright unethical practices of some email advertisers who use "misleading subject lines and invalid email addresses to thwart filtering attempts and get respondents to open them."[1] Whatever the explanation, the resistance is real. You will need to consider these objections any time you use this sales medium. As we shall note later, there are steps reputable advertisers can take to minimize this resistance.

● Email sales messages are even more unpopular, and for good reason.

Fortunately, a more acceptable form of email selling is emerging. Called *permission email* or *opt-in email marketing,* it permits potential customers to sign on a company's website or offer their email addresses to a catalog, phone marketer, or other such organization. The potential customers may be asked to indicate the products, services, and specific topics of their interest. Thus the marketers can tailor their messages to the customer, and the customer receives only what he or she wants. This form of marketing is growing rapidly. According to eMarketer, by 2005 companies will spend more than $4 billion on these marketing efforts.

● Permission email marketing is emerging.

Since this form of sales message is relatively new, directions for writing it have not yet been determined. As one authoritative source worded it, "Long held ideas about how to most effectively persuade an audience must be reexamined in light of email capabilities and limitations."[2] Whatever direction this form of sales messaging will take, it will no doubt embrace much of the persuasion and selling techniques reviewed in the following pages.

● Its techniques have not yet developed.

We take no stand on the issue. Our goal in the following paragraphs is to show you how to write sales messages. You will have to decide whether and when sales messages should be written. We can only suggest that you follow your conscience and practice good business ethics in whatever you do.

● We take no stand on the issue, covering only sales writing techniques.

---

[1] Rich Gray, "Spamitize Your Inbox," *Guide to E-Mail and More* 8, no.7 (2000): 66.

[2] Carol M. Lehman, Debbie D. DuFrene, Brian T. Engelland, and Rodney A. Pearson, "Persuasive Communication in the Information Age," *2003 Proceedings,* Association for Business Communication, Southwestern United States (Houston, TX): 42.

Benefiting from Sales Writing

INTRODUCTORY SITUATION

Sales Messages

Introduce yourself to the next message type by assuming the role of Anthony A. Killshaw, a successful restaurant consultant. Over the past 28 years, you have acquired an expert knowledge of restaurant operations. You have made a science of virtually every area of restaurant activity: menu design, food control, purchasing, kitchen organization, service. You also have perfected a simple system for data gathering and analysis that quickly gets to the heart of most operations' problems. Testimonials from a number of satisfied clients prove that the system works.

Knowing that your system works is one thing. Getting this knowledge to enough prospective clients is another. So you have decided to publicize your work by writing restaurant managers and telling them about what you have to offer.

At the moment your plan for selling your services is hazy. But you think you will do it by email. It's a fast and easy way to reach your potential customers, you think. They will be more likely to read your message than if you used direct mail. Probably you will use a basic message that will invite the readers to look at your website. The website conveys the details—much more than you could get into the message.

Because sales writing requires special skills, you have decided to use the help of a local advertising agency—one with good experience with this type of selling. However, you have a pretty good idea of what you want, so you will not leave the work entirely up to the agency's personnel. You will tell them what you want included, and you will have the final word on what is acceptable.

- Professionals usually do the sales writing, so why study the subject?

- The answer: Knowing selling techniques helps you in writing other types of messages.

Probably you will never write sales messages—real ones, that is. In business, professional writers usually write them. These professionals achieve their status by practicing long and hard, and usually they are blessed with a special talent for writing. Why, then, you might ask, should you study sales writing?

The answer is that even an amateurish effort to write sales messages gives you knowledge of selling techniques that will help you in many of your other activities. Especially will it help you in writing other business messages, for in a sense most of them involve selling something—an idea, a line of reasoning, your company, yourself. Sales techniques are more valuable to you than you might think. After you have studied the remainder of this chapter, you should see why.

Planning the Structure

- Usually brochures, leaflets, a letter, and such combine to form a sales mailing.

- Email sales emphasize the basic message but use support information.

- Our emphasis is on the basic sales message.

As you probably know from experience, most direct-mail sales efforts consist of a number of pieces. Typically, brochures, leaflets, foldouts, a letter, and so on combine to form a coordinated message. But usually a letter is the main piece. It carries the main message, and the other pieces carry the supporting details.

Sales efforts by email also use support information, usually enough to give the reader all that is needed to complete a sale. The information may be in the basic message, perhaps broken down into distinct subtopics in boxes, separate listings, or such. Or it may be in links or attachments skillfully arranged by subtopics. With the use of artwork, color, font selection, and such, the total email package can be as complete and attractive as the comparable direct-mail package.

The following discussion emphasizes the basic message, whether it is sent by mail or email. It would be beyond the scope of this book to cover more. But much of what is said about this basic message applies also to the other forms of sales literature. After you have studied the following material, you should have a general idea of how to sell by the written word.

Knowing the Product or Service and the Reader

Before you can begin writing, you must know about the product or service you are selling. You simply cannot sell most goods and services unless you know them and can tell the prospects what they need to know. Before prospects buy a product, they may want to know how it is made, how it works, what it will do, and what it will not do. Clearly, a first step in sales writing is careful study of your product or service.

In addition, you should know your readers. In particular, you should know about their needs for the product or service. Anything else you know about them can help: their economic status, age, nationality, education, and culture. The more you know about your readers, the better you will be able to adapt your sales message.

In large businesses, a marketing research department or agency typically gathers information about prospective customers. If you do not have such help, you will need to gather this information on your own. If time does not permit you to do the necessary research, you may have to follow your best logic. For example, the nature of a product can tell you something about its likely buyers. Industrial equipment would probably be bought by people with technical backgrounds. Expensive French perfumes and cosmetics would probably be bought by people in high-income brackets. Burial insurance would appeal to older members of the lower economic strata. If you are purchasing a mailing list, you usually receive basic demographics such as age, sex, race, education, income, and marital status of those on the list. Sometimes you know more—interests, spending range, consumption patterns, and such.

- Begin work on a sales message by studying the product or service to be sold.

- Also, study your readers.

- Research can help you learn about prospective customers. If research is not possible, use your best logic.

Determining the Appeal

With your product or service and your prospects in mind, you are ready to create the sales message. This involves selecting and presenting basic appeals. By *appeals*, we mean the strategies you use to present a product or service to the reader. You could, for example, present a product's beauty or its taste qualities. You could stress that a product will provide hours of fun or that it will make one more attractive to the opposite sex. Or you could present a product through an appeal to profits, savings, or durability.

For convenience in studying appeals, we can divide them into two broad groups. In one group are emotional efforts to persuade. Such efforts affect how we feel, taste, smell, hear, and see. They also include strategies that arouse us through love, anger, pride, fear, and enjoyment. Illustrating emotional appeal is the following example from a message selling a perfume through linking the romance of faraway places with the product's exotic scent:

- Next, decide on what appeals and strategies to use.

- Appeals may be emotional (to the feelings),

> Linger in castle corridors on court nights in London. Dance on a Budapest balcony high above the blue Danube. Seek romance and youth and laughter in charming capitals on five continents. And there you'll find the beguiling perfume that is fragrance Jamais.

In the other group are rational appeals. These are appeals to reason—to the thinking mind. Such appeals include strategies based on saving money, making money, doing a job better, and getting better use from a product. Illustrating a rational appeal (saving money) are these words from a message selling magazine subscriptions:

- or they may be rational (to the reason).

> I am going to slash the regular rate of $36 a year down to only $28, saving you a full 22 percent. That means you get 12 information-filled new issues of *Science Digest* for only $2.33 a copy. You save even more by subscribing for 2 or 3 years.

In any given case, many appeals are available to you. You should consider those that fit your product or service and those that fit your readers best. Such products as perfume, style merchandise, candy, and fine food lend themselves to emotional appeals. On the other hand, such products as automobile tires, tools, and industrial equipment are best sold through rational appeals. Automobile tires, for example, are not bought because they are pretty but because they are durable, because they grip the road, and because they are safe. Sometimes the appeals can be combined to support each other.

- Select the appeals that fit the product and the prospects.

A Basic Lesson for Sales Writing

The neophyte sales writer's first sales letter had failed miserably. In discussing the matter with the advertising manager, the neophyte offered this explanation: "I think I have demonstrated that you can lead a horse to water, but you cannot make it drink."

"That's not an appropriate explanation," the advertising manager replied. "Your primary goal is not to make your readers drink. It is to make them thirsty."

● The prospects' uses of the product often determine which appeal is best.

How the buyer will use the product may be a major basis for selecting a sales strategy. Cosmetics might well be sold to the final user through emotional appeals. Selling cosmetics to a retailer (who is primarily interested in reselling them) would require rational appeals. A retailer would be interested in their emotional qualities only to the extent that these make customers buy. A retailer's main questions about the product are: Will it sell? What turnover can I expect? How much money will it make for me?

Determining the Mechanics

● Writing sales messages involves imagination.

After selecting the appeal, you should write the sales message. At this point, your imagination comes into the picture. Writing sales messages is as creative as writing short stories, plays, and novels. In addition to imagination, it involves applied psychology and skillful word use. There are as many different ways of handling a sales message as there are ideas. The only sure measure of the effectiveness of each way is the sales that the message brings in.

● The makeup of sales messages differs somewhat from that of ordinary messages. For example, sales messages may use impersonal salutations, headlines for inside addresses, and attention-gaining devices.

When you write a sales message to be sent by mail, a part of your effort is in determining the makeup of the mailing. The physical arrangement of the hard-copy sales message as contrasted with email may be quite different. Typically, they are mass produced. Some use impersonal salutations, such as "Dear Student," "Dear Homeowner," or "Dear Sir or Madam." One technique eliminates the salutation and inside address and places the beginning words in the form of these parts. As shown below, this arrangement gives the message what appears at first glance to be a normal letter layout.

> IT'S GREAT FOR PENICILLIN.
> BUT YOU CAN DO WITHOUT IT
> ON YOUR ROOF . . .

> We're referring to roof fungus, which, like penicillin, is a moldlike growth. However, the similarity ends there. Unlike penicillin, roof fungus serves . . .

● Email sales messages can use all the creativity that computers can produce.

Email sales messages can use all the publishing features available on the computer. Typically, the heading appears in email formatting, but the message is presented creatively with color, font variations, box arrangements, art work, and such. The message may include links to support material as well as to the ordering procedure. And it may have attachments. Just as with a direct-mail package, the email sales package makes available everything a reader needs to know in order to complete the sale.

Gaining Attention

● The basic requirement of the beginning is to gain attention.

The beginnings of all sales messages have one basic requirement. They must gain attention. If they do not, they fail. The reason is apparent. Because sales messages are sent without invitation, they are not likely to be received favorably. In fact, they even may be unwanted. Unless they gain attention early, the messages are not read.

With direct mail, the envelope containing the message is the first attention getter. All too often the reader recognizes the mailing as an uninvited sales message and promptly discards it. For this reason many direct-mail writers place an attention getter on the envelope. It may be the offer of a gift ("Free gift inside"). It may present a brief sales message ("12 months of *Time* at 60% off the newsstand price"). It may present a picture and a message (a picture of a cruise ship and "Tahiti and more at 2-for-1 prices"). An official-appearing envelope sometimes is used. So are brief and simple messages such as "Personal," "Sensitive material enclosed," and "May we have the courtesy of a reply." The possibilities are limited only by the imagination.

- With direct mail, attention begins with the envelope.

With email, of course, there is no envelope. The attention begins with the from, to, and subject fields. As explained by one authority, you should clearly tell who you are and identify your company.[3] Many "spam" messages disguise these identities. And you should address the reader by name. Even though some readers will delete the message even with this clear identification, the honesty conveyed will induce some to read on.

- With email, it begins with the from, to, and subject fields. Be honest.

The subject line in email messages is the main place for getting attention. Here honesty and simplicity should be your guide. The subject line should tell clearly what your message is about, and it should be short. It should avoid sensationalism such as "How to earn $60,000 the first month." In addition, avoiding sensationalism involves limiting the use of solid caps, exclamation points, dollar signs, "free" offers, and such. One subject line that generally meets these requirements for the message selling a restaurant consultant's services is the following: "Subject: A proven way to increase your profits."

- Make the subject line clear and short. Avoid sensationalism.

Holding Attention in the Opening

The first words of your message also have a major need to gain attention. The reader must be moved to read on. What you do here is a part of your creative effort. But the method you use should assist in presenting the sales message. That is, it should help set up your strategy. It should not just gain attention for attention's sake. Attention is easy to gain if nothing else is needed. In a sales letter, a small explosion set off when the reader opens the envelope would gain attention. So would an electric shock or a miniature stink bomb. But these methods would not be likely to assist in selling your product or service.

- The opening sentence should hold attention and set up the strategy.

One of the most effective attention-gaining techniques is a statement or question that introduces a need that the product will satisfy. For example, a rational-appeal message to a retailer would clearly tap his or her strong needs with these opening words:

- Rational appeals stress logic.

> Here is a proven best-seller—and with a 12 percent greater profit.

Another rational-appeal attention getter is this beginning of an email sales message from eFax.com:

> Never type a fax again!

This paragraph of a message selling a fishing vacation at a lake resort illustrates a need-fulfilling beginning of an emotional-appeal approach:

> Your line hums as it whirs through the air. Your line splashes and dances across the smooth surface of the clear water as you reel. From the depth you see the silver streak of a striking bass. You feel a sharp tug. The battle is on!

As you can see, the paragraph casts an emotional spell, which is what emotional selling should do. It puts a rod in the reader's hand, and it takes the reader through the thrills of the sport. To a reader addicted to fishing, the need is clearly established. Now the reader will listen to see how the need can be fulfilled.

As mentioned previously, gimmicks are sometimes used to gain attention in direct-mail sales. But a gimmick is effective only if it supports the theme of the message. One company made effective use of a penny affixed to the top of a letter with these words:

- Gimmicks can gain attention and emphasize a theme in sales messages.

---

[3] John Sterne and Anthony Priore, *Email Marketing* (New York: John Wiley & Sons, 2001), 143.

Most pennies won't buy much today, but this penny can save you untold worry and money—and bring you new peace of mind.

A paper manufacturer fastened small samples of sandpaper, corrugated aluminum, and smooth glossy paper to the top of a letter that began with these words:

You've seen the ads—
You've heard the talk—
Now feel for yourself what we mean by level-smooth.

The story is another opening approach. Most people like to read stories, and if you can start one interestingly, your reader should want to read the rest of it. Here is the story beginning of an email sales message for Data Viz:

You're out of the office and need to review a file for a business meeting. Alas, you left the document on your hard drive. Don't sweat it. Documents To Go from Data Viz puts your most important data within easy reach—regardless of format.

- Summary messages are also effective.

Thus far, the attention-gaining techniques illustrated have been short. But longer ones have been used—and used effectively. In fact, a technique currently popular in direct-mail selling is to place a digest of the sales message at the beginning—usually before the salutation. The strategy is to quickly communicate the full impact of the sales message before the reader loses interest. If any of the points presented arouse interest, the reader is likely to continue reading.

Illustrating this technique is the beginning of a letter selling subscriptions to *Change*. These lines appeared before the salutation, which was followed by four pages of text.

A quick way to determine whether you should read this letter:

If you are involved in or influenced by higher education—and you simply don't have the time to read copiously in order to "keep up"—this letter is important. Because it offers you a money-shortcut (plus a *free gift* and a money-back guarantee).

As a subscriber to *CHANGE,* the leading magazine of higher learning, you'll have facts and feelings at your fingertips—to help *you* form opinions on today's topics: tenure, professors' unions, open admissions, the outlook for new PhDs . . . On just about any subject that concerns academe and you.

CHANGE has the largest readership of any journal among academic people. To find out why 100,000 people now read *CHANGE* every month, take three minutes to read the following letter.

Presenting the Sales Material

With the reader's attention gained, you proceed with the sales strategy that you have developed. In general, you establish a need. Then you present your product or service as fulfilling that need.

- Plans vary for presenting appeals. Emotional appeals usually involve creating an emotional need.

The plan of your sales message will vary with your imagination. But it is likely to follow certain general patterns determined by your choice of appeals. If you select an emotional appeal, for example, your opening has probably established an emotional atmosphere that you will continue to develop. Thus, you will sell your product based on its effects on your reader's senses. You will describe the appearance, texture, aroma, and taste of your product so vividly that your reader will mentally see it, feel it—and want it. In general, you will seek to create an emotional need for your product.

- Rational appeals stress fact and logic.

If you select a rational appeal, your sales description is likely to be based on factual material. You should describe your product based on what it can do for your reader rather than how it appeals to the senses. You should write matter-of-factly about such qualities as durability, savings, profits, and ease of operation. Differences in these two sharply contrasting types of appeals are shown in the illustrations near the end of the chapter.

Sales Letters (Using Emotional Appeal to Sell New Orleans) Sent to a select group of young business and professional people, this letter takes the readers through the experiences that they will enjoy if they accept the offer.

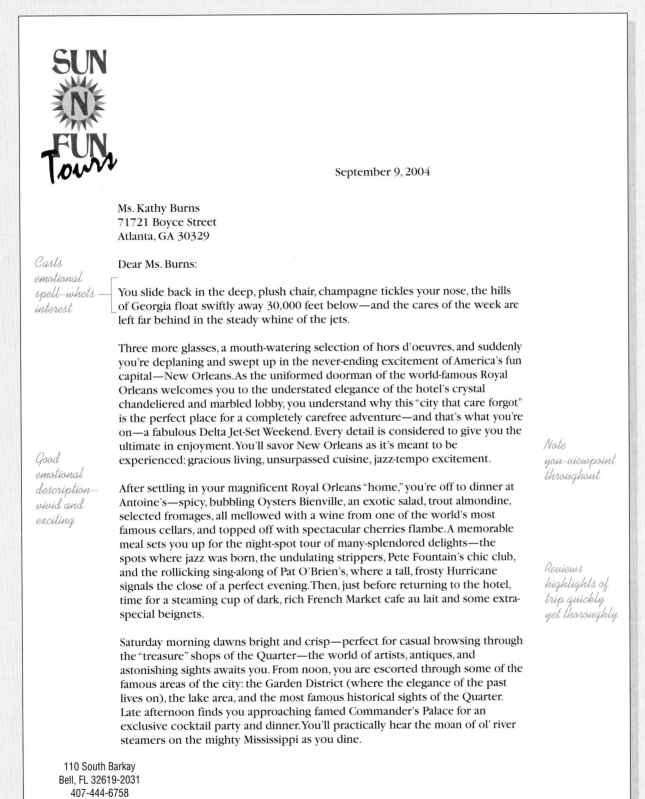

September 9, 2004

Ms. Kathy Burns
71721 Boyce Street
Atlanta, GA 30329

Dear Ms. Burns:

Casts emotional spell—whets interest

You slide back in the deep, plush chair, champagne tickles your nose, the hills of Georgia float swiftly away 30,000 feet below—and the cares of the week are left far behind in the steady whine of the jets.

Three more glasses, a mouth-watering selection of hors d'oeuvres, and suddenly you're deplaning and swept up in the never-ending excitement of America's fun capital—New Orleans. As the uniformed doorman of the world-famous Royal Orleans welcomes you to the understated elegance of the hotel's crystal chandeliered and marbled lobby, you understand why this "city that care forgot" is the perfect place for a completely carefree adventure—and that's what you're on—a fabulous Delta Jet-Set Weekend. Every detail is considered to give you the ultimate in enjoyment. You'll savor New Orleans as it's meant to be experienced: gracious living, unsurpassed cuisine, jazz-tempo excitement.

Note you-viewpoint throughout

Good emotional description—vivid and exciting

After settling in your magnificent Royal Orleans "home," you're off to dinner at Antoine's—spicy, bubbling Oysters Bienville, an exotic salad, trout almondine, selected fromages, all mellowed with a wine from one of the world's most famous cellars, and topped off with spectacular cherries flambe. A memorable meal sets you up for the night-spot tour of many-splendored delights—the spots where jazz was born, the undulating strippers, Pete Fountain's chic club, and the rollicking sing-along of Pat O'Brien's, where a tall, frosty Hurricane signals the close of a perfect evening. Then, just before returning to the hotel, time for a steaming cup of dark, rich French Market cafe au lait and some extra-special beignets.

Reviews highlights of trip quickly yet thoroughly

Saturday morning dawns bright and crisp—perfect for casual browsing through the "treasure" shops of the Quarter—the world of artists, antiques, and astonishing sights awaits you. From noon, you are escorted through some of the famous areas of the city: the Garden District (where the elegance of the past lives on), the lake area, and the most famous historical sights of the Quarter. Late afternoon finds you approaching famed Commander's Palace for an exclusive cocktail party and dinner. You'll practically hear the moan of ol' river steamers on the mighty Mississippi as you dine.

110 South Barkay
Bell, FL 32619-2031
407-444-6758
FAX: 407-444-6758

(concluded)

Ms. Kathy Burns
September 9, 2004
Page 2

Night ends back in the Quarter—with the particular pleasure of your choice. But don't sleep too late Sunday! Unforgettable "breakfast at Brennan's" begins at 11 a.m., and two hours later you'll know why it is the most famous breakfast in the world! Wrap up your relaxed visit with shopping in the afternoon; then the mighty Delta jet whisks you back to Atlanta by 7 p.m. This perfect weekend can be yours for the very special price of only $375, which includes transportation, lodging, and noted meals. For double occupancy, the price per person is only $335. Such a special vacation will be more fun with friends, so get them in on this bargain—you owe yourself the pleasures of a Jet-Set Weekend in America's fun capital.

Tells how need can be satisfied— gives details

Perhaps the action would be more effective if it were more direct, but it is persuasive

This Jet-Set Weekend to dream about becomes a reality starting right now—a free call to the Delta Hostell at 800-491-6700 confirms your reservation to escape to the fun, the food, and the fantasy of New Orleans, city of excitement. The city is swinging—waiting for you!

The final words link the action with the main appeal

Sincerely,

Mary Massey

Mary Massey
Travel Consultant

P.S. Check out our website at http://www.sun_n_fun.com/ for some sights and sounds you'll experience on this fabulous Jet-Set Weekend.

The writing that carries your sales message can be quite different from your normal business writing. Sales writing usually is highly conversational, fast moving, and aggressive. It even uses techniques that are incorrect or inappropriate in other forms of business writing: sentence fragments, one-sentence paragraphs, folksy language, and such. It uses mechanical emphasis devices (underscore, capitalization, boldface, italics, exclamation marks, color) to a high degree. It uses all kinds of graphics and graphic devices as well as a variety of type sizes and fonts. Its paragraphing often appears choppy. Apparently, the direct-mail professionals believe that whatever will help sell is appropriate.

- Sales writing is not ordinary writing.

Stressing the You-Viewpoint

In no area of business communication is the you-viewpoint more important than in sales writing. We human beings are selfish creatures. We are persuaded best through self-interest. Thus, in sales writing you should base your sales points on reader interest. You should liberally use and imply the pronoun *you* throughout the sales message.

- The you-viewpoint is important in sales writing. Use it.

The techniques of you-viewpoint writing in sales messages are best described through illustration. For example, assume you are writing a sales message to a retailer. One point you want to make is that the manufacturer will help sell the product with an advertising campaign. You could write this information in a matter-of-fact way: "Star mixers will be advertised in *Ladies' Home Journal* for the next three issues." Or you could write it based on what the advertising means to the reader: "Your customers will read about the new Star mixer in the next three issues of *Ladies' Home Journal*." For another example, you could quote prices in routine words such as "a four-ounce bottle costs $2.25, and you can sell it for $3.50." But you could emphasize the readers' interest with words like these: "You can sell the four-ounce size for $3.50 and make a 55 percent profit on your $2.25 cost." Using the you-viewpoint along with an explicit interpretation of how the facts benefit the reader will strengthen your persuasiveness. The following examples further illustrate the value of this technique:

MATTER-OF-FACT STATEMENTS	YOU-VIEWPOINT STATEMENTS
We make Aristocrat hosiery in three colors.	You may choose from three lovely shades.
The Regal has a touch as light as a feather.	You'll like Regal's featherlight touch.
Lime-Fizz tastes fresh and exciting.	You'll enjoy the fresh, exciting taste of Lime-Fizz.
Baker's Dozen is packaged in a rectangular box with a bright bull's-eye design.	Baker's Dozen's new rectangular package fits compactly on your shelf, and its bright bull's-eye design is sure to catch the eyes of your customers.

Choosing Words Carefully

In persuasive messages, your attention to word choice is extremely important, for it can influence whether the reader acts on your request. Try putting yourself clearly in your reader's place as you select words for your message. Some words, while closely related in meaning, have clearly different emotional effects. For example, the word *selection* implies a choice while the word *preference* implies a first choice. Here are some examples where a single adjective changes the effect of a sentence:

- Consider the effect of your words.

You'll enjoy the sensation our hot salsa gives you.

You'll enjoy the sensation our fiery salsa gives you.

You'll enjoy the sensation our burning salsa gives you.

Framing your requests in the positive is also a proven persuasive technique. Readers will clearly opt for solutions to problems that avoid negatives. Here are some examples.

An Email Sales Message (Using Rational Appeal) Note now complete coverage is made easier by using subheads, bullets, and short paragraphs.

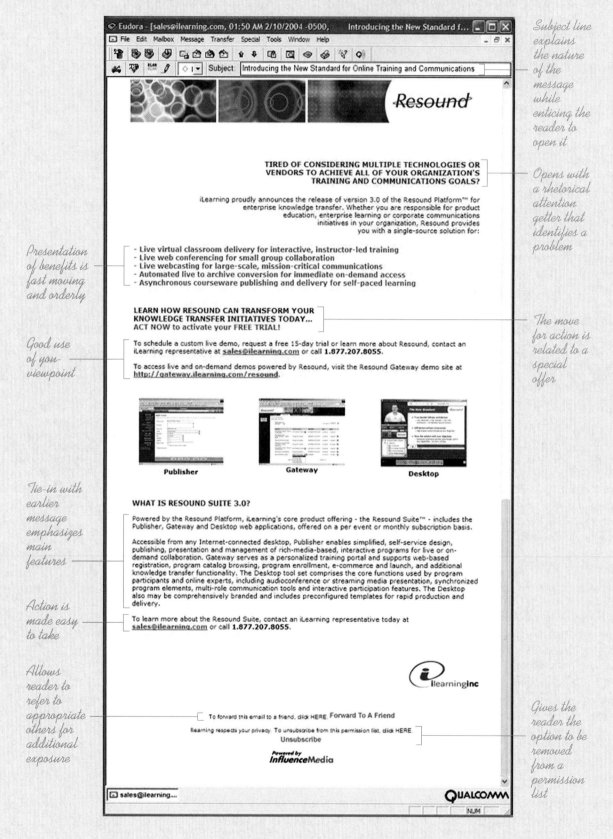

Subject line explains the nature of the message while enticing the reader to open it

Opens with a rhetorical attention getter that identifies a problem

Presentation of benefits is fast moving and orderly

Good use of you viewpoint

The move for action is related to a special offer

Tie-in with earlier message emphasizes main features

Action is made easy to take

Allows reader to refer to appropriate others for additional exposure

Gives the reader the option to be removed from a permission list

A Successful Sales Letter?

"Friend," the sales letter began, "let me show you how you can make an extra $25,000 a year. I am doing it this year—and you can do it, too. For detailed information, just send me $25."

One of the letters went to George Dimwitty. George was excited about the possibility of making money. So he mailed his $25. In a few days he got the following instructions:

"To make extra money just as I did, you first get a mailing list of suckers who want to make extra money. Then you write them 'Friend, let me show you how you can make an extra $25,000 a year. I am doing it this year—and you can do it, too. For detailed information, just send me $25.'"

ORIGINAL WORDING

Reorganization Plan A will cause 10 percent of the staff to lose their jobs.

Our new laser paper keeps the wasted paper from smudged copies to less than 2 percent.

POSITIVE WORDING

Reorganization Plan A will retain 90 percent of the workforce.

Our new laser paper provides smudge-free copies more than 98 percent of the time.

Including All Necessary Information

Of course, the information you present and how you present it are matters for your best judgment. But you must make sure that you present enough information to complete the sale. You should leave none of your reader's questions unanswered. Nor should you fail to overcome any likely objections. You must work to include all such basic information in your message, and you should make it clear and convincing.

- Give enough information to sell. Answer all questions; overcome all objections.

In your effort to include all necessary information in a direct-mail sales effort, you can choose from a variety of enclosures—booklets, brochures, leaflets, and the like. When you use such enclosures, you should take care to coordinate all the parts. All the parts in the mailing should form a unified sales message. As a general rule, you should use the letter to carry your basic sales message. This means your letter should not shift a major portion of your sales effort to an enclosure. Instead, you should use enclosures mainly to supplement the letter. The enclosures might cover descriptions, price lists, diagrams, and pictures—in fact, all helpful information that does not fit easily into the message. To ensure that all the parts in the mailing fit into a unified effort, you would be wise to direct your reader's attention to each of them. You can do this best through incidental references at appropriate places in the letter (for example, by saying "as shown on page 3 of the enclosed booklet" or "see page 7 of the enclosed brochure").

- Coordinate the sales letter with accompanying booklets, brochures, and leaflets. But make the letter carry the main sales message. Enclosures should serve as supplements.

When you send the sales message by email, the supporting information must be worked into the message or presented in links or attachments that you invite the reader to view. You must take care to avoid the appearance of too much length or clutter when working this material into the message. By skillfully cutting up the message visually (see Resound case illustration p. 206), you can reduce the effect of excessive length. And by making the boxes attractive with imaginative use of color, font selection, and formatting, you can enhance the effectiveness of the presentation. In either mail or email selling, your goal is to give the readers all they need to know to complete a sale, while allowing them the option of reading only as much as they desire.

- In email sales messages, the supporting information can be accessed through links or attachments.

Driving for the Sale

After you have caught your reader's interest in your product or service, the next logical step is to drive for the sale. After all, this is what you have been working for all along. It is a natural conclusion to the sales effort you have made.

- End with a drive for the sale.

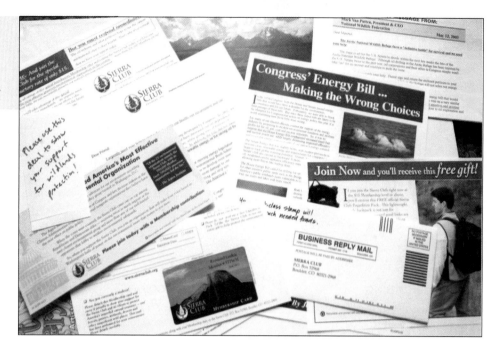

As in this Sierra Club example, most sales mailings consist of a letter and a coordinated group of support pieces.

• In strong selling efforts, a command is effective. For milder efforts, a request is appropriate. Take the reader through the motions.

How you should word your drive for the sale depends on your strategy. If your selling effort is strong, your drive for action also may be strong. It may even be worded as a command. ("Order your copy today—while it's on your mind.") If you use a milder selling effort, you could use a direct question. ("Won't you please send us your order today?") In any event, the drive for action should be specific and clear. In no way should it resemble a hint. For best effect, it should take the reader through the motions of whatever he or she must do. Here are some examples:

"Just check your preferences on the enclosed order form. Then fax it to us today at 888.755.5265!"

"Mail the enclosed card today—and see how right Fast Company is for you!"

Similarly, in email selling you will need to make the action easy. Make it a simple click—a click to an order form, to order instructions, or such. Words such as these do the job well: "Just click on the button below to order your customized PDA case now!" and "You can download our free, new catalog of business gifts at <http://thank youtoo.com>."

Urging the Action

• Urge action now.

Because readers who have been persuaded sometimes put things off, you should urge immediate action. "Do it now" and "Act today" are versions of this technique, although some people dislike the commanding tone of such words. Even so, this type of action is widely used. A milder and generally more acceptable way of urging action is to tie it in with a practical reason for doing it now. Here are some examples:

. . . to take advantage of this three-day offer.

. . . so that you can be ready for the Christmas rush.

. . . so that you will be the first in your community.

Recalling the Appeal

• Recalling the appeal in the final words is good technique.

Yet another effective technique for the close of a sales message is to use a few words that recall the basic appeal. Associating the action with the benefits that the reader will gain by taking it adds strength to your sales effort. Illustrating this technique is a message selling Maxell DVDs to retailers. After building its sales effort, the message asks for action and then follows the action request with these words:

. . . and start taking your profits from the fast-selling Maxell DVDs.

Another illustration is a message selling a fishing resort vacation that follows its action words with a reminder of the joys described earlier.

It's your reservation for a week of battle with the fightingest bass in the Southland.

Adding a Postscript

Unlike other business messages where a postscript (P.S.) appears like an afterthought, a sales message can use a postscript as a part of its design. It can be used effectively in a number of ways: to urge the reader to act, to emphasize the major appeal, to invite attention to other enclosures, to suggest that the reader pass along the sales message, and so on. Postscripts effectively used by professionals include the following:

- Postscripts are acceptable and effective.

PS: Don't forget! If ever you think that *Action* is not for you, we'll give you every cent of your money back. We are that confident that *Action* will become one of your favorite magazines.

PS: Hurry! Save while this special money-saving offer lasts.

PS: Our little magazine makes a distinctive and appreciated gift. Know someone who's having a birthday soon?

PS: Click now to order and automatically enter our contest for an Olympus digital camera.

Inviting Name Removal to Email Readers

In email selling, because you are entering the reader's private domain, the courteous thing to do is to offer to remove the reader from your mailing list if he or she desires. Such invitations help to soften the reader's attitude toward your intrusion. It even may make him or her tend to like you and your message. Regardless of the result, you should consider doing it. Consider also placing this invitation in a prominent place—perhaps even before the message text. According to one authority, "This is the equivalent of asking, 'Is it OK if we come in?' "[4] Unfortunately, many such offers to remove readers are fake and serve only to tell the sender that your address is valid. So they send your more junk email knowing that it will reach you.[5]

- Offer to remove reader from mailing as a courtesy gesture.

Illustrating this technique is the note at the bottom of the Resound example (p. 206). A similar note is used by Princess Cruises in their email sales messages: "If you do not wish to receive occasional email messages like this from Princess Cruises, please click the below link."

Reviewing the General Sales Plan

From the preceding discussion, a general plan for the sales message emerges. This plan is similar to the classic AIDA (attention, interest, desire, action) model developed almost a century ago. It should be noted, however, that in actual practice, sales messages vary widely. Creativity and imagination are continually leading to innovative techniques. Even so, the general prevailing plan is the following:

- Sales messages vary in practice, but this plan is used most often.

- Gain favorable attention.
- Create desire by presenting the appeal, emphasizing supporting facts, and emphasizing reader viewpoint.

---

[4] Nick Usbornn, as quoted in Sterne and Priore, *Email Marketing*, 151.

[5] One website where you can keep up on currently pending legislation in both the federal and state legislatures is <http://www.cauce.org/legislation/>.

- Include all necessary information—using a coordinated sales package (brochures, leaflets, links, appended parts, and such).
- Drive for the sale by urging action now and recalling the main appeal.
- Possibly add a postscript.
- In email writing, consider offering to remove name from list.

Evaluating Contrasting Examples

The following two email sales messages show good and bad efforts to sell Killshaw's restaurant consulting services. Clearly, the bad message is the work of an amateur and the better one was written by a professional.

Weakness in an Illogical Plan. Although the subject line of the amateur's sales message presents the main appeal, it is dull and general. The opening statement is little more than an announcement of what the consultant does. Then, as a continuation of the opening, it offers the services to the reader. Such openings do little to gain attention or build desire. Next comes a routine, I-viewpoint review of the consultant's services. The explanation of the specific services offered is little better. Although the message tells what the consultant can do, it is dull. The drive for action is more a hint than a request. The closing words do suggest a benefit for the reader, but the effort is too little too late.

The bad message is amateurish. It does little more than announce that services are available.

Subject: A plan to increase profits

Ms. Collins:

You have probably heard in the trade about the services I provide to restaurant management. I am now pleased to be able to offer these services to you.

From 28 years of experience, I have learned the details of restaurant management. I know what food costs should be. I know how to find other cost problems, be they the buying end or the selling end. I know how to design menu offerings for the most profitability. I have studied kitchen operations and organization. And I know how the service must be conducted for best results.

From all this knowledge, I have perfected a simple system for analyzing a restaurant and finding its weaknesses. This I do primarily from guest checks, invoices, and a few other records. As explained in my website <http://www.restaurantimp.com>, my system finds the trouble spots. It shows exactly where to correct all problems.

I can provide you with the benefits of my system for only $1,500—$700 now and $800 when you receive my final report on your operations. If you will fill out and return by email the information requested below, I will show you how to make more money.

Larry Kopel, Consultant

Skillful Presentation of a Rational Appeal. The better message follows the conventional sales pattern described in the preceding pages. Its appeal is rational, which is justified in this case. Its subject line gains interest with a claim of the main message presented in you-viewpoint language. The beginning sentence continues this appeal with an attention-holding testimonial. The following sentences explain the service quickly—and interestingly. Then in good you-viewpoint writing, the reader learns what he or she will get from the service. This part is loaded with reader benefits (profits, efficiency, cost cutting). Next, after the selling has been done, the message drives for action. The last sentence ties in the action with its main benefit—making money. A post note about how to "unsubscribe" courteously suggests the writer's good intentions.

Visuals Help Business Writers Add Interest to Sales Messages

Sales messages—both print and rich email—often include art and animation to increase the visual appeal as well as attract attention to the message. In one recent experiment comparing two types of visual email messages, an HTML and a video message, Holland America found that the video message resulted in a 33 percent higher click-through rate than the HTML mailing. Furthermore, once readers got to the site, the average stay was 9 minutes compared to 5 minutes for the HTML message. Additionally, the video message was cost effective, costing only 20 percent more than HTML message.*

Today's business writers need not be artists or professional photographers to use good visuals in their documents. Major software programs include bundled art, animation, photographs, and sounds; and scanners and easy-to-use programs are readily available to help writers create customized visuals. Additionally, on the web, writers can find a vast assortment of specialists with products and services to help enhance their sales messages.

Here is a short list of a few websites. You'll find more on the textbook website as well.

- http://webclipart.about.com/   A rich collection of links to websites for clip art, tutorials, hardware, and software.

- http://www.fotosearch.com/   A meta search tool for finding professional photographs, illustrations, and videos.

- http://www.flashcomponents.com/   A subscription website for finished and modifiable Flash files.

- http://www.freeaudioclips.com/   A site for free audio clips and links to software tools as well as a good search tool.

* Heidi Anderson, "Cruising to E-Mail Results," <http://www.clickz.com/em_mkt/case_studies/prnt.php/2232781> (July 10, 2003).

Subject: A proven plan that guarantees you more profits

Ms. Collins:

"Killshaw is adding $15,000 a year to my restaurant's profits!"

With these words, Bill Summers, owner of Boston's famed Pirate's Cove, joined the hundreds of restaurant owners who will point to proof in dollars in assuring you that I have a plan that can add to your profits.

My time-proven plan to help you add to your profits is a product of 28 years of intensive research, study, and consulting work with restaurants all over the nation. I found that where food costs exceed 40 percent, staggering amounts slip through restaurant managers' fingers. Then I tracked down the causes of these losses. I can find these trouble spots in your business—and I'll prove this to you in extra income dollars!

To make these extra profits, all you do is send me, for a 30-day period, your guest checks, bills, and a few other items I'll tell you about later. After these items have undergone my proven method of analysis, I will write you an eye-opening report that will tell you how much money your restaurant should make and how to make it.

From the report, you will learn in detail just what items are causing your higher food costs. And you will learn how to correct them. Even your menu will receive thorough treatment. You will know what "best-sellers" are paying their way—what "poor movers" are eating into your profits. All in all, you'll get practical suggestions that will show you how to cut costs, build volume, and pocket a net 10 to 20 percent of sales.

For a more detailed explanation of this service, you'll want to review the information presented at my website <http://www.restaurantimp.com/>. Then won't you let me prove to you, as I have to so many others, that I can add money to your income this year? This

Following the conventional plan, the better message uses good strategy and technique.

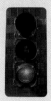

added profit can be yours for the modest investment of $1,500 ($700 now and the other $800 when our profit plan report is submitted). Just email the information requested below and I'll do the rest.

That extra $25,000 or more will make you glad you did!

Larry Kopel, Consultant

You were sent this message because of your status in the restaurant field. If you wish to be removed from our list, please send an email with the word "unsubscribe" in the subject line.

SUMMARY BY CHAPTER OBJECTIVES

1 Use imagination in writing skillful persuasive requests that begin indirectly, use convincing reasoning, and close with goodwill and action.

2 Describe the choices available in determining the structure of a direct-sales mailing or email sales messages.

3 Describe the preliminary steps of studying the product or service and selecting the appeals to use in a sales message.

4 Discuss the choices of mechanics available to the sales writer.

5 Compose sales messages that gain attention, persuasively present appeals, and effectively drive for action.

1. Requests that are likely to be resisted require an indirect, persuasive approach.
   - Such an approach involves developing a strategy—a plan for persuading.
   - Your opening words should set up this strategy and gain attention.
   - Follow with convincing persuasion.
   - Then make the request—clearly yet positively.
   - The request can end the message, or more persuasion can follow (whichever you think is appropriate).
2. Sales messages are a special type of persuasive request.
   - Typically, a sales mailing contains a number of pieces: brochures, reply forms, and such.
   - But our emphasis is on the basic sales message, which usually is the main item.
   - Email sales messages are creatively designed to include supporting information. They may refer to a website.
3. Begin work on the sales message by studying the product or service to be sold. Also, study your prospects, using marketing research information if available.
   - Then select an appropriate appeal (or appeals).
   - Appeals fall into two broad groups: emotional and rational.
     — Emotional appeals play on our senses (taste, hearing, and so on) and our feelings (love, anger, fear, and the like).
     — Rational appeals address the rational mind (thrift, durability, efficiency, and such).
   - Select the appeals that fit the product and prospects.
4. Before beginning to write, you determine the mechanics of the mailing.
   - Sales letters may use impersonal salutations (Dear Student), headlines rather than inside addresses, pictures, lines, and such to gain attention.
   - Email messages may include support information creatively worked into the message design or a reference to a website.
   - Your imagination is the major limitation on what you can choose to do.
5. Although innovations are frequently used, the basic sales message generally follows this traditional plan:
   - The opening seeks to gain attention and set up the sales presentation.
   - The sales message follows.
   - In emotional selling, the words establish an emotional atmosphere and build an emotional need for the product or service.
   - In rational selling, the appeal is to the thinking mind, using facts and logical reasoning.
   - Throughout the message, emphasis is on good sales language and the you-viewpoint.
   - All the information necessary for a sale (prices, terms, choices, and the like) is included in the message, though references are made to supporting information.

- Next comes a drive for a sale.
  — It may be a strong drive, even a command, if a strong sales effort is used.
  — It may be a direct question if a milder effort is desired.
  — In either case, the action words are specific and clear, frequently urging action *now*.
  — Taking the action may be associated with the benefits to be gained.
  — Postscripts often are included to convey a final sales message.
  — In email messages, opt-out links are often provided as a professional courtesy.

1. Explain why a persuasive request is usually written in the indirect order. Could the direct order ever be used for such messages? Discuss.

2. What is the role of the you-viewpoint in persuasive requests?

3. Discuss the relationship between a persuasive request and a sales message.

4. What appeals would be appropriate for the following products when they are being sold to consumers?

   a. Shaving cream.
   b. Carpenter's tools.
   c. Fresh vegetables.
   d. Software.
   e. Lubricating oil.
   f. Ladies' dresses.
   g. Perfume.
   h. Fancy candy.
   i. CD players.
   j. Hand soap.

5. With what products would you use strong negative appeals? Positive appeals?

6. When could you justify addressing sales letters to "occupant"? When to each reader by name?

7. Rarely should a sales letter exceed a page in length. Discuss this statement.

8. Should the traditional sales-message organization discussed in the text ever be altered? Discuss.

9. Discuss the relationship between the sales message and its accompanying support information.

10. When do you think a strong drive for action is appropriate in a sales message? When do you think a weak drive is appropriate?

1. Criticize the persuasive request message below. It was written by the membership chairperson of a chapter of the Service Corps of Retired Executives (SCORE), a service organization consisting of retired executives who donate their managerial talents to small businesses in the area. The recipients of the message are recently retired executives.

Dear Ms. Petersen:

As membership chair it is my privilege to invite you to join the Bay City chapter of the Service Corps of Retired Executives. We need you, and you need us.

We are a volunteer, not-for-profit organization. We are retired business executives who give free advice and assistance to struggling small businesses. There is a great demand for our services in Bay City, which is why we are conducting this special membership drive. As I said before, we need you. The work is hard and the hours can be long, but it is satisfying.

Please find enclosed a self-addressed envelope and a membership card. Fill out the card and return it to me in the envelope. We meet the first Monday of every month (8:30 at the Chamber of Commerce office). This is the fun part—strictly social. A lot of nice people belong.

I'll see you there Monday!

Sincerely yours,

2. Criticize the following sales message. It was written to people on a mailing list of fishing enthusiasts. The writer, a professional game fisher, is selling his book by direct mail. The nature of the book is evident from the letter.

Have you ever thought
why the pros catch fish
and you can't?

They have secrets. I am a pro, and I know these secrets. I have written them and published them in my book, *The Bible of Fishing*.

This 240-page book sells for only $29.95, including shipping costs, and it is worth every penny of the price. It tells where to fish in all kinds of weather and how the seasons affect fishing. It tells about which lures to use under every condition. I describe how to improve casting and how to set the hook and reel them in. There is even a chapter on night fishing.

I have personally fished just about every lake and stream in this area for over forty years and I tell the secrets of each. I have one chapter on how to find fish without expensive fish-finding equipment. In the book I also explain how to determine how deep to fish and how water temperature affects where the fish are. I also have a chapter on selecting the contents of your tackle box.

The book also has an extensive appendix. Included in it is a description of all the game fish in the area—with color photographs. Also in the appendix is a glossary that covers the most common lures, rods, reels, and other fishing equipment.

The book lives up to its name. It is a bible for fishing. You must have it! Fill out the enclosed card and send it to me in the enclosed stamped and addressed envelope. Include your check for $29.95 (no cash or credit cards, please). Do it today!

Sincerely yours,

3. Criticize each of the following parts of sales messages. The product or service being sold and the part identification are indicated in the headings.

Email Subject Lines

a. Earn BIG profits NOW!!!

b. Reduce expenses with an experienced consultant's help.

c. Free trial offer ends this week!

Openings

Product or Service: A Color Fax Machine

a. Now you can fax in color!

b. Here is a full-color fax that will revolutionize the industry.

c. If you are a manufacturer, ad agency, architect, designer, engineer, or anyone who works with color images, the Statz Color Fax can improve the way you do business.

Product or Service: A Financial Consulting Service

d. Would you hire yourself to manage your portfolio?

e. Are you satisfied with the income your portfolio earned last year?

f. Dimmitt-Hawes Financial Services has helped its clients make money for over a half century.

Parts of Sales Presentations

Product or Service: A Paging Service

a. Span-Comm Messaging is the only paging service that provides service coast to coast.

b. Span-Comm Messaging is the only paging service that gives you the freedom to go coast to coast and still receive text messages.

c. Span-Comm Messaging gives you coast-to-coast service.

Product or Service: A Color Fax Machine

d. The Statz Color Fax is extraordinary. It produces copies that are indistinguishable from the originals.

e. The extraordinary Statz Color Fax produces copies identical to the originals.

f. Every image the Statz Color Fax produces is so extraordinary you may not be able to tell a fax from an original.

Product or Service: Vermont Smoked Hams

g. You won't find a better-tasting ham than the old-fashioned Corncob Smoked Ham we make up here on the farm in Vermont.

h. Our Corncob Smoked Ham is tender and delicious.

i. You'll love this smoky-delicious Corncob Smoked Ham.

Product or Service: A Unique Mattress

j. Control Comfort's unique air support system lets you control the feel and firmness of your bed simply by pushing a button.

k. The button control adjusts the feel and firmness of Control Comfort's air support system.

l. Just by pushing a button you can get your choice of feel and firmness in Control Comfort's air support system.

Action Endings

Product or Service: An Innovative Writing Instrument

a. To receive your personal Airflo pen, you have but to sign the enclosed card and return it to us.

b. You can experience the writing satisfaction of this remarkable writing instrument by just filling out and returning the enclosed card.

c. Don't put it off! Now, while it's on your mind, sign and return the enclosed card.

Product or Service: A News Magazine

d. To begin receiving your copies of *Today's World,* simply fill out and return the enclosed card.

e. For your convenience, a subscription card is enclosed. It is your ticket to receiving *Today's World.*

f. If you agree that *Today's World* is the best of the news magazines, just sign and return the enclosed card.

Postscripts

a. You can also monogram items you order before November 1.

b. If you order before November 1, you can monogram your items.

c. Items ordered before November 1 can be monogrammed.

CRITICAL THINKING PROBLEMS

Persuasive Requests

1. Every year, (the local chapter of a professional society of your choice, real or imagined) holds an awards dinner to honor special members for their accomplishments. You're the new president of the organization, so it falls to you this year to invite people to attend.

It's pretty easy to persuade the award winners to come. After all, they're told in advance that they've won, and they usually look forward to being publicly honored for their achievements. Getting the other members to attend is more difficult. First, though the meal is usually quite nice, attendees have to pay for it themselves, even though your organization always gets a group rate that keeps the cost down a bit.

Another problem, you suspect, is that the nonwinners are somewhat jealous. Why should they go to the trouble and expense of going to see other members get the awards? Last year, attendance at the dinner was embarrassingly low. You want to make sure that this doesn't happen again; the awards lose much of their value when nobody comes to help congratulate the honorees.

As you consider what appeals to use in your message, keep a few facts in mind. The dinner will be held at the Carrousel Restaurant, a beautiful facility that's well known for its elegant fare. It will cost $25 per person. The program will consist of a welcome and society news from you, the president; a relatively short talk given by a guest speaker (make the specifics about this person attractive but realistic); and the awards (develop the details for three to five awards that will be given for certain accomplishments). You can come up with other interesting elements for the dinner, but remember that the budget is very tight.

Your message will need to include all the necessary information about the dinner while also persuading people to attend. See if you can make this awards dinner the best ever while not going over budget.

2. Assume the role of manager of the Apex Parking Garage in the heart of a major business district. In addition to the increased competition of a new garage just across the street, you are faced with a problem that requires your immediate attention. It seems that your customers who pay extra for the "reserved" spaces on the convenient ground floor are complaining. All too often, customers who pay only the reduced fee for less convenient parking take their spaces. You have documented these violations and have the names of 37 violators. They all work in nearby office buildings, and you have their email addresses.

Apparently your park-yourself honor system isn't working. You will have to do something about it. You could assign every customer a numbered spot so there could be no mistake. But you tried this system before and it proved to have unnecessary complications. A better approach, you think, is to try to appeal to the 37 violators to follow the simple rule: reserved parking for those paying for it, the rest of the garage for all others. You'll make your appeal in an email message, taking care to be as courteous but firm as the situation permits.

As you think through your message, you consider the need for backing up your appeal. Will you tow away the offenders' cars? Is there some other action that you could take? Or should you depend totally on persuasion now—reserving more threatening action for a follow-up appeal? Whatever your decision, you must try hard not to offend. These customers may be rule breakers, but they could just move their business to the garage across the street.

3. As a financial consultant with a major stock and bond brokerage firm, your specialty is making presentations to investor groups. Your goal, of course, is to persuade the investors through education to invest in your company's programs. You know your work well, and you are good at it.

Recently, you have been disappointed in the attendance at your presentations. Your procedure involves first selecting an investment group and then sending letter invitations to the members. Typically you make the presentations at hotels, country clubs, or such. You serve drinks, hors d'oeuvres, and sometimes full meals. You try hard to make the meetings both enjoyable and informative.

Your next meeting is scheduled for the first Wednesday evening of next month at 6:30. It will be at the Green Hills Club, which is located at the Green Hills Resort and Conference Center. Your audience will be largely modestly wealthy retirees living in the Green Hills area. Your presentation will revolve around a gourmet meal prepared by the club's chefs, and beverages will be offered as well. As usual, you will stress financial education, although investing with you is the desired result.

Now you must write the message that will get the prospects to attend. In doing so, you may use your logical imagination to supply any additional facts you may need. In the end you will produce a message that will make the readers want to attend. You will request RSVP responses by way of an enclosed card or a telephone number.

4. Project yourself about 10 years into the future and assume that you are your college's representative on the development committee of your alumni association. You earned this prestigious assignment through your loyalty to the association and your hard work on association projects. Today you received a packet of information from Kara Mariucci, the executive administrator of the alumni association. The packet includes plans for a new alumni house to be built on campus. This imposing structure will serve as a focal point for all alumni activities, and each college is to have its own room in the building for meetings, social gatherings, and other activities.

Funds for the building have been donated by an anonymous, wealthy friend of the university. But no funds were provided for furnishing it. So now each college will be asked to solicit donations from its own graduates to provide these furnishings for its room. And as your college's representative on the development committee, it will be your job to solicit these funds for your college's room. Ms. Mariucci notes in her message that the goal for your college's room is $30,000.

Ms. Mariucci suggests that you write each alumni member from your college a persuasive message seeking their support. "If you want help in composing this message, I'll be glad to provide it," she notes. But you don't need or want help. You'll rely on your course in business communication to carry you through. You feel confident of success. Since most of your college's graduates have done well in the real world of business, you know everyone can make a donation—and you will see to it that they do. But you also know that since they are traditionally tightfisted, you will have to be very persuasive.

Although your major appeal will be directed to the pride of graduates in their alma mater, you will include any other appeals that you think might be appropriate. Among possible appeals are the alumni's desire for their college's room to be first-class in every respect, the potential uses for the room, how they might benefit from the room when they're on campus, the potential for forming a private club to use the room year round, the public relations advantages of such a room, and so on.

The association will furnish the mailing list of your college's graduates. About 70 percent have email addresses; all have mailing addresses.

5. As sales manager for the regional office of Farmers' and Cattlemen's Insurance Company, you face a ticklish situation concerning your agents. More and more policy owners are writing your office and asking questions about their policies. Most of the questions could be answered better by the agents who sell the insurance. Reports reaching you indicate that many of your agents tell their clients to write headquarters for the answers.

The workload in answering these letters is becoming heavy. As you don't have sufficient qualified personnel in your office to do the work, you must try to put an end to this practice. So you decide to send an email message to all agents in the region persuading them to have their customers contact them—not your office—when the customers have questions or complaints. After all, answering questions and handling complaints is a part of their job. They shirk responsibility when they refer their customers to headquarters. Of course, you know that there may be some questions the agents can't answer. But they can check with headquarters for the answers and then inform their customers.

You know that some of your agents are rather sensitive. So you will work to be as diplomatic as possible in conveying your message. You will not command compliance, but you will be courteous, understanding, and convincing. Since the home office makes almost daily email contacts with the agents, you will send this message by email.

6. For this assignment, you are the president of Local 419, United Federation of Retail Workers. A few minutes ago you talked with Miguel Vasquez, the executive director for Blood for Life. Mr. Vasquez's organization collects blood, which it stores and dispenses as needed to local hospitals. As he explained the situation to you, the local supply is extremely low. At times the situation is desperate, as it is expected to be during the coming holiday season. Thus his organization is conducting a campaign to inform the public of the immediate need for more blood. He asked for your union's help, and you gave it.

Now you must inform the membership of your action. So you will write a message. It will be persuasive—one that will clearly explain the gravity of the situation and make the members want to give blood. In the message you will report that the Blood for Life van will be in the Hillside Shopping Mall parking lot all day next Saturday and the East Gate Mall the following Saturday. You will explain that qualified medical personnel will be present to ensure proper conduct of the operation. And you will assure the members that giving blood is painless and harmless. You will send the message to every member of Local 419. In addition, you will post the request on the union website and post copies on all available company bulletin boards.

7. A few months ago, the administration of Permian Oil Company, Inc., agreed to sponsor an educational program for employees.

The program that resulted consisted of a variety of course offerings. For those whose basic knowledge of mathematics, English, and science was weak, basic courses were offered after work hours in the company training center. Qualified public school teachers in the area were brought in to teach these courses. For those desiring college course work, the company offered to underwrite all tuition costs at the local university as well as many online courses. And for those wanting to study a variety of interesting and exciting topics, the company offered short courses at the training center. Currently, the company is offering courses in ceramics, music appreciation, and public speaking. It plans to offer courses in investments, automotive repair, nutrition, interior decorating, and landscaping soon.

Clearly, the plan was to offer something for everyone. In spite of the company's best efforts, however, very few of the employees have taken advantage of the courses. In fact, the whole program has been a miserable failure.

Before writing off the program as a lost cause, the company will make one last effort to increase participation. To this end, web announcements and a feature story in the company newsletter have been the primary means of promoting the courses. Now a persuasive written message to each worker will be used. And you, the training director, have been assigned the task of writing it.

In the message you will present your most persuasive arguments for why the workers should take advantage of the educational opportunities being offered. You will attach a brochure describing the courses scheduled for the coming months and giving the details of the program. (If you need additional facts, you may supply them as long as they are consistent with the information given.)

You will send the message to each of your employees. In addition, it will be posted on the company portal.

8. In your assignment as a management trainee at one of the Boyer Aluminum Company plants, you are presently assigned to the office of the works manager. Your job is to assist the works manager, Paul Adami, generally and to learn how he operates. Today you receive what you regard as your first real test.

Paul has just received a message from the president of the neighborhood association for the residential area adjacent to the plant. As explained in the message, Boyer employees speed and drive recklessly as they leave the plant at the end of each work shift. In the words of the association president, "One would think the 4:30 whistle is the starter's signal at the Indianapolis Speedway the way some workers speed out of the plant exits." Further down the message the president notes that "such driving through a residential neighborhood will someday lead to a fatality. Luckily, no one has been hurt yet, although one child was narrowly missed by a speeding car and one pet was killed." The message concluded with the request that Boyer "get the word to the drivers or we will reluctantly ask the police to correct the problem."

Barbara Calmes, the president and your boss, is busy with other work; so she delegates to you the task of informing the workers. She instructs you to write a message that will persuade employees to drive carefully and generally be good neighbors with the neighborhood people. "Use whatever appeal you think will be effective," she instructs, "but it wouldn't hurt to let them know what will happen if they don't shape up. Don't just make a blunt threat. Be positive and persuasive." You'll write the message for the president's signature. It will be sent by email to all workers with computer accessibility and by regular mail to all others.

9. Every fall the civic leaders of your city conduct a fund drive for United Givers. This umbrella organization is designed to reduce the number of fund-raising campaigns of the charity groups in the town to just one. The money collected in the United Givers drive is apportioned among the approved organizations in town—organizations such as Girl Scouts, International Red Cross, YMCA, and Cystic Fibrosis.

You are the chair of this year's United Givers committee at the local Ridgeway Chemical Company plant. Your committee's plan is to send contribution cards and a covering message to all 577 of the plant's employees. The message will persuade, and it will give all the information needed. Specifically, it will appeal to the reader's civic pride and responsibility. It will suggest a "fair-share" contribution of one day's pay. It will ask the reader to fill out his or her card and have it ready to be picked up by the United Givers worker who will come by later.

As the committee chair, you must write the message. You will begin by thinking through the situation to determine the very best strategy to use. Then you will do your best persuasive writing, and you will use good judgment in doing so.

10. As a sales copywriter, today you have been given a most unusual assignment. It is to write a message soliciting funds for Hire a Rehab (HARE). The main goal of this association is to help rehabilitating people, mainly recovering alcoholics and chemically dependent persons, to find employment after they are released from hospital treatment programs.

The writing task interests you because you strongly believe in HARE's goal. You know that a job and a feeling of self-worth are requisites for successful rehabilitation of these unfortunate people. And you know how difficult it is for such people to find jobs. Many people view them as degenerates who are looking for ways to support old lifestyles. You will have to overcome such impressions. Think through the situation carefully. What can you say that will overcome the resistance to your goal. The message you will write will be sent by email to all on HARE's mailing list with email addresses and by regular mail to the others.

11. As area sales manager for Alamo Insurance Company, you are experiencing difficulties with your salespeople. They are doing a great job of selling. But their effort in submitting the paperwork related to sales is far from great.

One of the papers the salespeople ignore submitting all too often is the sales-information report. This report records information about each customer—information such as how the prospect was obtained, the sales appeals used, and demographic data (age, income, education, marital status, and so on). The information in the report is useful to Alamo management primarily as a basis for planning advertising and selling strategies. Contrary to what some salespeople reportedly think, the information is used—and used extensively.

In an effort to get salespeople to submit their reports regularly, you will appeal to them in a message. No, you can't command them to submit the reports, for the salespeople are independent operators. But you should be able to show them how the information collected is used for their best interests.

The appeal you select will be the one you think will be the most effective in this case. Address the message to any of the salespeople on your list and send it to his or her email address, which is how you usually communicate with these people.

12. Yesterday you were elected president of the Centerville Humane Society, an organization devoted to bettering the lives of our animal friends. You were pleased because you believe in the organization's goals. You were also pleased because you know that your company will benefit from your election. Your performance as president will give you and your company exposure that will help in building good public relations.

    You were somewhat less pleased, however, when you attended your first meeting of the society's board of directors. At the meeting you learned that your new position involves some unexpected work. The board decided to attempt something new in this year's fund-raising. The Society will seek corporate donations. Specifically, it plans to persuade local companies to match the donations of their employees and to assist in soliciting from their employees. Your first task is to sell those companies on the idea.

    You will try to persuade the companies to participate in the fund-raising through a message that you will write. Participation means assisting in contacting their employees (you will supply the messages and paperwork needed for this purpose) and then matching dollar for dollar the money the employees contribute. Writing the message to the employees is a second chore for you, but this one can wait. At this time you are concerned with the message to the company heads.

    As you plan this message to the company heads, you think of possible persuasive strategies. Will you appeal to humane concerns about animal suffering? Can assisting in this campaign yield business benefits? What other benefits are involved? You will think through the situation carefully, arriving at the best possible strategy for this one case. You have the email addresses of most area managers. The remaining ones on your list you can reach by regular mail.

13. Recently your company moved its offices to centrally located downtown quarters in an attempt to attract more desirable clients and to make it easier for employees to reach. However, both the availability and cost of square footage has led to smaller, more compact workspaces.

    Although you love the new location, the closeness has led to an unexpected nuisance—distracting noise. The company recognized the importance of creating efficient work areas, so all old computer monitors were replaced with smaller, more compact flat panel displays. These flat panels are much quieter than the old monitors, but now you can hear the clicking of keyboards everywhere. So you researched quieter keyboards and discovered some fairly low-cost options—membrane keyboards.

    Membrane keyboards are quieter than mechanical ones because when the user presses a key on a membrane keyboard, it hits a rubbery material. Although these keyboards usually have a softer, spongier feel than the mechanical ones, some manufacturers use small plungers and springs to increase the tactile response some typists prefer. Companies from IBM to Keytronic to Belkin offer these keyboards at costs ranging from $30 to $50 each, a low price for improving productivity.

    You realize that your company has spent a lot in this move, so it's likely management won't be pleased with your request for spending even more. Therefore, you recognize you'll have to write a persuasive message in your attempt to get new keyboards as soon as possible. You decide to write this message to your boss, Kate Donnelly.

14. You love your job! Although it's hard to describe exactly, you do everything related to running the business side of a small business. You joined the company when there were just 25 employees; in less than two years, you've seen it grow to 50 employees. Not only is the business growing, even expanding into a new, company-owned headquarters building, but you are also beginning to hire employees with specialized expertise.

    In fact, the applicant you are planning to make an offer to today is a network specialist. During the interview process for this position, several candidates asked about your benefits. Until recently, you have been proud of your benefits package, considering it to be among the best offered by small businesses. But you realize that as your business grows, your benefits package will need to compete with those offered by larger companies.

    One ancillary benefit you have been reading about is the vision plan. This plan benefits both the employee and the employer. Employees benefit from the prevention and early detection of eye problems, problems that can be both costly and debilitating if not identified early. It benefits employers because it can generate a cash savings by reducing expenses for eye-related illnesses and stress. Many companies with this plan report reduced absenteeism due to vision-related problems such as headaches and neck strain. It is a tool for both employee recruitment and retention.

    Write a message to the owner and president, Jane Adami, persuading her to consider adding a vision plan to your current benefits package.

15. You are the operations manager for a small company in your area, SafePrint. SafePrint is the exclusive U.S. distributor of a German machine that prints on cords. Not only do you assemble them locally, but you also

sell and maintain these printers across the country. To reach many of your customers, you often exhibit at trade shows.

On one of your recent trips to a trade show in Chicago, you were reading a newspaper account of SBC Communications' success in reducing workplace injuries through prevention programs. In addition to requiring all office workers to take an interactive PC training course, SBC trains its managers in assessing workers' application of appropriate ergonomics. They have learned that often small, low-cost adjustments can reduce the chance of work-related musculoskeletal disorders. In fact, preventing just one case of carpal-tunnel syndrome saved over $20,000 in direct costs alone.

You believe injury prevention training would be good for your business and for employees too. Not only would it boost employee morale by showing you care about their safety, but it might even lower the costs to your company for the insurance premiums you pay for your employees. However, although you can pay for the training, you can't afford giving every employee half a day off to complete the training. So you'll have to persuade them to take the training online, at their own pace, but in addition to their regular work. Not only that, but 90 percent of the employees will have to complete the program by December 31 to allow you to expense the costs in this fiscal year and to qualify for the reduced insurance premiums in the next quarter.

Write a persuasive email to your employees. Be sure it is strong enough to convince everyone because you will need nearly full compliance to qualify for the reduced premiums.

Sales

16. Assume that you will be selling your services as (you decide what) in order to help finance your college education. You have gotten permission to distribute your message on campus, if you like, or you might choose a different audience. You'll need to decide how and to whom to deliver this sales pitch.

    If you feel that you don't yet have a skill that you could market, choose something you're good at or interested in and do some research to invent additional qualifications for yourself. For example, if you like landscaping, you could interview some professionals in this area or pick up some literature, either in hard copy or from the Internet, to be able to outline your credentials and your range of services knowledgeably. Or maybe your skills lie in the area of tutoring, childcare, car care, web design, house painting, home repairs, house cleaning, computer training . . . you name it. People need help with many tasks, and many of them are happy to hire a clever college student (especially if the charge is reasonable).

Using the strategies discussed in this chapter, put your best foot forward in your message in order to persuade people to hire you.

17. Select an advertisement from a current magazine for a product that could be sold profitably to business executives. Be careful to select one that contains a thorough description. Then write a sales message (email or letter, as your instructor specifies) for the product.

    In writing this message, be very careful that you do not just borrow the wording in the advertisement. Work hard to create an original approach. A major part of the evaluation of your work will depend on your personal contribution. You may assume that other information accompanies your sales message (brochure, attachments, or such). For class purposes, attach the advertisement to your work.

18. As a copywriter with a major agency you must write a sales message for Gulf Breeze Hotel. Located on the Mississippi Gulf coast, this is truly one of the nation's better resort hotels. It provides just about everything a vacationer would want—golfing on a beautiful 18-hole course, tennis on 12 Rubico courts, a marina with a wide assortment of rental boats, deep-sea fishing on the hotel's own *Magnolia Belle,* and fishing on the hotel's own pier. Bicycles are available for rent. And there are miles of hiking trails in the area. For those who like swimming, the hotel offers a long, sandy beach as well as a beautiful heated pool. To top it off, excellent food has earned the dining room a four-star rating from the International Gourmet Association. Truly, Gulf Breeze is a wonderful spot.

    The full facilities of the club are available at an affordable rate of $295 a day per couple ($215 for singles). This price includes room, breakfast, dinner, and use of most of the hotel's facilities. Golfing, tennis, bicycles, boating, and deep-sea fishing cost extra.

    Your message will be mailed to a select list of prospective vacationers and will be accompanied by a brochure that gives more of the details. It will refer to the hotel's website, which is more detailed and provides a reservation service. You may use your logical imagination to supplement the information given.

19. As the director of the Chamber of Commerce for _____ (your instructor will determine the city), your duties include attracting conventions. Next week the site selection committee of the State Teachers Association meets to determine where their group will meet next year, and you hope to sell them on your city.

    As the committee meeting will be behind closed doors, you will have to sell them by written message. Perhaps it won't be the typical sales message that you will write, but it will do a lot of selling. You plan to gather all the facts convention planners need (hotel capacities, meeting rooms, rates, transportation services, and such). Then you will mold the facts into a well-organized sales presentation.

For class purposes, you will need to search all the best sources of information—especially the websites of the local Chamber of Commerce, hotels, transportation facilities, and entertainment establishments. You will send your written sales message to each member of the STA's selection committee.

20. Take over as business manager for your school's football (or another sport) program. Attendance at home games has been lagging, and what is needed, you think, is some strategic promotion. So you have decided to conduct a direct-mail promotion to sell more season tickets for the coming year. You will write the sales message.

As you begin preparation for this assignment, you think of the advantages of a season ticket at $192 for six home games. Season-ticket holders enjoy certain advantages that other purchasers do not, such as a lower price per game (six tickets at $32 per game rather than the $35 per ticket for individual purchases). Another advantage is a first preference on any postseason classic your team might enter. Yet another is that season-ticket seat locations usually are better. Also, season-ticket holders have no problem when there are sell-outs; their seats are secured. Added to all these advantages are the underlying excitement and fun of intercollegiate athletics, guaranteed for all six home games.

Your sales message will make the reader see all these advantages and want to be a part of next year's

activities. Accompanying your message will be a drawing of your stadium, showing where seats may be selected, and a return order blank and envelope. In addition to the mailing, your letter will also be on your website where readers can also see the stadium seating plan and purchase tickets.

21. T. W. Bruyn of Brock in Waterland, Holland, has for years enjoyed good sales of his Edam cheese to the tourists who visit his small cheese factory. In traditional Dutch fashion, he makes the cheese right in his home, which he shares with his cows during the cold winter months.

While visiting this quaint dairy farm and cheese factory, you hit upon the idea of selling the cheeses by direct mail to the people back in the States. Without question, the cheese is unbelievably good; and Mr. Bruyn's guest registers over the past years provide a ready-made mailing list—a list of tourists who no doubt liked the cheese as well as you did.

You talk over the possibilities with Mr. Bruyn and get him excited, too. He'll furnish all the cheese you can sell—from neighbors, if necessary. (They all use the same manufacturing process.) And he and his family will handle all shipments for you.

So, with a few samples of Edam cheese and his mailing list of American tourists who have visited his place, you return to the states and begin plans for your direct-mail campaign. You plan to use a main selling message that will rekindle memories of the taste thrill of this exotic cheese. Accompanying this message will be an order card enclosure with a picture of the Bruyn home and factory and a price list. You may use your logical imagination to bring in additional facts needed but not given.

CHAPTER NINE

Strategies in the Job-Search Process

CHAPTER OBJECTIVES

Upon completing this chapter, you will be able to conduct an effective job search; compose effective cover messages, résumés, and follow-ups; and prepare for interviews. To reach these goals, you should be able to

1 Develop and use a network of contacts in your job search.

2 Assemble and evaluate information that will help you select a job.

3 Identify the sources that can lead you to an employer.

4 Compile print and electronic résumés that are strong, complete, and organized.

5 Write targeted cover messages that skillfully sell your abilities.

6 Explain how you can participate effectively in an interview.

7 Write application follow-up messages that are appropriate, friendly, and positive.

8 Maintain your job-search skills.

The Job-Search Process

Introduce yourself to this chapter by assuming a role similar to one you are now playing. You are Jason Andrews, a student at Olympia University. In a few months, you will complete your studies for work in marketing.

You believe that it is time to begin seeking the job for which those studies have been preparing you. But how do you do this? Where do you look? What does the search involve? How should you present yourself for the best results? The answers to these and related questions are reviewed in the following pages.

THE JOB SEARCH

Of all the things you do in life, few are more important than getting a job. Whether it involves your first job or one further down your career path, job seeking is directly related to your success and your happiness. It is vital that you conduct the job search properly—that you prepare wisely and carefully and proceed diligently. The following review of job-search strategies should help you succeed.

- For success in job seeking, use the following procedures.

Building a Network of Contacts

You can begin the job search long before you are ready to find employment. In fact, you can do it now by building a network of contacts. More specifically, you can build relationships with people who can help you find work when you need it. Such people include classmates, professors, and businesspeople.

- Begin the job search by building a network of contacts in this way:

At present, your classmates are not likely to be holding positions in which they make or influence hiring decisions. But in the future, when you may want to make a career change, they may hold such positions. Right now, some of them may know people who can help you. The wider your circle of friends and acquaintances, the more likely you are to make employment contacts.

- (1) Broaden your circle of friends.

Knowing your professors and making sure that they know you also can lead to employment contacts. Because professors often consult for business, they may know key executives and be able to help you contact them. Professors sometimes hear of position openings, and in such cases they can refer you to the hiring executives. Demonstrating your work ethic and your ability in the classroom is probably the best way to get your professors to know you and help you. Take advantage of opportunities to meet your professors outside the classroom, especially the professors in your major field.

- (2) Know your professors.

Obviously, meeting key business executives also can lead to employment contacts. You already may know some through family and friends. But broadening your relationships among businesspeople would be helpful. You can do this in various ways, but especially through college professional groups such as the Association for Information Technology Professionals, Delta Sigma Pi, and the Society for the Advancement of Management. By taking an active role in the organizations in your field of study, especially by working on program committees and by becoming an officer, you can get to know the executives who serve as guest speakers. You also might meet businesspeople online. If you share a particular interest on a listserv and are known to its members as one who contributes valuable comments, you may get some good job leads there. Members of newsgroups can sometimes be helpful, but you need to evaluate those leads carefully.

- (3) Meet executives.

If your school offers internships, you can make good career contacts through them. But you should find the one that is best for you, that offers you the best training for your career objective. And by all means, do not regard an internship as just a job. Regard it as a foundation step in your career plan. The experience you gain and the contacts you make in an internship might lead to your first career position. In fact, if you perform well, your internship could turn into full-time employment.

- (4) Make contacts through internships.

- (5) Work with community organizations.

In addition to these more common ways of making contacts, you can use some less common ones. By working in community organizations (charities, community improvement groups, fund-raising groups), you can meet community leaders. By attending meetings of professional associations (every field has them), you can meet the leaders in your field. In fact, participation in virtually any activity that provides contacts with business leaders can open doors for you now and in the future.

Identifying Appropriate Jobs

- Look at both your internal and external factors.

To find the right job, you need to investigate both internal and external factors. The best fit occurs when you have carefully looked at yourself: your education, personal qualities, experience, and any special qualifications. However, to be realistic, these internal qualities need to be analyzed in light of the external factors. Some of these factors may include the current and projected job market, economic needs, location preferences, and family needs.

- Begin with a self-analysis covering these background areas:

Analyzing Yourself. When you are ready to search for a job, you should begin the effort by analyzing yourself. In a sense, you should look at yourself much as you would look at a product or service that is for sale. After all, when you seek employment, you are really selling your ability to work—to do things for an employer. A job is more than something that brings you money. It is something that gives equal benefits to both parties—you and your employer. Thus, you should think about the qualities you have that enable you to do the work that an employer needs to have done. This self-analysis should cover the following categories.

- (1) Education. For specialized curricula, the career path is clear.

Education. The analysis might well begin with education. Perhaps you have already selected your career area such as accounting, finance, information systems, international business, management, or marketing. If you have, your task is simplified, for your specialized curriculum has prepared you for your goal. Even so, you may be able to note special points—for example, electives that have given you special skills or that show something special about you (such as psychology courses that have improved

"Do you have any other references besides these people in your chat room?"

SOURCE: © 2000 by Eli Stein. Reprinted with permission.

PART 3   Basic Patterns of Business Messages

your human-relations skills, communication courses that have improved your writing and speaking skills, or foreign language courses that have prepared you for international assignments).

If you have pursued a more general curriculum (general business, liberal arts, or such), you will need to look at your studies closely to see what they have prepared you to do. Perhaps you will find an emphasis on computers, written communication, human relations, foreign languages—all of which are sorely needed by some businesses. Or perhaps you will conclude that your training has given you a strong general base from which to learn specific business skills.

- For general curricula, a career choice must be made.

In analyzing your education, you should look at the quality of your record—grades, honors, special recognitions. If your record is good, you can emphasize it. But what if your work was only mediocre? As we will point out later, you will need to shift the emphasis to your stronger sales points—your willingness to work, your personality, your experience. Or perhaps you can explain, for example, by noting that while working your way through school may have limited your academic performance, it gave you valuable business skills.

- Consider quality of educational record (grades, honors, courses taken).

Personal Qualities. Your self-analysis also should cover your personal qualities. Qualities that relate to working with people are especially important. Qualities that show leadership or teamwork ability are also important. And if you express yourself well in writing or speaking, note this, for good communication skills are valuable in most jobs.

- (2) Personal qualities (people skills, leadership, and such).

Of course, you may not be the best judge of your personal qualities, for we do not always see ourselves as others see us. You may need to check with friends to see whether they agree with your assessments. You also may need to check your record for evidence supporting your assessments. For example, organization membership and participation in community activities are evidence of people and teamwork skills. Holding office in an organization is evidence of leadership ability. Participation on a debate team, college bowl, or collegiate business policy team is evidence of communication skills.

Work Experience. If you have work experience, you should analyze it. Work experience in your major deserves emphasis. In fact, such work experience becomes more and more important as you move along in your career. Work experience not related to the job you seek also can tell something important about you—even if the work was part-time. Part-time work can show willingness and determination, especially if you have done it to finance your education. And almost any work experience can help develop your skills in dealing with people.

- (3) Work experience (with interpretations).

Special Qualifications. Your self-analysis also should include special qualifications that might be valuable to an employer. The ability to speak a foreign language can be very helpful for certain business environments. Athletic participation, hobbies, and interests also may be helpful. To illustrate, athletic experience might be helpful for work for a sporting goods distributor, a hobby of automobile mechanics might be helpful for work with an automotive service company, and an interest in music might be helpful for work with a piano manufacturer or an online music website.

- (4) Special qualities (languages, communication skills, and such).

You also might take an interest inventory such as the Strong Campbell Interest Inventory or the Minnesota Vocational Interest Inventory. These tests help match your interests to those of others successful in their careers. Most college counseling and career centers make these tests available to their students, and some are available online. Getting good help in interpreting the results is critical to providing you with valuable information.

Analyzing Outside Factors. After you have analyzed yourself, you need to combine this information with the work needs of business and other external influences. Your goal in this process is to give realistic direction to your search for employment. Where is the kind of work you are seeking available? Are you willing to move? Is

- Combine internal and external factors.

such a move compatible with others in your life—your partner, your children, your parents? Does the location meet with your lifestyle needs? Although the availability of work may drive the answer to some of these questions, you should answer them as well as you can on the basis of what you know now and then conduct your job search accordingly. Finding just the right job should be one of the most important goals in your life.

Finding Your Employer

- Search for potential employers by using these sources:

You can use a number of sources in your search for an employer with whom you will begin or continue your career. Your choice of sources will probably be influenced by the stage of your career.

- (1) your school's career center,

Career Centers. If you are just beginning your career, one good possibility is the career center at your school. Most large schools have career centers, and these attract employers who are looking for suitable applicants. Many centers offer excellent job-search counseling and maintain databases on registrants containing school records, résumés, and recommendations for review by prospective employers. Most have directories listing the major companies with contact names and addresses. And most provide interviewing opportunities. Campus career centers often hold career fairs. They are an excellent place to find employers who are looking for new graduates as well as to gather information about the kinds of jobs different companies offer. By attending them early, you often find out about internships and summer jobs as well as gather ideas for selecting courses that might give you a competitive advantage when you do begin your career search.

- (2) your network of personal contacts,

Network of Personal Contacts. As has been noted, the personal contacts you make can be extremely helpful in your job search. In fact, according to some employment reports, personal contacts are the leading means of finding employees. Obviously, personal contacts are more likely to be a source of employment opportunities later in your career—when you may need to change jobs. Acquaintances, unlike close friends, may provide job leads outside those known to your friends.

- (3) classified advertisements,

Classified Advertisements. Help-wanted advertisements in newspapers and professional journals, both online or in print, provide good sources of employment opportunities for many kinds of work. Many are limited, however, in the opportunities they provide for new college graduates. Classified ads are good sources for experienced workers who are seeking to improve their positions, and they are especially good sources for people who are conducting a major search for high-level positions. However, they are only a partial list of jobs available.

- (4) online sources,

Online Sources. In addition to finding opportunities in classifieds, you also will find them in online databases. Monster.com, for example, lists jobs available throughout the country, with new opportunities posted regularly. Many companies even post job openings on the web, some with areas dedicated to new college graduates. If you are working now, you may want to check the company's intranet for positions there, too. And professional associations often maintain job databanks. Furthermore, you could query users of newsgroups or listservs about job openings they know exist. All of these online systems are sources for job opportunities. See the textbook website for links to many useful websites.

- (5) employment agencies,

Employment Agencies. Companies that specialize in finding jobs for employees can be useful. Of course, such companies charge for their services. The employer sometimes pays the charges, usually if qualified applicants are scarce. Executive search consultants (headhunters) are commonly used to place experienced people in executive positions. Employment agencies also can help job seekers gain temporary employment.

Since employers often search university web pages for prospective employees, posting a web page profile is a good idea. Not only can you add much more detail than on a print résumé, but you can also use colorful photos, videos, and sounds. You can show examples of real projects, documents, and presentations you have created as well as showcase your skills and creativity. A web page profile can range from a simple résumé as shown in Figure 9–6 to a sophisticated, interactive profile such as the Flash page you see here. In this section of the web profile, the author provides an overview of experience (Track Record). The reader can view the job candidate's résumé for more details and even link to examples of some work. Additionally, the author's clean design, easy navigation,

Site created by Will Weyer

and continuity in use of color help the reader find needed information easily and quickly. On the textbook website, you will find a link to this web page where you can explore its links.

Today, creating a simple web page profile is pretty easy, even for the beginner. In addition to full-featured website authoring tools such as FrontPage, Dreamweaver, and others, you already may have tools such as FrontPage Express or Netscape Composer. And websites such as GeoCities, Tripod, Homestead, Zy, and others offer inexpensive hosting as well as online web builder tools. You can link to some of these sites on your textbook website. Once you have posted your page profile, you will want to be sure to include its URL on your print résumé.

Temping can lead to permanent employment with a good fit. It allows the worker to get a feel for the company and the company to observe the worker before making a job commitment.

Personal Search Agents. In addition to searching online sources, you can request that job notices be sent to you. These tools, called personal search agents or job agents, will create a personal filter matched to a confidential profile you submit. They use this filter to search their websites and often many others to find jobs that might interest you, sending you email messages about the jobs. Starting with a very narrow search initially is wise. You can always modify your profile if you find you need more leads. If you learn of a job listing for a company visiting your campus or one with which you are already interviewing, you should ask about it. Not only will it show the employer you have done your homework, but it will also show that you have a sincere interest in working for the company.

● (6) personal search agents,

Web Page Profiles. To make yourself more visible to potential employers, you may want to consider posting your résumé to the web. Some employers actively search for new employees on university websites. Posting a web page profile is not difficult. Today's word processors let you save your documents in hypertext markup language (HTML), creating a basic web page for you. Additionally, easy-to-use web page building and generating tools are available on the web to help novices create personal web profiles. Once posted, it is a good idea to link your web page to your major department or to a business student club, allowing more potential employers to find your résumé. With a little extra effort, you can create a web page that greatly expands on the printed résumé. You will want to put your web page address on your printed résumé.

● (7) web page profiles,

● (8) prospecting techniques.

Prospecting. Some job seekers approach prospective employers directly, either by personal visit, mail, or email. Personal visits are effective if the company has an employment office or if a personal contact can set up a visit. Mail contacts typically include a résumé and a cover letter. An email contact can include a variety of documents and be sent in various forms. The construction of these messages is covered later in the chapter.

PREPARING THE APPLICATION DOCUMENTS

INTRODUCTORY SITUATION

Résumés and Applications

In your role as Jason Andrews, you consider yourself well qualified for a career in marketing. You know the field from both personal experience and classroom study. You grew up in a working-class neighborhood. From an early age, you worked at a variety of jobs, the most important of which was a job as a pollster. You were a restaurant host and a food server for two years. Your college studies were especially designed to prepare you for a career in marketing. You studied Olympia University's curriculum in marketing, and you carefully chose the electives that would give you the best possible preparation for this career. As evidenced by your grades, your preparation was good.

Now it is time to begin your career. Over the past weeks you followed good procedures in looking for employment (as reviewed in the preceding pages). Unfortunately, you had no success with the recruiters who visited your campus. Now you will send written applications to a select group of companies that you think might use a person with your skills. You have obtained the names of the executives you should reach at these companies. You will send them the application documents—résumé and cover message. The following discussion shows you how to prepare these documents for best results, both in hard copy and electronically.

● Pursue job openings by personal visit, online, mail, email, or fax.

After your search has uncovered a job possibility, you pursue it. How you pursue it depends on the circumstances of the case. When it is convenient and appropriate to do so, you make contact in person. It is convenient when the distance is not great, and it is appropriate when the employer has invited such a contact. When a personal visit is not convenient and appropriate, you apply online or by mail, email, or fax.

● You are likely to use résumés, cover messages, and reference sheets in your job search.

Whether or not you apply in person, you are likely to use some written material. If you apply in person, probably you will take a résumé with you to leave as a record of your qualifications. If you do not apply in person, of course, the application is completely in writing. Typically, it consists of a résumé, a cover message, and a reference sheet. At some point in your employment efforts, you are likely to use each of these documents.

● Prepare them as you would prepare a sales mailing.

Preparing these documents is much like preparing a sales document—both types involve selling. You are selling a product or services—your ability to do work. The résumé and reference sheet are much like the supporting material that accompanies the sales message. The cover message is much like the sales message. These similarities should become obvious to you as you read the following pages.

● Study the product (you) and the work.

As in preparing a sales campaign, you begin work on a written application for a job by studying what you are selling, and what you are selling is you. Then you study the work. Studying yourself involves taking personal inventory—the self-analysis discussed earlier in the chapter. You should begin by listing all the information about you that you believe an employer would want to know. Studying the work means learning as much as you can about the company—its plans, its policies, its operations. It also means learning the requirements of the work that the company wants done. Today, campus career centers and student organizations often invite employers to give information sessions. Reading about various careers in the Opportunity Outlook Handbook

<http://www.bls.gov/oco/> will tell you about the nature of the work as well as salary range and demand. Sometimes you can get this information through personal investigation. More often, you will have to develop it through logical thinking.

With this preliminary information assembled, you are ready to plan the application. First, you need to decide just what your application will consist of. Will it be just a cover message; a cover message and a résumé (also called a *vita, qualifications brief,* or *data sheet*), or a cover message, résumé, and reference sheet? The résumé is a summary of background facts in list form. You will probably select the combination of cover message and résumé, for this arrangement is likely to do the best job. Some people prefer to use the cover message alone. When you send a print cover message, it usually contains substantial detail, for it must do the whole sales job. When you send an electronic message, it can be adapted to the channel chosen. You will include the reference sheet when asked or when it supports your case.

- Next, decide on whether to send a message alone or with a résumé.

CONSTRUCTING THE RÉSUMÉ

After you have decided to use the résumé, you must decide whether to use a print or an electronic format. Although some smaller firms have begun demanding paper résumés to help them deal with a glut of electronic résumés, most companies are slowly refusing to take paper résumés.[1] The traditional print format is used in face-to-face interviews where you know it will be used exclusively there. If you have reason to believe the company will store your résumé electronically, you should use a scannable print format. Constructing these forms is similar, but they differ in some very important ways.

- Choose the print or electronic format.

The electronic format, on the other hand, is used when sending your application document by email or submitting or posting it via the web. Depending on the capabilities of the recipient's system and any forms an employer may specify, the documents can range from low-end ASCII text to midrange attached files, to high-end, full-featured HTML pages. In both the print and electronic formats, you set up the documents to present your credentials in the most favorable way.

After deciding what your form will be, you construct the parts. Perhaps you will choose to begin with the résumé, for it is a logical next step from the self-analysis discussed above. In fact, the résumé is a formal arrangement of that analysis.

- The résumé lists facts in some orderly way.

Traditional Print Résumé

You will want to include in the résumé all background information you think the reader should have about you. This means including all the information that a cover letter reviews plus supporting and incidental details. Designed for quick reading, the résumé lists facts that have been arranged for the best possible appearance. Rarely does it use sentences.

The arrangements of résumés differ widely, but the following procedures generally describe how most are written:

- Follow this plan in constructing a résumé.

- Logically arrange information on education (institutions, dates, degrees, major field); information on employment (dates, places, firms, duties, accomplishments); personal details (memberships, interests, achievements, and such—but not religion, race, and sex); and special information derived from other information (achievements, qualifications, capabilities). Add a reference sheet as needed.

- Construct a heading for the entire résumé and subheadings for the parts.

- Include other vital information such as objectives and contact information.

- Arrange the data for best eye appeal, making the résumé balance—not crowded and not strung out.

---

[1] Kris Maher, "Career Journal—The Jungle: How to Apply Online," *The Wall Street Journal,* January 29, 2002 <Online Proquest: ABI/Inform> (July 17, 2003).

Selecting the Background Facts. Your first step in preparing the résumé is to review the background facts you have assembled about yourself and then to select the facts that you think will help your reader evaluate you. You should include all the information covered in the accompanying cover message, for this is the most important information. In addition, you should include significant supporting details not covered in the accompanying cover message to avoid making that message too cluttered.

Arranging the Facts into Groups. After selecting the facts you want to include, you should sort them into logical groups. Many grouping arrangements are possible. The most conventional is the three-part grouping of *Education, Experience,* and *Skills* or *Personal Qualities.* Another possibility is a grouping by job functions or skills, such as *Selling, Communicating,* and *Managing.* You may be able to work out other logical groups.

You also can derive additional groups from the four conventional groups mentioned above. For example, you can have a group of *Achievements.* Such a group would consist of special accomplishments taken from your experience and education information. Another possibility is to have a group consisting of information highlighting your major *Qualifications.* Here you would include information drawn from the areas of experience, education, and skills or personal qualities. Illustrations of and instructions for constructing groups such as these appear later in the chapter.

Constructing the Headings. With your information organized, a logical next step is to construct the headings (captions) for the résumé. Probably you will begin by constructing the main head—the one that covers the entire document.

The most widely used form of main head is the topic, which consists only of words that describe what follows. Your name is usually the main heading. It should be presented clearly; usually this means using larger and bolder type so that the name stands out from the rest of the résumé. If an employer remembers only one fact from your résumé, that fact should be your name. It can be presented in either all caps or caps and lowercase:

Terrence P. Lenaghan

The next level of headings might be *Objective, Education, Experience,* and *Skills.* These headings can be placed to the left or centered above the text that follows.

A second and less widely used form is the talking head. This form uses words that tell the nature of what follows. For example, instead of the topic head, *Education,* a talking head might read *Specialized Training in Accounting* or *Computer Software Application Skills Acquired.* Obviously, these heads add to the information covered. They help the reader interpret the facts that follow.

As you can see from the illustrations in the chapter, the headings are distinguished from the other information in the résumé by the use of different sizes and styles of type. The main head should appear to be the most important of all (larger and heavier). Headings for the groups of information should appear to be more important than the information under them. Courtesy requires that you choose heading forms carefully, making sure they are neither so heavy and large that they offend nor so light and small that they show no distinctions. Your goal is to choose forms that properly show the relative importance of the information and are pleasing to the eye.

Including Contact Information. Your address, telephone number, and email address are the most likely means of contacting you. Thus, you should display them prominently somewhere in the résumé. You also may want to display your fax number or web page address. The most common location for displaying contact information is at the top, under the main head.

When it is likely that your address or telephone number will change before the job search ends, you would be wise to include two addresses and numbers: one current and the other permanent. If you are a student, for example, your address at the time of

---

- Begin by reviewing the background facts you have assembled. Select the facts that will help the reader evaluate you.

- Sort the facts by conventional groups, job functions, time, or a combination.

- Also, consider groups such as *Achievements* and *Qualifications.*

- Write headings for the résumé and its parts.

- Topic heads are most common.

- Talking heads interpret for the reader.

- Distinguish the headings from the other information by font selection.

- Display your contact information prominently.

- Anticipate changes in contact information.

applying for a job may change before the employer decides to contact you. Therefore, you may want to consider using the voice-mail on your cell phone or an Internet-based voice message service so that you can receive your messages wherever you go.

Including a Statement of Objective. Although not a category of background information, a statement of your objective is appropriate in the résumé. Headings such as *Career Objective, Job Objective,* or just *Objective* usually appear at the beginning.

● Consider a statement of your objective.

Not all authorities agree on the value of including the objective, however. Recommending that they be omitted from today's résumés, some authorities suggest that the résumé should concentrate instead on skills, experience, and credentials. They argue that the objective includes only obvious information that is clearly suggested by the remainder of the résumé. Moreover, they point out also that an objective limits the applicant to a single position and eliminates consideration for other jobs that may be available.

● However, note that some authorities oppose it.

Those favoring the use of a statement of objective reason that it helps the recruiter see quickly where the applicant might fit into the company. Since this argument appears to have greater support, at least for the moment, probably you should include the objective. When your career goal is unclear, you may use broad, general terms. And when you are considering a variety of employment possibilities, you may want to have different versions of your résumé for each possibility.

● Even so, probably you should use it.

Primarily, your statement of objective should describe the work you seek. When you know the exact job title of a position you want at the targeted company, use it.

● The statement should cover the job you seek and more, as in these examples.

> Objective: Marketing Research Intern

Another technique includes using words that convey a long-term interest in the targeted company, as in this example. However, using this form may limit you if the company does not have the career path you specify.

> Objective: Sales Representative for McGraw-Hill leading to sales management.

Also, wording the objective to point out your major strengths can be very effective. It also can help set up the organization of the résumé.

> Objective: To apply three years of successful ecommerce accounting experience at a small startup to a larger company with needs for careful attention to transaction management and analysis.

Presenting the Information. The information you present under each heading will depend on your good judgment. You should list all the facts that you think are relevant. You will want to include enough information to enable the reader to judge your ability to do the work you seek.

● List the facts under the headings.

Your coverage of work experience should identify completely the jobs you have held. Minimum coverage would include dates, places, firms, and responsibilities. If the work was part-time or volunteer, you should say so without demeaning the skills you developed on the job. In describing your duties, you should select words that highlight what you did, especially the parts of this experience that qualify you for the work you seek. Such a description will reflect your practice of good business ethics. For example, in describing a job as credit manager, you could write "Credit Analyst for Federated Stores, St. Petersburg, Florida, 2002–05." But it would be more meaningful to give this fuller description: "Credit Analyst for Federated Stores, St. Petersburg, Florida, 2002–05, supervising a staff of seven in processing credit applications and communications."

● When covering work experience, at a minimum include dates, places, firms, and responsibilities.

If your performance on a job shows your ability to do the work you seek, you should consider emphasizing your accomplishments in your job description. For example, an experienced marketer might write this description: "Marketing Specialist for Colgate-Palmolive, 2002–2005. Served in advisory role to company management. Developed marketing plan that increased profits 24 percent in two years." Or a successful advertising account executive might write this description: "Phillips-Ramsey

● When appropriate, show achievements.

Inc., San Diego, 2002–05. As account executive, developed successful campaigns for nine accounts and led development team in increasing agency volume 18 percent."

- Use action verbs to strengthen the appeal.

As you can see from the previous examples, the use of action verbs strengthens job descriptions. Verbs are the strongest of all words. If you choose them well, they will do much to sell your ability to do work. One strategy is to choose verbs that describe both the work you want to do as well as the work you have done, making it easier for the reader to see how you have transferable skills. A list of the more widely used action verbs appears in Figure 9–1.

- For education, include institutions, dates, degrees, and areas of study.

Because your education is likely to be your strongest selling point for your first job after college, you will probably cover it in some detail. (Education gets less and less emphasis in your applications as you gain experience.) At a minimum, your coverage of education should include institutions, dates, degrees, and areas of study. For some jobs, you may want to list specific courses, especially if you have little other information to present or if your coursework has uniquely prepared you for those jobs. If your grade-point average (GPA) is good, you may want to include it. Remember, for your résumé, you can compute your GPA in a way that works best for you as long as you label it accurately. For example, you may want to select just those courses in your major, labeling it Major GPA. Or if your last few years were your best ones, you may want to present your GPA for just that period. In any case, include GPA when it works favorably for you.

- For legal reasons, some personal information (on race, religion, sex) should probably not be listed.

What personal information to list is a matter for your best judgment. In fact, the trend appears to be toward eliminating such information. If you do include personal information, you should probably omit race, religion, sex, age, and marital status because current laws prohibit hiring based on them. But not everyone agrees on this matter. Some authorities believe that at least some of these items should be included. They argue that the law only prohibits employers from considering such information in hiring—that it does not prohibit applicants from presenting the information. They reason that if such information helps you, you should use it. The illustrations shown in this chapter support both viewpoints.

- Information on activities and interests tells about one's personal qualities.

Personal information that is generally appropriate includes all items that tell about your personal qualities. Information on your organization memberships, civic involvement, and social activities is evidence of experience and interest in working with people. Hobbies and athletic participation tell of your balance of interests. Such information can be quite useful to some employers, especially when personal qualities are important to the work involved.

- Consider listing references, but know that some authorities favor postponing using them.

Authorities disagree on whether to list references on the résumé. Some think that references should not be contacted until negotiations are further along. Others think that references should be listed because some employers want to check them early in the screening process. One recent study of human resource administrators in Fortune 500 organizations rated the importance of references on résumés of recent college graduates as the lowest of all major groupings—between not too important and somewhat important.[2] Clearly, both views have substantial support. You will have to make the choice based on your best knowledge of the situation.

- Good etiquette requires that you get permission.

When you do list someone as a reference, good business etiquette requires that you ask for permission first. Although you will use only those who can speak highly of you, sometimes asking for your reference's permission beforehand helps that person prepare better. And, of course, it saves you from unexpected embarrassment such as a reference not remembering you, being out of town, or, worse yet, not having anything to say.

- Consider using a separate sheet for references.

A commonly used tool is a separate reference sheet. When you use it, you close the résumé with a statement indicating references are available. Later, when the reader wants to check references, you give her or him this sheet. The type size and style of the main heading of this sheet should match that used in your résumé. It may say something like "References for [*your name*]." Below this heading is a listing of your

---

[2] Kevin L. Hutchinson and Diane S. Brefka, "Personnel Administrators' Preferences for Résumé Content: Ten Years After," *Business Communication Quarterly* (June 1997): 71–72.

FIGURE 9–1   A List of Action Verbs That Add Strength to Your Résumé

The underlined words are especially good for pointing out **accomplishments.**

Clerical/Detail Skills
approved
arranged
catalogued
checked
classified
collected
compiled
confirmed
copied
detected
dissected
executed
generated
implemented
inspected
monitored
operated
organized
prepared
processed
purchased
recorded
retrieved
scheduled
screened
specified
systematized
tabulated
validated

Communication Skills
addressed
arbitrated
arranged
articulated
authored
collaborated
composed
convinced
corresponded
developed
directed
drafted
edited
enlisted
formulated

influenced
interpreted
lectured
mediated
moderated
negotiated
persuaded
presented
promoted
publicized
reconciled
recruited
reported
spoke
translated
wrote

Creative Skills
acted
built
conceived
conceptualized
created
customized
designed
developed
devised
directed
established
fabricated
fashioned
founded
illustrated
initiated
instituted
integrated
introduced
invented
originated
performed
planned
revitalized
shaped

Financial Skills
administered
allocated
analyzed
appraised

audited
balanced
budgeted
calculated
computed
consolidated
converted
developed
dispensed (financial)
forecast
managed
marketed
planned
projected
researched

Helping Skills
advised
assessed
assisted
challenged
clarified
coached
counseled
demonstrated
diagnosed
educated
expedited
facilitated
guided
motivated
referred
rehabilitated
represented

Management Skills
accomplished
addressed
administered
allocated
analyzed
anticipated
approved
assigned
attained
chaired
completed

conserved
consolidated
contracted
controlled
coordinated
critiqued
decided
defined
delegated
delivered
developed
directed
evaluated
executed
guided
hired
implemented
improved
increased
initiated
led
organized
oversaw
planned
prioritized
produced
recommended
reviewed
scheduled
strengthened
supervised

Research Skills
analyzed
clarified
collected
compiled
conducted
critiqued
detected
diagnosed
discovered
evaluated
examined
experimented
extracted
gathered

identified
inspected
interpreted
interviewed
investigated
organized
reviewed
sampled
summarized
surveyed
systematized

Teamwork/ Interpersonal Skills
clarified
collaborated
coordinated
facilitated
harmonized
negotiated
networked

Technical Skills
accessed
assembled
built
calculated
charted
computed
configured
designed
devised
diagnosed
engineered
fabricated
installed
maintained
operated
overhauled
performed troubleshooting
programmed
remodeled
repaired
retrieved
solved
upgraded

Training/ Supervision Skills
adapted
advised
assembled
clarified
coached
communicated
conducted
coordinated
demonstrated
demystified
developed
enabled
encouraged
evaluated
explained
facilitated
guided
informed
instructed
lectured
persuaded
set goals
stimulated
trained
tutored

More Accomplishment Verbs
achieved
acquired
earned
eliminated (waste)
expanded
founded
improved
pioneered
reduced (losses)
resolved (problems)
restored
revamped
solved
spearheaded
transformed

SOURCE: Revised and updated from *The Damn Good Résumé Guide* by Yana Parker (Berkeley, California: Ten Speed Press, 2002).

references, beginning with the strongest one. In addition to solving the reference dilemma, use of this separate reference sheet allows you to change both the references and their order for each job. A sample reference sheet is shown in the example in Figure 9–4.

Sometimes you may have good reason not to list references, as when you are employed and want to keep the job search secret. If you choose not to list them, you should explain their absence. You can do this in the accompanying cover message; or you can do it on the résumé by following the heading "References" with an explanation, such as "Will be furnished on request."

- Select references that cover your background.

How many and what kinds of references to include will depend on your background. If you have an employment record, you should include one for every major job you have held—at least for recent years. You should include references related to the work you seek. If you base your application heavily on your education or your personal qualities, or both, you should include references who can vouch for these areas: professors, clergy, community leaders, and the like. Your goal is to list those people who can verify the points on which your appeal for the job is based. At a minimum, you should list three references. Five is a good maximum.

- Include accurate mailing and email addresses and job titles.

Your list of references should include accurate mailing addresses, with appropriate job titles. Complete addresses are important because the reader is likely to contact the references. Also useful are telephone and fax numbers as well as email addresses. Job titles (officer, manager, president, supervisor) are helpful because they show what the references are able to tell about you. It is appropriate to include forms of address: Mr., Mrs., Ms., Dr., and so on.

- Choose an organizational strategy that best presents your case.

Organizing for Strength. After you have identified the information you want to include on your résumé, you will want to organize or group items to present yourself in the best possible light. Three strategies for organizing this information are the *reverse chronological approach,* the *functional* or *skills approach,* and the *accomplishments/ achievements* or *highlights approach.*

- The reverse chronological approach is orderly.

The *reverse chronological* organizational layout (Figures 9–5 and 9–6) presents your education and work experience from the most recent to oldest. It emphasizes the order and time frame in which you have participated in these activities. It is particularly good for those who have progressed in an orderly and timely fashion through school and work.

- The functional or skills approach emphasizes relevant skills.

A *functional* or *skills* layout (Figure 9–7) organizes around three to five areas particularly important to the job you want. Rather than forcing an employer to determine that you developed one skill on one job and another skill on another job, this organizational plan does that for the reader. It is particularly good for those who have had many jobs, for those who have taken nontraditional career paths, and for those who are changing fields. Creating this kind of résumé takes much work and careful analysis of both jobs and skills to show the reader that you are a good match for the position.

- The accomplishments/ achievements approach shows you can perform.

An *accomplishments/achievements* layout (Figure 9–8) presents a picture of you as a competent worker. It puts hard numbers and precise facts behind skills and traits you have. Refer back to Figure 9–1 for some good verb choices to use in describing accomplishments. Here is an example illustrating this arrangement in describing work done at a particular company:

> Successfully managed the Austin store for two years in a period of low unemployment with these results:
>
> - Reduced employee turnover 55 percent.
> - Increased profits 37 percent.
> - Grew sales volume 12 percent.

- The highlights or summary approach shows you are a good fit for the position.

Information covered under a *Highlights* or *Summary* heading may include key points from the three conventional information groups: education, experience, and personal qualities. Typically, this layout emphasizes the applicant's most impressive background facts that pertain to the work sought, as in this example:

- **Experienced:** three years of practical work as programmer/analyst in designing and developing financial databases for the banking industry.
- **Highly trained:** B.S. degree with honors in management information systems.
- **Self-motivated:** proven record of successful completion of three online courses.

Although such items may overlap others in the résumé, using them in a separate group emphasizes strengths. See an example of an accomplishments layout in Figure 9–8.

Writing Impersonally and Consistently.

Because the résumé is a listing of information, you should write without personal pronouns (no *I*'s, *we*'s, *you*'s). You should also write all equal-level headings and the parts under each heading in the same grammatical form. For example, if one major heading in the résumé is a noun phrase, all the other major headings should be noun phrases. The following four headings illustrate the point. All but the third (an adjective form) are noun phrases. The error can be corrected by making the third a noun phrase, as in the examples to the right:

- List the information without use of personal pronouns (I, we, you).
- Use the same grammatical form for all equal-level headings and for the parts listed under each heading.

Not Parallel	**Parallel**
Specialized study	Specialized study
Experience in promotion work	Experience in promotion work
Personal and physical	Personal and physical qualities
Qualified references	Qualified references

The following items illustrate grammatical inconsistency in the parts of a group:

Have good health

Active in sports

Ambitious

Inspection of these items shows that they do not fit the same understood words. The understood word for the first item is *I* and for the second and third, the understood words are *I am*. Any changes that make all three items fit the same understood words would correct the error.

Making the Form Attractive.

The attractiveness of your résumé will say as much about you as the words. The appearance of the information that the reader sees plays a part in forming his or her judgment. While using a template is one solution, it will make you look like many other applicants. A layout designed with your reader and your unique data in mind will probably do a better job for you. Not only will your résumé have a distinctive appearance, but the design should sell you more effectively than one where you must fit your data to the design. A sloppy, poorly designed presentation, on the other hand, may even ruin your chances of getting the job. Thus, you have no choice but to give your résumé and your cover message an attractive physical arrangement.

- Make the résumé attractive.

Designing the résumé for eye appeal is no routine matter. There is no one best arrangement, but a good procedure is to approach the task as a graphic designer would. Your objective is to design an arrangement of type and space that appears good to the eye. You would do well to use the following general plan for arranging the résumé.

- Design it as a graphic designer would. Use balance and space for eye appeal.

Margins look better if at least an inch of space is left at the top of the page and on the left and right sides of the page and if at least 1½ inches of space are left at the bottom of the page. Your listing of items by rows (columns) appears best if the items are short and if they can be set up in two uncrowded rows, one on the left side of the page and one on the right side. Longer items of information are more appropriately set up in lines extending across the page. In any event, you would do well to avoid long and narrow columns of data with large sections of wasted space on either side. Arrangements that give a heavy crowded effect also offend the eye. Extra spacing between subdivisions and indented patterns for subparts are especially pleasing to the eye.

- Here are some suggestions on form.

While layout is important in showing your ability to organize and good spacing increases readability, other design considerations such as font and paper selection affect attractiveness almost as much. Commercial designers say that type size for headings should be at least 14 points and for body text, 10 to 12 points. They also recommend using fewer than four font styles on a page. Some word processing programs have a "shrink to fit" feature that allows the user to fit information on one page. It will automatically adjust font sizes to fit the page. Be sure the resulting type size is both appropriate and readable.

Another factor affecting the appearance of your application documents is the paper you select. The paper should be appropriate for the job you seek. In business, erring on the conservative side is usually better; you do not want to be eliminated from consideration simply because the reader did not like the quality or color of the paper. The most traditional choice is white, 100 percent cotton, 20- to 24-lb. paper. Of course, reasonable variations can be appropriate.

Contrasting Bad and Good Examples. The résumés in Figures 9–2 and 9–3 are at opposing ends of the quality scale. The first one, scant in coverage and poorly arranged, does little to help the applicant. Clearly the second one is more complete and better arranged.

Weakness in Incompleteness and Bad Arrangements. Shortcomings in the first example (Figure 9–2) are obvious. First, the form is not pleasing to the eye. The weight of the type is heavy on the left side of the page. Failure to indent wrapped lines makes reading difficult.

This résumé also contains numerous errors in wording. Information headings are not parallel in grammatical form. All are in topic form except the first one. The items listed under *Personal* are not parallel either. Throughout, the résumé coverage is scant, leaving out many of the details needed to present the best impression of the applicant. Under *Experience,* little is said about specific tasks and skills in each job; and under *Education,* high school work is listed needlessly. The references are incomplete, omitting street addresses and job titles.

Strength through Good Arrangement and Completeness. The next résumé (Figure 9–3) appears better at first glance, and it gets even better as you read it. It is attractively arranged. The information is neither crowded nor strung out. The balance is good. Its content is also superior to that of the other example. Additional words show the quality of Mr. Andrews's work experience and education, and they emphasize points that make him suited for the work he seeks. This résumé excludes trivial personal information and has only the facts that tell something about Andrews's personal qualities. Complete mailing addresses permit the reader to contact the references easily. Job titles tell how each is qualified to evaluate the subject.

Scannable Print Résumé

Although paper résumés are not obsolete, a recent addition to the job-search process is the scannable résumé. This résumé bridges the print-to-digital gap. It is simply one that can be scanned into a database and retrieved when a position is being filled. Since the objective is getting your résumé reviewed in order to be interviewed, you should use the following strategies to improve your chances of having it retrieved by the computer.

Include Keywords. One strategy, using keywords, is often recommended for use with electronic scanning software. These keywords are usually nouns or concrete words that describe skills and accomplishments precisely. Instead of listing a course in comparative programming, you would list the precise languages compared, such as VB.net, C#, and Java. Instead of saying you would like a job in information systems, you would name specific job titles such as systems analyst, network specialist, or application specialist. Using industry-specific terminology is highly recommended.

FIGURE 9–2

Incompleteness and Bad Arrangement in a Traditional Print Résumé. This résumé presents Jason Andrews ineffectively (see "Introductory Situation to Résumés and Applications"). It is scant and poorly arranged.

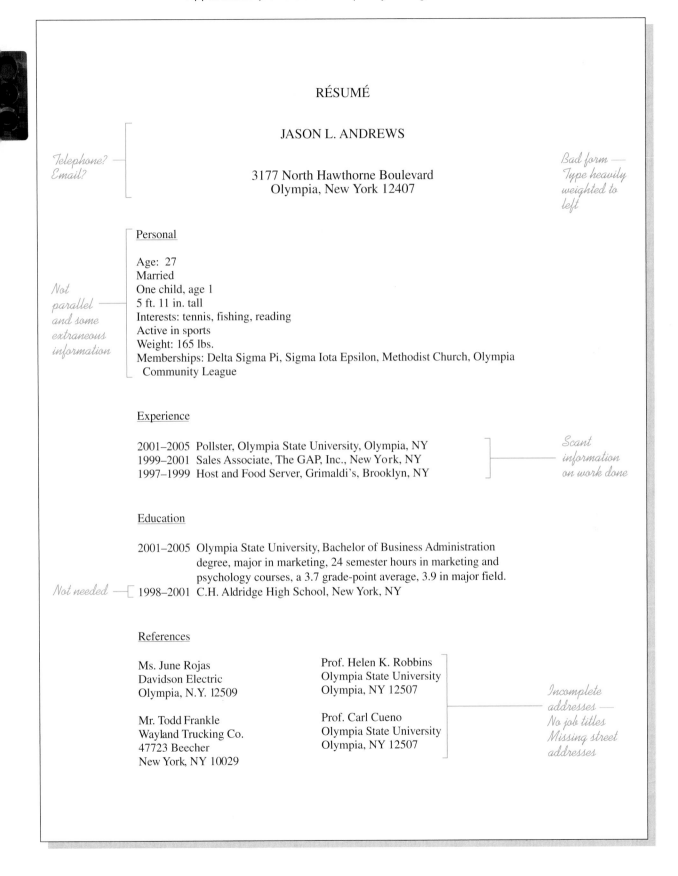

RÉSUMÉ

JASON L. ANDREWS

Telephone?
Email?

3177 North Hawthorne Boulevard
Olympia, New York 12407

Bad form —
Type heavily
weighted to
left

Personal

Not
parallel
and some
extraneous
information

Age: 27
Married
One child, age 1
5 ft. 11 in. tall
Interests: tennis, fishing, reading
Active in sports
Weight: 165 lbs.
Memberships: Delta Sigma Pi, Sigma Iota Epsilon, Methodist Church, Olympia
  Community League

Experience

2001–2005 Pollster, Olympia State University, Olympia, NY
1999–2001 Sales Associate, The GAP, Inc., New York, NY
1997–1999 Host and Food Server, Grimaldi's, Brooklyn, NY

Scant
information
on work done

Education

2001–2005 Olympia State University, Bachelor of Business Administration
           degree, major in marketing, 24 semester hours in marketing and
           psychology courses, a 3.7 grade-point average, 3.9 in major field.
Not needed — 1998–2001 C.H. Aldridge High School, New York, NY

References

Ms. June Rojas
Davidson Electric
Olympia, N.Y. 12509

Mr. Todd Frankle
Wayland Trucking Co.
47723 Beecher
New York, NY 10029

Prof. Helen K. Robbins
Olympia State University
Olympia, NY 12507

Prof. Carl Cueno
Olympia State University
Olympia, NY 12507

Incomplete
addresses —
No job titles
Missing street
addresses

FIGURE 9–3

Thoroughness and Good Arrangement in a Traditional Print Résumé. This complete and reverse chronologically organized résumé presents Jason Andrews's case effectively (see "Introductory Situation to Résumés and Applications").

Jason L. Andrews

3177 North Hawthorne Boulevard
Olympia, NY 12407-3278
914.967.3117 (Voice/Message)
jandrews@hotmail.com

Presents contact data clearly

Objective

A position in marketing that will lead to work as a marketing manager for an ebusiness.

Education

Bachelor of Business Administration	Major: Marketing
Olympia State University—May 2002	Minor: Psychology
GPA: 3.7/4.0	Dean's List

Emphasizes education by position

Related Coursework:

- Strategic Marketing
- Marketing Research
- Marketing Communications & Promotion
- Global Marketing

- Interpersonal Communication
- Statistical Analysis
- Consumer and Buyer Behavior
- Social Psychology

Highlights most relevant courses and subjects

- Research Projects: Cultural Influence on Purchasing, Customer Brand Preference, and Motivating Subordinates with Effective Performance Appraisals.

Experience

Pollster, Olympia State University, Olympia, NY, 2001–present

Sales Associate, The Gap, Inc., New York, NY (named top store sales associate four of eight quarters), 1999–2001

Host and Food Server, Grimaldi's, Brooklyn, NY (part-time), 1997–1999

Emphasizes positions; de-emphasizes dates

Personal Qualities

Interests: tennis, fishing, reading, and jogging.
Memberships: Delta Sigma Pi (professional); Sigma Iota Epsilon (honorary), served as treasurer and president; Board of Stewards for church; League of Olympia, served as registration leader.

Includes only most relevant information

References

Personal and professional references gladly furnished upon request.

Tells reader someone will speak for him

FIGURE 9–4

Thoroughness and Good Arrangement for a Reference Sheet. This reference sheet presents Jason Andrews's references completely.

Jason L. Andrews

3177 North Hawthorne Boulevard
Olympia, NY 12407-3278
914.967.3117 (Voice/ Message)
jandrews@hotmail.com

*Heading
format
matches
resume*

Ms. June Rojas, Polling Supervisor
Olympia State University
7114 East 71st Street
Olympia, NY 12509-4572
Telephone: 518.342.1171
Fax: 518.342.1200
Email: June.Rojas@osu.edu

Mr. Todd E. Frankle, Store Manager
The Gap, Inc.
Lincoln Square
New York, NY 10023-0007
Telephone: 212.466.9101
Fax: 212.468.9100
Email: tfrankle@gap.com

Professor Helen K. Robbins
Department of Marketing
Olympia State University
Olympia, NY 12507-0182
Telephone: 518.392.6673
Fax: 518.392.3675
Email: Helen.Robbins@osu.edu

Professor Carol A. Cueno
Department of Psychology
Olympia State University
Olympia, NY 12507-0234
Telephone: 518.392.0723
Fax: 518.392.7542
Email: Carol.Cueno@osu.edu

*Complete
information
and
balanced
arrangement*

Robert J. Montgomery

Emphasizes name

Woodland Village Apartments
2221 Bush River Road, #48
Columbia, SC 29210
Home 803.252.4946
robert_j_montgomery@hotmail.com

Includes complete contact information

OBJECTIVE
An internship position with a consulting firm.

Uses concise statement

SUMMARY OF SKILLS

Highlights strengths

Extensive experience in team-oriented projects and presentations. Capable of performing in-depth business research and analysis and preparing written deliverables. Proven skills in analytical thinking, problem solving, and conflict resolution. Able to pick up new concepts quickly and self-motivated to learn.

EDUCATION
Bachelor of Science in **Business Administration** with an emphasis in **Management Science, May 2005.**
University of South Carolina, Columbia
Major GPA: 3.7/4.0 scale; Overall GPA: 3.27/4.0 scale

RELATED COURSEWORK

Expands and emphasizes through detail

- **Computer Information Systems for Business:** Acquired a strong understanding of software applications such as the Microsoft Office Suite. Prepared numerous projects using Access, Excel, PowerPoint, and Word.
- **Business Information Systems:** Closely examined the fundamental concepts of operating systems, software applications, and programming languages. Created several programs using VB.net, C#, and SQL.
- **Architecture of Computer Hardware and Software Systems:** Established a sound foundation in computer organization, components, arithmetic, I/O processing, storage devices, and networking. Researched and prepared a presentation on multimedia processing.

COMPUTER SKILLS
- **Operating Systems:** Windows 98/2000/XP
- **Software Applications:** Access, Excel, PowerPoint, Visio, Word, Outlook, OneNote, InfoPath, Project, Explorer, Acrobat, SPSS, RefViz, Photoshop, and Internet Browsers.
- **Web-based Applications:** Survey Monkey, RefWorks
- **Programming Languages:** C#, HTML, and VB.net

WORK EXPERIENCE
Student Assistant
University of South Carolina   Columbia, SC   2003–Present
Prepared and processed student data into the school's payroll system. Created a database to track student employment eligibility. Verified invoices and assisted in the distribution of checks.

Emphasizes position held rather than place or date

Porter
United Parcel Services   Columbia, SC   2001–2003
Inspected warehouse to ensure accurate package inventory. Operated forklift and administered motor and conveyor belt inspections for proper functioning and safety compliance.

Uses descriptive action verbs

Sales Associate
Walgreen Drugs   Charleston, SC   1999–2000
Supervised inventory levels, resolved customer complaints, and operated cash registers. Prioritized and managed several co-existing critical issues.

REFERENCES
Available upon request.

Provides closure and says someone will speak for him

FIGURE 9–6

Electronic HTML Résumé Organized in Reverse Chronological Format and Sent as Rich Email. Presents the applicant's education and experience and highlights career-related experience. Links help provide detailed support. See this résumé on the textbook web page and explore its links.

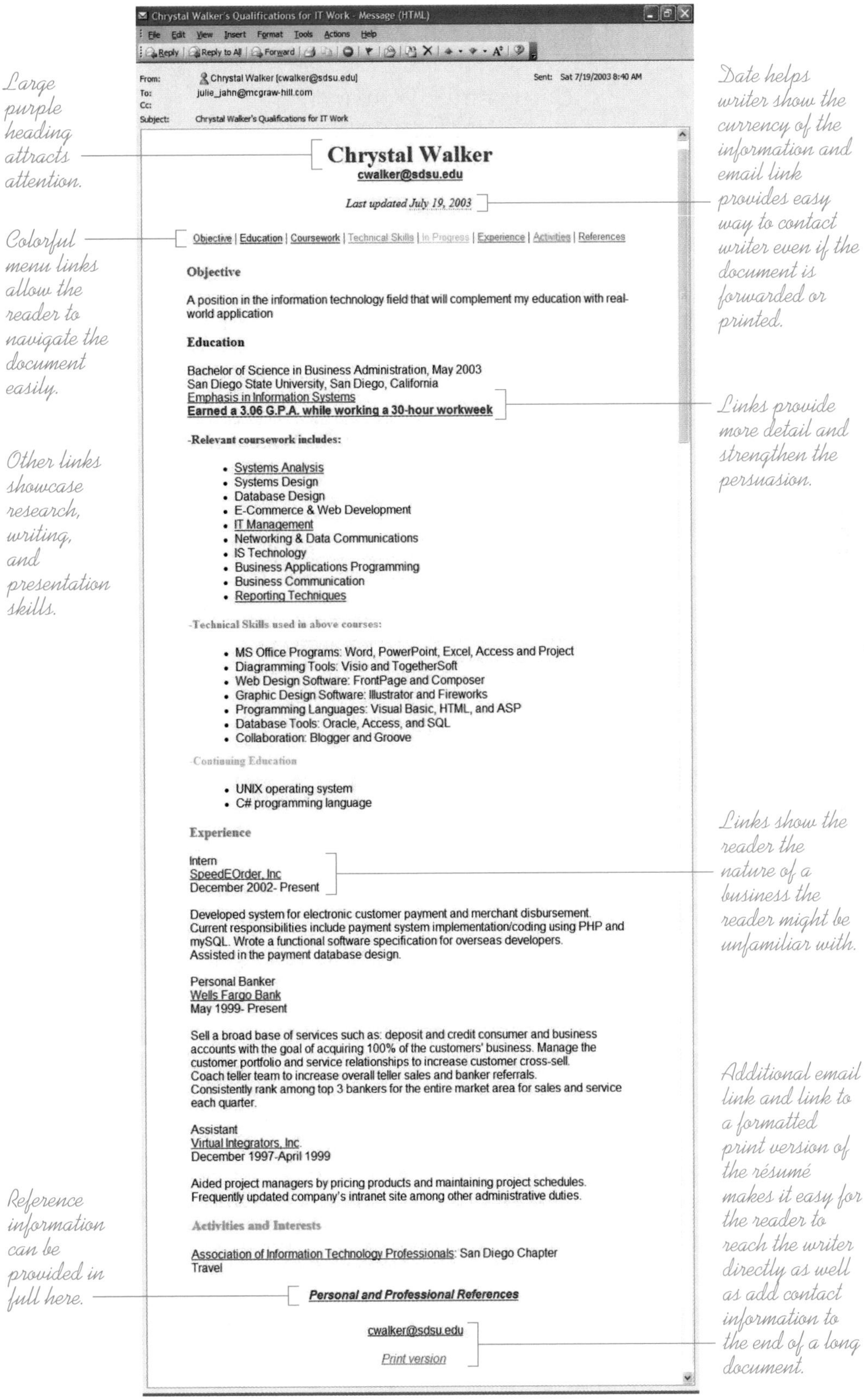

Large purple heading attracts attention.

Colorful menu links allow the reader to navigate the document easily.

Other links showcase research, writing, and presentation skills.

Reference information can be provided in full here.

Date helps writer show the currency of the information and email link provides easy way to contact writer even if the document is forwarded or printed.

Links provide more detail and strengthen the persuasion.

Links show the reader the nature of a business the reader might be unfamiliar with.

Additional email link and link to a formatted print version of the résumé makes it easy for the reader to reach the writer directly as well as add contact information to the end of a long document.

Chrystal Walker's Qualifications for IT Work - Message (HTML)

File Edit View Insert Format Tools Actions Help

Reply | Reply to All | Forward

From: Chrystal Walker [cwalker@sdsu.edu] Sent: Sat 7/19/2003 8:40 AM
To: julie_jahn@mcgraw-hill.com
Cc:
Subject: Chrystal Walker's Qualifications for IT Work

Chrystal Walker
cwalker@sdsu.edu

Last updated July 19, 2003

Objective | Education | Coursework | Technical Skills | In Progress | Experience | Activities | References

Objective

A position in the information technology field that will complement my education with real-world application

Education

Bachelor of Science in Business Administration, May 2003
San Diego State University, San Diego, California
Emphasis in Information Systems
Earned a 3.06 G.P.A. while working a 30-hour workweek

-Relevant coursework includes:

- Systems Analysis
- Systems Design
- Database Design
- E-Commerce & Web Development
- IT Management
- Networking & Data Communications
- IS Technology
- Business Applications Programming
- Business Communication
- Reporting Techniques

-Technical Skills used in above courses:

- MS Office Programs: Word, PowerPoint, Excel, Access and Project
- Diagramming Tools: Visio and TogetherSoft
- Web Design Software: FrontPage and Composer
- Graphic Design Software: Illustrator and Fireworks
- Programming Languages: Visual Basic, HTML, and ASP
- Database Tools: Oracle, Access, and SQL
- Collaboration: Blogger and Groove

-Continuing Education

- UNIX operating system
- C# programming language

Experience

Intern
SpeedEOrder, Inc
December 2002- Present

Developed system for electronic customer payment and merchant disbursement. Current responsibilities include payment system implementation/coding using PHP and mySQL. Wrote a functional software specification for overseas developers. Assisted in the payment database design.

Personal Banker
Wells Fargo Bank
May 1999- Present

Sell a broad base of services such as: deposit and credit consumer and business accounts with the goal of acquiring 100% of the customers' business. Manage the customer portfolio and service relationships to increase customer cross-sell. Coach teller team to increase overall teller sales and banker referrals. Consistently rank among top 3 bankers for the entire market area for sales and service each quarter.

Assistant
Virtual Integrators, Inc.
December 1997-April 1999

Aided project managers by pricing products and maintaining project schedules. Frequently updated company's intranet site among other administrative duties.

Activities and Interests

Association of Information Technology Professionals: San Diego Chapter
Travel

Personal and Professional References

cwalker@sdsu.edu

Print version

Carolynn W. Workman
12271 69th Terrace North
Seminole, FL 33772
727.399.2569 (Voice/Message)
cworkman@msn.com

Emphasizes tight organization through use of horizontal ruled lines

| **Objective** | An accounting position with a CPA firm |

Education

Emphasizes degree and GPA through placement

Bachelor of Science: University of South Florida, December 2004
Major: Business Administration
Emphasis: Accounting
GPA: 3.42 with Honors

Uses internal bullets to increase readability

Accounting-Related Course Work:
Financial Accounting ❖ Cost Accounting and Control ❖ Accounting Information Systems ❖ Auditing ❖ Concepts of Federal Income Taxation ❖ Financial Policy ❖ Communications for Business and Professions

Activities:
Vice-President of Finance, Beta Alpha Psi
Editor, Student Newsletter for Beta Alpha Psi
Member, Golden Key National Honors Society

Emphasizes key skills relevant to objective

Skills
Computer

▶ Assisted in installation of small business computerized accounting system using QuickBooks Pro.
▶ Prepared tax returns for individuals in the VITA program using specialty tax software.
▶ Experienced power user of Excel, designing data input forms, analyzing and interpreting results of most functions, generating graphs, and creating and using macros.

Accounting

▶ Experienced with financial statements and general ledger.
▶ Reconciled accounts for center serving over 1300 clients.
▶ Experienced in preparing income, gift, and estate tax returns.
▶ Processed expense reports for twenty professional staff.
▶ Experienced in using Great Plains and Solomon IV.

Varies use of action verbs

Business Communication

▶ Conducted client interviews and researched tax issues.
▶ Communicated both in written and verbal form with clients.
▶ Delivered several individual and team presentations on business cases, projects, and reports to business students.

Work History
Administrative Assistant

Office of Student Disability Services, University of South Florida
Tampa, FL. Spring 2004.

Tax Assistant

Rosemary Lenaghan, Certified Public Accountant. Seminole, FL 2003.

References available upon request

Kimberly M. VanLerBerghe

2411 27th Street
Moline, IL 61265
309.764.0017 (Mobile)
kmv@yahoo.com

JOB TARGET TRAINER/TRANSLATOR for a large, worldwide industrial company

HIGHLIGHTS OF QUALIFICATIONS

Emphasizes those qualifications most relevant to position sought

- Experienced in creating and delivering multimedia PowerPoint presentations.
- Enthusiastic team member/leader whose participation brings out the best in others.
- Excellent analytical ability.
- Skilled in gathering data and interpreting it.
- Bilingual—English/Spanish.

EDUCATION

Presents the most important items here

DEGREE	B.S. English—June 2005—Western Illinois University	
EMPHASIS	Education	MAJOR GPA—3.87/4.00
HONORS	Dean's List, four semesters Chevron Scholarship, Fall 2004	
MEMBER	Mortar Board, Women's Golf Team	

EMPLOYMENT

Identifies most significant places of work and de-emphasizes less important work

DEERE & COMPANY, INC.   CONGRESSMAN J. DENNIS HASTERT
Student Intern, Summer 2004   Volunteer in Computer Services, Fall 2003

Several years' experience in the restaurant business including supervisory positions.

ACCOMPLISHMENTS

Presents only selected accomplishments from various work and volunteer experience that relate to position sought

- ▸ Trained executives to create effective cross-cultural presentations
- ▸ Developed online training program for executive use of WebEx
- ▸ Designed and developed a database to keep track of financial donations
- ▸ Coded new screens and reports; debugged and revised screen forms for easier data entry
- ▸ Provided computer support to virtual volunteers on election committee

REFERENCES

Will gladly furnish personal and professional references on request.

One way to identify the keywords in your field is by reading ads, listening to recruiters, and listening to your professors. Start building a list of words you find used repeatedly. From this list, choose those words most appropriate for the kind of work you want to do. Amplify your use of abbreviations, acronyms, and jargon appropriate to the work you want to do. In the early days of preparing scannable résumés, some experts recommended using a separate keyword section at the beginning of the résumé, loading it with all the relevant terms. Reportedly this technique improved the odds of the résumé being retrieved. If this helps you ensure that your résumé includes all the appropriate terms, you might still use it. However, today most résumé writers are well aware of the importance of using keywords and consciously work to integrate them into their résumés. This is especially true of those who use the hybrid résumés to cover both the face-to-face and scanning purposes in one document.

● Use precise nouns on the scannable résumé.

● Use both precise nouns and action verbs in the hybrid résumé.

Choose Words Carefully. Unlike the traditional résumé, the scannable résumé is strengthened not by the use of action verbs but rather by the use of nouns. Informal studies have shown that those retrieving résumés from such databases tend to use precise nouns.

For the hybrid résumé, one you use in both face-to-face and scanning situations, you can combine the use of precise nouns with strong action verbs. The nouns will help ensure that the résumé gets pulled from the database, and the verbs help the face-to-face recruiter see the link to the kind of work you want to do.

Present the Information. Since you want your résumé to be read accurately, you will use a font most scanners can read without problem. Some of these fonts include Helvetica, Arial, Garamond, and Times Roman. Most scanners can easily handle fonts between 10 and 14 points. Although many handle bold, when in doubt use all caps for emphasis rather than bold. Also, because italics often confuse scanners, avoid them. Underlining is best left out as well. It creates trouble with descending letters such as *g* or *y* when the line cuts through the letter. In fact, you should use all lines sparingly. Also, avoid graphics and shading wherever possible; they just confuse the software. Use white paper to maximize the contrast, and always print in the portrait mode. The Kathryn Donnelly résumé in Figure 9–9 is a scannable résumé employing these guidelines.

Today companies accept résumés by mail, fax, and email. Be sure to choose the channel that serves you best. If a company asks for résumés by fax and email, it may prefer to capture them electronically. Others still prefer to see an applicant's ability to organize and lay out a printed page. Some employers give the option to the sender. Obviously, when speed gives you a competitive advantage, you'll choose the fax or email options. However, you do lose some control over the quality of the document. If you elect to print and send a scannable résumé, it is best not to fold it. Just mail it in a 9 × 12 envelope. For a little extra cost, you will help ensure that your résumé gets scanned accurately rather than wondering if your keywords were on a fold that a scanner might have had difficulty reading.

Electronic Résumé

Transmitting an electronic résumé involves making decisions about the receiver's preferences and capabilities for receiving them as well as leveraging the technology to present you in the best possible light. These documents range from low-end plain text files, to formatted word processor files, to full-blown multimedia documents and web pages.

While much of the content of an electronic résumé is similar to that of the print résumé, two important changes should be made. The first is to delete all contact information except your email address. Not only can you lose control over the distribution of the document since electronic files can be passed along easily and quickly, but your information could be added to databases and sold. Many experts recommend setting up a web-based email account that you use solely for your job search. Second, you

FIGURE 9–9 Scannable Print Résumé Can Be Used Both for Traditional and Scannable Purposes. Uses precise nouns and strong action verbs. Arranged for pleasant eye appeal and formatted for accurate scanning.

Avoids italics and underlines yet is pleasantly arranged for a human reader

Kathryn Suzanne Donnelly
2252 Felspar Street #1, San Diego, CA 92109
Phone: 858.775.8772 Email: katiedonnelly@hotmail.com

Objective

A position in marketing in a consumer-driven organization that will lead to work as a marketing manager. *Uses boldface and whitespace for emphasis*

Uses standard, widely used font to improve scanning accuracy

Education

Master of Business Administration, San Diego State University		May 2004
Emphasis: Marketing and Finance		GPA 3.88/4.0
Bachelor of Arts, University of California, Los Angeles		June 2000
Major: Communication Studies—Graduated Cum Laude		GPA 3.72/4.0
Language Immersion Program, Angers, France		June 1999
Study: French language, culture and history		GPA 4.0/4.0

Related Coursework

- Strategic Marketing
- Global Marketing
- Consumer and Buyer Behavior
- Financial Management
- Economics
- Management/Operations Mgmt.
- Social Psychology
- Interpersonal Communication
- Research Projects: New Product Development and Promotion, Economic Analysis of Fortune 500 Companies, Social Analysis and Implications of Theories of Behavioral Motivation.
- Computer Skills: Microsoft Word, Decision Systems, Excel, and PowerPoint

Integrates precise nouns and industry-specific jargon as keywords

Experience

Avoids graphics and extra lines

Sales Representative, George's at the Cove, San Diego   November 2001–Present
Recognized as top representative for the number one restaurant in San Diego; sold over $200,000 in goods in 2002; conducted marketing and suggestive up-selling to consumers; won two sales awards for product selling contests.

Operations Manager, Life a la Carte, San Diego   August 2000–October 2001
Coordinated production and post-production for the television magazine; assisted in development and execution of marketing plan for the production and sale of the pilot television show; conducted Q&A sessions with television executives; facilitated public relations; organized team and managed event staff at the NATPE 2001 Las Vegas Convention.

Assistant, MTV News, Los Angeles   August 1999–June 2000
Assisted in production; conducted Internet research; communicated with record labels; processed the written interviews on shoots; transcribed and dubbed tapes; supported Chris Connelly with story research.

Honors, Activities, and Interests

- Phi Beta Kappa Member, UCLA
- UCLA Honors Program
- Scuba Certified, NAUI
- Project Share (tutoring inner-city kids)
- Graduate Business Student Association, SDSU
- Alpha Phi Sorority: Director of COB, Director of New Member Development
- Project Angelfood (food delivery to HIV+ patients)

Uses laser ink on white paper for high contrast in scanning

References

Available upon request

should date the résumé. That way when an unscrupulous recruiter pulls it from a database and presents it to your boss two years later, you will be able to explain that you are truly happy working there and that the résumé is clearly dated before you went to work for your employer. These content changes should be made to all forms of the electronic résumé.

● (1) ASCII or text files;

The low-end electronic résumé is usually a document saved as an ASCII or text file. You will use it when an employer requests that form. Sometimes you will send it as an attached file and other times you will place it inside your email. Since you can create it in your word processor and run a spell checker on it, you will probably want to cut and paste from it when you are filling out online application forms. It is also a good idea to test it out by sending it to yourself and viewing it with as many different email programs as you can. Then you will know if you need to shorten lines, add spacing, or make other changes to improve its readability.

● (2) word processor, RTF, and PDF files;

To help ensure readability, you may want to send your résumé as a formatted attached file. Of course, you would only send it this way when you know the receiver welcomes getting them this way. You have a couple of choices of file format with attached files. You could send it in a standard word processing file format, one that is widely read by a variety of programs. Or you could send it as an RTF (rich text format) or PDF (portable document file). All these formats attempt to preserve the layout of your document. You also can help by using standard fonts most readers are likely to have installed or by embedding your font, so that the receiver's view is the one you intended.

● (3) multimedia HTM files.

The multimedia format can be a dramatic extension of the print résumé. Not only can you add links, color, and graphics, but you can also add sound, animation, and even video. If your receiver is like many others today, he or she is likely able to receive HTM files within the email program. You could use the email as a cover message with a link to a web page profile (an example is shown later in this chapter), or you could put the HTM résumé file inside the email (see Figure 9–6). An HTM file allows you to display links to supporting files as well as include color, graphics, photos, and so on on your résumé. If used effectively, you could enhance your strengths and showcase your knowledge, creativity, and skills.

Since length is not the issue it is with the print résumé, the electronic résumé should include all the detail needed to support your case. You also should take care to use the terms and keywords on which the document is likely to be searched, including nouns, buzzwords, jargon, and even acronyms commonly used in the field. You want your résumé retrieved when an appropriate position is available.

WRITING THE COVER MESSAGE

● Writing the cover message involves matching your qualifications with the job.

You should begin work on the cover message by fitting the facts from your background to the work you seek and arranging those facts in a logical order. Then you present them in much the same way that a sales writer would present the features of a product or service. Wherever logical, you adapt the points made to the reader's needs. Like those of sales messages, the organizational plans of cover messages vary depending on whether the print or electronic channel is chosen.

Print Cover Letters

The following procedure (discussed in detail below) is used in most successful print efforts:

● This plan for writing the letter has proved to be effective.

- Begin with words selected to gain attention appropriately and to set up the review of information.
- Present your qualifications, keeping like information together and adapting to the company and the job.
- Use good sales strategy, especially you-viewpoint and positive language.
- Drive for the appropriate action (request for interview, reference check, further correspondence).

Professorial Words of Wisdom

We can see, then, that using the Internet to recruit for managerial and non-managerial jobs offers many benefits. For example, turnaround times are considerably shorter than they are for traditional recruiting techniques. Also, the recruiters are sometimes able to recruit passive job candidates. Those who are not looking for another position are often more highly qualified than those who are. Furthermore, using Websites has turned out to be less expensive than other forms of job advertising.

C. Glenn Pearce, Virginia Commonwealth University
Tracy L. Tuten, Longwood College

C. Glenn Pearce and Tracy L. Tuten, "Internet Recruiting in the Banking Industry," *Business Communication Quarterly* 64, no. 1 (March 2001): 17.

Gaining Attention in the Opening. As in sales writing, the opening of the cover message has two requirements: It must gain attention and it must set up the review of information that follows.

• Gain attention and set up the information review in the opening.

Gaining attention is especially important in prospecting messages (cover messages that are not invited). Such letters are likely to reach busy executives who have many things to do other than read cover messages. Unless the writing gains favorable attention right away, the executives probably will not read them. Even invited messages must gain attention because they will compete with other invited messages. Invited messages that stand out favorably from the beginning have a competitive advantage.

• Gaining attention in the opening makes the letter stand out.

As the cover message is a creative effort, you should use your imagination in writing the opening. But the work you seek should guide your imagination. Take, for example, work that requires an outgoing personality and a vivid imagination such as sales or public relations. In such cases, you would do well to show these qualities in your opening words. At the opposite extreme is work of a conservative nature, such as accounting or banking. Openings in such cases should normally be more restrained.

• Use your imagination in writing the opening. Make the opening fit the job.

In choosing the best opening for your case, you should consider whether you are writing a prospecting or an invited message. If the message has been invited, your opening words should begin qualifying you for the work to be done. They also should refer incidentally to the invitation, as in this example:

• An invited application might refer to the job and the source of the invitation.

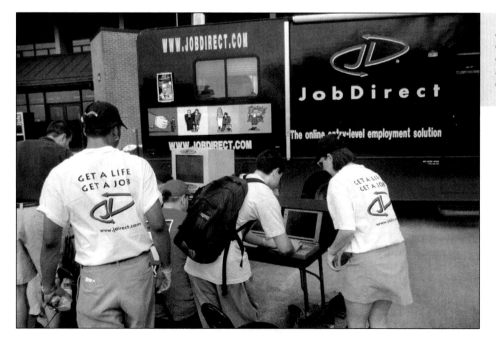

Job boards and career center websites are a good place to look for announcements of job openings.

Choice Lines Gleaned from Application Letters

"I have no influential father, uncles, or friends. I have no political ties, no drag, no pull. The result: no job. I am just an ambitious and intelligent young man who will work hard."

"Actually, I am looking for a big desk and an upholstered chair with a position attached. The duties (if any) must be amusing or interesting."

"I am familiar with all phases of office procedure, including bowling, coffee-breaking, working crossword puzzles, doodling, personal letter writing, and collection taking."

"I have answered all the questions on your application form except 'Sex.' This I think is a very personal matter."

"For three years I worked for Ms. Helen Simmons, who I am sending to you as a reference on the attached data sheet."

Will an honor graduate in accounting, with experience in tax accounting, qualify for the work you listed in today's *Times*?

In addition to fitting the work sought, your opening words should set up the review of qualifications. The preceding example meets this requirement well. It structures the review of qualifications around two areas: education and experience.

- You can gain attention by showing an understanding of the reader's operations.

You can gain attention in the opening in many ways. One way is to use a topic that shows understanding of the reader's operation or of the work to be done. Employers are likely to be impressed by applicants who have made the effort to learn something about the company, as in this example:

Now that Taggart, Inc., has expanded operations to Central America, can you use a broadly trained international business major who knows the language and culture of the region?

Another way is to make a statement or ask a question that focuses attention on a need of the reader that the writer seeks to fill. The following opening illustrates this approach:

- You can stress a need of the reader that you can fill.

When was the last time you interviewed a young college graduate who wanted to sell and had successful sales experience?

If you seek more conservative work, you should use less imaginative openings. For example, a message answering an advertisement for a beginning accountant might open with this sentence:

- Use conservative openings for applications in a conservative field.

Because of my specialized training in accounting at State University and my practical experience in cost-based accounting, I believe I have the qualifications you described in your *Journal* advertisement.

- Using an employee's name gains attention.

Sometimes one learns of a job possibility through a company employee. Mentioning the employee's name can gain attention, as in this opening sentence:

At the suggestion of Ms. Mary E. Adami of your staff, I am sending the following summary of my qualifications for work as your loan supervisor.

- Many opening possibilities exist, but avoid the old-style ones.

Many other possibilities exist. In the final analysis, you will have to use what you think will be best for the one case. But you should avoid the overworked beginnings that were popular a generation or two ago such as "This is to apply for . . ." and "Please consider this my application for . . ." Although the direct application these words make may be effective in some cases (as when answering an advertisement), the words are timeworn and dull.

FIGURE 9–10 Cover Letters (A Conservative Request for Work). Using a company executive's name to gain attention, this letter is conservative in style and tone.

Mildred E. Culpepper

2707 Green Street
Lincoln, NE 68505
Message: 402-594-6942
Fax: 402-594-1573
Email: mculpepper@creighton.edu

April 17, 2005

Ms. Marlene O'Daniel
Vice President for Administration
Continental Insurance Company
3717 Saylor Road
Des Moines, IA 50313-5033

Dear Ms. O'Daniel:

Gains attention with associate's name—opens door

On the suggestion of Mr. Victor O. Krause of your staff, here is a summary of my qualifications for work as your communications specialist.

Shows the writer knows the work in interpretations of experience

Employs conservative style and tone

Presently I am in my fifth year as communications specialist for Atlas Insurance. Primarily my work consists of writing to Atlas policyholders. This work has made me a convert of business writing, and it has sharpened my writing skills. And, more important, it has taught me how to gain and keep customers for my company through writing.

Uses subtle you-viewpoint—implied from writer's understanding of work

Additional experience working with businesspeople has given me an insight into the communication needs of business. This experience includes planning and presenting a communication improvement course for local civil service workers, a course in business writing for area business executives, and a course in bank communication for employees of Columbia National Bank.

References résumé

My college training was certainly planned to prepare me for work in business writing. Advertising and public relations were my areas of concentration for my B.S. degree from Creighton University. As you will see in the enclosed résumé, I studied all available writing courses in my degree plan. I also studied writing through English and journalism.

Brings review to a conclusion—fits qualifications presented to the job

Moves appropriately for action

In summary, Ms. O'Daniel, my experience and my studies have equipped me for work as your communication specialist. I know business writing. I know how it should be practiced to benefit your company. May I have the privilege of discussing this matter with you personally? Please contact me at 402-786-2575 so that I can arrange to be in your office at any time convenient to you.

Sincerely,

Mildred E. Culpepper

Mildred E. Culpepper

Enc.

4407 Sunland Avenue
Phoenix, AZ 85040-9321
July 8, 2005

Ms. Anita O. Alderson, Manager
Tompkins-Oderson Agency, Inc.
3901 Tampico Avenue
Los Angeles, CA 90032-1614

Dear Ms. Alderson:

Uses reader's words for good attention gainer

Sound background in advertising. . . well trained. . . works well with others. . . .

These key words in your July 6 advertisement in the *Times* describe the person you want, and I believe I am that person.

Demonstrates ability to write advertising copy through writing style used

Shows clearly what the writer can do on job through interpretation

I have gained experience in every phase of retail advertising while working for the *Lancer*, our college newspaper. I sold advertising, planned layouts, and wrote copy. During the last two summers, I gained firsthand experience working in the advertising department of Wunder & Son. I wrote a lot of copy for Wunder, some of which I am enclosing for your inspection; you will find numerous other examples on my web page at http://www.asu.edu/home/mjanek.htm. I also did just about everything else there is to do in advertising work. I enjoyed it, and I learned from it. This experience clearly helps me fit in and contribute to the work in your office.

Shows strong determination through good interpretation

In my concentrated curriculum at the university, I studied marketing with a specialization in advertising. I completed every course offered in advertising and related fields. My honor grades give some evidence that I worked hard and with sincerity. This educational background has definitely given me a firm foundation and stimulated my ability to be creative in working for you.

Understanding the importance of being able to get along well with people, I actively participated in Sigma Chi (social fraternity), the Race for the Cure (breast cancer), and Pi Tau Pi (honorary business fraternity). From the experience gained in these associations, I am confident that I can fit in well with the people in your advertising department.

Provides good evidence of social skills

Leads smoothly to action

As you can see from this description and the enclosed résumé, I am clearly qualified for a position in advertising. May I now meet with you to discuss this matter further? You can reach me at janek@hotmail.com or at 602-713-2199 to arrange a convenient time to talk about doing your advertising work.

Uses a clear and strong drive

Sincerely,

Michael S. Janek

Michael S. Janek

enclosures

12713 Sanchez Drive
San Bernardino, CA 92405
April 9, 2005

Mr. Conrad W. Butler
Office Manager
Darden, Inc.
14316 Butterfield Road
San Francisco, CA 94129

Dear Mr. Butler:

Gains attention with question

Can Darden, Inc., use a hardworking Mesa College business major who wants a career in office administration? My experience, education, and personal qualities qualify me well for this work.

Sets up rest of letter tightly

Justifies job search

My five years of work experience (see attached résumé) have taught me to do all phases of office work. For the past two years I have been in charge of payrolls at Gynes Manufacturing Company. As the administrator of payrolls, I have had to handle all types of office operations, including records management and general correspondence. Although I am happy at this job, it does not offer the career opportunity I seek with Darden.

Brings out highlights with review of experience

Complementing my work experience are my studies at Mesa College. In addition to studying the prescribed courses in my major field of business administration, I selected electives to help me in my career objective. And I believe I have succeeded. In spite of full-time employment through most of my time in college, I was awarded the Associate of Arts degree last May with a 3.3 grade point average (4.0 basis). But most important of all, I learned from my studies how office work should be done.

Interprets positively

In addition, I have the personal qualities that would fit me harmoniously into your organization. I like people, and through experience I have learned how to work with them as both a team leader and a player.

Sets up action and uses adaption in concluding statement

My preparation has been designed to prepare me for work in office administration, Mr. Butler. So may I talk to you about working for Darden? Please call me at 714-399-2569 or email me at jgoetz@hotmail.com to arrange an interview.

Requests action clearly and appropriately

Sincerely,

Jimmy I. Goetz

Jimmy I. Goetz

Enc.

FIGURE 9–13 Cover Letters (Persuasion in a Form Prospecting Letter). Written by a recent college graduate seeking her first job, this letter was prepared for use with a number of different types of companies.

MARY O. MAHONEY

May 17, 2005

Mr. Nevil S. Shannon
Director of Personnel
Snowdon Industries, Inc.
1103 Boswell Circle
Baltimore, MD 21202

Dear Mr. Shannon:

Effective attention-getting question

Will you please review my qualifications for work in your management trainee program? My training, work attitude, and personal skills qualify me for this program.

Good organization plan set-up

Good interpretation of education

My training for administration consists primarily of four years of business administration study at State University. The Bachelor of Business Administration degree I will receive in June has given me a broad foundation of business knowledge. As a general business major, I studied all the functional fields (management, marketing, information systems, finance, accounting) as well as the other core business subjects (communications, statistics, law, economics, production, and personnel). I have the knowledge base that will enable me to be productive now. And I can build upon this base through practical experience.

Skillfully handles lack of experience

As I am seeking my first full-time job, I must use means other than work experience to prove my work attitude. My grade point record at State is evidence that I took my studies seriously and that I worked hard. My 3.8 overall average (4.0 basis) placed me in the top 10 percent of the graduating class. I also worked diligently in student associations. My efforts were recognized by the special assignments and leadership roles you see listed in the enclosed résumé. I assure you that I would bring these work habits with me to Snowdon Industries.

Individually adapted

Good use of fact to back up personal qualities

Throughout college, I devoted time to the development of my personal skills. As an active member of the student chapter of the Society for the Advancement of Management, I served as treasurer and program chairperson. I participated in intramural golf and volleyball. And I was an active worker in the Young Republicans, serving as publicity chairperson for three years. All this experience has helped me to have the balance you seek in your administrative trainees.

These highlights and the additional evidence presented in the enclosed résumé present my case for a career in management. May I have an interview to continue my presentation? You can reach me at 301.594.6942 or marymahoney@yahoo.com. I could be in your office at your convenience to talk about working for Snowdon.

Clear request for action — flows logically from preceding presentation

Good ending message

Sincerely,

Mary O Mahoney

Mary O. Mahoney

Enclosure

1718 CRANFORD AVENUE • ROCKWELL, MD • 20854
VOICE/MESSAGE/FAX: 301.594.6942 • EMAIL: MARYMAHONEY@YAHOO.COM

The job interview is the final examination of the application process. Appropriate grooming and relaxed, yet enthusiastic behavior are helpful to the applicant's success.

Selecting Content. Following the opening, you should present the information that qualifies you to do the work. Begin this task by reviewing the job requirements. Then select the facts about you that qualify you for the job.

- Present your qualifications. Fit them to the job.

If your letter has been invited, you may learn about the job requirements from the source of the invitation. If you are answering an advertisement, study it for the employer's requirements. If you are following up an interview, review the interview for information about job requirements. If you are prospecting, your research and your logical analysis should guide you.

- You do this by studying the job. Use all available information sources.

In any event, you are likely to present facts from three background areas: education, experience, and skills and/or personal details. You also may include a fourth—references. But references are not exactly background information. If you include references, they will probably go on a separate reference sheet.

- Include education, experience, personal qualities, references.

How much you include from each of these areas and how much you emphasize each area should depend on the job and on your background. Most of the jobs you will seek as a new college graduate will have strong educational requirements. Thus, you should stress your education. When you apply for work after you have accumulated experience, you will probably need to stress experience. As the years go by, experience becomes more and more important—education, less and less important. Your personal characteristics are of some importance for some jobs, especially jobs that involve working with people.

- The emphasis each of these areas deserves varies by job. So consider the job in determining emphasis.

If a résumé accompanies the cover message, you may rely on it too much. Remember that the message does the selling and the résumé summarizes the significant details. Thus, the message should contain the major points around which you build your case, and the résumé should include these points plus supporting details. As the two are parts of a team effort, somewhere in the message you should refer the reader to the résumé.

- Do not rely too heavily on the résumé. The cover message should carry all the major selling points.

Organizing for Persuasion. You will want to present the information about yourself in the order that is best for you. In general, the plan you select is likely to follow one of three general orders. The most common order is a logical grouping of the information, such as education, skills and/or personal details, and experience. A second possibility is a time order. For example, you could present the information to show a year-by-year preparation for the work. A third possibility is an order based on the job requirements. For example, selling, communicating, and managing might be the requirements listed in an advertised job.

- In organizing the background facts, select the best of these orders: logical grouping, time, job requirements.

Merely presenting facts does not ensure conviction. You also will need to present the facts in words that make the most of your assets. You could say, for example, that

- Use words that present your qualifications most favorably.

you "held a position" as sales manager; but it is much more convincing to say that you "supervised a sales force of 14." Likewise, you do more for yourself by writing that you "earned a degree in business administration" than by writing that you "spent four years in college." And it is more effective to say that you "learned tax accounting" than to say that you "took a course in tax accounting."

Use the you-viewpoint wherever practical.

You also can help your case by presenting your facts in reader-viewpoint language wherever this is practical. More specifically, you should work to interpret the facts based on their meaning for your reader and for the work to be done. For example, you could present a cold recital like this one:

> I am 21 years old and have an interest in mechanical operations and processes. Last summer I worked in the production department of a container plant.

Or you could interpret the facts, fitting them to the one job:

> The interest I have held in things mechanical over most of my 21 years would help me fit into one of your technical manufacturing operations. And last summer's experience in the production department of Miller Container Company is evidence that I can and will work hard.

Avoid the tendency to overuse *I*'s, but use some.

Since you will be writing about yourself, you may find it difficult to avoid overusing I-references. But you should try. An overuse of *I*'s sounds egotistical and places too much attention on the often repeated word. Also, such overuse is not good business etiquette. Some *I*'s, however, should be used. The letter is personal. Stripping it of all I-references would rob it of its personal warmth. Thus, you should be concerned about the number of I-references. You want neither too many nor too few.

Driving for Action in the Close.

In the close, drive for whatever action is appropriate.

The presentation of your qualifications should lead logically to the action that the close proposes. You should drive for whatever action is appropriate in your case. It could be a request for an interview, an invitation to engage in further communication (perhaps to answer the reader's questions), or an invitation to contact references. Rarely would you want to ask for the job in a first message. You are concerned mainly with opening the door to further negotiations.

Make the action words clear and direct.

Your action words should be clear and direct. Preferably, you should put them in question form. As in the sales message, the request for action may be made more effective if it is followed by words recalling a benefit that the reader will get from taking the action. The following closes illustrate this technique, although some may think the second is overly aggressive:

> The highlights of my education and experience show that I have been preparing for a career in human resources. May I now discuss beginning this career with you? You can reach me at 727-921-4113 or by email at owensmith@att.com to talk about how I can help in your human resource work.

> I am very much interested in discussing with you how my skills will contribute to your company's mission. If I do not hear from you by Friday, October 22, I'll call on Monday to arrange a time for a mutually convenient meeting.

Contrasting Cover Messages.

The following two messages show bad and good application techniques.

Illustrating bad and good techniques, the following two cover messages present the qualifications of Jason L. Andrews, the job seeker described in the introductory situation at the beginning of the chapter. The first message follows few of the suggestions given in the preceding pages, whereas the second letter is in general accord with these suggestions.

A Bland and Artless Presentation of Information. The bad message begins with an old-style opening. The first words stating that this is an application letter are of little interest. The following presentation of qualifications is a matter-of-fact, uninterpreted review of information. Little you-viewpoint is evident. In fact, most of the message emphasizes the writer (note the *I*'s). The information presented is scant. The closing action is little more than an I-viewpoint statement of the writer's availability.

Websites Offer Valuable Interview Advice

Used with permission of Monster.com.

The web is a rich resource for help with interviewing. Your school's career center may have a website with interview schedules. Sites such as Monster.com and many of the other online job database sites offer tips on all aspects of interviewing. You can get ideas for questions to ask interviewers, techniques for staying calm, and methods of handling the telephone screening interview. They even include practice interactive virtual interviews with immediate feedback on your answers to questions as well as suggestions and strategies for handling difficult questions. This site includes a planner listing a host of good commonsense tips from polishing your shoes to keeping an interview folder to keeping track of all written and verbal communication. Using these sites to help you prepare for interviews not only will help you feel more confident and interview more effectively, but also can help you evaluate the company as well.

Dear Mr. Stark:

This is to apply for a position in marketing with your company.

At present, I am completing my studies in marketing at Olympia State University and will graduate with a Bachelor of Business Administration degree with an emphasis in marketing this May. I have taken all the courses in marketing available to me as well as other helpful courses such as statistics, organizational psychology, and ecommerce.

I have had good working experience as a host and food server, sales associate, and pollster. Please see details on the enclosed résumé. I believe that I am well qualified for a position in marketing and am considering working for a company of your size and description.

Because I must make a decision on my career soon, I request that you write me soon. For your information, I will be available for an interview on March 17 and 18.

Sincerely,

This bad one is dull and poorly written.

Skillful Selling of One's Ability to Work. The better message begins with an interesting question that sets the stage for the following presentation. The review of experience is interpreted by showing how the experience would help in performing the job sought. The review of education is similarly covered. Notice how the interpretations show that the writer knows what the job requires. Notice also that reader-viewpoint is stressed throughout. Even so, a moderate use of *I*'s gives the letter a personal quality. The closing request for action is a clear, direct, and courteous question. The final words recall a main appeal of the letter.

This better letter follows textbook instructions.

Dear Mr. Stark:

Is there a place in your marketing department for a person who is specially trained in the field and who knows working people and can talk with clients on their level? My background, experience, and education have given me these unique qualifications.

All my life I have lived and worked with a wide variety of people. I was born and reared by working parents in a poor section of New York City. While in high school, I worked mornings and evenings in New York's garment district, primarily as a host and food server. For two years, between high school and college, I worked full-time as a pollster for Olympia State University. Throughout my four years of college, I worked half-time as a sales associate for The Gap. From these experiences, I have learned to understand marketing. I speak marketing's language and listen carefully to people.

My studies at Olympia State University were specially planned to prepare me for a career in marketing. I studied courses in advertising, marketing communication, marketing research, and ecommerce. In addition, I studied a wide assortment of supporting subjects: economics, business communication, information systems, psychology, interpersonal communication, and operations management. My studies have given me the foundation of knowledge on which to learn the practical side of marketing work. I plan to begin the practical side of my development in June after I receive the Bachelor of Business Administration degree with honors (3.7 grade point average on a basis of 4.0).

These brief facts and the information in my résumé describe my diligent efforts to prepare for a position in marketing. May I now talk with you about beginning that position? You can reach me at 917.938.4449 to bring me to your office at your convenience to talk about how I could help in your marketing division.

Sincerely,

Email Cover Message

An email cover message can take different forms depending on the document file format it covers. Like other email messages, it needs a clear subject line; like print cover messages, it needs a formal salutation and closing. And its purpose is still to highlight your qualifications for the particular job you are applying for. While it could be identical to one you might create for print, most readers prefer shorter documents onscreen. And since the length of the résumé is not limited to a page as in print, much of the supporting detail could be included there. The primary job of the email cover message is to identify the job, highlight the applicant's strengths, and invite the reader to review the résumé.

Notice how the solicited cover message below quickly gains the reader's attention in the opening, highlights the skills in the body, and calls for action in the close.

To: Kate Troy <kate_troy@thankyoutoo.com>

From: Megan Adami <mmadami@msn.com>

Date: October 1, 2005

Subject: Web Design Intern Position

Dear Mrs. Troy:

Yesterday my advisor here at Brown University, Dr. Payton Kubicek, suggested I contact you about the summer intern position in web design you recently announced.

At Brown I have taken courses that have given me a good understanding of both the design aspects as well as the marketing functions a good website needs. Additionally, several of my course projects involved working with successful web-based businesses, analyzing the strengths and weaknesses of their business models.

I would enjoy applying some of these skills in a successful site targeted at high-end retail customers that Thankyoutoo.com attracts. You will see from my web page profile at http://www.meganadami.com/ my design skills complement those on your company's website, allowing me to contribute almost immediately. Please let me know as soon as possible when we can talk further about this summer position.

Sincerely,

Megan Adami

mmadami@msn.com

HANDLING THE INTERVIEW

Your initial contact with a prospective employer can be by mail, email, phone, or a personal (face-to-face) visit. Even if you contact the employer by mail, a successful application will eventually involve a personal visit—or an *interview,* as we will call it. Sometimes, before inviting candidates to a formal interview session, recruiters use phone interviews for preliminary screening. Much of the preceding parts of this chapter concerned the mail contact. Now our interest centers on the interview.

- Apply for the job—by mail or visit.

In a sense, the interview is the key to the success of the application—the "final examination," so to speak. You should carefully prepare for the interview, as the job may be lost or won in it. The following review of employment interview highlights should help you understand how to deal with the interview in your job search. You will find additional information about interviewing in the resource links on the textbook website.

- The interview is essential. For it, follow these procedures:

Investigating the Company

Before arriving for an interview, you should learn what you can about the company: its products or services, its personnel, its business practices, its current activities, its management. Such knowledge will help you talk knowingly with the interviewer. And perhaps more important, the interviewer is likely to be impressed by the fact that you took the time to investigate the company. That effort might even give you a competitive advantage.

- (1) Find out what you can about the employer.

Making a Good Appearance

How you look to the interviewer is a part of your message. Thus, you should work to present just the right image. Interviewers differ to some extent on what that image is, but you would be wise to present a conservative appearance. This means avoiding faddish, offbeat styles, preferring the conservative, conventional business colors such as black, brown, navy, and gray. Remember that the interviewer wants to know whether you fit into the role you are seeking. You should appear to look like you want the job.

- (2) Make a good appearance (conservative dress and grooming).

Some may argue that such an insistence on conformity in dress and grooming infringes on one's personal freedom. Perhaps it does. We will even concede that employers should not force such biases on you. But you will have to be realistic if you want a successful career. If the people who can determine your future have fixed views on matters of dress and grooming, it is good business sense to respect those views.

Anticipating Questions and Preparing Answers

You should be able to anticipate some of the questions the interviewer will ask. Questions about your education (courses, grades, honors, and such) are usually asked. So are questions about work experience, interests, career goals, location preferences, and activities in organizations. You should prepare answers to these questions in advance. Your answers will then be thorough and correct, and your words will display poise and confidence. Your preparation will reflect your concern for good business etiquette.

- (3) Anticipate the questions; plan the answers.

In addition to general questions, interviewers often ask more complicated ones. Some of these are designed to test you—to learn your views, your interests, and your ability to deal with difficult problems. Others seek more specific information about

- Be prepared to handle standard questions,

SOURCE: NON SEQUITUR © Wiley Miller. Dist. By UNIVERSAL PRESS SYNDICATE.
Reprinted with permission. All rights reserved.

your ability to handle the job in question. Although such questions are difficult to anticipate, you should be aware that they are likely to be asked. Following are questions of this kind that one experienced interviewer asks:

What can you do for us?

Would you be willing to relocate? To travel?

Do you prefer to work with people or alone?

How well has your performance in the classroom prepared you for this job?

What do you expect to be doing in 10 years? In 20 years?

What income goals do you have for those years (10 and 20 years ahead)?

Why should I rank you above the others I am interviewing?

Why did you choose _____ for your career?

How do you feel about working overtime? Nights? Weekends?

Did you do the best work you are capable of in college?

Is your college record a good measure of how you will perform on the job?

What are the qualities of the ideal boss?

What have you done that shows leadership potential? Teamwork potential?

What are your beginning salary expectations?

Sometimes interviewers will throw in tough or illegal questions to test your poise. These are naturally stressful, but being prepared for these kinds of questions will keep you cool and collected.[3] Here are some examples:

---

[3] Martin Yate, *Knock 'em Dead 2003* (Avon, MA: Adams Media Corp., 2003), 166–82.

What is your greatest weakness?

With hindsight, how could you have improved your progress?

What kind of decisions are most difficult for you?

What is the worst thing you have heard about this company?

See this pen I'm holding? Sell it to me.

Tell me about a time when you put your foot in your mouth.

What kinds of people do you find it difficult to deal with?

- tough questions,

What religion do you practice?

How old are you?

Are you married?

Do you plan to have children?

- illegal questions,

If you get through these types of questions, some brainteasers or puzzles may be thrown your way. Microsoft often gets credit for starting this trend because the company used it extensively in attempting to hire only the best and brightest employees. Other companies soon followed, often creating their own versions of some of these questions or creating some tougher ones of their own. Many of these questions do not have a right answer; rather, they are designed to elicit an applicant's thinking, logic, and creativity skills. In answering them, be sure that you reason aloud rather than sitting there silently so that you can show you are thinking. Feel free to make assumptions as well as to supply needed information. Giving a good answer the interviewer has not heard before is often a good strategy. Here are some real questions that have been asked in interviews by Microsoft and other companies.[4]

- brainteaser or critical thinking questions,

Why are manhole covers round?

Why do mirrors reverse right and left instead of up and down?

How many piano tuners are there in the world?

How many times a day do a clock's hands overlap?

Design a spice rack for a blind person.

Why are beer cans tapered at the top and bottom?

You have eight coins, and one of them is lighter than the others. Find the light coin in two weighings of a pan balance.

Recently, the behavioral interview style has become popular with campus recruiters. Rather than just determining your qualifications for the job, interviewers are attempting to verify if you can do the work. They ask questions about current situations because how you behave now is likely to transfer to similar situations in another job. Here are a few examples of behavioral questions:

- and behavioral questions.

What major problem have you faced in group projects and how have you dealt with it?

Do you tend more toward following the rules or toward stretching them?

What do you think your performance review will say one year from now?

For more practice preparing for questions, check the resource links on the textbook website.

Putting Yourself at Ease

Perhaps it is easier to say than to do, but you should be at ease throughout the interview. Remember that you are being inspected and that the interviewer should see a calm and collected person. How to appear calm and collected is not easy to explain. Certainly, it

- (4) Be at ease—calm, collected, confident.

---

[4] William Poundstone, *How Would You Move Mount Fuji?: Microsoft's Cult of the Puzzle: How the World's Smartest Companies Select the Most Creative Thinkers* (Boston, MA: Little, Brown and Company, 2003), 80–6, 118–20.

involves talking in a clear and strong voice. It also involves controlling your facial expressions and body movements. Developing such controls requires self-discipline—working at it. You may find it helpful to convince yourself that the stress experienced during an interview is normal. Or you may find it helpful to look at the situation realistically—as merely a conversation between two human beings. Other approaches may work better for you. Use whatever approaches work. Your goal is to control your emotions so that you present the best possible appearance to the interviewer.

Helping Control the Dialogue

● (5) Help bring out the questions that show your qualifications.

Just answering the questions asked is often not enough. Not only are you being evaluated, but you are evaluating others as well. The questions you ask and the comments you play off them should bring up what you want the interviewer to know about you. Your self-analysis revealed the strong points in your background. Now you should make certain that those points come out in the interview.

● Here are some examples of how to do it.

How to bring up points about you that the interviewer does not ask is a matter for your imagination. For example, a student seeking a job in advertising believed that a certain class project should be brought to the interviewer's attention. So she asked, "Do you attach any importance to business plans written as class projects in your evaluation?" The anticipated affirmative answer allowed her to show her successful project. For another example, a student who wanted to bring out his knowledge of the prospective employer's operations did so with this question: "Will your company's expansion in the Bakersfield area create new job opportunities there?" How many questions of this sort you should ask will depend on your need to supplement your interviewer's questioning. Your goal should be to make certain that the interviewer gets all the information you consider important.

FOLLOWING UP AND ENDING
THE APPLICATION

The interview is only an early step in the application process. A variety of other steps can follow. Conveying a brief thank-you message by letter, email, or telephone is an appropriate follow-up step. It shows good business etiquette, and because some of your competitors will not do this, it can give you an advantage. If you do not hear from the prospective employer within a reasonable time, it is appropriate to inquire by telephone, email, or letter about the status of your application. You should certainly do this if you are under a time limit on another employer's offer. The application process may end with no offer (frequently with no notification at all—a most discourteous way of handling applicants), with a rejection notice, or with an offer. How to handle these situations is reviewed in the following paragraphs.

- Follow up the interview with thank-you, status-inquiry, job-acceptance, and job-rejection messages.

Other Job-Search Messages

Writing a Thank-You Message. After an interview it is courteous to write a thank-you message, whether or not you are interested in the job. If you are interested, the message can help your case. It singles you out from the competition and shows your interest in the job.

Such messages are usually short. They begin with an expression of gratefulness. They say something about the interview, the job, or such. They take care of any additional business (such as submitting information requested). And they end on a good-will note—perhaps a hopeful look to the next step in the negotiations. The following letter does these things:

- Good business etiquette requires that you write a thank-you message following an interview.

- The typical order for such a message is as follows: (1) expression of gratefulness, (2) appropriate comments fitting the situation, (3) any additional information needed, and (4) a goodwill close.

Dear Mr. Woods:

I genuinely appreciate the time you gave me yesterday. You were most helpful. And you did a first-rate job of selling me on Sony Corporation of America.

As you requested, I have enclosed samples of the financial analysis I developed as a class project. If you need anything more, please let me know.

I look forward to the possibility of discussing employment with you soon.

Sincerely,

Constructing a Follow-up to an Application. When a prospective employer is late in responding or you receive another offer with a time deadline, you may need to write a follow-up message. Employers are often just slow, but sometimes they lose the application. Whatever the explanation, a follow-up message may help to produce action.

Such a message is a form of routine inquiry. As a reason for writing, it can use the need to make a job decision or some other good explanation. The following message is an example:

- When employers do not respond, you may write a follow-up message. It is ordered like the routine inquiry.

Dear Ms. Lambley:

Because the time is approaching when I must make a job decision, will you please tell me the status of my application with you?

You may recall that you interviewed me in your office November 7. You wrote me November 12 indicating that I was among those you had selected for further consideration.

SAIC remains one of the organizations I would like to consider in making my career decision. I will very much appreciate hearing from you by December 3.

Sincerely,

Planning the Job Acceptance.

- You may need to write to accept a job. Write it as you would a favorable response.

Planning the Job Acceptance. Job acceptances in writing are merely favorable response messages with an extra amount of goodwill. Because the message should begin directly, a yes answer in the beginning is appropriate. The remainder of the message should contain a confirmation of the starting date and place and comments about the work, the company, the interview—whatever you would say if you were face to face with the reader. The message need not be long. This one does the job well:

Dear Ms. Garcia:

Yes, I accept your offer of employment. After my first interview with you, I was convinced that Allison-Caldwell was the organization for me. It is good to know that you think I am right for Allison-Caldwell.

Following your instructions, I will be in your Toronto headquarters on May 28 at 8:30 AM ready to work for you.

Sincerely,

- To refuse a job offer, use the normal refusal pattern (indirect).

Writing a Message Refusing a Job. Messages refusing a job offer follow the normal refusal pattern. One good technique is to begin with a friendly comment—perhaps something about past relations with the company. Next, explain and present the refusal in clear yet positive words. Then end with more friendly comment. This example illustrates the plan.

Dear Mr. Chen:

Meeting you and the other people at Northern was a genuine pleasure. All that I saw and heard impressed me most favorably. I was especially impressed to receive the generous job offer that followed.

In considering the offer, I naturally gave some weight to these favorable impressions. Even though I have accepted a job with another firm, they remain strong in my mind.

Thank you for the time and the courteous treatment you gave me.

Sincerely,

- Job resignations are made in person, by letter, or both.

Writing a Resignation. At some point in your career you are likely to resign from one job to take another. When this happens, probably you will inform your employer of your resignation orally. But when you find it more practical or comfortable, you may choose to resign in writing. In some cases, you may do it both ways. As a matter of policy, some companies require a written resignation even after an oral resignation has been made. Or you may prefer to give a written resignation following your oral announcement of it.

- Make the letter as positive as circumstances permit.

Your resignation should be as positive as the circumstances permit. Even if your work experiences have not been pleasant, you will be wise to depart without a final display of anger. As an anonymous philosopher once explained, "When you write a resignation in anger, you write the best letter you will ever regret."

- Preferably use indirect order, for the situation is negative.

The best resignations are written in the indirect order. The situation is negative, and as you know, indirectness usually is advisable in such cases. But many are written in the direct order. They present the resignation right away, following it with expressions of gratitude, favorable comments about past working experiences, and the like. Either approach is acceptable. Even so, you would do well to use the indirect order, for it is more likely to build the goodwill and favorable thinking you want to leave behind you.

The example below shows the indirect order, which is well known to you. It begins with a positive point—one that sets up the negative message. The negative message follows, clearly yet positively stated. The ending returns to positive words chosen to build goodwill and fit the case.

- This illustration begins and ends positively.

Dear Ms. Shuster:

Working as your assistant for the past five years has been a genuinely rewarding experience. Under your direction I have grown as an administrator. And I know you have given me a practical education in retailing.

As you may recall from our past discussions, I have been pursuing the same career goals that you held early in your career. Thus I am sure you will understand why I now submit my resignation to accept a store management position with Lawson's in Belle River. I would like my employment to end on the 31st, but I could stay a week or two longer if needed to help train my replacement.

I leave with only good memories of you and the other people with whom I worked. Thanks to all of you for a valuable contribution to my career.

Sincerely,

Continuing Job-Search Activities

Some authorities recommend continuing your job search two weeks into a new job. It provides insurance if you should discover the new job isn't what you expected. In any case, continuously keeping your finger on the pulse of the job market is a good idea. Not only does it provide you with information about changes occurring in your field, but it also keeps you alert to better job opportunities as soon as they are announced.

- Keeping your attention on the job market alerts you to changes and opportunities in the field.

Maintaining Your Résumé. While many people intend to keep their résumés up-to-date, they just do not make it a priority. Some others make it easy by updating as changes occur. And a few update their résumés at regularly designated times such as a birthday, New Year's Day, or even the anniversary of their employment. No matter what works best for you, updating your résumé as you gain new accomplishments and skills is important.

- Update your résumé regularly to reflect new accomplishments and skills.

Reading Job Ads/Professional Journals. Nearly as important as keeping your résumé updated is keeping up on your professional reading. Most trade or professional journals have job notices or bulletin boards you should check regularly. These ads give you insight into what skills are in demand, perhaps helping you choose assignments where you get the opportunity to develop new skills. Staying up-to-date in your field can be stimulating; it can provide both challenges and opportunities.

- Keeping current in your professional reading brings many benefits.

SUMMARY BY CHAPTER OBJECTIVES

1. A good first step in your job search is to build a network of contacts.
   - Get to know people who might help you later: classmates, professors, business leaders, and such.
   - Use them to help you find a job.

Develop and use a network of contacts in your job search.

2. When you are ready to find work, analyze yourself and outside factors.
   - Look at your education, personal qualities, and work experience.
   - From this review, determine what work you are qualified to do.
   - Then select the career that is right for you.

Assemble and evaluate information that will help you select a job.

3. When you are ready to find a job, use the contact sources available to you.
   - Check university career centers, personal contacts, advertisements, online sources, employment agencies, personal search agents, and web page profiles.
   - If these do not produce results, prospect by mail.

Identify the sources that can lead you to an employer.

4. In your application efforts, you are likely to use résumés and cover messages. Prepare them as you would written sales material.
   - First, study your product—you.
   - Then study your prospect—the employer.
   - From the information gained, construct the résumé, cover message, and reference sheet.
   In writing the résumé (a listing of your major background facts), you can choose from two types.
   - The *print résumé*—traditional and scannable.
   - The *electronic résumé*—ASCII, attached file, and HTM file.
   In preparing the traditional résumé, follow this procedure:

Compile print and electronic résumés that are strong, complete, and organized.

- List all the facts about you that an employer might want to know.
- Sort these facts into logical groups: *experience, education, personal qualities, references, achievements, highlights.*
- Put these facts in writing. As a minimum, include job experience (dates, places, firms, duties) and education (degrees, dates, fields of study). Use some personal information, but omit race, religion, sex, marital status, and age.
- Authorities disagree on whether to list references. If you list them, use complete mailing addresses and have one for each major job.
- Include other helpful information: address, telephone number, email address, web page address, and career objective.
- Write headings for the résumé and for each group of information; use either topic or talking headings.
- Organize for strength in reverse chronological, functional/skills, or accomplishment/highlights approach.
- Preferably write the résumé without personal pronouns, make the parts parallel grammatically, and use words that help sell your abilities.
- Present the information for good eye appeal, selecting fonts that show the importance of the headings and the information.

In preparing the scannable résumé, follow these procedures:
- Include industry-specific keywords.
- Choose precise nouns over action verbs.
- Present the information in a form read accurately by scanners.

In preparing the electronic résumé, follow these procedures:
- Use the electronic format the receiver specifies or prefers.
- Remove all contact information except your email address.
- Consider adding a last updated notation.
- Extend the HTML format to include colors, graphics, video, and sound as appropriate.

5 Write targeted cover messages that skillfully sell your abilities.

5. As the cover message is a form of sales message, plan it as you would a sales message.
   - Study your product (you) and your prospect (the employer) and think out a strategy for presentation.
   - Begin with words that gain attention, begin applying for the job, and set up the presentation of your sales points.
   - Adapt the tone and content to the job you seek.
   - Present your qualifications, fitting them to the job you seek.
   - Choose words that enhance the information presented.
   - Drive for an appropriate action—an interview, further communication, reference checks.

6 Explain how you can participate effectively in an interview.

6. Your major contact with a prospective employer is the interview. For best results, you should do the following:
   - Research the employer in advance so you can impress the interviewer.
   - Present a good appearance through appropriate dress and grooming.
   - Try to anticipate the interviewer's questions and to plan your answers.
   - Make a good impression by being at ease.
   - Help the interviewer establish a dialogue with questions and comments that enable you to present the best information about you.

7 Write application follow-up messages that are appropriate, friendly, and positive.

7. You may need to write other messages in your search for a job.
   - Following the interview, a thank-you message is appropriate.
   - Also appropriate is an inquiry about the status of an application.
   - You also may need to write messages accepting, rejecting, or resigning a job.
   - Write these messages much as you would the messages reviewed in preceding chapters: direct order for good news, indirect order for bad.

8 Maintain your job-search skills.

8. To learn information about the changes occurring in their field and to be aware of better job opportunities, employees should
   - Maintain their résumés.
   - Read both job ads and professional journals.

1. "Building a network of contacts to help one find jobs appears to be selfish. It involves acquiring friendships just to use them for one's personal benefit." Discuss this view.

2. Maryann Brennan followed a broad program of study in college and received a degree in general studies. She did her best work in English, especially in the writing courses. She also did well in history, sociology, and psychology. As much as she could, she avoided math and computer courses.

   Her overall grade point average of 3.7 (4.0 basis) placed her in the top 10 percent of her class. What advice would you give her as she begins her search for a career job?

3. Discuss the value of each of the sources for finding jobs to a finance major (*a*) right after graduation and (*b*) after 20 years of work in his or her specialty.

4. Assume that in an interview for the job you want, you are asked the questions listed in the text under the heading "Anticipating Questions and Preparing Answers." Answer these questions.

5. The most popular arrangement of résumé information is the three-part grouping: education, experience, and personal details. Describe two other arrangements. When would each be used?

6. Distinguish between the print résumé and the electronic résumé. When would each be most appropriate?

7. What is meant by *parallelism of headings?*

8. Describe the cover message and résumé you would write (*a*) immediately after graduation, (*b*) 10 years later, and (*c*) 25 years later. Point out similarities and differences, and defend your decisions.

9. What differences would you suggest in writing cover messages for jobs in (*a*) accounting, (*b*) banking, (*c*) advertising copy writing, (*d*) management, (*e*) sales, (*f*) consulting, and (*g*) information systems?

10. Discuss the logic of beginning a cover message with these words: "This is to apply for . . ." and "Please consider this my application for the position of . . ."

11. "In writing cover messages, just present the facts clearly and without analysis and interpretation. The facts alone will tell the employer whether he or she wants you." Discuss this viewpoint.

12. When should the drive for action in a cover message (*a*) request the job, (*b*) request an interview, and (*c*) request a reference check?

13. Discuss some of the advantages that writing a thank-you note to the interviewer gives the writer.

14. Identify some of benefits one gains from continuing to read professional journals for job information after one is employed.

1. Criticize the following résumé parts. (They are not from the same résumé.)

   a. Work Experience

2002–2005	Employed as sales rep for Lloyd-Shanks Tool Company
1999–2002	Office manager, Drago Plumbing Supply, Toronto
1997–99	Matson's Super Stores. I worked part time as sales clerk while attending college.

   b. References

   Mr. Carl T. Whitesides
   Sunrise Insurance, Inc.
   317 Forrest Lane
   Dover, DE 19901-6452

   Patricia Cullen
   Cullen and Cullen Realtors
   2001 Bowman Dr.
   Wilmington, DE 19804

   Rev. Troy A. Graham
   Asbury Methodist Church
   Hyattsville, MD 20783

   D. W. Boozer
   Boozer Industries
   Baltimore, MD 21202

   c. Education

2001	Graduated from Tippen H.S. (I was in top 10 percent of class.)
2005	B.S. from Bradley University with major in marketing
2005 to present	Enrolled part time in M.B.A. program at the University of Phoenix

   d. Qualifications

   Know how to motivate a sales force. I have done it.
   Experienced in screening applicants and selecting salespeople.

Know the pharmaceutical business from 11 years of experience.

Knowledgeable of realistic quota setting and incentives.

Proven leadership ability.

2. Criticize these sentences from cover messages:

Beginning Sentences

    a. Please consider this my application for any position for which my training and experience qualify me.

    b. Mr. Jerry Bono of your staff has told me about a vacancy in your loan department for which I would like to apply.

    c. I am that accountant you described in your advertisement in today's *Times-Record.*

    d. I want to work for you!

Sentences Presenting Selling Points

    e. From 2001 to 2005 I attended Bradley University where I took courses leading to a B.S. degree with a major in finance.

    f. I am highly skilled in trading corporate bonds as a result of three years spent in the New York office of Collins, Bragg, and Weaver.

    g. For three years (2002–2005) I was in the loan department at Bank One.

    h. My two strongest qualifications for this job are my personality and gift of conversation.

Sentences from Action Endings

    i. I will call you on the 12th to arrange an interview.

    j. If my qualifications meet your requirements it would be greatly appreciated if you would schedule an interview for me.

    k. Please call to set up an interview. Do it now—while it is on your mind.

CRITICAL THINKING PROBLEMS

Applications

1. You have successfully prepared yourself for the career of your choice, but the recruiters visiting your school have not yet offered you a job. Now you must look on your own. So by searching newspapers, online job databases, and company website announcements, find the best job for which you believe you are qualified. Write two cover messages that you might use to present your qualifications for this job: one for print presentation and one for email. Attach a copy of the job description to the messages. (Assume that a résumé accompanies the cover message.)

2. Write the résumé and reference sheet to accompany the message for Problem 1.

3. Project yourself three years past your graduation date. During those years, you have had good experience working for the company of your choice in the field of your choice. (Use your imagination to supply this information.)

    Unfortunately, your progress hasn't been what you had expected. You think that you must look around for a better opportunity. Your search through the classified advertisements in your area newspapers, online, and in *The Wall Street Journal* turns up one promising possibility (you find it). Write a cover message that skillfully presents your qualifications for this job. (You may make logical assumptions about your experience over the three-year period.) For class purposes, attach the advertisement to your message.

4. Write the résumé and reference sheet to accompany the message in Problem 3.

5. Assume you are in your last term of school and graduation is just around the corner. Your greatest interest is in finding work that you like and that would enable you to support yourself now and to support a family as you win promotions.

    No job of your choice is revealed in the want ads of newspapers and trade magazines. No career center has provided anything to your liking. So you decide to do what any good salesperson does: survey the product (yourself) and the market (companies that could use a person who can do what you are prepared to do) and then advertise (send each of these companies a résumé with a cover letter). This procedure sometimes creates a job where none existed before; and sometimes it establishes a basis for negotiations for the "big job" two, three, or five years after graduation. And very frequently, it puts you on the list for the good job that is not filled through advertising or from the company staff. Write the cover message.

6. Write the résumé and reference sheet to accompany the message for Problem 5.

7. Move the calendar to your graduation date so that you are now ready to sell your working ability in the job market for as much as you can get and still hold your own. Besides canvassing likely firms with the help of prospecting letters and diligently following up family

contacts, you have decided to look into anything that appears especially good in the ads of newspapers, online sources, and magazines. The latest available issues of large city publications and online services list the following jobs that you think you could handle. (You may change publication and place names to fit your section of the country.)

a. *Office manager.* Currently seeking an office manager with initiative and flexibility for work in a fast-paced environment. Must have an outgoing personality and excellent communication skills and be a team player. Must be a "power user" of Word and Excel. Knowledge of PowerPoint a plus. Some overtime expected during crunch periods. Send application materials to Chris Eveland at ceveland@qconline.com.

b. *Assistant webmaster.* Outstanding information technology, organizational, and interpersonal skills are needed for work on a company portal. Mastery of HTML coding, website design including graphic design, and client server technology is vital. Candidates also must possess excellent writing skills and the ability to effectively manage multiple projects while interfacing with company employees. A bachelor's degree with a background in information systems, marketing, or communications is required. Please send résumé to Megan Adami in Human Resources, 7165 North Main Street, _(your city)_ , or fax it to 1-888-444-5047, or email it to megan_adami@cnet.com.

c. *Management trainee.* Named by *Fortune* magazine as one of the best places to work, this constantly expanding international company uses shared decision making and clear career paths so that employees can be productive and well rewarded. The challenging management training program requires candidates with good communications skills and high energy levels to be successful. Applicants must be computer literate and possess good interpersonal skills. Fax résumé to Don Zatyko at 1-888-399-2569.

d. *Staff accountant—payroll specialist.* We are looking for an accountant who desires to grow and move up the ladder. One should be motivated and willing to work in a fast-paced, multitasking environment. An associate's degree in accounting or finance is required. Additionally, the ideal candidate will be detail-oriented and able to meet deadlines. The job involves coordinating transfers of time worked data from time collection systems to payroll systems. Must have extended knowledge of Excel to compute withholdings and deductions, and must stay up to date on multiple state laws regarding payroll. Excellent compensation package and benefits. Apply to Carolynn Workman, accounting director, at carolynn_workman@adelphia.net.

e. *Staff accountant.* Successful candidate should have a B.S. in accounting and be proficient in QuickBooks and/or Excel. Would be responsible for performing account analysis for corporate accounts, assisting in consolidation of subsidiaries, and assisting in the preparation of annual and quarterly financial statements and financial reports for certain subsidiaries. Experience in the local environment of small business is desirable. If you are concerned with order, quality, and accuracy, please contact us by mail at Administrative Partner, Winship and Acord, P.C., 3013 Stonybrook Drive, _(your city)_ , or by email at CWA@msn.com, or by fax at 1-217-399-2569.

f. *Network specialist.* We seek someone who can help deliver reliable, secure, and integrated networks. Must be able to bring together data and voice, WAN and LAN, fiber optics and wireless. Opportunity to learn newest technologies. Must have network certification such as MCP, MCSE, CNA, or CNE as well as a college degree or the equivalent experience. Requires excellent interpersonal and problem-solving skills. Experience with multiplatform computing is preferred. Will be expected to develop technical documentation and help establish network policies, procedures, and standards to ensure comformance with information systems and client objectives and strategy. Qualified applicants should send application documents to Robert Edwards at redwards@tyt.com.

g. *Technology analyst/consultant.* A fast-growing, highly regarded information technology assessment/consulting firm has a position for someone with expertise in client/server technology and Oracle. Must have excellent written communications and interpersonal skills. Vendor or user organization experience is highly desirable. Position is in the Bay Area. Send or fax your résumé to director of human resources at 500 Airport Road, Suite 100, _(your city)_ or 415-579-1022.

h. *Financial analyst.* An eastern-based investment firm is seeking an analyst to help with the evaluation of potential private equity investments and marketing of an existing and new leveraged buyout fund. Should have a bachelor's degree from a good school and some experience in banking. Ideal candidates will have strong analytical capabilities and excellent computer skills, particularly spreadsheet, statistics, and database. Please fax résumé and cover letter to 203-869-1022 or send an email file to andrew-winston@fidelity.com.

i. *Trade show exhibits coordinator.* Position reports to the national sales manager and requires an individual who can work independently as well as part of a team. Professional telephone and computer skills are essential. Coordinator will maintain exhibitor contact databases, serve as an internal liaison to accounting and as an external liaison to vendors, and assist the on-site floor managers with various exhibitor-related responsibilities. Also must create exhibitor and attendee pre- and post-show surveys, collect data, and compile results. Trade show, association, or convention services experience is a plus. Some limited travel is expected. Send your résumé to lmiller@aol.com.

j. *Sales representative.* Major pharmaceutical company is expanding and looking for a sales representative in your area. Ideal candidate will have a successful record of sales experience, preferably in a business-to-business environment. Candidate must be well-versed in science and willing to continually learn about new products. Good knowledge of your area is highly desirable. Send your résumé to Jane_Adami@pfizer.com.

k. *Internet programmer.* Seeking a professional individual with experience in complex HTML/DHTML, strong web development, and a thorough understanding of Javascript and Perl. Will design, write, modify, test, and maintain programs and scripts for a suite of server applications. Must be comfortable in a UNIX environment and possess some competency in SQL. Any experience with data warehousing would be a plus. Additionally, a qualified candidate should be a team player and self-motivated and possess excellent speaking and writing skills. Send all application documents to James.Andrews@menshealth.com.

l. *Marketing professional.* An international, rapidly growing consumer and trade publisher is seeking a self-motivated individual to help us reach our goal of doubling revenues by the year 2010. Ideal candidate will be an innovative, results-oriented professional willing to take the challenge of developing new markets. Should be good at packaging and repackaging information products for a large and expanding customer base. We are looking for those with some experience, creative writing talent, leadership skills, good communications skills, and strong interpersonal skills. Sell yourself through your cover letter and résumé. Send a rich media text to Thomas McLaughlin, corporate vice president, Blackhawk Publishing at tjmclaughlin@blackhawk.com.

m. *Executive administrative assistant.* Vice president of a Fortune 500 manufacturing company seeks a highly competent, personable, organized, and dependable executive assistant. College degree

desired. Must have excellent communication skills and thorough command of Internet navigation as well as word processing and presentation programs. In addition to basic business knowledge in accounting, finance, marketing, and management, an understanding of manufacturing in a global market would be desirable. Apply to director of human resources, P.O. Box 3733, (your city) .

n. *Graphic artist.* An employee-owned systems integration firm has an immediate need for a graphic artist. A bachelor's degree or an associate's degree with some experience desired. Must be proficient in PhotoShop and Illustrator, preferably in a Windows environment. Will prepare presentation and curriculum support graphics for government customer. Knowledge of project management software is a plus. Must have a work portfolio. Send résumé to the attention of KML, P.O. Box 900, (your city) .

o. *MIS specialist.* A local medical clinic is seeking an individual to manage a multisite, multiplatform computer system. Will be responsible for troubleshooting and coordinating problems in a Windows XP environment and writing reports for management. A background in the health care/medical field combined with a good knowledge of computing is highly desirable. Send résumé to (your city's name) Community Clinic, 1113 Henderson, (your city) or fax to 888-316-1026.

p. *Financial manager.* Multispecialty medical group (60 doctors) needs dedicated professional to work in providing financial planning and control in growing organization. Join a team of financial specialists who bear responsibility for budgeting, general accounting, reimbursement, billing processes, and external reporting. Also responsible for development of long- and short-range financial goals and evaluation of their impact on strategic objectives and service mission. Degree in accounting/finance. Technical and team skills needed. Competitive salary and benefits package. Send letter and résumé to Mount Renault Medical Group, Box 14871, New York, NY 00146.

q. *Accountant.* A major real estate developer and property management company seeks an accountant. Must have a bachelor's degree in accounting. Will assist in financial reporting, tax preparation, cash flow projections, and year-end audit workpaper preparation. Mastery of Excel is required as are good communication skills. Some work experience in accounting is desirable; internship experience in an accounting or real estate environment is also desirable. Send your résumé and cover letter to TPL, P.O. Box 613, (your city) or email it to tpl@hotmail.com.

r. *Accounting majors.* Multinational consumer electronics firm seeks entry-level accountant for work in its controller's division. This person must be knowledgeable in financial and cost accounting, internal auditing, budgeting, and capital investments. A multinational orientation, degree in accounting, and progress toward completion of CPA or CMA are a plus. Good communication skills (written and oral) and computer applications are required. Interested applicants should send letter and résumé to hrdirector@circuitcity.com.

s. *Bank examiner.* Federal Reserve Bank (nearest to your location) seeks positions for career-oriented individuals. Persons hired will conduct on-site examinations of foreign banks operating in the U.S. in their lending activities, derivative products, bank operations, and financial information. Applicants must possess a bachelor's degree in accounting, finance, or economics. Evidence of cross-cultural sensitivity and foreign language proficiency is preferred. Travel 30–50 percent of the time. Excellent oral/written skills and U.S. citizenship required. Apply with letter, résumé, and reference sheets to Federal Reserve Board, Human Resources Department, (your region) .

t. *Proposal writer.* Global leader in high-technology asset management needs individual to prepare proposals for clients. Person selected must be a team player, thrive on high-tech challenges in fast-paced environment, and possess a state-of-the-art solution orientation. Excellent writing skills essential, along with BBA degree and experience with various hardware/software technologies. Job includes coordinating appropriate persons to define solutions and preparing program plans with cost estimation for clients. Send letter, résumé, and writing sample to Department SAS, (your city) .

u. *Assistant to operations manager.* Proven leader in the insurance industry seeks a highly motivated assistant to the operations manager of regional service center. Technical skills include proficiency in Internet use and Microsoft Word, Excel, PowerPoint, Access, and other database applications. College training preferred with good people skills. Person selected must be able to develop and maintain effective working relationships with internal and external customers. Apply to H R Department, Box 7438, (your city) or email to hrdirector@statefarm.com.

v. *Environmental safety and health assistant.* World leader in battery manufacturing is looking for an individual to work in safety and health area of production plant and distribution center. The successful candidate will need to have a business or environmental engineering degree and possess excellent organizational and people skills. Job duties involve administering health/safety programs, conducting training, and working with governmental agencies and regulatory personnel. Excellent opportunity for results-oriented individual seeking to work for a safe, attractive, and sanitary environment. Send cover message and résumé to Box SH, (your city) .

w. *Account executive for display advertising.* State business journal invites applications for career-oriented individuals. Qualified candidates must be college graduates (business preferred) and have work background to demonstrate reliability and commitment. Job scope involves selling display advertising in creative ways for specialized business print and online publications. Applicants should be of high energy, aggressive, and creative. Send applications to Drawer HBD, (your city) or salesmgr@busjrnl.com.

x. *Financial consultant.* Large communications services company needs qualified person to provide communication-based utility automation consulting to electric utilities. Must have comprehensive financial management knowledge. Perform economic analyses on current and proposed projects; assist in development of budgets; evaluate budget to actual performance; prepare monthly reports. Demonstrated knowledge of strategic planning, valuation techniques, accounting principles, and economic forecasts. Must communicate well orally and in writing. Email letter, résumé, and references to applications@alc.com.

y. *E-cruiter.* Must possess a fundamental knowledge of the web in order to search, target, and harvest quality business résumés and turn them into candidates for our placement firm. This job requires that one create, update, and track web activity through research, marketing, and promotion of our candidates and services on an in-house website. Combine your Internet savvy and research experience with an upbeat and helpful personality for a great career. Fax your résumé today to Carmen Sanchez at 800-594-6942 or email it to Carmen.Sanchez@pns.com.

z. *Corporate trainer.* Exciting opportunity is available for a professional with strong presentation skills, good organizational skills, and excellent written and oral communication skills. Successful trainer will be able to effectively communicate technical information to both technical and nontechnical users. Should be able to design classroom training modules and measure their effectiveness. Good time management and use of Outlook is required. Some travel to clients' sites may be required. Application documents including a sample PowerPoint presentation should be sent to Sharon

Garbett, president, Sedona Training, P.O. Box 1308, Moline, Illinois 61266.

Concentrate on the ad describing the job you would like most or could do best—and then write a cover message that will get you that job. Your message will first have to survive the filtering that eliminates dozens (sometimes hundreds) of applicants who lack the expected qualifications. Toward the end you will be getting into strong competition in which small details may give you the little extra margin of superiority that will get you an interview and a chance to campaign further.

Study your ad for what it says and even more for what it implies. Weigh your own preparation even more thoroughly than you weigh the ad. You may imagine far enough ahead to assure completion of all the courses that are planned for your degree. You may build up your case a bit on what you actually have. Sort out the things that line you up for the one job, organize them strategically, and then present them. Assume that you have attached a résumé.

8. Write the résumé and reference sheet to accompany the message for Problem 7.

9. You are looking ahead to your graduation soon. You've decided to begin to look for jobs online. Tap into a system that you know posts jobs in your major or a corporate website that posts job openings. (See textbook website for links to some of these sites.) Browse through the jobs until you see one that appeals to you and for which you will be qualified when you graduate. Print (or save) a copy of the ad so you will have it handy when you write your résumé and cover messages. Address the points covered in the ad and tell them that you learned about the position from a particular online system. Plan to send your résumé electronically, creating both an ASCII text and an HTM file.

10. Create a web page profile complete with links that provide supporting details. Take care that your design is easy to navigate as well as pleasing to view.

Jerry Yang's success stems from knowing what information is needed and packaging it in a user-friendly way.

"The ability for people to obtain information down the line is going to be the critical way for people to communicate with each other, the critical way for people to influence thought and opinion, and it is going to change the way we think about issues and the way we think about our lives."

Jerry Yang, Co-Founder and "Chief Yahoo," Yahoo

CHAPTER TEN

Basics of Report Writing

CHAPTER OBJECTIVES

Upon completing this chapter, you will be able to prepare well-organized, objective reports. To reach this goal, you should be able to

1 State a problem clearly in writing.

2 List the factors involved in a problem.

3 Explain the common errors in interpreting and develop attitudes and practices conducive to good interpreting.

4 Organize information in outline form, using time, place, quantity, factor, or a combination of these as bases for division.

5 Construct topic or talking headings that outline reports logically and meaningfully.

6 Write reports that are clear, objective, consistent in time viewpoint, smoothly connected, and interesting.

7 Prepare reports collaboratively.

Report Writing

Introduce yourself to the subject of report writing by assuming the role of administrative assistant to the president of Technisoft, Inc. Much of your work at this large software company involves getting information for your boss. Yesterday, for example, you looked into the question of excessive time spent by office workers web surfing. A few days earlier, you worked on an assignment to determine the causes of unrest in one of the local branches. Before that assignment you investigated a supervisor's recommendation to change an evaluation process. You could continue the list indefinitely, for investigating problems is a part of your work.

So is report writing, for you must write a report on each of your investigations. You write these reports for good reasons. Written reports make permanent records. Thus, those who need the information contained in these reports can review and study them at their convenience. Written reports also can be routed to a number of readers with a minimum of effort. Unquestionably, such reports are convenient and efficient means of transmitting information.

Your report-writing work is not unique in your job. In fact, report writing is common throughout the company. Sometimes reports are written by individuals. Increasingly, however, they are prepared in collaboration with others. For example, the engineers often report on the technical problems they encounter. The accountants regularly report to management on the company's financial operations. From time to time, production people report on various aspects of operations. The salespeople regularly report on marketing matters. And so it is throughout the company. Such reporting is vital to your company's operations—as it is to the operations of all companies. Organizations require information for many reasons. In a sense, they feed on information. Reports supply them with a vital portion of the information they need.

This chapter and the following two chapters describe the structure and writing of this vital form of business communication.

How often you write reports in the years ahead will depend on the size of the organization you work for. If you work for a very small organization (say, one with fewer than 10 employees), you will probably write only a few. But if you work for a midsize or larger organization, you are likely to write many. In fact, the larger the organization, the more reports you are likely to write. The explanation is obvious. The larger the organization, the greater is its complexity; and the greater the complexity, the greater is the need for information to manage the organization. As reports supply much of the information needed, the demand for them is great.

- Reports are vital to larger organizations. You will probably write them.

DEFINING REPORTS

You probably have a good idea of what reports are. Even so, you would be likely to have a hard time defining them. Even scholars of the subject cannot agree, for their definitions range from one extreme to the other. Some define reports to include almost any presentation of information; others limit reports to only the most formal presentations. For our purposes, this middle-ground definition is best: *A business report is an orderly and objective communication of factual information that serves a business purpose.*

The key words in this definition deserve emphasis. As an *orderly* communication, a report is prepared carefully. Thus, care in preparation distinguishes reports from casual exchanges of information. The *objective* quality of a report is its unbiased approach. Reports seek truth. They avoid human biases. The word *communication* is broad in meaning. It covers all ways of transmitting meaning: speaking, writing, drawing, and such. The basic ingredient of reports is *factual information*. Factual information is based on events, records, data, and the like. Not all reports are business reports. Research scientists, medical doctors, ministers, students, and many others write them. To be classified as a business report, a report must *serve a business purpose.*

This definition is specific enough to be meaningful, yet broad enough to take into account the variations in reports. For example, some reports (information reports) do

- A business report is an orderly and objective communication of factual information that serves a business purpose.

- The key words are *orderly, objective, communication, factual information,* and *serves a business purpose.*

nothing more than present facts. Others (analytical reports) go a step further by including interpretations, sometimes accompanied by conclusions and recommendations. There are reports that are highly formal both in writing style and in physical appearance. And there are reports that show a high degree of informality. Our definition permits all of these variations.

DETERMINING THE REPORT PURPOSE

Your work on a report logically begins with a need, which we refer to generally as the *problem* in the following discussion. Someone or some group (usually your superiors) needs information for a business purpose. Perhaps the need is for information only; perhaps it is for information and analysis; or perhaps it is for information, analysis, and recommendations. Whatever the case, someone with a need (problem) will authorize you to do the work. Usually the work will be authorized orally. But it could be authorized in a written message.

After you have been assigned a report problem, your first task should be to get your problem clearly in mind. Elementary and basic as this task may appear, all too often it is done haphazardly. And all too often a report fails to reach its goal because of such haphazardness.

The Preliminary Investigation

Getting your problem clearly in mind is largely a matter of gathering all the information needed to understand it and then applying your best logic to it. Gathering the right information involves many things, depending on the problem. It may mean gathering material from company files, talking over the problem with experts, searching through print and electronic sources, and discussing the problem with those who authorized the report. In general, you should continue this preliminary investigation until you have the information you need to understand your problem.

Need for a Clear Statement of the Problem

After you understand your problem, your next step is to state it clearly. Writing the problem statement is good practice for several reasons. A written statement is preserved permanently. Thus, you may refer to it time and again. In addition, a written statement can be reviewed, approved, and evaluated by people whose assistance may be valuable. Most important of all, putting the problem in writing forces you to think it through.

The problem statement normally takes one of three forms: infinitive phrase, question, or declarative statement. To illustrate each, we will use the problem of determining why sales at a certain store have declined:

1. *Infinitive phrase:* "To determine the causes of decreasing sales at Store X."

2. *Question:* "What are the causes of decreasing sales at Store X?"

3. *Declarative statement:* "Store X sales are decreasing, and management wants to know why."

These three forms are grammatical structures with which to state a report problem. As such, crystal-clear thinking must precede any grammatical statement, for clear problem statements are only as good as the thinking that guides them. Accordingly, one form is not better than another. You may use any of the three forms for stating the report problem. All of them should give a problem statement with equal clarity and with the same intended meaning.

One way to make sure you have the problem clearly in mind is to state it in one form (say the infinitive phrase) and then state it again in another form (say the question form). No differences in meanings should exist between the two problem statements. If there are differences, you should rethink the report problem for clarity before you proceed further in the report process.

- Work on a report begins with a business need (problem).

- Your first task is to get the problem clearly in mind.

- To do this, you should begin by gathering all the information you need to understand the problem.

- Then you should express the problem clearly, preferably in writing.

- The problem statement may be (1) an infinitive phrase, (2) a question, or (3) a declarative statement.

- One form is not superior to the others.

- State the problem in several forms. The meaning should be the same.

Report writing requires hard work and clear thinking in every stage of the process. To determine the problem and to gather facts, you will need to consult many sources of information.

DETERMINING THE FACTORS

After stating the problem, you determine what needs to be done to solve it. Specifically, you look for the factors of the problem. That is, you determine what subject areas you must look into to solve the problem.

- Next, you should determine the factors of the problem.

Problem factors may be of three types. First, they may be subtopics of the overall topic about which the report is concerned. Second, they may be hypotheses that must be tested. Third, in problems that involve comparisons, they may be the bases on which the comparisons are made.

- The factors may be subtopics of the overall topic, hypotheses, or bases for comparison.

Use of Subtopics in Information Reports

If the problem concerns a need for information, your mental effort should produce the main areas about which information is needed. Illustrating this type of situation is the problem of preparing a report that reviews Company X's activities during the past quarter. Clearly, this is an informational report problem—that is, it requires no analysis, no conclusion, no recommendation. It only requires that information be presented. The mental effort in this case is concerned simply with determining which subdivisions of the overall topic should be covered. After thoroughly evaluating the possibilities, you might come up with something like this analysis:

- Subtopics of the overall topic are the factors in information reports.

Problem statement: To review operations of Company X from January 1 through March 31.

Subtopics:

1. Production
2. Sales and promotion
3. Financial status
4. Computer systems
5. Product development
6. Human resources

Hypotheses for Problems Requiring Solution

Some problems concern why something bad is happening and perhaps how to correct it. In analyzing problems of this kind, you should seek explanations or solutions. Such explanations or solutions are termed *hypotheses.* Once formulated, hypotheses are tested, and their applicability to the problem is either proved or disproved.

To illustrate, assume that you have the problem of determining why sales at a certain store have declined. In preparing to investigate this problem, you would think of the possible explanations (hypotheses) for the decline. Your task would be one of studying, weighing, and selecting, and you would brainstorm such explanations as these:

- Hypotheses (possible explanations of the problem) may be the factors in problems requiring solution.

Problem statement: Sales at the Springfield store have declined, and management wants to know why.

Hypotheses:

- For example, these hypotheses could be suggested to explain a store's loss in sales.

1. Activities of the competition have caused the decline.
2. Changes in the economy of the area have caused the decline.
3. Merchandising deficiencies have caused the decline.
4. Changes in the environment (population shifts, political actions, etc.) have caused the decline.

In the investigation that follows, you would test these hypotheses. You might find that one, two, or all apply. Or you might find that none is valid. If so, you would have to advance additional hypotheses for further evaluation.

Bases of Comparison in Evaluation Studies

- For evaluation problems, the bases for evaluating are the factors.

When the problem concerns evaluating something, either singularly or in comparison with other things, you should look for the bases for the evaluation. That is, you should determine what characteristics you will evaluate. In some cases, the procedure may concern more than naming the characteristics. It also may include the criteria to be used in evaluating them.

- This illustration shows the bases for comparing expansion.

Illustrating this technique is the problem of a company that seeks to determine which of three cities would be best for expansion. Such a problem obviously involves a comparison of the cities. The bases for comparison are the factors that determine success for the type of work involved. After careful mental search for these factors, you might come up with a plan such as this:

Problem statement: To determine whether Y Company's new location should be built in City A, City B, or City C.

Comparison bases:

1. Availability of skilled workers
2. Tax structure
3. Community attitude
4. Transportation facilities
5. Nearness to markets

- The factors sometimes have factors of their own. That is, they also may be broken down.

Need for Subbreakdown. Each of the factors selected for investigation may have factors of its own. In the last illustration, for example, the comparison of transportation in the three cities may well be covered by such subdivisions as water, rail, truck, and air. Workers may be compared by using such categories as skilled workers and unskilled workers. Breakdowns of this kind may go still further. Skilled workers may be broken down by specific skills: engineers, programmers, technical writers, graphic designers, and such. The subdivisions could go on and on. Make them as long as they are helpful.

GATHERING THE INFORMATION NEEDED

- The next step is to conduct the research needed. A personal investigation is usually appropriate.

For most business problems, you will need to investigate personally. A production problem, for example, might require gathering and reviewing the company's production records. A sales problem might require collecting information through discussions with customers and sales personnel. A computer problem might require talking to both end users and programmers. A purchasing problem might require getting prod-

OneNote Helps Writers Integrate Ideas from Diverse Sources

Microsoft's recently introduced OneNote brings the flexibility of a paper pad and the power of digital technology together. It allows writers to use pages as blank sheets, typing or writing on them, drawing or doodling on them, and pasting graphics, photos, text, and even sounds on them. Additionally, users can also open the new research tool introduced with Office 2003. This tool gives users access to a variety of standard and subscription reference services. Furthermore, it allows users to combine information from its new sticky note application, Side Step.

In the example you see here, the writer is beginning to compile a list of resources on graphics. The notes are on a page titled Resources in a Uses section within a Graphics folder. It reveals a photo and some text describing an upcoming publication by Edward Tufte that was pasted from a website, which the software documented with the pasting. The writer noted in digital ink that the publication date needs to be checked. Additionally, the writer is using the Research tool to search for information on JASC, a major graphics software company. OneNote allows writers to integrate easily a variety of information formats. Once data is in place, writers can grab chunks of infor-

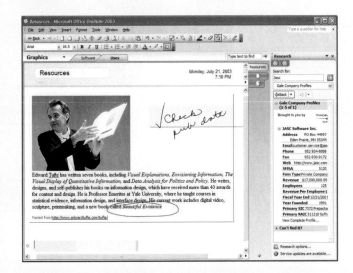

mation and reorganize them as needed. By giving writers a tool to integrate these diverse technologies, OneNote can help improve both a writer's efficiency and the quality of the end document.

---

uct information, finding prices, compiling performance statistics, and so on. Such a personal investigation usually requires knowledge of your field of work, which is probably why you were assigned the problem.

Some business problems require a more formal type of research, such as an experiment or a survey. The experiment is the basic technique of the sciences. Business uses experiments primarily in the laboratory, although experiments have some nonlaboratory applications in marketing. Surveys are more likely to be used in business, especially in marketing problems. If you are called on to use experiments or surveys, it will probably be because your training has prepared you to use them. If you should need these techniques in this course, you will find them summarized in Chapter 19.

> • Experiments or surveys are sometimes needed.

In some cases, you may use library and online research to find the information you need. Perhaps you have a good working knowledge of the techniques of research. If you do not, you will find these techniques also summarized in Chapter 19. To present facts from published sources in reports, you will need to use still other techniques: constructing a bibliography, citing references, quoting, paraphrasing, and so on. These techniques are covered in Appendix E.

> • Sometimes library research is used.

With the computer, you can search for electronically stored information. By using the Internet, a worldwide collection of networks, you can connect to information sources throughout the world. For example, you can work with others at different locations, you can access databases, you can use larger computers to help in your research, or you can browse any number of library catalogs. As noted in Chapter 19, the Internet is a vital source for information gathering in business reports. Information quality varies widely on the Internet, however. You should make sure the sources you consult are reliable. You will find more information on evaluating sources in Chapter 19.

> • The Internet gives you access to many information sources. Quality may vary.

Interpreting facts requires playing the role of a judge. To get to the truth, you must rise above the ordinary persona and think without bias, prejudice, and emotion. You should consider all sides of a problem in your search for the truth.

- Apply the research techniques needed for the problem.

In any event, your task is to apply whatever research techniques are required to get the information you need for your problem. When you have gathered that information, you are ready for the next step in report preparation.

INTERPRETING THE FINDINGS

- Next, apply the information collected to the problem. Interpret it.

With your research done, you are ready to prepare your findings for presentation. You will perform this task with your readers' convenience in mind. If your readers will want only the facts you have found, you need only organize by subtopics of the subject. But if your readers will want an analysis of the data with application to the problem, you must do much more. You must interpret the information as it affects the problem. Applying and interpreting your findings is obviously a mental process. Thus, we can give you only limited advice on how to do it. But even though this advice is limited, you can profit by following it.

- Interpreting is mental. You can profit from the following advice.

Advice for Avoiding Human Error

- Avoid human error by remembering these fundamentals:

The first advice is to avoid certain human tendencies that lead to error in interpretation. Foremost among these are the following:

- 1. Report the facts as they are.

1. *Report the facts as they are.* Do nothing to make them more or less exciting. Adding color to interpretations to make the report more interesting amounts to bias.

- 2. Do not think that conclusions are always necessary.

2. *Do not think that conclusions are always necessary.* When the facts do not support a conclusion, you should just summarize your findings and conclude that there is no conclusion. All too often report writers think that if they do not conclude, they have failed in their investigation.

- 3. Do not interpret a lack of evidence as proof to the contrary.

3. *Do not interpret a lack of evidence as proof to the contrary.* The fact that you cannot prove something is true does not mean that it is false.

- 4. Do not compare noncomparable data.

4. *Do not compare noncomparable data.* When you look for relationships between sets of data, make sure they have similarities—that you do not have apples and oranges.

- 5. Do not draw illogical cause–effect conclusions.

5. *Do not draw illogical cause–effect conclusions.* Just because two sets of data appear to affect each other does not mean they actually do. Use your good logic to determine whether a cause–effect relationship is likely.

You're right. This report does make you look like a fool.
SOURCE: Copyright, *USA Today*. Reprinted with permission.

6. *Beware of unreliable and unrepresentative data.* Much of the information to be found in secondary sources is incorrect to some extent. The causes are many: collection error, biased research, recording mistakes. Beware especially of data collected by groups that advocate a position (political organizations, groups supporting social issues, and other special interest groups). Make sure the sources you uncover are reliable. And remember that the interpretations you make are no better than the data you interpret.

• 6. Beware of unreliable and unrepresentative data.

7. *Do not oversimplify.* Most business problems are complex, and all too often we neglect some important parts of them.

• 7. Do not oversimplify.

Appropriate Attitudes and Practices

In addition to being alert to the most likely causes of error, you can improve your interpretation of findings by adopting the following attitudes and practices:

• Adopt the following attitudes and practices:

1. *Maintain a judicial attitude.* Play the role of a judge as you interpret. Look at all sides of every issue without emotion or prejudice. Your primary objective is to uncover truth.

• 1. Maintain a judicial attitude.

2. *Consult with others.* It is rare indeed when one mind is better than two or more. Thus, you can profit by talking over your interpretations with others.

• 2. Consult with others.

3. *Test your interpretations.* Unfortunately, the means of testing are subjective and involve the thinking process. Even so, testing is helpful and can help you avoid major error. Two tests are available to you.

• 3. Test your interpretations.

First is the test of experience. In applying this test, you use the underlying theme in all scientific methods—reason. You ponder each interpretation you make, asking yourself, "Does this appear reasonable in light of all I know or have experienced?"

• Use the test of experience—reason.

Second is the negative test, which is an application of the critical viewpoint. You begin by making the interpretation that is directly opposite your initial one. Next, you examine the opposite interpretation carefully in light of all available evidence, perhaps even building a case for it. Then you compare the two interpretations and retain the one that is more strongly supported.

• Use the negative test—question your interpretations.

Statistical Tools in Interpretation

In many cases, the information you gather is quantitative—that is, expressed in numbers. Such data in their raw form usually are voluminous, consisting of tens, hundreds, even thousands of figures. To use these figures intelligently, you first must find ways of simplifying them so that your reader can grasp their general meaning. Statistical techniques provide many methods for analyzing data. By knowing them, you can improve your ability to interpret. Although a thorough review of statistical techniques is

• Statistics permit you to examine a set of facts.

beyond the scope of this book, you should know the more commonly used methods described in the following paragraphs.

Possibly of greatest use to you in writing reports are *descriptive statistics*—measures of central tendency, dispersion, ratios, and probability. Measures of central tendency—the mean, median, and mode—will help you find a common value of a series that appropriately describes a whole. The measures of dispersion—ranges, variances, and standard deviations—should help you describe the spread of a series. Ratios (which express one quantity as a multiple of another) and probabilities (which determine how many times something will likely occur out of the total number of possibilities) also can help you convey common meaning in data analysis. Inferential and other statistical approaches are also useful but go beyond these basic elements. You will find descriptions of these and other useful techniques in the help documentation of your spreadsheet and statistics software as well as in any standard statistics textbook.

A word of caution, however: Your job as a writer is to help your reader interpret the information. Sometimes unexplained statistical calculations—even if elementary to you —may confuse the reader. Thus, you must explain your statistical techniques explicitly with words and visuals when needed. You must remember that statistics are a help to interpretation, not a replacement for it. Whatever you do to reduce the volume of data deserves careful explanation so that the reader will receive the intended meaning.

ORGANIZING THE REPORT INFORMATION

When you have finished interpreting your information, you know the message of your report. Now you are ready to organize this message for presentation. Your goal here is to present the information in the order that communicates best to your readers. You want not just what is easiest for you but what will best serve your readers. Organizing the report message, of course, is the procedure of constructing the outline. As you know, an outline is the plan for the writing task that follows. It is to you, the writer, what the blueprint is to the construction engineer or what the pattern is to the dressmaker. Constructing an outline forces you to think before you write. When you do this, your writing is likely to benefit.

Although your plan may be written or mental, using a written plan is advisable for all but the shortest problems. In a longer report, the outline forms the basis for the table of contents. Also, in most long reports, and even in some short ones, the outline topics serve as guides to the reader, as headings to the material they cover.

In constructing your outline, you probably will use either the conventional or the decimal symbol system to mark the levels. The conventional system uses Roman numerals to show the major headings and letters of the alphabet and Arabic numbers to show the lesser headings, as illustrated here:

Conventional System
I. First-level heading
  A. Second level, first part
  B. Second level, second part
     1. Third level, first part
     2. Third level, second part
       a. Fourth level, first part
         (1) Fifth level, first part
           (a) Sixth level, first part
II. First-level heading
  A. Second level, first part
  B. Second level, second part
  Etc.

The decimal system uses whole numbers to show the major sections. Whole numbers followed by decimals and additional digits show subsections. That is, the digits to the right of the decimal show each successive step in the outline. Illustration best explains this system:

- Descriptive statistics should help the most.

- Do not allow statistical calculations to confuse the reader; they should help interpret.

- After you know what your findings mean, you are ready to construct the outline.

- Outlines should usually be written. They serve as tables of contents and captions.

- This conventional symbol system is used in marking the levels of an outline.

Software Tools Assist the Writer in Both Identifying Factors and Outlining

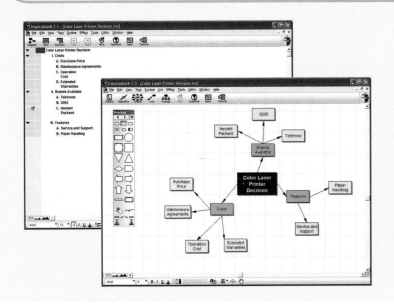

Inspiration is a concept mapping tool aimed at helping business executives create and outline business documents. The example shown here demonstrates how individuals or groups can brainstorm the factors of a report that investigates which color laser printer a product design department should purchase. Using either the diagram or outline view (or both), a report writer would list as many ideas as possible. Later the items and relationships can be rearranged by dragging and moving pointers.

The software will update the outline symbols as changes are made. Users can toggle between the different views to work with the mode that works best for them. When ready to write, users can export the outline or diagram to Word or rtf format.

Decimal System

1.0 First-level heading
   1.1 Second level, first part
   1.2 Second level, second part
      1.2.1 Third level, first part
      1.2.2 Third level, second part
         1.2.2.1 Fourth level, first part
            1.2.2.1.1 Fifth level, first part
               1.2.2.1.1.1 Sixth level, first part

2.0 First-level heading
   2.1 Second level, first part
   2.2 Second level, second part
   Etc.

- This decimal system is also used.

Whatever system you use, when you begin producing the final report, you also will show differences in the levels of headings by placement and form (font, size, or style). The placement and form options available to you are reviewed in Appendix B.

The Nature and Extent of Outlining

In general, you should build the outline around the objective of the report and the information you have gathered to meet that objective. With the objective and your information in mind, you build the structure of the report mentally. In this process, you shift facts and ideas about until the most workable order becomes clear. That order is the one that presents the findings in the clearest and most meaningful way.

How much work you will have to do at this stage varies by problem. In some cases, you may have little to do, for you may have determined the order of the report in preceding steps. For example, the problem factors that you determined early in the investigation may also be the main heads of your outline. Or perhaps you worked out an order for presenting your research findings when you analyzed and interpreted them. In all likelihood, when you reach the stage of consciously constructing the outline, you will find that you have already done some of the work. Even so, there will probably

- The outline is designed to meet the objective of the report.

- When you reach the outlining stage, you have probably done some of the work.

be much to do. In doing it, you would be wise to use the general procedure described in the following paragraphs.

Introductory and Concluding Parts

● The following discussion of outlining deals with the body of the report. Assume that an introduction and a conclusion will be added.

Outlining is concerned mainly with the part of the report commonly called the *body*. The body is the part of the report that presents the information gathered, with analyses and interpretations where needed. It is usually preceded by an introduction, which is common in all but the shortest reports. And it is usually followed by an ending section, which may be a summary, a conclusion, a recommendation, or some combination of the three. The introduction and the ending section are parts of the outline, of course, but the following discussion does not concern them. The structure and content of these parts are discussed where appropriate in the following chapters.

Organization by Division

● You may view organizing as a process of division. First, you divide the whole into parts.

The organizing procedure described in the following pages is based on a process of dividing. The subject you are dividing is all the information (facts) you have gathered and interpreted. Thus, you begin the task of organizing by looking over that information for some way of dividing it into logical parts. When you find a way, you divide it. This process gives you the major outline parts indicated in Figure 10–1 by the Roman numeral captions (II, III, IV, and so on).

● Then you divide the parts into subparts. You may subdivide further.

In short reports, one level of division may be enough. Long reports, however, may require that each level in the first division be divided. The parts in the second level of division are identified by capital letter headings (A, B, C). You may have to divide a third time (for the 1, 2, 3 outline parts). In fact, you may continue to subdivide as long as it is practical to do so. Each division makes a step in the outline.

Division by Conventional Relationships

● Time, place, quantity, and factor are the bases for the process of division.

In dividing your information into subparts, you have to find a way of dividing that will produce approximately equal parts. Time, place, quantity, and factor are the general bases for these divisions.

● When the information has a time basis, division by time is possible.

Whenever the information you have to present has some time aspect, consider organizing it by *time*. In such an organization, the divisions are periods of time. These time periods usually follow a sequence. Although a past-to-present or present-to-past sequence is the rule, variations are possible. The periods you select need not be equal in duration, but they should be about equal in importance.

A report on the progress of a research committee illustrates this possibility. The period covered by this report might be broken down into the following comparable subperiods:

The period of orientation, May–July

Planning the project, August

Implementation of the research plan, September–November

The happenings within each period might next be arranged in order of occurrence. Close inspection might reveal additional division possibilities.

● When the information is related to geographic location, a place division is possible.

If the information you have collected has some relation to geographic location, you may use a *place* division. Ideally, this division would be such that the areas are nearly equal in importance.

A report on the U.S. sales program of a national manufacturer illustrates a division by place. The information in this problem might be broken down by these major geographic areas:

New England

Atlantic Seaboard

South

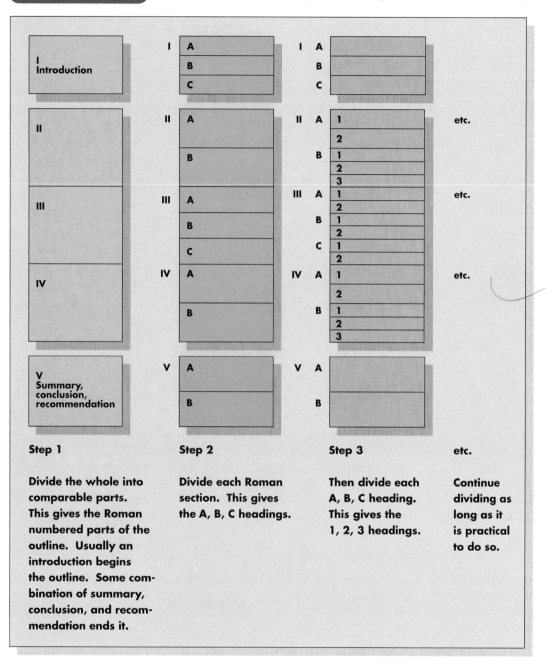

Step 1

Divide the whole into comparable parts. This gives the Roman numbered parts of the outline. Usually an introduction begins the outline. Some combination of summary, conclusion, and recommendation ends it.

Step 2

Divide each Roman section. This gives the A, B, C headings.

Step 3

Then divide each A, B, C heading. This gives the 1, 2, 3 headings.

etc.

Continue dividing as long as it is practical to do so.

Southwest

Midwest

Rocky Mountains

Pacific Coast

Another illustration of organization by place is a report on the productivity of a company with a number of customer service branches. A major division of the report might be devoted to each of the branches. The information for each branch might be broken down further, this time by sections, departments, divisions, or the like.

Quantity divisions are possible for information that has quantitative values. To illustrate, an analysis of the buying habits of potential customers could be divided by such income groups as the following:

- Division based on quantity is possible when the information has a number base.

Under $30,000

$30,000 to under $45,000

$45,000 to under $60,000

$60,000 to under $85,000

$85,000 to under $100,000

$100,000 and over

Another example of division on a quantitative basis is a report of a survey of men's preferences for shoes, in which an organization by age groups might be used to show variations in preference by ages. Perhaps the following divisions would be appropriate:

Youths, under 18

Young adults, 18–30

Adults, 31–50

Senior adults, 51–70

Elder adults, over 70

- Factors (areas to be investigated) are a fourth basis for dividing information.

Factor breakdowns are less easily seen than the preceding three possibilities. Problems often have few or no time, place, or quantity aspects. Instead, they require that certain information areas be investigated. Such areas may consist of questions that must be answered in solving a problem, or of subjects that must be investigated and applied to the problem.

An example of a division by factors is a report that seeks to determine which of three locations is the best for a new office for property management. In arriving at this decision, one would need to compare the three locations based on the factors affecting the office location. Thus, the following organization of this problem would be a possibility:

Location accessibility

Rent

Parking

Convenience to current and new customers

Facilities

Another illustration of organization by factors is a report advising a manufacturer whether to begin production of a new product. The solution of this problem will be reached by careful consideration of the factors involved. Among the more likely factors are these:

Production feasibility

Financial considerations

Strength of competition

Consumer demand

Marketing considerations

Combination and Multiple Division Possibilities

- Combinations of time, place, quantity, and factor are sometimes logical.

Not all division possibilities are clearly time, place, quantity, or factor. In some instances, combinations of these bases of division are possible. In a report on the progress of a sales organization, for example, the information collected could be arranged by a combination of quantity and place:

Areas of high sales activity

Areas of moderate sales activity

Areas of low sales activity

Some reports on sales of cyclical products might use the following combination of time and quantity:

Periods of low sales

Periods of moderate sales

Periods of high sales

Some problems can be organized in more than one way. For example, take the problem of determining the best of three locations for an annual sales meeting. It could be organized by site or by the bases of comparison. Organized by sites, the bases of comparison would probably be the second-level headings:

II.   Site A
    A. Airport accessibility
    B. Hotel accommodations
    C. Meeting facilities
    D. Favorable weather
    E. Costs
    F. Restaurant/entertainment options
III. Site B
    A. Airport accessibility
    B. And so on
IV.   Site C
    A. Airport accessibility
    B. And so on

Organized by bases of comparison, cities would probably be the second-level headings:

II.   Airport accessibility
    A. Site A
    B. Site B
    C. Site C
III. Hotel accommodations
    A. Site A
    B. Site B
    C. Site C
IV.   Meeting facilities
    A. Site A
    B. Site B
    C. Site C

At first glance, both plans appear logical. Close inspection, however, shows that organization by cities separates information that has to be compared. For example, three different parts of the report must be examined to find out which city has the best hotel accommodations. In the second outline, the information that has to be compared is close together. You can determine which city has the best hotel accommodations after reading only one section of the report.

Nevertheless, these two plans show that some problems can be organized in more than one way. In such cases, you must compare the possibilities carefully to find the one that best presents the report information.

Wording of the Outline

The outline in its finished form is the table of contents. Its parts serve as headings to the sections of the report (which is why we refer to these parts as *headings* in the following discussion). Because the outline is an important part of the report, you should construct its final wording carefully. In this regard, you should consider the conventional principles of construction reviewed in the following pages.

- Multiple organization possibilities can occur.

- This meeting problem is organized by place.

- Here, it is organized by factors (the bases of comparison).

- The second plan is better because it makes comparison easy.

- When the outline will appear in the report, take care in its wording.

Topic or Talking Headings. In selecting the wording for outline headings, you have a choice of two general forms: topic headings and talking headings. *Topic headings* are short constructions, frequently consisting of one or two words. They merely identify the topic of discussion. Here is a segment of a topic-heading outline:

II. Present armor unit
    A. Description and output
    B. Cost
    C. Deficiencies
III. Replacement effects
    A. Space
    B. Boiler setting
    C. Additional accessories
    D. Fuel

Like topic headings, *talking headings* (or *popular headings* as they are sometimes called) identify the subject matter covered. But they go a step further. They also indicate what is said about the subject. In other words, talking headings summarize the material they cover, as in this illustration:

II. Operation analyses of armor unit
    A. Recent lag in overall output
    B. Increase in cost of operation
    C. Inability to deliver necessary steam
III. Consideration of replacement effects
    A. Greater space requirements
    B. Need for higher boiler setting
    C. Efficiency possibilities of accessories
    D. Practicability of firing two fuels

The following report outline is made up of headings that talk:

I. Orientation to the problem
    A. Authorization by board action
    B. Problem of locating a woolen mill
    C. Use of miscellaneous government data
    D. Factors as bases of problem solution
II. Community attitudes toward the woolen industry
    A. Favorable reaction of all towns to new mill
    B. Mixed attitudes of all towns toward labor policy
III. Labor supply and prevailing wage rates
    A. Lead of San Marcos in unskilled labor
    B. Concentration of skilled workers in San Marcos
    C. Generally confused pattern of wage rates
IV. Nearness to the raw wool supply
    A. Location of Ballinger, Coleman, and San Marcos in the wool area
    B. Relatively low production near Big Spring and Littlefield
V. Availability of utilities
    A. Inadequate water supply for all towns but San Marcos
    B. Unlimited supply of natural gas for all towns
    C. Electric rate advantage of San Marcos and Coleman
    D. General adequacy of all towns for waste disposal
VI. Adequacy of existing transportation systems
    A. Surface transportation advantages of San Marcos and Ballinger
    B. General equality of airway connections
VII. A final weighting of the factors
    A. Selection of San Marcos as first choice
    B. Recommendation of Ballinger as second choice
    C. Lack of advantages in Big Spring, Coleman, and Littlefield

This report outline is made up of topic headings:

I. Introduction
   A. Authorization
   B. Purpose
   C. Sources
   D. Preview
II. Community attitudes
   A. Plant location
   B. Labor policy
III. Factors of labor
   A. Unskilled workers
   B. Skilled workers
   C. Wage rates
IV. Raw wool supply
   A. Adequate areas
   B. Inadequate areas
V. Utilities
   A. Water
   B. Natural gas
   C. Electricity
   D. Waste disposal
VI. Transportation
   A. Surface
   B. Air
VII. Conclusions
   A. First choice
   B. Alternative choice
   C. Other possibilities

Parallelism of Construction. As a general rule, you should write headings at each level of the outline in the same grammatical form. In other words, equal-level headings should be parallel in structure. This rule is not an exercise in grammar; its purpose is to show similarity. As you will recall from the discussion of conventional relationships of data, equal-level headings are divided consistently using time, place, quantity, factor, or combinations. You want to show consistently such equal-level divisions through parallel headings. For example, if the heading for Roman numeral I is a noun phrase, all other Roman numeral headings should be noun phrases. If the heading for A under I is a sentence, the A, B, C headings throughout the outline should be sentences. However, authorities also permit varying the form from one part to another (example: sentences for A, B, and C under II and noun phrases for A, B, and C under III).

- Headings making up a level of division should be parallel grammatically.

The following segment of an outline illustrates violations of parallelism:

A. Programmer output is lagging (sentence).
B. Increase in cost of labor (noun phrase)
C. Unable to deliver necessary results (decapitated sentence)

You may correct this violation in any of three ways: by making the headings all sentences, all noun phrases, or all decapitated sentences. If you desire all noun phrases, you could construct such headings as these:

A. Lag in programmer output
B. Increase in cost of labor
C. Inability to deliver necessary results

Or you could make all the headings sentences, like this:

A. Programmer output is lagging.
B. Cost of labor is increasing.
C. Information systems cannot deliver necessary results.

Conciseness in Wording. Your talking captions should be the shortest possible word arrangement that also can meet the talking requirement. Although the following captions talk well, their excessive lengths obviously affect their roles in communicating the report information:

Personal appearance enhancement is the most desirable feature of contact lenses that wearers report.

The drawback of contacts mentioned by most people who can't wear them is that they are difficult to put in.

More comfort is the most desired improvement suggested by wearers and nonwearers of contact lenses.

Obviously, the captions contain too much information. Just what should be left out, however, is not easily determined. Much depends on the analysis the writers have given the material and what they have determined to be most significant. One analysis, for example, would support these revised captions:

Personal appearance most desirable feature

Difficulty of insertion prime criticism

Comfort most desired improvement

Variety of Expression. In the report outline, as in all other forms of writing, you should use a variety of expressions. You should not overwork words, for repeating words too frequently makes for monotonous writing; and monotonous writing is not pleasing to the reader. The following outline excerpt illustrates this point:

A. Oil production in Texas
B. Oil production in California
C. Oil production in Louisiana

As a rule, if you make the headings talk well, there is little chance of monotonous repetition. Since your successive sections would probably not be presenting similar or identical information, headings really descriptive of the material they cover would not be likely to use the same words. The headings in the preceding example can be improved simply by making them talk:

A. Texas leads in oil production.
B. California holds runner-up position.
C. Rapidly gaining Louisiana ranks third.

WRITING THE REPORT

After you have collected and organized your information, you are ready to begin writing. Much of what you should do in writing the report was covered in the review of clear writing techniques in Chapters 2 and 3. All of these techniques apply to report writing, and you would do well to keep them in mind as you write. As in all the business messages discussed previously, in report writing you have an obligation to communicate as easily, as clearly, and as quickly as possible. Your reader's time is valuable to his or her understanding of your message, and this understanding is vital to work performance.

You can further help your reader to receive the report message clearly by giving your report some specific characteristics of well-written reports. These characteristics are objectivity, consistency in time viewpoint, transition, and interest. We review each of them in the following pages.

Requirement of Objectivity

Good report writing presents facts and interprets them logically. It avoids presenting the writer's opinions, biases, and attitudes. In other words, it is objective.

You can make your report objective by putting aside your prejudices and biases, by approaching the problem with an open mind and looking at all sides of every issue, and by fairly reviewing and interpreting the information you have uncovered. Your role should be much like that of a fair-minded judge presiding over a court of law. You will leave no stone unturned in your search for truth.

- Keep out all bias. Seek truth.

Objectivity as a Basis for Believability. An objective report has an ingredient that is essential to good report writing—believability. Biased writing in artfully deceptive language may at first glance be believable. But if bias is evident at any place in a report, the reader will be suspicious of the entire report. Maintaining objectivity is, therefore, the only sure way to make report writing believable.

- Objective writing is believable.

Objectivity and the Question of Impersonal versus Personal Writing. Recognizing the need for objectivity, the early report writers worked to develop an objective style of writing. Since the source of bias in reports was people, they reasoned objectivity was best attained by emphasizing facts rather than the people involved in writing and reading reports. So they tried to take the human beings out of their reports. The result was impersonal writing, that is, writing in the third person—without *I*'s, *we*'s, or *you*'s.

- Historically, objective writing has meant writing impersonally (no I's, we's, you's).

In recent years, some writers have questioned impersonal report writing. They argue that personal writing is more forceful and direct than impersonal writing. They point out that writing is more conversational and, therefore, more interesting if it brings both the reader and the writer into the picture. They contend that objectivity is an attitude—not a matter of person—and that a report written in personal style can be just as objective as a report written in impersonal style. These writers argue that impersonal writing frequently leads to an overuse of the passive voice and a dull writing style. This last argument, however, lacks substance. The style of impersonal writing can and should be interesting. Any dullness that impersonal writing may have is the fault of the writer. As proof, one has only to look at the lively style of writers for newspapers, newsmagazines, and journals. Most of this writing is impersonal—but it is usually not dull.

- Recently, some writers have argued that personal writing is more interesting than impersonal writing and just as objective.

As in most controversies, the arguments of both sides have merit. In some situations, personal writing is better. In other situations, impersonal writing is better. And in still other situations, either type of writing is good.

- There is merit to both sides. You would be wise to do what your reader expects of you.

Your decision should be based on the facts of each report situation. First, you should consider the expectations of those for whom you are preparing the report. More than likely, you will find a preference for impersonal writing, for businesspeople have been slow to break tradition. Then you should consider the formality of the situation. You should use personal writing for informal situations and impersonal writing for formal situations.

- Good advice is to use personal style for routine reports and impersonal style for more formal reports.

Perhaps the distinction between impersonal and personal writing is best made by illustration.

Personal

Having studied the advantages and disadvantages of using coupons, I conclude that your company should not adopt this practice. If you use the coupons, you would have to pay out money for them. You also would have to hire additional employees to take care of the increase in sales volume.

Impersonal

A study of the advantages and disadvantages of using coupons supports the conclusion that the Mills Company should not adopt this practice. The coupons themselves would cost extra money. Also, use of coupons would require additional personnel to take care of the increase in sales volume.

Consistency in Time Viewpoint

Presenting information in the right place in time is a major problem in keeping order in a report. Not doing so confuses the reader. Thus, it is important that you maintain a proper time viewpoint.

- Keep a consistent time viewpoint throughout the report.

An Example of Objective Reporting?

The story is told of the sea captain who once found his first mate drunk on duty. A man of the old school, the captain dutifully recorded the incident in his daily report to the ship's owners. He wrote: "Today First Mate Carlos E. Sperry was drunk on duty."

The first mate, unhappy about the incident, was determined to get revenge at the first opportunity. Some days later, his chance came. The captain was so ill that he could not leave his quarters, and First Mate Sperry was now in charge. At the end of the day it was Sperry's duty to write the daily report. This is what he wrote: "Today Captain Eli A. Dunn was sober."

The words were literally true, of course. But what a second meaning they carried!

- There are two time viewpoints: past and present. Select one, and do not change.

- The past-time viewpoint views the research and the findings as past, and prevailing concepts and proven conclusions as present.

You have two choices of time viewpoint: past and present. Although some authorities favor one or the other, either viewpoint can produce a good report. The important thing is to be consistent—to select one time viewpoint and stay with it. In other words, you should view all similar information in the report from the same position in time.

If you adopt the past-time viewpoint, you treat the research, the findings, and the writing of the report as past. Thus, you would report the results of a recent survey in past tense: "Twenty-two percent of the managers *favored* a change." You would write a reference to another part of the report this way: "In Part III, this conclusion *was reached.*" Your use of the past-time viewpoint would have no effect on references to future happenings. It would be proper to write a sentence like this: "If the current trend continues, 30 percent *will favor* a change by 2009." Prevailing concepts and proven conclusions are also exceptions. You would present them in present tense. For examples, take the sentences: "Solar energy *is* a major potential source of energy" and "The findings *show* conclusively that managers are not adequately trained."

- The present-time viewpoint presents as current all information that can be assumed to be current at the time of writing.

Writing in the present-time viewpoint presents as current all information that can logically be assumed to be current at the time of writing. All other information is presented in its proper place in the past or future. Thus, you would report the results of a recent survey in these words: "Twenty-two percent of the managers *favor* a change." You would refer to another part of the text like this: "In Part III, this conclusion *is reached.*" In referring to an old survey, you would write: "In 2003 only 12 percent *held* this opinion." And in making a future reference, you would write: "If this trend continues, 30 percent *will hold* this opinion by 2009."

Need for Transition

- You should use transitions to connect the parts of the report.

A well-written report reads as one continuous story. The parts connect smoothly. Much of this smoothness is the result of good, logical organization. But more than logical order is needed in long reports. As you will see in Chapter 12, a coherence plan may be needed in such reports. In all reports, however, lesser transitional techniques are useful to connect information.

- *Transition* means a "bridging across."

By *transition* we mean a "bridging across." Transitions are words or sentences that show the relationships of succeeding parts. They may appear at the beginning of a part as a way of relating this part to the preceding part. They may appear at the end of a part as a forward look. Or they may appear within a part as words or phrases that help move the flow of information.

- *Transitions* should be used where there is a need to connect the parts of the report.

Whether you use transitional words or a transitional sentence in a particular place depends on need. If there is need to relate parts, you should use a transition. Because good, logical organization frequently clarifies the relationships of the parts in a short report, such reports may need only a few transitional words or sentences. Longer and more involved reports, on the other hand, usually require more.

Before we comment more specifically on transitions, we should make one point clear. You should not use transitions mechanically. You should use them only when they are needed—when leaving them out would produce abruptness. Transitions should not appear to be stuck in. They should blend naturally with the surrounding writing. For example, avoid transitions of this mechanical form: "The last section discussed Topic X. In the next section, Y will be analyzed."

Sentence Transitions. Throughout the report you can improve the connecting network of thought by the wise use of sentence transitions. You can use them especially to connect parts of the report. The following example shows how a sentence can explain the relationship between Sections A and B of a report. Note that the first words draw a conclusion for Section B. Then, with smooth tie-in, the next words introduce Section C and relate this part to the report plan. The words in brackets explain the pattern of the thought connections.

[Section B, concluded] . . . Thus, the data show only negligible differences in the cost for oil consumption [subject of Section B] for the three models of cars.

[Section C] Even though the costs of gasoline [subject of Section A] and oil [subject of Section B] are the more consistent factors of operation expense, the picture is not complete until the costs of repairs and maintenance [subject of Section C] are considered.

In the following examples, succeeding parts are connected by sentences that make a forward-looking reference and thus set up the next subject. As a result, the shift of subject matter is smooth and logical.

These data show clearly that alternative fuel cars are the most economical. Unquestionably, their operation by gas and hydrogen and their record for low-cost maintenance give them a decided edge over gas-fueled cars. *Before a definite conclusion about their merit is reached, however, one more vital comparison should be made.*

(The final sentence clearly introduces the subsequent discussion of an additional comparison.)

. . . At first glance the data appear convincing, but a closer observation reveals a number of discrepancies.

(Discussion of the discrepancies is logically set up by this sentence.)

Placing topic sentences at key points of emphasis is another way of using sentences to link the various parts of the report. Usually the topic sentence is best placed at the paragraph beginning. Note in the following example how topic sentences maintain the flow of thought by emphasizing key information.

The Acura accelerates faster than the other two brands, both on a level road and on a 9 percent grade. According to a test conducted by *Consumer Reports,* Acura reaches a speed of 60 miles per hour in 13.2 seconds. To reach the same speed, Toyota requires 13.6 seconds, and Volkswagen requires 14.4 seconds. On a 9 percent grade, Acura reaches the 60-miles-per-hour speed in 29.4 seconds, and Toyota reaches it in 43.3 seconds. Volkswagen is unable to reach this speed.

Because it carries more weight on its rear wheels than the others, Acura has the best traction of the three. Traction, which means a minimum of sliding on wet or icy roads, is important to safe driving, particularly during the cold, wet winter months. Since traction is directly related to the weight carried by the rear wheels, a comparison of these weights should give some measure of the safety of the three cars. According to data released by the Automobile Bureau of Standards, Acura carries 47 percent of its weight on its rear wheels. Nissan and Toyota carry 44 and 42 percent, respectively.

Transitional Words. Although the most important transition problems concern connection between the major parts of the report, transitions are needed between the lesser parts. If the writing is to flow smoothly, you will need to connect clause to clause, sentence to sentence, and paragraph to paragraph. Transitional words and phrases generally serve to make such connections.

Numerous transitional words are available. The following list shows such words and how you can use them. With a little imagination to supply the context, you can easily see how these words relate ideas. For better understanding, the words are grouped by the relationships they show between what comes before and what follows.

- This partial list shows how words explain relationships.

Relationship	Word Examples
Listing or enumeration of subjects	In addition
	First, second, and so on
	Besides
	Moreover
Contrast	On the contrary
	In spite of
	On the other hand
	In contrast
	However
Likeness	In a like manner
	Likewise
	Similarly
Cause–result	Thus
	Because of
	Therefore
	Consequently
	For this reason

Relationship	Word Examples
Explanation or elaboration	For example
	To illustrate
	For instance
	Also
	Too

Maintaining Interest

Like any other form of writing, report writing should be interesting. Actually, interest is as important as the facts of the report, for communication is not likely to occur without interest. Readers cannot help missing parts of the message if their interest is not held—if their minds are allowed to stray. Interest in the content is not enough to ensure communication. The writing itself must be interesting. This should be evident to you if you have ever tried to read dull writing in studying for an examination. How desperately you wanted to learn the subject, but how often your mind strayed!

Perhaps writing interestingly is an art. But if so, it is an art in which you can develop ability by working at it. To develop this ability, you need to avoid the rubber-stamp jargon so often used in business and instead work to make your words build concrete pictures. You need to cultivate a feeling for the rhythmic flow of words and sentences. You need to remember that in back of every fact and figure there is life—people doing things, machines operating, a commodity being marketed. A technique of good report writing is to bring that life to the surface by using concrete words and active-voice verbs as much as possible. You also should work to achieve interest without using more words than are necessary.

Here a word of caution should be injected. You can overdo efforts to make report writing interesting. Such is the case whenever your reader's attention is attracted to how something has been said rather than to what has been said. Effective report writing simply presents information in a clear, concise, and interesting manner. Perhaps the purpose and definition of report-writing style are best summarized in this way: Report-writing style is at its best when the readers are prompted to say "Here are some interesting facts" rather than "Here is some beautiful writing."

- Report writing should be interesting. Interesting writing is necessary for good communication.

- Interesting writing is the result of careful word choice, rhythm, concreteness—in fact, all the good writing techniques.

- But efforts to make writing interesting can be overdone. The writing style should never draw attention away from the information.

COLLABORATIVE REPORT WRITING

In your business career, you are likely to participate in collaborative writing projects. That is, you will work on a report with others. Group involvement in report preparation is becoming increasingly significant for a number of reasons. For one, the specialized knowledge of different people can improve the quality of the work. For another, the combined talents of the members are likely to produce a document better than any one of the members could produce alone. A third reason is that dividing the work can reduce the time needed for the project. And fourth, new software tools allow groups to collaborate from different places.

- Collaborative report preparation is common for good reasons.

Determination of Group Makeup

As a beginning step, the membership of the group should be determined. In this determination, the availability and competencies of the people in the work situation involved are likely to be the major considerations. As a minimum, the group will consist of two. The maximum will depend on the number actually needed to do the project. As a practical matter, however, a maximum of five is a good rule, for larger groups tend to lose efficiency. More important than size, however, is the need to include all major areas of specialization involved in the work to be done.

In most business situations the highest ranking administrator in the group serves as leader. In groups made up of equals, a leader usually is appointed or elected. When no

- Groups should have five or fewer members and include all pertinent specialization areas.

- Preferably, the group has a leader, but there are exceptions.

Professorial Words of Wisdom

The first benefit of group work in the classroom is that it teaches students how to work collaboratively in the business environment. Business organizations repeatedly indicate that the increased use of teams in the real world has increased students' need for exposure and experience with teams. Companies that use teams creatively spend many hours and dollars training individuals to work in teams and training managers to manage teams.

Jacqueline K. Eastman, Valdosta State University

Cathy Owens Swift, Georgia Southern University

Jacqueline K. Eastman and Cathy Owens Swift, "Enhancing Collaborative Learning: Discussion Boards and Chat Rooms as Project Communication Tools," *Business Communication Quarterly* 65, no. 3 (September 2002): 30.

leader is so designated, the group works together informally. In such cases, however, an informal leader usually emerges.

Techniques of Participation

- Leaders and participants have clear duties to make the procedure work.

The group's work should be conducted much the way a meeting should be conducted. As described in Chapter 14, leaders and members of meetings have clear roles and duties. Leaders must plan the sessions and follow the plan. They must move the work along. They must control the discussion, limiting those who talk too much and encouraging input from those who are reluctant to participate. Group members should actively participate, taking care not to monopolize. They should be both cooperative and courteous in their work with the group.

- Groups often experience results that are less than ideal. Consult references on effective groups.

All too often, groups experience results that vary from these patterns. Although a discussion of group development and processes is beyond the scope of this book, you might want to consult one of the many references on the subject.[1] Group members should recognize that effective groups do not just happen. They have unique characteristics and processes that are planned for and managed explicitly.

Procedure of the Work

- At least two meetings and a work period are needed.

As a general rule, groups working together on report projects need a minimum of two meetings with a work period between meetings. But the number of meetings required will vary with the needs of the project. For a project in which data gathering and other preliminary work must be done, additional meetings may be necessary. On the other hand, if only the writing of the report is needed, two meetings may be adequate.

Activities Involved

- The following activities normally occur, usually in this sequence.

Whatever number of meetings are scheduled, the following activities typically occur, usually in the sequence shown. As you review them, it should be apparent that because of the differences in report projects, these activities vary in their implementation.

- First, determine the report purpose.

Determine the Purpose. As in all report projects, the participants must determine just what the report must do. Thus, the group should follow the preliminary steps of problem determination discussed previously.

---

[1] Two especially good resources are Allan R. Cohen and Stephen L. Fink, *Effective Behavior in Organizations,* 7th ed. (New York: McGraw-Hill/Irwin, 2001) and Gerald L. Wilson, *Groups in Context: Leadership and Participation in Small Groups,* 6th ed. (New York: McGraw-Hill, 2001).

Some reports written in business are produced in collaboration with others. Although you will do some work individually, you can expect to plan, organize, and revise the report as a group.

Derive the Factors. The group next determines what is needed to achieve the purpose. This step involves determining the factors of the problem, as described earlier in the chapter. An advantage of collaboration is that several minds are available for the critical thinking that is so necessary for identifying the factors of the problem.

- Next, derive the factors involved.

Gather the Information Needed. Before the group can begin work on the report, it must get the information needed. This activity could involve conducting any of the research designs mentioned earlier in this chapter and in Chapter 19. In some cases, group work begins after the information has been assembled, thus eliminating this step.

- If necessary, make a plan for gathering the information needed.

Interpret the Information. Determining the meaning of the information gathered is the next logical step for the group. In this step, the participants apply the findings to the problem, thereby selecting the information to be used in the report. In applying the findings to the problem, they also give meaning to the facts collected. The facts do not speak for themselves. Rather, group participants must think through the facts, apply the facts to the problem, and derive logical meaning from the facts. Interpretations are no better than the thinking of the people in the group.

- The members interpret the information, applying it to the problem.

Organize the Material. Just as in any other report-writing project, the group next organizes the material selected for presentation. They will apply time, place, quantity, factor (or combinations) relationships to the data collected in steps as shown in Figure 10–1.

- They organize the information for presentation in the report.

Plan the Writing. A next logical step is that of planning the makeup of the report. In this step the formality of the situation and the audience involved determine the

- They plan the writing of the report.

Comment and Review Tools Help Track Others' Changes to Your Documents

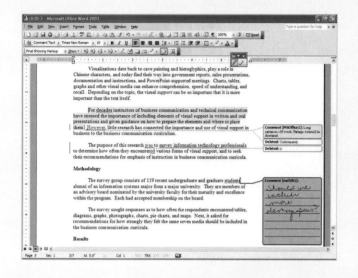

The commenting and reviewing tools in most word processors help people work together on documents asynchronously. When others review content and edit your document electronically, the commenting tool allows them to express opinions and concerns while the tracking tool makes their editing changes clearly visible. In fact, the tools allow you to accept or reject their suggestions individually or en masse.

In the example shown here, the reviewer turned on the reviewing toolbar to put frequently used tools at hand. Using this tool on a Tablet PC enabled the reviewer to choose from a variety of input methods—keyboard, digital ink, or voice. The tracking system allows reviewers to use a variety of colors, so others can easily determine who the changes belong to and the commenting tool inserts identifying information, too. If a reviewer had entered a voice comment, the user would have simply clicked on the speaker icon to listen to the comment.

---

decision. In addition, matters of writing such as tone, style, and formality are addressed. Needs for coherence, time consistency, and interesting writing are usually reinforced.

- They assign themselves report parts to write.

Assign Parts to Be Written. After the planning has been done, the group next turns its attention to the writing. The usual practice is to assign each person a part of the report.

- The members then write their parts.

Write Parts Assigned. Following comes a period of individual work. Each participant writes his or her part. Each will apply the ideas in Chapters 2 and 3 about word selection, sentence design, and paragraph construction to writing the assigned parts.

- The group members collaboratively review the writing.

Revise Collaboratively. The group meets and reviews each person's contribution and the full report. This should be a give-and-take session with each person actively participating. It requires that every person give keen attention to the work of each participant, making constructive suggestions wherever appropriate. It requires courteous but meaningful criticisms. It also requires that the participants be open-minded, remembering that the goal is to construct the best possible document. In no case should the group merely give automatic approval to the work submitted. In cases of controversy, the majority views of the group should prevail.

- A selected member edits the final draft.

Edit the Final Draft. After the group has done its work, one member usually is assigned the task of editing the final draft. This gives the document consistency. In addition, the editor serves as a final proofreader. Probably the editor should be the most competent writer in the group.

If all the work has been done with care and diligence, this final draft should be a report better than anyone in the group could have prepared alone. Those who study groups use the word *synergistic* to refer to groups that function this way. The final report is better than the sum of the individual parts.

SUMMARY BY CHAPTER OBJECTIVES

1. Your work on a report begins with a problem (purpose, goal, objective).
   - Get the problem in mind by gathering all the information you need about it.
   - Then develop a problem statement from the information.
   - Phrase this statement as an infinitive phrase, a question, or a declarative statement.

2. From the problem statement, determine the factors involved.
   - These may be subtopics in information reports.
   - They may be hypotheses (possible explanations) in problems requiring a solution.
   - They may be bases of comparison in problems requiring evaluations.

3. After you have gathered the information needed, interpret it as it applies to the problem.
   - Interpreting is mental and thus difficult to describe.
   - Heed this advice for avoiding human error:
     — Report the facts as they are.
     — Do not think that conclusions are always necessary.
     — Do not interpret a lack of evidence as proof to the contrary.
     — Do not compare noncomparable data.
     — Do not draw illogical cause–effect conclusions.
     — Beware of unreliable and unrepresentative data.
     — Do not oversimplify.
   - Adopt these attitudes and practices:
     — Maintain a judicial attitude.
     — Consult with others.
     — Test your interpretations by applying the test of experience (reason) and the negative test (question them).

4. Next, organize the information (construct an outline).
   - Probably you will use the conventional outline symbols (I, A, 1, a) or numeric symbols (1, 1.1, 1.1.1, 1.1.1.1) in structuring the outline.
   - Probably you will begin with an introduction and end with a summary, conclusion, or recommendation.
   - Organize the report body (the part between the introduction and the ending section) by a process of division.
     — Look over the findings for ways of dividing on the basis of time, place, quantity, factor, or combinations.
     — Then divide, forming the major parts of the report (Roman numeral headings).
     — Next, look at these divisions for ways of dividing them (making the capital letter headings).
     — Continue to subdivide as far as necessary.
     — The end result is your outline.

5. Construct headings for each part in the outline.
   - Use the topic form (identifies topic).
   - Or use the talking form (identifies topic and says something about it).
   - Make the wording of comparable parts parallel grammatically.
   - Prune each caption for conciseness.
   - Avoid excessive repetition of words.

6. From the outline, write the report.
   - Follow the rules of clarity discussed previously in this book.
   - Maintain objectivity (no bias).

1 State a problem clearly in writing.

2 List the factors involved in a problem.

3 Explain the common errors in interpreting and develop attitudes and practices conducive to good interpreting.

4 Organize information in outline form, using time, place, quantity, factor, or a combination of these as bases for division.

5 Construct topic or talking headings that outline reports logically and meaningfully.

6 Write reports that are clear, objective, consistent in time viewpoint, smoothly connected, and interesting.

- Impersonal writing style (third person) has long been associated with objectivity.
        - But some authorities question this style, saying personal style is more interesting.
        - The argument continues, although most formal reports are written in impersonal style.
    - Be consistent in time viewpoint—either past or present.
        - Past-time viewpoint views the research and findings as past and prevailing concepts and conclusions as present.
        - Present-time viewpoint presents as current all that is current at the time of writing.
    - Use transitions to make the report parts flow smoothly.
        - Between large parts, you may need to use full sentences to make connections.
        - Topic sentences also can help the flow of thought.
        - Use transitional words and phrases to connect the lesser parts.
    - Work to make the writing interesting.
        - Select words carefully for best effect.
        - Follow techniques of good writing (correctness, rhythmic flow of words, vigorous words, and such).
        - Do not overdo these efforts by drawing attention to how you write rather than what you say.

7. Expect that you will sometimes prepare reports collaboratively in groups.
    - Groups (two to five members) may produce better reports than individuals if all things go well.
    - Members of groups (leaders and participants) should have clear roles.
    - Groups should plan two or more meetings with a work period.
    - Groups should follow this procedure in writing reports collaboratively:
        - Determine report purpose.
        - Derive factors.
        - Collect facts for the report.
        - Interpret the facts.
        - Organize the facts.
        - Plan for writing.
        - Assign parts to members.
        - Write assigned parts.
        - Revise members' contributions collaboratively.
        - Edit the final draft.

7
Prepare reports collaboratively.

CRITICAL THINKING QUESTIONS

1. Explain the concept of outlining as a division process.
2. You are writing a report on the progress of your local cable company's efforts to increase sales of five of its products through extensive advertising in print and online newspapers and magazines and on television and radio. Discuss the possibilities for major headings. Evaluate each possibility.
3. Not all business reports are written objectively. In fact, many are deliberately biased. Why, then, should we stress objectivity in a college course that includes report writing?
4. Explain how the question of personal and impersonal writing is related to objectivity.
5. Explain the differences between the present-time viewpoint and the past-time viewpoint.
6. Is it incorrect to have present, past, and future tense in the same report? In the same paragraph? In the same sentence? Discuss.
7. "Transitional sentences are unnecessary. They merely add length to a report and thus are contrary to the established rules of conciseness." Discuss.
8. "Reports are written for business executives who want them. Thus, you don't have to be concerned about holding your reader's interest." Discuss.
9. Collaborative reports are better than reports written by an individual because they use many minds rather than one. Discuss.

CRITICAL THINKING EXERCISES

1. For each of the following problem situations, write a clear statement of the problem and list the factors involved. When necessary, you may use your imagination logically to supply any additional information needed.

    a. A manufacturer of breakfast cereals wants to determine the characteristics of its consumers.

    b. The manufacturer of a toothpaste wants to learn what the buying public thinks of its product in relation to competing products.

    c. Wal-Mart wants to give its stockholders a summary of its operations for the past calendar year.

    d. A building contractor engaged to build a new office for Company X submits a report summarizing its monthly progress.

    e. The Able Wholesale Company must prepare a report on its credit relations with the Crystal City Hardware Company.

    f. The supervisor of Department X must prepare a report evaluating the performance of a secretary.

    g. Baker, Inc., wants a study made to determine why its employee turnover is high.

    h. An executive must rank three subordinates on the basis of their suitability for promotion to a particular job.

    i. The supervisor of production must compare three competing machines that are being considered for use in a particular production job.

    j. An investment consultant must advise a client on whether to invest in the development of a lake resort.

    k. A consultant seeks to learn how a restaurant can improve its profits.

2. Select a hypothetical problem with a time division possibility. What other division possibilities does it have? Compare the two possibilities as the main bases for organizing the report.

3. Assume that you are writing the results of a survey conducted to determine what styles of shoes are worn throughout the country on various occasions by women of all ages. What division possibilities exist here? Which would you recommend?

4. For the problem described in the preceding exercise, use your imagination to construct topic headings for the outline.

5. Point out any violations of grammatical parallelism in these headings:

    a. Region I sales lagging.

    b. Moderate increase seen for Region II.

    c. Region III sales remain strong.

6. Point out any error in grammatical parallelism in these headings:

    a. High cost of operation.

    b. Slight improvement in production efficiency.

    c. Maintenance cost is low.

7. Which of the following headings is logically inconsistent with the others?

    a. Agricultural production continues to increase.

    b. Slight increase is made by manufacturing.

    c. Salaries remain high.

    d. Service industries show no change.

8. Select an editorial, feature article, book chapter, or the like that has no headings. Write talking headings for it.

9. Assume that you are writing a report that summarizes a survey you have conducted. Write a paragraph of the report using the present-time viewpoint; then write the paragraph using the past-time viewpoint. The paragraph will be based on the following information:

Answers to the question about how students view the proposed Aid to Education Bill in this survey and in a survey taken a year earlier (in parentheses).

For, 39 percent (21); Against, 17 percent (43).
No answer, undecided, etc., 44 percent (36).

CHAPTER ELEVEN

Report Structure: The Shorter Forms

CHAPTER OBJECTIVES

Upon completing this chapter, you will be able to write well-structured short reports. To reach this goal, you should be able to

1 Explain the structure of reports relative to length and formality.

2 Discuss the four major differences involved in writing short and long reports.

3 Write clear and well-organized short reports.

4 Write clear and well-organized letter and email reports.

5 Adapt the procedures for writing short reports to staff, audit, and progress reports as well as minutes of meetings.

6 Write clear, well-organized, and effective proposals.

The Structure of Short Reports

Assume again the position of assistant to the president of Technisoft and the report-writing work necessary in this position. Most of the time, your assignments concern routine, everyday problems: human resource policies, administrative procedures, work flow, and the like. Following what appears to be established company practice, you write the reports on these problems in simple email form.

Occasionally, however, you have a more involved assignment. Last week, for example, you investigated a union charge that favoritism was shown to the nonunion workers on certain production jobs. As your report on this very formal investigation was written for the benefit of ranking company administrators as well as union leaders, you dressed it up.

Then there was the report you had helped prepare for the board of directors last fall. That report summarized pressing needs for capital improvements. A number of executives contributed to this project, but you were the coordinator. Because the report was important and was written for the board, you made it as formal as possible.

Clearly, reports vary widely in structure. How report structures vary is the first topic of this chapter. Because the shorter reports are more important to you, they are discussed next.

Before you can put your report in finished form, you will need to decide on its structure. Will it be a simple email? Will it be a long, complex, and formal report? Or will it fall between these extremes?

AN OVERVIEW OF REPORT STRUCTURE

- Length and formality determine report structure.

Your decision about report structure will be based on the needs of your situation. Those needs are related to report length and the formality of the situation. The longer the problem and the more formal the situation, the more involved the report structure is likely to be. The shorter the problem and the more informal the situation, the less involved the report structure is likely to be. Such adjustments of report structure to length and formality help meet the reader's needs in each situation.

- The following classification plan provides a general picture of report structure.

To help you understand the various report structures, we will review the possibilities. The following classification plan provides a very general picture of how reports are structured. This plan does not account for all the possible variations, but it does acquaint you with the general structure of reports. It should help you construct reports that fit your specific need.

- It pictures report structure as a stairway (Figure 11–1). Long, formal reports are at the top. Prefatory pages dress up these reports.

The classification plan arranges all business reports as a stairway, as illustrated by the diagram in Figure 11–1. At the top of the stairway are the most formal, full-dress reports. Such reports have a number of pages that come before the text material, just as this book has pages that come before the first chapter. These pages serve useful purposes, but they also dress up the report. Typically, these *prefatory pages*, as they are called, are included when the problem situation is formal and the report is long. The exact makeup of the prefatory pages may vary, but the most common arrangement includes these parts: title fly, title page, letter of transmittal, table of contents, and executive summary. Flyleaves (blank pages at the beginning and end that protect the report) also may be included.

- Prefatory pages consist of the title fly, title page, letter of transmittal, table of contents, and executive summary.

These parts are explained in Chapter 12, but a brief description of them at this point should help you understand their roles. The first two pages (title fly and title page) contain identification information. The *title fly* carries only the report title. The *title page* typically contains the title, identification of the writer and reader, and usually the date. As the words imply, the *letter of transmittal* is a letter that transmits the report. It is a personal message from the writer to the reader. The *table of contents*, of course, is a listing of the report contents. It is the report outline in finished form, with page

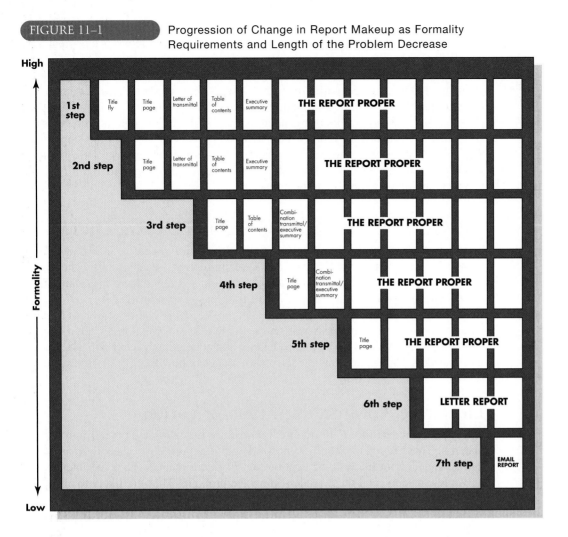

numbers to indicate where the parts begin. It also may include a list of illustrations (tables, figures, diagrams), which may be a separate part. The *executive summary* summarizes whatever is important in the report—the major facts and analyses, conclusions, and recommendations.

As the need for formality decreases and the problem becomes smaller, the makeup of the report changes. The changes primarily occur in the prefatory pages. As we have noted, these pages give the report a formal appearance. So it is not surprising that they change as the report situation becomes less formal. Usually, such reports are shorter.

- As reports become shorter and less formal, changes occur in this general order.

Although the changes that occur are far from standardized, they follow a general order. First, the title fly drops out. This page contains only the report title, which also appears on the next page. Obviously, the title fly is used primarily for reasons of formality.

- The title fly drops out.

Next in the progression, the executive summary and the letter of transmittal are combined. When this stage is reached, the report problem is short enough to be summarized in a short space. As shown in Figure 11–1, the report at this stage has three prefatory parts: title page, table of contents, and combination transmittal letter and executive summary.

- The executive summary and the letter of transmittal are combined.

At the fourth step, the table of contents drops out. The table of contents is a guide to the report text, and a guide has limited value in a short report. Certainly, a guide to a 100-page report is necessary. But a guide to a one-page report is not. Somewhere between these extremes a dividing point exists. You should follow the general guide of including a table of contents whenever it appears to be of some value to the reader.

- Next, the table of contents is omitted.

Another step down, as formality and length requirements continue to decrease, the combined letter of transmittal and executive summary drops out. Thus, the report commonly called the *short report* now has only a title page and the report text. The title

- The combined letter of transmittal and executive summary drops out, and what is left forms the popular short report.

page remains to the last because it serves as a very useful cover page. In addition, it contains the most important identifying information. The short report is a popular form in business.

Below the short-report form is a form that reinstates the letter of transmittal and summary and presents the entire report as a letter—*thus*, the *letter report*. And finally, for short problems of more informality, the *email* form is used.

As mentioned earlier, this is a general analysis of report change; it probably oversimplifies the structure of reports. Few actual reports coincide with the steps in the diagram. Most reports, however, fit generally within the framework of the diagram. Knowledge of the general relationship of formality and length to report makeup should help you understand and plan reports.

CHARACTERISTICS OF SHORTER REPORTS

The shorter report forms (those at the bottom of the stairway) are by far the most common in business. These are the everyday working reports—those used for the routine information reporting that is vital to an organization's communication. Because these reports are so common, our study of report types begins with them.

The techniques for organizing discussed in the preceding chapter cover all forms of reports. But there the emphasis was on organizing the information gathered—on the body of the report. As we noted, introductory and concluding parts would be attached when needed. Thus, the following discussion relates to how these parts are used in the shorter reports.

Little Need for Introductory Information

Most of the shorter, more informal reports require little (sometimes no) introductory material. These reports typically concern day-to-day problems. Their lives are short; that is, they are not likely to be kept on file for future readers. They are intended for only a few readers, and these readers know the problem. They are likely to need little introduction to it.

This is not to say that all shorter reports have no need for introductory material. Some do need it. In general, however, the need is likely to be small.

Determining what introductory material is needed is simply a matter of answering one question: What does my reader need to know before receiving this report? In very short reports, sufficient introductory material is provided by an incidental reference to the problem, authorization of the investigation, or the like. In extreme cases, however, you may need a detailed introduction comparable to that of the more formal reports.

Reports need no introductory material if their very nature explains their purpose. This holds true for personnel actions. It also holds true for weekly sales reports, inventory reports, and some progress reports.

Predominance of the Direct Order

Because the shorter reports usually solve routine problems, they are likely to be written in the direct order. By *direct order* we mean that the report begins with its most important information—usually the conclusion and perhaps a recommendation. Business writers use this order because they know that their readers' main concern is to get the information needed to make a decision. So they present this information right away.

As you will see in Chapter 12, the longer report forms also may use the direct order. Many longer reports do, but most do not. Most follow the traditional logical order (introduction, body, conclusion). As one moves down the structural ladder toward the more informal and shorter reports, however, the need for the direct order increases. At the bottom of the ladder, the direct order is more the rule than the exception.

Deciding whether to use the direct order is best based on a consideration of your readers' likely use of the report. If your readers need the report conclusion or recommendation as a basis for an action that they must take, directness will speed their effort by enabling them to quickly receive the most important information. If they have

- The next step is the letter report, and the step after that is the email report.

- This progression of structure is general.

- The shorter report forms are the most common in business.

- Their need for introductions and conclusions varies.

- Shorter reports have little need for introductory material.

- Some shorter reports need introductory material. Include as much introductory material as is necessary to prepare the reader for the report.

- The shorter reports usually begin directly—with conclusions and recommendations.

- Sometimes, but not often, longer reports are written in the direct order.

- Use the direct order when the conclusion or recommendation will serve as a basis for action.

Most short reports are personal, direct, and without formal introductions. Although exceptions exist, they provide everyday working information to organizations that is essential to survival.

confidence in your work, they may choose not to read beyond this point and to quickly take the action that the report supports. Should they desire to question any part of the report, however, the material is there for their inspection.

On the other hand, if there is reason to believe that your readers will want to arrive at the conclusion or recommendation only after a logical review of the analysis, you should organize your report in the indirect (logical) order. This arrangement is especially preferable when your readers do not have reason to place their full confidence in your work. If you are a novice working on a new assignment, for example, you would be wise to lead them to your recommendation or conclusion by using the indirect order. As you can see, the indirect and direct orders are ways of relating to the information needs of the reader.

- Use the indirect order when you need to take the readers through the analysis.

Because order is so vital a part of constructing the shorter reports, let us be certain that the difference between the direct arrangement and the indirect arrangement is clear. To make it clear, we will go through each, step by step.

The direct arrangement presents right away the most important part of the report. This is the answer—the achievement of the report's goal. Depending on the problem, the direct beginning could consist of a summary of facts, a conclusion, a recommendation, or some combination of summary, conclusion, and recommendation.

- The direct order gives the main message first.
- Then it covers introductory material (if any), findings and analyses, conclusions, and recommendations.

Whatever introductory material is needed usually follows the direct opening. As noted previously, sometimes little or none is needed in the everyday, routine reports.

FRANK & ERNEST ©
SOURCE: Reprinted by permission of *United Features Syndicate, Inc.*

There are specific concepts that the students should learn and skills that they should improve by completing the business report assignment. These include organizing, writing, editing, revising, formatting, data gathering and evaluation, audience analysis, understanding how the report will be used for decision-making, and the need to pay careful attention to detail when writing so that their report is mechanically correct.

Kathleen M. Hiemstra, John Carroll University

Kathleen M. Hiemstra, "Instructor and Student Perceptions of What Is Learned by Writing the Business Report," *Business Communication Quarterly* 64, no. 2 (June 2002): 50.

Next come the report findings, organized in good order (as described in Chapter 10). From these facts and analyses comes the conclusion, and perhaps a recommendation.

Illustrating this arrangement is the following report of a short and simple personnel problem. For reasons of space economy, only the key parts of the report are shown here.

> Clifford A. Knudson, administrative assistant in the accounting department, should be fired. This conclusion has been reached after a thorough investigation brought about by numerous incidents during the past two months . . .
>
> The recommended action is supported by this information from his work record for the past two months:
>
> - He has been late to work seven times.
> - He has been absent without acceptable excuse for seven days.
> - Twice he reported to work in a drunken and disorderly condition.
> - [And so on].

- **The indirect order has this sequence: introduction, facts and analyses, conclusions, and recommendations.**

The indirect arrangement begins with whatever introductory material is needed to prepare the reader for the report. Then comes the presentation of facts, with analyses when needed. Next comes the part that accomplishes the goal of the report. If the goal is to present information, this part summarizes the information. If the goal is to reach a conclusion, this part reviews the analyses and draws a conclusion from them. And if the goal is to recommend an action, this part reviews the analyses, draws a conclusion, and, on the basis of the conclusion, makes a recommendation.

Using the simple personnel problem from the last example, the indirect arrangement would appear like this:

> Numerous incidents during the past two months appear to justify an investigation of the work record of Clifford A. Knudson, administrative assistant in the accounting department.
>
> The investigation of his work record for the past two months reveals these points:
>
> - He has been late to work seven times.
> - He has been absent without acceptable excuse for seven days.
> - Twice he reported to work in a drunken and disorderly condition.
> - [And so on to the conclusion that Knudson should be fired].

More Personal Writing Style

- **Personal writing is common in the shorter reports.**

Although the writing for all reports is much the same, writing in shorter reports tends to be more personal. That is, the shorter reports are likely to use the personal pronouns *I, we,* and *you* rather than only the third person.

The reasons for this tendency toward personal writing in shorter reports should be

Templates Help Writers Format Reports

Templates for word processors help report writers format reports easily and consistently. Once a template is selected, report writers can concentrate on the report message and let the software create a professional-looking document.

These templates contain margin settings, font type and size for headings and text, and even graphic layouts. Most are designed to help the writer present a report that communicates its message with a professional look. Although standard templates can be used, some companies design their own templates to give their reports consistent and distinct images.

Word and WordPerfect have templates that set up both short and long reports. In addition to the standard templates, you can find more on the web. Here you see a list of templates found in Microsoft's Template Gallery after a search on *reports* followed by view of the template before downloading. Finally, you see the template loaded in Word.

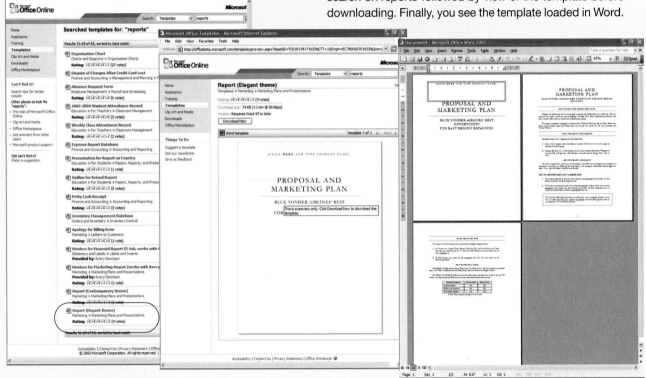

obvious. In the first place, short-report situations usually involve personal relationships. Such reports tend to be from and to people who know each other and who normally address each other informally when they meet. In addition, shorter reports are apt to involve personal investigations and to represent the observations, evaluations, and analyses of their writers. Finally, shorter reports tend to deal with day-to-day, routine problems. These problems are by their very nature informal. It is logical to report them informally, and personal writing tends to produce this informal effect.

- The reasons are that the shorter reports usually (1) involve personal relationships, (2) concern a personal investigation, and (3) are routine.

As explained in Chapter 10, your decision about whether to write a report in personal or impersonal style should be based on the situation. You should consider the expectations of those who will receive the report. If they expect formality, you should write impersonally. If they expect informality, you should write personally. If you do not know their preferences, you should consider the formality of the situation. Convention favors impersonal writing for the most formal situations. Like the direct and indirect order, the question of personal versus impersonal style involves the matter of relating to the reader in ways that he or she prefers.

- Write impersonally (1) when your reader prefers it and (2) when the situation is formal.

Constructing short reports requires many of the same organizational skills used to develop longer, more formal reports.

From this analysis, it should be clear that either personal or impersonal writing can be appropriate for reports ranging from the shortest to the longest types. The point is, however, that short-report situations are most likely to justify personal writing.

Less Need for a Structured Coherence Plan

As you will see in Chapter 12, long and formal reports usually require a structured coherence plan. Short reports do not. This is not to say that coherence is not essential to short reports. It is. The point is that a *structured* plan is not needed. By structured coherence plan we mean an arrangement of summarizing, forward looking, and backward looking parts that tie together the report presentation. When you study this plan, you will understand why it has little use in short reports. We mention it now primarily for the sake of completeness in covering differences between long and short reports.

FORMS OF SHORTER REPORTS

- Following is a review of the more popular shorter reports.

As noted earlier, the shorter report forms are by far the most numerous and important in business. In fact, the three forms represented by the bottom three steps of the stairway (Figure 11–1) make up the bulk of the reports written. Thus, a review of each of these three types is in order.

The Short Report

- The short report consists of a title page and the report text.

One of the more popular of the less formal report forms is the short report. Representing the fifth step in the diagram of report progression, this report consists of only a title page and text. Its popularity may be explained by the middle-ground impression of formality that it conveys. Including the most important prefatory part gives the report at least some appearance of formality. And it does this without the tedious work of preparing the other prefatory pages. The short report is ideally suited for the short but somewhat formal problem.

Like most of the less formal report forms, the short report may be organized in either the direct or indirect order. But the direct order is far more common. As illustrated by Figure 11–2, this plan begins with a quick summary of the report, including and emphasizing conclusions and recommendations. Such a beginning serves much the same function as the executive summary (described in Chapter 12) of a long, formal report.

● It is usually in the direct order, beginning with the conclusion.

Following the summary come whatever introductory remarks are needed. (See Chapter 12 for a more detailed discussion of the introduction.) Sometimes this part is not needed. Usually, however, a single paragraph covers the facts of authorization and a brief statement of the problem and its scope. After the introductory words come the findings of the investigation. As in the longer report forms, the findings are presented, analyzed, and applied to the problem. From all this comes a conclusion and, if needed, a recommendation. These last two elements—conclusions and recommendations—may come at the end even though they also appear in the beginning summary. Omitting a summary or a conclusion would sometimes end the report abruptly. It would stop the flow of reasoning before reaching the logical goal.

● The introduction comes next, then the findings and analyses, and finally the conclusions.

The mechanics of constructing the short report are much the same as the mechanics of constructing the more formal, longer types. The short report uses the same form of title page and page layout. Like the longer reports, it uses headings. But because of the short report's brevity, the headings rarely go beyond the two-division level. In fact, one level of division is most common. Like any other report, the short report uses graphics, an appendix, and a bibliography when these are needed.

● See Figure 11–2 for this report form.

Letter Reports

The second of the more common shorter report forms is the letter report, that is, a report in letter form. Letter reports are used primarily to present information to persons outside the organization, especially when the information is to be sent by mail or fax. For example, a company's written evaluation of its experience with a particular product may be presented in letter form and sent to the person who requests it. An outside consultant may write a report of analyses and recommendations in letter form. Or the officer of an organization may report certain information to the membership in a letter.

● Letter reports are reports in letter form.

Typically, the length of letter reports is three or four pages or less. But no hard-and-fast rule exists on this point.

● They usually cover short problems.

As a general rule, letter reports are written personally, using *I, you,* and *we* references. Exceptions exist, of course, such as letter reports for very important readers—for example, a company's board of directors. Otherwise, the writing style recommended for letter reports is much the same as that recommended for any other reports. Certainly, clear and meaningful expression is a requirement for all reports (see Figure 11–3).

● They are usually written in personal style.

Letter reports may be in either the direct order or the indirect order. If such a report is to be mailed, there is some justification for using the indirect order. Because such reports arrive unannounced, it is logical to begin with a reminder of what they are, how they originated, and the like. A letter report written to the membership of an organization, for example, might appropriately begin as follows:

● Most of them begin indirectly.

> As authorized by your board of directors last January 6, this report reviews member company expenditures for travel.

If a letter report is begun in the direct order, a subject line is appropriate. The subject line consists of identifying words appearing at the top of the letter, usually right after the salutation. Another common practice is to omit the word *subject* and the colon and to type the entire subject description in capital letters. Although subject lines may be formed in many ways, one acceptable version begins with the word *subject* and follows it with words that identify the situation. As the following example illustrates, this identifying device helps overcome any confusion that the direct beginning might otherwise create.

● Subject lines are appropriate to begin them.

FIGURE 11–2

Illustration of a Short Report. Designed for the busy reader who wants the main message quickly, this report begins with the recommendations. Then it presents the report in logical order, following a brief introduction with a comparison of three methods of depreciation for delivery trucks (the subject of the investigation). The somewhat formal style is appropriate for reports of this nature.

743 Beaux Avenue
New Orleans, LA 70118-4913

Brewington and Karnes, CPAs

5 Ws and
1 H produce
complete title

Recommendations for Depreciating Delivery Trucks

An Analysis of Three Plans Proposed for the Bagget Laundry Company

Use of three-spot title page gives good emphasis to writer–reader relationship and balances page.

FIGURE 11–2   Continued

• • • • • • •

Recommendations for Depreciating Delivery Trucks

An Analysis of Three Plans Proposed for the Bagget Laundry Company

Recommendation of Reducing Charge Method

The Reducing Charge method appears to be the best method to depreciate Bagget Laundry Company delivery trucks. The relative equality of cost allocation for depreciation and maintenance over the useful life of the trucks is the prime advantage under this method. Computation of depreciation charges is relatively simple by the Reducing Charge plan but not quite so simple as computation under the second best method considered.

The second best method considered is the Straight-Line depreciation plan. It is the simplest to compute of the plans considered, and it results in yearly charges equal to those under the Reducing Charge method. The unequal cost allocation resulting from increasing maintenance costs in successive years, however, is a disadvantage that far outweighs the method's ease of computation.

Third among the plans considered is the Service Hours method. This plan is not satisfactory for depreciating delivery trucks primarily because it combines a number of undesirable features. Prime among these is the complexity and cost of computing yearly charges under the plan. Also significant is the likelihood of poor cost allocation under this plan. An additional drawback is the possibility of variations in the estimates of the service life of company trucks.

The Whats and Whys of the Problem

Authorization by President Bagget. This report on depreciation methods for delivery trucks of the Bagget Laundry Company is submitted on April 16, 2005, to Mr. Ralph P. Bagget, President of the Company. Mr. Bagget orally authorized Brewington and Karnes, Certified Public Accountants, to conduct the study on March 15, 2005.

Problem of Selecting Best Depreciation Method. Having decided to establish branch agencies, the Bagget Laundry Company has purchased delivery trucks to transport laundry back and forth from the central cleaning plant in downtown New Orleans. The Company's problem is to select from three alternatives the most advantageous method to depreciate the trucks. The three methods concerned are the Reducing Charge, Straight-Line, and Service-Hours. The trucks have an original cost of $25,000, a five-year life, and trade-in value of $10,000.

1

FIGURE 11–2   Continued

Preview paragraph gives sequence of body divisions and justifies it.

Use of Company Records to Solve Problem. In seeking an optimum solution to the Company's problem, we studied Company records and reviewed authoritative literature on the subject. We also applied our best judgment and our experience in analyzing the alternative methods. We based all conclusions on the generally accepted business principles in the field. Clearly, studies such as this involve subjective judgment, and this one is no exception.

Illustrations of Methods to Analyze Problem. In the following analysis, our evaluations of the three depreciation methods appear in the order in which we rank the methods. Since each method involves different factors, direct comparison by factors is meaningless. Thus our plan is that we evaluate each method in light of our best judgment.

Marked Advantages of the Reducing Charge Method

Sometimes called Sum-of-the-Years'-Digits, the Reducing Charge method consists of applying a series of decreasing fractions over the life of the property. To determine the fraction, first compute the sum of years of use for the property. This number becomes the denominator. Then determine the position number (first, second, etc.) of the year. This number is the numerator. Then apply the resulting fractions to the depreciable values for the life of the property. In the case of the trucks, the depreciable value is $15,000 ($25,000 – $10,000).

Sub-ordinate reference to graphic allows main sentence to begin interpretation.

As shown in Table I, this method results in large depreciation costs for the early years and decreasing costs in later years. But since maintenance and repair costs for trucks are higher in the later years, this method provides a relatively stable charge over the life of the property. In actual practice, however, the sums will not be as stable as illustrated, for maintenance and repair costs will vary from those used in the computation.

Table I				
Depreciation and Maintenance Costs for Delivery Trucks of Bagget Laundry for 2001–2005 Using Reducing Charge Depreciation				
End of Year	Depreciation		Maintenance	Sum
1	5/15 ($15,000) =	$ 5,000	$ 200	$ 5,200
2	4/15 ($15,000) =	4,000	1,000	5,000
3	3/15 ($15,000) =	3,000	1,800	4,800
4	2/15 ($15,000) =	2,000	2,600	4,600
5	1/15 ($15,000) =	1,000	3,400	4,400
	Totals	$15,000	$9,000	$24,000

In summary, the Reducing Charge method uses the most desirable combination of factors to depreciate trucks. It equalizes periodic charges, and it is easy to compute. It is our first choice for Bagget Laundry Company.

2

FIGURE 11–2   Continued

Incidental reference to graphic ties text and illustration together.

Runner-up Position of Straight-Line Method

The Straight-Line depreciation method is easiest of all to compute. It involves merely taking the depreciable value of the trucks ($15,000) and dividing it by the life of the trucks (5 years). The depreciation in this case is $3,000 for each year.

As shown in Table II, however, the increase in maintenance costs in later years results in much greater periodic charges in later years. The method is not usually recommended in cases such as this.

Table II				
Depreciation and Maintenance Costs for Delivery Trucks of Bagget Laundry for 2001–2005 Using Straight-Line Depreciation				
End of Year	Depreciation		Maintenance	Sum
1	1/5 ($15,000) =	$ 3,000	$ 200	$ 3,200
2	1/5 ($15,000) =	3,000	1,000	4,000
3	1/5 ($15,000) =	3,000	1,800	4,800
4	1/5 ($15,000) =	3,000	2,600	5,600
5	1/5 ($15,000) =	3,000	3,400	6,400
	Totals	$15,000	$9,000	$24,000

Summary statements at section endings provide reader with time to see solution unfold.

In addition, the Straight-Line method generally is best when the properties involved are accumulated over a period of years. When this is done, the total of depreciation and maintenance costs will be about even. But Bagget Company has not purchased its trucks over a period of years. Nor is it likely to do so in the years ahead. Thus, Straight-Line depreciation will not result in equal periodic charges for maintenance and depreciation over the long run.

Poor Rank of Service-Hours Depreciation

The Service-Hours method of depreciation combines the major disadvantages of the other ways discussed. It is based on the principle that a truck is bought for the direct hours of service that it will give. The estimated number of hours that a delivery truck can be used efficiently according to automotive engineers is computed from a service total of 100,000 miles. The depreciable cost ($15,000) for each truck is allocated pro rata according to the number of service hours used.

Completeness and detail in analysis give objectivity.

The difficulty and expense of maintaining additional records of service hours is a major disadvantage of this method. The depreciation cost for the delivery trucks under this method will fluctuate widely between the first and last years. It is reasonable to assume that as the trucks get older more time will be spent on maintenance. Consequently, the larger depreciation costs will occur in the initial years. As can be seen by Table III, the periodic

3

FIGURE 11–2   Concluded

charges for depreciation and maintenance hover between the two previously discussed methods.

Table III				
Depreciation and Maintenance Costs for Delivery Trucks of Bagget Laundry for 2001–2005 Using Service-Hours Depreciation				
End of Year	Estimated Service Miles	Depreciation	Maintenance	Sum
1	30,000	$ 4,500	$ 200	$ 4,700
2	25,000	3,750	1,000	4,750
3	20,000	3,000	1,800	4,800
4	15,000	2,250	2,600	4,850
5	10,000	1,500	3,400	4,950
	100,000	$15,000	$9,000	$24,000

The periodic charge for depreciation and maintenance increases in the later years of ownership. Another difficulty encountered is the possibility of a variance between estimated service hours and the actual service hours. The wide fluctuation possible makes it impractical to use this method for depreciating the delivery truck.

The difficulty of maintaining adequate records and increasing costs in the later years are the major disadvantages of this method. Since it combines the major disadvantages of both the Reducing Charge and Straight-Line methods, it is not satisfactory for depreciating the delivery trucks.

Completeness and detail in analysis give objectivity.

4

FIGURE 11–3

Illustration of a Letter Report. This direct-order letter report compares two hotels for a meeting site. Organized by the bases used in determining the choice, it evaluates the pertinent information and reaches a decision. The personal style is appropriate.

INTERNATIONAL COMMUNICATION ASSOCIATION

314 N Capitol St. NW • Washington, DC 20001 • 202.624.2411

October 26, 2005

Professor Helen Toohey
Board of Directors
International Communication Association
Thunderbird American Graduate School of International Management
15249 N. 59th Ave.
Glendale, AZ 85306-6000

Dear Professor Toohey:

Subject: Recommendation of Convention Hotel for the 2006 Meeting

RECOMMENDATION OF THE HYATT

Direct order emphasizes decision.

The Hyatt Hotel is my recommendation for the International Communication Association meeting next October. My decision is based on the following summary of the evidence I collected. First, the Hyatt has a definite downtown location advantage, and this is important to convention goers and their spouses. Second, accommodations, including meeting rooms, are adequate in both places, although the Marriott's rooms are more modern. Third, Hyatt room costs are approximately 15 percent lower than those at the Marriott. The Hyatt, however, would charge $500 for a room for the opening session. Although both hotels are adequate, because of location and cost advantages the Hyatt appears to be the better choice from the members' viewpoint.

Preview gives transition lead.

ORIGIN AND PLAN OF THE INVESTIGATION

In investigating these two hotels, as was my charge from you at our October 7 board meeting, I collected information on what I believed to be the three major factors of consideration in the problem. First is location. Second is adequacy of accommodations. And third is cost. The following findings and evaluations form the basis of my recommendation.

THE HYATT'S FAVORABLE DOWNTOWN LOCATION

Bases of comparison (factors) permit hotels (units) to be compared logically.

The older of the two hotels, the Hyatt is located in the heart of the downtown business district. Thus it is convenient to the area's major mall as well as the other downtown shops. The Marriott, on the other hand, is approximately nine blocks from the major shopping area. Located in the periphery of the business and residential area, it provides little location advantage for those wanting to shop. It does, however, have shops within its walls that provide virtually all of the guest's normal needs. Because many members will bring spouses, however, the downtown location does give the Hyatt an advantage.

Short sentences and transitional words increase readability and move ideas forward.

FIGURE 11–3   Concluded

Alternate placement of topic sentences offers pattern variety.

Board of Directors   -2-   October 26, 2005

ADEQUATE ACCOMMODATIONS AT BOTH HOTELS

Talking captions (all noun phrases) help interpretation.

Both hotels can guarantee the 600 rooms we will require. Because the Marriott is newer (since 2001), its rooms are more modern and, therefore, more appealing. The 9-year-old Hyatt, however, is well preserved and comfortable. Its rooms are all in good condition, and the equipment is up-to-date.

The Marriott has 11 small meeting rooms and the Hyatt has 13. All are adequate for our purposes. Both hotels can provide the 10 we need. For our opening session, the Hyatt would make available its Capri Ballroom, which can easily seat our membership. It would also serve as the site of our presidential luncheon. The assembly facilities at the Marriott appear to be somewhat crowded, although the management assures me that it can hold 600. Pillars in the room, however, would make some seats undesirable. In spite of the limitations mentioned, both hotels appear to have adequate facilities for our meeting.

Paragraph length shows good organization.

LOWER COSTS AT THE HYATT

Both the Hyatt and the Marriott would provide nine rooms for meetings on a complimentary basis. Both would provide complimentary suites for our president and our executive director. The Hyatt, however, would charge $500 for use of the room for the opening session. The Marriott would provide this room without charge.

Text analysis relates facts to problem.

Convention rates at the Hyatt are $169 for singles, $179 for double-bedded rooms, and $229 for suites. Comparable rates of the Marriott are $189, $199, and $350. Thus, the savings at the Hyatt would be approximately 15 percent per member.

Cost of the dinner selected would be $35 per person, including gratuities, at the Hyatt. The Marriott would meet this price if we would guarantee 600 plates. Otherwise, they would charge $38. Considering all of these figures, the total cost picture at the Hyatt is the more favorable one.

Sincerely,

Willard K Mitchell

Willard K. Mitchell
Executive Secretary

Subject: Travel Expenditures of Association Members, Authorized by Board of Directors, January 2005

Association members are spending 11 percent more on travel this year than they did the year before. Current plans call for a 10 percent increase for next year.

Regardless of which type of beginning is used, the organizational plans for letter reports correspond to those of longer, more formal types. Thus, the indirect-order letter report follows its introduction with a logical presentation and analysis of the information gathered. From this presentation, it develops a conclusion or recommendation, or both, in the end. The direct-order letter report follows the initial summary-conclusion-recommendation section with whatever introduction is appropriate. For example, the direct beginning illustrated previously could be followed with these introductory sentences:

> These are the primary findings of a study authorized by your board of directors last January. Because they concern information vital to all of us in the Association, they are presented here for your confidential use.

Following such an introduction, the report would present the supporting facts and their analyses. The writer would systematically build up the case supporting the opening comment. With either the direct or indirect order, a letter report may close with whatever friendly, goodwill comment fits the occasion.

Email Reports

As we noted in Chapter 5, email is the most widely used form of written communication in business. Although heavily used for communicating with outside parties, email dominates internal written communication. That is, email is written by and to people in an organization, as Figure 11–4 illustrates.

Because email is primarily communication between people who know each other, it is usually informal. In fact, many are hurried, casual messages. Some email, however, is formal, especially reports directed to readers high in the administration of the organization.

As indicated in Chapter 5, some email resembles letters. Others, however, are more appropriately classified as reports. Most email reports tend to be more formal and factual. In fact, some email reports rival the longer forms in formality. Like the longer forms, they may use headings to display content and graphics to support the text. Email reports tend to be problem related.

SPECIAL REPORT FORMS

As noted previously, this review describes only generally the report forms used in business. Many variations exist, a few of which deserve emphasis.

Staff Report

One of the more popular forms of reports used in business is the staff report. Usually written in memorandum form, it can be adapted to any structural type, including the long, formal report.

The staff report differs from other forms of reports primarily in the organization of its contents. It arranges contents in a fixed plan. The plan remains the same for all problems. Because this arrangement leads systematically to conclusions and recommendations, it is especially useful for business problems.

Although the organization of staff reports varies by company, this plan used by a major metals manufacturer is typical:

Identifying information: Because the company's staff reports are processed with templates, the conventional identification information (*To, From, Date, Subject*) appears at the beginning.

- The organizational plans of letter reports are much like those of longer reports.

- Supporting facts and analyses follow an appropriate introduction.

- Email (internal written messages) is widely used.

- Most email messages are written informally.

- Some resemble letters and follow letter form.

- Some are reports. Such email reports tend to be formal, factual, and problem related.

- Some special report forms deserve review.

- One is the staff report.

- Staff reports follow a fixed organization plan that leads to a conclusion.

- A typical plan for staff reports has these parts:

- Identifying information.

FIGURE 11–4

Illustration of a Progress Report in Email Form. This email report summarizes a sales manager's progress in opening a new district. It begins with highlight information—all a busy reader may need to know. Organized by three categories of activity, the factual information follows. The writer–reader relationship justifies personal style.

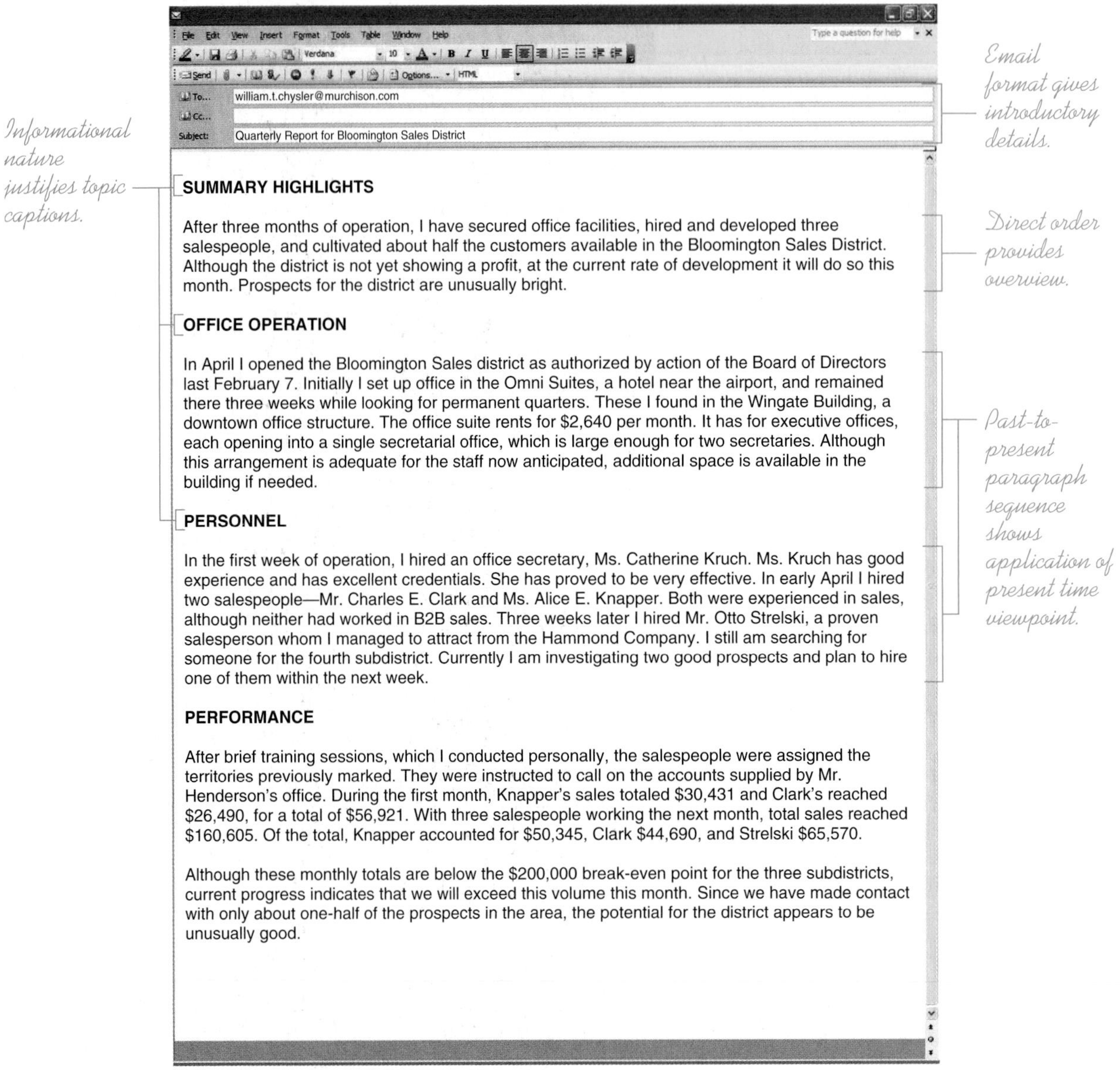

Email format gives introductory details.

Informational nature justifies topic captions.

Direct order provides overview.

Past-to-present paragraph sequence shows application of present time viewpoint.

To... william.t.chysler@murchison.com

Cc...

Subject: Quarterly Report for Bloomington Sales District

SUMMARY HIGHLIGHTS

After three months of operation, I have secured office facilities, hired and developed three salespeople, and cultivated about half the customers available in the Bloomington Sales District. Although the district is not yet showing a profit, at the current rate of development it will do so this month. Prospects for the district are unusually bright.

OFFICE OPERATION

In April I opened the Bloomington Sales district as authorized by action of the Board of Directors last February 7. Initially I set up office in the Omni Suites, a hotel near the airport, and remained there three weeks while looking for permanent quarters. These I found in the Wingate Building, a downtown office structure. The office suite rents for $2,640 per month. It has for executive offices, each opening into a single secretarial office, which is large enough for two secretaries. Although this arrangement is adequate for the staff now anticipated, additional space is available in the building if needed.

PERSONNEL

In the first week of operation, I hired an office secretary, Ms. Catherine Kruch. Ms. Kruch has good experience and has excellent credentials. She has proved to be very effective. In early April I hired two salespeople—Mr. Charles E. Clark and Ms. Alice E. Knapper. Both were experienced in sales, although neither had worked in B2B sales. Three weeks later I hired Mr. Otto Strelski, a proven salesperson whom I managed to attract from the Hammond Company. I still am searching for someone for the fourth subdistrict. Currently I am investigating two good prospects and plan to hire one of them within the next week.

PERFORMANCE

After brief training sessions, which I conducted personally, the salespeople were assigned the territories previously marked. They were instructed to call on the accounts supplied by Mr. Henderson's office. During the first month, Knapper's sales totaled $30,431 and Clark's reached $26,490, for a total of $56,921. With three salespeople working the next month, total sales reached $160,605. Of the total, Knapper accounted for $50,345, Clark $44,690, and Strelski $65,570.

Although these monthly totals are below the $200,000 break-even point for the three subdistricts, current progress indicates that we will exceed this volume this month. Since we have made contact with only about one-half of the prospects in the area, the potential for the district appears to be unusually good.

- Summary.

  Summary: For the busy executive who wants the facts fast, the report begins with a summary. Some executives will read no further. Others will want to trace the report content in detail.

- Problem (or objective).

  The problem (or objective): As with all good problem-solving procedures, the report text logically begins with a clear description of the problem: what it is, what it is not, what its limitations are, and the like.

- Facts.

  Facts: Next comes the information gathered in the attempt to solve the problem.

- Discussion.

  Discussion: This is followed by analyses of the facts and applications of the facts and the analyses to the problem. (The statement and discussion of the facts often can be combined.)

- Conclusions.

  Conclusions: From the preceding discussion of the facts come the final meanings as they apply to the problem.

- Recommendation.

  Recommendation: If the problem's objective allows for it, a course of action may be recommended on the basis of the conclusions.

Unexpected Findings in a Report

A successful businessman fell in love with a woman who he felt might not meet the requirements of a person in his position. So he hired a detective agency to investigate her background.

After weeks of intensive checking, the detective agency submitted this report:

Ms. Stoner has an excellent reputation. She has high morals, lives within her means, and is well respected in the community. The only blemish on her record is that in recent months she has been seen repeatedly in the company of a business executive of doubtful repute.

One of the major users of staff reports is the Armed Forces, all branches of which use a standardized form. As shown in Figure 11–5, the military version of the staff report differs somewhat from the plan just described.

- See Figure 11–5 for the military form of staff reports.

Anytime you use a standardized form, you will want to consider developing a template macro or merge document with your word processing software. A macro would fill in all the standard parts for you, pausing to let you enter the variable information. It would be most suitable for periodic reports, such as progress reports or quarterly sales reports. A template merge document would prompt you for the variables first, merging them with the primary document later. You'll find this feature most useful when you have to write several reports in short time intervals. For example, performance appraisal for several employees illustrate good application of the merge.

Meeting Minutes

Minutes provide a written record of a group's activities and decisions, a history that includes announcements, reports, significant discussions, and decisions. Minutes might report who will do what and when, but they are primarily a summary that reports the gist of what happened, not a verbatim transcript. Minutes include only objective data; their writer carefully avoids using descriptive adjectives such as brilliant, intelligent, reasonable, and so on. However, if the group passes a resolution that specific wording be officially recorded, a writer would then include it. Accurate minutes are important because they can have some legal significance as to whether decisions are binding.

- Minutes provide a written record of a group's activities

The physical form is typically a memo or email, but the layout varies among organizations. Basically, it should enable the reader to easily focus on the content as well as easily retrieve it. Some writers find numbering items in the minutes to agree with the numbering of a meeting's agenda helps in retrieving and reviewing specific discussions. Subheads are often useful, especially if they are bold, italicized, or underlined to make them stand out. Most importantly, minutes should provide an adequate record.

- Most are distributed by memo or email but their layout varies among organizations.

Figure 11–6 illustrates typical minutes. The following preliminary, body, and closing items may be included.

- Typical minutes include common preliminary, body, and closing items.

Preliminary Items

- Name of the group.
- Name of document.
- Type of meeting (monthly, emergency, special).
- Place, date, and time called to order.
- Names of those attending including guests (used to determine if a quorum is present).
- Names of those absent and reasons for absence.

FIGURE 11–5   Military Form of Staff Study Report

DEPARTMENT OF THE AIR FORCE
HEADQUARTERS UNITED STATES AIR FORCE
WASHINGTON, DC 20330

REPLY TO
ATTN OF   AFODC/Colonel Jones

SUBJECT   Staff Study Report

TO:

PROBLEM

1. --
--.

FACTORS BEARING ON THE PROBLEM

2. Facts.

    a.---
--.
    b--.

3. Assumptions.

4. Criteria.

5. Definitions.

DISCUSSION

6. --.

7. --.

8. --.

CONCLUSION

9. --.

ACTION RECOMMENDED

10. ---.

11. -----------------------------------.

JOHN J. JONES, Colonel, USAF   2 Atch
Deputy Chief of Staff, Operations   1. -----------------------
                                                      2. -----------------------

Use only those portions of this format necessary for your particular report. If you omit certain paragraphs, renumber subsequent paragraphs accordingly.

Only long enough for identification.

Normally this caption is left blank on the staff study report.

Clear, but brief, statement of the problem.

Pertinent facts, assumptions (if necessary), criteria, and definitions (if necessary) used to solve the problem.

Briefly state background of problem.

List possible solutions that are most probable; test each possible solution, using criteria listed under FACTORS BEARING ON THE PROBLEM; compare all solutions; and select the best possible solution, giving reasons for choice. No set number of paragraphs is prescribed.

Restate the best possible solution to the problem, using only one paragraph.

Indicate clearly the action necessary to implement the solution.

Body Items

- Approval of minutes of previous meeting.
- Meeting announcements.
- Old business—Reports on matters previously presented.
- New business—Reports on matters presented to the group.

Closing Items

- Place and time of next meeting.
- Notation of the meeting's ending time.
- Name and signature of the person responsible for preparing the minutes.

- Preparing ahead of time makes the job easier and encourages more complete notes.

When you are responsible for preparing the minutes of a meeting, you can take several steps to make the task easier. First, get an agenda in advance. Use it to complete as much of the preliminary information as possible, including the names of those expected to attend. If someone is not present, you can easily move that person's name to the absentee list. You might even set up a table in advance with the following column headings to encourage you to take complete notes.

Topic	Summary of Discussion	Action/Resolution

FIGURE 11–6   Illustration of Meeting Minutes

Minutes of the Policy Committee
Semiannual Meeting
November 21, 2004, 9:30–11:30 A.M., Conference Room A

Present: Megan Adami (chair), D'Marie Simon, DeAnne Overholt, Michelle Lum, Joel Zwanziger, Rebecca Shuster, Jeff Merrill, Donna Wingler, Chris Woods, Tim Lebold (corporate attorney, guest).

Absent: Joan Marian, Jeff Horen (excused), Leonna Plummer (excused)

Complete preliminary information provides a good record.

Minutes

Minutes from the May 5, 2004, meeting were read and approved.

Subheads help readers retrieve information.

Announcements

Chris Woods invited the committee to a reception for Milton Chen, Director in our Asia region. It'll be held in the executive dining room at 3:00 P.M. tomorrow. Chris reminded us that Asia is ahead of the United States in its use of wireless technology. He suggested that perhaps we can get some idea of good policies to implement now.

Old Business—Email Policy

Joel Zwanziger reported the results of his survey on the proposed new email policy. While 16 percent of the employees approved implementing the policy, 84 percent were not opposed. The committee approved a January 1, 2005, implementation subject to its distribution to all employees before the Christmas break.

Discussions are summarized and actions taken are included.

Web Surfing Policy

D'Marie Simon reported on the preliminary findings of other companies in the industry. Most have informal guides but no official policies. The guidelines generally are that all surfing must be related to the job and that personal surfing should be done on breaks. The committee discussed the issue at length. It approved a policy that reflects the current general guidelines.

Temp Policy

Tim Lebold presented the legal steps we need to take to get our old and new temporary employees to sign a nondisclosure agreement prior to working here as we've been discussing in relation to a new temp policy. The committee directed Tim to begin the process so that the policy could be put in force as soon as possible.

New Business—Resolution

Michelle Lum proposed that a resolution of thanks be added to the record recognizing Megan for her terrific attention to detail as well her clear focus on keeping the committee abreast of policy issues. It was unanimously approved.

Resolutions often include descriptive language.

Next Meeting

The next meeting of the committee will be May 3, 2005, from 9:30–11:30 A.M. in Conference Room A.

Closing gives reader complete needed facts.

Adjournment

The meeting was adjourned at 11:25 A.M.

Respectfully submitted,

Megan Adami
Megan Adami

Signing signifies the minutes are official records.

Progress Report

• Progress reports review progress on an activity.

As its name implies, a progress report presents a review of progress made on an activity. For example, a fund-raising organization might prepare weekly summaries of its efforts to achieve its goal. Or a building contractor might prepare a report on progress toward completing a building for a customer. Typically, the contents of these reports concern progress made, but they also may include such related topics as problems encountered or anticipated and projections of future progress.

• Most are informal and narrative; some are formal.

Progress reports follow no set form. They can be quite formal, as when a contractor building a large manufacturing plant reports to the company for whom the plant is being built. Or they can be very informal, as in the case of a worker reporting by email to his or her supervisor on the progress of a task being performed. Some progress reports are quite routine and structured, sometimes involving filling in blanks on forms devised for the purpose. Most, however, are informal, narrative reports, as illustrated by the example in Figure 11–4.

Audit Report

• Short- and long-form audit reports are well known in business.

Short-form and long-form audit reports are well known in business. The short-form audit report is perhaps the most standardized of all reports—if, indeed, it can be classified as a report. Actually, it is a standardized statement verifying an accountant's inspection of a firm's financial records. Its wording seldom varies. Illustrations of this standard form are found in almost any corporate annual report.

• Long-form audit reports vary in their makeup.

Long-form audit reports vary greatly in their makeup. In fact, a national accounting association that studied the subject exhaustively found the makeup of these reports to be so varied that it concluded that no typical form existed.

Proposal

• Proposals vary in length.

Whether proposals belong in a discussion of shorter reports is debatable, for they are not always short. In fact, they range in length from just a few pages to several volumes. We discuss them here primarily as a matter of convenience.

• A proposal is a presentation for consideration of something.

Proposals Defined. By definition, a *proposal* is a persuasive presentation for consideration of something. In actual practice, some proposals fit this definition well—for example, one company's proposal to merge with another company, an advertising agency's proposal to promote a product, or a city's proposal to induce a business to locate within its boundaries. But other proposals are more precisely described as appeals or bids for grants, donations, or sales of products or services. To illustrate, a college professor submits a request for research funds to a government agency, a community organization submits a request to a philanthropic foundation for help in establishing a drug rehabilitation facility, or a company submits a bid for the sale of its products or services.

Proposals are usually written, but they can be oral presentations or a combination of both. They may be made by individuals or organizations, including business organizations, and they may be made to any of a variety of individuals or organizations such as government agencies, foundations, businesses. They can even be made internally—by one part of a business to another part or to the management of the business. For example, a department might outline its needs for new equipment in a proposal to management.

- Proposals are made by individuals or organizations to individuals or organizations.

Invited or Prospecting. Proposals may be invited or prospecting. By *invited* we mean that the awarding organization announces to interested parties that it will make an award and that it is soliciting proposals. To illustrate, a government agency might have funds to award for research projects, a foundation might wish to make grants for educational innovations, or a business might want competing suppliers to bid on a product or service that it needs. In their announcements, the awarding organizations typically describe their needs and specify the unique requirements that the proposals should cover.

- They may be invited or prospecting.

In business situations, invited proposals usually follow preliminary meetings between the parties involved. For example, if a business has a need for certain production equipment, its representatives might initiate meetings with likely suppliers of this equipment. At these meetings the representatives would discuss the need with suppliers. Each supplier would then be invited to submit a proposal for fulfilling the need with its equipment. In a sense, such a proposal is a bid supported by the documentation and explanation needed for conviction.

- In business, invited proposals usually follow meetings.

Prospecting proposals are much like rational sales letters. They amount to descriptions of what the writer or the writer's organization could do if given an award by the reader's organization. For example, a university department that wishes to seek funding for the development of a new online degree in entrepreneurship might write proposals to philanthropic foundations describing the curriculum, outlining its financial needs for instituting the curriculum, and proposing that the foundation award the funds needed. Or a business supplying unique services might submit an unsolicited description of the services to a business that might use them. Such proposals differ from rational sales messages primarily in their physical form (they are in report form). Such proposals also may differ from rational sales messages by being specifically adapted to the reader's business.

- Prospecting proposals are like sales messages.

Format and Organization. The physical arrangement and organization of proposals vary widely. The simplest proposals resemble formal email reports. Internal proposals (those written for and by people in the same organization) usually fall into this category, though exceptions exist. The more complex proposals may take the form of full-dress, long reports, including prefatory pages (title pages, letter of transmittal, table of contents, executive summary), text, and an assortment of appended parts. Most proposals have arrangements that fall somewhere between these extremes.

- Their formats vary from email reports to long-report forms.

Because of the wide variations in the makeup of proposals, you would be wise to investigate carefully before designing a particular proposal. In your investigation, try to determine what format is conventional among those who will read it. Look to see what others have done in similar situations. In the case of an invited proposal, review the request thoroughly, looking for clues concerning the preferences of the inviting organization. If you are unable to follow any of these courses, design a format based on your knowledge of report structure. Your design should be the one that you think is best for the one situation.

- Select the format appropriate for your one case.

Formality Requirements. The formality requirements of proposals vary. In some cases (a university's proposal for a research grant, for example), strict formality is expected. In other cases (such as a manufacturing department's proposal that the plant manager change a production procedure), informality is in order. As with other reports, the decision should be based primarily on the relationship between the parties involved. If the parties are acquainted with each other, informality is appropriate. If they are not, a formal report is usually expected. An exception would be made in any case in which formality is expected regardless of the relationship of the parties.

Content. You should consider the needs of the individual case in determining the content of a proposal. In the case of an invited (solicited) proposal, review the proposal request if the request is in writing. If the proposal results from a meeting, review your announcement of the meeting or the notes you took at the meeting. Such a review will usually tell you what is wanted. In fact, some written invitations even give a suggested plan for the proposal. It is highly important that you follow such guidelines, for in competitive situations the selection procedure frequently involves a checklist and rating for each item stated in the invitation.

If you are submitting an uninvited proposal, you will have to determine what your readers need to know. Because each case will involve different needs, you will have to use your best judgment in making that determination.

Although the number of content possibilities is great, you should consider including the eight topics listed below. They are broad and general, and you can combine or subdivide them as needed to fit the facts of your case. (See Figure 11–7 for one logical application.)

1. *Writer's purpose and the reader's need.* An appropriate beginning is a statement of the writer's purpose (to present a proposal) and the reader's need (to reduce turnover of field representatives). If the report is in response to an invitation, that statement should tie in with the invitation (as described in the July 10 announcement). The problem should be stated clearly, in the way described in Chapter 10. This proposal beginning illustrates these recommendations:

   As requested at the July 10 meeting with Alice Burton, Thomas Cheny, and Victor Petrui in your Calgary office, the following pages present Murchison and Associates' proposal for reducing turnover of field representatives. Following guidelines established at the meeting, the proposal involves determining the job satisfaction of the current sales force, analyzing exit interview records, and comparing company compensation and human resource practices with industry norms.

   If a proposal is submitted without invitation, its beginning has an additional requirement: it must gain attention. As noted previously, uninvited proposals are much like sales messages. Their intended readers are not likely to be eager to read them. Thus, their beginnings must overcome the readers' reluctance. An effective way of doing this is to begin by briefly summarizing the highlights of the proposal with emphasis on its benefits. This technique is illustrated by the beginning of an unsolicited proposal that a restaurant consultant sent to prospective clients:

   The following pages present a proven plan for operations review that will (1) reduce food costs, (2) evaluate menu offerings for maximum profitability, (3) increase kitchen efficiency, (4) improve service, and (5) increase profits. Mattox and Associates proposes to achieve these results through its highly successful procedures, which involve analysis of guest checks and invoices and observational studies of kitchen and service work.

   Your clear statement of the purpose and problem may be the most important aspect of the proposal. In order to win a contract, you must convince your reader that you have a clear understanding of what needs to be done.

2. *Background.* A review of background information promotes an understanding of the problem. Thus, a college's proposal for an educational grant might benefit from a review of the college's involvement in the area to which the grant would be applied. A

Marginal notes (left column):

- The formality requirements of proposals vary. Do what is appropriate.

- Determine the content of a proposal by reviewing the needs of the case. If the proposal has been invited, review the invitation.

- If the proposal is uninvited, use judgment in determining the readers' needs.

- Consider including these eight topics:

- 1. Writer's purpose and the reader's need (good beginning topics).

- Uninvited proposals must gain attention.

- 2. Background.

FIGURE 11–7

Illustration of a Short Proposal. This simple proposal seeks organization membership for its writer. It begins with a quick introduction that ties in with the reader's invitation for the proposal. Then it presents the case, logically proceeding from background information to advantages of membership, to costs. It concludes with the recommendation to sponsor membership.

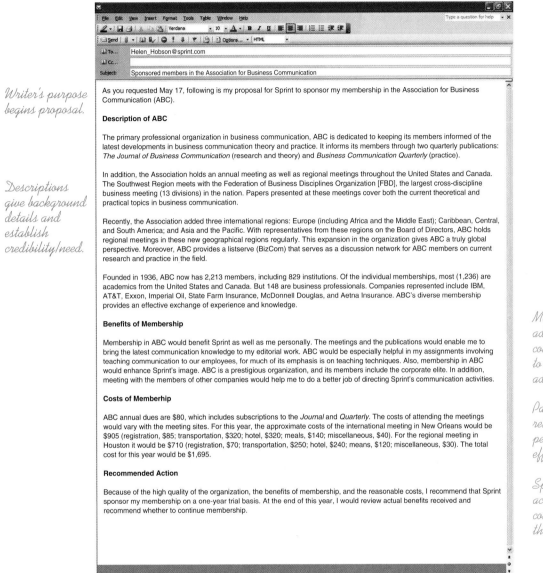

Writer's purpose begins proposal.

Descriptions give background details and establish credibility/need.

Membership advantages to company and to individual add connection.

Particulars reinforce persuasive effort.

Specified action completes the plan.

---

company's proposal of a merger with another company might review industry developments that make the merger desirable. Or a chief executive officer's proposal to the board of directors that a company's administration be reorganized might present the background information that justifies the proposal.

3. *Need.* Closely related to the background information is the need for what is being proposed. In fact, background information may well be used to establish need. But because need can be presented without such support, we list it separately.

4. *Description of plan.* The heart of a proposal is the description of what the writer proposes to do. This is the primary message of the proposal. It should be concisely presented in a clear and orderly manner.

5. *Particulars.* Although the particulars of the proposal are a part of the plan description, they are discussed separately for reasons of emphasis. By *particulars* we mean the

- 3. Need.

- 4. Plan description.

- 5. Particulars (time schedules, costs, performance standards, equipment and supplies needed, and such).

specifics: time schedules, costs, performance standards, means of appraising performance, equipment and supplies needed, guarantees, personnel requirements, and such. What is needed in a given case depends on its unique requirements. But in any event, the particulars should anticipate and answer the readers' questions.

● 6. Ability to deliver.

6. *Evidence of ability to deliver.* The proposing organization must sometimes establish its ability to perform. This means presenting information on such matters as the qualifications of personnel, success in similar cases, the adequacy of equipment and facilities, operating procedures, and financial status. Whatever information will serve as evidence of the organization's ability to carry out what it proposes should be used.

● 7. Benefits of the proposal (especially if selling is needed).

7. *Benefits of the proposal.* The proposal also might describe good things that it would bring about, especially if a need exists to convince the readers. Reader benefits were what we stressed in sales writing, but as we have noted, proposals can be much like sales presentations. The greater the need to persuade, the more you should stress benefits. As noted in an earlier chapter, however, proposal writing is more objective and less flamboyant than sales writing.

As an example of benefits logically covered in proposals, a college's request for funding to establish a program for retaining the older worker could point to the profitability that such funding would give local businesses. And a proposal offering a consulting service to restaurants could stress such benefits as improved work efficiency, reduced employee theft, savings in food costs, and increased profits.

● 8. Concluding comments (words directed toward the next step).

8. *Concluding comments.* The proposal should end with words directed to the next step—acting on the proposal. One possibility is to present a summary review of the highlights. Another is to offer additional information that might be needed. Yet another is to urge (or suggest) action on the proposal.

SUMMARY BY CHAPTER OBJECTIVES

1
Explain the structure of reports relative to length and formality.

1. Length and formality determine the following general progression of report structure:
   • The very long ones have prefatory pages (title fly, title page, letter of transmittal, table of contents, executive summary).
   • As reports become shorter and less formal, the composition of the prefatory parts section changes, generally in this order:
     — First, the title fly drops out.
     — Then, in succession, the executive summary and letter of transmittal are combined,
     — The table of contents is omitted, and
     — The combined letter of transmittal and executive summary is dropped.
   • Below these steps are the letter report and the email report.

2
Discuss the four major differences involved in writing short and long reports.

2. The shorter and by far the most common reports are much like the longer ones except for these four differences:
   • They have less need for introductory material.
   • They are more likely to begin directly (conclusion and recommendation first).
   • They are more likely to use personal style.
   • They have less need for a formal coherence plan.

3
Write clear and well-organized short reports.

3. One of the more popular forms of less formal reports is the short report.
   • It consists of a title page and report text.
   • Usually it begins with a summary or conclusion.
   • Then it presents findings and analyses.

4
Write clear and well-organized letter and email reports.

4. Letter reports are another popular short form.
   • Usually they are written in the indirect order.
   • They are organized much like longer reports.
   Email reports are like letter reports.
   • They are usually written for and by people within an organization.
   • They are the most common report form.

5. Among the various special reports, four stand out.
   - The staff report follows a fixed organization plan (for example, identifying information, summary, problem, facts, discussion, conclusions, recommendation).
   - Meeting minutes provide a written record of a group's activities and decisions.
   - A progress report reviews the progress on an activity and follows no set form.
   - The audit report presents the results of an audit and follows a variety of forms.
     — The longer ones may follow a specified order.
     — One such order is introduction, methodology, facts, discussion, conclusion, recommendation.
6. A proposal is a persuasive presentation for the consideration of something: a merger, a bid for an account, a research grant, and so on.
   - Individuals and organizations make them to other individuals and organizations.
   - Some are made internally from one department to another.
   - They may be invited or prospecting. They range from the very short to the very long.
   - They vary in form, from simple email to full-dress reports.
   - They may be formal or informal.
   The contents of proposals vary with need, but one should consider these topics:
   - Writer's purpose and reader's need.
   - Background.
   - Need.
   - Plan description.
   - Particulars (time, schedule, costs, performance standards, and such).
   - Ability to deliver.
   - Benefits.
   - Concluding comments.

5 Adapt the procedures for writing short reports to staff, audit, and progress reports as well as minutes of meetings.

6 Write clear, well-organized, and effective proposals.

1. Discuss the effects of formality and problem length on the model of report makeup described in the chapter.
2. Which of the prefatory pages of reports appear to be related primarily to the length of the report? Which to the need for formality?
3. Explain why some routine report problems require little or no introduction.
4. Why is the direct order generally used in the shorter reports? When is the indirect order desirable for such reports?
5. Give examples of short report forms that are appropriately written in personal style. Do the same for impersonal style.
6. Describe the organization of the conventional short report.
7. What types of problems are written up as letter reports? As email reports? Explain the differences.
8. Why is the order of the staff report said to be a problem-solving order?
9. Discuss the pros and cons of including a list of absentees in meeting minutes.
10. "To be successful, a proposal must be persuasive. This quality makes the proposal different from most short reports (which stress objectivity)." Discuss.

1. Review the following report situations and determine for each the makeup of the report you would recommend for it:
   a. A professional research organization has completed a survey of consumer attitudes toward BankOne. The survey results will be presented to the bank president in a 28-page report, including seven charts and three tables.
   b. Joan Marion was asked by her department head to inspect the work area and report on safety conditions. Her report is two pages long and written in personal style.
   c. Bill Wingler has an idea for improving a work procedure in his department at McLaughlin Body Company. His department head suggested that Bill present his idea in a report to the production superintendent. The report is almost five pages long, including a full-page diagram. It is written in personal style.
   d. Karen Canady, a worker in the corporate library of Accenture, was asked by Doug Edmunds, its president, for current inventory information on a number of subscriptions. Her report is less than a full page and consists mostly of a list of items and numbers.
   e. Bryan Toups, a sales manager for Johnson and Johnson, was asked by the vice president of marketing to prepare an analysis of the results of a promotional campaign conducted in Toups's district. The report is six pages long (including one chart) and is written in the personal style.
2. Following is a report that was written for the manager of a large furniture retail store by the manager's assistant.

The manager was concerned about customer complaints of late deliveries of furniture purchased and wanted to know the cause of the delays. Critique this report.

11-17-04

TO: Martina Kalavoda

FROM: Anthony Dudrow

SUBJECT: Investigation requested 11-17-04

This morning at staff meeting it was requested that an investigation be made of the status of home deliveries and of the causes of the delays that have occurred. The investigation has been made with findings as follows.

Now that a new driver's helper, Morris Tunney, has been hired, there should be no more delays. This was the cause of the problem.

Over the past two weeks (10 working days), a total of 143 deliveries were made; and of these, 107 were made on or before the date promised. But some of the deliveries were late because of the departure two weeks ago of the driver's helper, Sean Toulouse, who had to be fired because of dishonesty and could not be replaced quickly with a permanent, qualified helper. Now that a permanent, qualified helper has been hired, there should be no more delays in delivery as this was the cause of the problem.

The driver was able to find a temporary helper, a man by the name of Rusty Sellers, for some help in the unloading work, but he got behind and couldn't seem to catch up. He could have caught up by working overtime, in the opinion of the writer, but he refused to do so. Of the 36 deliveries that were late, all were completed within two days. The problem is over now that the driver has a helper, so there should be no additional delays.

Short-Length Reports

1. *Recommending discharge of an errant subordinate.* Brandon Ludden has left you no alternative. You will have to report him for improper conduct and neglect of duty.

   Mr. Ludden joined the Triton Marine Products sales force about 11 months ago and was assigned the task of calling on retailers in a three-state area. For the first six months he performed well. In fact, at the end of this period you wrote him a letter of commendation for exceeding his quota for the period.

   In the past five months, however, his performance has been deteriorating. At first you noticed a sudden drop in sales. The drop became more severe with each passing month. In time, you began to receive reports from old customers that they were not getting good service—that Mr. Ludden's calls were becoming too irregular to be depended upon. At least six of the better customers in his area shifted their business to competitors. Reports also began to reach you that the man has a drinking problem.

   So you called Mr. Ludden to your office, confronting him directly with the question. He readily admitted his drinking problem, but he insisted that it was over. He laid the blame on marital troubles, which he said were ironed out. You decided to give him another chance.

   It is now a week later, and you have evidence that Mr. Ludden's problem is not behind him. Two of his better customers called in to complain of bad service (he failed to make his regular calls on them; so they had to buy elsewhere). A quick check revealed that he failed to call on seven other customers during the week. You suspect the number is larger.

   As Triton's sales manager, you must take action now. You will recommend that the man be relieved of his duties immediately. Following company policy, you will make your recommendation, and you will justify it in a report that you will send by company email to the vice president of human resources. (For class purposes, you may assume additional information, but do not alter the nature of the situation.) Ms. Maria Ayala is your vice president for human resources.

2. *Investigating a problem in Department 377.* As a trainee in the human resources department of Bimmerle Aircraft, Inc., you must investigate a problem in Department 377. Matt Pringle, the union steward, has charged that the union workers in this department have been discriminated against. He charges that overtime work, considered an extra benefit by the workers, has been given primarily to nonunion workers. He charges further that this discrimination is consistent with management's plan to get the union out of the plant. (Currently, about 42 percent of the production employees are union members.)

   After hearing the complaint, you visited Department 377 and talked with Taylor Bilbo, the department head. Bilbo's version of the story goes like this. Of the eight workers in the department, five are members of the union and three are not. The three nonunion workers have had more overtime than the others, but they deserve it. Bilbo claims that he gives overtime on the basis of seniority and productivity—nothing else. This approach, he points out, is permitted by company policy. If the nonunion workers got most of the overtime, Bilbo says it is because they have seniority and are better workers.

   After talking with Bilbo, you go to the files that contain the department's records. Here you find data that should prove or disprove Pringle's claim and, in fact, should point to the solution of the problem. After an hour or more of poring over these records, you arrange your notes in this neat tabular form:

Employee and Union Status	Hours of Overtime	Years Employed	Productivity (average units per day)	Rejection rate (percent rejected)
Rod Kennedy (U)	0	16	30	0.08
Kara Borg (U)	0	1	21	0.09
Roslyn Unitis (U)	10	3	32	0.07
Rod Roban (U)	60	8	26	0.01
Melissa Torno (NU)	40	35	30	0.03
Sean O'Grady (NU)	72	17	26	0.02
Calvin Webb (NU)	88	11	45	0.03

   Now your task is to analyze these data and present your findings in report form to Ms. Trish Benton, vice president for human resources. You will send your report by company email. In addition to analyzing the data, you will recommend a course of action if one is justified.

3. *Presenting and analyzing differences in grades of dorm and nondorm students.* As director of the Office of Campus Housing at your university, your current task is to report on grade-point averages of students who live in dormitories and students who do not. You have the data neatly assembled (see table below). Now you must organize it for analysis and presentation in a report for your Dean of Students. The dean is concerned about reports that studying is difficult in the dormitories and he wants evidence of it.

Grade-point averages (4.0 basis)

	Freshmen	Sophomores	Juniors	Seniors
Men				
Dormitory	2.15	2.40	2.51	2.78
Off-campus	1.90	2.14	2.37	2.56
Women				
Dormitory	2.34	2.54	2.68	3.06
Off-campus	2.13	2.31	2.55	2.92

As you review the data, you quickly see that the dean's information is wrong. Dorm students are the better performers. You will present this information fully, of course, and you will give your explanation of why. Certainly your explanation will be subjective, and you will make this clear. But by giving it you will attempt to assist the dean in making sense of your findings.

You will present this report in memorandum form and will send it the way you send most of your campus messages—by email.

4. *Recommending dress and grooming regulations.* Move into the role of administrative trainee at First International Bank and write a memorandum report on dress and grooming regulations for employees of your sex. At last week's executive meeting the discussion centered on the inappropriate attire and grooming of too many of the employees. The general thought was that the bank's image is suffering.

The meeting concluded with President Karen Devillier directing you to prepare appropriate dress and grooming regulations for your sex. Another trainee got the assignment for the opposite sex. "Be careful not to make us appear to be prudes," she warns, "but give us something that will protect the bank image. Send your recommendations to me first. We'll discuss them at the next executive meeting."

Now you must use your best judgment in preparing these regulations. Be careful to cover all important matters. And make the regulations so clear that all will understand. Write them in a memorandum report to the president.

5. *Reporting an accident at Permian Oil.* As safety director at the Permian Oil refinery, you must write a report on every accident that results in injury at the plant. Today such an accident occurred.

The accident happened on C Street, the street running from the entrance gate to the administration building. Duane Moss was hit by a private automobile driven and owned by Pansy Crittenden, who works in the payroll department. Mr. Moss, who works in plant maintenance, was taken to Mission General Hospital. He suffered two broken ribs, multiple bruises on the left forearm and left thigh, and a cut requiring nine stitches on the forehead. He remains hospitalized but is in good condition and should be released in a day or two.

You interviewed the two participants and Burl Felton (the gate guard and the only known witness to the accident). These comments summarize their reports:

Moss: I was on my way from my office to the parking lot to get the lunch I had left in my car. As I left the Administration Building I started to cross the street. No, it wasn't at a crosswalk. But since it was midmorning, I didn't expect any traffic. Just as I was crossing, I heard this car coming. I looked, but it was too late. It was moving fast—real fast. I heard a horn—then brakes squealing. That's all I remember. Next thing I knew, I was in the hospital.

Crittenden: I overslept that morning, so I was late—very late coming to work. Yes, I was in a hurry, but I was being very careful. I saw this man come out of the building and start to cross the street in front of me. I honked my horn because I wanted to make sure he knew I was there. He looked my way. I thought surely he would stop. But he didn't. He wasn't at a crosswalk. He just kept walking. I tried hard to stop, but it was too late. Was I going fast? Perhaps. But I was careful—always am. He saw me and just kept walking.

Felton: I had just admitted Ms. Crittenden to the plant. She had told me she was late; so she was in a hurry. She left the gate kinda fast. She clearly was in a hurry. Next thing I knew she was approaching the Administration Building. I saw this man (Moss) crossing the street. She was going right at him. She honked her horn and applied the brakes—but too late. I don't think he knew what hit him. I couldn't leave my post; so I called 911. Help was here in a few minutes.

Now you must write your report on the incident. (You may supply any incidental details you think are needed as long as they are consistent with the information given.) Your report will present an objective account of what happened and any conclusions and/or recommendations you think are needed. Address the report to the plant manager and send it by company email.

6. *Writing an objective report on an incompetent subordinate.* As supervisor of the shipping department of Buyitwholesale.com, you have been putting up with the antics of Jermaine Vanhoozer for six weeks. When he first came to you six weeks ago, he appeared to be

well qualified for his assignment of marking packages for their destinations. Even though you know he was hired primarily because his father and the company founder are good friends, you were satisfied with his selection. But soon after he began work, you saw problems.

A few days after beginning employment, Mr. Vanhoozer started missing a day or two. Always he explained that he had had a virus. But rumor around the office had it that the man has a drug problem. This rumor soon became fact when he began to report for work stoned. On three occasions you had to send him home. In all, he missed work nine days in the first month of employment, including the three days you sent him home.

Mr. Vanhoozer's problem involved much more than just missing some days. It involved making some embarrassing errors. In the first month, he made 14 errors that resulted in merchandise being sent to wrong destinations. Your other shipping workers rarely if ever make such errors. Some of the lost goods could not be traced, and the result was a loss of $1,744.35 to the company. Obviously, the company also lost in goodwill.

You have had three long discussions with Vanhoozer about his work, and each time he promised to do better. The last time (five days ago), you warned him that he would have no more chances—that it was the last. But today he showed up high. You sent him home and told him you were recommending that he be fired. Now you must carry out the action.

Following company procedure, you will write a report recommending that Vanhoozer be fired and providing supporting reasons. (You may supply additional supporting information as long as it is consistent with the information given.) Address the report to Jose Cruz, the president. Send it by company email.

7. *Determining whether Guardian Insurance should use a cleaning service.* For this problem assume the role of administrative trainee for Guardian Insurance Company, Inc. You are assigned duties as the president's assistant. Today the president gave you your first real assignment—the task of looking into the question of whether Guardian should employ a cleaning service rather than the three janitors it now employs. In recent years, the company has had great difficulty keeping janitors. In fact, seven people have filled the three $360-per-week positions within the past two years. The three janitors currently employed have been with the company for only three, five, and seven weeks, respectively. And in the past five years, only one janitor stayed on the job longer than a year.

As you gather the facts, you learn that in addition to the three salaries, the company must spend about $30 a week on cleaning supplies. Then, of course,

there are the workers' fringe benefits, which amount to an additional 34 percent. And throughout the year, extra help sometimes is needed. Over the past five years this help has averaged a cost of around $2,200 a week. The Plummer Cleaning Service has offered to do all of the company's janitorial work for $1,360 a week.

Your task is to analyze all of the facts involved and arrive at a recommendation. You will give the cost factors heavy weight, of course, but you must remember that there may be other less tangible factors to be considered. You will write up your analysis and recommendation in a memorandum report addressed to Giles W. Thornton, the president.

8. *Investigating abuses of sick-leave policy at Bastion Insurance.* Bastion Insurance Company has a rather lenient sick-leave policy—one day per month with pay. Employees may accumulate sick leave as long as they work for Bastion. Most do and find it helpful during extended periods of illness. Unfortunately, a few do not. They use it like vacation. This practice is encouraged by Bastion's lax policy of taking the worker's word for short (one-day or less) illnesses.

Justin Thibodaux, director of human resources at the home office, suspects that the company has more of a problem than most of the other executives think. He has asked you, his executive assistant, to investigate the facts of the matter. "Give me your findings in a report," he instructed. "If there is an obvious conclusion, point it out. Make copies for all six staff members as I plan to bring the matter before them at the next staff meeting."

Your investigation involved going through the leave records for one year of all 269 employees at the headquarters office. As most of the questionable sick leaves are assumed to be taken on Fridays and Mondays (to make long weekends), you looked especially at these absences. And as longer absences required medical doctor approval, you excluded absences over one day. Thus you come up with this picture of one-day sick leaves by day of the week: Mondays, 417; Tuesdays, 35; Wednesdays, 30; Thursdays, 37; Fridays, 521.

Then you determined the number of employees who have taken 12 one-day sick leaves, 11 one-day sick leaves, 10 one-day sick leaves, and so on. This information, you reason, should tell the extent of the sick-leave violators. Your findings are as follows: 12 days, 41; 11 days, 22; 10 days, 14; 9 days, 5; 8 days, 3; 7 days, 1; 6 days, 0; 5 days, 3; 4 days, 2; 3 days, 17; 2 days, 31; 1 day 33; 0 days, 97.

Now you must analyze these findings and write the report.

9. *Writing a personnel action report on a dishonest employee.* You don't like to do such things, but you must report one of your subordinates for cheating on

his expense claims. In fact, you must recommend his discharge.

One of your duties as sales manager of Techsystems, Inc., is to review and approve the expense vouchers of your salespeople. For the past seven months you have been concerned about the expenses claimed by Bryan Collier. They have been high—about 35 percent above the norm. You talked to Bryan about the matter three times. He took offense each time, saying that his expenses were legitimate and noting that he had the receipts required (he did). So each time you took no action and asked only that he watch his expenses in the future.

Friday before last you made a startling observation. You were having dinner at the exclusive Rapson's Restaurant when you caught a glimpse of Bryan, his wife, and his two teenage daughters being escorted to a dining room at the rear of the restaurant. You don't think he saw you.

You thought nothing of the incident until you reviewed Brad's expense vouchers at the end of the next week. He had submitted a receipt for $144.50 from Rapson's Restaurant, and it was for the night you saw him. On the voucher he had noted that this claim was for entertaining Lisa Bankston, Gerry Cutshaw, and Scott Petruy of the Bentley-Havens Manufacturing Company, one of his customers.

You wondered how often this has happened. Checking past records, you found two other vouchers for Friday night entertainment of customers. As Friday night is not a normal time for customer entertaining, you became suspicious. On one of the vouchers you noticed that Sid Butler, an old acquaintance from your selling days, was named as one of the customers. You telephoned Sid. He reported that Bryan had never entertained him—that he didn't even know the man.

You confronted Brad with the evidence. At first, he denied any wrongdoing. Then he admitted his guilt and promised that it would never happen again. He even promised to pay back "every cent I owe." But you do not tolerate such behavior. So, following company procedure, you will recommend to Gabriela Domingo (vice president for sales and your immediate superior) that Brad Collier be fired. You will present your recommendation in a report by company email. You will follow company standard practice of beginning with a conclusion (or a recommendation) and continuing with supporting facts and analyses. And, yes, you will recommend that $485.50 (the amount that Brad admitted was fraudulent) be deducted from the final paycheck.

10. *Reporting your academic progress to your future employer.* Assume that last summer you worked as an intern for _____ (the company with which you would like to work after college). You liked them. And they liked you so much that they promised you a job

after graduation and have awarded you a scholarship to help you through your program. A condition of the scholarship grant was the annual submission of an annual report on your academic progress. It is time for this report.

So now you must prepare a summary of your academic progress over the past 12 months. You will also cover any extracurricular activities that you think have contributed to your personal development, for the people you worked with at this company made it clear that they were concerned about the whole person, not just coursework. Using the facts of your own record, write this report. If there are any shortcomings, include them and explain them convincingly. Address the report to _____ (your supervisor for your internship). You have the email address.

11. *Evaluating the potential of city art projects.* The cities of Chicago and Cincinnati have earned national attention with their bold and whimsical public art projects. In 1999, Chicago featured "Cows on Parade," which consisted of brightly, and sometimes beautifully, decorated cow sculptures scattered throughout the downtown area, each masterpiece with its own clever theme and title (for example, "PiCOWso," "Holy Cow!," and "Moooonwalk"). Cincinnati followed suit the next year with the "Big Pig Gig," featuring such pig sculptures as "Hamlet," "Frankenswine," and "Squeal of Fortune."

You work as an intern for a public-relations consulting firm hired by the city of (you name it) to bolster its public image. The city is in a nice location, but its population (and, therefore, its tax base) has been declining, and some businesses have left town. The city leaders feel that potential visitors and residents bypass their city for others nearby that are perceived to have more charm. Your boss has asked you to report on the potential of public art projects like Cows on Parade and the Big Pig Gig to draw positive attention to a city. Specifically, your boss wants you to gather the details about these two events and any other similar ones that you can find. Who came up with and supervised these projects? Who paid for them? How did they work, exactly (for example, how were the artists recruited or chosen)? Did they cost the city anything? And, most importantly, what benefits do the cities claim to have reaped as a result of these projects?

Write a short report giving your boss the background information that he or she needs in order to decide whether or not to pursue this kind of project as one solution to the city's problem.

12. *Identifying and evaluating productivity incentives.* In today's business environment, keeping employees productive is extremely important. One technique many businesses are using for maintaining productivity is performance recognition awards. Not

only are these awards effective in terms of productivity, but they also reduce absenteeism as well as provide an extremely high return on investment (ROI).

You have recently read of ABC Communications' success in improving productivity through employee recognition programs held at regular intervals. In addition to allowing all workers to participate in both the competition and the selection of the winners, ABC ties all the awards to cash or other product incentives. ABC management believes these programs improve both employee morale and customer service. Management has learned that often small, low-cost programs can maintain or even increase productivity substantially. In fact, dropping just one regular program resulted in decreasing profits over $20,000.

You believe starting a small incentive and awards program is worth doing. Write a short report to your boss identifying and evaluating some incentives you believe would be effective productivity motivators as well as the costs to implement the program. Also, suggest ways to evaluate the success of the program.

13. *Determining best online training program for workplace injury prevention.* In today's competitive business environment, keeping costs down is extremely important. One area many businesses are targeting for cost cutting is workplace injuries. Not only are these injuries costly in terms of paid sick leave, but they deprive businesses of valuable assets—their workers.

You have recently read of SBC Communications' success in reducing injuries through prevention programs. In addition to requiring all office workers to take an interactive PC training course, SBC trains its managers in assessing workers' application of appropriate ergonomics. Managers then assess all employees' ergonomics at regular intervals. They have learned that often small, low-cost adjustments can reduce the chance of work-related musculoskeletal disorders. In fact, preventing just one case of carpal-tunnel syndrome saved over $20,000 in direct costs alone.

You believe injury prevention training would be good for your business and employees, too. Identify three appropriate online courses and explain their strengths and weaknesses to your boss in a short report.

14. *Evaluating web-based survey tools.* You work for a small start-up company with about 25 employees selling major medical insurance for pets. It's a new market niche, but one you believe in because you know that others must care for their pets as much you care for your 10-year-old golden retriever. Many of the drugs and medical procedures once available only for humans are now also available for pets. And most people would treat their pets with the best alternative if cost were not an issue. That's where your company

steps in, protecting people's finances from the high cost of major expenses for their pets while ensuring that pets get the best care available.

You've only been in business three years, and your business has been growing steadily until recently, when growth began to level off. You wonder if the market is saturated, whether your customers are not satisfied, or whether you are missing any cross-selling opportunities. So you decide to survey your current customers to get more insight so you can get the growth rate back on track.

As a small company, you don't have any specialists on staff to conduct the survey or any special survey tools. However, you know there are many web-based applications that might help you. These applications would email the survey or a link to it to your customers; you'd have data back pretty quickly—especially since you plan to offer a prize to one lucky respondent to encourage participation. But you have not used any of the web-based tools before, although you know other small businesspeople who have. Tom McLaughlin, president of McLaughlin Body, mentioned Zoomerang during a recent golf game. He said, "It's the easiest way to get good customer feedback fast that I've ever used." Another friend, Sharon Garbett of the Sedona Group, swears by Surveymonkey. She tells you that it's one of the most intuitive and easiest to use tools she's ever used. That has big appeal to you. And you know there are other tools, too.

So you decide to review the websites of three to five of these tools to find one that might fit your needs. Then you'll write up a comparison and recommend one tool for the company to use. You'll present the short report to the directors at the next board meeting.

15. *Determining the appropriateness of a web-based collaboration tool.* You feel so lucky today since you accidentally found what looks like an excellent web-based collaboration tool. It is called Enlista and is found at < http://www.enlista.com/>. You found it when you were reading an online response an Oscar Pouce had written to a business article on building better lists. Oscar reported he used Enlista to create and organize lists and share them with other users. Since it works over the web, it doesn't need your server. And it is free, requiring no subscription fee.

You checked it out at the website. There you saw a demo and learned that the classic version has even more features. Some of these additional features are instant messaging, contact management, and solid security. But although "free" is tempting, you know there's always some cost. So before recommending it to your friend, Lisa Miller, for use in her work as coordinator of the local program for employing the disabled, you decide to download it and test it out yourself. You'll document your procedures, tests, and results in a short report. If you think it's flexible enough to meet Lisa's needs and easy to learn and use, you'll suggest she download it. If you determine it's not appropriate for your needs, you'll report that conclusion.

Middle-Length Reports

16. *Determining the best customer-focused cell phone policy.* You are the manager of an upscale ethnic restaurant (you choose) near your campus. The customers include an equal mix of students, faculty, staff, and businesspeople serving the campus community. After years of hearing both pro and con comments from customers on cell phone use in your establishment, you realize you need to establish an electronic devices policy since cell phones, pagers, and PDAs are becoming ubiquitous

   On one hand, you see other restaurants near your campus embracing the use of technology. Starbucks, of course, is one of these. More recently, Schlotzsky's Deli announced it would allow customers to surf the net while enjoying its muffuletta-style sandwiches. Subway is using GIS systems to send text message coupons and special offers to its nearby customers, experiencing an excellent draw on this permission-based advertising. And the more casual Papa John's and Dairy Queen restaurants are testing the use of technology, too.

   However, the fine dining restaurants in your area seem to be taking the exact opposite action, forbidding the use of these electronic devices. In general, they view this policy as an extension of no-smoking policies and others designed for the comfort and well-being of their customers.

   Since this decision is one that may dramatically affect the revenues of the restaurant, you realize you need to make your decision based on good information drawn from both the literature and from your current and potential customers. So you will gather this information, analyze it, and conclude from it. Then you will present your work in a recommendation report to the restaurant's owner, Terry Lenaghan. Terry is the new owner. He recently expanded his business, diversifying from a small successful chain of pizza restaurants also serving the campus community

17. *Recommending a car-rental company for Techsystems, Inc.* For the past five years the executives and salespeople of Techsystems, Inc., have rented automobiles from Avis whenever they needed out-of-town transportation. Techsystems has been well satisfied with Avis equipment and service. But recent advertising of a number of competing rental companies has prompted the administration to take a comparative look at what the other rental companies have to offer. You, a management trainee working

under the vice president for administration, Cory Schmidt, have been assigned the task of investigating the matter.

   Specifically, Mr. Schmidt has asked you to gather all pertinent information from the other leading automobile rental companies—information on costs, services, equipment, and whatever else should be considered. Then he wants you to evaluate this information in terms of Techsystems' needs and make a recommendation. "We made such a study five years ago and selected Avis," he told you, "but the situation can change over time. We want to view things as they are today."

   Much of the information you will find on the Internet, although you may also find brochures and other printed matter to be helpful. You will present your findings and analyses in a report appropriate for the situation. Address the report to Mr. Schmidt.

18. *Recommending a purchase for Granite Insurance, Inc.* For this assignment, you are a management trainee working in the purchasing department of Granite Insurance Company, Inc., under Hans Durflinger, the department head. The company needs to purchase a quantity of _____ (you may choose, or your instructor will specify). Mr. Durflinger has assigned you the task of gathering the pertinent information, analyzing it, and making a recommendation.

   You began the task by collecting all pertinent information (prices, features, maintenance problems, dependability, and so on) on three brands by searching the Internet, gathering brochures, and consulting knowledgeable people. Now you must compare the three on the basis of the appropriate factors to be considered in making a choice. Then you will reach your conclusion. You will write up your conclusion and supporting analyses in an appropriate report addressed to Mr. Durflinger.

19. *Evaluating a client's portfolio and recommending action.* Play the role of a financial consultant working in your own consulting firm. Today you were visited by Miguel Villarreal, a man whose father recently died, leaving him with a substantial portfolio. Mr. Villarreal explained to you that he has little interest in investments—that he has spent most of his life in the U.S. Navy. He retired last year at the age of 51 and has obtained a good job as a manager of a fast-food restaurant.

   Mr. Villarreal told you that his father's holdings came as a complete surprise. "I had no idea he had anything saved. But he lived frugally, never spending much on himself, especially after his wife died about ten years ago. I suppose he was doing it for me, his only child." Mr. Villarreal further told you that he didn't know what to do with these inherited securities. "Are they good investments? he asked. "How have they been performing? Should I sell some of them?

All of them? If I sell some, what should I do with the money? I don't need the money now. With my pension and salary, I have more than enough to live on. I wouldn't mind keeping them for my daughter's education. She'll start college next year."

Your job now is to answer the man's questions. Using the Internet, you'll look at past performances of the stocks. And you'll gather information that might foretell the future. When you have finished, you'll write your findings in a report that will be easy to read for this man who isn't well acquainted with financial language. His portfolio looks like this:

Common Stocks

Hydrogenics Corp. (HYGS)	2,500 shares
General Electric Company (GE)	1,600 shares
Bristol Myers Squibb Company (BMY)	1,200 shares
Unisys Corp. (UIS)	900 shares
Kaneb Pipe Line Partners (KPP)	1,000 shares
Healthsouth Corp. (HRC)	7,500 shares

Mutual Funds

Seligman Communication & Information Fund., Inc. Class A (SLMCX)	9,558 units
ING High Yield Opportunity Fund, Class B (NAHBX)	7,544 shares

(NOTE: These securities were active at the time this problem was written. If any have become defunct, please replace with securities of a similar nature.)

Now you must get the information you need. Then you will analyze it and present your findings and analyses to Mr. Villarreal in a report appropriate for the situation

20. *Recommending a business book for Bell executives.* You are a management trainee working directly under Forrest W. Bell, the founder and CEO of Bell Computers, Inc. Your task at the moment is to help Mr. Bell select a business book to give his 77 top executives as a Christmas gift. He wants a book that will really help make the recipients better managers. So he asks you to survey the books that have come out in the past year—reviewing their contents, evaluating their contributions—and then choose the best three.

Although Mr. Bell will make the final selection, he wants you to rank the three.

You welcome this assignment, for it appears to be a good opportunity to show your intellect and business acumen to the top administrator. You know that general business publications such as *Business Week* periodically review business books. And you know that some newspapers review and rate them, too. So you will start by searching these sources. Then you

will search the Internet to see what it provides. If possible, you will find copies of the better books and review them personally.

When you have completed your research, you will present an analysis of the three books. You will emphasize what each can do to make the 77 executives better administrators. You will present your work to Mr. Bell in appropriate report form. How well you do this report just might determine your future with this company.

21. *Assessing the moonlighting of Bigg City police.* For some time the mayor and council members of Bigg City have been concerned about reports that members of their police force are working at second jobs (moonlighting). Some of the reports suggest that the police are working because their low pay forces them to seek extra income. Some suggest that police administration is bad—that the resulting low morale moves the police to look elsewhere for satisfaction. And some suggest that the police lack dedication and don't like their work.

As a research specialist for your own company, (your name) Research, Inc., you have been hired to find out the true status of things. To get the information needed, you constructed a questionnaire on Surverymonkey.com and anonymously surveyed 371 members of the Bigg City police force. From each you determined whether they were working at extra jobs. You also got information designed to show how satisfied they are with their chosen work. And you got their opinions about the quality of their administration. In general, you got the information that you think will tell the Bigg City leadership what they want to know.

After completing the interviews, you assembled the findings neatly in a summary table (Table 1). Now you are ready to determine the meaning of what you have found. You will review the information and apply your best logic to it. Then you will present your analysis with the supporting facts to the Bigg City leaders. And you will make any conclusions and/or recommendations that appear to be supported.

You will present your work in short-report form (title page followed by text) Because you want to give added emphasis to the main facts and conclusions, you will write the text in the direct order (highlights first). Address the report jointly to Mayor Cristy Erickson and the council members.

22. *Analyzing performance of the Metroville store.* As an administrative assistant to Wayne Witherspoon, president of Nottingham's, Inc., you have been assigned the task of reviewing the year's operating record of each of the food chain's 51 stores. Your instructions were to compare each store's performance, by departments, with the all-store averages. Your work should inform the store manager

TABLE 1   Responses of Police to Moonlighting Questionnaire

Do you have a second job?
   Yes: 119
   No: 252

Police moonlighting and departmental administration:

1. In general, how well do you think the department has been run in the past five years?	Answer Selection	Percent*	N(336)
	Very Well	29	97
	Pretty Well	53	179
	Not So Well	13	42
	Poorly	5	18

2. Do you think the department has given you a chance to show what you can do?	Answer Selection	Percent	N(341)
	Good Chance	42	145
	Fair Chance	39	133
	Poor Chance	15	50
	No Chance	4	13

3. Duty assignments are passed out fairly in the department.	Answer Selection	Percent	N(342)
	Agree Strongly	23	80
	Agree Somewhat	38	131
	Disagree Somewhat	23	80
	Disagree Strongly	15	51

4. Promotions in the department are too slow.	Answer Selection	Percent	N(339)
	Agree Strongly	9	31
	Agree Somewhat	27	93
	Disagree Somewhat	38	128
	Disagree Strongly	25	87

5. Politics plays a vital role in promotions and duty assignments.	Answer Selection	Percent	N(341)
	Agree Strongly	16	55
	Agree Somewhat	17	58
	Disagree Somewhat	34	116
	Disagree Strongly	33	112

Police moonlighting and general job satisfaction.

1. How would you rate your present job?	Answer Selection	Percent*	N(342)
	Excellent	30	104
	Good	44	151
	Fair	21	73
	Poor	4	14

2. Compared to other city agencies, how do you think the police department is treated by city government?	Answer Selection	Percent	N(340)
	Better than most	21	73
	About the same	49	168
	Not as good as most	23	78
	Much worse than most	6	21

3. How would you rate this police department compared with departments in comparable cities?	Answer Selection	Percent	N(338)
	Better than most	60	205
	About the same	25	84
	Not as good as most	11	37
	Much worse than most	4	12

4. If starting over again, would you become a police officer again?	Answer Selection	Percent	N(334)
	Yes, no reservations	47	159
	Yes, some reservations	40	134
	No, some reservations	6	20
	No, no reservations	6	21

*Percentages have been rounded.

of his or her performance and the performance of his or her departments. You will prepare a report for each store.

The report you will write on each store will be in short-report form (title page followed by text) with copies for Mr. Witherspoon and the store manager involved. You will organize each report in the direct style of presentation (with the major points at the beginning. And you will use graphics wherever they help communicate the report message. As you will try hard to be objective in your work, you will take care to point out good as well as bad performances.

First of the 51 stores that will be included in your report is the one at Metroville, which is managed by Andy Bradburry. The store's performance summary and the all-chain averages are presented in Tables 2 and 3.

TABLE 2   Profit and Loss, Metroville Store by Departments

	Total Store	Groceries	Meats	Produce	Dairy	Baked Goods	Frozen Foods	H&BA	Other Nonfoods
Sales	100%	100%	100%	100%	100%	100%	100%	100%	100%
Margin on sales	18.1	16.7	18.8	23.2	14.4	16.4	27.1	31.3	25.8
Expenses:									
Personnel	7.2	5.9	11.8	14.1	3.2	4.5	6.6	7.2	4.0
Wrapping, supplies	.7	.4	1.4	.7	.5	.5	.3	.3	.2
Utilities	.4	.2	.4	.8	.7	.1	2.4	.2	.3
Laundry	.1	—	.1	—	—	—	—	—	—
Insurance, outside service, telephone, bad checks, over-short, miscellaneous	.2	.2	.2	.2	.2	.1	.2	.2	.2
Repairs, maintenance	.2	.1	.2	.3	.4	.1	2.5	.1	.1
Rent, depreciation of lease-hold improvements	1.8	1.6	1.2	2.8	1.4	1.2	2.1	1.2	1.5
Licenses, taxes	.2	.2	.2	.2	.2	.2	.2	.2	.3
Depreciation equipment	.5	.4	.6	1.3	.9	.3	3.3	.3	.2
Advertising, promotion	.4	.8	.5	.5	.4	.5	.3	.5	.7
Stamps	2.1	2.0	2.0	2.0	2.0	2.0	2.0	2.0	2.0
All other overhead	1.1	1.3	1.2	1.2	1.2	1.2	1.2	1.2	1.2
Total expenses	14.9	13.1	19.8	24.1	11.1	10.7	21.1	13.4	10.7
NOP (before taxes)	3.2	3.6	(–1.0)	(–.9)	4.3	5.7	6.0	17.9	15.1

23. *Reporting on the progress of women in the International Academy of Communication.* Ten years ago the leadership of the International Academy of Communication (IAC) was chastised by a group of its women members for permitting men to dominate this scholarly organization. The women cited some convincing statistics that showed that the men did, in fact, run the organization to a much greater extent than their numbers justified. The leadership at that time promised the women that the problem would be corrected. And soon thereafter some changes occurred.

Now, ten years later, IAC has its first woman president. As one of her first acts, she appointed a special committee to study and report on the progress of women in the organization over the past ten years. She made you the chairperson of this committee.

As is often the case with committees, the chairperson must do most of the work. And that's the way it is for you. You got a little help in conducting a survey of a random sample of members (Table 4), but you had to gather the information on male–female participation yourself (Table 5). And now you'll have do the rest. The rest, of course, means preparing the report.

The data collected are quite adequate for your needs, for they cover the primary areas of concern. You must review them and analyze them—from your analyses you will determine just how much progress the organization has made on women's rights. If your analysis justifies it, you will also recommend actions to be taken to give the women justice.

You will write the report in short-report form (title page and text, with conclusions–recommendations coming first). Although the report will be duplicated and distributed to the entire membership, you will address it to President Kisha Cleveland. Wherever it will help tell the report story, you will use the appropriate graphics.

TABLE 3 Average for All Nottingham Stores,
Profit and Loss Statement by Department

	Total Store	Groceries	Meats	Produce	Dairy	Baked Goods	Frozen Foods	H&BA	Other Nonfoods
Sales	100%	100%	100%	100%	100%	100%	100%	100%	100%
Margin on sales	18.8	16.7	18.3	28.9	15.2	16.1	25.7	32.1	26.0
Expenses:									
Personnel	6.0	4.9	8.3	12.8	3.8	4.9	5.7	3.8	3.1
Wrapping, supplies	.7	.4	1.5	.8	.5	.5	.3	.2	.2
Utilities	.5	.2	.5	.9	.7	.1	2.4	.2	.3
Laundry	.1	—	.1	—	—	—	—	—	—
Insurance, outside service, telephone, bad checks, over-short, miscellaneous	.2	.2	.2	.2	.2	.1	.2	.2	.2
Repairs, maintenance	.2	.1	.2	.3	.4	.1	1.6	.1	.1
Rent, depreciation of leasehold improvements	1.4	1.4	1.0	2.7	.9	1.0	1.8	1.2	1.6
Licenses, taxes	.2	.2	.2	.2	.2	.2	.2	.2	.3
Depreciation equipment	.7	.4	.7	1.4	1.0	.3	3.2	.3	.2
Advertising, promotion	.8	.6	.9	1.0	.9	.8	.5	1.0	1.3
Stamps	2.0	2.0	2.0	2.0	2.0	2.0	2.0	2.0	2.0
All other overhead	1.2	1.2	1.2	1.2	1.2	1.2	1.2	1.2	1.2
Total expenses	14.0	11.6	16.8	23.5	11.9	11.2	19.0	10.4	10.5
NOP (before taxes)	4.8	5.1	1.5	5.4	3.3	4.9	6.6	22.0	15.5

24. *Reporting on income benefits of education.* As secretary to the Board of Regents (or similar governing body) of your school, you have been asked to gather information for the board's next meeting. Specifically, the regents want information on the relationship of income and education. As explained by Dr. Annette Easton, the board's chair, "We want information that will tell us just how valuable education is to our students. We'd like to be able to point out whether they can expect to be better off financially if they pursue an education. If the information is persuasive, we'll work up a brochure for prospective students. See what you can find."

Your search is soon rewarded. From the Census Bureau, you find the median earnings for people 25 and older by level of education. (See Table 6.) The data do indeed show what Dr. Easton hopes to find.

Now you will carefully analyze the data and make

TABLE 4 Percent of Academy Members Answering Yes to Questions on Sex Discrimination

			Females by Level of Participation		
	Females (n = 152)	Males (n = 101)	Low (n = 79)	Medium (n = 34)	High (n = 39)
1. Do you think the Academy has worked to include more women as members?	33.6%	72.0%	30.8%	34.4%	38.5%
2. Do you think your divisions have worked to include more women as members?	23.0	62.5	16.9	28.1	30.8
3. Do you think there is adequate representation of women in the Academy in general?	15.1	40.0	18.8	18.8	18.9
4. Have you experienced any discrimination professionally in the Academy due to sex?	8.8	8.0	3.8	7.4	19.4
5. Have you experienced any discrimination professionally in your current job due to sex?	46.6	8.0	44.2	51.6	47.4
6. Have you experienced any discrimination professionally in any previous job due to sex?	72.1	8.0	73.1	61.3	78.8

TABLE 5 Male–Female Participation in Academy of Communication, Current Year versus Ten Years Ago

	Ten Years Ago		Current Year	
	Males	**Females**	**Males**	**Females**
Membership (number)	2,117	947	2,707	1,743
Participation in				
Academy affairs				
Administration	97.4	2.6	75.7	24.3
Editorial board	87.3	12.7	78.8	21.2
Committee chairs	88.7	11.3	73.5	26.5
Committee work	86.5	13.5	59.4	40.6
Participation in national meetings				
Chair	92.8	7.2	78.5	21.5
Paper presenter	84.6	15.4	71.2	28.8
Discussant	87.2	12.8	77.3	22.7
Panelist	90.3	9.7	70.1	29.9
Invited speaker	100.0	0	100.0	0
Participation (all forms) in regional meetings				
Eastern	81.4	18.6	66.7	33.3
Central	87.8	12.2	71.5	28.5
Western	90.1	9.9	74.6	25.4
Southern	94.3	5.7	79.9	20.1

the interpretations they suggest. Then you will present your findings in a report appropriate for the board. You will send the report by email to each member. Address the report you submit for class to Dr. Easton.

25. *Determining the best email protection software for a biotech company.* New software programs promise to help protect companies from nasty email-related lawsuits, lawsuits that sealed the fate of Arthur Andersen, Merrill Lynch, WorldCom, and even

TABLE 6 Median Earnings for Full-Time Workers 25 and Older by Sex and Education Level

Education Level	Men	Women
Less than 9th grade	$18,150	$12,055
Some high school	22,047	13,595
High school graduate	30,659	19,286
Some college	35,756	23,020
Associate degree	39,863	25,810
Bachelor's degree	50,730	33,662
Master's degree	61,808	41,799
Professional degree	86,741	50,308
Doctorate degree	75,005	51,628

SOURCE: U.S. Census Bureau, Current Population Survey, March 2002.

Note: Details can be found at <http://ferret.bls.census.gov/macro/032002/perinc/new03_000.htm>.

Microsoft. However, the current programs seemed targeted at large companies. These companies will pay millions for this protection as a form of insurance.

The software both complies with new laws and solves a variety of problems. It ranges from preventing deletion of messages (meeting the requirements of the Sarbanes-Oxley Act), to reducing the chance that a writer will send email messages when annoyed or tired, to retracting sent messages. Although many of the features of these high-end programs are extremely sophisticated, some can be done manually.

One software package controls which workers can read, copy, or print email. Another scans emails for banned words and phrases while another encrypts messages. Others determine which messages need to be retained for long-term archival purposes as well as which messages should be deleted at regular intervals. Under court order as a result of a privacy lawsuit, Eli Lilly rewrote its email software to cloak addresses in bulk emails after an employee carelessly sent out a message to over 600 users of Prozac with all addresses visible to all recipients.

As a medium-sized biotech company, two areas that concern you most are the protection of both privacy and trade secrets. Identify some software programs that will give you this kind of protection. Write a short report comparing these products and recommending the one that is most appropriate for your company.

Following are topics that may be developed into reports of varying length and difficulty. In each case, you will need to create the facts of the situation through your (or the instructor's) imagination to indicate that a business-type problem exists. The information needed in most cases should be available on the Internet or in the library.

1. Recommend for X Company a city and hotel for holding its annual meeting of sales representatives.

2. Determine the problem areas and develop a set of policies for employees who work at home during business hours for X Company.

3. For an investment service, determine which mutual funds do better: those that invest for the long run or those that emphasize market timing.

4. What can X Company (you choose the name and industry) do to improve the quality of its product or service?

5. Investigate the problem of employee absenteeism and recommend ways to decrease it.

6. Using the data found at three major reporting agencies, evaluate your own credit for the ability to get a new car once you graduate.

7. Determine the problems of recycling and recommend ways to overcome them.

8. Investigate the advantages and disadvantages of requiring workers to wear uniforms and recommend whether X Company should require them.

9. Advise X Company on the advantages and disadvantages of hiring student interns from the local college.

10. Evaluate and compare the economic forecasts of three leading forecasters over the past five years.

11. Advise Company X on the desirability of establishing a child care center for the children of its employees.

12. Report to Company X management what other leading companies are doing to increase ethics consciousness among employees.

13. Report to a large ecommerce site on current means of reducing online fraud.

14. Determine the effects of fitness programs on worker health and/or productivity.

15. Determine whether Company X should ban personal web surfing in the workplace.

16. Advise your student government association on whether a social-norm marketing campaign to curb drinking would be effective on your campus.

17. Report on the office design of the future for Company X.

18. What can Company X (you choose the type of company) do to improve employee retention?

19. Determine how Company X should cope with the problem of an aging workforce.

20. Evaluate the advantages and disadvantages of flextime.

21. Determine the advantages and disadvantages of fixed-rate and variable-rate mortgages.

22. Study the benefits and problems of adding a competitive intelligence division, and draw conclusions on the matter.

23. Study and report on the more popular forms of creative financing being used in real estate today.

24. Review the literature to determine the nature and causes of executive burnout and remedies for it.

25. What should Company X do about employees who have been made obsolete by technological change?

26. Your company (to be specified by your instructor) is considering the purchase of _____ (number) smart phones for its sales representatives. Evaluate three brands, and recommend one for purchase.

27. Evaluate the use of the Tablet PC's handwriting input for use by sales reps in completing sales reports for Company X.

28. Advise Company X (a national grocery chain) on whether to add online shopping.

29. Investigate and report on the demand for college-trained people in the coming years in _____ (a major of your choice).

30. Report to Company X which major hotel chain offers the best value in Internet access for your employees when they travel domestically.

31. Determine the recent developments in, current status of, and outlook for _____ industry.

32. Investigate and report on the criminal liability of corporate executives.

33. Investigate whether hiring physically challenged workers is charity or good business for Company X.

34. Assess the status of pollution control in _____ industry for an association of firms in that industry.

35. Review the status of consumer protection laws, and recommend policies for Company X.

36. Review current developments in technology and determine whether we are truly moving toward the "paperless office."

37. Advise Company X (your choice of a specific manufacturer) on the problems and procedures involved in exporting its products to _____ (country or countries of your choice).

38. Report to Company X on the quality of life in your city. The company may open an office there and would move some executives to it.

39. Report to Company X on the ethics and effectiveness of subliminal advertising.

40. Compare the costs, services, and other relevant factors of the major automobile rental firms, and recommend which of these firms Company X should use.

41. Survey the franchise possibilities for _____ (fast foods, automotive services, or such), and select one of these possibilities for a business client.

42. Advise Company X on developing a wellness (preventive health) program.

Additional topics are listed at the end of the long-length problem section following Chapter 12. Many of these topics are suitable for intermediate-length reports, just as some of the topics above are suitable for long reports.

CHAPTER TWELVE

Long, Formal Reports

CHAPTER OBJECTIVES

Upon completing this chapter, you will be able to construct long, formal reports for important projects. To reach this goal, you should be able to

1 Describe the roles and contents and construct the prefatory parts of a long, formal report.

2 Organize each introduction of a long report by considering the likely readers and selecting the appropriate contents.

3 Determine, based on the report's purpose, the most effective way to end a report: a summary, a conclusion, a recommendation, or a combination of the three.

4 Describe the role and content of the appendix and bibliography of a report.

5 Prepare a structural coherence plan for a long, formal report.

Long, Formal Reports

Assume the role of associate director of research, Midwestern Research, Inc. As your title indicates, research is your business. Perhaps it would be more accurate to say that research and reports are your business. Research is your primary activity, of course. But you must present your findings to your customers. The most efficient way of doing so is through reports.

Typical of your work is your current assignment with Nokia, a manufacturer of mobile phones. The sales division of Nokia wants information that will help improve the effectiveness of its salespeople. Specifically, it wants answers to the question of what its salespeople can do to improve their performance. The information gathered will be used in revising the curriculum of Nokia's sales training program.

To find the answer to the basic question, you plan to investigate three areas of sales activities: how salespeople use their time, how they find prospects, and how they make sales presentations. You will get this information for two groups of Nokia salespeople: the successful and the unsuccessful. Next, you will compare the information you get from these two groups. You will compare the groups on the three areas of sales activity (the bases of comparison). The differences you detect in these comparisons should identify the effective and the ineffective sales practices.

Your next task will be to determine what your findings mean. When you have done this, you will present your findings, analyses, conclusions, and recommendations in a report to Nokia. Because Nokia executives will see the report as evidence of the work you did for the company, you will dress the report up. You know that what Nokia sees will affect what it thinks of your work.

So you will use the formal arrangement that is traditional for reports of this importance. You will include the conventional prefatory pages. You will use headings to guide the readers through the text. And you will use graphics liberally to help tell the report story. If the situation calls for them, you may use appended parts. In other words, you will construct a report that matches the formality and importance of the situation. How to construct such reports is the subject of this chapter.

Although not numerous, long, formal reports are highly important in business. They usually concern major investigations, which explains their length. They are usually prepared for high-level executives, which explains their formality.

- Long, formal reports are important but not numerous in business.

ORGANIZATION AND CONTENT OF LONGER REPORTS

In determining the structure of longer, more formal reports, you should view your work much as architects view theirs. You have a number of parts to work with. Your task is to design from those parts a report that meets your reader's needs.

- Needs should determine the structure of long, formal reports.

The first parts in your case are the prefatory pages. As noted in Chapter 11, the longest, most formal reports contain all of these. As the length of the report and the formality of the situation decrease, certain changes occur. As the report architect, you must decide which arrangement of prefatory parts meets the length and formality requirements of your situation.

- The need for the prefatory parts decreases as reports become shorter and less formal.

To make this decision, you need to know these parts. Thus, we will describe them in the following pages. In addition, we will describe the remaining structure of the longest, most formal report. As you proceed through these descriptions, it will be helpful to trace the parts through the illustration report at the end of this chapter. In addition, it will help to consult Appendix B for illustrations of page form.

- In determining which prefatory parts to include, you should know their roles and contents.

For convenience in the following discussion, the report parts are organized by groups. The first group comprises the prefatory parts, the parts that are most closely related to the formality and length of the report. Then comes the report proper, which, of course, is the meat of all reports. It is the report story. The final group comprises the

- Thus, they are reviewed in the following pages.

The introduction to long reports greets readers and prepares them for the facts and interpretations that will follow.

appended parts. These parts contain supplementary materials, information that is not essential to the report but may be helpful to some readers. In summary, the presentation follows this pattern:

Prefatory parts: Title fly. Title page. Authorization message. Transmittal message, preface, or foreword. Table of contents and list of illustrations. Executive summary.

The report proper: Introduction. The report findings (presented in two or more divisions). Summary, conclusion, or recommendation.

Appended parts: Appendix. Bibliography.

THE PREFATORY PARTS

As you know from preceding discussion, there may be many variations in the prefatory parts of a formal report. Even so, the six parts covered in the following pages are generally included in longer reports.

Title Fly

- The title fly contains only the report title.

- Construct titles to make them describe the report precisely.

The first of the possible prefatory report pages is the title fly (see page 357). It contains only the report title, and it is included solely for reasons of formality. Since the title appears again on the following page, the title fly is somewhat repetitive. But most books have one, and so do most formal reports.

Although constructing the title fly is simple, composing the title is not. In fact, on a per-word basis, the title requires more time than any other part of the report. This is as it should be, for titles should be carefully worded. Their goal is to tell at a glance what the report does and does not cover. A good title fits the report like a glove. It covers all the report information tightly.

For completeness of coverage, you should build your titles around the five Ws: *who, what, where, when, why*. Sometimes *how* may be important. In some problems, you will not need to use all the Ws. Nevertheless, they serve as a good checklist for completeness. For example, you might construct a title for the report described at the chapter beginning as follows:

Who: Nokia

What: Sales training recommendations

Where: Implied (Nokia regional offices)

When: 2005

Why: Understood (to improve sales training)

How: Based on a 2005 study of company sales activities

● As a checklist, use who, what, where, when, why, and sometimes how.

From this analysis comes this title: "Sales Training Recommendations for Nokia Based on a 2005 Study of Company Sales Activities."

For another example, take a report analyzing the Petco's 2005 advertising campaigns. This analysis would be appropriate:

Who: Petco

What: Analysis of advertising campaigns

Where: Not essential

When: 2005

Why: Implied

How: Not essential

Thus, this title emerges: "Analysis of Petco's 2005 Advertising Campaigns."

Obviously, you cannot write a completely descriptive title in a word or two. Extremely short titles tend to be broad and general. They cover everything; they touch nothing. Even so, your goal is to be concise as well as complete. So you must seek the most economical word pattern consistent with completeness. In your effort to be concise and complete, you may want to use subtitles. Here is an example: "A 2004 Measure of Employee Morale at Florida Human Resource Offices: A Study Based on a Survey Using the Semantic Differential."

● One- or two-word titles are too broad. Subtitles can help conciseness.

Title Page

Like the title fly, the title page presents the report title. In addition, it displays information essential to identification of the report. In constructing your title page, you should include your complete identification and that of the authorizer or recipient of the report. You also may include the date of writing, particularly if the date is not in the title. An example of a three-spot title page appears in the report at the end of the chapter. You can see a four-spot arrangement (used when writer and reader are within the same organization) in Appendix B.

● The title page displays the title, identification of the writer and authorizer, and the date.

Authorization Message

Although not illustrated in the diagram of report structure in Chapter 11 or in the report at the end of this chapter, an authorization message can be a prefatory part. It was not shown in the diagram (Figure 11–1) because its presence in a report is not determined by formality or length but by whether the report was authorized in writing. A report authorized in writing should include a copy of the written authorization. This part usually follows the title page.

As the report writer, you would not write the authorization message. But if you ever have to write one, handle it as you would a direct-order message. In the opening, authorize the research. Then cover the specific information that the reader needs to conduct it. This might include a clear description of the problem, time and money

● Include the authorization message if the report was authorized in writing.

● Write the authorization message in the direct order: authorization, information about the problem, goodwill close.

limitations, special instructions, and the due date. Close the message with appropriate goodwill comment.

Transmittal Message, Foreword, Preface

Most formal reports contain a personal message of some kind from the writer to the reader. In most business reports, the transmittal message performs this function. In some cases, particularly where the report is written for a group of readers, a foreword or preface is used instead.

The transmittal message transmits the report to the reader. In less formal situations, the report is transmitted personally (orally). In more formal situations, a message usually does the job. But keep in mind that the message merely substitutes for a face-to-face meeting. What you write in it is much like what you would say if you were face to face with the reader. Meeting your reader's needs enhances the communication effect of your report. It involves doing what is best for the reader.

Because the goal of transmitting the report is positive, you should begin the transmittal message directly, without explanation or other delaying information. Your opening words should say, in effect, "Here is the report." Tied to or following the transmittal of the report, you should briefly identify the report goal, and you can refer to the authorization (who assigned the report, when, why).

What else you include in the transmittal message depends on the situation. In general, you should include anything that would be appropriate in a face-to-face presentation. What would you say if you were handing the report to the reader? It would probably be something about the report—how to understand, use, or appreciate it. You might make suggestions about follow-up studies, warnings about limitations of the report, or comments about side issues. In fact, you might include anything that helps the reader understand and value the report. Typically, the transmittal message ends with appropriate goodwill comment. An expression of gratefulness for the assignment or an offer to do additional research if necessary makes good closing material.

When you combine the transmittal message with the executive summary (an acceptable arrangement), you follow the opening transmittal statement with a summary of the report highlights. In general, you follow the procedure for summarizing described in the discussion of the executive summary. Following the summary, you include appropriate talk about the report. Then you end with a goodwill comment.

Because the transmittal message is a personal note to the reader, you may write in a personal style. In other words, you may use personal pronouns (*you, I, we*). In addition, you may write the message in conversational language that reflects the warmth

- The transmittal message is a personal message from the writer to the reader.

- It substitutes for a face-to-face meeting.

- Its main goal is to transmit the report.

- In addition, it includes helpful comments about the report. The close is goodwill.

- A summary follows the opening when the executive summary and the transmittal message are combined.

- The transmittal message is usually in personal style.

Playing possum doesn't work anymore,
Stephmeyer! I want that report by 5 P.M. or else!

A Questionable Example of Effective Reporting

"How could I have hired this fellow Glutz?" the sales manager moaned as he read this first report from his new salesperson: "I have arrive in Detroit. Tomorry I will try to sell them companys here what ain't never bought nothing from us."

Before the sales manager could fire this stupid fellow, Glutz's second report arrived: "I done good here. Sold them bout haff a millun dollars wirth. Tomorry I try to sell to them there Smith Company folks what threw out that last feller what sold for us."

Imagine how the sales manager's viewpoint changed when he read Glutz's third report: "Today I seen them Smith folks and sole them bout a millun dollars wirth. Also after dinner I got too little sails mountin to bout half a millun dollars. Tomorry I going to do better."

The sales manager was so moved that he tacked Glutz's reports on the company bulletin board. Below them he posted his note to all the salespeople: "I want all you should reed these reports wrote by Glutz who are on the road doin a grate job. Then you should go out and do like he done."

and vigor of your personality. You may not want to use the personal style in very formal cases. For example, if you were writing a report for a committee of senators or for other high-ranking dignitaries, you might elect to write the transmittal message impersonally. But such instances are rare. In whatever style, you should convey genuine warmth to the contact with another human being.

As noted previously, you may transmit reports to broad audiences in a foreword or a preface. Minor distinctions are sometimes drawn between forewords and prefaces. But for all practical purposes, they are the same. Both are preliminary messages from the writer to the reader. Although forewords and prefaces usually do not formally transmit the report, they do many of the other things transmittal messages do. Like transmittal messages, they seek to help the reader appreciate and understand the report. They may, for example, include helpful comments about the report—its use, interpretation, follow-up, and the like. In addition, they frequently contain expressions of indebtedness to those helpful in the research. Like transmittal messages, they are usually written in the first person. But they are seldom as informal as some transmittal messages. There is no established pattern for arranging the contents of forewords and prefaces.

- For broad audiences, a foreword (or preface) is used. Forewords do not transmit the report—they comment about it.

Table of Contents, List of Illustrations

If your report is long enough to need a guide to its contents, you should include a table of contents. This table is the report outline in finished form with page numbers. As noted in the discussion of outlining in Chapter 10, the outline headings appear in the text of the report as headings of the various parts. Thus, a list showing the pages where the headings appear helps the reader find the parts of the report. A table of contents is especially helpful to the reader who wants to read only a few selected parts of the report.

- Include a table of contents when the report is long enough to need a guide to its contents.

In addition to listing the text headings, the table of contents lists the parts of the report that appear before and after the report proper. Thus, it lists the prefatory parts, but usually only those that follow the table of contents. It also lists the appended parts (bibliography, appendix) and the figures and tables that illustrate the report. Typically, the figures and tables appear as separate listings following the listings reviewed above. See the textbook website for instructions on how to generate a table of contents easily using Word.

- The table of contents lists text headings, prefatory parts, appended parts, and figures and tables. It gives page numbers.

Executive Summary

The executive summary (also called *synopsis, abstract, epitome, précis, digest*) is the report in miniature. It concisely summarizes whatever is important in the report. For some readers, the executive summary serves as a preview to the report. But it is written primarily for busy executives who may not have time to read the whole report. Perhaps they can get all they need to know by reading the executive summary. If they need to know more about any part, they can find that part through the table of contents. Thus, they can find out whatever they need to know quickly and easily.

You construct the executive summary simply by reducing the parts of the report in order and in proportion. More specifically, you go through the report, selecting whatever is essential. You should include all the major items of information—the facts of the report. You should include all the major analyses of the information presented. And you should include all the conclusions and recommendations derived from these analyses. The finished product should be a miniature of the whole, with all the important ingredients. As a general rule, the executive summary is less than an eighth as long as the writing it summarizes.

Because your goal is to cut the report to a fraction of its length, much of your success will depend on your skill in word economy. Loose writing is costly. But in your efforts to be concise, you are more likely to write in a dull style. You will need to avoid this tendency.

The traditional executive summary reviews the report in the indirect order (introduction, body, conclusion). In recent years, however, the direct order has gained in popularity. This order shifts the conclusions and/or recommendations (as the case may be) to the major position of emphasis at the beginning. Direct-order executive summaries resemble the short reports described in Chapter 11. From this direct beginning, the summary moves to the introductory parts and then through the major highlights of the report in normal order.

Diagrams of both arrangements appear in Figure 12–1. Whichever arrangement you choose, you will write the executive summary after the report proper is complete.

THE REPORT PROPER

As noted in Chapter 11, most longer reports are written in the indirect order (introduction, body, conclusion). But there are exceptions. Some longer reports are in the direct order—with summaries, conclusions, or recommendations at the beginning. And some are in a prescribed order similar to that of the staff reports described in Chapter 11. Even though the orders of longer reports may vary, the ingredients of all these reports are similar. Thus, the following review of the makeup of a report in the indirect order should help you in writing any report.

Introduction

The purpose of the introduction of a report is simply to prepare the readers to receive the report. Whatever will help achieve this goal is appropriate content. Giving your readers what they need makes a good first impression as well as displays your concern.

In determining what content is appropriate, consider all the likely readers of your report. As we noted earlier, the readers of many shorter reports are likely to know the problem well and have little or no need for an introduction. But such is not often the case for longer reports. Many of these reports are prepared for a large number of readers, some of whom know little about the problem. These reports often have long lives and are kept on file to be read in future years. Clearly, they require some introductory explanation to prepare the readers.

Determining what should be included is a matter of judgment. You should ask yourself what you would need or want to know about the problem if you were in your readers' shoes. As the report's author, you know more about the report than anyone else. So you will work hard not to assume that readers have the same knowledge of the problem that you do. In selecting the appropriate information, you would do well to

FIGURE 12–1

Diagram of the Executive
Summary in Indirect and
Direct Order

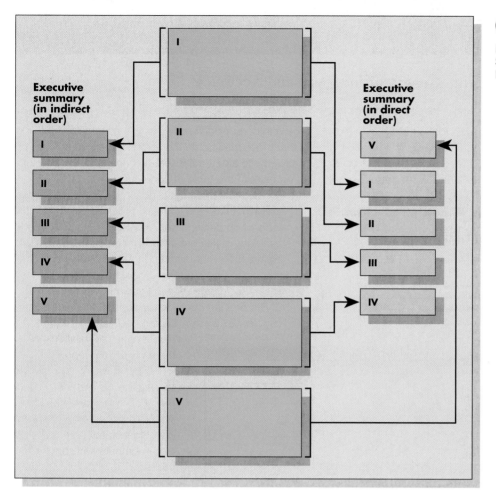

use the following checklist of likely introduction contents. Remember, though, that it is only a checklist. Only on rare occasions, such as in the longest, most complex reports, would you include all the items.

Origin of the Report. The first part of your introduction might well include a review of the facts of authorization. Some writers, however, leave this part out. If you decide to include it, you should present such facts as when, how, and by whom the report was authorized; who wrote the report; and when the report was submitted. Information of this kind is particularly useful in reports that have no transmittal message.

● 1. Origin—the facts of authorization.

Problem and Purpose. A vital part of almost every report is a statement of its problem. The *problem* is whatever the report seeks to do. It is the satisfaction of the need that prompted the investigation.

● 2. Problem—what the report seeks to do.

You may state the problem of your report in three ways, as shown in Chapter 10. One common way is to word it in the infinitive form: "To determine standards for corporate annual reports." Another common way is to word it as a question: "What retail advertising practices do Springfield consumers disapprove of?" Still another way is to word it as a declarative statement: "Company X wants to know the characteristics of the buyers of Y perfume as a guide to its advertising planning." Any of the three should give your reader a clear picture of what your report seeks to do. But the problem statement is not the only item you include. You will need to elaborate on what you are going to do.

● The problem is commonly stated in infinitive, question, or declarative form.

Closely related to *what* you are doing is *why* you are doing it. The *purpose* (often called by other names such as *objective, aim, goal*) tells the reason of the report. For example, you might be determining standards for the corporate annual report *in order*

● The purpose is the reason for the report.

Using a Table of Contents Generator for Speed and Accuracy

The table of contents generator tool in today's word processors frees writers from both the physical formatting and the accuracy tasks. Just a few clicks produces and formats the table of contents, along with leaders and page numbers. Additionally, today's generators add links so that those reading on the screen rather paper can easily navigate to a particular section or page by simply clicking on them in the table of contents.

The table of contents generator works with styles, using them as tags for marking items to include in the table of contents. If you are using a standard report template, styles are already incorporated in it. If you are creating your own report from a blank document, you could use predefined styles or define your own styles to create titles, headings, and subheads. Styles provide consistency so that headings at certain levels always appear the same, helping the reader see the relationship of the parts of your report.

Furthermore, if you decide to change the material in your report after you have generated the table of contents, you simply regenerate it to update page numbers with only a few clicks.

to streamline the production process. You will need to weave the why and what of the report together for a smooth flow of thoughts.

- 3. Scope—the boundaries of the problem.

Scope. If the scope of the problem is not clearly covered in any of the other introductory parts, you may need to include it in a separate part. By *scope* we mean the boundaries of the problem. In this part of the introduction—in plain, clear language—you should describe what is included in the problem. You also should identify the delimitations—what you have not included.

- 4. Limitations—anything that impairs the quality of the report.

Limitations. In some reports, you will need to explain limitations. By *limitations* we mean things that impair the quality of your report. For example, you may not have been given enough time to do the work thoroughly. Or perhaps a small budget prevented you from doing everything that should have been done. And there are other limitations: unavoidable conditions, restrictions within the problem, absence of historical information. In general, this part of the introduction should include whatever you think might explain possible shortcomings in your report.

- 5. History—how the problem developed and what is known about it.

Historical Background. Knowledge of the history of the problem is sometimes essential to understanding the report. Thus, you may need to cover that history in your introduction. You will need to do more than merely list and present facts. You will need to organize and interpret them for the readers. Your general aim in this part is to acquaint the readers with how the problem developed and what has been done about it. Your discussion here should bring out the main issues. It should review what past investigations have determined about the problem, and it should lead to what still needs to be done.

Sources and Methods of Collecting Information. You usually need to tell the readers how you collected the information in the report. That is, you explain your research methodology and you justify it. You specify whether you used published research, surveys, experiments, or what not. And you describe the steps you followed. In general, you describe your work in enough detail to allow your readers to judge it. You tell them enough to convince them that your work was done competently.

In a simple case in which you gathered published research, you need to say little. If most of your findings came from a few sources, you could name the sources. If you used a large number of sources, you would be wise to note that you used secondary research and refer to the bibliography in the report appendix.

More complex research usually requires a more detailed description. If you conducted a survey, for example, you probably would need to explain all parts of the investigation. You would cover sample determination, construction of the questionnaire, interview procedure, and checking techniques. In fact, you would include as much detail as is needed to gain the readers' confidence in your work.

Definitions, Initialisms, and Acronyms. If you use words, initialisms, or acronyms that are likely to be unfamiliar to readers of the report, you should define these words and initials. You can do this in either of two ways: you can define each term in the text or as a footnote when it is first used in the report, or you can define all unfamiliar terms in a separate part of the introduction. This part begins with an introductory statement and then lists the terms with their definitions. If the list is long, you may choose to arrange the terms alphabetically.

Report Preview. In very long reports, a final part of the introduction should preview the report presentation. In this part you tell the readers how the report will be presented—what topics will be taken up first, second, third, and so on. Of even greater importance, you give your reasons for following this plan. That is, you explain the *strategy* of your report. In short, you give your readers a clear picture of the road ahead. As you will see later in the chapter, this part of the introduction is a basic ingredient of the coherence plan of the long report. Illustrations of report previews appear in the discussion of this plan (page 353) and in the report at the end of the chapter (see Fig. 12–3 on page 364).

The Report Body

In the report body, the information collected is presented and related to the problem. Normally, this part of the report comprises most of its content. In a sense, the report body is the report. With the exception of the conclusion or recommendation part, the other parts of the report are attached parts.

Although the body makes up most of the report, practically all that we need to say about it has already been said. Its organization was discussed extensively in Chapter 10. It is written in accord with the instructions on clear writing presented in Chapters 2 and 3 and the writing techniques covered in Chapter 10. Sources used must be appropriately noted and documented as illustrated in Appendix E. It uses good presentation form, with figures, tables, and caption display, discussed and illustrated at various places in this book. In fact, most of our discussion of report writing has concerned this major part of the report.

The Ending of the Report

You can end your report in any of a number of ways: with a summary, a conclusion, a recommendation, or a combination of the three. Your choice should depend on the purpose of your report. You should choose the way that enables you to satisfy that purpose.

- 6. Sources and methods—how you got the information.

- Sometimes it is necessary to cite sources.

- More complex research requires thorough description.

- 7. Definitions of unfamiliar words, acronyms, or initialisms used.

- 8. Preview—a description of the route ahead.

- The report body presents and analyzes the information gathered.

- Writing this part involves instruction covered elsewhere in the book.

- Reports can end in various ways.

Technical Writer's Report on Humpty Dumpty

A 72-gram brown Rhode Island Red country-fresh candled egg was secured and washed free of feathers, blood, dirt, and grit. Held between thumb and index finger, about 3 ft. or more from an electric fan (GE Model No. MC-2404, Serial No. JC23023, nonoscillating, rotating on "Hi" speed at approximately 1045.23 plus or minus 0.02 rpm), the egg was suspended on a pendulum (string) so that it arrived at the fan with essentially zero velocity normal to the fan rotation plane. The product adhered strongly to the walls and ceiling and was difficult to recover. However, using putty knives a total of 13 grams was obtained and put in a skillet with 11.2 grams of hickory-smoked Armour's old-style bacon and heated over a low Bunsen flame for 7 min. 32 sec. What there was of it was of excellent quality.

"The DP Report," Du Pont Explosives Department, Atomic Energy Division, Savannah River Laboratories, July 12, 1954.

- Informational reports usually end with a summary of the major findings.

Ending Summary. When the purpose of the report is to present information, the ending is logically a summary of the major findings. There is no attempt to interpret. Any interpretations of the information in the report occur on the reader's part, but not the writer's. Such reports usually have minor summaries at the end of the major sections. When this arrangement is followed, the ending summary recapitulates these summaries.

- The ending summary is not as complete as the executive summary.

You should not confuse the ending summary with the executive summary. The executive summary is a prefatory part of the report; the ending summary is a part of the report text. Also, the executive summary is more complete than the ending summary. The executive summary reviews the entire report, usually from the beginning to the end. The ending summary reviews only the highlights of the report.

- Reports that seek an answer end with a conclusion.

- The structure of the conclusion varies by problem.

Conclusions. Some reports must do more than just present information. They must analyze the information in light of the problem; and from this analysis, they must reach a conclusion. Such reports typically end with this conclusion.

The makeup of the conclusion section varies from case to case. In problems for which a single answer is sought, the conclusion section normally reviews the preceding information and analyses and, from this review, arrives at the answer. In problems with more than one goal, the report plan may treat each goal in a separate section and draw conclusions in each section. The conclusion section of such a report might well summarize the conclusions previously drawn. There are other arrangements. In fact, almost any plan that brings the analyses together to reach the goals of the report is appropriate.

- Include recommendations when the readers want or expect them.

Recommendations. When the goal of the report is not only to draw conclusions but also to present a course of action, a recommendation is in order. You may organize it as a separate section following the conclusion section. Or you may include it in the conclusion section. In some problems, the conclusion is the recommendation—or at least a logical interpretation of it. Whether you include a recommendation should be determined by whether the readers want or expect one.

Appended Parts

- Add an appendix or a bibliography when needed.

Sometimes you will need to include an appendix, a bibliography, or both at the end of the report. Whether you include these parts should be determined by need.

- The appendix contains information that indirectly supports the report.

Appendix. The appendix, as its name implies, is a tacked-on part. You use it for supplementary information that supports the body of the report but has no logical place within the body. Possible appendix contents are questionnaires, working papers, summary tables, additional references, and other reports.

As a rule, the appendix should not include the charts, graphs, and tables that directly support the report. These should be placed in the body of the report, where they support the findings. Reports should be designed for the convenience of the readers. Obviously, it is not convenient for readers to look to the appendix for illustrations of the facts they read in the report body. They would have to thumb back and forth in the report, thus losing their concentration. Such a practice would not help the reader.

- Information that directly supports the report belongs in the text of the report.

Bibliography. When your investigation makes heavy use of published sources, you normally include a bibliography (a list of the publications used). The construction of this list is described in Appendix E of this book.

- Include a bibliography if you make heavy use of published sources.

STRUCTURAL COHERENCE HELPERS

As we have noted, the writing in the longer reports is much like the writing in the shorter ones. In general, the instructions given in earlier chapters apply to the longer reports. But the longer reports have one writing need that is not present in the shorter ones—the need for structural coherence helpers.

- Longer reports need structural coherence helpers.

By *structural coherence helpers* we mean a network of explanations, introductions, summaries, and conclusions that guide the reader through the report. You should use these helpers wherever they will help relate the parts of the report or move the message along. Although you should not use them mechanically, you will find that they are likely to follow the general plan described in Figure 12–2.

- These are a network of explanations, introductions, summaries, and conclusions.

The coherence plan begins with the report preview in the introduction. As you will recall, the preview tells the readers what lies ahead. It covers three things: the topics to be discussed, their order, and the logic of that order. With this information in mind, the readers know how the parts of the report relate to one another. They know the overall strategy of the presentation. The following paragraphs do a good job of previewing

- The coherence plan begins with the preview, which describes the route ahead.

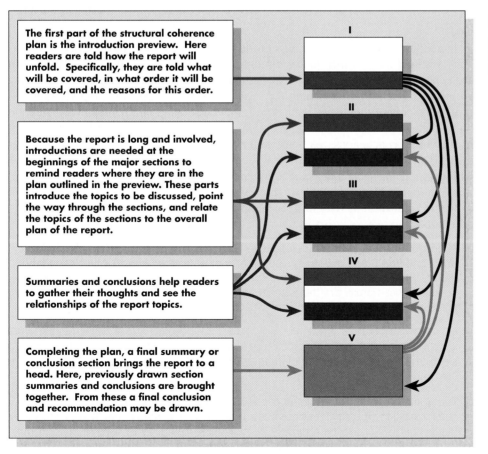

FIGURE 12–2

Diagram of the Structural Coherence Plan of a Long, Formal Report

The first part of the structural coherence plan is the introduction preview. Here readers are told how the report will unfold. Specifically, they are told what will be covered, in what order it will be covered, and the reasons for this order.

Because the report is long and involved, introductions are needed at the beginnings of the major sections to remind readers where they are in the plan outlined in the preview. These parts introduce the topics to be discussed, point the way through the sections, and relate the topics of the sections to the overall plan of the report.

Summaries and conclusions help readers to gather their thoughts and see the relationships of the report topics.

Completing the plan, a final summary or conclusion section brings the report to a head. Here, previously drawn section summaries and conclusions are brought together. From these a final conclusion and recommendation may be drawn.

Structural coherence helpers guide readers through the report. Helpers are similar to today's car navigational systems. Readers can clearly see where they have been, where they are, and where they will go next. By constructing paragraphs, sentences, and words at important positions throughout the report, readers can be guided skillfully to the report's ending.

a report comparing four automobiles to determine which is the best for a company's sales fleet.

> The decision as to which light car Allied Distributors should buy is reached by comparing the cars on the basis of three factors: cost, safety, and performance. Each of these factors is broken down into its component parts, which are applied to the specific makes being considered.

> Because cost is the most tangible factor, it is examined in the first major section. In this section, the four automobiles are compared for initial and trade-in values. Then they are compared for operating costs, as determined by mileage, oil use, repair expense, and the like. In the second major section, the safety of the four makes is compared. Driver visibility, special safety features, brakes, steering quality, acceleration rate, and traction are the main considerations here. In the third major section, the dependability of the four makes is compared on the basis of repair records and salespersons' time lost because of automobile failure. In the final major section, weights are assigned to the foregoing comparisons, and the automobile that is best suited to the company's needs is recommended.

● Introductions to and summaries of the report sections keep readers informed of where they are in the report.

In addition to the preview in the introduction, the plan uses introductory and summary sections at convenient places throughout the report. Typically, these sections are at the beginning and end of major divisions, but you should use them wherever they are needed. Such sections remind the readers where they are in the report. They tell the readers where they have been, where they are going, and perhaps why they are going there. You will need to keep section introductions neutral; that is, you will not include facts, conclusions, references to graphics, and such in them. Other report elements (facts, conclusions, etc.) follow.

Illustrating this technique is the following paragraph, which introduces a major section of a report. Note how the paragraph ties in with the preceding discussion, which concerned industrial activity in three geographic areas. Note also how it justifies covering secondary areas.

> Although the great bulk of industry is concentrated in three areas (Grand City, Milltown, and Port Starr), a thorough industrial survey needs to consider the secondary, but nevertheless important, areas of the state. In the rank of their current industrial potential, these areas are the Southeast, with Hartsburg as its center; the Central West, dominated by Parrington; and the North Central, where Pineview is the center of activities.

The following summary-conclusion paragraph is a good ending to a major section. The paragraph brings to a head the findings presented in the section and points the way to the subject of the next section.

> These findings and those pointed out in preceding paragraphs all lead to one obvious conclusion. The small-business executives are concerned primarily with subject matter that will assist them directly in their work. That is, they favor a curriculum slanted in favor of the practical subjects. They insist, however, on some coverage of

the liberal arts, and they also are convinced of the value of studying business administration. On all these points, they are clearly *out of tune* with the bulk of the big-business leaders who have voiced their positions on this question. Even the most dedicated business administration professors would find it difficult to support such an extremely practical concept. Nevertheless, these are the opinions of the small-business executives. Because they are the consumers of the business-education product, their opinions should at least be considered. Likewise, their specific recommendations on courses (the subject of the following section) deserve careful review.

Completing the coherence plan is the final major section of the report. In this section, you achieve the goal of the report. Here you recall from the preceding section summaries all the major findings and analyses. Then you apply them to the problem and present the conclusion. Sometimes you will make recommendations. Thus, you complete the strategy explained in the introduction preview and recalled at convenient places throughout the report.

- The final major section of the report brings together the preceding information and applies it to the goal.

Wise use of coherence helpers can form a network of connections throughout the report. You should keep in mind, however, that these helpers should be used only when they are needed. That is, you should use them when your readers need help in seeing relationships and in knowing where they are and where they are going. If you use them well, they will appear as natural parts of the report story. They should never appear to be mechanical additions. When paragraphs are combined with sentence and word transitions, as discussed in Chapter 10, the total plan should guide your readers smoothly and naturally through the report.

- Use coherence helpers naturally—when they are needed.

THE LONG ANALYTICAL REPORT ILLUSTRATED

Illustrating the long analytical report is the report presented at the end of this chapter (Figure 12–3). The report's structure parallels that of the formal type described in the preceding pages.

- Figure 12–3 is an illustration of a long, formal report.

SUMMARY BY CHAPTER OBJECTIVES

1. The prefatory section of the long, formal report consists of these conventional parts:
   - Title fly—a page displaying only the title.
     — As a checklist for constructing the title, use the 5 Ws (*who, what, where, when, why*).
     — Sometimes *how* is important.
   - Title page—a page displaying the title, identification of writer and recipient, and date.
   - Authorization message—included only when a message authorized the report.
   - Transmittal message—a message transmitting the report (a *foreword* or *preface* in very long and highly formal papers).
     — This part takes the place of a face-to-face presentation.
     — Begin it with a presentation of the report.
     — Include comments about the report you would have made in a face-to-face presentation.
     — In some cases you may combine it with the executive summary.
     — Write the message in personal style (first and second person).
   - Table of contents, list of illustrations—a listing of the report parts and illustrations with page numbers.
   - Executive summary—the report in miniature.
     — Include, in proportion, everything that is important—all the major facts, analyses, and conclusions.
     — Write it in either direct or indirect order.

Describe the roles and contents and construct the prefatory parts of a long, formal report.

2
Organize each introduction of a long report by considering the likely readers and selecting the appropriate contents.

3
Determine, based on the report's purpose, the most effective way to end a report: a summary, a conclusion, a recommendation, or a combination of the three.

4
Describe the role and content of the appendix and bibliography of a report.

5
Prepare a structural coherence plan for a long, formal report.

2. The report introduction prepares the readers to receive the report.
   • Include whatever helps reach this goal.
   • Use these items as a checklist for content: purpose, scope, limitations, problem history, methodology, definitions, preview.
   • A preview telling the order and reasoning for the order is useful in longer, more involved reports.
3. The ending of the report achieves the report purpose.
   • Use a summary if the purpose is to review information.
   • Use a conclusion if the purpose is to reach an answer.
   • Use a recommendation if the purpose is to determine a desirable action.
4. An appendix and/or bibliography can follow the report text.
   • The appendix contains items that support the text but have no specific place in the text (such as questionnaires, working papers, summary tables).
   • The bibliography is a descriptive list of the secondary sources that were used in the investigation.
5. The longer reports need various structural helpers to give them coherence.
   • These helpers consist of a network of explanations, introductions, summaries, and conclusions that guide the reader through the report.
   • Begin the coherence plan with the introduction preview, which tells the structure of the report.
   • Then use the introductions and summaries in following parts to tell readers where they are in this structure.
   • At the end, bring together the preceding information, analyses, and conclusions to reach the report goal.
   • Make these coherence helpers inconspicuous—that is, make them appear to be a natural part of the message.

FIGURE 12–3

Illustration of a Long, Formal Report. This long, formal report presents the findings of an observational study of successful and unsuccessful salespeople to determine the differences in how each group works. The results will be used to revise the content of the company's sales training program. Because the report is extensive and the situation formal, the report has all the major prefatory parts. The significant statistical findings are effectively emphasized by graphics. Whenever secondary sources are used, they are appropriately noted and listed in the bibliography. Its physical presentation uses the Word contemporary report template. Its documentation and figures use the *Chicago Manual of Style,* 15th edition.

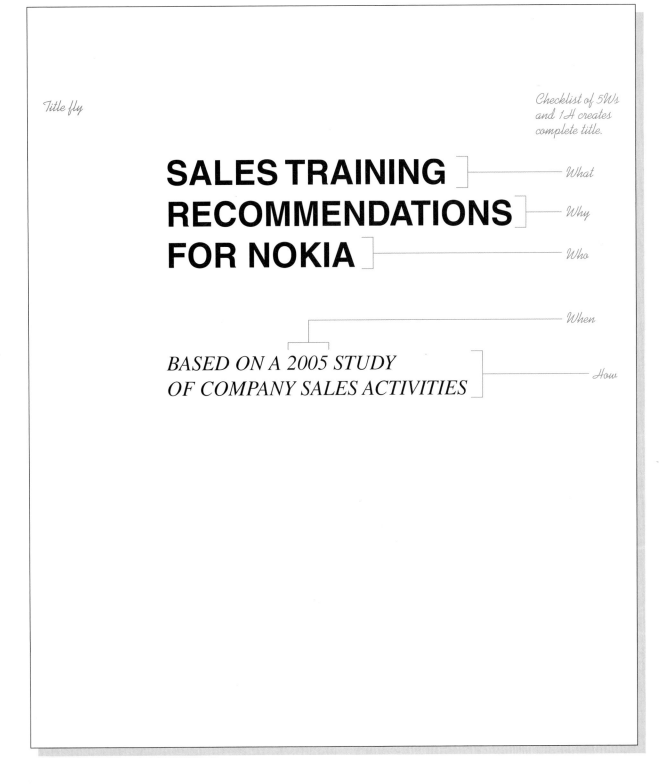

Title fly

Checklist of 5Ws and 1H creates complete title.

SALES TRAINING RECOMMENDATIONS FOR NOKIA

— *What*

— *Why*

— *Who*

— *When*

BASED ON A 2005 STUDY OF COMPANY SALES ACTIVITIES

— *How*

FIGURE 12–3   (Continued)

Three-spot title page

SALES TRAINING RECOMMENDATIONS FOR NOKIA

BASED ON A 2005 STUDY OF COMPANY SALES ACTIVITIES

Recipient of report receives prime position on page.

Prepared for
Mr. Peter R. Simpson, Vice President for Sales
Nokia Inc.
72117 North Musselman Road
Dearborn, MI 48126-2351

Writer receives subordinate page position.

Prepared by
Ashlee P. Callahan
Midwestern Research Associates
Suite D, Brownfield Towers
212 North Bedford Avenue
Detroit, MI 48219-6708

November 17, 2005

FIGURE 12–3   (Continued)

Midwestern Research Associates

Suite D, Brownfield Towers
212 North Bedford Avenue
Detroit, MI 48219-6708
312-222-2575 research@midwestern.com

Transmittal message

November 17, 2005

Mr. Peter R. Simpson
Vice President for Sales
Nokia Inc.
72117 North Musselman Road
Dearborn, MI 48126-2351

Dear Mr. Simpson:

Begins directly, with the transmittal.

Here is the report on the observational study of your salespeople you asked us to conduct last August 17.

Pertinent comments help the reader understand and appreciate the research.

As you will see, our observations pointed to some specific needs for sales training. Following the procedure we agreed to, we will prepare an outline of these needs in a revised curriculum plan that we will submit to your training director December 4. We are confident that this curriculum plan will help correct the shortcomings in your sales force.

Goodwill comment ends letter.

At Midwestern we appreciate having this assignment. If you should need any assistance in interpreting this report or in implementing our recommendations, please contact us at acallahan@midwestern.com or 312-222-2575.

Sincerely yours,

Ashlee P. Callahan

Ashlee P. Callahan
Senior Research Associate

FIGURE 12–3 (Continued)

Table of contents

TABLE OF CONTENTS

Background details of the problem prepare the reader to receive the report.

Three areas of sales work investigated logically form main headings.

Subfactors of the work areas make logical second-level headings.

First- and second-level headings are parallel.

Conciseness in headings improve readability.

Divisions of main body parts by factors (and subdivisions) show good thought and logical solution to problem.

Talking captions avoid monotonous repetition in wording.

FIGURE 12–3　(Continued)

List of figures (a continuation of the table of contents)

LIST OF FIGURES

Titles use 5 Ws and 1 H in title construction.

FIGURE 12–3   (Continued)

Executive summary

EXECUTIVE SUMMARY

The recommendations that result from this study are to add the following topics to Nokia's sales training program:

Following the direct-order plan, this executive summary places the recommendations first. Highlights of the supporting findings follow.

- Negative effects of idle time
- Techniques of cultivating prospects
- Development of bird dog networks
- Cultivation of repeat sales
- Projection of integrity image
- Use of moderate persuasion
- Value of product knowledge

Supporting these recommendations are the following findings and conclusions drawn from an observational study comparing three types of sales activities of productive and marginal salespeople.

Remaining paragraphs summarize the major findings in the order presented in the report.

The data show that the productive salespeople used their time more effectively than did the marginal salespeople. Compared with marginal salespeople, the productive salespeople spent less time in idleness (28% vs. 53%). They also spent more time in contact with prospects (31.3% vs. 19.8%) and more time developing prospects (10.4% vs. 4.4%).

Investigation of how the salespeople got their prospects showed that because field assignments were about equal, both groups profited about the same from unsolicited web inquiries. The productive group got 282; the marginal group got 274. The productive group used bird dogs more extensively, having 64 contacts derived from this source during the observation period. The marginal group had 8. Productive salespeople also were more successful in turning these contacts into sales.

Significant comparisons and conclusions are emphasized throughout.

Observations of sales presentations revealed that productive salespeople displayed higher integrity, used pressure more reasonably, and knew the product better than marginal salespeople. Of the 20 productive salespeople, 16 displayed images of moderately high integrity (Group II). Marginal group members ranged widely with 7 in Group III (questionable) and 5 each in Group II (moderately high integrity) and Group IV (deceitful). Most (15) of the productive salespeople used moderate pressure, whereas the marginal salespeople tended toward extremes (10 high pressure, 7 low pressure). On the product knowledge test, 17 of the productive salespeople scored excellent and 3 fair. Of the marginal members, 5 scored excellent, 6 fair, and 9 inadequate.

FIGURE 12–3 (Continued)

SALES TRAINING RECOMMENDATIONS FOR NOKIA

BASED ON A 2005 STUDY OF COMPANY SALES ACTIVITIES

Report proper (introduction)

THE PROBLEM AND THE PLAN

Incidentals of Authorization and Submittal

Authorization facts identify participants in the report.

This study of Nokia salespeople's sales activities is submitted to Mr. Peter R. Simpson, Vice President for Sales, on November 17, 2005. As authorized on August 28, the investigation was conducted under the direction of Ashlee P. Callahan of Midwestern Research Associates.

Objective of Sales Training Improvement

Purpose section explains the problem clearly and precisely.

The objective of the study was to find means of improving the effectiveness of Nokia salespeople. For achieving this objective, the plan involved first determining the techniques and characteristics of effective selling. This information then will be used in improving Nokia 's sales training program.

Use of Observational Techniques

Thorough review of methodology permits reader to judge credibility of research.

The methodology used in this investigation was an observational study of Nokia salespeople. Specifically, the study employed the contrived observation technique, which is a unique means of observing work performance under real conditions.[1] A detailed description of this technique is a part of the proposal approved at the August meeting and is not repeated here. Specific items relative to the application of this method in this case are summarized below.

Two groups of 20 Nokia salespeople were selected for the observation—a productive and a marginal group. The productive group was made up of the company's top producers for the past year; the marginal group comprised the lowest producers. Only salespeople with three years or more of experience were eligible.

A team of two highly trained observers observed each of the salespeople selected for a continuous period of five working days. Using specially designed forms, the observers recorded the work activities of the salespeople. At the end of the observation period, the

All sources used are appropriately credited and thoroughly documented.

---

[1] William G. Zikmund, *Business Research Methods,* 7th ed. (Cincinnati, OH: South-Western, 2003), 240.

1

FIGURE 12–3   (Continued)

2

observers conducted an exit interview, recording certain demographic data and administering a test of the salesperson's knowledge of Nokia 's mobile phones.

A Preview of the Presentation

Preview prepares reader for what follows in body sections.

In the following pages, the findings and analysis appear in the arrangement discussed at the August meeting. First comes a comparison of how the productive and the marginal salespeople spend their work time. Second is an analysis of how the productive and the marginal salespeople find their prospects. Third is a comparative analysis of the observable differences in sales presentations of the two groups. Conclusions drawn from these comparisons form the bases for recommendations of content emphasis in Nokia 's sales training program.

ANALYSIS OF WORK TIME USE

Body sections contain facts, interpretations, and solutions to report problems.

The time-duty observation records were examined to determine whether differences exist between the productive and marginal salespeople in their use of work time. Activities were grouped into four general categories: (1) idleness, (2) contacting prospects, (3) finding prospects, and (4) miscellaneous activities. This examination revealed the following results.

Section introductions tell what follows in subdivisions.

Negative Effect of Idle Time

Subordinate reference to figure ties text and graphic together and allows interpretation to begin in main sentence.

As shown in Figure 1, the productive salespeople spent less work time in idleness (28%) than did the marginal salespeople (53%). Further examination of the observations reveals that the top five of the 20 productive salespeople spent even less time in idleness (13%), and the bottom five of the marginal salespeople spent more time in idleness (67%). Clearly, these observations suggest the predictable conclusion that successful salespeople work more than their less productive counterparts.

Sentence conclusions complement formal coherence plan.

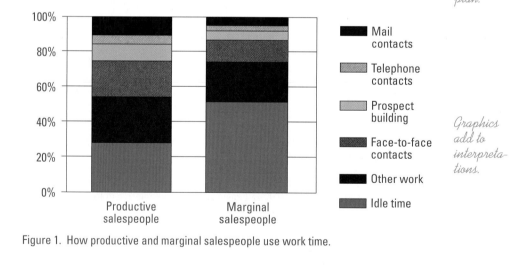

Figure 1. How productive and marginal salespeople use work time.

Graphics add to interpretations.

FIGURE 12–3   (Continued)

3

Correlation of Prospect Contacting and Success

Report text presents data thoroughly yet concisely — and with appropriate comparisons.

Productive salespeople spent more time contacting prospects face to face, by telephone, and by mail (31.3%) than did marginal salespeople (19.8%). The specific means of making these contacts show similar differences. Productive and marginal salespeople spent their work time, respectively, 23.2% and 13.5% in face-to-face contacts, 4.8% and 2.0% in mail contacts, and 8.3% and 4.6% in telephone contacts. These data lend additional support to the conclusion that work explains sales success.

Report length and situation formality justify third-person writing.

Vital Role of Prospect Building

During the observation period, productive salespeople spent more than twice as much time (10.5%) as marginal salespeople (4.4%) in building prospects. Activities observed in this category include contacting bird dogs (people who give sales leads) and other lead sources and mailing literature to established and prospective customers.

Necessity of Miscellaneous Activities

Section summary helps the reader identify and remember the major findings.

Both productive and marginal salespeople spent about a fourth of their work time in miscellaneous activities (tending to personal affairs, studying sales literature, attending sales meetings, sending and responding to email, and such). The productive group averaged 25.2%; the marginal group averaged 22.5%. As some of this time is related to mobile phone sales, productive salespeople would be expected to spend more time in this category.

The preceding data reveal that the way salespeople spend their time affects their productivity. Productive salespeople work at selling. In sharp contrast with the marginal salespeople, they spend little time in idleness. They work hard to contact prospects and to build prospect lists. Like all mobile phone salespeople, they spend some time in performing miscellaneous duties.

Tense consistency places concepts in appropriate time frames and gives a present time viewpoint.

DIFFERENCES IN FINDING PROSPECTS

Section introduction continues formal coherence plan.

A comparison of how productive and marginal salespeople find prospects and measurement of the productivity of these methods were a second area of investigation. For this study, the observations were classified by the four primary sources of prospects: (1) unsolicited web inquiries, (2) bird dogs and other referrals, (3) repeat customers, and (4) other. Only prospects that were contacted in person or by telephone during the observation period were included. Prospects were counted only once, even though some were contacted more than once.

Key transitional words used in emphasis positions keep ideas moving.

Near Equal Distribution of Web Inquiries

As expected, most of the contacts of both productive and marginal salespeople were web inquiries. Because both groups had about equal field assignments, they got about the same number of prospects from this source. As illustrated in Figure 2, productive members got 282 (an average of 14.1 each) and marginal members got 274 (an average of 13.7 each).

Variety in sentence design helps maintain reader interest.

Although both groups got about the same number of prospects from web inquiries, productive salespeople got better results. A review of sales records shows that productive salespeople averaged 260 units per week from web inquiries; marginal salespeople averaged 220 units. The difference, although appearing slight, represents roughly 40 mobile phones per week.

FIGURE 12–3   (Continued)

4

Color adds interest and helps reader visualize comparisons in graphics.

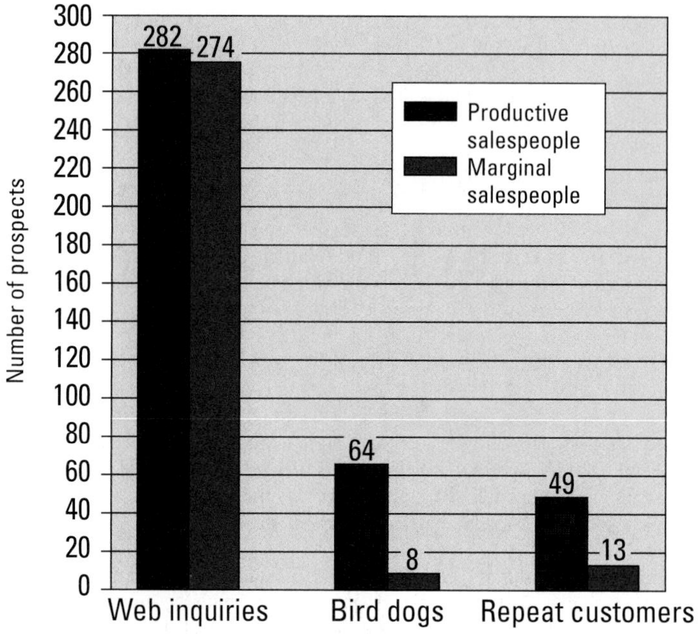

Use of graphics allows only important details to be emphasized in report text.

Figure 2. Prospects contacted during observation period by productive and marginal salespeople by method of obtaining them.

Value of Cultivating Repeat Customers

Predominance of active voice verbs provide flow and concreteness in text.

Repeat customers and friends referred by them constitute the second most productive source of prospects. During the observation period, productive salespeople had contacts with 49 such prospects; marginal salespeople had 13. Productive salespeople also had better sales success with these prospects, turning 40 of them into sales—an average of two per week. Marginal group members made sales to seven of these prospects—an average of 0.35 per person. These findings agree with those of a recent study reported in the *American Salesman.*[2] These differences appear to be a direct result of effort (or lack of it) in maintaining contacts with customers after the sale.

---

[2] Alex Hatzivassilis and Igor Kotlyar, "Increase the Number of Top Performers on Your Team," *American Salesman* 48, no. 7 (2003): 17.

FIGURE 12–3   (Continued)

5

Limited Effectiveness of Using Bird Dogs

Contacts from bird dogs comprise the third largest group, producing 64 total contacts for the productive and 8 for the marginal salespeople. Sales from this source totaled 9 for productive salespeople and 2 for marginal salespeople—an average of 0.45 and 0.1 sales per person, respectively. Although not large in terms of volume, these data explain much of the difference between the two groups. The use of bird dogs involves work,[3] and the willingness to work varies sharply between the two groups.

Scant Use of Other Techniques

Other prospect-gaining techniques were little used among the salespeople observed. Techniques long discussed in industry sales literature such as cold spearing, placing written messages on automobile windshields, and random telephoning produced no prospects for either group during the observation period.[4] All of the salespeople observed noted that they had used these techniques in the past, but with little success. The lack of evidence in this study leaves unanswered the question of the effectiveness of these techniques.

The obvious conclusion drawn from the preceding review of how prospects are found is that the productive salespeople work harder to get them. Although both groups get about the same number of web inquiries, the successful ones work harder at maintaining contacts with past customers and at getting contacts from a network of bird dogs and friends.

OBSERVABLE VARIATIONS IN PRESENTATIONS

Differences in the sales presentations used constituted the third area of study. Criteria used in this investigation were (1) integrity, (2) pressure, and (3) product knowledge. Obviously, the first two of these criteria had to be evaluated subjectively. Even so, highly trained observers who used comprehensive guidelines made the evaluations. These guidelines are described in detail in the approved observation plan.

Positive Effect of Integrity

Evaluations of the salespeople's integrity primarily measured the apparent degree of truthfulness of the sales presentations. The observers classified the images of integrity they perceived during the sales presentations into four groups: Group I—Impeccable (displayed the highest degree of truthfulness), Group II—Moderately High (generally truthful, some exaggeration), Group III—Questionable (mildly deceitful and tricky); and Group IV—Deceitful (untruthful and tricky).

Of the 20 productive salespeople observed, 16 were classified in Group II, as shown in Figure 3. Of the remaining four, 2 were in Group I and 2 in Group III.

---

[3] Julie Jahn, "Big Business Encourages Effective Use of Bird Dogs throughout Their Organizations," *BusinessWeek* (April 22, 2003), under "Advantages," <http://:www.businessweek.com/bwdaily/dnflash/ap203126__085.htm> (accessed October 22, 2004).

[4] James Poon Teng Fatt, "Criteria Used for Evaluating Sales Persons," *Management Research News* 23, no. 1 (2000): 27.

FIGURE 12–3   (Continued)

6

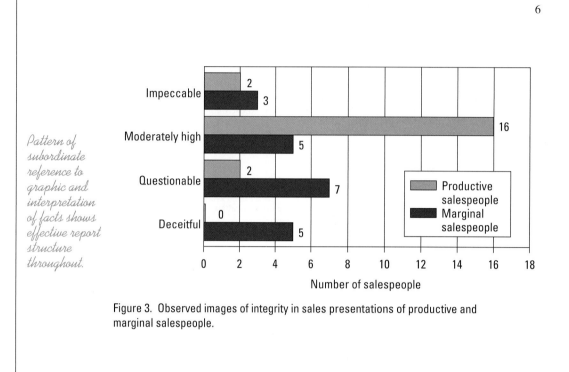

Figure 3. Observed images of integrity in sales presentations of productive and marginal salespeople.

Pattern of subordinate reference to graphic and interpretation of facts shows effective report structure throughout.

Distribution of the marginal salespeople was markedly different: 3 in Group I, 5 in Group II, 7 in Group III, and 5 in Group IV. Clearly, integrity was more apparent among the productive salespeople.

Apparent Value of Moderate Pressure

Measurements (by observation) of pressure used in the sales presentations were made in order to determine the relationship of pressure to sales success. Using the guidelines approved at the August meeting, the observers classified each salesperson's presentations into three categories: (1) high pressure, (2) moderate pressure, and (3) low pressure. Observers reported difficulties in making some borderline decisions, but they felt that most of the presentations were easily classified.

Of the 20 productive salespeople, 15 used moderate pressure, 3 used low pressure, and 2 used high pressure, as depicted in Figure 4. The 20 marginal salespeople presented a different picture. Only 3 of them used moderate pressure. Of the remainder, 10 used high pressure and 7 used low pressure. The evidence suggests that moderate pressure is most effective.

Interpretation of significant report facts follows subordinate reference to graphic.

FIGURE 12–3   (Continued)

7

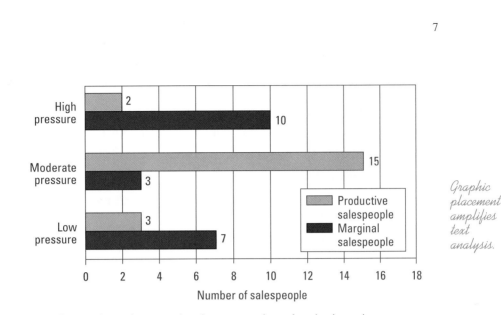

Figure 4. Observed use of pressure in sales presentations of productive and marginal salespeople.

Graphic placement amplifies text analysis.

The facts are not just presented. They are compared and conclusions are drawn from them.

Central idea and factual support demonstrate paragraph unity.

Necessity of Product Knowledge

Product knowledge, a widely accepted requirement for successful selling, was determined during the exit interview.[5] Using the 30 basic questions developed by Nokia management from sales literature, observers measured the salespeople's product knowledge. Correct responses to 27 or more of the questions were determined to be excellent, 24 through 26 was fair, and below 24 was classified as inadequate.

Productive salespeople displayed superior knowledge of the product with 17 of the 20 scoring excellent. As shown in Figure 5, the remaining 3 scored fair.

Balanced, short paragraphs indicate good organization of thought and improve readability.

---

[5] Barton Weitz, Stephen B. Castleberry, and John F. Tanner, *Selling: Building Partnerships,* 5th ed. (New York: McGraw-Hill, 2004), 247.

FIGURE 12–3   (Continued)

8

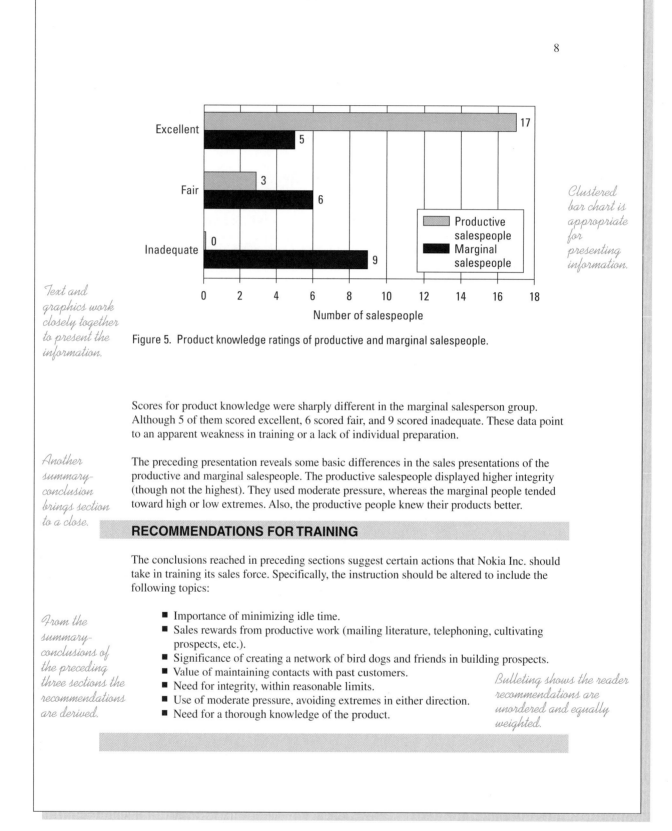

Clustered bar chart is appropriate for presenting information.

Figure 5. Product knowledge ratings of productive and marginal salespeople.

Text and graphics work closely together to present the information.

Scores for product knowledge were sharply different in the marginal salesperson group. Although 5 of them scored excellent, 6 scored fair, and 9 scored inadequate. These data point to an apparent weakness in training or a lack of individual preparation.

Another summary-conclusion brings section to a close.

The preceding presentation reveals some basic differences in the sales presentations of the productive and marginal salespeople. The productive salespeople displayed higher integrity (though not the highest). They used moderate pressure, whereas the marginal people tended toward high or low extremes. Also, the productive people knew their products better.

RECOMMENDATIONS FOR TRAINING

The conclusions reached in preceding sections suggest certain actions that Nokia Inc. should take in training its sales force. Specifically, the instruction should be altered to include the following topics:

From the summary-conclusions of the preceding three sections the recommendations are derived.

- Importance of minimizing idle time.
- Sales rewards from productive work (mailing literature, telephoning, cultivating prospects, etc.).
- Significance of creating a network of bird dogs and friends in building prospects.
- Value of maintaining contacts with past customers.
- Need for integrity, within reasonable limits.
- Use of moderate pressure, avoiding extremes in either direction.
- Need for a thorough knowledge of the product.

Bulleting shows the reader recommendations are unordered and equally weighted.

FIGURE 12–3 (Concluded)

9

BIBLIOGRAPHY

Fatt, James Poon Teng. "Criteria Used for Evaluating Sales Persons," *Management Research News* 23, no. 1 (2000).

Hatzivassilis, Alex, and Igor Kotlyar. "Increase the Number of Top Performers on Your Team," *American Salesman* 48, no. 7 (2003).

Jahn, Julie. "Big Business Encourages Effective Use of Bird Dogs throughout Their Organizations," *BusinessWeek,* April 22, 2003. http://:www.businessweek.com/ bwdaily/dnflash/ap203126__085.htm (accessed October 22, 2003).

Weitz, Barton, Stephen B. Castleberry, and John F. Tanner. *Selling: Building Partnerships.* 5th ed. New York: McGraw-Hill, 2004.

Zikmund, William G. *Business Research Methods,* 7th ed. Cincinnati, OH: South-Western, 2003.

Bibliography sources are presented alphabetically and completely. They present last name first and use the hanging indent format.

1. Long, formal reports are not often written in business. So why should you know how to write them?

2. A good title should be complete and concise. Are not these requirements contradictory? Explain.

3. Discuss the relative importance of the title fly and the title page in a report.

4. Distinguish among the transmittal message, the foreword, and the preface.

5. Describe the role and content of a transmittal message.

6. Why is personal style typically used in the transmittal message?

7. What is the basis for determining whether a report should have a table of contents?

8. Discuss the construction of the executive summary.

9. Why does the executive summary include the facts and figures in addition to the analyses and conclusions drawn from them?

10. Some reports need little or no introduction; others need a very long introduction. Why is this so?

11. Give examples of report problems that require introductory coverage of methods of collecting data, historical background, and limitations.

12. Give examples of report problems that require, respectively, (a) an ending summary, (b) an ending conclusion, and (c) an ending recommendation.

13. Using as a guide the diagram in Figure 12–2, summarize the coherence plan of the long, formal report.

1. Making any assumptions needed, construct complete yet concise titles for the reports described below:

   a. A report writer reviewed records of exit interviews of employees at Marvel-Floyd Manufacturing Company who quit their jobs voluntarily. The objective of the investigation was to determine the reasons for leaving.

   b. A researcher studied data from employee personnel records at Magna-Tech, Inc., to determine whether permanent (long-term) employees differ from short-term employees. Any differences found would be used in hiring employees in the future. The data studied included age, education, experience, sex, marital status, test scores, and such.

   c. A report writer compared historical financial records (1935 to the present) of Super Saver Foods to determine whether this grocery chain should own or rent store buildings. In the past it did both.

2. Criticize the following beginning sentences of transmittal messages:

   a. "In your hands is the report you requested January 7 concerning . . ."

   b. "As you will recall, last January 7 you requested a report on . . ."

   c. "That we should open a new outlet in Bragg City is the conclusion of this report, which you authorized January 7."

3. In a report comparing four automobiles (Alpha, Beta, Gamma, and Delta) to determine which one is the best buy for a company, section II of the report body covered these cost data: (a) initial costs, (b) trade-in values, and (c) operating expenses. Section III presented a comparison of these safety features of the automobiles: (a) standard safety features, (b) acceleration data, (c) weight distribution, and (d) braking quality.

   a. Criticize this introductory paragraph at the beginning of section III:

   In the preceding section was presented a thorough analysis of the cost data. Now safety of the cars will be compared. Although costs are important, Warren-Burke also is concerned about the safety of its salespeople, who spend almost half their work time driving.

   b. Write a more appropriate introductory paragraph.

4. The next section of the report (section IV) covered these topics: (a) handling, (b) quality of ride, and (c) durability.

   a. Criticize this introductory paragraph for the section:

   This section of the report presents a comparison of the overall construction of the four automobiles. These considerations also are important because they affect how a car rides, and this is important. Thus, we will take up in this order: handling, general riding quality, and construction qualities.

   b. Write a more appropriate introductory paragraph.

5. Criticize this final paragraph (a preview) of the introduction of the report described above:

   This report compares the automobiles by three factors. These are costs, safety, and comfort and construction, in that order. Costs include initial expenditure, trade-in value, and operating expense. Safety covers safety devices, acceleration, weight distribution, and braking. Comfort and construction includes handling, ride quality, and durability. A ranking is derived from this comparison.

Long Reports

1. *Selecting a university for accounting scholarships.* In your role as training director for Sanderson-Bowes, Inc., a major, nationwide accounting firm, you have been asked by the company president (Edwin J. Toohey) to help select a university to receive three scholarships to be funded by the company. The company wants to establish these scholarships in the hope that the recipients will consider signing on after graduation. But there would be no legal obligation to do so.

   Of course, the scholarships will be in accounting. They will cover all expenses: tuition, supplies, incidentals, room and board. They will be awarded to entering freshmen selected on the basis of academic ability. And they will continue for four years as long as the student makes satisfactory progress toward graduation.

   Your role is to find the university that will receive these scholarships. "We want a school in this general area," Mr. Toohey told you. "We want to select the one that will give us the very best training in this curriculum. Find three leading schools. Review their curricula. Evaluate their offerings, their faculties, their reputations, their standards, their students—everything that will help us select the best ones. Find out what it costs to go there. This includes tuition, fees, living cost estimates—all we need to know in determining the amount to put in the scholarships. Cost is important because we'll have to come up with an amount for the scholarships. But it is not the only consideration. Equally important is the quality of the education obtained. You might help us if you ranked the three schools for us. Of course, there is no guarantee we'll follow your rankings."

   You will get most of what you need on the websites of the schools. But you may use other sources as well: opinions of knowledgeable people, catalogs, brochures, and such. When you have the information you need, you'll study it, make comparisons, and organize your findings and analyses in report form. You will address the report to Mr. Toohey, but he wants additional copies for the other executives who will be in on the decision.

2. *Determining what business will be like in the months ahead.* Rick M. Novotny, president of Continental Department Stores, Inc., has assigned you, his assistant, the task of writing a consensus business forecast for presentation at the next board of directors meeting. Continental does not have an economist. "Why should we pay for one," Mr. Novotny reasons. "We can't afford such frills. We can get all we need from current business periodicals, newspapers, and the Internet."

   Since Mr. Novotny's instructions were—as usual— quite vague, much of what you do will depend on your good judgment. All he said was that he wanted you to survey the predictions of the leading economic forecasters for the months ahead and to present your findings in a clear and meaningful report to the board. And he wants the forecasts consolidated—that is, he does not want a mere succession of individual forecasts. Your report, covering the entire economy, will be largely general in nature. But you will give special emphasis to forecasts pertaining to retailing.

   Of course, your report will be in a form appropriate for the board. Because the members will want to get at the most important material quickly, be sure to include a fast-moving executive summary. Address the report to the board. Mr. Novotny chairs the board.

3. *Recommending a resort as the site of Granite Insurance's annual sales meeting.* As a management trainee with Granite Insurance Company, Inc., you have your first major assignment. It is to gather information and recommend to Kalle Huber a resort for the next annual sales meeting. Ms. Huber is the Granite vice president for sales and your immediate superior. This five-day meeting (Monday through Friday) is scheduled for early September, and it will be held at a resort of her choosing. A number of resorts have been recommended to her, but she has eliminated all but three. She wants you to investigate these three, evaluate them, and recommend one of them.

   "I may not go along with your recommendation," Ms. Huber tells you, "so give me enough information to permit me to evaluate them myself. Cost is important, but not the major factor. We will negotiate price after we have selected the preferred place. But give me their listed cost information, and make it a part of our evaluation. Our general plan is to hold our sales meetings in the mornings. We'll need a meeting room that holds 74 people. The afternoons and evenings will be fun times. We want to reward our people for their work. They will be free to do whatever they like. We have a good number of golfers and tennis players. A few like swimming. Of course, they all like to eat and party. If you can think of any other things to consider, bring them in. I want a full report."

   Ms. Huber then gives you the identities of the three resorts: Broadmoor Hotel in Colorado Springs, Colorado; Wintergreen Resort in the Blue Ridge Mountains of Virginia; and La Quinta Resort and Club in Palm Springs, California. She suggests that you go to their web pages for the information you need. You find them to be as follows: <www.broadmoor.com>; <www.wintergreenresort.com>; and <www.laquintaresort.com>. (These sites were correct at the time this case was written. If any have become obsolete, please substitute a comparable resort.)

You will present your findings, analyses, and recommendations in a formal report to Ms. Huber. If she approves of what you do, she will make copies for the top brass who will make the decision.

4. *Solving a problem on your campus.* Certain problems exist on many college campuses. At least, they exist in the minds of many of the faculty, students, and staff. From the following list of such problems, you (or your instructor) will select one that needs attention on your campus.

Library operation
Campus security
Policies on sales of tickets to athletic events
Regulation of social activities
Student government
Registration procedure
Faculty-student relations
Orientation program for freshmen
Curriculum improvement
Increasing enrollments
Scholastic honesty
Campus crime
Improving cultural atmosphere on campus
Class attendance policies
Scholastic-probation policies
Parking, traffic control
Grade inflation
Student government
Emphasis on athletics
Campus beautification
Fire prevention
Admission policies (including diversification practices)

You will first gather all the significant facts regarding the problem you select. When you are thoroughly acquainted with them, you will gather authoritative opinions concerning the solution.

Obtaining such information may involve looking through bibliographic sources to find out what has been done on other campuses. It may involve interviewing people on campus who are attempting to deal with the problem. Next you will carefully analyze your problem in light of all you have learned about it. Then you will develop a solution to the problem.

To make the situation appear realistic, place yourself in the proper role at your school. Write a formal report, with all the conventional prefatory arts. Address the report to the appropriate administrator.

5. *Determining how prices at near-campus stores compare with prices at stores away from campus.* As a member of the student government at your school, you have heard many complaints about the high prices

students must pay at stores in the campus area. Many of the complaints you heard suggest that the local stores are gouging students—that prices at stores far off campus are lower. After long debate, the student government members agreed that they needed more information on the question. They agreed to form a special committee to study and report on the question. And you were elected to serve as chairperson of this committee.

Working with your committee members, you selected a few campus stores and some comparable off-campus stores (in a mall or shopping district some distance away). You then worked out a student's market basket—products frequently bought by students. Next, you got prices for these items at the two groups of stores. Of course, you ignored specials, promotions, or the like.

When you have gathered this information, you are ready to give it meaning. You will carefully analyze it and organize it for presentation. Then you will present it in the formal report form you learned in your business communication course. As the information is largely statistical, you will present the major facts in graphic form. Your conclusion will determine whether there is truth to the complaint that campus stores have higher prices. You will not only address the general question but also look into differences in the major categories of items in your shopping basket. Address the report to your student-body president.

6. *Evaluating an experiment with flextime.* For the past year Sentry Securities, Inc., has been experimenting with flexible working hours. Accounting, clerical, and financial employees at each of its 44 sites in the United States and Canada have been allowed to start and finish work at their discretion, as long as they complete the number of hours required (usually 40 hours per week). In preparation for an annual review of the procedure, known informally as *flextime,* you, the director of human resources, asked the supervisors of the departments involved to evaluate how the employees responded to the experiment. Their responses are now in. You have counted them and arranged them neatly in tabular form (see Table 1).

Now you must review these data, analyze them, conclude from them, and report your work to Tucker Perrin (the CEO) and the board of directors. They are eager to know the results of this experiment. Has it worked? What are its apparent strengths and weaknesses? Should it be continued, ended, amended? You will give them what they need in the form of a complete and clearly written report. Because of the importance of its content and the status of the readers, your completed report will have all the trappings of formality. Your report must be ready by Friday for it will be the sole topic on the agenda for the board meeting on that date.

TABLE 1   (Problem 6) Sentry Securities Employees on Flextime

Clerical Staff	Accounting Staff	Financial Staff
1. Quantity of work	**1. Quantity of work**	**1. Quantity of work**
Much higher	Much higher	Much higher
43% Somewhat higher	48% Somewhat higher	25% Somewhat higher
57% No change	54% No change	67% No change
Somewhat lower	Somewhat lower	8% Somewhat lower
Much lower	Much lower	Much lower
2. Quality of work	**2. Quality of work**	**2. Quality of work**
Much higher	Much higher	4% Much higher
32% Somewhat higher	55% Somewhat higher	25% Somewhat higher
65% No change	42% No change	71% No change
3% Somewhat lower	Somewhat lower	Somewhat lower
Much lower	Much lower	Much lower
3. Absenteeism	**3. Absenteeism**	**3. Absenteeism**
Much higher	Much higher	Much higher
2% Somewhat higher	Somewhat higher	Somewhat higher
55% No change	40% No change	63% No change
35% Somewhat lower	42% Somewhat lower	25% Somewhat lower
8% Much lower	18% Much lower	12% Much lower
4. Amount of overtime	**4. Amount of overtime**	**4. Amount of overtime**
Much higher	3% Much higher	Much higher
6% Somewhat higher	Somewhat higher	Somewhat higher
59% No change	39% No change	84% No change
29% Somewhat lower	40% Somewhat lower	16% Somewhat lower
6% Much lower	18% Much lower	Much lower
5. Job satisfaction	**5. Job satisfaction**	**5. Job satisfaction**
40% Much higher	38% Much higher	37% Much higher
52% Somewhat higher	55% Somewhat higher	63% Somewhat higher
8% No change	7% No change	No change
Somewhat lower	Somewhat lower	Somewhat lower
Much lower	Much lower	Much lower
6. Degree of efficiency	**6. Degree of efficiency**	**6. Degree of efficiency**
6% Much higher	4% Much higher	4% Much higher
50% Somewhat higher	48% Somewhat higher	25% Somewhat higher
44% No change	45% No change	71% No change
Somewhat lower	3% Somewhat lower	Somewhat lower
Much lower	Much lower	Much lower
7. Degree of effectiveness	**7. Degree of effectiveness**	**7. Degree of effectiveness**
29% Very good results	21% Very good results	21% Very good results
68% Good results	65% Good results	67% Good results
3% No change	6% No change	7% No change
Poor results	8% Poor results	Poor results
Very poor results	Very poor results	Very poor results

7. *Evaluating the quality of life in your city.* Sentinel Insurance, Inc., is considering moving its headquarters to _____ (your city or a city selected by your instructor). The company has completed a study considering the economic advantages in relocating, and this study was positive. But before finally deciding, the firm's leaders want to know more about the quality of life they and their employees could expect there. They have hired you and your research organization to get the information they need.

Although *quality of life* is a very general term, you and the company's executive president, Tony Luvisi, have agreed that housing, educational institutions, recreational and cultural facilities, and climate would be considered. You may think of other factors as you get into the problem.

Your first step is to gather the information available for the factors involved. Some of it you can get from Internet sources—the website of the chamber of commerce in particular. More may come from local libraries, the telephone directory, travel brochures, and such. Some you may get by personal observation. And some you may know from experience.

After you have gathered, assembled, and analyzed the information you gather, you will organize it for presentation in a formal report. You will present the information and interpret it objectively, remembering your professional obligation for objectivity. In the end, you will arrive at a recommendation on whether your city would offer a good quality of life for the 85 employees and their families who would move there.

You will address the report to Mr. Luvisi, as he is the one who authorized you to do the work. As you hope to do additional work for these people in the years to come, you will do your very best work. Your finished product will be a formal report complete with helpful graphics wherever they help to tell the report story.

8. *Evaluating three charities for a philanthropist.* As business manager for Ms. Frida Voglesang, owner-operator of a number of successful businesses, a multimillionaire, and a philanthropist of the first order, you received the following from your boss.

"I have decided that I should make more informed decisions about the money I give to various charities. I want my money to go to the most deserving ones. I want it to do the most good for the most people. I hear stories about how some of them are run—how high their administrative costs are. And there are reports that much of the money some charities raise goes to the people who solicit it. Specifically, I want you to check out the three I have favored in recent years: American Cancer Society, Habitat for Humanity, and Alzheimer's Association. (or other groups specified by your instructor). Find out what good they do, how efficient they are—and anything else that will help me decide on whether to favor them. Your goal will be to determine how deserving they are. When you have gathered all this information, analyze it, compare, and conclude. You might even rank these three. I might decide to give all to one, divide equally, vary among them. I'll do whatever appears to be right."

Now you must follow your boss' instructions. You will present the results of your work in a formal report (she has liked these in past assignments). As usual, you will include a fast-moving executive summary that will give her answers right off.

9. *Determining what makes an Auto Care service center successful.* The management of Auto Care, Inc., wants to know why some of its service centers are doing much better than others. And it is your job to find out.

You, a research associate with Probst Research Associates, have been working on the problem for the past four weeks. As orally authorized by Auto Care's vice president for sales, Marisa DeSpain, you and your assistants have visited 200 manager-owned Auto Care operations in the 39-state area served by the company. The stations visited were selected by Auto Care executives to be about equal insofar as physical facilities and location are concerned. All are predominantly community stations—that is, they are off main highways. All are about equal in traffic flow past the station, and all have nearly equal competitive situations. But they differ in one major respect—sales volume. One half (100) have had low volumes.

To find the reasons for high or low volumes, you worked out a detailed plan for collecting data. First you had your investigators visit each station posing as customers. They then observed and recorded such things as the attendants' courtesy, services rendered, and conditions of the stations. Some of these observations were factual. Others were subjective. But the subjective evaluations were based on definite guide points on which each observer was very carefully instructed. Later, the investigators returned to the stations to observe and interview the managers. From the managers they received some pertinent factual information on the personnel employed at each station.

Now the research is done and you have the summary tabulations before you. Your next step is to put these data into some meaningful order. Then you will analyze them in the light of your problem. From these analyses you hope to be able to draw conclusions as to why some stations are successful and others are not.

Your summary findings are presented in Table 2. If you require other information, you may use your good logical imagination. For example, in describing your research procedure you may fill in with steps that are consistent with good research methodology. Now you must analyze the data, organize your work, and prepare the report that will give Auto Care what it needs. Your report will be in a form befitting the formality of this situation.

10. *Determining the best Internet source for buying office furniture.* Play the role of assistant to the purchasing manager for Gibraltar Insurance, Inc. In response to criticisms that the company's current source of office furniture is not giving the company the best deals, you have been asked to help correct the situation. Specifically, you have been asked to "survey the major office furniture outlets on the Internet, get their prices

	S	U
Courtesy of attendants:		
Unusually courteous	18	3
Above average	44	23
Average	32	42
Below average	4	20
Discourteous	2	12
Customer services:		
Muffler	100	100
Wash and lube	7	23
Brakes	74	37
Carburetor	54	32
Ignition, tune-up	61	33
Wheels and shocks	81	34
Heavy repairs	2	21
Condition of stations:		
Overall appearance:		
Clean and neat	82	10
Fair, but could be improved	18	62
Dirty	0	28
Rest rooms:		
Clean and neat	92	22
Fair	8	47
Dirty	0	31
Age of building:		
Less than 5 years	31	33
5–10 years	41	38
Over 10 years	38	29
Overall appearance of stock:		
Neatly arranged	68	11
Fair	30	63
Poorly arranged	2	26
Qualifications of managers:		
Education:		
Grade school or less	2	12
Some high school	28	44
High school graduate	56	42
Some college	14	2
Experience:		
Less than 1 year	0	11
1 to 5 years	52	41
6 to 10 years	36	38
Over 10 years	12	20
Marital status:		
Married	6	24
Single	6	24

	S	U
Qualifications of managers (continued):		
Age:		
Under 21	—	3
21–25	4	12
26–30	10	19
31–40	51	36
41–50	19	20
Over 50	16	10
Grades on Auto Care's Manager's Aptitude Test:		
Below 40 (not qualified)	0	9
40–59 (acceptable)	17	43
60–79 (good)	42	30
80–100 (outstanding)	41	18
Attended Auto Care Manager's School (two weeks' duration)	43	21
Qualifications of service workers:		
Education:		
Grade school or less	18	27
Some high school	43	57
High school graduate	39	16
Experience (similar work):		
Less than 1 year	9	19
1 to 5 years	36	44
6 to 10 years	27	22
Over 10 years	28	15
Grade on Auto Care Aptitude Test:		
Below 40 (not qualified)	10	34
40–59 (acceptable)	17	43
60–79 (good)	36	7
80–100 (outstanding)	7	2
Marital status:		
Married	62	65
Single	38	35
Age:		
Under 21	13	14
21–30	66	33
31–40	17	31
41–50	4	20
Over 50	—	2
Attended Auto Care's Service School (one week's duration)	59	27

on the items Gibraltar buys, and recommend a source for us." Currently, Gibraltar gets its office furniture from Office Furniture USA, at <www.officefurniture-usa.com> .

You will begin your effort by making a list of the items Gibraltar typically purchases. Use your best judgment here, but certainly the list will include those items of furniture common to most offices: computer desks, desk chairs, executive desks, filing cabinets, bookcases, conference tables, and such. But since these items vary widely in quality and style, select only items that are comparable to items carried by most office furniture outlets. That is, you will want to be certain that you are not comparing apples to oranges.

With your list completed, you will then search for office supply outlets on the Internet. Then you will record the prices for the items on our list. As you will see, there are many outlets, but make certain that you find at least two. (Two possibilities are

<www.beckofficefurniture.com> and <www.abcofurniture.com>.) Of course, in addition you will include Gibraltar's current supplier.

After you have gathered the information you need, you will make your recommendation. (Gibraltar prefers to do business primarily with one supplier.) Because the report will be extensive and will likely be read by various top management people, you will dress it up. Wherever they help, you will use appropriate graphics. This is your first chance to display your ability to those who can help determine your future with the company.

TOPIC SUGGESTIONS FOR INTERMEDIATE-LENGTH AND LONG REPORTS

Following are suggestions for additional report problems ranging from the simple to the highly complex. You can convert them into realistic business problems by supplying details and/or adapting them to real-life business situations. For most of these problems, you can obtain the needed information through secondary research. The topics are arranged by business field, although many of them cross fields.

Accounting

1. Report on current depreciation accounting practices, and recommend depreciation accounting procedures for Company X.

2. Design an inventory control system for X Company.

3. Report to Company X executives on how tax court decisions handed down over the past six months will affect their firm.

4. What security measures should Company X take regarding access to its accounting data online?

5. Advise the managers of X Company on the accounting problems that they can anticipate when the company begins overseas operations.

6. Analyze break-even analysis as a decision-making tool for X Company.

7. Explain to potential investors which sections in Company X's most recent annual report they should review most carefully.

8. Analyze the relative effects on income of the first-in, first-out (FIFO) and last-in, first-out (LIFO) methods of inventory valuation during a prolonged period of inflation.

9. Write a report for the American Accounting Association on the demand for accountants with computer systems training.

10. Develop for accounting students at your college information that will help them choose between careers in public accounting and careers in private accounting.

11. Advise the management of X Company on the validity of return on investment as a measure of performance.

12. Report on operations research as a decision-making tool for accountants and managers.

13. Report to the management of X Company on trends in the content and design of corporate annual reports.

14. Report to an association of accountants the status of professional ethics in accounting.

15. Report to management of X Company on the communication skills important to accounting.

16. Investigate the matching principle and its effects on financial statements for Company X.

17. Report to the board of directors at X Company whether the balance sheet fails to recognize important intangible assets.

18. Explain the extent to which accounting reflects the intent of Company X's business decisions.

19. Review for Company X whether disclosure could be an effective substitute for recognition in financial statements.

20. Report to the management of Company X whether intangible assets have finite or infinite lives.

21. Advise the founders of new Company X on income tax considerations in the selection of a form of business organization.

22. Review for Company X the pros and cons of current methods of securities evaluation.

General Business

23. Evaluate the adequacy of current college programs for developing business leadership.

24. Which business skills should schools and colleges teach, and which should companies teach?

25. What should be the role of business leaders in developing courses and curricula for business schools?

26. Report on ways to build and use good teams in the workplace.

27. Identify the criteria Company X should use in selecting a public relations firm.

28. Report on the advisability of including business internships in a business degree program.

29. Investigate the impact of electronic signatures on the business community.

30. How does today's business community regard the master of business administration (MBA) degree?

31. Evaluate the contribution that campus business and professional clubs make to business education.

32. How effective is online training in education for business?

33. Should education for business be specialized, or should it provide a generalized, well-rounded education?

34. Determine how to get and use permission for music added to business presentations.

35. Determine which of three franchises (your instructor will select) offer the best opportunity for investment.

36. Determine guidelines for avoiding sexual harassment for Company X.

37. Determine cultural problems likely to be encountered by employees going to work in _____ (a foreign country).

38. Investigate the pros and cons of international business majors studying abroad for one term.

39. Should Company X use the U.S. Postal Service or a private courier (Federal Express, United Parcel Service)?

40. For an instructor, answer the question of whether IM should be used as a class teaching tool.

41. Advise a client on whether to invest in a company producing renewable energy (wind, solar, etc.).

Labor

42. For the executives of the National Association of Manufacturers (or some such group), report on the outlook for labor–management relations in the next 12 months.

43. For the officers of a major labor union, research and report progress toward decreasing job discrimination against minorities.

44. For X Union, project the effects that a particular technology (you choose) will have on traditionally unionized industries by the year 2012.

45. Advise the management of X Company on how to deal with Y Union, which is attempting to organize the employees of X Company.

46. Interpret the change in the number of union members over the past _____ years.

47. Report on the successes and failures of employee-run businesses.

48. Report on the status and effects of "right to work" laws.

49. Evaluate the effects of a particular strike (your choice) on the union, the company, the stockholders, and the public. Write the report for a government investigating committee.

50. For Union X, prepare an objective report on union leadership in the nation during the past decade.

51. Layoffs based on seniority are causing a disproportionate reduction in the number of women and minority workers at Company X. Investigate alternatives that the company can present to the union.

52. Investigate recent trends relative to the older worker and the stands that unions have taken in this area.

53. Review the appropriateness of unionizing government workers, and recommend to a body of government leaders the stand they should take on this issue.

54. Report on the role of unions (or management) in politics, and recommend a course for them to follow.

55. Reevaluate _____ (unions or employment relations—your instructor will specify) for the management of X Company.

56. Analyze the changing nature of work for the leaders of _____ union (your instructor will designate).

57. Report on the blending of work and family issues for X Union.

Finance

58. As a financial consultant, evaluate a specific form of tax shelter for a client.

59. Review the customer-relations practices of banks and recommend customer relations procedures for Bank X.

60. Review current employee loan practices and recommend whether Company X should make employee loans.

61. Report on what Company X needs to know about financial matters in doing business with _____ (foreign country).

62. Give estate planning advice to a client with a unique personal situation.

63. Advise X Company on whether it should lease capital equipment or buy it.

64. Advise Company X on whether it should engage in a joint venture with a company overseas or establish a wholly owned foreign subsidiary.

65. Compare the costs for X Company of offering its workers child care or elder care benefits.

66. Should Company X accept national credit cards or set up its own credit card system?

67. Advise Company X on how to avoid a hostile takeover.

68. Which will be the better investment in the next three years: stocks or bonds?

69. Advise Company X on whether it should list its stock on a major stock exchange.

70. Advise Company X, which is having problems with liquidity, on the pros and cons of factoring accounts receivable.

71. Recommend the most feasible way to finance a start-up restaurant.

Management

72. Develop for Company X a guide to ethics in its highly competitive business situation.

73. After reviewing pertinent literature and experiences of other companies, develop a plan for selecting and training administrators for an overseas operation for Company X.

74. Survey the current literature and advise Company X on whether its management should become politically active.

75. After reviewing the pros and cons, advise X Company on whether it should begin a program of hiring individuals with disabilities or the disadvantaged.

76. Report on the behavioral and psychological effects of introducing wellness programs to Company X.

77. The executives of X Company (a manufacturer of automobile and truck tires) want a report on recent court decisions relating to warranties. Include any recommendations that your report justifies.

78. Report on the problems involved in moving Company X headquarters from _____ (city) to _____ (city).

79. After reviewing current practices with regard to worker participation in management, advise Company X on whether it should permit such participation.

80. Should Company X outsource for _____ (service) or establish its own department?

81. Review the advantages and disadvantages of rotating executive jobs at Company X, and then make a recommendation.

82. What should be Company X's policy on office romances?

83. Develop an energy conservation or recycling plan for X Company.

84. Evaluate the effectiveness of a portal for handling internal communications for Company X.

85. Design a security system for preventing computer espionage at Company X, a leader in the highly competitive _____ industry.

86. Evaluate the various methods for determining corporate performance and select the one most appropriate for Company X.

87. Advise X Company on the procedures for incorporating in _____ (state or province).

88. Report to Company X on the civil and criminal liabilities of its corporate executives.

89. Report on the quality awards being given to businesses.

90. Determine how diversity enrichment is addressed at Company X.

91. Determine for a legislative committee the extent of minority recruiting, hiring, and training in the industry.

92. As a consultant for an association of farmers, evaluate the recent past and project the future of growing, raising, or bioengineering _____ (your choice—cattle, poultry, wheat, soybeans, or the like).

93. Develop a plan for reducing employee turnover for Company X.

94. Report to a labor union on recent evidence of sexual harassment, and recommend steps that the union should take to correct any problems you find.

95. Investigate the feasibility of hiring older workers for part-time work for Company X.

Personnel/Human Resource Administration

96. Report on and interpret for Company X the effects of recent court decisions on the testing and hiring of employees.

97. Survey company retirement practices and recommend retirement policies for Company X.

98. Report on practices in compensating key personnel in overseas assignments and recommend for Company X policies for the compensation of such personnel.

99. Report on what human resource executives look for in application documents.

100. Report on the advantages and disadvantages of Company X's providing on-site day care for children of employees.

101. After reviewing the legal and ethical questions involved, recommend whether Company X should use integrity tests in employee hiring.

102. Review what other companies are doing about employees suffering from drug or alcohol abuse, and recommend a policy on the matter for Company X.

103. Report on effective interviewing techniques used to identify the best people to hire.

104. Investigate the impact of the Family Leave Act on Company X.

105. Compare the pros and cons of alternative methods of dispute resolution.

106. Report on ways Company X can link performance improvement plans to discipline and pay.

107. Investigate the impact of the legal aspects of human resource management (EEO, ADA, wrongful termination, harassment, family care and medical leave, workplace violence—your instructor will select one or several) on Company X.

108. Analyze the impact of changing work priorities in a culturally diverse workplace for Company X.

109. Report on recent issues in employee communication for Company X.

Marketing

110. Review the available literature and advise Company X on whether it should franchise its _____ business.

111. Select a recent national marketing program and analyze why it succeeded or failed.

112. Advise the advertising vice president of Company X on whether the company should respond to or ignore a competitor's direct attack on the quality of its product.

113. Review the ethical considerations involved in advertising to children and advise Company X on the matter.

114. Determine for Company X the social and ethical aspects of pricing for the market.

115. Explore the possibilities of trade with _____ (a foreign country) for Company X.

116. Determine for a national department store chain changing trends in the services that customers expect when shopping online.

117. Prepare a report to help a contingent of your legislature decide whether current regulation of advertising should be changed.

118. Determine the problems X Company will encounter in introducing a new product to its line.

119. Report on the success of rebates as a sales stimulator and advise Company X on whether it should use rebates.

120. Should Company X buy or lease minivans for distributing its products?

121. Determine the trends in packaging in the _____ industry.

122. Should X Company establish its own sales force, use manufacturer's agents, or use selling agents?

123. How should Company X evaluate the performance of its salespeople?

124. Determine for X Company how it can evaluate the effectiveness of its (online, print, or radio) advertising.

125. Select the best channel of distribution for new product Y and justify your choice.

126. Should X Company establish its own advertising department or use an advertising agency?

127. Conduct a market study of _____ (city) to determine whether it is a suitable location for _____ (a type of business).

128. Report to X Company on drip marketing and recommend whether it should use drip marketing to increase sales.

129. Investigate the factors to consider when marketing online through the Internet to children.

130. Compare the effectiveness of three different types of online advertising and recommend one for Company X.

131. Determine whether any of the products of Company X are good candidates for infomercials.

Computer Applications

132. Recommend a handheld computer for use by the salespeople of Company X.

133. Advise Company X about the steps it can take to protect its computer files from internal sabotage.

134. Determine whether Company X should purchase or lease its computer equipment.

135. Report to the president of Company X the copyright and contract laws that apply to the use of computer programs.

136. Investigate the possibility of using the majority of office applications from the Internet rather than continually purchasing and upgrading programs.

137. Determine which positions Company X should designate as possible telecommuting candidates.

138. Report to the CIO on the impact of wireless technology on Company X.

139. Report on the future developments of robotics in the _____ industry.

140. Review and rank for possible adoption three software programs that Company X might use for its _____ work (name the field of operations).

141. Determine for Company X the factors it should consider in selecting computer insurance.

142. Compare three online programs for training your employees on _____ (name the software application) and recommend one.

143. Report on the collaborative electronic meeting tools used in businesses similar to Company X.

144. Explore the procedures and methods for measuring information system effectiveness and productivity for Company X.

145. Investigate how to improve information security and control for Company X.

146. Identify and recommend web-based survey tools that would be appropriate for Company X.

147. Should _____ (a small company) use the Internet as a marketing tool?

Business Education

148. Evaluate the effect of remodeling your new office site with both ergonomic and feng shui principles applied.

149. Report on ways companies now use and plan to use desktop videoconferencing.

150. Analyze the possibility of instituting companywide training on etiquette, covering everything from handling telephone calls, to sexual harassment, to dining out.

151. Advise management on the importance of the air quality in its offices.

152. Investigate ways to complete and submit company forms on the web or the company portal.

153. Evaluate the reprographic services and practices at your school from an environmental perspective.

154. Report on ways to hire and keep the best employees in the computer support center.

155. Report on ways to improve literacy in the workplace.

156. Report on the availability and quality of online training programs.

157. Report on ways to improve the communication of cross-cultural work groups.

158. Analyze the possibility of using voice-recognition software with the products available today.

159. Determine for Company X whether it should replace the laptop computers of its sales reps with tablet PCs.

160. Evaluate at least three data visualization programs and recommend one for use at Company X.

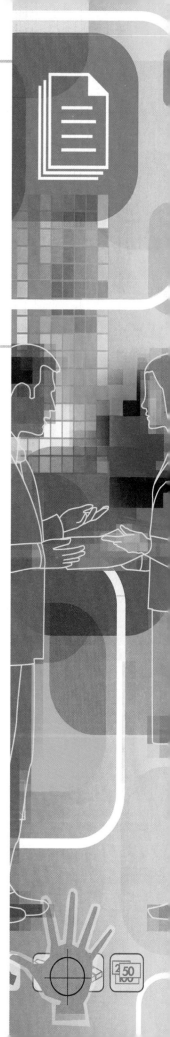

CHAPTER THIRTEEN

Graphics

CHAPTER OBJECTIVES

Upon completing this chapter, you will be able to use graphics effectively in business reports. To reach this goal, you should be able to

1 Determine which parts of your report should be communicated by graphics and where in the report the graphics should appear.

2 Explain the general mechanics of constructing graphics—size, layout, type, rules and borders, color and cross-hatching, clip art, background, numbering, titles, title placement, and footnotes and acknowledgments.

3 Construct textual graphics such as tables, pull quotes, flowcharts, and process charts.

4 Construct and use visual graphics such as bar charts, pie charts, line charts, scatter diagrams, and maps.

5 Avoid common errors in constructing and using graphics.

Graphics

In your management job at Pinnacle, you proofread reports prepared by your co-workers. Because Pinnacle uses chemicals in its products, many of the reports are highly technical and complex. Many others, especially those coming from finance and sales, are filled with facts and figures. In your judgment, most of the reports you have proofread are hard to understand.

The one you are looking at now is packed with page after page of sales statistics. Your mind quickly gets lost in the mass of details. Why didn't the writer take the time to summarize the more important figures in a chart? And why didn't the writer put some of the details in tables? Many of the other reports you have been reading, especially the technical ones, are in equal need of graphics. Bar charts, pie charts, and maps would certainly help explain some of the concepts discussed. If only report writers would understand that words alone sometimes cannot communicate clearly—that words sometimes need to be supplemented with visual communication techniques. If the writers of your reports studied the following review of graphics, your job would be easier and more enjoyable. So would the jobs of the readers of those reports.

- A graphic is any form of illustration.

In many of your reports you will need to use graphics to help convey information quickly and accurately. By *graphics* we mean any form of illustration: charts, pictures, diagrams, maps. Although tables and bulleted lists are predominantly text, their format permits us to include them here. Also, most computer presentation programs include these formats.

PLANNING THE GRAPHICS

- You should plan the use of graphics.

You should plan the graphics for a report soon after you organize your findings. Your planning of graphics should be based on the need to communicate. Graphics serve one purpose—to communicate—and you should use them primarily for that purpose. Graphics can clarify complex or difficult information, emphasize facts, add coherence, summarize data, and provide interest. Additionally, today's data visualization tools help writers filter the vast amount of data that are collected and warehoused. Of course, well-constructed graphics also enhance the appearance of a report.

- In planning their use, look for parts that they should communicate.

In selecting graphics, you should review the information that your report will contain, looking for any possibility of improving communication of the report through the use of graphics. Specifically, you should look for complex information that visual presentation can make clear, for information too detailed to be covered in words, and for information that deserves special emphasis.

- Plan graphics with your reader in mind.

Of course, you will want to plan with your reader in mind. You will choose graphics appropriate to both the content and context where they are presented. The time and money you spend on gathering information or creating a graphic should be balanced in terms of the importance of the message you want to convey. Thus, you construct graphics to help the reader understand the report quicker, easier, and more completely.

- But remember that graphics supplement and do not replace the writing

As you plan the graphics, remember that unlike info graphics that stand alone, report graphics should supplement the writing or speaking—not take its place. They should help the wording by covering the more difficult parts, emphasizing the important points, and presenting details. But the words should carry the main message—all of it.

PLACING THE GRAPHICS IN THE REPORT

- Place the graphics near the first place in the text in which you refer to them.

For the best communication effect, you should place each graphic near the place where it is covered in writing. Exactly where on the page you should place it, however, should be determined by its size. If the graphic is small, you should place it within the text that covers it. If it is a full page, you should place it on the page following the first reference to the information it covers.

Some writers like to place all graphics at the end of the report, usually in the appendix. This arrangement may save time in preparing the report, but it does not help the readers. They have to flip through pages every time they want to see a graphic. Common sense requires that you place graphics in such a way as to help readers understand the report.

Sometimes you may need to include graphics that do not fit a specific part of the report. For example, you may have a graphic that is necessary for completeness but is not discussed in the report. Or you may have summary charts or tables that apply to the entire report but to no specific place in it. When such graphics are appropriate, you should place them in the appendix. And you should refer to the appendix somewhere in the report.

Graphics communicate most effectively when the readers see them at the right place in the report. Thus, you should refer the readers to them at the right place. That is, you should tell the readers when to look at a graphic and what to see. You can do this best through an incidental reference to the information in the graphic. Of the many wordings used for this purpose, these are the most common:

. . . , as shown in Figure 4, ...

. . . , indicated in Figure 4, ...

. . . , as a glance at Figure 4 reveals, . . .

. . . (see Figure 4) . . . .

When you refer to graphics subordinately, the main parts of your sentences can interpret the meaning of the graphics for your reader.

- Placing graphics at the end of the report does not help the readers.

- Graphics not discussed in the report belong in the appendix.

- At the right place, incidentally invite the readers to look at the graphics.

DETERMINING THE GENERAL MECHANICS OF CONSTRUCTION

In constructing graphics, you will be concerned with various mechanical matters. The most common are summarized in the following paragraphs.

Size Determination

One of the first decisions you must make in constructing a graphic is determining its size. This decision should not be arbitrary, and it should not be based on convenience. You should give the graphic the size its contents justify. If a graphic is simple (with only two or three quantities), a quarter page might be more than enough and a full page would be too much. But if a graphic must display complex or detailed information, a full page might be justified.

With extremely complex, involved information, you may need to use more than a full page. When you do, make certain that this large page is inserted and folded so that the readers can open it easily. The fold you select will be determined by the size of the page. You simply have to experiment until you find a convenient fold.

- Make each graphic the size its contents justify.

- Graphics larger than a page are justified if they contain enough information.

Layout Arrangement

You should determine the layout (shape) of the graphic by size and content requirements. Sometimes a tall, narrow rectangle (portrait) is the answer; sometimes the answer is a short, wide rectangle or a full-page rectangle (landscape). You simply consider the logical possibilities and select the one that appears best.

- Size and contents determine the shape of graphics.

Type

Type used in graphics throughout a report is generally consistent in both style and font. Style refers to the look of the type such as bold or italics; font refers to the look of the letters such as with or without feet (*serif* or *sans serif*). Occasionally you may

- Choose a type to help convey the message clearly.

On the Fast Track by Bill Holbrook

SOURCE: On the Fast Track cartoon by Bill Holbrook. © 2001 King Features Syndicate. © Reprinted with special permission of King Features Syndicate.

want to vary the type, but do so by design for some special reason. Be aware that even the design of the font you choose will convey a message, a message that should work with the text content and design.

Size is another variable to watch. The size you choose should look appropriate in the context you use it. Your top priority in choosing type style, font, and size should be readability.

- Choose a type size that is readable.

Rules and Borders

- Use rules and borders when they help appearance.

You should use rules and borders when they help the appearance of the graphic. Rules help distinguish one section or graphic from another, while borders help separate graphics from the text. In general, you should place borders around graphics that occupy less than a full page. You also can place borders around full-page graphics, but such borders serve little practical value. Except in cases in which graphics simply will not fit into the normal page layout, you should not extend the borders of graphics beyond the normal page margins.

Color and Cross-Hatching

- Color and cross-hatching can improve graphics.

Color and cross-hatching, appropriately used, help readers see comparisons and distinctions. In fact, research has found that color in graphics improves the comprehension, retention, and ease of extracting information. Also, both color and cross-hatching add to the attractiveness of the report. Because color is especially effective for this purpose, you should use it whenever practical and appropriate.

Clip Art

- Use clip art to help your reader understand your message.

Today you can get good-looking clip art easily—so easily in fact that some writers often overuse it. Although clip art can add interest and bring the reader into a graphic effectively, it also can overpower and distract the reader. The general rule is to keep in mind the purpose your clip art is serving: to help the reader understand the content. It should be appropriate in both its nature and size. It also should be appropriate in its representation of gender. One study revealed that much of the clip art bundled with today's software programs is biased.[1] Be sure to select your clip art to avoid the gender, race, and age bias. Also, if it is copyrighted, you need permission to use it.

Background

- Background color, photos, and art should enhance the message of the graphic.

Background colors, photos, and art for your graphics should be chosen carefully. The color should provide high contrast with the data and not distract from the main message. Photos, especially faded photos, that are well chosen can add interest and draw the reader in. However, photos as well as other art can send other messages and evoke

---

[1] Marilyn A. Dyrud, "An Exploration of Gender Bias in Computer Clip Art," *Business Communication Quarterly* 60, no. 4 (December 1997): 30–51.

emotions not appropriate or desirable for the message the graphic conveys. Additionally, when graphics are used cross-culturally, you will want to be sure the message your background sends is the one you intended by testing or reviewing it with the intended receivers.

Numbering

Except for minor tabular displays, pull quotes, and clip art, you should number all the graphics in the report. Many schemes of numbering are available to you, depending on the makeup of the graphics.

- Number graphics consecutively by type.

If you have many graphics that fall into two or more categories, you may number each of the categories consecutively. For example, if your report is illustrated by six tables, five charts, and six maps, you may number these graphics Table I, Table II, . . . Table VI; Chart 1, Chart 2, . . . Chart 5; and Map 1, Map 2, . . . Map 6.

But if your graphics comprise a wide mixture of types, you may number them in two groups: tables and figures. Figures, a miscellaneous grouping, may include all types other than tables. To illustrate, consider a report containing three tables, two maps, three charts, one diagram, and one photograph. You could number these graphics Table I, Table II, and Table III and Figure 1, Figure 2, . . . Figure 7. By convention, tables are not grouped with other types of graphics. But it would not be wrong to group and number as figures all graphics other than tables even if the group contained sufficient subgroups (charts, maps, and the like) to permit separate numbering of each of them.

- Figures are a miscellaneous grouping of types. Number tables separately.

Construction of Titles and Captions

Every graphic should have a title or caption that adequately describes its contents. A title is used with graphics displayed in oral presentations; a caption is used with graphics included in print documents. Like the headings used in other parts of the report, the title or caption of the graphic has the objective of concisely covering the contents. As a check of content coverage, you might well use the journalist's five Ws: *who, what, where, when, why,* and sometimes you also might use *how* (the classification principle). But because conciseness also is desired, it is not always necessary to include all the Ws in the title. The title or caption of a chart comparing the annual sales volume of the Texas and California territories of the Dell Company for the years 2003–04 might be constructed as follows:

- The titles should describe content clearly (consider the five Ws: who, what, where, when, why).

Who: Dell Company

What: Annual sales

Where: Texas and California branches

When: 2003–04

Why: For comparison

The title or caption might read, "Comparative Annual Sales of Texas and California Territories of the Dell Company, 2003–04." For even more conciseness, you could use a major title and subtitle. The major title might read, "A Texas and California Sales Comparison"; the subtitle might read, "Dell Company 2003–04." Similarly, the caption might read "A Texas and California Sales Comparison: Dell Company 2003–2004."

Placement of Titles and Captions

- The conventional placement of titles is at the top for tables and at the bottom for charts. But many place all titles at the top.

In documents, titles of tables conventionally appear above the tabular display; captions of all other types of graphics conventionally appear below it. In presentations, titles of both tables and other charts and illustrations are usually placed above the graphic. There has been a trend toward the use of lowercase type for all illustration titles and to place the titles of both tables and figures at the top. In fact, most presentation programs default to the top. These practices are simple and logical; yet you should follow the conventional practices for the more formal reports.

Footnotes and Acknowledgments

- Use footnotes to explain or elaborate.

Parts of a graphic sometimes require special explanation or elaboration. When this happens, as when similar situations arise in connection with the text of the report, you should use footnotes. Such footnotes are concise explanations placed below the illustration and keyed to the part explained by means of a superscript (raised) number or symbol (asterisk, dagger, double dagger, and so on). Footnotes for tables are best placed immediately below the graphic presentation. Footnotes for other graphic forms follow the illustration when the title or caption is placed at the bottom of the graphic.

- Acknowledge source of data with note below.

Usually, a source acknowledgment is the bottom entry made in the graphic context. By *source acknowledgment* we mean a reference to the body or authority that deserves the credit for gathering the data used in the illustration. The entry consists simply of the word *Source* followed by a colon and the source name. A source note for data based on information gathered by the U.S. Department of Commerce might read like this:

Source: U.S. Department of Commerce

- "Source: Primary" is the proper note for data you gathered.

If you or your staff collected the data, you may either omit the source note or give the source as "Primary," in which case the note would read like this:

Source: Primary

CONSTRUCTING TEXTUAL GRAPHICS

- Graphics fall into two general categories: (1) textual (words and numerals) and (2) visual (pictures).

Graphics for communicating report information fall into two general categories: those that communicate primarily by their textual content (words and numerals) and those that communicate primarily by some form of picture. Included in the textual group are tables, pull quotes, and a variety of flow and process charts (Gantt, flow, organization, and such).

Tables

- A table is an orderly arrangement of information.
- You may use general-purpose tables (those containing broad information),

A *table* is an orderly arrangement of information in rows and columns. As we have noted, tables are not truly graphic (not really pictures). But they communicate like graphics, and they have many of the characteristics of graphics.

Two basic types of tables are available to you: the general-purpose table and the special-purpose table. General-purpose tables cover a broad area of information. For

FIGURE 13–1

Table number and title

Spanner heads
Column heads

Row heads

Footnote
Source
acknowledgment

Table I Average Annual Returns of Various Hedge Fund Categories*				
	Short term		Long term	
Category	*1-year*	*3-year*	*5-year*	*10-year*
Aggressive Growth	80.40	39.66	33.74	24.94
Distressed Securities	3.30	5.22	10.12	14.99
Managed Futures	−1.20	7.05	8.76	7.69
Market Timing	39.80	31.11	23.20	20.27
Short Selling	−19.40	−9.57	−10.51	−3.09
Value	42.00	24.14	24.47	19.54

*For years ending September 30

Source: Van Hedge Fund Advisors International Inc.

example, a table reviewing the answers to all the questions in a survey is a general-purpose table. Such tables usually belong in the appendix.

Special-purpose tables are prepared for one special purpose: to illustrate a particular part of the report. They contain information that could be included with related information in a general-purpose table. For example, a table presenting the answer to one of the questions in a survey is a special-purpose table. Such tables belong in the report text near the discussion of their contents.

- or you may use special-purpose tables (those covering a specific area of information).

Aside from the title, footnotes, and source designation previously discussed, a table contains heads, columns, and rows of data, as shown in Figure 13–1. Row heads are the titles of the rows of data, and spanner heads are the titles of the columns. The spanner heads, however, may be divided into column heads, as they are often called.

- See Figure 13–1 for details of table arrangement.

The construction of text tables is largely influenced by their purpose. Nevertheless, a few general construction rules may be listed:

- If rows are long, the row heads may be repeated at the right.

- The em dash (—) or the abbreviation *n.a.* (or *N.A.* or *NA*), but not the zero, is used to indicate data not available.

- Footnote references to numbers in the table should be keyed with asterisks, daggers, double daggers, and such. Numbers followed by footnote reference numbers may cause confusion. Small letters of the alphabet can be used when many references are made.

- Totals and subtotals should appear whenever they help the purpose of the table. The totals may be for each column and sometimes for each row. Row totals are usually placed at the right; but when they need emphasis, they may be placed at the left. Likewise, column totals are generally placed at the bottom of the column, but they may be placed at the top when the writer wants to emphasize them. A ruled line (usually a double one) separates the totals from their components.

- The units in which the data are recorded must be clear. Unit descriptions (bushels, acres, pounds, and the like) appropriately appear above the columns, as part of the headings or subheadings. If the data are in dollars, however, placing the dollar mark ($) before the first entry in each column is sufficient.

Tabular information need not always be presented in formal tables. In fact, short arrangements of data may be presented more effectively as parts of the text. Such arrangements are generally made as either leaderwork or text tabulations.

- Tabular information also can be presented as (1) leaderwork (as illustrated here), or

Leaderwork is the presentation of tabular material in the text without titles or rules. (*Leaders* are the repeated dots with intervening spaces.) Typically, a colon precedes the tabulation, as in this illustration:

The August sales of the representatives in the Western Region were as follows:

Charles B. Brown. $33,517

Thelma Capp 39,703

Bill E. Knauth 38,198

Text tabulations are simple tables, usually with column heads and some rules. But they are not numbered, and they have no titles. They are made to read with the text, as in this example:

- (2) text tabulations (as illustrated here).

In August the sales of the representatives in the Western Region increased sharply from those for the preceding month, as these figures show:

Representative	July Sales	August Sales	Increase
Charles B. Brown	$32,819	$33,517	$ 698
Thelma Capp	37,225	39,703	2,478
Bill E. Knauth	36,838	38,198	1,360

Pull Quotes

- Pull quotes emphasize key concepts.

The pull quote is a textual visual that is often overlooked yet extremely useful in emphasizing key points. It is also useful when the text or content of the report does not lend itself naturally or easily to other graphics. By selecting a key sentence, copying it to a text box, enlarging it, and perhaps even enhancing it with a new font, style, or color, a writer can break up the visual boredom of a full page or screen of text. Drawing software lets users easily wrap text around shapes as well as along curves and irregular lines. Figure 13–2 shows an example that is simple yet effective in both drawing the reader's attention to a key point and adding visual interest to a page.

Bullet Lists

- Bullet lists show points set off by a bullet symbol.

Bullet lists are listings of points arranged with bullets (•) to set them off. These lists can have a title that covers all the points, or they can appear without titles, as they appear at various places in this book. When you use this arrangement, make the points grammatically parallel. If the points have subparts, use sub-bullets for them. Make the

FIGURE 13–2

Illustration of a Pull Quote on a Curved Line

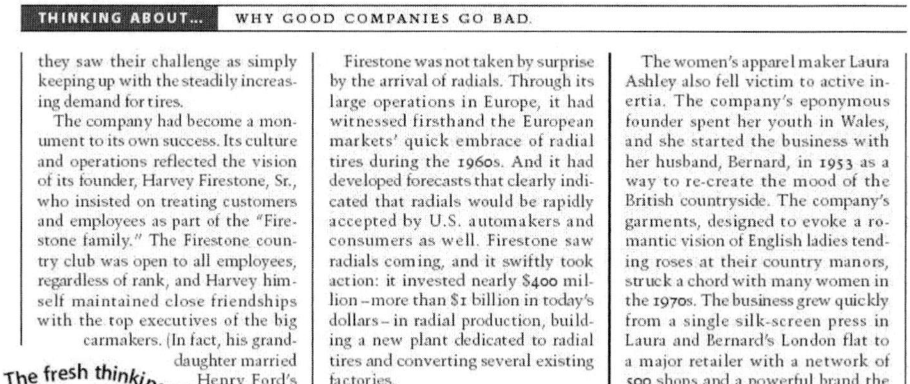

THINKING ABOUT... WHY GOOD COMPANIES GO BAD

they saw their challenge as simply keeping up with the steadily increasing demand for tires.

The company had become a monument to its own success. Its culture and operations reflected the vision of its founder, Harvey Firestone, Sr., who insisted on treating customers and employees as part of the "Firestone family." The Firestone country club was open to all employees, regardless of rank, and Harvey himself maintained close friendships with the top executives of the big carmakers. (In fact, his granddaughter married Henry Ford's grandson.) Firestone created fiercely loyal managers, steeping them in the company's family values and in its Akron-centered worldview.

The company's operating and capital allocation processes were designed to exploit the booming demand for tires by quickly bringing new production capacity on line. In the capital-budgeting process, for example, frontline employees identified market opportunities and translated them into proposals for investing in additional capacity.

Firestone was not taken by surprise by the arrival of radials. Through its large operations in Europe, it had witnessed firsthand the European markets' quick embrace of radial tires during the 1960s. And it had developed forecasts that clearly indicated that radials would be rapidly accepted by U.S. automakers and consumers as well. Firestone saw radials coming, and it swiftly took action: it invested nearly $400 million – more than $1 billion in today's dollars – in radial production, building a new plant dedicated to radial tires and converting several existing factories.

Although Firestone's response was quick, it was far from effective. Even as it invested in the new product, it clung to its old ways of working. Rather than redesign its production processes, it just tinkered with them – even though the manufacture of radial tires required much higher quality standards. In addition, the company delayed closing many of its factories that produced bias tires, despite clear indications of their impending

The women's apparel maker Laura Ashley also fell victim to active inertia. The company's eponymous founder spent her youth in Wales, and she started the business with her husband, Bernard, in 1953 as a way to re-create the mood of the British countryside. The company's garments, designed to evoke a romantic vision of English ladies tending roses at their country manors, struck a chord with many women in the 1970s. The business grew quickly from a single silk-screen press in Laura and Bernard's London flat to a major retailer with a network of 500 shops and a powerful brand the world over.

Laura Ashley expanded her tiny operation not to maximize profits but to defend and promote traditional British values, which she felt were under siege from sex, drugs, and miniskirts in the 1960s. From the beginning, she and Bernard exercised tight control over all aspects of the business, keeping design, manufacturing, distribution, and retailing in-house. The couple opened a central manufacturing and distribution center in Wales,

The fresh thinking that led to a company's initial success is often replaced by a rigid devotion to the status quo.

SOURCE: *Harvard Business Review,* July–August, 1999, 42.

FIGURE 13–3   Illustration of an Organization Chart

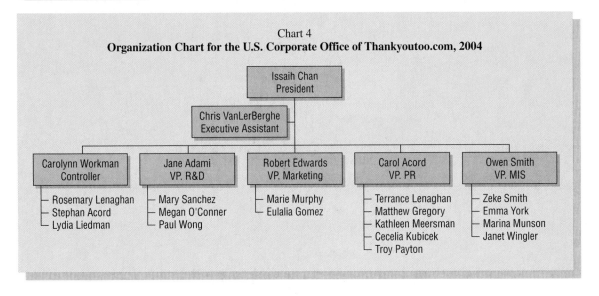

Chart 4
Organization Chart for the U.S. Corporate Office of Thankyoutoo.com, 2004

sub-bullets different by color, size, shape, or weight. Darts, check marks, squares, or triangles can be used for the secondary bullets.

Flowcharts and Process Charts

If you have studied business management, you know that administrators use a variety of specialized charts in their work. Often these charts are a part of the information presented in reports. Perhaps the most common of these is the *organization chart* (see Figure 13–3). These charts show hierarchy of positions, divisions, departments, and such in an organization. *Gantt charts* are graphic presentations that show planning and scheduling activities. As the word implies, a *flowchart* (see Figure 13–4) shows the sequence of activities in a process. Traditionally, flowcharts use specific designs and symbols to show process variations. A variation of the organization and flowchart is the *decision tree.* This chart helps one follow a path to an appropriate decision. You can easily construct these charts with presentation and drawing software.

- Various specialized management charts are useful in reports—for example, organization charts, Gantt charts, and flowcharts.

CONSTRUCTING VISUAL GRAPHICS

The truly visual types of graphics include a variety of forms: charts and illustrations. Charts are graphics built with raw data and include bar, pie, and line charts and all their variations and combinations. Illustrations includes maps, diagrams, drawings, cartoons, and such.

- Visual graphics include data-generated charts, photographs, and artwork.

Bar and Column Charts

Simple bar and column charts compare differences in quantities by differences in the lengths of the bars representing those quantities. You should use them primarily to show comparisons of quantity changes at a moment in time.

As shown in Figure 13–5, the main parts of the horizontal bar chart are the bars and the grid (the field on which the bars are placed). The bars, which may be arranged horizontally or vertically (also called a column chart), should be of equal width. You should identify each bar or column, usually with a caption at the left or bottom. The grid (field) on which the bars are placed is usually needed to show the magnitudes of the bars, and the units (dollars, pounds, miles, and such) are identified by the scale caption below.

- Simple bar and column charts compare differences in quantities by varying bar lengths.

FIGURE 13–4   Illustration of a Flowchart

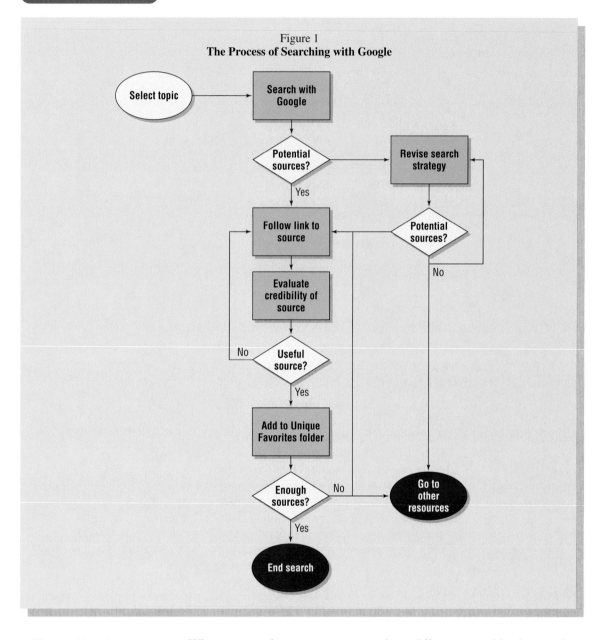

Figure 1
The Process of Searching with Google

- Clustered bar charts are useful in comparing two or three kinds of quantities.

  When you need to compare two or three different quantities in one chart, you can use a *clustered* (or *multiple*) *bar chart*. In such a chart, bars show the values of the quantities compared. Cross-hatching, colors, or the like on the bars distinguish the different kinds of information (see Figure 13–6). Somewhere within the chart, a legend (explanation) gives a key to the differences in the bars. Because clustered bar charts can become cluttered, usually you should not compare more than three kinds of information on one of them.

- When you need to show plus and minus differences, bilateral column charts are useful.

  When you need to show plus and minus differences, you can use *bilateral column charts*. The columns of these charts begin at a central point of reference and may go either up or down, as illustrated in Figure 13–7. Bar titles appear either within, above, or below the bars, depending on which placement fits best. Bilateral column charts are especially good for showing percentage changes, but you may use them for any series in which plus and minus quantities are present.

- To compare subdivisions of columns, use a stacked bar chart.

  If you need to compare subdivisions of columns, you can use a *stacked* (*subdivided*) *column chart*. As shown in Figure 13–8, such a chart divides each column into its parts. It distinguishes these parts by color, cross-hatching, or the like; and it explains

FIGURE 13–5

Illustration of a Bar Chart

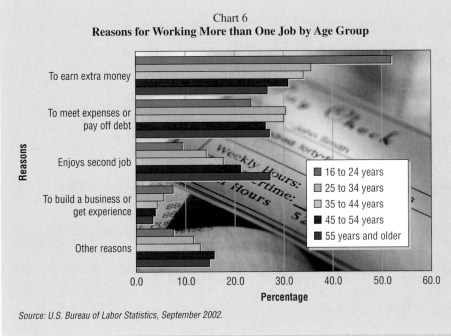

FIGURE 13–6

Illustration of a Clustered Bar Chart

these differences in a legend. Subdivided columns may be difficult for your reader to interpret since both the beginning and ending points need to be found. Then the reader has to subtract to find the size of the column component. Clustered column charts or pie charts do not introduce this possibility for error.

Another feature that can lead to reader error in interpreting bar and column chart data is the use of three dimensions when only two variables are being compared. One study evaluated the speed and accuracy of readers' interpretation of two-dimensional columns on two-dimensional axes with three-dimensional columns on two-dimensional axes and three-dimensional columns on three-dimensional axes. The results showed that readers were able to extract information from the column chart fastest and most accurately when it was presented in the simple two-dimensional column on the two-dimensional axis.[2] Therefore, unless more than two variables are used, choosing the two-dimensional presentation over the three-dimensional form is usually best.

- Two-dimensional columns on two-dimensional axes are easiest for readers to use.

[2] Theophilus B. A. Addo, "The Effects of Dimensionality in Computer Graphics," *The Journal of Business Communication* 31, no. 4 (1994): 253.

FIGURE 13–7

Illustration of a Bilateral
Column Chart

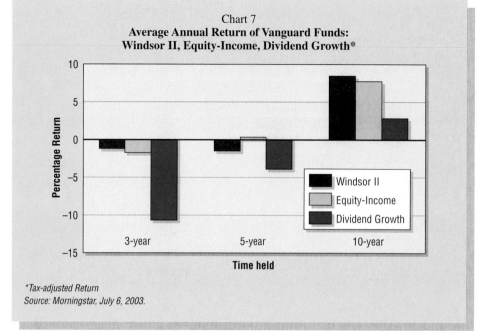

Chart 7
**Average Annual Return of Vanguard Funds:
Windsor II, Equity-Income, Dividend Growth***

*Tax-adjusted Return
Source: Morningstar, July 6, 2003.

FIGURE 13–8

Illustration of a Stacked
Column Chart

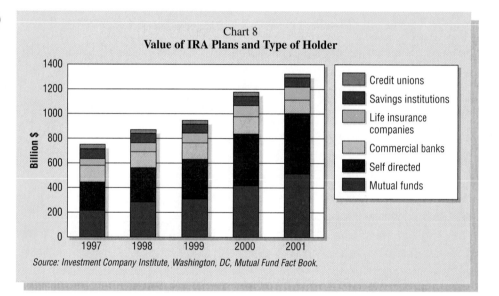

Chart 8
Value of IRA Plans and Type of Holder

Source: Investment Company Institute, Washington, DC, Mutual Fund Fact Book.

● You also can use such a chart for comparing subdivisions of percentages.

A special form of stacked (subdivided) column chart is used to compare the subdivisions of percentages. In this form, all the bars are equal in length, for each represents 100 percent. Only the subdivisions within the bars vary. The objective of this form is to compare differences in how wholes are divided. The component parts may be labeled, as shown in Figure 13–9, but they also may be explained in a legend.

Pictographs

● Pictographs are bar or column charts made with pictures.

A *pictograph* is a bar or column chart that uses bars made of pictures. The pictures are typically drawings of the items being compared. For example, a company's profits over a period of years, instead of being shown by ordinary bars (formed by straight lines), could be shown by bar drawings of stacks of coins. This type of column chart is a pictograph (see Figure 13–10).

● In constructing pictographs, follow the procedure for making bar and column charts.

In constructing a pictograph, you should follow the procedures you used in constructing bar and column charts and two special rules. First, you must make all the picture units equal in size. That is, you must base the comparisons wholly on the number

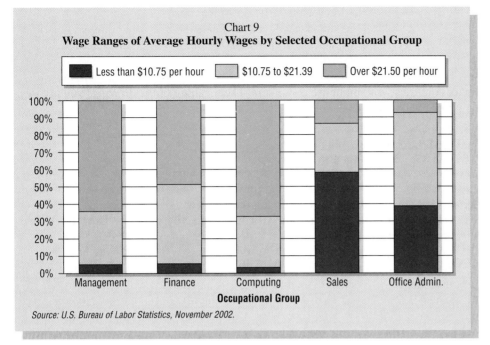

Chart 9
Wage Ranges of Average Hourly Wages by Selected Occupational Group

Less than $10.75 per hour $10.75 to $21.39 Over $21.50 per hour

Occupational Group

Source: U.S. Bureau of Labor Statistics, November 2002.

FIGURE 13–9

Illustration of a 100 Percent Stacked Column Chart

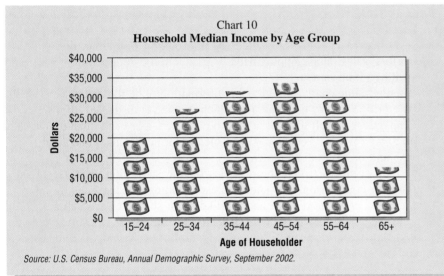

Chart 10
Household Median Income by Age Group

Age of Householder

Source: U.S. Census Bureau, Annual Demographic Survey, September 2002.

FIGURE 13–10

Illustration of a Pictograph

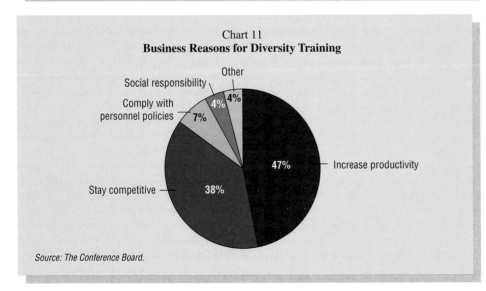

Chart 11
Business Reasons for Diversity Training

Source: The Conference Board.

FIGURE 13–11

Illustration of a Pie Chart

of picture units used and never on variation in the areas of the units. The reason for this rule is obvious. The human eye is grossly inadequate in comparing geometric designs that vary in more than one dimension. Second, you should select pictures or symbols that fit the information to be illustrated. In comparing the cruise lines of the world, for example, you might use ships. In comparing computers used in the world's major countries, you might use computers. The meaning of the drawings you use must be immediately clear to the readers.

Pie Charts

- Pie charts show subdivisions of a whole.

The most frequently used chart in comparing the subdivisions of wholes is the *pie chart* (see Figure 13–11). As the name implies, pie charts show the whole of the information being studied as a pie (circle), and the parts of this whole as slices of the pie. The slices may be distinguished by labeling and color or cross-hatching. A single slice can be emphasized by exploding—pulling out—a piece. Because it is hard to judge the values of the slices with the naked eye, it is good to include the percentage values within or near each slice. Also, placing a label near each slice makes it quicker for the reader to understand the items being compared than using a legend to identify components. A good rule to follow is to begin slicing the pie at the 12 o'clock position and then to move around clockwise. It is also good to arrange the slices in descending order from largest to smallest.

Line Charts

- Line charts show changes over time.

Line charts are useful in showing changes of information over time. For example, changes in prices, sales totals, employment, or production over a period of years can be shown well in a line chart.

- The line appears on a grid (a scaled area) and is continuous.

In constructing a line chart, you draw the information to be illustrated as a continuous line on a grid. The grid is the area in which the line is displayed. It is scaled to show time changes from left to right across the chart (X-axis) and quantity changes from bottom to top (Y-axis). You should mark clearly the scale values and the time periods. They should be in equal increments.

- Two or more lines may appear on one chart.

You also may compare two or more series on the same line chart (see Figure 13–12). In such a comparison, you should clearly distinguish the lines by color or form (dots, dashes, dots and dashes, and the like). You should clearly label them on the chart or by a legend somewhere in the chart. But the number of series that you may compare on one line chart is limited. As a practical rule, the maximum number is five to seven.

FIGURE 13–12

Illustration of a Line Chart

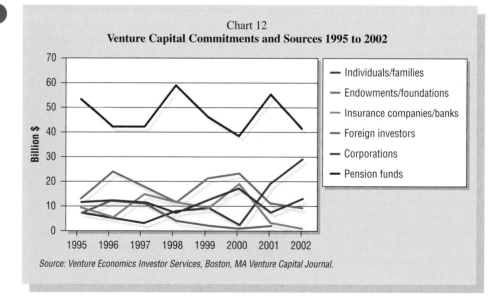

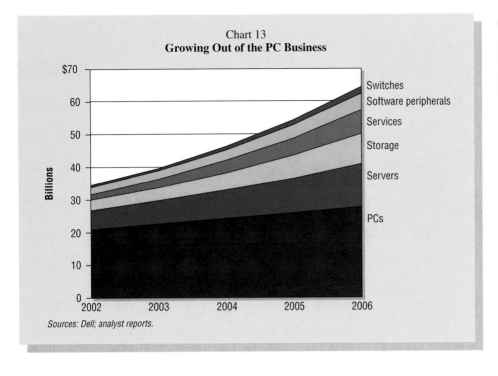

Chart 13
Growing Out of the PC Business

Billions

Switches
Software peripherals
Services
Storage
Servers
PCs

2002 2003 2004 2005 2006

Sources: Dell; analyst reports.

FIGURE 13–13

Illustration of an Area Chart

SOURCE: *Forbes,* June 10, 2002, 112.

It is also possible to show parts of a series by use of a *surface* chart—sometimes called an *area* chart. Such a chart, however, can show only one series. You should construct this type of chart, as shown in Figure 13–13, with a top line representing the total of the series. Then, starting from the base, you should cumulate the parts, beginning with the largest and ending with the smallest. You may use cross-hatching or coloring to distinguish the parts.

Line charts that show a range of data for particular times are called *variance* or *hi-lo* charts. Some variance charts show high and low points as well as the mean, median, or mode. When used to chart daily stock prices, they typically include closing price in addition to the high and low. When you use points other than high and low, be sure to make it clear what these points are.

● Surface charts show the makeup of a series.

● Variance charts show high and low points— sometimes more.

Scatter Diagrams

Scatter diagrams are often considered another variation of the line chart. Although they do use X and Y axes to plot paired values, the points stand alone without a line drawn through them. For example, a writer might use a scatter diagram in a report on digital cameras to plot values for price and resolution of several cameras. While clustering the points allows users to validate hunches about cause and effect, they can only be interpreted for correlation—the direction and strength relationships. The points can reveal positive, negative, or no relationships. Additionally, by examining the tightness of the points, the user can see the strength of the relationship. The closer the points are to a straight line, the stronger the relationship. In Figure 13–14, the paired values are *Cover Hardness* and *Compression.* The directions show a positive and strong relationship.

● Scatter diagrams show direction and strength of paired values.

Maps

You also may use *maps* to communicate quantitative as well as physical (or geographic) information. Statistical maps are useful primarily when quantitative information is to be compared by geographic areas. On such maps, the geographic areas are clearly outlined, and some graphic technique is used to show the differences between areas (see Figure 13–15). Quantitative maps are particularly useful in illustrating and analyzing complex data. Traffic patterns on a website could be mapped as well as patterns in a retail store. Physical or geographic maps (see Figure 13–16) can show

● Maps show quantitative and geographic information.

FIGURE 13–14   Illustration of a Scatter Diagram

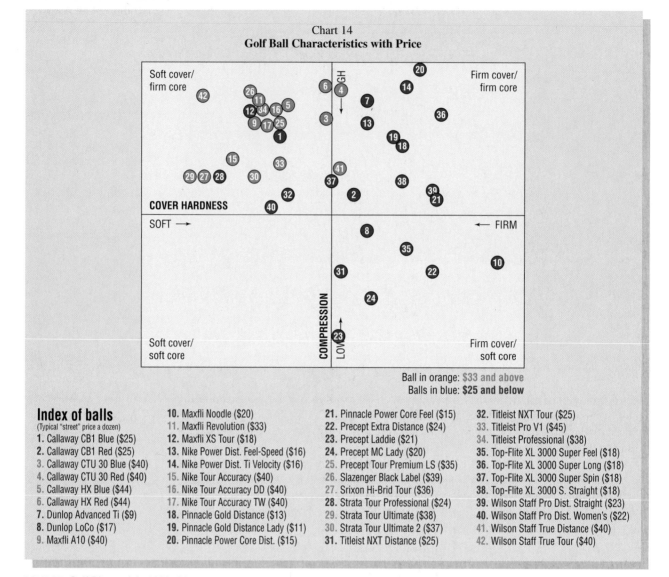

Chart 14
Golf Ball Characteristics with Price

Ball in orange: **$33 and above**
Balls in blue: **$25 and below**

Index of balls
(Typical "street" price a dozen)

1. Callaway CB1 Blue ($25)
2. Callaway CB1 Red ($25)
3. Callaway CTU 30 Blue ($40)
4. Callaway CTU 30 Red ($40)
5. Callaway HX Blue ($44)
6. Callaway HX Red ($44)
7. Dunlop Advanced Ti ($9)
8. Dunlop LoCo ($17)
9. Maxfli A10 ($40)

10. Maxfli Noodle ($20)
11. Maxfli Revolution ($33)
12. Maxfli XS Tour ($18)
13. Nike Power Dist. Feel-Speed ($16)
14. Nike Power Dist. Ti Velocity ($16)
15. Nike Tour Accuracy ($40)
16. Nike Tour Accuracy DD ($40)
17. Nike Tour Accuracy TW ($40)
18. Pinnacle Gold Distance ($13)
19. Pinnacle Gold Distance Lady ($11)
20. Pinnacle Power Core Dist. ($15)

21. Pinnacle Power Core Feel ($15)
22. Precept Extra Distance ($24)
23. Precept Laddie ($21)
24. Precept MC Lady ($20)
25. Precept Tour Premium LS ($35)
26. Slazenger Black Label ($39)
27. Srixon Hi-Brid Tour ($36)
28. Strata Tour Professional ($24)
29. Strata Tour Ultimate ($38)
30. Strata Tour Ultimate 2 ($37)
31. Titleist NXT Distance ($25)

32. Titleist NXT Tour ($25)
33. Titleist Pro V1 ($45)
34. Titleist Professional ($38)
35. Top-Flite XL 3000 Super Feel ($18)
36. Top-Flite XL 3000 Super Long ($18)
37. Top-Flite XL 3000 Super Spin ($18)
38. Top-Flite XL 3000 S. Straight ($18)
39. Wilson Staff Pro Dist. Straight ($23)
40. Wilson Staff Pro Dist. Women's ($22)
41. Wilson Staff True Distance ($40)
42. Wilson Staff True Tour ($40)

SOURCE: *Golf Digest,* July 2002, 61.

distributions as well as specific locations. Of the numerous techniques available to you, these are the most common:

- Here are some specific instructions for statistical maps.

- Showing differences of areas by color, shading, or cross-hatching is perhaps the most popular technique (see Figure 13–15). Of course, maps using this technique must have a legend to explain the quantitative meanings of the various colors, cross-hatchings, and so forth.

- Graphics, symbols, or clip art may be placed within each geographic area to depict the quantity for that area or geographic location.

- Placing the quantities in numerical form within each geographic area is another widely used technique.

Combination Charts

- Sometimes a combination of chart types is effective.

Combination charts often serve readers extremely well by allowing them to see relationships of different kinds of data. The example in Figure 13–17 shows the reader the price of stock over time (the trend) as well as the volume of sales over time (compar-

FIGURE 13–15   Illustration of a Map (quantitative)

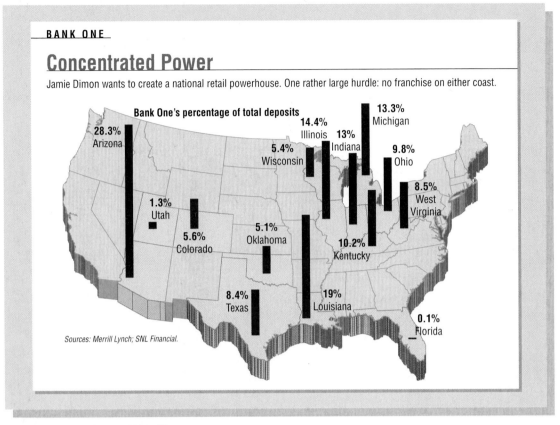

BANK ONE

Concentrated Power

Jamie Dimon wants to create a national retail powerhouse. One rather large hurdle: no franchise on either coast.

Bank One's percentage of total deposits

- 28.3% Arizona
- 1.3% Utah
- 5.6% Colorado
- 5.1% Oklahoma
- 8.4% Texas
- 5.4% Wisconsin
- 14.4% Illinois
- 13% Indiana
- 13.3% Michigan
- 9.8% Ohio
- 8.5% West Virginia
- 10.2% Kentucky
- 19% Louisiana
- 0.1% Florida

Sources: Merrill Lynch; SNL Financial.

SOURCE: *Forbes*, May 13, 2002, 66.

isons). It allows the reader to detect whether the change in volume affects the price of the stock. This kind of information would be difficult to get from raw data.

Three-Dimensional Graphics

Today three-dimensional 1 (3-D) graphics are beginning to make their way from science labs into business settings. Several factors seem to be driving the trend. Businesses large and small are collecting and attempting to analyze extremely large amounts of detailed data. Not only are they analyzing their own data but also data on their competitors. And advances in both the hardware and software tools have made it easier to graphically represent data—both quantitative and qualitative data.

- Three-dimensional graphics facilitate analyze large data sets.

Although 3-D graphics help writers deploy the results of their data analysis, they change how readers look at information and may take some getting used to. These tools enable users to both see data from new perspectives and interact with it. They allow users to free themselves from two dimensions and gives them ways to stretch their insights and see new possibilities. These graphics can help businesses make timely decisions by leveraging their corporate information assets.

- 3-D graphics facilitate seeing data from new perspectives.

The example in Figure 13–18 is a static image of a 3-D data visualization of business communication literature, and the actual tool, OmniViz Platinum <www.omniviz. com>, allows the user to interact with the data in many ways. This image was created in seconds from a data file of nearly 900 scholarly business communication publications captured from the most recent five years in ABI/Inform database. That is a small file for OmniViz Platinum, which can handle a million or more records, yet the graphic displays most of the work done by business communication scholars in five years. Using its algorithm, it reads and sorts the publications. The peaks show where the most research has been and the volume around the peak shows related work.

- Tools allow users to interact with their data.

FIGURE 13–16   Illustration of a Map (Physical)

U.S. Clean Cities

*Connecticut Clean Cities Include:
– New Haven
– CT Southwestern Area
– Capitol Clean Cities of CT
– Norwich

Map Date: 6/9/03

SOURCE: DOE Alternative Fuels Data Center.

FIGURE 13–17

Illustration of a
Combination Chart

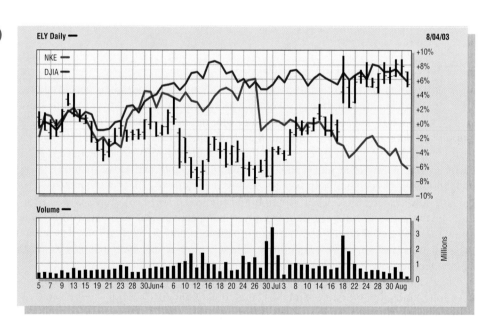

If you were to interact with the graphic, you would be able to see a detailed list of every item under any point you clicked on. If you clicked near your area of research, you would have identified the most relevant research to your study. Just think how long it would have taken to manually review and sort 900 sources. The list would help you identify other scholars in the area, major journals where this kind of research ap-

FIGURE 13–18

An Illustration of a Three-Dimensional Graphic

SOURCE: OmniViz, Inc.

pears, and much more. Additionally the graphic provides other important information—it shows you where no or little research has been done, where the boundaries of the published literature are, what type of articles there are, and in which journals they appear. Furthermore, it can be rotated and colored to help one analyze, interpret, and present results.

Using 3-D graphics clearly has its place and use, the most appropriate of which seem to be helping one analyze large data sets, query them, and interpret them. As more of these tools become readily available, either bundled with analytic tools or standalone products such as RefViz <www.refviz.com>, writers should take care to use them appropriately.

Other Graphics

The types of graphics discussed thus far are the ones most commonly used. Other types also may be helpful. *Photographs* may serve a useful communication purpose. You could use the photo in Figure 13–19 as a metaphor for the concept of a hole in a company's computer security (someone getting in) or the loss of corporate intelligence (something getting out). *Diagrams* (see Figure 13–20) and drawings (see Figure 13–21) may help simplify a complicated explanation or description. *Icons* are another useful type of graphic. You can create new icons and use them consistently, or you can draw from an existing body of icons with easily recognized meanings, such as ●. Even carefully selected *cartoons* can be used effectively. *Video clips* and *animation* are now used in electronic documents. See the text website for some examples. For all practical purposes, any graphic is acceptable as long as it helps communicate the true story. The possibilities are almost unlimited.

- Other graphics available to you are diagrams, drawings, and photographs—even cartoons.

Visual Integrity[3]

In writing an objective report, you are ethically bound to present data in ways the reader can extract easily and accurately. By being aware of some of the common errors made in presenting graphics, you learn how to avoid them as well as how to spot

- Business writers are ethically bound to present data readers can extract easily and accurately.

[3] For an excellent expanded discussion of graphic errors, see Gerald E. Jones, *How to Lie with Charts* (San Jose, CA: iUniverse.com, 2001).

FIGURE 13–19

Illustration of a Photo

FIGURE 13–20

Illustration of a Diagram

SOURCE: U.S. Department of Transportation's Share the Road Safely Program.

FIGURE 13–21

Illustration of a Drawing

Illustration by Zeke Smith © 2003.

Professorial Words of Wisdom

Students must be sensitized in the importance of pictures that accompany written messages to the same extent that they are sensitized to the importance of nonverbal communication that accompanies oral messages.

Shirley Kuiper, The University of South Carolina
Rosemary Booth, The University of North Carolina at Charlotte
Charles D. Bodkin, The University of North Carolina at Charlotte

Shirley Kuiper, Rosemary Booth, and Charles D. Bodkin, "The Visual Portrayal of Women in IBM's *Think*: A Longitudinal Analysis," *The Journal of Business Communication,* 35, no. 2 (April 1998): 259.

them in other documents. Even when errors are not deliberately created to deceive a reader, they cause loss of credibility with the reader—casting doubt on the document as well as other work you have completed.

Two categories of common errors are errors of scale and errors of format. Another category of more difficult error is inaccurate or misleading presentation of context.

- Common errors are errors of scale, format, and context presentation.

Errors of scale include problems with uniform scale size, scale distortion, and zero points. You need to be sure that all the dimensions from left to right (X axis) are equal, and the dimensions from the bottom to the top (Y axis) are equal. Otherwise, as you see here, an incorrect picture would be shown.

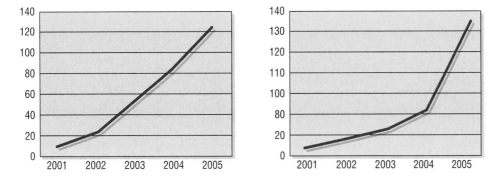

Scale distortion occurs when a graphic is stretched excessively horizontally or vertically to change the meaning it conveys to the reader. Expanding a scale can change the appearance of the line. For example if the values on a chart are plotted one-half unit apart, changes appear much more suddenly. Determining the distances that present the most accurate picture is a matter of judgment. Notice the different looks the graphic here shows when stretched vertically and horizontally.

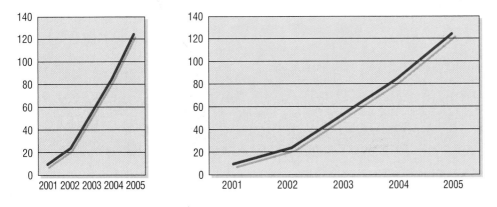

CHAPTER 13   Graphics

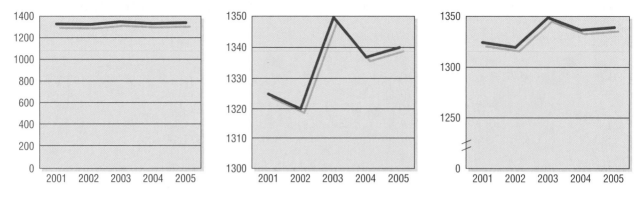

Finally, another type of error is violating the zero beginning of the series. For accuracy, you should begin the scale at zero. But when all the information shown in the chart has high values, it is awkward to show the entire scale from zero to the highest value. For example, if the quantities compared range from 1320 to 1350 and the chart shows the entire area from zero to 1350, the line showing these quantities would be almost straight and very high on the chart. Your solution in this case is not to begin the scale at a high number (say 1300), for this would distort the information, but to begin at zero and show a scale break. Realize, however, that while this makes the differences easier to see, it does exaggerate the differences. You can see this here.

Errors of format come in a wide variety. Some of the more common ones include choice of wrong chart type, distracting use of grids and shading, misuse of typeface, and problems with labels. If a company used pie charts to compare expenses from one year to the next, readers might be tempted to draw conclusions that would be inappropriate because, although the pies both represent 100 percent of the expenses, the size of the business and the expenses may have grown or shrunk drastically in a year's

Software programs are available that enable writers to create all common forms of graphics.

Practicing Visual Ethics

As you have learned in this chapter, graphics can serve several useful purposes for the business writer. However, the writer needs to be accountable in using graphics to present graphics that in the eye and mind of the reader communicate accurately and completely. To do this, the careful writer pays attention to both the design and content of the graphic. These are particularly important, for readers often skim text but see the graphics. Research shows that people remember images much better and longer than text.

The following guides will help you in evaluating the graphics you use:

- Does the document's design create accurate expectations?
- Does the story told match the data?
- Is the implied message congruent with the actual message?
- Will the impact of the visual on your audience be appropriate?
- Does the visual convey all critical information free of distortion?
- Are the data depicted accurately?

Adapted from Donna S. Kienzler, "Visual Ethics," *The Journal of Business Communication* (April 1997): 171–87.

time. If one piece of the pie had been colored or shaded in such a way as to make it stand out from the others, it could mislead readers. And, of course, small type or unlabeled, inconsistent, or inappropriate labels clearly confuse readers. You need to be careful to present graphics that are both complete and accurate.

Another ethical dilemma is accurately presenting context. Politicians are often deliberately guilty of this, framing the issue to suit their cause. Business writers can avoid this error by both attempting to frame the data objectively and presenting the data with the reader in mind. For example, one might look at the cost of attending college for the past 30 years. A line chart of the actual dollar cost over the years would show a clear upward trend. However, to present the costs without factoring in inflation during that 30-year period would distort the results. In Figure 13–22, you can see that the actual cost of college tuition and fees in dollars adjusted for inflation would show costs that are lower or equal to today's costs.

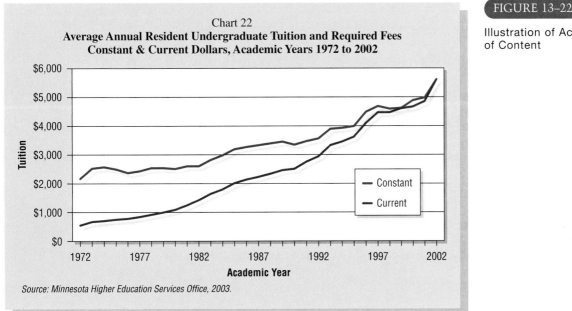

Chart 22
**Average Annual Resident Undergraduate Tuition and Required Fees
Constant & Current Dollars, Academic Years 1972 to 2002**

Source: Minnesota Higher Education Services Office, 2003.

FIGURE 13–22

Illustration of Accuracy of Content

SUMMARY BY CHAPTER OBJECTIVES

1 Determine which parts of your report should be communicated by graphics and where in the report the graphics should appear.

2 Explain the general mechanics of constructing graphics—size, layout, type, rules and borders, color and cross-hatching, clip art, background, numbering, titles, title placement, and footnotes and acknowledgments.

3 Construct textual graphics such as tables, pull quotes, flowcharts, and process charts.

4 Construct and use visual graphics such as bar charts, pie charts, scatter diagrams, and maps.

5 Avoid common errors in constructing and using graphics.

1. Because graphics are a part of the communication in a report, you should plan for them.
   - But remember that they supplement the writing; they do not replace it.
   - Use them wherever they help communicate the report information.
   - Place them near the text part they illustrate.
   - Invite the readers to look at them at the appropriate place.
   - Place in the appendix those that you do not discuss in the text.

2. Construct each graphic carefully, following these general instructions:
   - Give each the size and arrangement its contents justify.
   - Choose a readable type.
   - Use rules, borders, and color when they help.
   - Use clip art and background appropriately.
   - Number the graphics consecutively by type.
   - Construct titles for them using the five Ws (*who, what, where, when, why*) and one H (*how*) as a checklist.
   - Use footnotes and acknowledgments when needed, placing them below the graphic.

3. Choose textual graphics to display data that are largely text-based.
   - Use general-purpose tables for information that is broad in scope.
   - Use special-purpose tables for information that is specific in scope.
   - See Figure 13–1 for the details of table construction.
   - Use leaderwork or tabulations for short arrangement of data.
   - Use pull quotes to emphasize a key idea.
   - Use bullet lists to set off points.
   - Use flowcharts and process charts to show activity sequences.

4. In selecting a graphic, consider these primary uses of each:
   - *Simple bar or column chart*—shows quantity comparisons over time or over geographic distances.
   - *Clustered bar or column chart*—shows two or three quantities on one chart.
   - *Bilateral column chart*—shows plus and minus differences and is especially good for showing percentage changes.
   - *Subdivided* (or *stacked*) *bar chart*—used to compare differences in the division of wholes.
   - *Pictograph*—shows quantitative differences in picture form.
   - *Pie chart*—used to show how wholes are divided.
   - *Line chart*—useful in showing changes over time. Variations include belt charts, surface charts, and variance charts.
   - *Scatter diagram*—compares pairs of values.
   - *Map*—shows quantitative and geographic differences by area.
   - *Combination chart*—used to show relationships between separate data sets.
   - *Three-dimensional graphic*—used to analyze and interpret large data sets.

   Apply other graphics to serve special needs:
   - Photographs.
   - Diagrams and drawings.
   - Icons.
   - Cartoons.
   - Video clips and animation.

5. Avoid these common errors to present data objectively:
   - *Errors of scale*—uniform scale size, scale distortion, zero point.
   - *Errors of format*—wrong chart type, distracting use of grids and shading, misuse of typeface, and problems with labels.
   - *Errors of context presentation.*

CRITICAL THINKING QUESTIONS

1. For the past 20 years, Professor Clark Kupenheimer has required that his students include five graphics in the long, formal report he assigns them to prepare. Evaluate this requirement.

2. Because it was easier to do, a report writer prepared each of the graphics on a full page. Some of these graphics were extremely complex; some were very simple. Comment on this practice.

3. "I have placed every graphic near the place I write about it. The reader can see the graphic without any *additional* help from me. It just doesn't make sense to direct the reader's attention to the graphics with words." Evaluate this comment.

4. A report has five maps, four tables, one chart, one diagram, and one photograph. How would you number these graphics?

5. How would you number these graphics in a report: seven tables, six charts, nine maps?

6. Discuss the techniques that may be used to show quantitative differences by area on a statistical map.

7. Select data that are ideally suited for presentation in three dimensions. Explain why use of a data visualization is good for this case.

8. Discuss the advantages and disadvantages of using pictographs.

9. Find a graph that uses scale breaks. Discuss the possible effects of its use on the reader.

10. Find a graphic with errors in format. Tell how you would correct the errors to present the chart's data more clearly to the reader.

CRITICAL THINKING EXERCISES

1. Construct a complete, concise title for a bar chart showing annual attendance at home football (or basketball, or hockey) games at your school from 1994 to the present.

2. The chart prepared in Question 1 requires an explanation for the years 1999 to the present. In each of those years, one extra home game was played. Explain how you would provide the necessary explanation.

3. For each of the areas of information described below, which form of graphic would you use? Explain your decision.

   a. Record of annual sales for the Kenyon Company for the past 20 years.

   b. Comparison of Kenyon Company sales, by product, for this year and last year.

   c. Monthly production of the automobile industry in units.

   d. Breakdown of how the average middle-income family in your state (or province) disposes of its income dollar.

   e. How middle-income families spend their income dollar as compared with how low-income families spend their income dollar.

   f. Comparison of sales for the past two years for each of the B&B Company's 14 sales districts. The districts cover all 50 states, Canada, and Puerto Rico.

   g. National production of automobiles from 1930 to present, broken down by manufacturer.

   h. Relationship between list price and gas mileage of alternative and gasoline-fueled cars.

4. For each of the following sets of facts, (a) determine the graphic (or graphics) that would be best, (b) defend your choice, and (c) construct the graphic.

   a. Average (mean) amount of life insurance owned by Fidelity Life Insurance Company policyholders. Classification is by annual income.

Income	Average Life Insurance
Under $30,000	$ 15,245
$30,000–34,999	24,460
$35,000–39,999	36,680
$40,000–44,999	49,875
$45,000–49,999	61,440
$50,000 and over	86,390

   b. Profits and losses for D and H Food Stores, by store, 2000–2004, in dollars.

Store				
Year	Able City	Baker	Charleston	Total
2000	234,210	132,410	97,660	464,280
2001	229,110	−11,730	218,470	435,850
2002	238,430	−22,410	216,060	432,080
2003	226,730	68,650	235,510	530,890
2004	230,080	91,450	254,820	576,350

c. Share of real estate tax payments by ward for Bigg City, 1999 and 2004, in thousands of dollars.

	1999	2004
Ward 1	17.1	21.3
Ward 2	10.2	31.8
Ward 3	19.5	21.1
Ward 4	7.8	18.2
City total	54.6	92.4

d. Percentage change in sales by employee, 2003–2004, District IV, Abbott, Inc.

Employee	Percentage Change
Joan Abraham	+ 7.3
Helen Calmes	+ 2.1
Edward Sanchez	− 7.5
Clifton Nevers	+ 41.6
Wilson Platt	+ 7.4
Clara Ruiz	+ 11.5
David Schlimmer	− 4.8
Phil Wirks	− 3.6

5. The basic blood types are O, A, B, and AB. These can be either positive or negative. With some basic research, determine what percentage of each type people in the United States have. Choose an appropriate graph type and create it to convey the data.

6. Through your research, find the approximate milligrams of caffeine in the following items and create an appropriate graphic for Affiliated Food Products, Inc., to illustrate your findings.

5-oz. cup of coffee (drip brewed)

7-oz. glass of iced tea

6-oz. glass of soda with caffeine

1-oz. dark chocolate, semisweet

7. Choose five or six outdoor summer sport activities. In a graphic identify the activity and whether it affects cardiovascular, arms, legs, back, or abdominals. You can assume these activities can affect more than one fitness zone. You work for the Parks and Recreation Department of a city of your choosing.

PART FIVE

Other Forms of Business Communication

Considered one of Fortune 500's "Most Powerful Black Executives" at age 39, Pamela Thomas-Graham was the first black woman to become a partner at management consulting firm McKinsey & Company. Thomas-Graham recognizes the importance of communicating informally to gather information and harvest good ideas.

"It's very important to have a lot of interaction with people at every level of the company. You should spend time walking around talking with people, and have meetings that bring together different groups of people, either from different areas of the company or from different levels within the company. And my basic philosophy is, 'The best idea wins.' It doesn't matter where it comes from."

Pamela Thomas-Graham, CEO and President, CNBC, Executive Vice President NBC

CHAPTER FOURTEEN

Informal Oral
Communication

CHAPTER OBJECTIVES

Upon completing this chapter, you will be able to understand and use good talking techniques, lead and participate in meetings, communicate effectively by telephone, dictate messages effectively, listen well, and understand nonverbal communication. To reach these goals, you should be able to

1 Discuss talking and its key elements.

2 Explain the techniques for conducting and participating in meetings.

3 Describe good telephone and voice mail techniques.

4 Describe the techniques of good dictating.

5 Explain the listening problem and how to solve it.

6 Describe the nature and role of nonverbal communication.

Informal Oral Communication on the Job

Your job as assistant director in the Public Relations Department at Mastadon Chemicals, Inc., seems somewhat different from what you expected. It makes full use of your specialized college training, as you expected; but it also involves duties for which you did not train because you did not expect them. Most of these duties seem to involve some form of oral communication. In fact, you probably spend more of your work time in talking and listening than in any other activity.

To illustrate, take today's activities. Early this morning, you discussed a morale problem with some of your supervisors. You don't think they understood what you said. After that, you conducted a meeting of the special committee to plan the department's annual picnic. As chairperson, you ran the meeting. It was a disaster, you felt—everybody talking at once, interrupting, arguing. It was a wonder that the committee made any progress. It seemed that everybody wanted to talk but nobody wanted to listen.

In the afternoon, you had other job duties involving oral communication. After you returned from lunch, you must have had a telephone conversation every 20 minutes or so. You felt comfortable with most of these calls, but you thought some of the callers needed a lesson or two in telephone etiquette. Also, you dictated a few messages and emails (using voice recognition on your computer) between telephone calls.

You most certainly do a lot of talking (and listening) on your job, as do most of the people at Mastadon (and just about everywhere else). Oral communication is a vital part of your work. Perhaps you can become better at it by studying the following review of oral communication techniques.

As you know, your work will involve oral as well as written communication. The written communication will probably give you more problems, but the oral communication will take up more of your time. In fact, you are likely to spend more time in oral communication than in any other work activity.

- You will spend more time talking than writing in business.

Much of the oral communication that goes on in business is the informal, person-to-person communication that occurs whenever people get together. Obviously, we all have experience with this form of communication, and most of us do it reasonably well. But all of us can improve our informal speaking and listening with practice.

- Most of your oral communication will be informal.

In addition to informal talking and listening, various kinds of other more formal oral communication take place in business. Sometimes businesspeople conduct and participate in committee meetings, conferences, and group discussions. Often they call one another on the telephone. Even their messages and reports may begin orally as spoken dictation. And frequently, they are called upon to make formal presentations: speeches, lectures, oral reports, and the like. All of these kinds of oral communication are a part of the work that businesspeople do.

- But some of it will be formal, as in meetings, telephone calls, dictation, speeches, and oral reports.

This and the following chapter cover these kinds of oral communication. This chapter reviews the somewhat less formal kinds: informal talking, listening, participating in meetings, talking by telephone, and dictating. The following chapter presents the two most formal kinds: public speaking and oral reporting. Together, the two chapters should give you an understanding of the types of oral communication situations you will encounter in business.

- This and the following chapter cover these types of oral communication.

INFORMAL TALKING

As noted previously, most of us do a reasonably good job of informal talking. In fact, we do such a good job that we often take talking for granted and overlook the need for improving our talking ability. Most of us could stand to improve. To improve our talking ability, we need to be aware of its nature and qualities. We need to assess our abilities. Then we need to work to overcome our shortcomings.

- Most of us talk reasonably well, but probably we can do better.

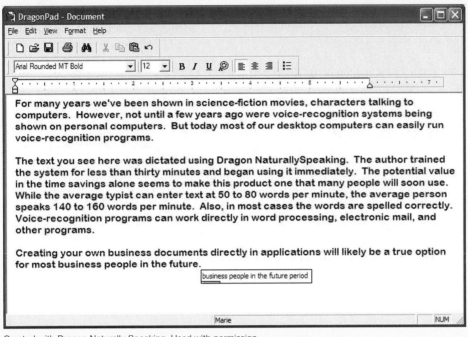

Created with Dragon Naturally Speaking. Used with permission.

Definition of Talking

- Think about having no words to speak. If you try to express yourself, you probably become frustrated.

Imagine for a few moments what it would be like to have no words. All that you have to express your thoughts are grunts, groans, and other such utterances. Of course, you have various nonverbal symbols such as pointing your fingers, nodding your head, and the like. As you find yourself increasingly in need of expressing yourself, you probably become more and more emotional and frustrated—to the point of exaggerating the nonverbal symbols and experiencing many physical symptoms such as redness of the face, heavy breathing, and an increased heartbeat.

- Thus, we learn words to control ourselves and the world about us.

- Talking, then, is the oral expression of knowledge, viewpoints, and emotions through words.

- Think about the best and worst speakers you can imagine. This contrast should give you the qualities of good talking: voice quality, speaking style, word choice, adaptation.

More than likely, the foregoing analogy describes the way you learned to talk. As a dependent child, you expressed yourself with screams, cries, and nonverbal symbols. But as you matured, you learned words, and the words greatly reduced the frustrations of the past. They enabled you to communicate with others more exactly. They enabled you to relate better to the world about you and to some extent to control it.

The foregoing review of how you learned to talk gives us the basis for defining talking. From it we can derive this definition: *Talking* is the oral expression of knowledge, viewpoints, and emotions through words. Also, from this review we can see that talking replaces many of the body movements we made before we were able to talk. And as we will see, it is supplemented by various body movements we have acquired as we learned to talk: gestures, facial expressions, body positions, and such.

As a first step in improving your talking ability, think for a moment about the qualities you like in a good talker—one with whom you would enjoy talking in ordinary

Professorial Words of Wisdom

Oral communication was consistently identified as the most important competency in evaluating entry-level candidates. The four oral communication skills identified as most important for entry-level jobs are following instructions, listening, conversing, and giving feedback.

Jeanne D. Maes, University of South Alabama
Teresa G. Weldy, University of South Alabama
Marjorie L. Icenogle, University of South Alabama

Jeanne D. Maes, Teresa G. Weldy, Marjorie L. Icenogle, "A Managerial Perspective: Oral Communication Is Most Important for Business Students in the Workplace," *Journal of Business Communication* 34, no. 1 (January 1997): 78.

conversation. Then think about the opposite—the worst conversationalist you can imagine. If you will get these two images in mind, you will have a good picture of the characteristics of good talking. Probably this mental picture includes good voice quality, excellence in talking style, accuracy of word choice, and adaptation. As these elements control the overall quality of oral expression, we will now review them.

Elements of Good Talking

The techniques of good talking may be summarized by four basic elements: (1) voice quality, (2) style, (3) word choice, and (4) adaptation.

Voice Quality. It should be obvious that good voice quality is central to good talking. By voice quality we mean the vocal sounds one hears when another speaks. Primarily voice quality refers to the pitch and resonance of the sounds made. But for our purposes, speed and volume are included. Because we cover these topics in Chapter 15, our review here is brief. We need only to say that voices vary widely—from the unpleasant to the melodious. Each of us is saddled with the voice given us. But we can work for improvement.

- Good voice quality helps one communicate. It involves pitch, delivery speed, and volume.

Perhaps the best way of improving voice quality is to first refer to your life experiences. From your life experiences you know good voice quality when you hear it. You know bad voice quality when you hear it. You know the effect received from talking that is too fast or too slow. You know the effect of talking in a monotone. You know the effect of a high-pitched voice, a guttural voice, a melodious voice. With this knowledge in mind, you should analyze your own voice, perhaps with the assistance of a recorder. Listen carefully to you. Fit what you hear into impressions you have gained from your life experiences. Then do what you can to improve. It will take conscious effort.

- Study the quality of your voice and compare it with what experience tells you is good. Then correct the shortcomings.

Style. Talking style refers to how the three parts of voice quality—pitch, speed, and volume—blend together. It is the unique way these parts combine to give personality to one's oral expression. As such, style refers to a set of voice behaviors that give uniqueness to a person.

- Style is the blending of pitch, speed, and volume to form a unique talking personality.

From the self-analysis described in our review of voice quality, you also should have a good idea of your talking style. What is the image your talking projects? Does it project sincerity? Is it polished? Smooth? Rough? Dull? After your honest

- A self-analysis of your talking should show you your talking style and the image it projects.

Good talking is the foundation for other types of discourse— interviewing, conducting meetings, telephoning, etc. You should develop good voice quality, perfect effective style, and select words that fit the mind of the listener.

assessment, you should be able to determine your style deficiencies. Then you should work to improve.

- Choose words in your listener's vocabulary. Select those that appropriately convey the morality and courtesy you intend and respect the listener's knowledge.

Word Choice. A third quality of talking is word choice. Of course, word choice is related to one's vocabulary. The larger the vocabulary, the more choices one has. Even so, you should keep in mind the need for the recipient to understand the words you choose. You should choose words you know are in his or her vocabulary. In addition, the words you choose should be appropriate. They should convey the morality and courtesy you desire. And they should respect the listener's knowledge of the subject matter—that is, they should not talk down to or above the listener.

- Adaptation is fitting the message to the listener. It includes word selection, but here we refer to the combined effect of words, voice, and style.

Adaptation. Adaptation is the fourth quality of good talking. It is an extension of our discussion in the paragraphs above. Adaptation means fitting the message to the intended listener. Primarily this means fitting the words to the listener's mind. But it also can include voice and style. To illustrate, the voice, style, and words might vary in an oral message aimed at children and the same message aimed at adults. Similarly, these qualities might vary in messages delivered in different cultures as well as different social situations, work situations, and classrooms.

Courtesy in Talking

- Good talkers are courteous. They don't attempt to dominate.

Our review of talking would not be complete without a comment about the need for courtesy. Good relations between human beings require courtesy. We all know talkers who drown out others with their loud voices, who butt in while others are talking, who attempt to dominate others in conversation. They are universally disliked. Do not be one of them. Good talkers encourage others to make their voices heard. They practice courtesy in their conversations.

- They are aggressive, but they treat others as they want to be treated.

This emphasis on courtesy does not suggest that you should be submissive in your conversations—that you should not be aggressive in pressing your points. It means that you should accord others the courtesy that you expect of them. What we are suggesting is simply the Golden Rule applied to conversation.

Collaborative Tools Support Virtual Meetings

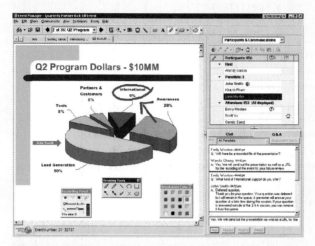

SOURCE: WebEx.com.

Virtual meetings are becoming common in small and large business alike. No longer do businesses need sophisticated teleconferencing equipment to work together from different locations. A typical desktop or laptop with an Internet connection will work nicely. With the proper system configuration, meeting participants can both see and hear others as well as see and work with various software applications.

Businesses are using this technology with their employees, their suppliers, and their customers. Some of the uses include training, sales presentations, review meetings, product demonstrations, and much more—sometimes even holding just-in-time meetings. All uses help the businesspeople do their jobs while saving both time and travel costs.

One such meeting tool is WebEx, a web-based tool that currently has over 60 percent of the web conferencing market share. The screen shown here shows a meeting with WebEx that involves three panelists and 852 attendees. Because the technology is scalable, meeting size can vary widely. The screen lists the participants and indicates that both the chat and Q&A tools are enabled. Participants appear to be discussing the International component, using annotation tools to highlight it.

CONDUCTING AND PARTICIPATING IN MEETINGS

From time to time, you will participate in business meetings. They will range from extreme formality to extreme informality. On the formal end will be conferences and committee meetings. On the informal end will be discussions with groups of fellow workers. Whether formal or informal, the meetings will involve communication. In fact, the quality of the communication will determine their success. As noted in Chapter 10, collaborative report-writing groups should use the suggestions for conducting effective meetings.

- Meetings involve oral communication.

Your role in a meeting will be that of either leader or participant. Of course, the leader's role is the primary one, but good participation is also vital. The following paragraphs review the techniques of performing well in either role.

- In a meeting you will be either a leader or a participant.

Techniques of Conducting Meetings

How you conduct a meeting depends on the formality of the occasion. Meetings of such groups as formal committees, boards of directors, and professional organizations usually follow generally accepted rules of conduct called *parliamentary procedure.* These very specific rules are too detailed for review here. When you are involved in a formal meeting, you would do well to study one of the many books covering parliamentary procedure before the meeting. In addition, you should know and practice the following techniques. For less formal meetings, you can depart somewhat from parliamentary procedure and those techniques. But you should keep in mind that every meeting has goals and that such departures should never hinder you from reaching them.

- To lead some formal meetings, you should know parliamentary procedure. So study the subject.

Plan the Meeting. A key to conducting a successful meeting is to plan it thoroughly. That is, you develop an agenda (a list of topics to be covered) by selecting the items that need to be covered to achieve the goals of the meeting. Then arrange these items in the most logical order. Items that explain or lead to other items should come before the items that they explain or lead to. After preparing the agenda, if the meeting is formal, make it available to those who will attend. For informal meetings, you may find keeping the agenda in mind satisfactory.

- In addition, you should do the following: (1) plan the items to be covered (the agenda),

Follow the Plan. You should follow the plan for the meeting item by item. In most meetings the discussion tends to stray and new items tend to come up. As leader, you should keep the discussion on track. If new items come up during the meeting, you can take them up at the end—or perhaps postpone them to a future meeting.

- (2) follow the plan item by item,

Move the Discussion Along. As leader, you should control the agenda. When one item has been covered, bring up the next item. When the discussion moves off subject, move it back on subject. In general, do what is needed to proceed through the items efficiently. But you should not cut off discussion before all the important points have been made. Thus, you will have to use your good judgment. Your goal is to permit complete discussion on the one hand and to avoid repetition, excessive details, and useless comments on the other.

- (3) move the discussion along,

Control Those Who Talk Too Much. Keeping certain people from talking too much is likely to be one of your harder tasks. A few people usually tend to dominate the discussion. Your task as leader is to control them. Of course, you want the meeting to be democratic, so you will need to let these people talk as long as they are contributing to the goals of the meeting. However, when they begin to stray, duplicate, or bring in useless matter, you should step in. You can do this tactfully and with all the decorum of business etiquette by asking for other viewpoints or by summarizing the discussion and moving on to the next topic.

- (4) allow no one to talk too much,

Encourage Participation from Those Who Talk Too Little. Just as some people talk too much, some talk too little. In business groups, those who say little are often in positions lower than those of other group members. Your job as leader is to encourage these people to participate by asking them for their viewpoints and by showing respect for the comments they make, even though the comments may be illogical.

- (5) encourage everybody to take part,

Control Time. When your meeting time is limited, you need to determine in advance how much time will be needed to cover each item. Then, at the appropriate times, you should end discussion of the items. You may find it helpful to announce the time goals at the beginning of the meeting and to remind the group members of the time status during the meeting.

- (6) control time when time is limited, and

Summarize at Appropriate Places. After a key item has been discussed, you should summarize what the group has covered and concluded. If a group decision is needed, the group's vote will be the conclusion. In any event, you should formally conclude each point and then move on to the next one. At the end of the meeting, you can summarize the progress made. You also should summarize whenever a review will help the group members understand their accomplishments. For some formal meetings, minutes kept by a secretary provide this summary.

- (7) at appropriate places, summarize what the group has covered and concluded.

Techniques for Participating in a Meeting

From the preceding discussion of the techniques that a leader should use, you know something about the things that a participant should do. The following review emphasizes them.

- As a participant in a meeting you should

Follow the Agenda. When an agenda exists, you should follow it. Specifically, you should not bring up items not on the agenda or comment on such items if others bring them up. When there is no agenda, you should stay within the general limits of the goal for the meeting.

● (1) follow the agenda,

Participate. The purpose of meetings is to get the input of everybody concerned. Thus, you should participate. Your participation, however, should be meaningful. You should talk only when you have something to contribute, and you should talk whenever you have something to contribute. Practice your professional etiquette skills as you work courteously and cooperatively with others in the group.

● (2) participate in the meeting,

Do Not Talk Too Much. As you participate in the meeting, be aware that other people are attending. You should speak up whenever you have something to say, but do not get carried away. As in all matters of etiquette, always respect the rights of others. As you speak, ask yourself whether what you are saying really contributes to the discussion. Not only is the meeting costing you time, but it is costing other people's time and salaries as well as the opportunity costs of other work they might be doing.

● (3) avoid talking too much,

Cooperate. A meeting by its very nature requires cooperation from all the participants. So keep this in mind as you participate. Respect the leader and her or his efforts to make progress. Respect the other participants, and work with them in every practical way.

● (4) cooperate with all concerned, and

Be Courteous. Perhaps being courteous is a part of being cooperative. In any event, you should be courteous to the other group members. Specifically, you should respect their rights and opinions, and you should permit them to speak.

● (5) practice courtesy.

USING THE TELEPHONE

A discussion of business telephone techniques may appear trivial at first thought. After all, most of us have had long experience in using the telephone and may feel that we have little to learn about it. No doubt, some of us have excellent telephone skills. But you have only to call a few randomly selected businesses to learn that not everyone who talks on the telephone is proficient in its use. You will get some gruff, cold greetings, and you will be subjected to a variety of discourtesies—those that break standards of business etiquette. And you will find instances of inefficient use of time (which, of course, is costly). This is not to say that the problem is major, for most progressive businesses are aware of the need for good telephone habits and do something about it. But poor telephone techniques are found often enough to justify reviewing the subject of telephone use in a business communication textbook.

● Many businesspeople are discourteous and inefficient in telephone communication.

Need for Favorable Voice Quality

In reviewing good telephone techniques, keep in mind that a telephone conversation is a unique form of oral communication. Only voices are heard; the speakers are not seen. Impressions are received only from the words and the quality of the voices. Thus, when speaking by telephone, it is extremely important that you work to make your voice sound cheerful and friendly.

● Because only sound is involved, friendly voices are important.

One often-suggested way of improving your telephone voice is to talk as if you were face to face with the other person—even smiling and gesturing as you talk, if this helps you be more natural. In addition, you would do well to put into practice the suggestions given earlier in this chapter concerning the use of the voice in speaking (voice quality, variation in pitch, and speed). Perhaps the best instructional device for this problem is to record one of your telephone conversations. Then judge for yourself how you come across and what you need to do to improve.

● So talk as if you were in a face-to-face conversation.

Techniques of Courtesy

- Be courteous.

If you have worked in business for any length of time, you have probably experienced most of the common telephone discourtesies. You probably know that most of them are not intended as discourtesies but result from ignorance or unconcern. The following review should help you avoid them and incorporate the qualities of business etiquette into your telephone conversations.

- When calling, immediately introduce yourself and ask for the person you want (or explain your purpose).

The recommended procedure when you are calling is to introduce yourself immediately and then to ask for the person with whom you want to talk:

"This is Wanda Tidwell of Tioga Milling Company. May I speak with Mr. José Martinez?"

If you are not certain with whom you should talk, explain the purpose of your call:

"This is Wanda Tidwell of Tioga Milling Company. We have a question about your service warranty. May I talk with the proper executive about it?"

- When receiving a call, identify your company or office; then offer assistance.

When a secretary or someone else who is screening calls answers the telephone, the recommended procedure is to first identify the company or office and then to make a cheerful offer of assistance:

"Rowan Insurance Company. How may I help you?"

"Ms. Santo's office. May I help you?"

When a call goes directly into the office of the executive, the procedure is much the same, except that the executive identifies herself or himself:

"Bartosh Realty. Toby Bartosh speaking. May I help you?"

- Assistants should avoid offending callers by asking misleading questions, by making misleading comments, or

When an assistant answers for an executive (the usual case), special care should be taken not to offend the caller. Following a question like "Who is calling?" by "I am sorry, but Mr. Gordon is not in" leaves the impression that Gordon may be in but does not want to talk with this particular caller. A better procedure would be to state directly "Mr. Gordon is not in right now. May I ask him to return your call?" Or perhaps "May I tell him who called?" or "Can someone else help you?" could be substituted for the latter sentence.

- by being inconsiderate in placing callers on hold. Let the callers choose, and check on the hold status continually.

Especially irritating to callers is being put on hold for unreasonable periods of time. If the person being called is on another line or involved in some other activity, it may be desirable to place the caller on hold. But good business etiquette dictates that the choice should be the caller's. If the hold continues for a period longer than anticipated, the assistant should check back with the caller periodically showing concern and offering assistance. Equally irritating is the practice of having an assistant place a call for an executive and then put the person called on hold until the executive is free to talk. Although it may be efficient to use assistants for such work, as a matter of courtesy and etiquette the executive should be ready to talk the moment the call goes through.

- Assistants often screen calls. They should do this courteously and honestly.

Assistants to busy executives often screen incoming calls. In doing so, they should courteously ask the purpose of the calls. The response might prompt the assistant to refer the caller to a more appropriate person in the company. It also might reveal that the executive has no interest in the subject of the call, in which case the assistant should courteously yet clearly explain this to the caller. If the executive is busy at the moment, the assistant should explain this and either suggest a more appropriate time for a call or promise a callback by the executive. But in no case should the assistant promise a callback that will not be made. Such a breach of etiquette would likely destroy any goodwill between the caller and the company.

Effective Telephone Procedures

- When calling, state your purpose early. Then cover your points systematically. Plan important calls.

At the beginning of a telephone conversation that you have initiated, it is good practice to state the purpose of the call. Then you should cover systematically all the points involved. For really important calls, you should plan your call, even to the point of making notes of the points to cover. Then you should follow your notes to make certain you cover them all.

Courteous procedure is much the same in a telephone conversation as in a face-to-face conversation. You listen when the other person is talking. You refrain from interrupting. You avoid dominating the conversation. And perhaps most important of all, you cover your message quickly, saving time (and money) for all concerned.

- Be considerate, listen, and do not dominate. Use time efficiently.

Effective Voice Mail Techniques

Sometimes when the person you are calling is not available, you will be able to leave a voice message in an electronic voice mailbox. Not only does this save you the time involved in calling back the person you are trying to reach, but it also allows you to leave a more detailed message than you might leave with an assistant. However, you need to be prepared for this to be sure your message is both complete and concise.

- Voice mail is becoming common in business.

You begin the message nearly the same way you would a telephone call. Be as courteous as you would on the telephone and speak as clearly and distinctly as you can. Tell the listener in a natural way your name and affiliation. Begin with an overview of the message and continue with details. If you want the listener to take action, call for it at the end. If you want the listener to return your call, state that precisely, including when you can be reached. Slowly give the number where your call can be returned. Close with a brief goodwill message. For example, as a program coordinator for a professional training organization, you might leave this message in the voice mailbox of one of your participants:

- Use it much as you would any other telephone call.

> This is Ron Ivy from Metroplex Development Institute. I'm calling to remind Ms. Melanie Wilson about the Chief Executive Round Table (CERT) meeting next week (Wednesday, July 20) at the Crescent Hotel in Dallas. Dr. Ken Cooper of the Dallas Aerobics Center will present the program on Executive Health in the 21st Century. We will begin with breakfast at 7:30 AM and conclude with lunch at noon. Some of the CERT members will play golf in the afternoon at Dallas Country Club. If Ms. Wilson would like to join them, I will be glad to make a tee time for her. She can contact me at 940-240-1003 before 5:00 PM this Friday. We look forward to our Chief Executive Round Table meeting next Wednesday.

Wireless Telephones and Their Courteous Use

In recent years the use of wireless telephones has become obiquitous. In fact, according to Cingular Wireless (a major equipment and service provider) by the time this book goes to press, more than half of all Americans will have a wireless telephone. To say the least, the benefits of this technology have greatly expanded our ability to communicate. Even so, their use has become an annoyance to many people. Each of us should be aware of these annoyances and do what we can to reduce them. We can do this by following these suggestions, any one of which can be broken in cases of emergency:

- Wireless telephones are widely used. Their use can be annoying.

1. Turn off the ringer in meetings and other places where it would be disruptive.

2. Do not use the wireless telephone at social gatherings.

3. Do not place the telephone on the table while eating.

4. Avoid talking whenever it will annoy others. (Usually this means when within earshot of others.)

5. Avoid discussing personal or confidential matters when others can hear you.

6. Do not talk in an excessively loud voice.

7. Preferably call from a quiet place, away from other people.

8. If you must talk while around people, be conscious of them. (Don't hold up lines, obstruct the movements of others, or such.)

9. Avoid using the telephone while driving (the law in some states).

- You can reduce these annoyances by following these suggestions.

DICTATING MESSAGES AND REPORTS

Dictating messages and reports is probably one of the most underutilized input methods for writers today. Voice recognition software has been improved to allow continuous speech and short setup periods with little training. Additionally, it works with most standard software applications, and it is inexpensive compared to the value it offers writers. Not only does such technology spell correctly, it can quickly learn specialized vocabularies. And it is generally faster for most people than writing by hand or keying information because most people can speak 140 to 160 words per minute. Although proofreading dictated documents is a bit different because it involves looking for homophones (words that sound alike) rather than misspelled or misused words, some programs offer the user the ability to play back the dictation.

If you haven't started dictating documents yet, one of the best ways to learn is to use voice recognition software to handle your email. If you are using Office XP or higher, you already have the software; you simply need a microphone and a few minutes for training. Two other excellent programs are Dragon NaturallySpeaking and IBM ViaVoice. Once you have the tools, following the steps below will help you could become proficient at dictating.

Techniques of Dictating

Gather the Facts. Your first logical step in dictating is to get all the information you need for the message. This step involves such activities as getting past correspondence from files, consulting with other employees, and ascertaining company policy. Unless you get all the information you need, you will be unable to work without interruption.

Plan the Message. With the facts of the case before you, you next plan the message. You may prefer to do this step in your mind or to jot down a few notes or an outline. Whatever your preference, your goal in this step is to decide what your message will be and how you will present it. In this step, you apply the procedures covered in our earlier review of message and report writing.

Make the Words Flow. Your next step is to talk through the message. Simple as this step appears, you are likely to have problems with it. Thinking out loud even to the computer frightens most of us at first. The result is likely to be slow and awkward dictation.

Overcoming this problem requires self-discipline and practice. You should force yourself to concentrate and to make the words flow. Your goal should be to get the words out—to talk through the message. You need not be too concerned about producing a polished work on the first effort. You will probably need to revise, perhaps several times. After you have forced your way through several messages, your need to revise will decrease and the speed and quality of your dictation will improve.

Speak Clearly. Because your dictation must be heard clearly by your system, you should speak as distinctly as you can. Even small improvements in accuracy—say from 95 percent to 98 percent—will have big payoffs in the time it takes you to complete documents.

Give Paragraphing, Punctuation, and Other Instructions as Needed. How much of the paragraphing, spelling, punctuation, and other mechanics you dictate depends on how well trained your system is. The more often you use the software, the more it knows your dictation style and fewer instructions will be needed. If you take care to spell out words unknown to your system in addition to training your system, it will serve you better. You can see how to dictate effectively in the following illustration.

Play Back Intelligently. Although you should try to talk through the message without interruption, you will sometimes need to stop and get a playback of what you have dictated. But do this only when necessary. More than likely, the need for a

---

- Dictation is an underutilized input method.

- Today's software make the process easy . . .

- and inexpensive.

- You should (1) get all the information you need to avoid interruption later;

- (2) plan the message following the procedures described in preceding chapters);

- (3) talk through the message,

- forcing the words to flow if necessary (you can revise later);

- (4) speak distinctly for improved accuracy;

- (5) give the paragraphing, punctuation, and other instructions as the system needs;

- (6) play back when necessary; and

playback results from confused thinking. When you are learning to dictate, however, some confused thinking is normal. And until you gain experience, you may profit from playbacks.

Proofread for Accuracy. You will find a playback especially helpful at the end of the message to give you a check on the overall effect of your words. Additionally, conducting playbacks while visually reading your final document will help you proofread your document for homophone errors.

● (7) play back to proofread for accuracy, especially checking for homophone errors.

Illustration

Many of the preceding techniques are illustrated in the following transcript of a dictated routine email message. This example shows all the dictator's words, including punctuation, paragraphing, and corrections, that were spoken after the microphone was activated. Note that the dictator spells out words that might not be in the program's vocabulary. However, if the word were the name of a client one expected to have for a long time, the name could be added to the program for future use. Also, note that the program attempts to learn your usage patterns, even the usage of homophones (words that sound alike). For example, if most of the time you used the word *sweet* rather than *suite,* the program would first supply *sweet.* As the software improves and as your dictation speed improves, the program may be able to select the correct word forms based on context. For now, though, careful proofreading is essential.

● Here is the exact transcript of a short confirmation message.

> Dear Payton *spell that* p-a-y-t-o-n *cap that comma new paragraph* Three crates of orchard *hyphen* fresh Florida oranges should be in your store sometime Wednesday morning as they were shipped today by Greene *spell that* g-r-e-e-n-e *cap that* motor *cap that* freight *cap that period new paragraph* As you requested in your August 29 order *comma* the three hundred sixty-one dollars and sixty cents *left paren* invoice *cap that* 14721 *right paren* was credited to your account *period new paragraph* Your customers will go for these large *comma* tasty oranges *comma* I am sure *period* They are the best we have handled in months *period new paragraph* Thanks *comma* Payton *comma* for another opportunity to serve you *period new paragraph* Sincerely *comma new line* Alex

LISTENING

Up to this point, our review of oral communication has been about sending information (talking). Certainly, this is an area in which businesspeople need help. But evidence shows that the receiving side (listening) causes more problems.

● Poor listening is a major cause of miscommunication.

The Nature of Listening

When listening is mentioned, we think primarily of the act of sensing sounds. In human communication, of course, the sounds are mainly spoken words. Viewed from a communication standpoint, however, the listening process involves the addition of filtering and remembering.

● Listening involves sensing, filtering, and remembering.

Sensing. How well we sense the words around us is determined by two factors. One factor is our ability to sense sounds—how well our ears can pick them up. As you know, we do not all hear equally well, although mechanical devices (hearing aids) can reduce our differences in this respect.

The other factor is our attentiveness to listening. More specifically, this is our mental concentration—our will to listen. As noted in Chapter 1, our mental concentration on the communication symbols that our senses can detect varies from moment to moment. It can range from almost totally blocking out those symbols to concentrating on them very intensely. From your own experience, you can recall moments when you were oblivious to the words spoken around you and moments when you listened with all the intensity you could muster. Most of the time, your listening fell somewhere between these extremes.

● How well we sense spoken words is determined by (1) our ability to sense sounds and

● (2) our attentiveness.

Listening Error in a Chain of Communication

Colonel to the executive officer:	"As the general feels the soldiers are unaware of the dangers of drinking impure water, he wishes to explain the matter to them. Have all personnel fall out in fatigues at 1400 hours in the battalion area, where the general will address them. In the event of rain, assemble them in the theater."
Executive officer to company commander:	"By order of the colonel, tomorrow at 1400 hours all personnel will fall out in fatigues in the battalion area if it rains to march to the theater. There the general will talk about their unawareness of the dangers of drinking."
Company commander to lieutenant:	"By order of the colonel, in fatigues the personnel will assemble at the theater at 1400 hours. The general will appear if it rains to talk about the dangers of the unawareness of drinking."
Lieutenant to sergeant:	"Tomorrow at 1400 hours the troops will assemble at the theater to hear the general talk about unawareness of drinking dangerously."
Sergeant to the enlisted personnel:	"Tomorrow at 1400 hours the drunken general will be at the theater in his underwear talking dangerously. We have to go and hear him."

- Filtering is the process of giving symbols meanings through the unique contents of each person's mind.

Filtering. From your study of the communication process in Chapter 1, you know that the filtering process enables you to give meanings to the symbols you sense. In this process, the contents of your mind serve as a sort of filter through which you give meaning to incoming messages. This filter is formed by the unique contents of your mind: your knowledge, emotions, beliefs, biases, experiences, expectations, and such. Thus, you sometimes give messages meanings different from the meanings that others give them.

- Remembering what we hear is a part of listening.

Remembering. Remembering what we hear is the third activity involved in listening. Unfortunately, we retain little of what we hear. We remember many of the comments we hear in casual conversation for only a short time—perhaps for only a few minutes or hours. Some we forget almost as we hear them. According to authorities, we even quickly forget most of the message in formal oral communications (such as speeches), remembering only a fourth after two days.

Improving Your Listening Ability

- To improve your listening, you must want to improve it.

Improving your listening is largely a matter of mental conditioning—of concentrating on the activity of sensing. You have to want to improve it, for listening is a willful act. If you are like most of us, you are often tempted not to listen or you just find it easier not to listen. We human beings tend to avoid work, and listening may be work.

- Be alert. Force yourself to pay attention.

After you have decided that you want to listen better, you must make an effort to pay attention. How you do this will depend on your mental makeup, for the effort requires disciplining the mind. You must force yourself to be alert, to pay attention to the word spoken. Active listening is one technique individuals can use successfully. It involves focusing on what is being said and reserving judgment. Other components include sitting forward and acknowledging with "um-hm" and nodding. Back-channeling is a variation of this technique that groups can use. Users leverage technologies such as chat and blogs to comment on and enhance presentations in real time, which helps keep a sharp focus on what is being said. Whatever technique you choose, improvement requires hard work.

Improve your listening skills by focusing your attention on the speaker and listening actively.

In addition to working on the improvement of your sensing, you should work on the accuracy of your filtering. To do this, you will need to think in terms of what words mean to the speakers that use them rather than what the dictionary says they mean or what they mean in your mind. You must try to think as the speaker thinks—judging the speaker's words by the speaker's knowledge, experiences, viewpoints, and such. Like improving your sensing, improving your filtering requires conscious effort.

- Concentrate on improving your mental filtering.

- Think from the speaker's viewpoint.

Remembering what you hear also requires conscious effort. Certainly, there are limits to what the mind can retain, but authorities agree that few of us come close to them. By taking care to hear what is said and by working to make your filtering process give more accurate meanings to the words you hear, you add strength to the messages you receive. The result should be improved retention.

- Consciously try to remember.

In addition to the foregoing advice, various practical steps may prove helpful. Assembled in a classic document titled, "The Ten Commandments of Listening,"[1] the following list summarizes the most useful of them:

- In addition, follow these practical guidelines (summarized in italics).

1. *Stop talking.* Unfortunately, most of us prefer talking to listening. Even when we are not talking, we are inclined to concentrate on what to say next rather than on listening to others. So you must stop talking before you can listen.

2. *Put the talker at ease.* If you make the talker feel at ease, he or she will do a better job of talking. Then you will have better input to work with.

3. *Show the talker you want to listen.* If you can convince the talker that you are listening to understand rather than oppose, you will help create a climate for information exchange. You should look and act interested. Doing things like reading, looking at your watch, and looking away distracts the talker.

4. *Remove distractions.* The things you do also can distract the talker. So don't doodle, tap with your pencil, shuffle papers, or the like.

5. *Empathize with the talker.* If you place yourself in the talker's position and look at things from the talker's point of view, you will help create a climate of understanding that can result in a true exchange of information.

6. *Be patient.* You will need to allow the talker plenty of time. Remember that not everyone can get to the point as quickly and clearly as you. And do not interrupt. Interruptions are barriers to the exchange of information.

---

[1] To some anonymous author goes a debt of gratitude for these classic and often-quoted comments about listening.

Voice input systems allow writers to concentrate on word choice and message composition, freeing them from typing and spelling concerns. But careful proofreading is still necessary.

7. *Hold your temper.* From our knowledge of the workings of our minds, we know that anger impedes communication. Angry people build walls between each other. They harden their positions and block their minds to the words of others.

8. *Go easy on argument and criticism.* Argument and criticism tend to put the talker on the defensive. He or she then tends to "clam up" or get angry. Thus, even if you win the argument, you lose. Rarely does either party benefit from argument and criticism.

9. *Ask questions.* By frequently asking questions, you display an open mind and show that you are listening. And you assist the talker in developing his or her message and in improving the correctness of meaning.

10. *Stop talking!* The last commandment is to stop talking. It was also the first. All the other commandments depend on it.

From the preceding review it should be clear that to improve your listening ability, you must set your mind to the task. Poor listening habits are ingrained in our makeup. We can alter these habits only through conscious effort.

THE REINFORCING ROLE
OF NONVERBAL COMMUNICATION

● Nonverbal communication accounts for more of a total message than words do.

In your role of either speaker or listener in oral communication, you will need to be aware of the nonverbal—nonword—part of your communication. In both roles, nonverbal communication accounts for a larger part of the total message than do the words you send or receive. Usually, we use nonverbal communication to supplement and reinforce our words. Sometimes, nonverbal communication communicates by itself. Because it is so important to our communication, we will look at the nature of nonverbal communication and some types of it.

Nature of Nonverbal Communication

Nonverbal or nonword communication means all communication that occurs without words. As you can see, the subject is a broad one. And because it is so broad, nonverbal communication is quite vague and imprecise. For instance, a frown on someone's forehead is sometimes interpreted to mean worry. But could it be that the person has a headache? Or is the person in deep thought? No doubt, there could be numerous meanings given to the facial expression.

The number of possible meanings is multiplied even more when we consider the cross-cultural side of communication. As noted in Chapter 16, culture teaches us about body positions, movements, and various factors that affect human relationships (intimacy, space, time, and such). Thus, the meanings we give to nonverbal symbols will vary depending on how our culture has conditioned us.

Because of these numerous meanings, you need to be sensitive to what others intend with nonverbal communication. And you need to make some allowance for error in the meanings you receive from nonverbal symbols. As a listener, you need to go beyond the obvious to determine what nonword symbols mean. As we have said about word symbols, you need to see what people intend with their nonverbal symbols as well. Perhaps one good way to grasp the intent of this suggestion is to look at the intended meanings you have for the nonverbal symbols you use.

Think for a few moments about the smile on your face, a gesture, or such. What do you mean by it? What could it mean to others? Is it exactly as you intend? Could it be interpreted differently? Could someone from a different culture give a different meaning to it? Only if you look at nonverbal symbols through the prism of self-analysis and realize their multiple meaning potential can you get some idea of how they might be interpreted differently. And when you become aware of the many differences, you then can become sensitive to the meaning intended by the nonverbal communication.

In order to become sensitive to the myriad of nonverbal symbols, we will look at some types of nonverbal communication. Specifically, we will study four types of communication that occur without words.

- Nonverbal (nonword) communication means all communication without words. It is broad and imprecise.

- Cross-cultural aspects give many meanings to nonverbal communication.

- Be sensitive to intended nonverbal meanings. Go beyond the obvious.

- Realize that nonverbal symbols can have many meanings.

Types of Nonverbal Communication

Although there are many ways to classify nonverbal communication, we will examine four of the more common types: body language, space, time, and paralanguage. These four types are especially important to our discussion of speaking and listening.

Body Language. Much of what we send to others without using words is sent through the physical movements of our bodies. When we wave our arms and fingers, wrinkle our foreheads, stand erect, smile, gaze at another, wear a coat and tie, and so on, we convey certain meanings; and others convey meanings to us in return. In particular, the face and eyes, gestures, posture, and physical appearance reflect the inner workings of emotions in our bodies.

The face and eyes are by far the most important features of body language. We look to the face and eyes to determine much of the meaning behind body language and nonverbal communication. For example, happiness, surprise, fear, anger, and sadness usually are accompanied by definite facial expressions and eye patterns. You should be aware of these two aspects of body language as you speak and listen to others.

Gestures are another way we send nonword messages through our body parts. *Gestures* are physical movements of our arms, legs, hands, torsos, and heads. Through the movement of each of these body parts, we can accent and reinforce our verbal messages. And we can observe how others punctuate their verbal efforts with gestures. For example, observe the hand movements of another person while he or she is talking. As you observe these gestures, you will get a good picture of the internal emotional state of the person. Moreover, speaking and gestures appear to be linked. In general, the louder someone speaks, the more emphatic the gestures used, and vice versa.

Another area of body language is physical appearance—our clothing, hair, and adornments (jewelry, cosmetics, and such). The appearance of our bodies indicates

- We will look at four common types of nonverbal communication: (1) body language, (2) space, (3) time, and (4) paralanguage.

- Our bodies send nonword messages— through arms, fingers, expressions, posture, and so on.

- The face and eyes are the most important.

- Gestures (physical movements of the arms, legs, torso, and head) send nonword messages.

- Physical appearance— clothing, hair, jewelry, cosmetics, and so on— also communicates.

how our body movements are seen. Consider, for example, how you might perceive a speaker at a formal banquet dressed in faded blue jeans. No doubt, the speaker's gestures, facial features, posture, and such would be perceived in relation to attire. Accordingly, you want to make sure that your appearance fits the situation. And you want to remember that appearance is an important part of the body messages that are sent and received in oral communication.

- Space is another type of nonverbal language.

Space. Another type of nonverbal communication involves space and how it communicates meaning in speaking and listening. How we use space and what we do in certain spaces we create tell much about us. Thus, each of us has a space language just as we do a body language. This space language is crafted by our culture.

- Four types of space exist: (1) intimate, (2) personal, (3) social, and (4) public. Communication behavior differs in each.

Authorities tell us that we create four different types of space: intimate (physical contact to 18 inches); personal (18 inches to 4 feet); social (4 to 12 feet); and public (12 feet to range of seeing and hearing). In each of these spaces, our communication behaviors differ and convey different meanings. For example, consider the volume of your voice when someone is 18 inches from you. Do you shout? Whisper? Now contrast the tone of your voice when someone is 12 feet away. Unquestionably, there is a difference, just because of the distance involved.

- Communication behaviors are learned from cultures.

Our behaviors in each type of space are learned from our cultures. Thus, you will need to be sensitive to the spaces of others—especially those from different cultures. As noted in Chapter 16, when people's attitudes toward space are different, their actions are likely to be misinterpreted.

- Time is a third type of nonverbal communication.

Time. A third type of nonverbal communication involves time. Just as there are body language and space language, there is also a time language. That is, how we give meaning to time communicates to others. To illustrate, think about how you manage your daily schedule. Do you arrive early for most appointments? Do you prioritize telephone calls? Do you prepare agendas for meetings? Your response to time in these ways communicates to others and, of course, others' use of time communicates to you. In terms of nonverbal communication, you should recognize that time orientations are not always the same—especially in the cross-cultural arena—but they do communicate. For Americans, Canadians, and many others from English-speaking countries, time values are monochronic. Monochronic people tend to view time as linear and always moving ahead. They expect events to happen at scheduled times. Polychronic people—such as those from Asian, Arabic, and Spanish-speaking countries—have a more indefinite view of time. Unlike the monochronic person who expects a meeting to start precisely at 9:00 AM, the polychronic person sees a 9:00 AM meeting as an objective to be accomplished if possible. Nevertheless, time orientations become parts of the messages we send to and receive from one another.

- Paralanguage involves *how* we say something.

Paralanguage. *Paralanguage*, meaning "like language," is a fourth type of nonverbal communication. Of all the types, it is the closest to communication with word symbols. It has to do with the sound of a speaker's voice, the "how" of it—those hints and signals in the way words are delivered.

To illustrate, read the following series of statements, emphasizing the underscored word in each.

I am a good communicator.

I am a good communicator.

I am a good communicator.

I am a good communicator.

I am a good communicator.

- You can change the meaning of spoken sentences by accenting different words in each.

By emphasizing the underscored word in each statement, you change the meaning of that statement from the others even though you used the same words. You do so by the way in which the word sequence sounds. As another example, try counting from 1 to 10 a number of times, each time expressing a different emotional state—say anxiety, anger, or happiness. The way you state each sequence of numbers will show what you intend quite accurately.

Paralanguage is the communication effect of the speed, pitch, volume, and connectivity of spoken words. Are they fast or slow? Are they high pitched or deep? Are they loud and forceful or barely audible? Are they smooth or disjointed? These questions are examples of the types you would ask to analyze the nonverbal symbols of paralanguage. The symbols become a part of the meaning that is filtered from a spoken message.

Paralanguage meanings also are conveyed by consistencies and inconsistencies in what is said and how it is said. Depending on the circumstance, a person's voice may or may not be consistent with the intended word meanings. But you should make every effort to avoid inconsistencies that will send a confusing message. Consistency among the words you choose and how you deliver them to create clear meaning should be your goal.

Senders and receivers have certain expectancies about how a message should sound. Whether real or imagined, people infer background factors (race, occupation, etc.); physical appearance (age, height, gender); and personality (introversion, social orientation, etc.) when they receive and filter voice patterns. When you speak, you should do whatever you can to influence these expectancies positively. Many of the suggestions in this chapter and the following one should help you deliver a consistent and effective message. Active listeners will also want to listen between the lines of a spoken message to determine the true meaning a speaker is sending.

- Paralanguage creates meanings because of speed, pitch, volume, and connection of words.

- Degrees of consistency between what and how someone says something convey meaning.

- Expectancies about background, appearance, and personality are part of paralanguage.

Other Types of Nonverbal Communication. Other types of nonverbal communication exist. But the preceding four types are the primary forms. For example, color communicates different meanings to us. Artists, interior decorators, and "image consultants" believe that different colors project different meanings. What meanings do you get from red, yellow, black, blue? That you can answer at all should prove that colors produce meanings in our minds. Applications of the idea to speaking and listening include visual-aid construction, wardrobe, office decor, and the like. Thus, you should give more than casual attention to color as a type of nonverbal communication. Indeed, you will want to create a specific and intended meaning with it.

Still another type of nonverbal communication involves the structure of our physical context—its layout and design. In an office, the physical arrangements—furniture, carpeting, size, location, and decorations—all communicate meaning to us and to others. These elements provide the context for many of our speaking and listening activities. As such, we should consider them as part of the messages we send and receive.

- Two other nonverbal types exist, but they are minor. One is color.

- Another is physical context—office, carpeting, decorations, and such.

SUMMARY BY CHAPTER OBJECTIVES

1. Talking is the oral expression of our knowledge, viewpoints, and emotions. It depends on four critical factors:
   - Voice quality—talking that varies in pitch, delivery, and volume.
   - Speaking style—blending voice quality and personality.
   - Word choice—finding the right word or words for the listener.
   - Adaptation—fitting a message to the mind of a unique listener.
2. In business, you are likely to participate in meetings, some formal and some informal.
   - If you are in charge of a meeting, follow these guidelines.
     — Know parliamentary procedure for formal meetings.
     — Plan the meeting; develop an agenda and circulate it in advance.
     — Follow the plan.
     — Keep the discussion moving.
     — Control those who talk too much.
     — Encourage participation from those who talk too little.
     — Control time, making sure the agenda is covered.
     — Summarize at appropriate times.

1 Discuss talking and its key elements.

2 Explain the techniques for conducting and participating in meetings.

- If you are a participant at a meeting, follow these guidelines:
  — Stay with the agenda; do not stray.
  — Participate fully.
  — But do not talk too much.
  — Cooperate.
  — Be courteous.

3. To improve your telephone and voice mail techniques, consider the following:
   - Cultivate a pleasant voice.
   - Talk as if in a face-to-face conversation.
   - Follow courteous procedures.
     — When calling, introduce yourself and ask for the person you want.
     — State your purpose early.
     — Cover points systematically.
     — When receiving a call, identify your company or office and offer assistance.
     — When answering for the boss, do not offend by asking questions or making comments that might give a wrong impression; and do not neglect callers placed on hold.
     — When screening calls for the boss, be courteous and honest.
     — Listen when the other person is talking.
     — Do not interrupt or dominate.
     — Plan long conversations, and follow the plan.
   - For good communication using voice mail, follow these suggestions:
     — Identify yourself by name and affiliation.
     — Deliver a complete and accurate message.
     — Speak naturally and clearly.
     — Give important information slowly.
     — Close with a brief goodwill message.

4. In dictating messages and reports, follow these suggestions.
   - First, gather all the information you will need so you will not have to interrupt your dictating to get it.
   - Next, plan (think through) the message.
   - Begin the dictation by giving the transcriptionist any special information or instructions needed (enclosures, forms, address, and the like).
   - Then talk through the message.
   - Until you are experienced, force the words to flow—then revise.
   - Remember, also, to speak in a strong, clear voice.
   - Give punctuation and paragraphing in the dictation.
   - Play back only when necessary.
   - Proofread for accuracy.

5. Listening is just as important as talking in oral communication, but it causes more problems.
   - Listening involves how we sense, filter, and retain incoming messages.
   - Most of us do not listen well because we tend to avoid the hard work that good listening requires.
   - You can improve your listening with effort.
   - Put your mind to it and discipline yourself to be attentive.
   - Make a conscious effort to improve your mental filtering of incoming messages; strive to retain what you hear.
   - Follow the practical suggestions offered in "The Ten Commandments of Listening."

6. Nonverbal (nonword) communication is the communication that occurs without words.
   - One major type is body language—the movements of our arms, fingers, facial muscles, and such.
     — Our face and eyes are the most expressive parts of body language.
     — Gestures also send messages.

— Our physical appearance (clothing, cosmetics, jewelry, hairstyle) communicates about us.
- Space is a second major type of nonverbal communication.
  — We create four unique types of spaces: (1) intimate, (2) physical, (3) social, and (4) public.
  — We communicate differently in each space, as determined by our culture.
- How we give meaning to time is a third type of nonverbal communication.
- Meanings the sounds of our voices convey (paralanguage) are a fourth type.
- Color and physical context are minor nonverbal forms.
- In our speaking, we should use nonverbal communication to accent our words.
- In listening, we need to "hear" the nonverbal communication of others.

1. Talking is a natural occurrence, so we should give it little attention. Discuss.

2. How do the elements of talking help us communicate better?

3. Being able to start a conversation is especially important when meeting clients in social settings. Discuss the types of topics that would and would not be appropriate.

4. The people attending a meeting—not the leader—should determine the agenda. Discuss.

5. As meetings should be democratic, everyone present should be permitted to talk as much as he or she wants without interference from the leader. Discuss.

6. Describe an annoying telephone practice that you have experienced or know about (other than the ones discussed in the chapter). Explain and/or demonstrate how it should be corrected.

7. Describe the strengths and weaknesses of voice mail systems with which you are familiar.

8. Use the Internet to gather information and present a report on recent developments in voice recognition.

9. Discuss why we have difficulty in listening.

10. What can you do to improve your listening?

11. Explain how each type of nonverbal communication relates to speaking and to listening.

Meetings

Because group meetings are meaningful only when they concern problems that the participants know about and understand, the following topics for meetings involve campus situations. For one of these topics, develop a specific problem that would warrant a group meeting. (Example: For student government, the problem might be "To determine the weaknesses of student government on this campus and what should be done to correct them.") Then lead the class (or participate) in a meeting on the topic. Class discussion following the meeting should reinforce the text material and bring out the good and bad of the meeting.

a. Student discipline

b. Scholastic dishonesty

c. Housing regulations

d. Student–faculty relations

e. Student government

f. Library

g. Grading standards

h. Attendance policies

i. Varsity athletics

j. Intramural athletics

k. Degree requirements

l. Parking

m. Examination scheduling

n. Administrative policies

o. University calendar

p. Homework requirements

q. Tuition and fees

r. Student evaluation of faculty

s. Community–college relations

t. Maintaining files of old examinations for students

u. Computer availability

Telephoning

Make a list of bad telephone practices that you have experienced or heard about. With a classmate, first demonstrate the bad practice and then demonstrate how you would handle it. Some possibilities: putting a caller on hold tactlessly, harsh greeting, unfriendly voice quality, insulting comments (unintended), attitude of unconcern, cold and formal treatment.

Dictating

Working with the voice recognition feature in Office XP (or any other your instructor specifies) select a writing case from the problems following the chapters on writing, Chapters 6, 7, and 8. Then dictate a message. You may need to train the software before using it. After you have finished your dictation, proofread it carefully. (If you have access to voice recognition software that will play back the message to you, review it one final time.)

Listening

After the class has been divided into two (or more) teams, the instructor reads some factual information (newspaper article, short story, or the like) to only one member of each team. Each of these team members tells what he or she has heard to a second team member, who in turn tells it to a third team member—and so on until the last member of each team has heard the information. The last person receiving the information reports what she or he has heard to the instructor, who checks it against the original message. The team able to report the information with the greatest accuracy wins.

Nonverbal

Using a digital camera or pictures from magazines, get three to five pictures of men and women with different facial expressions (happiness, sadness, anger, etc.) or gestures. Ask those native to your area to identify the emotions or the meanings of the gestures the pictures convey. Then ask at least three others from different countries (preferably different continents) to identify the emotions. Report your results to the class.

CHAPTER FIFTEEN

Public Speaking and Oral Reporting

CHAPTER OBJECTIVES

Upon completing this chapter, you will be able to use good speaking and oral-reporting techniques. To reach this goal, you should be able to

1 Select and organize a subject for effective formal presentation to a specific audience.

2 Describe how personal aspects and audience analysis contribute to formal presentations.

3 Explain the use of voice quality and physical aspects such as posture, walking, facial expression, and gestures in effective oral communication.

4 Plan for visuals (graphics) to support speeches and oral reports.

5 Work effectively with a group in preparing and making a team presentation.

6 Define oral reports and differentiate between them and written reports on the basis of their advantages, disadvantages, and organization.

Formal Speaking

In addition to your informal speaking and listening activities at Mastadon Chemicals, you have more formal ones involving oral communication.

Take last week, for example. Marla Cody (your boss) asked you to do something very special for the company. It seems that each year Mastadon Chemicals awards a $5,000 scholarship to a deserving business student at State University. The award is presented at the business school's annual Honors Day Convocation, usually by Ms. Cody. To show the business school's appreciation for the award, its administration requested that Ms. Cody be the speaker at this year's convocation. But Ms. Cody has a conflicting engagement, so you got the assignment. You responded to the challenge as well as you could, but you were not pleased with the results.

Then, at last month's meeting, Mastadon's executive committee asked you for a special oral report from your department for about the fifth time. This time the report concerned the results of a survey that your department conducted to determine local opinions about a dispute between Mastadon and its union. You did your best, but you felt uneasy about what you were doing.

Such assignments are becoming more and more a part of your work as you move up the administrative ladder at Mastadon. You must try to do them better, for your future promotions are involved. The following review of formal oral presentations (speeches and reports) should help you in this effort.

MAKING FORMAL SPEECHES

The most difficult kind of oral communication for many people is a formal speech. Most of us do not feel comfortable speaking before others, and we generally do a poor job of it. But it need not be this way. With effort, we can improve our speaking. We can do this by learning what good speaking techniques are and then putting those techniques into practice.

- Speeches are difficult for most of us. The following techniques should help you.

Selection of the Topic

Your first step in formal speechmaking is to determine the topic of your presentation. In some cases, you will be assigned a topic, usually one within your area of specialization. In fact, when you are asked to make a speech on a specified topic, it is likely to be because of your knowledge of the topic. In some cases, your choice of topic will be determined by the purpose of your assignment, as when you are asked to welcome a group or introduce a speaker.

- Your topic may be assigned.

If you are not assigned a topic, then you must find one on your own. In your search for a suitable topic, you should be guided by three basic factors. The first is your background and knowledge. Any topic you select should be one with which you are comfortable—one within your areas of proficiency. The second basic factor is the interests of your audience. Selecting a topic that your audience can appreciate and understand is vital to the success of your speech. The third basic factor is the occasion of the speech. Is the occasion a meeting commemorating a historic event? A monthly meeting of an executives' club? An annual meeting of a hairstylists' association? Whatever topic you select should fit the occasion. A speech about Japanese management practices might be quite appropriate for the members of the executives' club, but not for the hairstylists. Your selection should be justified by all three factors.

- If you must select a topic, consider (1) your knowledge, (2) your audience, and (3) the occasion.

Preparation of the Presentation

After you have decided what to talk about, you should gather the information you need for your speech. This step may involve searching through your mind for experiences or ideas, conducting research in a library or in company files, gathering information

- Conduct research to get the information you need.

**"My multimedia presentation is voice-activated.
If it hears a yawn from the audience, it automatically
switches to heavy metal music and throbbing dayglo colors."**

SOURCE: Copyright 2002 by Randy Glasbergen. www.glasbergen.com.

online, or consulting people in your own company or other companies. In short, you do whatever is necessary to get the information you need.

> • Then organize the information.

When you have that information, you are ready to begin organizing your speech. Although variations are sometimes appropriate, you should usually follow the time-honored order of a speech: *introduction, body, conclusion*. This is the order described in the following paragraphs.

> • The greeting usually comes first.

Although not really a part of the speech, the first words usually spoken are the greeting. Your greeting, of course, should fit the audience. "Ladies and gentlemen" is appropriate for a mixed audience; "gentlemen" fits an all-male audience; and "my fellow Rotarians" fits an audience of Rotary Club members. Some speakers eliminate the greeting and begin with the speech, especially in more informal and technical presentations.

> • Gain attention in the opening.

Introduction. The introduction of a speech has much the same goal as the introduction of a written report: to prepare the listeners (or readers) to receive the message. But it usually has the additional goal of arousing interest. Unless you can arouse interest at the beginning, your presentation is likely to fail. The situation is somewhat like that of the sales message. At least some of the people with whom you want to communicate are not likely to be interested in receiving your message. As you will recall from your study of listening, it is easy for a speaker to lose the audience's attention. To prove the point, ask yourself how many times your mind has drifted away from the speaker's words when you have been part of an audience. There is no question about it: You, the speaker, will have to work to gain and hold the attention of your audience.

> • There are many opening possibilities: human interest,

The techniques of arousing interest are limited only by the imagination. One possibility is a human-interest story, for storytelling has strong appeal. For example, a speaker presenting a message about the opportunities available to people with original ideas might open this way: "Nearly 150 years ago, an immigrant boy of 17 walked the streets of our town. He had no food, no money, no belongings except the shabby clothes he wore. He had only a strong will to work—and an idea."

> • humor,

Humor, another possibility, is probably the most widely used technique. To illustrate, an investment broker might begin a speech on investment strategy as follows: "What you want me to give you today is some 'tried and trusted' advice on how to make money in the stock market. This reminds me of the proverbial 'tried and trusted' bank teller. He was trusted; and when they caught him, he was tried." Humor works best and is safest when it is closely related to the subject of your presentation.

> • quotations, questions, and so on.

Other effective ways for gaining attention at the opening are by using quotations and questions. By quoting someone the audience would know and view as credible, you build interest in your topic. You also can ask questions. One kind of question is the rhetorical question—the one everyone answers the same, such as "Who wants to

A Speaker's Classic Putdown of an Unruly Audience

The speaker had covered his subject carefully and thoroughly. But his conclusion, which followed logically from his presentation, was greeted with loud hisses by some members of his audience. Because hisses leave little trace of their origin, the speaker did not know who the dissenters were and could not respond directly to them. So he skillfully handled the situation by saying: "I know of only three creatures that hiss—snakes, geese, and fools. I will leave it to you to determine which of the three we have here."

be freed of burdensome financial responsibilities?" Another kind of question gives you background information on how much to talk about different aspects of your subject. With this kind of question, you must follow through your presentation based on the response. If you had asked "How many of you have IRAs?" and nearly everyone put a hand up, you wouldn't want to talk about the importance of IRAs. You could skip that part of your presentation, spending more time on another aspect, such as managing your IRA effectively.

Yet another possibility is the startling statement, which presents facts and ideas that awaken the mind. Illustrating this possibility is the beginning of a speech to an audience of merchants on a plan to reduce shoplifting: "Last year, right here in our city, in your stores, shoplifters stole over $3.5 million of your merchandise! And most of you did nothing about it."

In addition to arousing interest, your opening should lead into the theme of your speech. In other words, it should set up your message as the examples above do.

- The opening should set up your subject.

Following the attention-gaining opening, it is appropriate to tell your audience the subject (theme) for your speech. In fact, in cases where your audience already has an interest in what you have to say, you can begin here and skip the attention-gaining opening. Presentations of technical topics to technical audiences typically begin this way. Whether you lead into a statement of your topic or begin with it, that statement should be clear and complete.

- Tell the subject of your speech . . .

Because of the nature of your subject, you may find it undesirable to reveal a position early. In such cases, you may prefer to move into your subject indirectly—to build up your case before revealing your position. This inductive pattern may be especially desirable when your goal is to persuade—when you need to move the views of your audience from one position to another. But in most business-related presentations you should make a direct statement of your theme early in the speech.

- unless you have reason not to, as when you must persuade.

Body. Organizing the body of your speech is much like organizing the body of a report (see Chapter 10). You take the whole and divide it into comparable parts. Then you take those parts and divide them. You continue to divide as far as it is practical to do so. In speeches, however, you are more likely to use factors rather than time, place, or quantity as the basis of division because in most speeches your presentation is likely to be built around issues and questions that are subtopics of the subject. Even so, time, place, and quantity subdivisions are possibilities.

- Organize most speeches by factors, as you would a report.

You need to emphasize the transitions between the divisions because, unlike the reader who can see them, the listener may miss them if they are not stressed adequately. Without clear transitions, you may be talking about one point and your listener may be relating those ideas to your previous point.

- Emphasize transitions between parts.

Conclusion. Like most reports, the speech usually ends by drawing a conclusion. Here you bring all that you have presented to a head and achieve whatever goal the speech has. You should consider including these three elements in your close: (1) a

- The ending usually (1) restates the subject, (2) summarizes key points, and (3) draws a conclusion.

Good speakers project their personal qualities—confidence, sincerity, friendliness, enthusiasm, and interest.

restatement of the subject, (2) a summary of the key points developed in the presentation, and (3) a statement of the conclusion (or main message). Bringing the speech to a climactic close—that is, making the conclusion the high point of the speech—is usually effective. Present the concluding message in strong language—in words that gain attention and will be remembered. In addition to concluding with a summary, you can give an appropriate quote, use humor, and call for action. The following close of a speech comparing Japanese and American management techniques illustrates this point: "These facts make my conclusion crystal clear. We are not Japanese. We do not have the Japanese culture. Most Japanese management methods have not worked—cannot work—will not work in our society."

Determination of the Presentation Method

- Choose one of these presentation methods:

With the speech organized, you are ready to prepare its presentation. At this time, you need to decide on your method of presentation—that is, whether to present the speech extemporaneously, to memorize it, or to read it.

- (1) extemporaneous presentation (thorough preparation, uses notes, rehearsed),

Presenting Extemporaneously. Extemporaneous presentation is by far the most popular and effective method. With this method, you first thoroughly prepare your speech, as outlined above. Then you prepare notes and present the speech from them. You usually rehearse, making sure you have all the parts clearly in mind, but you make no attempt to memorize. Extemporaneous presentations generally sound natural to the listeners, yet they are (or should be) the product of careful planning and practice.

- (2) memorizing, or

Memorizing. The most difficult method is memorizing. If you are like most people, you find it hard to memorize a long succession of words. And when you do mem-

436   PART 5   Other Forms of Business Communication

Presentation Delivery Tools Help You Convey Your Message Effectively

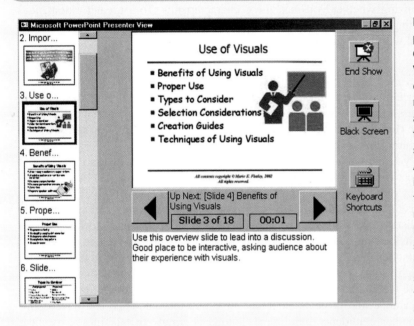

Delivery tools can help you to a better job preparing and delivering oral presentations. One tool within PowerPoint, Presenters View, should help you plan, practice, and deliver good presentations. You can see its major tools in the screenshot here. As your audience sees only the slide, you are seeing the presenters view. You see the current slide being projected and its slide notes. Additionally, you see the title to the upcoming slide as well as the elapsed time since the beginning of the presentation. Furthermore, along the right column are several buttons that allow you to start or end the show on one click, blackout that screen to bring the attention back to you, and other shortcut keys. As the presenter, you have the flexibility to skip slides or change the ordering on the fly. The slider bar at the left enables you easily to pull up slides during question and answer sessions as well.

orize, you are likely to memorize words rather than meanings. Thus, when you make the speech, if you miss a word or two, you become confused—and so does your speech. You even may become panic-stricken.

Probably few of the speakers who use this method memorize the entire speech. Instead, they memorize key passages and use notes to help them through the speech. A delivery of this kind is a cross between an extemporaneous presentation and a memorized presentation.

Reading. The third presentation method is reading. Unfortunately, most of us tend to read aloud in a dull monotone. We also miss punctuation marks, fumble over words, lose our place, and so on. Of course, many speakers overcome these problems, and with effort you can too. One effective way is to practice with a recorder and listen to yourself. Then you can be your own judge of what you must do to improve your delivery. You would be wise not to read speeches until you have mastered this presentation method. In most settings, it is a breach of etiquette to read. Your audience is likely to be insulted, and reading is unlikely to be as well received as an extemporaneous delivery. However, when you are in a position where you will be quoted widely, such as president of the United States or the CEO of a major company, reading from a carefully prepared speech is recommended.

- (3) reading.

Consideration of Personal Aspects

A preliminary to good speechmaking is to analyze yourself as a speaker. In oral presentations you, the speaker, are a very real part of the message. The members of your audience take in not only the words you communicate but also what they see in you.

- A logical preliminary to speechmaking is to analyze yourself as a speaker. You are a part of the message.

And what they see in you can significantly affect the meanings that develop in their minds. Thus, you should carefully evaluate your personal effect on your message. You should do whatever you can to detect and overcome your shortcomings and to sharpen your strengths.

The following summary of characteristics that should help you as a speaker may prove useful, but you probably already know what they are. To some extent, the problem is recognizing whether you lack these characteristics. To a greater extent, it is doing something about acquiring them. The following review should help you pinpoint and deal with your problem areas.

- You should seek the following four characteristics:

Confidence.
A primary characteristic of effective oral reporting is confidence—your confidence in yourself and the confidence of your audience in you. The two are complementary, for your confidence in yourself tends to produce an image that gives your audience confidence in you; and your audience's confidence in you can give you a sense of security that increases your confidence in yourself.

- (1) Having confidence in yourself is important. So is having the confidence of your audience.

Typically, you earn your audience's confidence over periods of association. But there are things you can do to project an image that builds confidence. For example, preparing your presentation diligently and practicing it thoroughly gives you confidence in yourself. That confidence leads to more effective communication, which increases your listeners' confidence in you. Another confidence-building technique is an appropriate physical appearance. Unfair and illogical as it may seem, certain types of dress and hairstyles create strong images in people's minds, ranging from highly favorable to highly unfavorable. Thus, if you want to communicate effectively, you should analyze the audience you seek to reach. And you should work to develop the physical appearance that projects an image in which that audience can have confidence. Yet another confidence-building technique is simply to talk in strong, clear tones. Such tones do much to project an image of confidence. Although most people can do little to change their natural voice, they can use sufficient volume.

- You must earn the confidence of your audience, project the right image, and talk in a strong, clear voice.

Sincerity.
Your listeners are quick to detect insincerity. And if they detect it in you, they are likely to give little weight to what you say. On the other hand, sincerity is valuable to conviction, especially if the audience has confidence in your ability. The way to project an image of sincerity is clear and simple: You must *be* sincere. Pretense of sincerity is rarely successful.

- (2) Sincerity is vital. You convey an image of sincerity by being sincere.

Thoroughness.
Generally, a thorough presentation is better received than a scanty or hurried presentation. Thorough coverage gives the impression that time and care have been taken, and this tends to make the presentation believable. But thoroughness can be overdone. Too much detail can drown your listeners in a sea of information. The secret is to leave out unimportant information. This, of course, requires good judgment. You must ask yourself just what your listeners need to know and what they do not need to know. Striking such a balance is the secret to achieving integrity in your presentation.

- (3) Thoroughness—giving your listeners all they need—helps your image.

Friendliness.
A speaker who projects an image of friendliness has a significant advantage in communicating. People simply like friendly people, and they are generally receptive to what such people say. Like sincerity, friendliness is hard to feign and must be honest to be effective. Both are parts of the conventions of business etiquette. Most people are genuinely friendly. Some, however, are just not able to project a genuinely friendly image. With a little self-analysis and a little mirror watching as you practice speaking, you can find ways of improving your projection of your friendliness.

- (4) Projecting an image of friendliness helps your communication effort.

These are but a few of the characteristics that should assist you as a speaker. There are others: *interest, enthusiasm, originality, flexibility*, and so on. But the ones dis-

cussed are the most significant and the ones that most speakers need to work on. Through self-analysis and dedicated effort, you can improve your speaking ability.

Audience Analysis

One requirement of good speechmaking is to know your audience. You should study your audience both before and during the presentation.

Preliminary Analysis. Analyzing your audience before the presentation requires that you size it up—that you search for audience characteristics that could affect how you should present your speech.

For example, the size of your audience is likely to influence how formal or informal your speech should be. As a rule, large audiences require more formality. Personal characteristics of your audience, such as age, gender, education, experience, and knowledge of subject matter, also should influence how you make your speech— affecting the words, illustrations, and level of detail you use. Like writing, speeches should be adapted to the audience. And the more you know about the audience, the better you will adapt your presentation to them.

Analysis during Presentation. Your audience analysis should continue as you make the speech. *Feedback* is information about how your listeners are receiving your words. Armed with this information, you can adjust your presentation to improve the communication result.

Your eyes and ears will give you feedback information. For example, facial expressions will tell you how your listeners are reacting to your message. Smiles, blank stares, and movements will give you an indication of whether they understand, agree with, or accept it. You can detect from sounds coming (or not coming) from them whether they are listening. If questions are in order, you can learn directly how your

- You should know your audience.

- Size up the audience in advance. Look for audience characteristics that will affect your speech—things like the size, gender, age, education, and knowledge of the audience.

- Analyze audience reactions during the speech (called *feedback*). Facial expressions, movements, and noises give you feedback information that helps you adapt to the audience.

message is coming across. In general, you can learn much from your audience by being alert; and what you learn can help you make a better speech.

Appearance and Physical Actions

- Your audience forms impressions from these six factors:

As your listeners hear your words, they are looking at you. What they see is a part of the message and can affect the success of your speech. What they see, of course, is you and what surrounds you. In your efforts to improve the effects of your oral presentations, you should understand the communication effects of what your listeners see. Some of the effects that were mentioned in Chapter 14 are expanded on here because they are particularly important to speeches and oral reports.

The Communication Environment. Much of what your audience sees is the physical things that surround you as you speak: the stage, lighting, background, and so on. These things tend to create a general impression. Although not visual, outside noises have a related influence. For the best communication results, the factors in your communication environment should contribute to your message, not detract from it. Your own experience as a listener will tell you what factors are important.

- (1) all that surrounds you (stage, lighting, and the like),

- (2) your personal appearance,

Personal Appearance. Your personal appearance is a part of the message your audience receives. Of course, you have to accept the physical traits you have, but most of us do not need to be at a disadvantage in appearance. All that is necessary is to use what you have appropriately. Specifically, you should dress in a manner appropriate for the audience and the occasion. Be clean and well groomed. Use facial expressions and physical movements to your advantage. Just how you should use facial expressions and physical movements is described in the following paragraphs.

- (3) your posture,

Posture. Posture is likely to be the most obvious of the things that your audience sees in you. Even listeners not close enough to detect such things as facial expressions and eye movements can see the general form of the body.

You probably think that no one needs to tell you about good posture. You know it when you see it. The trouble is that you are not likely to see it in yourself. One solution is to have others tell you whether your posture needs improvement. Another is to practice speaking before a mirror or watch yourself on video.

In your efforts to improve your posture, keep in mind what must go on within your body to form a good posture. Your body weight must be distributed in a way consistent with the impression you want to make. You should keep your body erect without appearing stiff and comfortable without appearing limp. You should maintain a poised, alert, and communicative bearing. And you should do all this naturally. The great danger with posture is an appearance of artificiality.

- (4) your manner of walking,

Walking. Your audience also forms an impression from the way you walk before it. A strong, sure walk to the speaker's position conveys an impression of confidence. Hesitant, awkward steps convey the opposite impression. Walking during the presentation can be good or bad, depending on how you do it. Some speakers use steps forward and to the side to emphasize points. Too much walking, however, attracts attention and detracts from the message. You would be wise to walk only when you are reasonably sure that this will have the effect you want. You would not want to walk away from a microphone.

- (5) facial expressions (smiles, frowns, eye contact), and

Facial Expression. As noted in Chapter 14, probably the most apparent and communicative physical movements are facial expressions. The problem, however, is that you may unconsciously use facial expressions that convey unintended meanings. For example, if a frightened speaker tightens the jaw unconsciously and begins to grin, the effect may be an ambiguous image that detracts from the entire communication effort. A smile, a grimace, and a puzzled frown all convey clear messages. Without question, you should use these effective communication devices.

Eye contact is important. The eyes, which have long been considered "mirrors of the soul," provide most listeners with information about the speaker's sincerity, goodwill, and flexibility. Some listeners tend to shun speakers who do not look at them. On the other hand, discriminate eye contact tends to show that you have a genuine interest in your audience.

Gestures. Like posture, gestures contribute to the message you communicate. Just what they contribute, however, is hard to say, for they have no definite or clear-cut meanings. A clenched fist, for example, certainly adds emphasis to a strong point. But it also can be used to show defiance, make a threat, or signify respect for a cause. And so it is with other gestures. They register vague meanings, as discussed in Chapter 14.

● (6) gestures.

Even though gestures have vague meanings, they are strong, natural helps to speaking. It appears natural, for example, to emphasize a plea with palms up and to show disagreement with palms down. Raising first one hand and then the other reinforces a division of points. Slicing the air with the hand shows several divisions. Although such gestures are generally clear, we do not all use them in exactly the same way.

● Gestures have vague meanings, but they communicate.

In summary, it should be clear that physical movements can help your speaking. Just which physical movements you should use, however, is hard to say. The appropriateness of physical movements is related to personality, physical makeup, and the size and nature of the audience. A speaker appearing before a formal group should generally use relatively few physical movements. A speaker appearing before an informal group should use more. Which physical movements you should use on a given occasion is a matter for your best judgment.

● In summary, your physical movements help your speaking.

Use of Voice

Good voice is an obvious requirement of good speaking. Like physical movements, the voice should not hinder the listener's concentration on the message. More specifically, it should not detract attention from the message. Voices that cause such difficulties generally fall into these areas of fault: (1) lack of pitch variation, (2) lack of variation in speed, (3) lack of vocal emphasis, and (4) unpleasant voice quality. Although these areas are mentioned in Chapter 14, we will examine them here because of their key significance to formal oral communication.

● Good voice is a requirement of good speaking. Four faults affect voice:

Lack of Pitch Variation. Speakers who talk in monotones are not likely to hold the interest of their listeners for long. Since most voices are capable of wide variations in pitch, the problem usually can be corrected. The failure to vary pitch generally is a matter of habit—of voice patterns developed over years of talking without being aware of their effect.

● (1) lack of variation in pitch (usually a matter of habit),

Lack of Variation in Speaking Speed. Determining how fast to talk is a major problem. As a general rule, you should present the easy parts of your message at a fairly fast rate and the hard parts and the parts you want to emphasize at a slower rate. The reason for varying the speed of presentation should be apparent: it is more interesting. A slow presentation of easy information is irritating; hard information presented fast may be difficult to understand.

● (2) lack of variation in speed (cover the simple quickly, the hard slowly),

A problem related to the pace of speaking is the incorrect use of pauses. Properly used, pauses emphasize upcoming subject matter and are effective means of gaining attention. But frequent pauses for no reason are irritating and break the listeners' concentration. Pauses become even more irritating when the speaker fills them in with distracting nonwords such as *uh, you know,* and *OK.*

Lack of Vocal Emphasis. A secret of good speaking is to give words their proper emphasis by varying the manner of speaking. You can do this by (1) varying the pitch of your voice, (2) varying the pace of your presentation, and (3) varying the volume of your voice. As the first two techniques have already been discussed, only the use of voice volume requires comment here.

● (3) lack of vocal emphasis (gain emphasis by varying pitch, pace, and volume), and

You must talk loudly enough for your entire audience to hear you, but not too loudly. Thus, the loudness—voice volume—for a large audience should be greater

Mark Twain on "Knowing When to Stop Talking"

This Mark Twain story carries a vital message for windy speakers:

> Some years ago in Hartford, we all went to church one hot sweltering night to hear the annual report of Mr. Hawley, a city missionary who went around finding people who needed help and didn't want to ask for it. He told of the life in cellars, where poverty resided; he gave instances of the heroism and devotion of the poor. "When a man with millions gives," he said, "we make a great deal of noise. It's noise in the wrong place, for it's the widow's mite that counts." Well, Hawley worked me up to a great pitch. I could hardly wait for him to get through. I had $400 in my pocket. I wanted to give that and borrow more to give. You could see greenbacks in every eye. But instead of passing the plate then, he kept on talking and talking, and as he talked it grew hotter and hotter, and we grew sleepier and sleepier. My enthusiasm went down, down, down, down—$100 at a clip—until finally, when the plate did come around, I stole ten cents out of it. It all goes to show how a little thing like this can lead to crime.

than that for a small audience. Regardless of audience size, however, variety in voice volume is good for interest and emphasis. It produces contrast, which is one way of emphasizing the subject matter. Some speakers incorrectly believe that the only way to show emphasis is to get louder and louder. But you can also show emphasis by going from loud to soft. The contrast with what has gone on earlier provides the emphasis. Again, variety is the key to making the voice more effective.

- (4) unpleasant voice (improvement is often possible).

Unpleasant Voice Quality. It is a hard fact of communication that some voices are more pleasant than others. Fortunately, most voices are reasonably pleasant. But some are raspy, nasal, or unpleasant in another way. Although therapy often can improve such voices, some speakers must live with them. But concentrating on variations in pitch, speed of delivery, and volume can make even the most unpleasant voice acceptable.

- You can correct the foregoing faults through self-analysis and work.

Improvement through Self-Analysis and Imitation. You can overcome any of the foregoing voice faults through self-analysis. In this day of recorders, it is easy to hear yourself talk. Since you know good speaking when you hear it, you should be able to improve your vocal presentation. One of the best ways to improve your presentation skills is through watching others. Watch your instructors, your peers, television personnel, professional speakers, and anyone else who gives you an opportunity. Analyze these speakers to determine what works for them and what does not. Imitate those good techniques that you think would help you and avoid the bad ones. Take advantage of any opportunity you have to practice speaking.

Use of Visuals (Graphics)

- Visuals (graphics) can sometimes help overcome the limitations of spoken words.

The spoken word is severely limited in communicating. Sound is here briefly and then gone. A listener who misses the vocal message may not have a chance to hear it again. Because of this limitation, speeches often need strong visual support: charts, tables, film, and the like. Visuals (graphics) may be as vital to the success of a speech as the words themselves.

- Use visuals for the hard parts of the message.

Proper Use of Design. Effective visuals are drawn from the message. They fit the one speech and the one audience.

In selecting visuals, you should search through your presentation for topics that appear vague or confusing. Whenever a visual of some kind will help eliminate vagueness or confusion, you should use it. You should use visuals to simplify complex information and improve cohesiveness, as well as to emphasize or add interest. Visuals are truly a part of your message, and you should look at them as such.

After deciding that a topic deserves visual help, you determine what form that help should take. That is, should the visual be a chart, a diagram, a picture, or what? You should select your visuals primarily on the basis of their ability to communicate content. Simple and obvious as this suggestion may appear, people violate it all too often. They select visuals more for appearance and dramatic effect than for communication effect.[1]

- Use the type of visual (chart, diagram, picture) that communicates the information best.

Types to Consider. Because no one type of visual is best for all occasions, you should have a flexible attitude toward visuals. You should know the strengths and weaknesses of each type, and you should know how to use each type effectively.

In selecting visuals, you should keep in mind the available types. You will mainly consider the various types of graphics—the charts, line graphs, tables, diagrams, and pictures—discussed in Chapter 13. Each of these types has its strengths and weaknesses and can be displayed in various ways, generally classified as nonprojected or projected. Nonprojected techniques include such media as posters, flip charts, models, handouts, and such; projected techniques include slides, transparencies, computer projections, and such.

- Select from the various available types of visuals.

Audience Size, Cost, and Ease of Preparation Considerations. Your choice of visuals also should be influenced by the audience size and formality, the cost of preparing and using the media (visuals), and the ease and time of preparation. The table below illustrates how the different media fare on these dimensions, helping guide you to the best choice for your particular needs.

	Media	Image Quality	Audience Size	Cost	Ease of Preparation
Nonprojected	Poster	Very good	Small	$$	Medium
	Flip chart	Good	Small	$	Short
	Presentation board	Good	Small	$	Short
	Real object or model	Very good	Small	$–$$$$	Short to long
	Chalkboard or whiteboard	Fair	Medium	$	None
	Photos	Very good	Medium	$$	Short to medium
	Handouts	Excellent	Large	$–$$	Short to long
Projected	35mm slides	Very good	Large	$	Medium
	Overhead transparencies	Very good	Medium	$	Short
	Visual presenters	Very good	Medium	None	None
	TVs/VCRs	Excellent	Medium to large	$–$$$$	Short to long
	Computer projection	Good	Medium to large	None	Short to long

Techniques in Using Visuals. Visuals usually carry key parts of the message. Thus, they are points of emphasis in your presentation. You blend them in with your words to communicate the message. How you do this is to some extent an individual matter, for techniques vary. They vary so much, in fact, that it would be hard to present a meaningful summary of them. It is more meaningful to present a list of dos and don'ts. Such a list follows:

- Make the visuals points of interest in your presentation.

- Make certain that everyone in the audience can see the visuals. Too many or too-light lines on a chart, for example, can be hard to see. An illustration that is too small can be meaningless to people far from the speaker.

- Here are specific suggestions for using visuals.

- Explain the visual if there is any likelihood that it will be misunderstood.

- Organize the visuals as a part of the presentation. Fit them into the presentation plan.

---

[1] For a revealing review on the strengths and weaknesses of slideware, see "Learning to Love PowerPoint" by David Byrne and "Power Corrupts. PowerPoint Corrupts. Absolutely." by Edward R. Tufte, both in *Wired,* September 2003.

- Emphasize the visuals. Point to them with physical action and words.
- Talk to the audience—not to the visuals. Look at the visuals only when the audience should look at them.
- Avoid blocking the listeners' views of the visuals. Make certain that the listeners' views are not blocked by lecterns, pillars, chairs, and such. Take care not to stand in anyone's line of vision.

A Summary List of Speaking Practices

- This review has covered the high points of speaking.

The foregoing review of business speaking has been selective, for the subject is broad. In fact, entire books have been devoted to it. But this review has covered the high points, especially those that you can easily transfer into practice. Perhaps even more practical is the following list of what to do and not to do in speaking.

- This summary checklist of good and bad speaking practices should prove helpful.

- Organize the speech so that it leads the listeners' thoughts logically to the conclusion.
- Use language specifically adapted to the audience.
- Articulate clearly, pleasantly, and with proper emphasis. Avoid mumbling and the use of nonwords such as *ah, er, uh,* and *OK.*
- Speak correctly, using accepted grammar and pronunciation.
- Maintain an attitude of alertness, displaying appropriate enthusiasm and confidence.
- Employ body language to best advantage. Use it to emphasize points and to assist in communicating concepts and ideas.
- Be relaxed and natural. Avoid stiffness or rigidity of physical action.
- Look the listeners in the eye and talk directly to them.
- Keep still. Avoid excessive movements, fidgeting, and other signs of nervousness.
- Punctuate the presentation with reference to visuals. Make them a part of the speech text.
- Even when faced with hostile questions or remarks, keep your temper. To lose your temper is to lose control of the presentation.
- Move surely and quickly to the conclusion. Do not leave a conclusion dangling, repeat unnecessarily, or appear unable to close.

TEAM (COLLABORATIVE) PRESENTATIONS

- Group presentations require individual speaking skills plus planning for collaboration. Adapt the ideas on collaborative writing in Chapter 10 to team presentations.

Another type of presentation you may be asked to give is a group or team presentation. To give this type of presentation, you will need to use all you have learned about giving individual speeches. Also, you will need to use many of the topics discussed in Chapter 10 on collaborative writing groups. But you will need to adapt the ideas to an oral presentation setting. Some of the adaptations should be obvious. We will mention others to which you should give special thought in your team presentation.

- Plan for the order of the presentation and each member's part.

First, you will need to take special care to plan the presentation—to determine the sequence of the presentation as well as the content of each team member's part. You also will need to select carefully supporting examples to build continuity from one part of the presentation to the next.

- Plan for the physical factors.

Groups should plan for the physical aspects of the presentation, too. You should coordinate the type of delivery, use of notes, graphics, and styles and colors of attire to present a good image of competence and professionalism. And you should plan transitions so that the team will appear coordinated.

- Plan for the physical staging.

Another presentation aspect—physical staging—is important as well. Team members should know where to sit or stand, how visuals will be handled, how to change or adjust microphones, and how to enter and leave the speaking area.

In oral presentations, appropriately handled visuals can be effective in communicating messages clearly.

Attention to the close of the presentation is especially strategic. Teams need to decide who will present the close and what will be said. If a summary is used, the member who presents it should attribute key points to appropriate team members. If there is to be a question-and-answer session, the team should plan how to conduct it. For example, will one member take the questions and direct them to a specific team member? Or will the audience be permitted to ask questions to specific members? Some type of final note of appreciation or thanks needs to be planned with all the team nodding in agreement or acknowledging the final comment in some way.

- Plan for the close.

In all of their extra planning activities, teams should not overlook the need to plan for rehearsal time. Teams should consider practicing the presentation in its entirety several times as a group before the actual presentation. During these rehearsals, individual members should critique thoroughly each other's contributions, offering specific ways to improve. After first rehearsal sessions, outsiders (nonteam members) might be asked to view the team's presentation and critique the group. Moreover, the team might consider videotaping the presentation so that all members can evaluate it. In addition to a more effective presentation, the team can enjoy the by-products of group cohesion and *esprit de corps* by rehearsing the presentation. Successful teams know the value of rehearsing and will build such activity into their presentation planning schedules.

- Plan to rehearse the presentation.

These points may appear trivial, but careful attention to them will result in a polished, coordinated team presentation.

REPORTING ORALLY

A special form of speech is the oral report. You are more likely to make oral reports than speeches in business, and the oral reports you make are likely to be important to you. Unfortunately, most of us have had little experience and even less instruction in oral reporting. Thus, the following review should be valuable to you.

- The oral report is a form of speech.

A Definition of Oral Reports

- An oral report is defined as an oral presentation of factual information.

In its broadest sense, an oral report is any presentation of factual information and its interpretation using the spoken word. A business oral report would logically limit coverage to factual business information. By this definition, oral business reports cover much of the information and analysis exchanged daily in the conduct of business. They vary widely in formality. At one extreme, they cover the most routine and informal reporting situations. At the other, they include highly formal and proper presentations. Because the more informal oral exchanges are little more than routine conversations, the emphasis in the following pages is on the more formal ones. Clearly, these are the oral reports that require the most care and skill and are the most deserving of study.

Differences between Oral and Written Reports

- Oral reports differ from written reports in three ways:

Oral reports are much like written reports, so there is little need to repeat much of the previously presented material on reports. Instead, we will focus on the most significant differences between oral and written reports. Three in particular stand out.

- (1) writing and speaking each has special advantages and disadvantages;

Visual Advantages of the Written Word. The first significant difference between oral and written reports is that writing permits greater use of visuals to communication than does speaking. With writing, you can use paragraphing to show readers the structure of the message and to make the thought units stand out. In addition, you can use punctuation to show relationships, subordination, and qualification. These techniques improve the communication effect of the entire message.

On the other hand, when you make an oral presentation, you cannot use any of these techniques. However, you can use techniques peculiar to oral communication. For example, you can use inflection, pauses, volume emphasis, and changes in the rate of delivery. Depending on the situation, the techniques used in both oral and written reports are effective in assisting communication. But the point is that the techniques are different.

- (2) the speaker controls the pace of an oral report, and the reader controls the pace of a written report; and

Reader Control of Written Presentation. A second significant difference between oral and written reports is that the readers of a written report, unlike the listeners to an oral report, control the pace of the communication. They can pause, reread, change their rate of reading, or stop as they choose. Since the readers set the pace, writing can be complex and still communicate. However, since the listeners to an oral report cannot control the pace of the presentation, they must grasp the intended meaning as the speaker presents the words. Because of this limiting factor, good oral reporting must be relatively simple.

- (3) written reports place more stress on correctness.

Emphasis on Correctness in Writing. A third significant difference between oral and written reports is the different degrees of correctness that they require. Because written reports are likely to be inspected carefully, you are likely to work for a high degree of correctness when you prepare them. That is, you are likely to follow carefully the recognized rules of grammar, punctuation, sentence structure, and so on. When you present oral reports, on the other hand, you may be more lax about following these rules. One reason is that usually oral reports are not recorded for others to inspect at their leisure. Another is that oral communication standards of correctness are less rigid than written communication standards. This statement does not imply that you should avoid good language in oral communication, however.

The differences between writing and speaking—visual aspects, reader control, and correctness—can become planning parts to improve your oral report. You will need to identify these advantages of written reports as barriers to your oral report. You will then need to think of ways to overcome them. Such a process is an essential preliminary step to the actual planning of oral reports.

Planning the Oral Report

As with written reports, planning is the logical first step in your work on oral reports. For short, informal oral reports, planning may be minimal. But for the more formal oral reports, particularly those involving audiences of more than one, proper planning is likely to be as involved as that for a comparable written report.

• Planning is the first step in preparing oral reports.

Determination of Report Objective. Logically, your first task in planning an oral report is to determine your objective. As described for the written report in Chapter 10, you should state the report objective in clear, concise language. Then you should clearly state the factors involved in achieving this objective. This procedure gives you a guide to the information you must gather and to the framework around which you will build your presentation.

• First determine the objective and what must be done to reach it.

In determining your report objective, you must be aware of your general objective. That is, you must decide on your general purpose in making the presentation. Is it to persuade? To inform? To recommend? This decision will have a major influence on your development of material for presentation and perhaps even on the presentation itself.

Organization of Content. The procedure for organizing oral reports is similar to that for organizing written reports. You have the choice of using either the direct or indirect order. Even so, the same information is not necessarily presented in the same way orally and in writing. Time pressure, for example, might justify direct presentation for an oral report on a problem that, presented in writing, might be better arranged in the indirect order. Readers in a hurry can always skip to the conclusion or ending of the report. Listeners do not have this choice.

• Next organize content. Either the indirect or direct order is all right,

Although oral reports may use either the direct or indirect order, the indirect is the most logical order and by far the most widely used order. Because your audience is not likely to know the problem well, introductory remarks are needed to prepare it to receive your message. In addition, you may need such remarks to arouse interest, stimulate curiosity, or impress the audience with the importance of the subject. The main goals of the introductory remarks are to state the purpose, define unfamiliar terms, explain limitations, describe scope, and generally cover all the necessary introductory subjects (see discussion of introduction, Chapter 11).

• but the indirect order is more common.

In the body of the oral report, you should work toward the objective you have set. Here, too, the oral report closely resembles the written report. Division of subject matter into comparable parts, logical order, introductory paragraphs, concluding paragraphs, and the like are equally important to both forms.

• The organization of oral and written reports is much the same, except that oral reports usually have a closing summary.

The major difference in the organization of the written and the oral report is in the ending. Both forms may end with a conclusion, a recommendation, a summary, or a combination of the three. But the oral report is likely to have a final summary, whether or not it has a conclusion or a recommendation. In a sense, this final summary serves the purpose of an executive summary by bringing together all the really important information, analyses, conclusions, and recommendations in the report. It also assists the memory by emphasizing the points that should stand out. Oral and nonverbal emphasis techniques should help memory as well.

SUMMARY BY CHAPTER OBJECTIVES

1. Consider the following suggestions in selecting and organizing a speech.
   - Begin by selecting an appropriate topic—perhaps one in your area of specialization and of interest to your audience.
   - Organize the message (probably by introduction, body, conclusion).
   - Consider an appropriate greeting ("Ladies and Gentlemen," "Friends").
   - Design the introduction to meet these goals:
     — Arouse interest with a story, humor, or such.
     — Introduce the subject (theme).
     — Prepare the reader to receive the message.

1 Select and organize a subject for effective formal presentation to a specific audience.

- Use indirect order presentation to persuade and direct order for other cases.
- Organize like a report: divide and subdivide, usually by factors.
- Select the most appropriate ending, usually restating the subject and summarizing.
- Consider using a climactic close.
- Choose the best manner of presentation.
  — Extemporaneous is usually best.
  — Memorizing is risky.
  — Reading is difficult unless you are skilled.

2. To improve your speaking, take these steps:
   - Work on these characteristics of a good speaker:
     — Confidence.
     — Sincerity.
     — Thoroughness.
     — Friendliness.
   - Know your audience.
     — Before the presentation, size them up—looking for characteristics that affect your presentation (gender, age, education).
     — During the presentation, continue to analyze them, looking at facial expressions, listening to noises, and such—and adapt to them.

3. What the listeners see and hear affects the communication.
   - They see the physical environment (stage, lighting, background), personal appearance, posture, walking, facial expressions, gestures, and such.
   - They hear your voice.
     — For best effect, vary the pitch and speed.
     — Give appropriate vocal emphasis.
     — Cultivate a pleasant quality.

4. Use visuals (graphics) whenever they help communicate.
   - Select the types that do the best job.
   - Blend the visuals into your speech, making certain that the audience sees and understands them.
   - Organize your visuals as a part of your message.
   - Emphasize the visuals by pointing to them.
   - Talk to the audience, not the visuals.
   - Do not block your audience's view of the visuals.

5. Group presentations have special problems.
   - They require all the skills of individual presentation.
   - In addition, they require extra planning to
     — Reduce overlap and provide continuity.
     — Improve transition between presentations.
     — Coordinate questions and answers.

6. Business oral reports are spoken communications of factual business information and its interpretation.
   - Written and oral reports differ in three significant ways.
     — Written reports permit more use of visual helps to communication (paragraphing, punctuation, and such); oral reports allow voice inflection, pauses, and the like.
     — Oral reports permit the speaker to exercise greater control over the pace of the presentation; readers of a written report control the pace.
     — Written reports place more emphasis on writing correctness (grammar, punctuation, etc.).
   - Plan oral reports just as you do written ones.
     — First, determine your objective and state its factors.
     — Next, organize the report, using either indirect or direct order.
     — Divide the body based on your purpose, keeping the divisions comparable and using introductory/concluding paragraphs, logical order, and the like.
     — End the report with a final summary—a sort of ending executive summary.

1. Assume that you must prepare a speech on the importance of making good grades for an audience of college students. Develop some attention-gaining ideas for the introduction of this speech. Do the same for a climactic close for the speech.

2. When is an extemporaneous presentation desirable? When should a speech be read? Discuss.

3. Explain how a speaker's personal characteristics influence the meanings of his or her spoken words.

4. An employee presented an oral report to an audience of 27 middle- and upper-level administrators. Then she presented the same information to three top executives. Note some of the probable differences between the two presentations.

5. Explain how feedback can be used in making a speech.

6. One's manner of dress, choice of hairstyle, physical characteristics, and the like are personal. They should have no influence on any form of oral communication. Discuss.

7. By description (or perhaps by example), identify good and bad postures and walking practices for speaking.

8. Explain how facial expressions can miscommunicate.

9. Give some illustrations of gestures that can be used to communicate more than one meaning. Demonstrate them.

10. "We are born with voices—some good, some bad, and some in between. We have no choice but to accept what we have been given." Comment.

11. What should be the determining factors in the use of visuals (graphics)?

12. Discuss (or demonstrate) some good and bad techniques of using visuals.

13. In presenting an oral report to a group composed of fellow workers as well as some bosses, a worker is harassed by the questions of a fellow worker who is trying to embarrass him. What advice would you give the worker? Would your advice be different if the critic were one of the bosses? What if the speaker were a boss and the critic a worker? Discuss.

14. Give examples of ways a team could provide continuity between members through the use of supporting examples. Be specific.

15. Explain the principal differences between written and oral reports.

16. Compare the typical organization plans of oral and written reports. Note the major differences between the two kinds of plans.

Speeches

Since a speech can be made on almost any topic, it is not practical to list topics for speeches. You or your instructor can generate any number of interesting and timely topics in a short time. Whatever topic you select, you will need to determine the goals clearly, to work out the facts of the situation, and to set a time limit.

Oral Reports

Most of the written report problems presented in the problem section following Chapter 11 also can serve as oral report problems. The following problems, however, are especially suitable for oral presentation.

1. Survey the major business publications for information about the outlook for the national (or world) economy for the coming year. Then present a summary report to the directors of Allied Department Stores, Inc.

2. Select a current technological innovation that is for business use and report it to a company's top administrators (you select the company). You will describe the innovation and point out how it will benefit the company. If appropriate, you may recommend its purchase.

3. Report to a meeting of a wildlife-protection organization on the status of an endangered species. You will need to gather the facts through research, probably in wildlife publications.

4. A national chain of _____ (your choice) is opening an outlet in your city. You have been assigned the task of reviewing site possibilities. Gather the pertinent information and make an oral recommendation to the board of directors.

5. The Future Business Leaders Club at your old high school has asked you to report to it on the nature and quality of business study at your college. You will cover all the factors that you think high school students need to know. Include visuals in your presentation.

6. As representative of a travel agency, present a travel package on _____ (place or places of your choice) to the members of the Adventurer Travel Club. You will describe places to be visited, and you will

cover all the essential details: dates, hotels, guide service, meals, costs, manner of travel, and so on.

7. As a member of an investment club, report to the membership on whether the club should purchase shares of Time Warner (TWX), Clear Channel Communications (CCU), and Yahoo (YHOO). Your report will cover past performance, current status, and future prospects for the short and long run. (You can get the information needed from the Internet.)

8. Look through current newspapers, magazines, the web, and so on, and get the best available information on the job outlook for this year's college graduates. You will want to look at each major field separately. You also may want to show variations by geographic area, degree, and schools. Present your findings in a well-organized and illustrated oral report.

9. Present a plan for improving some phase of operation on your campus (registration, scholastic honesty, housing, grade appeals, library, cafeteria, traffic, curricula, athletics, computer labs, or the like).

10. Present an objective report on some legislation of importance to business (right-to-work laws, environmental controls, taxes, or the like). Take care to present evidence and reasoning from all the major viewpoints. Support your presentation with facts, figures, and so on whenever they will help. Prepare visual supports.

11. Assume that you are being considered by a company of your choice for a job of your choice. Your prospective employer has asked you to make a _____-minute report (your instructor will specify) on your qualifications. You may project your education to the date you will be in the job market, making assumptions that are consistent with your record to date.

12. Prepare and present a report on how individuals may reduce their federal or state income tax payments. You probably will want to emphasize the most likely sources of tax savings, such as tax sheltering and avoiding common errors.

13. Make a presentation to a hypothetical group of investors that will get you the investment money you need for a purpose of your choice. Your purpose could be to begin a new business, to construct a building, to develop land—whatever interests you. Make your presentation as real (or realistic) as you can. And support your appeal with visuals.

14. As chairperson of the site-selection committee of the National Federation of Business Executives, present a report on your committee's recommendation. The committee has selected a city and a convention hotel (you may choose each). Your report will give your recommendation and the reasons that support it. For class purposes, you may make up whatever facts you may need about the organization and its convention requirements and about the hotel. But use real facts about the city.

15. As a buyer of men's (or women's) clothing, report to the sales personnel of your store on the fashions for the coming season. You may get the necessary information from publications in the field.

16. The top administrators of your company have asked you to look into the matter of whether the company should own automobiles, lease automobiles, or pay mileage costs on employee-owned automobiles. (Automobiles are used by sales personnel.) Gather the best available information on the matter and report it to the top administrators. You may make up any company facts you need, but make them realistic.

Cross-Cultural, Correctness, Technology, Research

Dawn C. Meyerriecks continuously seeks out emerging technologies to support command, control, communications, and intelligence for the U.S. military. In this critical position, Meyerriecks must negotiate a shared vision among leaders with very different backgrounds and concerns. "Today's successful individuals are broad thinkers who can apply what they know in a number of disciplines. I work at communicating across those boundaries by participating in cross-disciplinary groups so that I understand what people with different backgrounds bring to the table. And I constantly work to be at the peak of my own profession so that I'm not wasting others' time."

Dawn Meyerriecks, Chief Technology Officer
U.S. Defense Information Systems Agency

CHAPTER SIXTEEN

Techniques of Cross-Cultural Communication

CHAPTER OBJECTIVES

Upon completing this chapter, you will be able to describe the major barriers to cross-cultural communication and how to overcome them. To reach this goal, you should be able to

1 Explain why communicating clearly across cultures is important to business.

2 Define culture and explain its effects on cross-cultural communication.

3 Describe cultural differences in body positions and movements and use this knowledge effectively in communicating.

4 Describe cultural differences in views and practices concerning time, space, odors, and such and use this knowledge effectively in communicating.

5 Explain the language equivalency problem as a cause of miscommunication.

6 Describe what one can do to overcome the language equivalency problem.

Cross-Cultural Communication

To introduce yourself to this chapter, assume the position of assistant to the president of Thatcher-Stone and Company, a small manufacturer of computer components. Your boss, gregarious old Vernon Thatcher, invited you to join him at a luncheon meeting with a group of Asian business executives in which negotiations for the sale of Thatcher-Stone products would be opened. Because Thatcher-Stone's domestic sales have been lagging, the company badly needs these customers.

The Asian guests entered the room, bowing as introductions were made. Mr. Thatcher attempted to put them at ease. "No need to do that," he said. "I'm just plain Vernon Thatcher. Just relax and make yourself at home." You noticed that the Asians appeared bewildered. They appeared even more bewildered when early in the meeting Mr. Thatcher made this statement: "We've only got the lunch hour, gents. I know you'll appreciate getting right down to business."

Throughout the meeting Mr. Thatcher was in his best conversational mood—laughing, backslapping, telling jokes. But none of this seemed to make an impression on the guests. They seemed confused to you. They smiled and were extremely polite, but they seemed to understand little of what Mr. Thatcher was saying. Although he tried again and again to move to business talk, they did not respond. The meeting ended pleasantly, but without a sale.

"They're a strange people," Mr. Thatcher commented when he got back to his office. "They have a lot to learn about doing business. It doesn't look like they're going to deal with us, does it?" Mr. Thatcher was right in his last comment. They did not.

As you review the meeting, you cannot help but feel that Mr. Thatcher spoiled the deal, for he failed miserably in communicating with the Asians. The fact is that there is much to know about communicating in cross-cultural settings. The goal of this chapter is to introduce you to this issue.

Technological advances in communication, travel, and transportation have made business increasingly global. This trend is expected to continue in the foreseeable future. Thus, the chances are good that you will have to communicate with people from other cultures.

- Business has become more global.

Both large and small businesses want you to be able to communicate clearly with those from other cultures for several reasons. A primary reason is that businesses sell their products and services both domestically and internationally. Being able to communicate with others helps you be more successful in understanding customers' needs, communicating how your company can meet these needs, and winning their business. Another reason is that in addition to being a more effective worker, you will be more efficient both within and outside your company. You will be able to work harmoniously with those from other cultures, creating a more comfortable and productive workplace. Furthermore, if cultural barriers are eliminated, you will be able to hire good people despite their differences. Also, you will avoid problems stemming solely from misinterpretations. A final reason is that your attention to communicating clearly with those from other cultures will enrich your business and personal life.

- Communicating across cultures effectively improves your productivity and efficiency and promotes harmonious work environments.

In preparing to communicate with people from other cultures, you might well begin by reviewing the instructions given in this book. Most of them fit all people. But many do not, especially those involving message writing. To determine which do not, you must study the differences among cultures, for cultural differences are at the root of the exceptions. In addition, you must look at the special problems that our language presents to those who use it as a second language. It is around these two problem areas that this review of cross-cultural communication is organized.

- Cross-cultural communication involves understanding cultural differences and overcoming language problems.

PROBLEMS OF CULTURAL DIFFERENCES

A study of the role of culture in international communication properly begins with two qualifying statements. First, culture is often improperly assumed to be the cause of miscommunication. Often it is confused with the other human elements involved. We

- Two qualifying statements begin this study of culture: (1) It is improperly blamed for some miscommunication.

Web Tools for Cross-Cultural Communication

The Internet is a rich source for cross-cultural information for business communicators. Not only can you find information about places where you might be doing business, but you can use some interactive websites to help you with information and tools for your communication. One of these is a currency converter, allowing you to convert from one currency to another. In this example, U.S. dollars are converted to Japanese yen. These converters are set up to use regularly updated exchange rates, so you can quote prices in both U.S. dollars and other currency. The second web page example at the bottom right is part of a site that helps you learn some of the language of your customers. This site shows a word or phrase in English and the second language, as well as giving you an audio pronunciation of it. Learning a few words in your cus-tomers' language is both helpful and courteous. The other sites you see listed here include a site where you can get world time, a resource desk that provides updated site reviews regularly, a site on idioms and slang, and a site with helpful cultural information and some discussion groups on doing business in various countries.

Other good sites:

http://www.timeticker.com/main.htm

http://globaledge.msu.edu/ibrd/ibrd.asp

http://iteslj.org/links/ESL/Idioms_and_Slang/

http://executiveplanet.com/

must remember that communication between people of different cultures involves the same problems of human behavior that are involved when people of the same culture communicate. In either case, people can be belligerent, arrogant, prejudiced, insensitive, or biased. The miscommunication these types of behavior cause is not a product of culture.

- **(2) It is easy to overgeneralize cultural practices.**

Second, one must take care not to overgeneralize the practices within a culture. We say this even though some of the statements we make in the following paragraphs are overgeneralized. But we have little choice. In covering the subject, it is necessary to make generalizations such as "Latin Americans do this" or "Arabs do that" in order to emphasize a point. But the truth of the matter is that in all cultures, subcultures are present; and common practice in one segment of a culture may be unheard of by other segments. Within a culture townspeople differ from country dwellers, the rich differ from the poor, and the educated differ from the uneducated. Clearly, the subject of culture is highly complex and should not be reduced to simple generalizations.

- **Culture is the shared ways groups of people view the world.**

Culture has been defined in many ways. The classic definition most useful in this discussion is one derived from anthropology: *Culture* is "a way of life of a group of people . . . the stereotyped patterns of learning behavior, which are handed down from

A squatting position is quite natural for this woman as she conducts business.

one generation to the next through means of language and imitation."[1] Similarly, a modern definition is that culture is "the shared ways in which groups of people understand and interpret the world."[2]

While we can all talk on wireless phones and drink Coca-Cola at McDonald's, these activities can be interpreted very differently in different cultures. A Coke at McDonald's in America and a conversation on a wireless phone in Israel may be common occurrences, but in Moscow a trip to McDonald's is a status symbol, as is a wireless phone. In other words, people living in different countries have developed not only different ways to interpret events; they have different habits, values, and ways of relating to one another.

These differences are a major source of problems when people of different cultures try to communicate. Unfortunately, people tend to view the ways of their culture as normal and the ways of other cultures as bad, wrong, peculiar, or such. Specifically, these problems are related to two kinds of cultural differences: (1) differences in body positions and movements and (2) differences in views and practices concerning various factors of human relationships (time, space, intimacy, and so on).

- Two major kinds of cultural differences affect communication.

Body Positions and Movements

One might think that the positions and movements of the body are much the same for all people. But such is not the case. These positions and movements differ by culture, and the differences can affect communication. For example, in our culture most people sit when they wish to remain in one place for some time, but in much of the world people squat. Because we do not squat, we tend to view squatting as primitive. This view obviously affects our communication with people who squat, for what we see when we communicate is a part of the message. But how correct is this view? Actually, squatting is a very normal body position. Our children squat quite naturally—until their elders teach them to sit. Who is to say that sitting is more advanced or better?

- Body positions and movements differ among cultures. For example, in some cultures, people sit; in other cultures, they squat.

[1] V. Barnouw, *Culture and Personality* (Chicago: Dorsey Press, 1963), 4.

[2] Fons Trompenaars and Peter Woolliams, *Business across Cultures* (London: Capstone, 2003), 53.

Carefully Present and Receive a Business Card in Japan

In Japan, it is considered bad manners to go to a business meeting without a business card, or *meishi*. There are a number of ways to present the card, but receiving it is an art, too. If you want to make a good impression on the presenter, receive it in both hands, especially when the other party is senior in age or status or a potential customer. Be careful not to fiddle with the card or put it in your rear pocket—that is considered crude. Put it in some distinctive case. Those who do business in both countries often have their business cards translated on the back, as the examples here show.

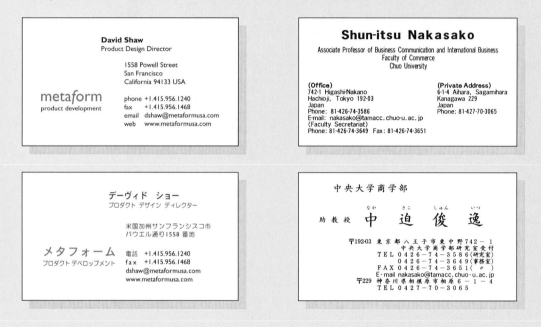

- Manners of walking differ among cultures.

For another example, people from our culture who visit certain Asian countries are likely to view the fast, short steps taken by the inhabitants as peculiar or funny and to view our longer strides as normal. And when people from our culture see the inhabitants of these countries bow on meeting and leaving each other, they are likely to interpret the bowing as a sign of subservience or weakness. Similarly, people from our culture see standing up as the appropriate thing to do on certain occasions (as when someone enters the room), whereas people from some other cultures do not.

- Communication with body parts (hands, arms, head, etc.) varies by culture.

As you know, movements of certain body parts (especially the hands) are a vital form of human communication. Some of these movements have no definite meaning even within a culture. But some have clear meanings, and these meanings may differ by culture. To us an up-and-down movement of the head means yes and a side-to-side movement of the head means no. These movements may mean nothing at all or something quite different to people from cultures in which thrusting the head forward, raising the eyebrows, jerking the head to one side, or lifting the chin are used to convey similar meanings.

- Hand gestures differ by culture.

In addition, the two-fingered "victory" sign is as clear to us as any of our hand gestures. To an Australian, whose culture is not vastly different from ours, the sign has a most vulgar meaning. The "OK" sign is terribly rude and insulting in such diverse places as Russia, Germany, and Brazil.[3] In Japan, a similar sign represents money. If

---

[3] Roger E. Axtell, *Gestures: The Dos and Taboos of Body Language around the World* (New York: John Wiley & Sons, 1998), 43.

a businessperson completing a contract gave this sign, the Japanese might think they needed to give more money, perhaps even a bribe. Even the widely used "thumbs up" sign for "things are going well" could get you into trouble in countries from Nigeria to Australia. In our culture a side-by-side hand movement can be interpreted to mean "hello." The same movement can be interpreted to mean "go away" or "no" in India.[4] And so it is with many of our other body movements. They differ widely, even within cultures.

The meanings that movements of our eyes convey also vary by culture. In North America, we are taught not to look over the heads of our audience but to maintain eye contact in giving formal speeches. In informal talking, we are encouraged to look at others but not to stare. In Indonesia, looking directly at people, especially those in higher positions and older, is considered to be disrespectful. On the other hand, our practices of eye contact are less rigorous than those of the British and Germans. Unless one understands these cultural differences, how one uses eye movement can be interpreted as being impolite on the one hand or being shy on the other.

- So do eye movements,

Touching and particularly handshaking differences are important to understand in cross-cultural communication. This is made difficult by other cultures adopting Western greetings. However, some cultures, like the Chinese, do not like much touching. They will give a handshake you might perceive as weak. Other cultures that like touching will give you greetings ranging from full embraces and kisses to nose rubbing. If you can avoid judging others from different cultures on their greeting based on your standards for others like you, you can seize the opportunity to access the cultural style of another. Here are some types of handshakes by culture.

- touching, and handshaking.

Culture	Handshakes
Americans	Firm
Germans	Brusque, firm, repeated upon arrival and departure
French	Light, quick, not offered to superiors, repeated upon arrival and departure
British	Soft
Hispanics	Moderate grasp, repeated frequently
Latin Americans	Firm, long-lasting
Middle Easterners	Gentle, repeated frequently
Asians	Gentle; for some, shaking hands is unfamiliar and uncomfortable (an exception to this is the Korean, who generally has a firm handshake)

In our culture, smiles are viewed positively in most situations. But in some other cultures (notably African cultures), a smile is regarded as a sign of weakness in certain situations (such as bargaining). Receiving a gift or touching with the left hand is a serious breach of etiquette among Muslims, for they view the left hand as unclean. We attach no such meaning to the left hand. And so it is with other body movements—arching the eyebrows, positioning the fingers, raising the arms, and many more. All cultures use body movements in communicating, but in different ways.

- A smile can be a sign of weakness, and the left hand may be taboo.

Views and Practices Concerning Factors of Human Relationships

Probably causing even more miscommunication than differences in body positions and movements are the different attitudes of different cultures toward various factors of human relationships. For illustrative purposes, we will review seven major factors: time, space, odors, frankness, intimacy of relationships, values, and expression of emotions.

- Differing attitudes toward various factors of human relationships cause communication problems.

---

[4] Jane Lasky, "Watch Your Body Language in Asia," *Austin American-Statesman* (October 17, 1999): D2.

A Classic Defense of Cultural Difference

The classic "ugly American" was traveling in a faraway land. He had been critical of much of what he experienced—the food, the hotels, the customs in general. One day he came upon a funeral. He observed that the mourners placed food on the grave—and left it there.

"What a stupid practice!" he exclaimed to his native host. "Do your people actually think that the dead person will eat the food?"

At this point, the host had taken all the insults he could handle for one day. So he replied, "Our dead will eat the food as soon as your dead smell the flowers you place on their graves."

- Views about time differ widely. Some cultures stress punctuality; some do not.

Time. In our culture, people tend to be monochronic. They regard time as something that must be planned for the most efficient use. They strive to meet deadlines, to be punctual, to conduct business quickly, and to work on a schedule.

In some other cultures (especially those of the Middle East and some parts of Asia), people are polychronic, viewing time in a more relaxed way. They see planning as unwise and unnecessary. Being late to a meeting, a social function, or such is of little consequence to them. In fact, some of them hold the view that important people should be late to show that they are busy. In business negotiations, the people in these cultures move at a deliberately slow pace, engaging in casual talk before getting to the main issue. It is easy to see how such different views of time can cause people from different cultures to have serious miscommunication problems.

- Space is viewed differently by different cultures. In some cultures, people want to be far apart; in other cultures, they want to be close.

Space. People from different cultures often vary in their attitudes toward space. Even people from the same culture may have different space preferences, as noted in Chapter 14. North Americans tend to prefer about two feet or so of distance between themselves and those with whom they speak. But in some cultures (some Arabian and South American cultures), people stand closer to each other; not following this practice is considered impolite and bad etiquette. For another example, North Americans view personal space as a right and tend to respect this right of others; thus, they stand in line and wait their turn. People from some other cultures view space as belonging to all. Thus, they jostle for space when boarding trains, standing at ticket counters, shopping in stores, and such. In encounters between people whose cultures have such different attitudes toward space, actions are likely to be misinterpreted.

- Some cultures view body odors as bad; others view them as normal.

Odors. People from different cultures may have different attitudes toward body odors. To illustrate, Americans work hard to neutralize body odors or cover them up and view those with body odors as dirty and unsanitary. On the other hand, in some Asian cultures people view body odors not as something to be hidden but as something that friends should experience. Some of the people from these cultures believe that it is an act of friendship to "breathe the breath" of the person with whom they converse and to feel their presence by smelling. Clearly, encounters between people with such widely differing attitudes could lead to serious miscommunication.

- High-context cultures are more frank and explicit than low-context cultures.

Frankness. North Americans tend to be relatively frank or explicit in their relationships with others, quickly getting to the point and perhaps being blunt and sharp in doing so. Germans and Israelis are even more frank than Americans. Asians tend to be far more reticent or implicit and sometimes go to great lengths to save face or not to offend. Americans belong to a high-context culture, a culture that explicitly shares all relevant background information in our communication. Asians, on the other hand, belong to a low-context culture, extracting limited background information and thus

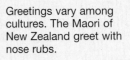
Greetings vary among cultures. The Maori of New Zealand greet with nose rubs.

communicating more implicitly.[5] Thus, Asians may appear evasive, roundabout, and indecisive to North Americans; and North Americans may appear harsh, impolite, and aggressive to Asians. Telephone customs may be an exception, especially among the Chinese, who tend to end telephone calls abruptly after their purpose has been accomplished. North Americans, on the other hand, tend to move on to friendly talk and clearly prepare the listener for the end of the call.

Intimacy of Relationships. In many cultures, strict social classes exist, and class status determines how intimately people are addressed and treated in communication. For this reason, a person from such a culture might quiz a person from another culture to determine that person's class status. Questions concerning occupation, income, title, and such might be asked. People from cultures that stress human equality are apt to take offense at such questioning about class status. This difference in attitude toward class status also is illustrated by differences in the familiarity of address. Some Americans are quick to use first names. This practice is offensive to people from some other cultures, notably the English and the Germans, who expect such intimate address only from long-standing acquaintances.

- Intimacy among people varies in different cultures.

Similarly, how people view superior–subordinate relations can vary by culture. The dominant view in Latin America, for example, is a strong boss with weak subordinates doing as the boss directs. In sharp contrast is the somewhat democratic work arrangement of the Japanese in which much of the decision making is by consensus. Most in our culture view as appropriate an order between these extremes. These widely differing practices have led to major communication problems in joint business ventures involving people from these cultures.

- How people view superior–subordinate relations also differs.

The role of women varies widely by culture. In North America, we continue to move toward a generally recognized goal of equality. In many Islamic cultures, the

- So does the role of women.

[5] Charles W. L. Hill, *International Business: Competing in the Global Marketplace*, 4th ed. (New York: McGraw-Hill/Irwin), 10.

role of women is quite different. To many in our culture, the practices of the people of these other cultures suggest severe restriction of human rights. In the view of the people of these cultures, their practices are in accord with their religious convictions. They see us as being the ones out of step.

Values. Also differing by culture are our values—how we evaluate the critical matters in life. Americans, for example, have been indoctrinated with the Protestant work ethic. It is the belief that if one puts hard work ahead of pleasure, success will follow. The product of this thinking is an emphasis on planning, working efficiently, and maximizing production. Of course, not all of us subscribe to this ethic, but it is a strong force in the thinking of many in our culture. The prevailing view in some other cultures is quite different. In some, the major concern is for spiritual and human well-being. The view of work is relaxed, and productivity is, at best, a secondary concern.

Views about the relationships of employers and employees also may differ by culture. North American workers expect to change companies in their career a number of times; and they expect companies to fire them from time to time. Employees expect to move freely from job to job, and they expect employers to hire and fire as their needs change. Expectations are quite different in some other cultures. In Japan, for example, employment tends to be for a lifetime. The workplace is viewed much like a family, with loyalty expected from employees and employer. Such differences have caused misunderstandings in American–Japanese joint ventures.

How employees view authority is yet another question that cultures view differently. We North Americans generally accept authority, yet we fiercely maintain the rights of the individual. In many Third World cultures, workers accept a subservient role passively. Autocratic rule is expected—even wanted.

Expression of Emotions. From culture to culture, differences in social behavior develop. To illustrate, some Asian cultures strongly frown upon public displays of affection—in fact, they consider them crude and offensive. Westerners, on the other hand, accept at least a moderate display of affection. To Westerners, laughter is a spontaneous display of pleasure, but in some cultures (Japanese, for one), laughter also can be a controlled behavior—to be used in certain social situations. Even such emotional displays as sorrow are influenced by culture. In some Middle Eastern cultures, sorrow is expressed with loud, seemingly uncontrolled wailing. In similar situations, Westerners typically respond with subdued and controlled emotions, which could be seen as cold and uncaring by Middle Easterners.

We all have observed the emotion and animation people of the Mediterranean cultures display as they communicate. And we have seen the more subdued communication of others—notably northern Europeans. The first group tends to see the second as disinterested and lacking in friendliness. The second sees the first as excitable, emotional, perhaps even unstable.

Many more such practices exist. Some cultures combine business and social pleasure; others do not. Some expect to engage in aggressive bargaining in business transactions; others prefer straightforward dealings. Some talk loudly and with emotion; others communicate orally in a subdued manner. Some communicate with emphasis on economy of expression; others communicate with an abundance of verbiage.

The comparisons could go on and on, for there are countless differences in cultures. But it is not necessary to review them all. What is important is that we recognize their existence, that we look for them, and that we understand them. We should guard against ethnocentrism, the use of cultural practices as standards for determining meaning in cross-cultural communication.

Effects on Business Communication Techniques

The foregoing examples illustrate only a few of the numerous differences that exist among cultures. Books have been written on the subject. Our objective here is only to establish the point that the differences among cultures affect communication between people of different cultures.

Margin notes:

• Each culture has different values concerning such matters as attitude toward work,

• employee–employer relations,

• and authority.

• Social behavior varies by culture, such as practices concerning affection, laughter, and emotion.

• Included is the degree of animation displayed.

• Many more such practices exist.

• We must recognize them, look for them, and understand them.

• Cultural differences affect communication.

460   PART 6   Cross-Cultural, Correctness, Technology, Research

The communication techniques presented in this book should be modified to fit the culture involved. Keep in mind that this book was written for our culture. Much of what we say does not apply to other cultures, especially our coverage of the basic message situations—those concerning directness and indirectness. People in Asian cultures, for example, generally favor a somewhat indirect approach for messages we would treat directly. They begin with an identification of context—that is, a description of the situation the message concerns.[6] They use what appears to us as exaggerated politeness and slowness in moving the message. In fact, some of our direct messages would be regarded as rude by people in these cultures.[7]

● Our communication techniques are not universally acceptable.

Our persuasive appeals may be rejected in India, where views of an older, more highly developed morality lead to thinking different from ours.[8] Even the British, whose culture we think of as resembling our own, have message practices that differ from ours. They especially differ in the treatment of negative situations. They prefer an approach that we would regard as blunt and calloused. They would regard our goodwill strategies as insincere and evasive.[9]

● The Indians and even the British have practices different from ours.

And so it is with the many other cultures of the world. Our practices just do not fit into them. What to do about this problem? You have no choice but to become a student of culture. You must learn the cultures of those with whom you communicate. Don't expect them to understand your culture, although many of them do. With your recipient's culture in mind, you then modify your communication accordingly.

● You must modify your communications to fit the culture of your recipient.

PROBLEMS OF LANGUAGE

The people on earth use more than 3,000 languages. Because few of us can learn more than one or two other languages well, problems of miscommunication are bound to occur in international communication.

● Communication problems are caused by the existence of many languages.

Lack of Language Equivalency

Unfortunately, wide differences among languages make precisely equivalent translations difficult. One reason for such differences is that languages are based on the concepts, experiences, views, and such of the cultures that developed them. And different cultures have different concepts, experiences, views, and such. For example, we think of a florist as someone who sells flowers and related items in a store. In some cultures, however, flowers are sold by street vendors, mainly women and children. Obviously, our *florist* does not have a precise equivalent in the language of such cultures.

● Differences among languages make equivalent translations difficult.

Similarly, our *supermarket* has no equivalent in some languages. The French have no word to distinguish between *house* and *home, mind* and *brain,* and *man* and *gentleman.* The Spanish have no word to distinguish between a *chairman* and a *president,* while Italians have no word for *wishful thinking.* And Russians have no words for *efficiency, challenge,* and *having fun.* However, Italians have nearly 500 words for types of pasta. And so it is with words for many other objects, actions, concepts, and such (for example, *roundup, interview, strike, tough, monopoly, domestic, feminine, responsible, aloof*).

● Examples prove the point.

Another explanation for the lack of language equivalency is the grammatical and syntactic differences among languages. Some languages (Urdu, for example) have no gerunds, and some have no adverbs and/or adjectives. Not all languages deal with verb mood, voice, and tense in the same way. The obvious result is that even the best translators often cannot find literal equivalents between languages.

● Grammar and syntax differences add to the difficulty.

Adding to these equivalency problems is the problem of multiple word meanings. Like English, other languages have more than one meaning for many words. Think, for

● So do the multiple meanings of words.

---

[6] Linda Beamer and Iris Varner, *Intercultural Communication in the Global Workplace* (New York: McGraw-Hill/Irwin, 2001), 133.

[7] Richard M. Hodgetts and Fred Luthans, *International Management* (New York: McGraw-Hill/Irwin, 2000), 206.

[8] Beamer and Varner, *Intercultural Communication in the Global Workplace,* 137–38.

[9] Hodgetts and Luthans, *International Management,* 207.

example, of our numerous meanings for the simple word *run* (to move fast, to compete for office, a score in baseball, a break in a stocking, a fading of colors, and many more). Or consider the multiple meanings of such words as *fast, cat, trip, gross, ring,* and *make.* The Oxford English Dictionary uses over 15,000 words to define *what.* Unless one knows a language well, it is difficult to know which of the meanings is intended.

Within a culture, certain manners of expression may be used in a way that their dictionary translations and grammatical structures do not explain. Those within the culture understand these expressions; those outside may not. For example, we might say, "Business couldn't be better," meaning business is very good. One from another culture might understand the sentence to mean "Business is bad" (impossible to improve). Or we might say, "We could never be too nice to our customers," meaning try as we may, we couldn't be overly nice. To one from another culture, the sentence might mean "We cannot be nice to our customers."[10]

Similarly, like-meaning words can be used in different ways in different cultures. One example is the simple word *yes,* a word that has an equivalent in all languages. "The Chinese *yes,* like the Japanese *yes,* can often be understood by Americans and British as their English *yes.* But the Chinese *yes* often means 'I am listening.' Or it may be understood in English as the opposite. For example, when an American says to a Chinese counterpart, "I see you don't agree with this clause," the Chinese will usually reply, "Yes" meaning a polite agreement with the negative question: 'Yes, you are right. I do not agree with the clause.' "[11]

Overcoming such language problems is difficult. The best way, of course, is to know more than one language well, but the competence required is beyond the reach of many of us. Thus, your best course is first to be aware that translation problems exist and then to ask questions—to probe—to determine what the other person understands. For very important oral messages, documents, or such, you might consider using a procedure called *back translating.* This procedure involves using two translators, one with first-language skills in one of the languages involved and one with first-language skills in the other language. The first translator translates the message into his or her language, and the second translator then translates the message back into the original. If the translations are good, the second translation matches the original.

Difficulties in Using English

Fortunately for us, English is the primary language of international business. This is not to say that other languages are not used in international business, for they are. When business executives from different countries have a common language, whatever it may be, they are likely to use it. For example, an executive from Iraq and an executive from Saudi Arabia would communicate with each other in Arabic, for Arabic is their common language. For the same reason, an executive from Venezuela would use Spanish in dealing with an executive from Mexico. However, when executives have no common language, they are likely to use English. The members of the European Free Trade Association conduct all their business in English even though not one of them is a native English speaker. In the words of one international authority, "English has emerged as the *lingua franca* of world commerce in much the same way that Greek did in the ancient world of the West and China did in the East."[12]

Although we can take comfort from knowing that ours is the primary language of international business, we must keep in mind that it is not the primary language of many of those who use it. Since many of these users have had to learn English as a second language, they are likely to use it less fluently than we and to experience prob-

The margin notes read:

- Certain of our expressions don't mean what their dictionary and grammatical structures say they mean.

- Even words with the same meaning can differ in usage by culture.

- Overcome such language problems by knowing languages well and by questioning.

- Use back translating for important communications.

- English is the primary language of international business.

- But many nonnatives have problems using English.

---

[10] Jensen J. Zhao, "The Chinese Approach to International Business Negotiation," *Journal of Business Communication* (July 2000): 225.

[11] *Ibid.*

[12] Naoki Kameda, *Business Communication toward Transnationalism: The Significance of Cross-Cultural Business English and Its Role* (Tokyo: Kindaibungeisha Co., 1996), 34.

lems in understanding us. Some of their more troublesome problems are reviewed in the following pages.

Two-Word Verbs. One of the most difficult problems for nonnative speakers of English involves the use of two-word verbs. By *two-word verbs* we mean a wording consisting of (1) a verb and (2) a second element that, combined with the verb, produces a meaning that the verb alone does not have. For example, take the verb *break* and the word *up*. When combined, they have a meaning quite different from the meanings the words have alone. And look how the meaning changes when the same verb is combined with other words: *break away, break out, break in, break down.* Dictionaries are of little help to nonnatives who are seeking the meanings of these word combinations.

There are many two-word verbs—so many, in fact, that a special dictionary of them has been compiled.[13] Figure 16–1 lists some of the more common words that combine with verbs.

- Two-word verbs are hard for nonnatives to understand,

- as in these combinations.

FIGURE 16–1   Some Two-Word Verbs That Confuse Nonnative Speakers

Verb Plus *Away*	**Verb Plus *In***	**Verb Plus *Out***	**Verb Plus *Up***
give away	cash in	blow out	blow up
keep away	cave in	clean out	build up
lay away	close in	crowd out	call up
pass away	dig in	cut out	catch up
throw away	give in	die out	cover up
Verb Plus *Back*	run in	dry out	dig up
cut back	take in	even out	end up
feed back	throw in	figure out	fill up
keep back	**Verb Plus *Off***	fill out	get up
play back	break off	find out	hang up
read back	brush off	give out	hold up
take back	buy off	hold out	keep up
turn back	check off	lose out	look up
win back	clear off	pull out	mix up
Verb Plus *Down*	cool off	rule out	pick up
calm down	cut off	tire out	save up
die down	finish off	wear out	shake up
hand down	let off	work out	shut up
keep down	mark off	**Verb Plus *Over***	slow up
let down	pay off	check over	wrap up
lie down	run off	do over	**Verb Plus Miscellaneous Words**
mark down	send off	hold over	
pin down	show off	pass over	bring about
play down	shut off	put over	catch on
put down	sound off	roll over	get across
run down	start off	run over	pass on
shut down	take off	stop over	put across
sit down	write off	take over	put forth
wear down		talk over	set forth
		think over	
		win over	

[13] George A. Meyer, *The Two-Word Verb* (The Hague, Netherlands: Mouton, 1975).

- Use two-word verbs sparingly. Find substitutes, as shown here.

Of course, nonnatives studying English learn some of these word combinations, for they are part of the English language. But many of them are not covered in language textbooks or listed in dictionaries. It is apparent that we should use these word combinations sparingly when communicating with nonnative speakers of English. Whenever possible, we should substitute for them words that appear in standard dictionaries. Following are some two-word verbs and suggested substitutes:

Two-Word Verbs	Suggested Substitutes
give up	surrender
speed up, hurry up	accelerate
go on, keep on	continue
put off	defer
take off	depart, remove
come down	descend
go in, come in, get in	enter
go out, come out, get out	exit, leave
blow up	explode
think up	imagine
figure out	solve
take out, take away	remove
go back, get back, be back	return

- Some two-word verbs have noun and adjective forms. Use these sparingly.

Additional problems result from the fact that some two-word verbs have noun and adjective forms. These also tend to confuse nonnatives using English. Examples of such nouns are *breakthrough, cover-up, drive-in, hookup, show-off,* and *sit-in.* Examples of such adjectives are *going away* (a going-away gift), *cover-up* (cover-up tactics), *cleanup* (cleanup work), and *turning-off* (turning-off place). Fortunately, some nouns and adjectives of this kind are commonly used and appear in standard dictionaries (words such as *hookup, feedback, breakthrough, lookout,* and *takeover*). In writing to nonnative readers, you will need to use sparingly those that do not appear in standard dictionaries.

- Culturally derived words, especially slang, cause problems.

Culturally Derived Words. Words derived from our culture also present problems. The most apparent are the slang expressions that continually come into and go out of use. Some slang expressions catch on and find a place in our dictionaries (*brunch, hobo, blurb, bogus*). But most are with us for a little while and then are gone. Examples of such short-lived slang expressions are the "twenty-three skiddoo" and "oh you kid" of the 1920s and the *ritzy, scram, natch, lousy, soused, all wet, hep, in the groove,* and *tops* of following decades. More recent slang words that are probably destined for the same fate include *nerd, wimp, earth pig, pig out, couch potato, squid, airhead,* and *cool.* Perhaps you are not aware of just how much slang we use. For an eye-opener, you have only to visit ESL: Idioms and Slang Page <http://ites/j.org/links/ESL/Idioms_and_slang/> for links to many lists.

- So avoid slang.

Most slang words are not in dictionaries or on the word lists that non–English-speaking people study to learn English. The obvious conclusion is that you should not use slang in cross-cultural communication.

- Words derived from sports, social activities, and so on cause problems.

Similar to and in fact overlapping slang are the words and expressions that we derive from our various activities—sports, social affairs, work, and the like. Sports especially have contributed such words, many of which are so widely used that they are part of our everyday vocabulary. From football we have *kickoff, goal-line stand,* and *over the top.* Baseball has given us *out in left field, strike out, touch base, off base, right off the bat, a steal, squeeze play, balk,* and *go to bat for.* From boxing we have *knockout, down for the count, below the belt, answer the bell,* and *on the ropes.* From other sports and from sports in general we have *jock, ace, par, stymie, from scratch, ballpark figure,* and *get the ball rolling.*

FIGURE 16–2

head for home	tuckered out	tote (carry)
have an itching palm	gumption	in a rut
grasp at straws	crying in his beer	priming the pump
flat-footed	in orbit	make heads or tails of it
on the beam	a honey	tearjerker
out to pasture	a flop	countdown
sitting duck	dope (crazy)	shortcut
in the groove	hood (gangster)	educated guess
nuts (crazy)	up the creek without a paddle	all ears
circle the wagons	a fish out of water	slower than molasses
shoot from the hip	a chicken with its head cut off	

Similar to these words and expressions are words and expressions developed within our culture (colloquialisms). Some of these have similar meanings in other cultures, but most are difficult for nonnatives to understand. You will find some examples in Figure 16–2.

- Colloquialisms also cause problems.

If you are like most of us, many of these words and expressions are a part of your vocabulary. You use them in your everyday communicating, which is all right. They are colorful, and they can communicate clearly to those who understand them. Nonnative English speakers are not likely to understand them, however; so you will need to eliminate such words and expressions in communicating with them. You will need to use words that are clearly defined in the dictionaries that these people are likely to use in translating your message. Following are some examples:

- We use such words in everyday communication. But avoid them in cross-cultural correspondence.

Not This	**But This**
We were caught flat-footed.	We were surprised.
He frequently shoots from the hip.	He frequently acts before he thinks.
We would be up the creek without a paddle.	We would be in a helpless situation.
They couldn't make heads or tails of the report.	They couldn't understand the report.
The sales campaign was a flop.	The sales campaign was a failure.
I'll touch base with you on this problem in August.	I'll talk with you about this problem in August.
Take an educated guess on this question.	Answer this question to the best of your knowledge.
Your sales report put us in orbit.	Your sales report pleased us very much.
We will wind down manufacturing operations in November.	We will end manufacturing operations in November.
Your prediction was right on the beam.	Your prediction was correct.

A GENERAL SUGGESTION FOR COMMUNICATING ACROSS CULTURES

In addition to the specific suggestions for improving your communication in English with nonnative English speakers, you should follow one general suggestion: Write or talk simply and clearly. Talk slowly and enunciate each word. Remember that because most nonnative speakers learned English in school, they are acquainted mainly with primary dictionary meanings and are not likely to understand slang words or shades

- Use simple, basic English.

Professorial Words of Wisdom

The lexical differences between American English and British English can be traced to the sixteenth and seventeenth centuries when early settlers brought to North America the language of their homelands. British settlers found that their language was not adequate for life on a different continent. The new things they encountered necessitated their adapting the meanings of existing English words or finding new words.

James Calvert Scott, Utah State University

James Calvert Scott, "Differences in American and British Vocabulary: Implications for International Business Communication," *Business Communication Quarterly* 63, no. 4 (December 2000): 28.

of difference in the meanings we give words. They will understand you better if you avoid these pitfalls. In the words of two highly regarded scholars in the field, you should "educate yourself in the use of Simplified English."[14]

- Word questions carefully to elicit the response intended.

You also will communicate better if you carefully word your questions. Be sure your questions are not double questions. Avoid "Do you want to go to dinner now or wait until after the rush hour is over?" Also, avoid the yes/no question that some cultures may have difficulty answering directly. Use more open-ended questions such as "When would you like to go to dinner?" Also, avoid negative questions such as "Aren't you going to dinner?" In some cultures a yes response confirms whether the questioner is correct; in other cultures the response is directed toward the question being asked.

- Continually check the accuracy of the communication.

Finally, try to check and clarify your communication through continuous confirmation. Summarizing in writing also is a good idea, and today's technology enables parties to do this on the spot. It allows you to be certain you have conveyed your message and received theirs accurately. Even in Britain, a culture similar to ours, similar words can have vastly different meanings. For example, we use a billion to mean 1,000,000,000 whereas the British use it to mean 1,000,000,000,000. Continually checking for meaning and using written summaries can help ensure the accuracy of the communication process.

SUMMARY BY CHAPTER OBJECTIVES

1
Explain why communicating clearly across cultures is important to business.

2
Define culture and explain its effects on cross-cultural communication.

3
Describe cultural differences in body positions and movements and use this knowledge effectively in communicating.

1. Businesses are becoming increasingly global in their operations.
   - Being able to communicate across cultures is necessary in these operations.
   - Specifically, it helps in gaining additional business, in hiring good people, and generally in understanding and satisfying the needs of customers.
2. *Culture* may be defined as "the way of life of a group of people."
   - Cultures differ.
   - People tend to view the practices of their culture as right and those of other cultures as peculiar or wrong.
   - These views cause miscommunication.
3. Variations in how people of different cultures use body positions and body movements is a cause of miscommunication.
   - How people walk, gesture, smile, and such varies from culture to culture.
   - When people from different cultures attempt to communicate, each may not understand the other's body movements.

[14] Robert Sellers and Elaine Winters, *Cultural Issues in Business Communication.* Available at <http://www.bena.com/ewinters/sect1.html> (November 3, 2003).

4. People in different cultures differ in their ways of relating to people.
   - Specifically, they differ in their practices and thinking concerning time, space, odors, frankness, relationships, values, and social behavior.
   - We should not use our culture's practices as standards for determining meaning.
   - Instead, we should try to understand the other culture.
5. Language equivalency problems are another major cause of miscommunication in cross-cultural communication.
   - About 3,000 languages are used on earth.
   - They differ greatly in grammar and syntax.
   - Like English, most have words with multiple meanings.
   - As a result, equivalency in translation is difficult.
6. Overcoming the language equivalency problems involves hard and tedious work.
   - The best advice is to master the language of the nonnative English speakers with whom you communicate.
   - Also, you should be aware of the problems caused by language differences.
   - Ask questions carefully to make sure you are understood.
   - For important communications, consider back translation—the technique of using two translators, the first to translate from one language to the other and the second to translate back to the original.
   - Check the accuracy of the communication with written summaries.

4 Describe cultural differences in views and practices concerning time, space, odors, and such and use this knowledge effectively in communicating.

5 Explain the language equivalency problem as a cause of miscommunication.

6 Describe what one can do to overcome the language equivalency problem.

CRITICAL THINKING QUESTIONS

1. "Just as our culture has advanced in its technological sophistication, it has advanced in the sophistication of its body signals, gestures, and attitudes toward time, space, and such. Thus, the ways of our culture are superior to those of most other cultures." Discuss this view.

2. What are the prevailing attitudes in our culture toward the following, and how can those attitudes affect our communication with nonnatives? Discuss.
   a. Negotiation methods
   b. Truth in advertising
   c. Company–worker loyalty
   d. Women's place in society

3. Some of our message-writing techniques are said to be unacceptable to people from such cultures as those of Japan and England.
   a. Which techniques in particular do you think would be most inappropriate in these cultures?
   b. Why?

4. Think of English words (other than text examples) that probably do not have a precise equivalent in some other culture. Tell how you would attempt to explain each of these words to a person from that culture.

5. Select a word with at least five meanings. List those meanings and tell how you would communicate each of them to a nonnative.

6. From newspapers or magazines, find and bring to class 10 sentences containing words and expressions that a nonnative English speaker would not be likely to understand. Rewrite the sentences for this reader.

7. Is conversational style appropriate in writing to nonnative readers? Discuss.

8. Interview a nonnative speaker of English about communication differences between cultures he or she has experienced. Report your findings to the class in a 10-minute presentation.

9. Research a non–English-speaking country on the Internet or in your library. Look for ways in which business communication can vary by culture. Report your work to the class in a short presentation.

CRITICAL THINKING EXERCISES

Instructions: Rewrite the following sentences for a nonnative English speaker.

1. Last year our laboratory made a breakthrough in design that really put sales in orbit.

2. You will need to pin down Mr. Wang to put across the need to tighten up expenses.

3. Recent losses have us on the ropes now, but we expect to get out of the hole by the end of the year.

4. We will kick off the advertising campaign in February, and in April we will bring out the new products.

5. Maryellen gave us a ballpark figure on the project, but I think she is ready to back down from her estimate.

6. We will back up any of our products that are not up to par.

7. Mr. Maghrabi managed to straighten out and become our star salesperson.

8. Now that we have cut back on our telemarketing, we will have to build up our radio advertising.

9. If you want to improve sales, you should stay with your prospects until they see the light.

10. We should be able to bring about a savings of 8 or 10 grand.

CHAPTER SEVENTEEN

Correctness of Communication

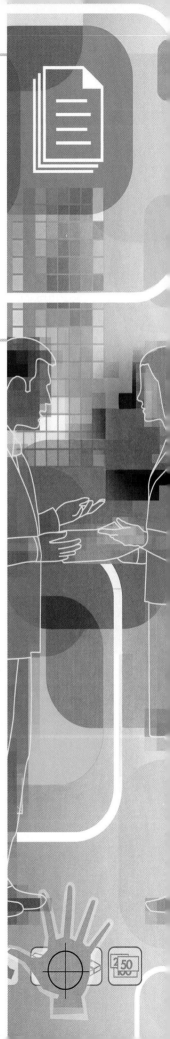

CHAPTER OBJECTIVES

Upon completing this chapter, you will be able to use the accepted standards of English grammar and punctuation in written business communications. To reach this goal, you should be able to

1 Punctuate messages correctly.

2 Write complete, grammatically correct sentences, avoiding such problems as awkward construction, dangling modifiers, and misuse of words.

3 Determine when to spell out numbers and when to express them in numeral form according to standards of correctness.

4 Spell words correctly by applying spelling rules and using a dictionary or spell checker.

5 Use capital letters for all proper names, first words of sentences, and first words of complimentary closes.

The Effects of Correctness on Communication

Play the role of Mike Rook, a purchasing agent for Hewlett-Packard, and read through today's mail. The first letter comes from Joe Spivey, sales manager, B and B Manufacturing Company. You have not met the writer, though you talked to him on the telephone a few days ago. At that time, you were favorably impressed with Spivey's enthusiasm and ability, and with B and B. In fact, you assumed that after he gave you the information you needed about B and B's products and services, you would begin buying from it.

As you read Spivey's letter, however, you are startled. "Could this be the same person I talked with?" you ask yourself. There in the first paragraph is an *it don't,* a clear error of subject–verb agreement. Farther down, an *it's* is used to show possession rather than *its.* Spivey apparently uses the sprinkle system for placing commas—that is, he sprinkles them wherever his whims direct. His commas often fall in strange places. For example, he writes, "Our salespeople, say the Rabb Company engineers, will verify the durability of Ironskin protective coating," but you think he means "Our salespeople say the Rabb Company engineers will verify the durability of Ironskin protective coating." The two sentences, which differ only in their punctuation, have distinctly different meanings. Spivey's message is filled with such errors.

In general, you now have a lower opinion of Spivey and his company. Perhaps you'll have to take a long look at B and B's products and services. After all, the products and services that a company provides are closely related to the quality of its people.

The problem just described is a very real one in business. Image does influence the success of both companies and people. And correctness in writing influences image. Thus, you will want to make certain that your writing is correct, so that it helps form a favorable image both of you and of your company. The material presented in the pages that follow should help you in that effort.

- People judge you and your company by the correctness of your communication.

The correctness of your communication will be important to you and your company. It will be important to you because people will judge you by it, and how they judge you will help determine your success in life. It will be important to your company because it will help convey the image of competence that companies like. People judge a company by how its employees act, think, talk, and write. Company executives want such judgments to be favorable.

THE NATURE OF CORRECTNESS

- Businesspeople expect you to follow the generally accepted standards of English.

Not all people agree that there are standards for correct communication. In fact, some people think there should be no general standards of this kind, that whatever communicates in a given case is all right. Businesspeople, however, generally accept the standards for correct usage that educated people have developed over the years. These are the standards that you have studied in your English composition classes and that appear in textbooks. Businesspeople expect you to follow them.

- These standards of correctness assist in communicating.

These standards of correctness have one basic purpose: to assist in communicating. To some people the standards of correctness appear arbitrary or unnecessary. But such is not the case. They are designed to reduce misunderstanding—to make communication more precise. When you communicate precisely, you practice good ethics by meeting your reader's needs for understandable messages. It is only in this light that we can justify studying them.

The practical value of these standards is easily illustrated. Take, for example, the following two sentences. Their words are the same; only their punctuation differs. But what a difference the punctuation makes!

"The teacher," said the student, "is stupid."

The teacher said, "The student is stupid."

Can You Detect the Differences in Meaning the Punctuation Makes?

What's the latest dope?

What's the latest, dope?

The groom was asked to call the guests names as they arrived.

The groom was asked to call the guests' names as they arrived.

A clever dog knows it's master.

A clever dog knows its master.

Everyone, I know, has a problem.

Everyone I know has a problem.

Do not break your bread or roll in your soup.

Do not break your bread, or roll in your soup.

She ate a half-fried chicken.

She ate a half fried chicken.

I left him convinced he was a fool.

I left him, convinced he was a fool.

In the parade will be several hundred children, carrying flags and many important officials.

In the parade will be several hundred children, carrying flags, and many important officials.

The play ended, happily.

The play ended happily.

Thirteen people knew the secret, all told.

Thirteen people knew the secret; all told.

Or what about the following pair of sentences? Who is speaking, the Democrats or the Republicans? The commas make a difference.

The Democrats, say the Republicans, will win.

The Democrats say the Republicans will win.

Here are two more sentences. The difference here needs no explanation.

He looked at her stern.

He looked at her sternly.

Because the standards of correctness are important to your communication in business, this chapter will review them. The review is not complete, for much more space would be needed for complete coverage. But the major standards are covered, those that most often present problems in your writing. For your convenience, the standards are coded with symbols (letters and numbers). You should find these symbols useful in identifying the standards. Your instructor should find them useful as grading marks to identify errors in your writing.

- The following review covers the major standards. They are coded for your convenience.

You probably already know many of the standards of correctness, so the following information will not all be new to you. To help you determine how much you know and do not know, you should take the self-analysis test at the end of the chapter or on the textbook website. This will enable you to study the standards selectively. Because the self-analysis test covers only the more frequently used standards, however, you would be wise to review the entire chapter.

- Take the self-analysis test to determine your present knowledge of the standards.

CHAPTER 17   Correctness of Communication

STANDARDS FOR PUNCTUATION

The following explanations cover the most important standards for correctness in punctuation. For reasons of accuracy, the explanations use some technical words. Even so, the illustrations should make the standards clear.

Apostrophe: Apos 1

- Use the apostrophe to show possession.

Use the apostrophe to show the possessive case of nouns and indefinite pronouns. If the word does not end in *s*, add an apostrophe and an *s*. If the word ends in *s*, add only an apostrophe.

Nominative Form	Possessive Form
company	company's
employee	employee's
companies	companies'
employees	employees'

Proper names and singular nouns ending in *s* sounds are exceptions. To such words you may add either an apostrophe and an *s* or just an apostrophe. Add only an apostrophe to the nominative plural.

Nominative Form	Possessive Form
Texas (singular)	Texas's, Texas'
Jones (singular)	Jones's, Jones'
Joneses (plural)	Joneses'
countess (singular)	countess's, countess'

Apos 2

- Mark omissions in contractions with the apostrophe.

Use an apostrophe to mark the place in a contraction where letters are omitted.

it is = it's

has not = hasn't

cannot = can't

Brackets: Bkts

- Use brackets to set off words that you insert in a quotation.

Set off in brackets words that you wish to insert in a quotation.

"The use of this type of mentor [the personal coach] may still be increasing."

"Direct supervision has diminished in importance during the past decade [the report was written in 2002], when 63 percent of the reporting business firms that started programs used teams."

Colon: Cln 1

- Use the colon to introduce formal statements.

Use the colon to introduce an enumeration, a formal quotation, or a statement of explanation.

Enumeration: Working in this department are three classes of support: clerical support, computer support, and customer support.

Formal quotation: President Hartung had this to say about the proposal: "Any such movement that fails to get the support of the workers from all divisions fails to get my support."

Explanation: At this time the company was pioneering a new marketing idea: It was attempting to sell customized products directly to consumers through its website.

Adam@Home by Brian Basset

Cln 2

Do not use the colon when the thought of the sentence should continue without interruption. If introducing a list by a colon, the colon should be preceded by a word that explains or identifies the list.

Not this: Cities in which new sales offices are in operation are: Fort Smith, Texarkana, Lake Charles, Jackson, and Biloxi.

But this: Cities in which new sales offices are in operation are Fort Smith, Texarkana, Lake Charles, Jackson, and Biloxi.

Or this: Cities with new sales offices are as follows: Fort Smith, Texarkana, Lake Charles, Jackson, and Biloxi.

- Do not use the colon when it breaks the thought flow.

Comma: Cma 1

Use the comma to separate principal clauses connected by a coordinating conjunction. Some coordinating conjunctions are *and, but, or,* and *nor.* (A principal clause has a subject and a verb and stands by itself. A coordinating conjunction connects clauses, words, or phrases of equal rank.)

Only two components of the index declined, and these two account for only 12 percent of the total weight of the index.

New automobiles are moving at record volumes, but used-car sales are lagging behind the record pace set two years ago.

Make exceptions to this rule, however, in the case of compound sentences consisting of short and closely connected clauses.

We sold and the price dropped.

Sometimes we win and sometimes we lose.

- Use the comma to separate clauses connected by *and, but, or,* and *nor.*

Cma 2–1

Separate the items listed in a series by commas. In order to avoid misinterpretation of the rare instances in which some of the items listed have compound constructions, it is always good to place the comma between the last two items (before the final conjunction).

Good copy must cover facts with accuracy, sincerity, honesty, and conviction.

Direct advertising can be used to introduce salespeople, fill in between salespeople's calls, cover territory where salespeople cannot be maintained, and keep pertinent reference material in the hands of prospects.

A survey conducted at the 2004 automobile show indicated that silver, white, blue, and black cars were favored by the public.

- Use the comma to separate (1) items in a series and

Cma 2–2

● (2) adjectives in a series.

Separate coordinate adjectives in a series by commas if they modify the same noun and if no *and* connects them. A good test to determine whether adjectives are coordinate is to insert an *and* between them. If the *and* does not change the meaning, the adjectives are coordinate.

Miss Pratt has been a reliable, faithful, efficient employee for 20 years.

We guarantee that this is a good, clean car.

Blue office furniture is Mr. Orr's recommendation for the new conference room. (Office furniture is practically a compound noun; blue modifies both words.)

A big crescent wrench proved to be best for the task. (The *and* won't fit between *big* and *crescent*.)

Cma 3

● Use commas to set off nonrestrictive modifiers (those that could be left out without changing the meaning of the sentence).

Set off nonrestrictive modifiers by commas. By a *nonrestrictive modifier* we mean a modifier that could be omitted from the sentence without changing its meaning. Restrictive modifiers (those that restrict the words they modify to one particular object) are not set off by commas. A restrictive modifier cannot be left out of the sentence without changing its meaning.

Restrictive: The salesperson who sells the most will get a bonus. (*Who sells the most* restricts the meaning to a particular salesperson.)

Nonrestrictive: Diana Chan, who was the company's top salesperson for the year, was awarded a bonus. (If the clause *who was the company's top salesperson for the year* is omitted, the meaning of the sentence is not changed.)

Restrictive: J. Ward & Company is the firm that employs most of the physically disabled in this area.

Nonrestrictive: J. Ward & Company, the firm that employs most of the physically disabled in this area, has gained the admiration of the community.

Notice that some modifiers can be either restrictive or nonrestrictive, depending on the writer's intended meaning.

Restrictive: All the suits that were damaged in the fire were sold at a discount. (Implies that some of the suits were not damaged.)

Nonrestrictive: All the suits, which were damaged by the fire, were sold at a discount. (Implies that the entire stock of suits was damaged.)

Cma 4–1

● Use commas to set off (1) parenthetic expressions (comments "stuck in"),

Use commas to set off parenthetic expressions. A parenthetic expression consists of words that interrupt the normal flow of the sentence. In a sense, they appear to be "stuck in." In many instances, they are simply words out of normal order. For example, the sentence "A full-page, black-and-white advertisement was run in the *Daily Bulletin*" contains a parenthetic expression when the word order is altered: "An advertisement, full-page and in black and white, was run in the *Daily Bulletin*."

This practice, it is believed, will lead to financial ruin.

Pfizer, so the rumor goes, has sharply reduced its acquisition activity.

● Use dashes or parentheses to set off long material or explanatory words.

Although in such cases you may use dashes or the parentheses in place of commas, the three marks differ in the degree to which they separate the enclosed words from the rest of the sentence. The comma is the weakest of the three, and it is best used when the material set off is closely related to the surrounding words. Dashes are stronger marks than commas and are used when the material set off tends to be long or contains internal punctuation marks. Parentheses, the strongest of the three, are primarily used to enclose material that helps explain or supplement the main words of the sentence.

Cma 4–2

Use commas to set off an appositive (a noun or a noun and its modifiers inserted to explain another noun) from the rest of the sentence. In a sense, appositives are parenthetic expressions, for they interrupt the normal flow of the sentence.

- (2) apposition words (words explaining another word),

Oracle, our database software, is releasing a new version.

St. Louis, home office of our Midwest district, will be the permanent site of our annual sales meeting.

President Cartwright, a self-educated woman, is the leading advocate of online training for employees.

But appositives that identify very closely are not set off by commas.

The word *liabilities* is not understood by most people.

Our next shipment will come on the ship *Alberta.*

Cma 4–3

Set off parenthetic words such as *however, in fact, of course, for example,* and *consequently* with commas.

- (3) certain parenthetic words (*in fact, however*), and

It is apparent, therefore, that the buyers' resistance was caused by an overvigorous sales campaign.

After the first experiment, for example, the traffic flow increased 10 percent.

The company, however, will be forced to adopt a more competitive pricing strategy.

Included in this group of parenthetic words may be introductory interjections (*oh, alas*) and responsive expressions (*yes, no, surely, indeed, well,* and so on). But if the words are strongly exclamatory or are not closely connected with the rest of the sentence, they may be punctuated as a sentence. (*No. Yes. Indeed.*)

Yes, the decision to increase production has been made.

Oh, contribute whatever you think is appropriate.

Cma 4–4

When more than one unit appears in a date or an address, set off the units by commas.

- (4) units in a date or address.

One unit: December 30 is the date of our annual inventory.

One unit: The company has one outlet in Ohio.

More than one unit: December 30, 1906, is the date the Johnston Company first opened its doors.

More than one unit: Richmond, Virginia, is the headquarters of the new sales district.

Cma 5–1

Use the comma after a subordinate clause that precedes the main clause.

- Use the comma after (1) introductory subordinate clauses and

Although it is durable, this package does not have eye appeal.

Since there was little store traffic on aisle 13, the area was converted into storage space.

Cma 5–2

Place a comma after an introductory verbal phrase. A verbal phrase is one that contains some verb derivative: a gerund, a participle, or an infinitive.

- (2) introductory verbal phrases.

Gerund phrase: After gaining the advantage, we failed to press on to victory.

Participle phrase: Realizing his mistake, Ron instructed his subordinates to keep a record of all salvaged equipment.

Infinitive phrase: To increase the turnover of automobile accessories, we must first improve their display area.

Cma 6–1

- Do not use the comma without good reason, such as between the subject and the verb.

Use the comma only for good reason. It is not a mark to be inserted indiscriminately at the writer's whim. As a rule, the use of commas should be justified by one of the standard practices previously noted.

Do not be tricked into putting a comma between the subject and the verb.

The thought that he could not afford to fail spurred him on. (No comma after *fail*.)

Cma 6–2

- Use the comma wherever it helps clarity.

Take exception to the preceding standards wherever the insertion of a comma will help clarity of expression.

Not this: From the beginning inventory methods of Hill Company have been haphazard.

But this: From the beginning, inventory methods of Hill Company have been haphazard.

Not this: Ever since she has been a model worker.

But this: Ever since, she has been a model worker.

Dash: Dsh

- Use the dash to show interruption or emphasis.

Use the dash to set off an element for emphasis or to show interrupted thought. In particular, use it with long parenthetic expressions or parenthetic expressions containing internal punctuation (see Cma 4–1). Most word processing software will usually allow you to insert a dash with a special character code. Depending on the software, you either insert the code through a combination of keystrokes or by selecting the character from a character map. You can also make the dash by striking the hyphen twice, without spacing before or after.

Budgets for some past years—2003, for example—were prepared without consulting the department heads.

The test proved that the new process is simple, effective, accurate—and more expensive.

Only one person—the supervisor in charge—has authority to approve a policy exception.

If you want a voice in the government—vote.

Exclamation Mark: Ex

- Use exclamation marks to show strong feeling.

Use the exclamation mark at the end of a sentence or an exclamatory fragment to show strong emotion. But use it sparingly; never use it with trivial ideas.

We've done it again!

Congratulations! Your outstanding performance review qualifies you for merit pay.

Hyphen: Hpn 1

- Mark word divisions with hyphens.

Use the hyphen to indicate the division of a word at the end of the line. You must divide between syllables. It is generally impractical to leave a one-letter syllable at the end of a line (*a-bove*) or to carry over a two-letter syllable to the next line (*expens-es*).

If you turn on the hyphenation feature of your word processing software, you can let it automatically take care of hyphenating words. This feature permits you to set a hyphenation range. The wider the range, the fewer words that will be hyphenated and the more ragged your margin; the narrower the range, the more words that will be hyphenated and the smoother your right margin. You also have the option of controlling the hyphenation you desire. You can accept what the program recommends, suggest a different place to hyphenate, or tell it not to hyphenate.

Hpn 2–1

Place hyphens between the parts of some compound words. Generally, the hyphen is used whenever its absence would confuse the meaning of the words.

Compound nouns: brother-in-law, cure-all, city-state, foreign-born

Compound numbers twenty-one through ninety-nine: fifty-five, eighty-one

Compound adjectives (two or more words used before a noun as a single adjective): *long-term* contract, *50-gallon* drum, *five-day* grace period, *end-of-month* clearance.

Prefixes (most have been absorbed into the word): co-organizer, ex-chairperson, anti-inflation, self-sufficient

- Place hyphens between the parts of compound words.

Hpn 2–2

A proper name used as a compound adjective needs no hyphen or hyphens to hold it together as a visual unit for the reader. The capitals perform that function.

Correct: A Lamar High School student.

Correct: A United Airlines pilot.

- Do not place hyphens between (1) proper names and

Hpn 2–3

Two or more modifiers in normal grammatical form and order need no hyphens. Particularly, a phrase consisting of an unmistakable adverb (one ending in *ly*) modifying an adjective or participle that in turn modifies a noun shows normal grammatical order and is readily grasped by the reader without the benefit of the hyphen. But an adverb not ending in *ly* is joined to its adjective or participle by the hyphen.

No hyphen needed: A poorly drawn chart.

Use the hyphen: A well-prepared chart.

- (2) words that only follow each other.

Italics: Ital 1

For the use of italics for book titles, see QM 4. Note that italics also are used for titles of periodicals, works of art, long musical compositions, and names of naval vessels and aircraft.

- Use italics for (1) publication titles,

Ital 2

Italicize rarely used foreign words—if you must use them (*wunderbar, keiretsu, oobeya*). After a foreign word is widely accepted, however, it does not need to be italicized (carpe diem, faux pas, verboten). A current dictionary is a good source for information on which foreign words are italicized.

- (2) foreign words and abbreviations, and

Ital 3

Italicize a word, letter, or figure used as its own name. Without this device, we could not write this set of rules. Note the use of italics throughout to label name words.

The little word *sell* is still in the dictionary.

The pronoun *which* should always have a noun as a clear antecedent. (Without the italics, this one becomes a fragment.)

- (3) a word used as its own name.

Software Enhances the Usefulness of Reference Tools

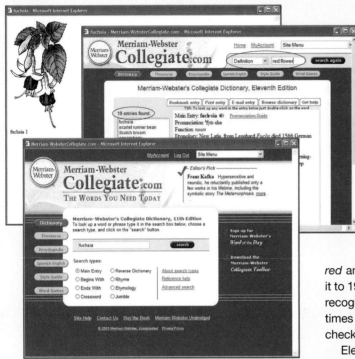

Reference software, like reference books, allows writers to look up facts when they need them. All kinds of reference materials are available electronically, from dictionaries to grammar and style guides, encyclopedias, ZIP code directories, quotation databases, maps, and much, much more. These programs vary widely in their similarities to and differences from traditional reference books.

Often they enhance the printed form, giving the user more ways to use them. Electronic dictionaries let you search for words the traditional way, with wildcards, as soundalikes (homophones), by words in their definition, and more. In the bottom example here, you see a search for the meaning of the word *fuchsia* in the traditional way at the Merriam-Webster website. However, if you were unsure of the spelling, you could search by its beginning or ending letters. Also, you may know the word begins with *fu* and ends with *a*, but not know the middle of the spelling. You could use the asterisk (*) wildcard, searching with *fu*a* to help find it. Furthermore, as you can see in the middle example, the author searched for the word by definition entering *red* and *flower* in the search field. The software narrowed it to 19 words with these search terms. Sometime you may recognize the word the minute you see it on the list; other times you'll need to review the definitions and perhaps check any illustrations.

Electronic dictionaries go beyond the printed dictionary by providing audio as well. The user here, looking up the word *fuchsia,* would simply click on the sound icon to hear the word pronounced. Additionally, electronic dictionaries often link to other definitions to help users understand the meaning when words in the definition are unclear. Such dictionaries, as well as all reference software, help writers to choose words that communicate clearly and to provide correctness in their writing.

Parentheses: Parens

- Set off parenthetic words with parentheses.

Use the parenthesis to set off words that are parenthetic or are inserted to explain or supplement the principal message (see Cma 4–1).

Robert Levine's phenomenal illustrations (*The Power of Persuasion,* 2003) show readers people are more gullible than they believe.

As soon as Owen Smith was elected chairperson (the vote was almost 2 to 1), he introduced his plan for reorganization.

Period: Pd 1

- End a declarative sentence, an imperative statement, or a courteous request with a period.

Use the period to indicate the end of a declarative sentence, an imperative statement, or a courteous request.

Declarative sentence: The survey will be completed and returned by October 26.

Imperative statement: Complete and return the survey by October 26.

Courteous request: Will you please complete and return the survey by October 26.

Pd 2

Use periods after abbreviations or initials.

Ph.D., Co., Inc., a.m., etc.

But omit the periods and use all capitals in the initials or acronyms of agencies, networks, associations, and such: IRS, NBC, OPEC, EEC.

- Use periods in abbreviations.

Pd 3

Use ellipses (a series of periods) to indicate the omission of words from a quoted passage. If the omitted part consists of something less than a sentence, three periods are customarily placed at the point of omission (a fourth period is added if the omission is a sentence or more). If the omitted part is a paragraph or more, however, a full line of periods is used. In all cases, the periods are separated by spaces.

- Use a series of periods to show omissions.

Logical explanations, however, have been given by authorities in the field. Some attribute the decline . . . to recent changes in the state's economy. . . .

. . . .

Added to the labor factor is the high cost of raw material, which has tended to eliminate many marginal producers. Moreover, the rising cost of electric power in recent years may have shifted the attention of many industry leaders to other forms of production.

Question Mark: Q

Place a question mark at the end of sentences that are direct questions.

- End direct questions with the question mark.

What are the latest quotations on Disney common stock?

Will this campaign help sell Microsoft products?

But do not use the question mark with indirect questions.

The president was asked whether this campaign would help sell Microsoft products.

He asked me what the latest quotations on Disney common stock were.

Quotation Marks: QM 1

Use quotation marks to enclose the exact words of a speaker or, if the quotation is short, the exact words of a writer.

Short written quotations are quotations of four lines or less, although authorities do not agree on this point. Some suggest three lines—others up to eight. Longer written quotations are best displayed without quotation marks and with indented right and left margins.

- Use quotation marks to enclose a speaker's or writer's exact words.

Short written quotation: H. G. McVoy sums up his presentation with this statement: "All signs indicate that change will be evolutionary, not revolutionary."

Oral quotation: "This really should bring on a production slowdown," said Ms. Kuntz.

If a quotation is broken by explanation or reference words, each part of the quotation is enclosed in quotation marks.

"Will you be specific," he asked, "in recommending a course of action?"

QM 2

Enclose a quotation within a quotation with single quotation marks.

- Use single quotation marks for a quotation within a quotation.

Professor Dalbey said, "It has been a long time since I have heard a student say, 'Prof, we need more writing assignments.' "

QM 3

- Periods and commas go inside quotation marks; semicolons and colons go outside; question marks and exclamation points go inside when they apply to the quoted part and outside when they apply to the entire sentence.

Always place periods and commas inside quotation marks. Place semicolons and colons outside the quotation marks. Place question marks and exclamation points inside if they apply to the quoted passage only and outside if they apply to the whole sentence.

"If we are patient," he said, "we will reach this year's goals." (The comma and the period are within the quotation marks.)

"Is there a quorum?" he asked. (The question mark belongs to the quoted passage.)

Which of you said, "I know where the error lies"? (The question mark applies to the entire sentence.)

I conclude only this from the union's promise to "force the hand of management": A strike will be its trump card.

QM 4

- Use quotation marks to enclose titles of parts of a publication.

Enclose in quotation marks the titles of parts of publications (articles in a magazine, chapters in a book). But italicize the titles of whole publications or underline if you are handwriting.

The third chapter of the book *Elementary Statistical Procedure* is titled "Concepts of Sampling."

Anne Fisher's timely article, "How Can I Negotiate a Fair Salary on My First Job?" appears in the current issue of *Fortune*.

Semicolon: SC 1

- Use the semicolon to separate independent clauses not connected by a conjunction.

Use the semicolon to separate independent clauses that are not connected by a conjunction.

The new contract provides wage increases; the original contract emphasized shorter hours.

Covered by this standard are independent clauses connected by conjunctive adverbs such as *however, nevertheless, therefore, then, moreover,* and *besides.*

The survey findings indicated a need to revise the policy; nevertheless, the president did not approve the proposed revision.

Small-town buyers favor the old model; therefore, the board concluded that both models should be marketed.

SC 2

- You may choose to separate with a semicolon independent clauses joined by a conjunction.

You may use the semicolon to separate independent clauses joined by *and, but, or,* or *nor* (coordinating conjunctions) if the clauses are long or if they have other punctuation in them. In such situations, you may also use the semicolon for special emphasis.

The OCAW and the NUPNG, rivals from the beginning of the new industry, have shared almost equally in the growth of membership; but the OCAW predominates among workers in the petroleum-products crafts, including pipeline construction and operation, and the NUPNG leads in memberships of chemical workers.

The market price was $6; but we paid $10.

SC 3

- Use the semicolon to separate items in a list when the items contain commas.

Separate by semicolons the items in a list when the items have commas in them.

The following gains were made in the February year-to-year comparison: Fort Worth, 7,300; Dallas, 4,705; Lubbock, 2,610; San Antonio, 2,350; Waco, 2,240; Port Arthur, 2,170; and Corpus Christi, 1,420.

Spell Check

Eye halve a spelling chequer
It came with my pea sea
It plainly marques four my revue
Miss steaks eye kin knot sea.
Eye strike a key and type a word
And weight four it two say
Weather eye am wrong oar write
It shows me strait a weigh.
As soon as a mist aches is maid
It nose bee fore two long
And eye can put the error rite
Its rare lea ever wrong.
Eye have run this poem threw it
I am shore your pleased two no
Its letter perfect awl the weigh
My chequer tolled me sew.

—Sauce unknown

Elected for the new term were Anna T. Zelnak, attorney from Cincinnati; Wilbur T. Hoffmeister, stockbroker and president of Hoffmeister Associates of Baltimore; and William P. Peabody, a member of the faculty of the University of Georgia.

SC 4

Use the semicolon between equal (coordinate) units only. Do not use it to attach a dependent clause or phrase to an independent clause.

● Use the semicolon only between equal units.

Not this: The flood damaged much of the equipment in Building 113; making it necessary for management to close the area and suspend some employees.

But this: The flood damaged much of the equipment in Building 113, making it necessary for management to close the area and suspend some employees.

Or this: The flood damaged much of the equipment in Building 113; thus, it was necessary for management to close the area and suspend some employees.

STANDARDS FOR GRAMMAR

Like the review of punctuation standards, the following summary of grammatical standards is not intended as a complete handbook on the subject. Rather, it is a summary of the major trouble spots business writers encounter. If you learn these grammatical principles, you should be able to write with the correctness expected in business.

Adjective–Adverb Confusion: AA

Do not use adjectives for adverbs or adverbs for adjectives. Adjectives modify only nouns and pronouns; and adverbs modify verbs, adjectives, or other adverbs.

● Do not use adjectives for adverbs.

   Possibly the chief source of this confusion occurs in statements in which the modifier follows the verb. If the modifier refers to the subject, an adjective should be used. If it refers to the verb, an adverb is needed.

Not this: She filed the records *quick.*

But this: She filed the records *quickly.* (Refers to the verb.)

Not this: John doesn't feel *badly.*

But this: John doesn't feel *bad.* (Refers to the noun.)

Not this: The new cars look *beautifully.*

But this: The new cars look *beautiful.* (Refers to the noun.)

It should be noted that many words are both adjective and adverb (*little, well, fast, much*). And some adverbs have two forms, of which one is the same as the adjective and the other adds *ly* (*slow* and *slowly, cheap* and *cheaply, quick* and *quickly*).

Acceptable: All our drivers are instructed to drive slow.

Acceptable: All our drivers are instructed to drive slowly.

Subject–Verb Agreement: Agmt SV

- Verbs must agree in number with their subjects.

Nouns and their verbs must agree in number. A plural noun must have a plural verb form; a singular noun must have a singular verb form.

Not this: Expenditures for miscellaneous equipment *was* expected to decline. (Expenditures is plural, so its verb must be plural.)

But this: Expenditures for miscellaneous equipment *were* expected to decline.

Not this: The *president,* as well as the staff, were not able to attend. (*President* is the subject, and the number is not changed by the modifying phrase.)

But this: The *president,* as well as the staff, *was* not able to attend.

- Compound subjects require plural verbs.

Compound subjects (two or more nouns joined by *and*) require plural verbs.

Not this: The *salespeople* and their *manager is* in favor of the proposal. (*Salespeople* and *manager* are compound subjects of the verb, but *is* is singular.)

But this: The *salespeople* and their *manager are* in favor of the proposal.

Not this: Received in the morning delivery *was* an *ink cartridge* and two *reams* of copy paper. (*Ink cartridge* and *reams* are the subjects; the verb must be plural.)

But this: Received in the morning delivery *were* an *ink cartridge* and two *reams* of copy paper.

- Collective nouns may be singular or plural.

Collective nouns may be either singular or plural, depending on the meaning intended.

The *committee have* carefully *studied* the proposal. (*Committee* is thought of as separate individuals.)

The *committee has* carefully *studied* the proposal. (The *committee* is thought of as a unit.)

- The pronouns listed here are singular.

As a rule, the pronouns *anybody, anyone, each, either, everyone, everybody, neither, nobody, somebody,* and *someone* take a singular verb. The word *none* may be either singular or plural, depending on whether it is used to refer to one unit or to more than one unit.

Either of the advertising campaigns *is* costly.

Nobody who watches the clock *is* successful.

None of the workers *understands* his assignment.

None of the workers *understand* their assignments.

Adverbial Noun Clause: AN

- Do not use an adverbial clause as a noun clause.

Do not use an adverbial clause as a noun clause. Clauses beginning with *because, when, where, if,* and similar adverbial connections are not properly used as subjects, objects, or complements of verbs.

Not this: The reason was *because* he did not submit a report.

But this: The reason was *that* he did not submit a report.

Not this: A time-series graph is *where* (or *when*) changes in an index such as wholesale prices are indicated.

But this: A time-series graph is the picturing of . . .

Awkward: Awk

Avoid awkward writing. By *awkward writing* we mean word arrangements that are unconventional, uneconomical, or simply not the best for quick understanding.

- Avoid awkward writing.

Dangling Modifiers: Dng

Avoid the use of modifiers that do not logically modify a word in the sentence. Such modifiers are said to dangle. They are both illogical and confusing. You can usually correct sentences containing dangling constructions by inserting the noun or pronoun that the modifier describes or by changing the dangling part to a complete clause.

- Avoid dangling modifiers (those that do not clearly modify a specific word).

Not this: Believing that credit customers should have advance notice of the sale, special letters were mailed to them.

But this: Believing that credit customers should have advance notice of the sale, we mailed special letters to them. (Improvement is made by inserting the pronoun modified.)

Or this: Because we believed that credit customers should have advance notice of the sale, we mailed special letters to them. (Improvement is made by changing the dangling element to a complete clause.)

Dangling modifiers are of four principal types: participial phrases, elliptical clauses, gerund phrases, and infinitive phrases.

Not this: Believing that District 7 was not being thoroughly covered, an additional salesperson was assigned to the area. (Dangling participial phrase.)

But this: Believing that District 7 was not being thoroughly covered, the sales manager assigned an additional salesperson to the area.

Not this: By working hard, your goal can be reached. (Dangling gerund phrase.)

But this: By working hard, you can reach your goal.

Not this: To succeed at this job, long hours and hard work must not be shunned. (Dangling infinitive phrase.)

But this: To succeed at this job, one must not shun long hours and hard work.

Not this: While waiting on a customer, the watch was stolen. (Dangling elliptical clause — a clause without a noun or verb.)

But this: While the salesperson was waiting on a customer, the watch was stolen.

However, several generally accepted introductory phrases are permitted to dangle. Included in this group are *generally speaking, confidentially speaking, taking all things into consideration,* and such expressions as *in boxing, in welding,* and *in farming.*

- Some introductory phrases are permitted to dangle.

Generally speaking, business activity is at an all-time high.

In farming, the land must be prepared long before planting time.

Taking all things into consideration, this applicant is the best for the job.

Sentence Fragment: Frag

Avoid the sentence fragment. Although the sentence fragment may sometimes be used to good effect, as in sales writing, it is best avoided by all but the most skilled writers. The sentence fragment consists of any group of words that are used as if they were a sentence but are not a sentence. Probably the most frequent cause of sentence fragments is the use of a subordinate clause as a sentence.

- Avoid sentence fragments (words used as a sentence that are not a sentence).

Not this: Believing that you will want an analysis of sales for November. We have sent you the figures.

But this: Believing that you will want an analysis of sales for November, we have sent you the figures.

Not this: He declared that such a procedure would not be practical. And that it would be too expensive in the long run.

But this: He declared that such a procedure would not be practical and that it would be too expensive in the long run.

Pronouns: Pn 1

- A pronoun should refer clearly to a preceding word.

Make certain that the word each pronoun refers to (its antecedent) is clear. Failure to conform to this standard causes confusion, particularly in sentences in which two or more nouns are possible antecedents or the antecedent is far away from the pronoun.

Not this: When the president objected to Mr. Carter, he told him to mind his own business. (Who told whom?)

But this: When the president objected to Mr. Carter, Mr. Carter told him to mind his own business.

Not this: The mixture should not be allowed to boil; so when you do it, watch the temperature gauge. (It doesn't have an antecedent.)

But this: The mixture should not be allowed to boil; so when conducting the experiment, watch the temperature gauge.

Not this: The Model V is being introduced this year. Ads in *USA Today, The Wall Street Journal,* and big-city newspapers over the country are designed to get sales off to a good start. It is especially designed for the novice boater who is not willing to pay a big price.

But this: The Model V is being introduced this year. Ads in *USA Today, The Wall Street Journal,* and big-city newspapers over the country are designed to get sales off to a good start. The new model is especially designed for the novice boater who is not willing to pay a big price.

Confusion may sometimes result from using a pronoun with an implied antecedent.

Not this: Because of the disastrous freeze in the citrus belt, it is necessary that most of them be replanted.

But this: Because of the disastrous freeze in the citrus belt, most of the citrus orchards must be replanted.

- Usually avoid using *which, that,* and *this* to refer to broad ideas.

Except when the reference of *which, that,* and *this* is perfectly clear, it is wise to avoid using these pronouns to refer to the whole idea of a preceding clause. Many times you can make the sentence clear by using a clarifying noun following the pronoun.

Not this (following a detailed presentation of the writer's suggestion for improving the company suggestion plan): This should be put into effect without delay.

But this: This suggestion plan should be put into effect right away.

Confusion may also result when using a pronoun with a group noun as the antecedent.

For reference to the group as a singular entity:

Not this: The committee gave their decision on the new proposal they reviewed.

But this: The committee gave its decision on the new proposal it reviewed.

For reference to the group as individual units:

Not this: The judge polled the jury for its decision on the charge.

But this: The judge polled the jury for their decision on the charge.

Pn 2

The number of the pronoun should agree with the number of its antecedent (the word it stands for). If the antecedent is singular, its pronoun must be singular. If the antecedent is plural, its pronoun must be plural.

Not this: Taxes and insurance are expenses in any business, and it must be considered carefully in anticipating profits.

But this: Taxes and insurance are expenses in any business, and they must be considered carefully in anticipating profits.

Not this: Everybody should plan for their retirement. (Such words as *everyone, everybody,* and *anybody* are singular.)

But this: Everybody should plan for his or her retirement.

Pn 3

Take care to use the correct case of the pronoun. If the pronoun serves as the subject of the verb, or if it follows a form of the infinitive *to be,* use a pronoun in the nominative case. (The nominative personal pronouns are *I, you, he, she, it, we,* and *they*).

He will record the minutes of the meeting.

I think it will be he.

If the pronoun is the object of a preposition or a verb, or if it is the subject of an infinitive, use the objective case. (The objective personal pronouns are *me, you, him, her, it, us, them.*)

Not this: This transaction is between you and he. (*He* is nominative and cannot be the object of the preposition *between.*)

But this: This transaction is between you and him.

Not this: Because the investigator praised Ms. Smith and *I,* we were promoted.

But this: Because the investigator praised Ms. Smith and *me,* we were promoted.

The case of a relative pronoun (*who, whom*) is determined by the pronoun's use in the clause it introduces. One good way of determining which case to use is to substitute the personal pronoun for the relative pronoun. If the case of the personal pronoun that fits is nominative, use *who.* If it is objective, use *whom.*

George Cutler is the salesperson *who* won the award. (*He,* nominative, could be substituted for the relative pronoun; therefore, nominative *who* should be used.)

George Cutler is the salesperson *whom* you recommended. (Objective *him* could be substituted; thus, objective *whom* is used.)

The possessive case is used for pronouns that immediately precede a gerund (a verbal noun ending in *ing*).

Our selling of the stock frightened some of the conservative members of the board.

Her accepting the money ended her legal claim to the property.

Parallelism: Prl

Parts of a sentence that express equal thoughts should be parallel (the same) in grammatical form. Parallel constructions are logically connected by the coordinating conjunctions *and, but,* and *or.* Care should be taken to see that the sentence elements connected by these conjunctions are of the same grammatical type. That is, if one of the parts is a noun, the other parts also should be nouns. If one of the parts is an infinitive phrase, the other parts also should be infinitive phrases.

Not this: The company objectives for the coming year are to match last year's sales volume, higher earnings, and improving customer relations.

But this: The company objectives for the coming year are to match last year's sales volume, to increase earnings, and to improve customer relations.

Not this: Writing copy may be more valuable experience than to make layouts.

But this: Writing copy may be more valuable experience than making layouts.

Not this: The questionnaire asks for this information: number of employees, what is our union status, and how much do we pay.

But this: The questionnaire asks for this information: number of employees, union affiliation, and pay rate.

Tense: Tns

- The tense of each verb should show the logical time of happening.

The tense of each verb, infinitive, and participle should reflect the logical time of happening of the statement: Every statement has its place in time. To communicate that place exactly, you must select your tenses carefully.

Tns 1

- Use present tense for current happenings.

Use present tense for statements of fact that are true at the time of writing.

Not this: Boston was not selected as a site for the headquarters because it *was* too near the coast. (Boston is still near the coast, isn't it?)

But this: Boston was not selected as a site for the headquarters because it *is* too near the coast.

Tns 2

- Use past tense for past happenings.

Use past tense in statements covering a definite past event or action.

Not this: Mr. Burns *says* to me, "Bill, you'll never become an auditor."

But this: Mr. Burns *said* to me, "Bill, you'll never become an auditor."

Tns 3

- The past participle (*having been . . .*) indicates a time earlier than that of the governing verb, and the present participle (*being . . .*) indicates the same period as that of the governing verb.

The time period reflected by the past participle (*having been . . .*) is earlier than that of its governing verb. The present participle (*being . . .*) reflects the same time period as that of its governing verb.

Not this: These debentures are among the oldest on record, *being* issued in early 1937.

But this: These debentures are among the oldest on record, *having been* issued in early 1937.

Not this: Ms. Sloan, *having been* the top salesperson on the force, was made sales manager. (Possible but illogical.)

But this: Ms. Sloan, *being* the top salesperson on the force, was made sales manager.

Tns 4

- Verbs in the principal clause govern those in subordinate clauses.

Verbs in subordinate clauses are governed by the verb in the principal clause. When the main verb is in the past tense, you should usually also place the subordinate verb in a past tense (past, past perfect, or present perfect).

I *noticed* [past tense] the discrepancy, and then I *remembered* [same time as main verb] the incidents that had caused it.

If the time of the subordinate clause is earlier than that of the main verb in past tense, use past perfect tense for the subordinate verb.

Not this: In early July, we *noticed* [past] that he *exceeded* [logically should be previous to main verb] his quota three times.

But this: In early July, we *noticed* that he *had exceeded* his quota three times.

The present perfect tense is used for the subordinate clause when the time of this clause is subsequent to the time of the main verb.

Not this: Before the war we *contributed* [past] generously, but lately we *forget* [should be a time subsequent to the time of the main verb] our duties.

But this: Before the war we *contributed* generously, but lately we *have forgotten* our duties.

● Present perfect tense (*have . . .*) refers to the indefinite past.

Tns 5

The present perfect tense does not logically refer to a definite time in the past. Instead, it indicates time somewhere in the indefinite past.

Not this: We *have audited* your records on July 31 of 2002 and 2003.

But this: We *audited* your records on July 31 of 2002 and 2003.

Or this: We *have audited* your records twice in the past.

● Use of present perfect tense indicates time somewhere in the indefinite past.

Word Use: WU

Misused words call attention to themselves and detract from the writing. The possibilities of error in word use are infinite; the following list contains only a few of the common errors of this kind.

● Use words correctly.

Don't Use	Use
a long ways	a long way
and etc.	etc.
anywheres	anywhere
continue on	continue
different than	different from
have got to	must
in back of	behind
in hopes of	in hope of
in regards to	in regard to
inside of	within
kind of satisfied	somewhat satisfied
nowhere near	not nearly
nowheres	nowhere
over with	over
seldom ever	seldom
try and come	try to come

Wrong Word: WW

Wrong words refer to meaning one word and using another. Sometimes these words are confused by their spelling and sometimes by their meanings. Since the spell checker won't find these errors, you need to proofread carefully to eliminate them. Here are a few examples:

● Check the spelling and meanings of words carefully.

affect	effect
among	between
bow	bough
capital	capitol
cite	sight, site

collision	collusion
complement	compliment
cooperation	corporation
deferential	differential
desert	dessert
except	accept
implicit	explicit
imply	infer
plane	plain
principal	principle
stationary	stationery

STANDARDS FOR THE USE OF NUMBERS: NO

Quantities may be spelled out or expressed as numerals. Whether to use one form or the other is often a perplexing question. It is especially perplexing to business writers, for much of their work deals with quantitative subjects. Because the proper expression of quantities is vital to business writers, the following notes on the use of numbers are presented.

No 1

- Spell out numbers nine and under, and use figures for higher numbers, except as follows:

Although authorities do not agree on number usage, business writers would do well to follow the rule of nine. By this rule, you spell out numbers nine and below. You use figures for numbers above nine.

The auditor found 13 discrepancies in the stock records.

The auditor found nine discrepancies in the stock records.

Apply the rule to both ordinal and cardinal numbers:

She was the seventh applicant.

She was the 31st applicant.

No 2

- Spell out numbers that begin a sentence.

Make an exception to the rule of nine when a number begins a sentence. Spell out all numbers in this position.

Seventy-three bonds and six debentures were destroyed.

Eighty-nine strikers picketed the north entrance.

No 3

- Keep in the same form all numbers in comparisons.

In comparisons, keep all numbers in the same form. If any number requires numeral form, use numerals for all the numbers.

We managed to salvage 3 printers, 1 scanner, and 13 monitors.

No 4

- Use numerals for percentages.

Use numerals for all percentages.

Sales increases over last year were 9 percent on automotive parts, 14 percent on hardware, and 23 percent on appliances.

On whether to use the percent sign (%) or the word, authorities differ. One good rule to follow is to use the percentage sign in papers that are scientific or technical and the word in all others. Also, it is conventional to use the sign following numbers in graphics. The trend in business appears to be toward using the sign. Consistent use of either is correct.

No 5

Present days of the month in figure form when the month precedes the day.

June 29, 2005.

When days of the month appear alone or precede the month, they may be either spelled out or expressed in numeral form according to the rule of nine.

I will be there on the 13th.

The union scheduled the strike vote for the eighth.

Ms. Millican signed the contract on the seventh of July.

Sales have declined since the 14th of August.

- Use figures for days of the month when the month precedes the day.

No 6

Use either of the two orders for date information. One, preferred by *The Chicago Manual of Style,* is day, month, and year:

On 29 June 2005 we introduced a new product line.

The other is the conventional sequence of month, day, and year. This order requires that the year be set off by commas:

On June 29, 2005, we introduced a new product line.

- For dates, use either day, month, year or month, day, year sequence, the latter with year set off by commas.

No 7

Present money amounts as you would other numbers. If you spell out the number, also spell out the unit of currency.

Twenty-seven dollars

If you present the number as a figure, use the $ with U.S. currency and the appropriate abbreviation or symbol with other currencies.

U.S., Canada, and Mexico	$27.33, Can $27.33, Mex $27.33
Euro countries	€202.61
Japan	¥2,178.61
Thailand	฿7,489.91

- Present amounts like other numbers, spelling units when numbers are spelled and using appropriate symbols or abbreviations when in figures.

No 8

Usually spell out indefinite numbers and amounts.

Over a million people live there.

The current population is about four hundred thousand.

Bill Gates's net worth is in the billions.

- Usually spell indefinite numbers and amounts.

No 9

Spell out a fraction such as one-half that stands alone (without a whole number) or begins a sentence. However, if this results in long and awkward wording or if it is technical, use the numeric form.

- Spell out fractions that stand alone or begin a sentence. Use numerics with whole numbers and in technical contexts.

Two-thirds of all jobs in the United States are jobs in the information industry.

The median price of a home rose by 6½ percent this year.

No 10

● Only use both words and figures for legal reasons.

Except in legal documents, do not express amounts in both figures and words.

For legal purposes: 25 (twenty-five)

For business use: either the figure or the word, depending on circumstance

SPELLING: SP

● Spell words correctly. Use the dictionary.

Misspelling is probably the most frequently made error in writing. And it is the least excusable. It is inexcusable because all one needs to do to virtually eliminate the error is to use a dictionary and a spell checker. Unfortunately, spell checkers cannot detect a correctly spelled, but misused, word.

● See Figure 17–1 for the 80 most commonly misspelled words.

We must memorize to spell. Thus, becoming a good speller involves long, hard work. Even so, you can improve your spelling significantly with relatively little effort. Studies show that fewer than 100 words account for most spelling errors. So if you will learn to spell these most troublesome words, you will go a long way toward solving your spelling problems. Eighty of these words appear in Figure 17–1. Although English spelling follows little rhyme or reason, a few helpful rules exist. You would do well to learn and use them.

Rules for Word Plurals

● These three rules cover plurals for most words.

1. To form the plurals of most words, add *s*.

price, prices

quote, quotes

2. To form the plurals of words ending in *s, sh, ch,* and *x,* usually add *es* to the singular.

boss, bosses

relinquish, relinquishes

glitch, glitches

tax, taxes

3. To form the plural of words ending in *y,* if a consonant precedes the *y,* drop the *y* and add *ies*. But if the *y* is preceded by a vowel, add *s*.

company, companies

medley, medleys

key, keys

Other Spelling Rules

● These rules cover four other trouble areas of spelling.

1. Words ending in *ce* or *ge* do not drop the *e* when adding *ous* or *able*.

charge, chargeable

change, changeable

notice, noticeable

service, serviceable

2. Words ending in *l* do not drop the *l* when adding *ly*.

final, finally

principal, principally

FIGURE 17–1 — Eighty of the Most Frequently Misspelled Words

absence	desirable	irritable	pursue
accessible	despair	leisure	questionnaire
accommodate	development	license	receive
achieve	disappear	misspelling	recommend
analyze	disappoint	necessary	repetition
argument	discriminate	ninety	ridiculous
assistant	drunkenness	noticeable	seize
balloon	embarrassment	occasionally	separate
benefited	equivalent	occurrence	sergeant
category	exceed	panicky	sheriff
cede	existence	parallel	succeed
changeable	forty	paralyze	suddenness
committee	grammar	pastime	superintendent
comparative	grievous	persistent	supersede
conscience	holiday	possesses	surprise
conscious	incidentally	predictable	truly
deductible	indispensable	privilege	until
definitely	insistent	proceed	vacuum
dependent	irrelevant	professor	vicious
description	irresistible	pronunciation	weird

3. Words ending in silent *e* usually drop the *e* when adding a suffix beginning with a vowel.

have, having

believe, believable

dine, dining

time, timing

4. Place *i* before *e* except after *c*.

relieve   conceive

believe   receive

Exception: when the word is sounded as long *a*.

neighbor   weigh

Exceptions:

either	Fahrenheit	height
seize	surfeit	efficient
sufficient	neither	foreign
leisure	ancient	seizure
weird	financier	codeine
forfeit	seismograph	sovereign
deficient	science	counterfeit

CAPITALIZATION: CAP

- Capitalize all proper names and the beginning words of sentences.

Use capitals for the first letters of proper names. Exceptions include names designed or used by the owner to begin with lowercase such as eBay, iOmega, and nVidia. Common examples are these:

Streets: 317 East Boyd Avenue

Geographic places: Chicago, Indiana, Finland

Companies: Yahoo!

Title preceding names: President Watkins

Titles of books, articles, poems: Lesikar's *Basic Business Communication*

First words of sentences and complimentary closes

The word **number** *(or its abbreviation) when used with a figure to identify something:* Our supply of No. 10 envelopes is running low.

As noted earlier, other standards are useful in clear communication. But those covered in the preceding pages will help you through most of your writing problems. By using them, you can give your writing the precision that good communication requires. For further references on this topic, you will find several links to more detailed sources on the textbook website. You also will find some interactive self-tests there to help you review this material.

Correct any punctuation or grammar errors you can find in the following sentences. Explain your corrections.

1. Charles E. Baskin the new member of the advisory committee has been an employee for seven years.

2. The auditor asked us, "If all members of the work group had access to the petty cash fund?"

3. Our January order consisted of the following items; two dozen Post-it pads, cube size, one dozen desk blotters, 20 by 32 inches, and one dozen gel roller pens, permanent black.

4. The truth of the matter is, that the union representative had not informed the workers of the decision.

5. Sales for the first quarter were the highest in history, profits declined for the period.

6. We suggest that you use a mild soap for best results but detergents will not harm the product.

7. Employment for October totaled 12,741 an increase of 3.1 percent over September.

8. It would not be fair however to consider only this point.

9. It is the only shrink resistant antiwrinkle and inexpensive material available.

10. Todd Thatcher a supervisor in our company is accused of the crime.

11. Mr. Goodman made this statement, "Contrary to our expectations, Smith and Company will lose money this year."

12. I bought and he sold.

13. Soon we saw George Sweeney who is the auditor for the company.

14. Sold in light medium and heavy weight this paper has been widely accepted.

15. Because of a common belief that profits are too high we will have to cut our prices on most items.

16. Such has been the growth of the cities most prestigious firm, H.E. Klauss and Company.

17. In 2003 we were advised in fact we were instructed to accept this five year contract.

18. Henrys goofing off has gotten him into trouble.

19. Cyrus B. Henshaw who was our leading salesperson last month is the leading candidate for the position.

20. The sales representative who secures the most new accounts will receive a bonus.

21. The word phone which is short for telephone should be avoided in formal writing.

22. In last weeks issue of Fortune appeared Johnson's latest article Tiger! The Sky's the Limit for Golf.

23. Yes he replied this is exactly what we mean.

24. Why did he say John it's too late?

25. Place your order today, it is not too late.

26. We make our plans on a day to day basis.

27. There is little accuracy in the 60 day forecast.

28. The pre Christmas sale will extend over twenty six days.

29. We cannot tolerate any worker's failure to do their duty.

30. An assortment of guns, bombs, burglar tools, and ammunition were found in the seller.

31. If we can be certain that we have the facts we can make our decision soon.

32. This one is easy to make. If one reads the instructions carefully.

33. This is the gift he received from you and I.

34. A collection of short articles on the subject were printed.

35. If we can detect only a tenth of the errors it will make us realize the truth.

36. She takes criticism good.

37. There was plenty of surprises at the meeting.

38. It don't appear that we have made much progress.

39. The surface of these products are smooth.

40. Everybody is expected to do their best.

41. The brochures were delivered to John and I early Sunday morning.

42. Who did he recommend for the job.

43. We were given considerable money for the study.

44. He seen what could happen when administration breaks down.

45. One of his conclusions is that the climate of the region was not desirable for our purposes.

46. Smith and Rogers plans to buy the Moline plant.

47. The committee feels that no action should be taken.

48. Neither of the workers found their money.

49. While observing the employees, the work flow was operating at peak perfection.

50. The new building is three stories high, fifteen years old, solid brick construction, and occupies a corner lot.

51. They had promised to have completed the job by noon.

52. Jones has been employed by Kimberly Clark for twenty years.

53. Wilson and myself will handle the job.

54. Each man and woman are expected to abide by this rule.

55. The boiler has been inspected on April 1 and May 3.

56. To find problems and correcting them takes up most of my work time.

57. The case of canned goods were distributed to the homeless.

58. The motor ran uneven.

59. All are expected except John and she.

60. Everyone here has more ability than him.

A SELF-ADMINISTERED DIAGNOSTIC TEST OF CORRECTNESS

The following test is designed to give you a quick measure of your ability to handle some of the most troublesome punctuation and grammar situations. First, correct all the errors in each sentence. Then turn to Appendix A for the recommended corrections and the symbols for the punctuation and grammar standards involved. Next, study the standards that you violate.

1. An important fact about this keyboard is, that it has the patented "ergonomic design".

2. Goods received on Invoice 2741 are as follows; 3 dozen blue denim shirts, size 15–33, 4 mens gortex gloves, brown, size large, and 5 dozen assorted socks.

3. James Silver president of the new union had the priviledge of introducing the speaker.

4. We do not expect to act on this matter however until we hear from you.

5. Shipments through September 20, 2004 totaled 69,485 pounds an increase of 17 percent over the year ago total.

6. Brick is recommended as the building material but the board is giving serious consideration to a substitute.

7. Markdowns for the sale total $34,000, never before has the company done anything like this.

8. After long experimentation a wear resistant high grade and beautiful stocking has been perfected.

9. Available in white green and blue this paint is sold by dealers all over the country.

10. Julie Jahn who won the trip is our most energetic salesperson.

11. Good he replied, sales are sure to increase.

12. Hogan's article Retirement? Never!, printed in the current issue of Management Review, is really a part of his book A Report on Worker Security.

13. Formal announcement of our Labor Day sale will be made in thirty two days.

14. Each day we encounter new problems. Although they are solved easily.

15. A list of models, sizes, and prices of both competing lines are being sent to you.

16. The manager could not tolerate any employee's failing to do their best.

17. A series of tests were completed only yesterday.

18. There should be no misunderstanding between you and I.

19. He run the accounting department for five years.

20. This report is considerable long.

21. Who did you interview for the position?

22. The report concluded that the natural resources of the Southwest was ideal for the chemical industry.

23. This applicant is six feet in height, 28 years old, weighs 165 pounds, and has had eight years' experience.

24. While reading the report, a gust of wind came through the window, blowing papers all over the room.

25. The sprinkler system has been checked on July 1 and September 3.

CHAPTER EIGHTEEN

Technology-Enabled Communication

CHAPTER OBJECTIVES

Upon completing this chapter, you will be able to describe the role of technology in business communication. To reach this goal, you should be able to

1 Explain how technology helps in constructing messages.

2 Identify appropriate tools for different stages in the writing process.

3 Discuss how technology helps in the presentation of messages.

4 Explain basic concepts of document layout and design.

5 Discuss various ways to transmit messages and the hardware currently used.

6 Describe how technology assists in collaboration.

7 Discuss what impact future developments in technology might have on business communication.

Business Communication Is Technology . . . Is Lesikar

In today's competitive work environment, technology and business communication go hand in hand. That's why the chapter you are about to read in Lesikar's *Basic Business Communication* is also featured as an enhanced chapter with more material on the web. It will be regularly updated by the authors to ensure the inclusion of the latest developments in technology and how they impact the world of business communication.

So visit our website often at **www.mhhe.com/lesikar05** to get the most up-to-date information about the technological changes that affect the way we communicate in business. We look forward to your feedback.

Using Technology in Communication Tasks

The company that hired you after your recent graduation is looking into ways the information technology (IT) department can empower its employees with technological support. Your new boss has asked you to be on the team that is to propose new ideas. The boss has told you that this team, composed of employees from a variety of divisions, will discuss hardware, software, and the Internet. One of the main focuses will be on identifying ways to help employees improve their day-to-day communication.

This chapter is designed to help you—to give you a picture of where we are now and where we may be going. It provides a structure for continuing to build your understanding of how future technology will assist you in communication tasks.

• Technology assists with both the tedious and creative writing tasks.

Technological tools can enhance the uniquely human ability to communicate. But as with any set of tools, how one uses them determines their degree of effectiveness. By using your mind both to create messages and to focus the technology appropriately, you can improve the quality of your communication.

Appropriately used, technology can assist individuals and groups with both the routine work related to writing as well as the creative, thinking aspects. William Zinsser, author of *On Writing Well,* compares one tool—the word processor—to a dishwasher. He describes it as liberating one from a chore that's not creative and that saps one's energy. As you'll learn, several technological tools assist you in this fashion. George Gilder, publisher of the *Gilder Technology Report,* believes the new technologies affirm our intellectual power and creativity. And Bill Gates, chairman and chief software architect of Microsoft, predicts that technology will bring us both improved voice recognition and enhanced graphics. He also believes we will be making more use of the computer to read, search, and make notations, predicting that the tablet PCs will be ubiquitous on college campuses in three years. As bandwidth increases infinitely and videogaming collaboration pushes genres, Gates believes that technology will change the dynamics of all kinds of work—not just IT. Andrew Grove, chairman of Intel Corporation, concurs; he believes IT's potential for changing the way people live and work is immense.

When you think of enhancing the communication process with technology, you probably first think of using word processing software on a personal computer. While that is one important tool, there are numerous hardware, software, and web-based tools that can help improve your messages. These tools help with the construction, presentation, and transmission of messages as well as with collaboration.

TOOLS FOR CONSTRUCTING MESSAGES

• Computer tools can be used throughout the writing process.

Computer tools for constructing written messages can be associated with the different stages of the writing process: planning, gathering and collecting information, analyzing and organizing information, and writing and rewriting. In the past, many of these tools were discrete tools. But today, as we move toward greater integration, they often work seamlessly with each other. And, of course, many of the formerly discrete tools have become integral parts of today's word processors. The more skilled you become with each of these tools, the better they serve you.

Computer Tools for Planning

• Outlining or brainstorming programs help in planning the content of a message.

Whether you are writing a short message or a long report, you can use a computer to help you plan both the document and the writing project. In planning the content of the document, *outlining* or *brainstorming* tools are useful. You can brainstorm, listing

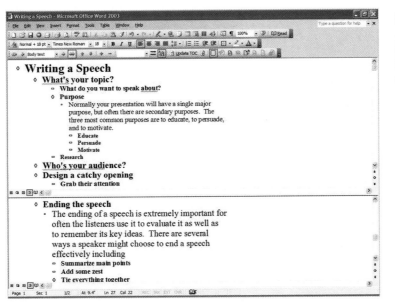

FIGURE 18-1

Illustration of the Fully
Expanded Outline Tool in
Word Using a Split
Screen

your ideas as they occur to you. Later you tag related ideas, asking the computer to group them. Outlining tools are included in most word processors. One way to use an outliner is with a split screen, as shown in Figure 18–1. In one part of the screen you'll see one part of your outline and in the other part, another section of the document you are writing. Today's large-screen monitors make this an effective use. Another way you can use an outliner is as a separate document. In this case your outline is held in memory; you can toggle back and forth to view it or work with the outline and document side by side using a widescreen display. Another discrete or specialty tool for planning is a concept-mapping/idea-generation program. As you see in Figure 18–2, below, the program Inspiration provides both a visual and an outlining mode, which allows users to toggle back and forth or work primarily in the mode that suits their

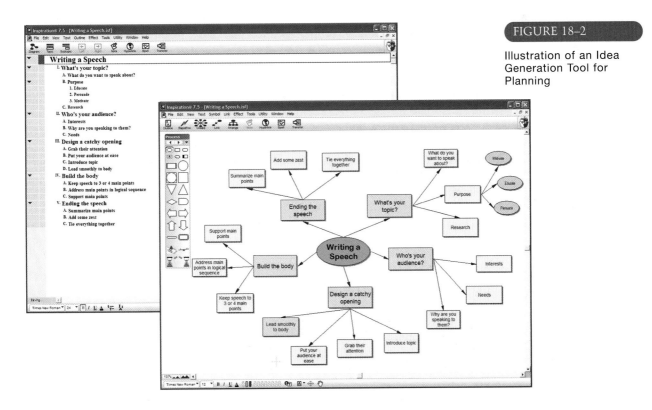

FIGURE 18-2

Illustration of an Idea
Generation Tool for
Planning

SOURCE: www.aceproject.com

particular tasks. You can also use these tools on your handheld personal digital assistant (PDA).

- **Project management programs assist in identifying tasks and allocating resources.**

When you are working on a long writing project, several projects, or one carried over a long time, *project management programs* are excellent for planning the project. They allow you to identify all the tasks needed to complete the project, to determine how much time each task might take, and to generate a time-and-task chart (commonly called a Gantt chart). Also, they help you keep track of your progress and determine how to reallocate your resources to complete the project on time or within budget. You can see an example of a Gantt chart created using a web-based tool in Figure 18–3.

- **Personal information management programs assist with time management.**

Finding time for writing, of course, is one of the major challenges for businesspeople. By using *personal information management (PIM)* tools, you can plan time for completing writing projects. These time-management tools are essentially annotated electronic calendars. However, they are excellent planning tools for scheduling your writing tasks. They will remind you of tasks to complete and days remaining before a document needs to be finished. These tools are readily available. One such desktop tool is Microsoft Outlook. It can be synced with many handheld PDAs as well as Internet-based PIM sites. But you can choose from a slew of other time-management tools as well. These offer a variety of ways to help you plan time for writing tasks, from day-to-day scheduling to longer-term planning. Figure 18–4 on page 499 shows the way one tool looks. The bell icon shows that this writer set an alarm to let the computer remind him or her when it was time to write. The alarm sounds and the window opens at the designated time with a precise message of what needs to be done.

Some research identifies planning as the primary step that separates good writers from others. However, few writers have discovered the power of electronic planning tools. Using the powerful features that both project management and PIM tools provide will give you the potential to produce high-quality work in a timely fashion.

Computer Tools for Gathering and Collecting Information

Before you can write, you have to have something to say. Sometimes you may be writing about your own ideas, but often you will supplement them with facts. Gathering facts or data is one of the most important jobs of the writer. Today you will want to combine your manual search for facts with electronic searches. The computer can help you find a variety of information quickly and accurately because today much of our published information is available electronically. In fact, some kinds of information are only available electronically. In Chapter 19, you will learn ways to evaluate the information you find online.

● When you need
information for a writing
task, consider
conducting an electronic
search.

While technology makes
constructing documents
with graphics easy,
writers still need to
carefully review the
messages they send.

What you are looking for are facts. These facts can be stored in databases, which can be either internal or external. Your report due today at 1:00 PM might be on the current inventory of your off-site manufacturing product line. You could simply connect to your company's computer at noon and download the most recent data before completing your report. However, if you need to project the number of completed units by the end of the month, you also may need to connect to your supplier's computer to check the inventory of the parts you will need to complete your units. In this case, you will be using your computer to find facts both internally (from within your company) and externally (from your suppliers).

Most libraries now allow both internal and external access to their online catalogs and databases. This means you can use the online catalog from within the library or from anywhere outside the library. Most college networks also allow you to connect to the library resources from campus computer labs, dormitories, and remote offices. And many colleges are installing wireless networks, allowing users within range and with wireless capabilities on laptops and PDAs to access their library resources.

You also can gather facts on the Internet. This expands your resources immensely beyond your local library. Not only can you reach the Library of Congress, but you also can search libraries in other countries. You can gather information from sources not available in any library anywhere. While you do need to be especially critical of the sources of your facts, knowing how to use the Internet effectively to gather information can give you a tremendous competitive advantage. Chapter 19 gives you more details on using the Internet to gather business information.

Currently you can use technology such as Google News Alert to push the information you want to your desktop. By completing a profile at a content provider's website, you will create a filter so the kind of information pushed to you is the kind you want. You also can use software agents to monitor sources and notify you when information you specify is available. And, of course, you can rerun the results page that you have saved from a search using a well-designed search strategy. The new results page will be updated to reflect the information available at the moment.

Once you have gathered the facts, you will want to store them in some organized fashion so you can retrieve them readily when needed. *Database tools* will help you immensely here. If your company is interested in developing a new product for a newly defined market niche, you may want to collect information about the targeted market, potential suppliers of components of your new product, sites for producing the product, projected labor costs, and so on. You could do this simply by entering the facts of publication and abstracted information in your individually designed form created with database tools. The source information you have collected will be available whenever you need it. You can search and sort it on any of the categories (called fields) you set up on your data entry screen.

Variations of the generic database are specialty tools such as EndNote, ProCite, Reference Manager, RefWorks, and others. These specialty programs allow you to enter information automatically as you download from a wide variety of online databases. Figure 18–5 gives you an example of this type of data manager, EndNote. You will find a trial version of EndNote on your student CD. Or you may want to use RefWorks, a web-based tool for data collection.

In Chapter 19, which discusses business research methods, you will learn about other online information providers for business information. The major point to remember is that in business it is not necessarily what you know that really counts, but what you can find out. No one can know all there is to know about a subject, but those who are skilled at using a computer to gather information will find it a real asset.

Computer Tools for Analyzing and Organizing

Three tools that writers find useful in analyzing data are statistics, graphics, and spreadsheet tools. Since sometimes you cannot say very much about raw numbers, combining them or viewing them in different ways gives you a clearer picture of their meaning. Today, some very sophisticated *statistical programs* have been made user-

FIGURE 18–5

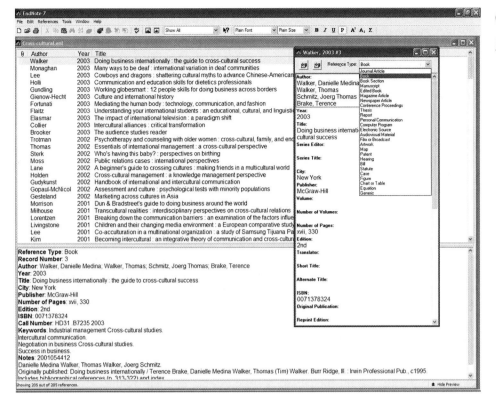

friendly, allowing those with little computer expertise to use them easily. Some programs will even query you about the nature of your data and recommend which statistical tests to use. Also, most *spreadsheet programs* will compute a broad range of statistics to help writers give meaningful interpretations to data.

Graphics programs help writers in several ways. First, graphics reveal trends and relationships in data that are often hard to cull from raw data. This helps writers understand clearly the meaning of their data. New data visualization tools, which allow users to graph and parse huge amounts of data, go further. These tools give users both the power to explore what their data means from multiple perspectives, as well as revealing where no data exists. These tools help users gain insights other tools cannot provide. Second, graphics programs help writers explain more clearly to readers what the data mean. For example, you can direct the reader to look at the red and blue lines for the last five years on a line chart, noting the trend of increasing rate of return. You can create graphics easily with all three tools. Also, most of these tools have features that allow you to annotate the graphic, directing the reader's attention to some particular aspect of the graph. You no longer have to be a graphic artist to create clear, good-looking graphics.

- Graphics programs help you understand the data and create graphics.

Outlining or *brainstorming programs* are an organizing tool for the writer as well as a planning tool. Once you have captured your ideas and grouped related ideas, you can rearrange items into a meaningful order, organizing with the reader in mind. You also can collapse or expand the outline to view as few or as many levels as you want. This lets you see a macro view or big picture of your document as well as a micro or detailed view, so you can check for consistency at all levels.

- Outlining and brainstorming programs help you organize your information.

Computer Tools for Writing

Word processing software is clearly the dominant writing tool of most writers. Today's word processors allow you to use other writing tools from within the word processor or that integrate seamlessly with it. Other computer writing tools that help writers include *spelling checkers, electronic thesauruses, grammar and style checkers, electronic references, graphics, drawing packages, voice recognition tools,* and *information rights management.* The following discussion of these computer writing tools will point out how they can be used as well as caution you about any limitations.

Word Processing Software. By liberating you from tiresome chores, word processing gives you time to spend on revising, editing, and other document-polishing efforts. Some of the most common features of word processing software for revising and editing include insert/delete, move and copy, and search and replace.

Insert allows the writer to add characters at any point, while *delete* lets the writer delete characters. You can change your mind and undo the most recent insert and delete changes. Some writers rarely delete text, moving the text to the end of the file or to another file for possible future use. The search and replace feature can be used in several ways. One way might be to search for the name in a file of someone who got married, retired, or was promoted and replace that name with the new name. Usually the writer decides whether to replace automatically every occurrence of the item or to check each occurrence. The search feature is usually used to find a particular word, name, or place. However, sometimes writers add asterisks or other symbols to mark copy or to add remarks or reminders—similar to the way one would use the bookmark feature. Later they search for those symbols to find the points in the document that need attention. You will find that these common features will be useful over and over.

Two other useful features of word processing are basic math and simple sorting. The basic math feature lets the writer enter columns or rows of numbers, leaving the calculation job for the program. The sorting feature lets the writer enter columns or rows of words, leaving the alphabetic sorting for the program. While these are useful features of word processing programs, the writer has to be careful to enter or mark the copy exactly the way the software needs it to do the proper calculating or sorting.

The tables feature is another tool that enables you to do simple math and sort. It works similarly to a spreadsheet by allowing you to enter formulas in table cells, freeing you from the math. You also can link a table to a spreadsheet. When numbers change in the linked spreadsheet, they are automatically changed in the table with which they are linked. The tables feature allows formatting individual cells, rows, and columns. It is useful for presenting both data and textual material in rows and columns.

Another nice feature of many word processing programs is the hidden text or comment feature. If you insert the proper symbol, the comments that follow will be recorded in the file but not printed unless you tell the software to print them. Teachers can use this feature to put test answers in files but not on the test; later they can print a second copy and direct the software to print the comments. This feature can be used for reminders, detailed information, and such. For example, one might note that the vice president directed that an exception to company policy be granted under some special circumstances. Or one might leave a reminder to verify the statistics presented at a particular point in a document. In Figure 18–6, you can see both the display of a comment and the printed document without the comment.

Two additional editing features involve the physical presentation of documents. These features are hyphenation and format change. Both help you change how the physical output looks. Hyphenation, for example, is a feature that helps the right margin appear less ragged than when it is not used. A ragged margin does not usually bother most people on a full page with full-length lines; however, when one is using a short line without hyphenating, the right margin can be distracting if it appears ragged. The example of column text in Figure 18–7, with and without hyphenation, illustrates how hyphenation can smooth out a ragged right margin. Word's reveal formatting feature and WordPerfect's reveal codes also help you change margins, tabs, spacing, and so on. Formatting is particularly useful when you are changing letterheads, paper sizes, type styles, or binding. It allows you to experiment easily to find the most appropriate form to present the document to the reader.

Since revising and editing are extremely important to turning out well-written business documents, these are tools you will use often.

- Word processing helps you capture, manipulate, edit, and revise your messages.

- Insert, delete, move and copy, and search and replace enable you to do what the terms suggest.

- Basic math calculates columns and sorting arranges information in an order.

- The tables feature also allows you to do simple math with data and to sort them.

- The hidden text feature permits inserting information that is not printed until you choose to print it.

- Hyphenation and format change enable you to control evenness of right margin.

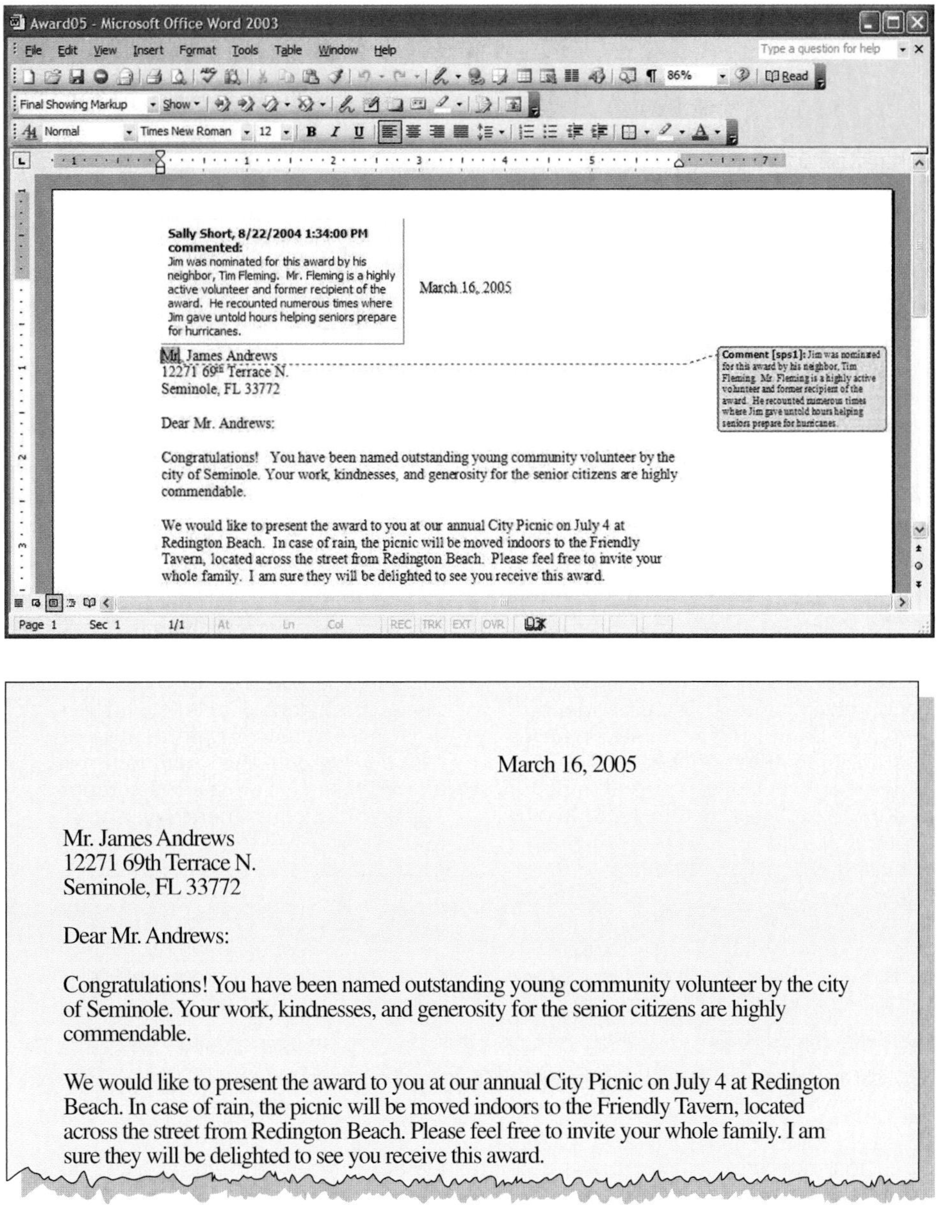

March 16, 2005

Mr. James Andrews
12271 69th Terrace N.
Seminole, FL 33772

Dear Mr. Andrews:

Congratulations! You have been named outstanding young community volunteer by the city of Seminole. Your work, kindnesses, and generosity for the senior citizens are highly commendable.

We would like to present the award to you at our annual City Picnic on July 4 at Redington Beach. In case of rain, the picnic will be moved indoors to the Friendly Tavern, located across the street from Redington Beach. Please feel free to invite your whole family. I am sure they will be delighted to see you receive this award.

FIGURE 18-6

Illustration of the Comment Tool for Writing

Some other word processing features that make the writing job easier are footnoting, table of contents generating, and index building. Most high-end word processors include the footnoting feature. It allows the writer to mark the place where the footnote occurs, entering the footnote at that point. The software then keeps track of the line count, placing each footnote at the bottom of the page on which it occurs, as well as numbering the footnotes consecutively. Also, the program will move a footnote if the text associated with it is moved. Another chore word processing software assists with is table of contents generation. Using the particular tagging system your program requires, you simply tell the software to generate the table of contents. In some cases you get to select from a variety of formats, and in other cases you can define the format. Closely related to the table of contents generator is the index builder. The writer simply tags the words to be indexed, includes cross-references, and creates a list of words and the program builds an alphabetic index with associated page numbers. This procedure is particularly helpful with long, frequently referenced documents.

- Footnoting, table of contents generating, and index building are features that make writing easier.

Word processing also has four other features that save the writer from having to reenter the same information: merge, macros, QuickWords and AutoText, and headers and footers. The merge feature permits you to combine one form document with a document containing variable data. Merge is particularly useful in early- and late-stage

- Using advanced word processing features saves time.

FIGURE 18–7

Computers, Human Intellect, and Organizational Nervous Systems

An executive provides vision and direction, makes decisions, diagnoses and solves problems, negotiates, convinces, and selects and coaches people. All these actions depend on the executive's ability to think creatively and communicate clearly; clear communication and creative thinking can be enhanced by the use of computers.

Unfortunately, most people don't realize this. The computer's role as a valuable thinking tool

seems to be a secret. Instead, many intelligent people, even today, believe that computers are best suited to clerical and administrative tasks. They see the computer as only a convenience or an operational necessity. I see the computer as an extension of the human brain.

An understanding of the connection between the evolution of the human mind and computers takes us back in time.

Note the ragged margin before the hyphenation feature is turned on.

Computers, Human Intellect, and Organizational Nervous Systems

An executive provides vision and direction, makes decisions, di-agnoses and solves problems, nego-tiates, convinces, and selects and coaches people. All these actions depend on the executive's ability to think creatively and communicate clearly; clear communication and creative thinking can be enhanced by the use of computers.

Unfortunately, most people don't realize this. The computer's role as a valuable thinking tool

seems to be a secret. Instead, many intelligent people, even to-day, believe that computers are best suited to clerical and adminis-trative tasks. They see the comput-er as only a convenience or an op-erational necessity. I see the com-puter as an extension of the hu-man brain.

An understanding of the con-nection between the evolution of the human mind and computers takes us back in time.

Note that after the hyphenation feature is used, the right margin is smoothed out.

collection messages, where names and amounts are variable but the message content is the same. Another feature, called *macros,* allows you to enter any characters you want to call up at the command of a few keystrokes. This feature is useful for calling up form paragraphs for answering commonly occurring questions as well as for bringing up repeatedly used memo headings or letter closings. QuickWords and AutoText features in WordPerfect and Word help users automatically complete frequently entered, long, or difficult terms and phrases. You simply begin entering the phrase and the software gives you the option of completing it for you. Headers and footers also let the program enter repeated information at the top and bottom of pages as well as count and print the page numbers.

Other special features of word processing programs help with using columns and fonts, importing graphics and spreadsheet files, and so on. Knowing how to apply fully the features of the word processing software you use will definitely make writing and revising easier for you.

- Learn to apply fully the features of your word processor.

Spelling Checkers. Along with AutoText and QuickWords, spelling checkers are relied on daily by business writers. However, they are effective only if the writer uses them. And they are only effective at identifying words that are not in their dictionary. Therefore, spellers could miss some of your mistakes. Mistakes you will want to watch out for include wrong word errors such as "compliment" for "complement" or "imply" for "infer." A spell checker also will miss errors such as "desert" for "dessert"

- Spelling checkers supplement proofreading but do not replace it.

Backing up Frequently Is the Writer's Responsibility

Most writers know how difficult it is to create a document, much less re-create it, so they are willing to spend a little time to protect their investment. In the Save Options dialog box of Word, a writer can set up the program to fit his or her needs. Here a writer elected to have Word always create a backup file, to run these backups every 10 minutes, and to do it in the background. This writer could have also asked Word to allow fast saves, which only save the changes but take more disk space. This type of saving helps protect from systems that go down unexpectedly whether from crashes, power outages, accidents, or viruses.

To protect your documents further, you might want to vary the backup media you use. If your computer is damaged or becomes infected with a computer virus, you still have copies of your files. This media could range from simple backups on disks or USB drives to backups at offsite locations. Individuals can do this with subscriptions on Internet hosts such as X-drive, idrive, and others, or on a smaller scale one can find free space at Yahoo Briefcase, school computers, and sometimes an Internet service provider.

Backing up is an easy, inexpensive form of insurance for a writer.

---

or misused words such as "good" for "well." In addition, if any misspelled words have inadvertently been added to its dictionary, the speller will skip those words too. Therefore, careful proofreading is still in order after a document has been checked with a spelling program. Taking care to proofread carefully is a simple courtesy your reader will appreciate.

Thesaurus Software. While some serious writers have a bound thesaurus on hand, many use an electronic thesaurus with great ease and efficiency. The ease of popping up a window with suggested synonyms is hard to beat. Most word processors include a thesaurus; however, several good web-based programs are available. You may have noticed that the Merriam-Webster website includes an online thesaurus; you can access it on the site or through the Merriam-Webster toolbar if you have installed it. The thesaurus is a powerful tool, and the computer has made it faster to use and easier to access.

- The electronic thesaurus gives easy access to synonyms.

Grammar and Style Checkers. The value of grammar and style checkers is often debated. Unlike spelling programs, which are easily able to identify "wrong" words (words that are not in their dictionaries), grammar and style checkers identify "possible problems" with "suggestions" for revision. It is then your responsibility to decide whether the "possible problem" is a problem and whether the "suggestion" is the best solution. Making this decision requires that you have a good understanding of basic grammar. One recent study of accounting students' writing identified their most common writing errors. When a grammar checker was run on these common errors, less than half were detected. Microsoft Word found only 3 of the 13 errors and suggested 3 correct revisions; WordPerfect found 6 of the 13 errors, but only 5 of the 6 revisions were appropriate.[1] However, these programs are improving rapidly, adding expert system techniques to identify "possible problems" in context more accurately.

- Grammar and style checkers are only suggestion systems.

---

[1] G. E. Whittenburg and Marie E. Flatley, "The Most Common Writing Errors Made by Accounting Students," *Proceedings of the Western Decision Sciences Institute* (Reno, NV) (April 1998).

FIGURE 18–8

Illustration of a Spelling
and Grammar Checker
for Writing

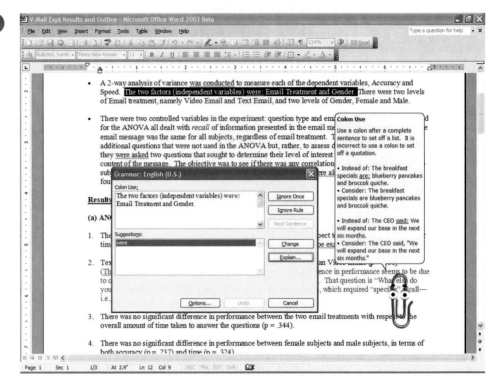

- They also evaluate a variety of other elements of writing quality.

In addition to checking grammar, style, word usage, and punctuation, these programs now report readability, strength, descriptive, and jargon indexes. They also perform sentence structure analysis, suggesting that you use simpler sentences, vary the sentence beginnings, use more or fewer prepositional phrases, and make various other changes. Grammar and style checkers also identify "possible problems" with specific words that might be slang, jargon, misspelled, misused, negative, or difficult for readers to understand. A complementary feature, Word Count, reports statistics for number of pages, words, characters, paragraphs, and lines. An example of the interactive use of one grammar checker is shown in Figure 18–8.

- Although often criticized, this tool is improving.

While the debate goes on, the tool is getting better. Recent versions address some of the issues concerning writers. For example, recent versions of grammar and style checkers are much more flexible than older versions. If you are writing in an informal environment where your boss finds beginning sentences with "And" and "But" acceptable, you can turn off the rule that would identify those beginnings as problems. Also, you can choose the level of writing your intended audience wants. These are just a few examples of the flexibility in the newest versions of grammar and style checkers.

Grammar and style checkers are definitely important for the business writer. But, like all tools, the more appropriately you use them the better job they do for you.

- A wide variety of reference books are available for easy access.

Reference Programs. Reference programs are just what its name suggests—programs that present reference books such as dictionaries, style manuals, ZIP code directories, and so on. While a few of these reference programs are on CDs, many dictionaries, thesauruses, books of quotations, ZIP code directories, world almanacs, and other references are on the web. They include such things as pronunciation of words in audio form and pictures, including video and animation. The Merriam-Webster website includes two good reference sources—an encyclopedia and a style guide. Chapter 19 and the textbook website identify many of these locations.

- Graphics and draw programs assist in supplementing textual materials with visuals.

Graphics and Drawing Tools. Graphics and drawing tools are becoming more important for the writer every day. Not only are these programs becoming easier to use, but you also can now launch them from within your word processor. In most cases, your drawing is pasted in your document at the point you left it. The introduction of ready-made graphs and pictures (called clip art), low-cost scanners and digital cameras, and photo libraries have made it easier to supplement text with professional-looking graphics. You learned how to use graphics effectively in Chapter 13. The important point to remember here is that the computer enables you to enhance textual communication easily with graphics.

Voice Recognition Tools. Recently several companies have introduced some good tools for continuous voice input. Although they are priced favorably, they have not yet gained wide acceptance in most businesses. However, as businesspeople begin to realize how easily they can compose their messages by talking to their computer systems and even editing through voice commands, their acceptance is likely to grow.

- Voice input is new technology that will free the writer from keying messages.

Information Rights Management (IRM). Beginning with Microsoft's Office Professional 2003, the software gave writers the ability to specify how their documents are shared, controlled, and used. Until this time writers had little control over a document once it was transmitted; one could password protect a document or perhaps encrypt it but both were awkward and a bit complicated to use. The new set of IRM tools are easy to use and much more powerful than these old methods. As you can see in Figure 18–9, the permission dialog box allows users to easily set a variety of features.

Writers can determine how their documents are shared by specifying who can read, change, or have full control over them. Additionally, the writer can set an expiration date on these permissions. Not only do these features help businesses prevent sensitive information from getting into the wrong hands either accidentally or intentionally, but they also give writers control over documents once they leave their computers. If only certain people have permissions, forwarded and copied files will be protected from unauthorized use just as print copies can be.

IRM tools will likely cause many businesses to establish practices or policies on the kinds of permissions required for various types of information. Perhaps this will help decrease in-box clutter as writers begin to think about who really needs the document and for how long.

As you have learned, technology is certainly an important tool for the writer in constructing messages. While word processing is the writer's primary tool in constructing a message, a wide variety of other tools will help in the planning, gathering and collecting, analyzing and organizing, and writing stages.

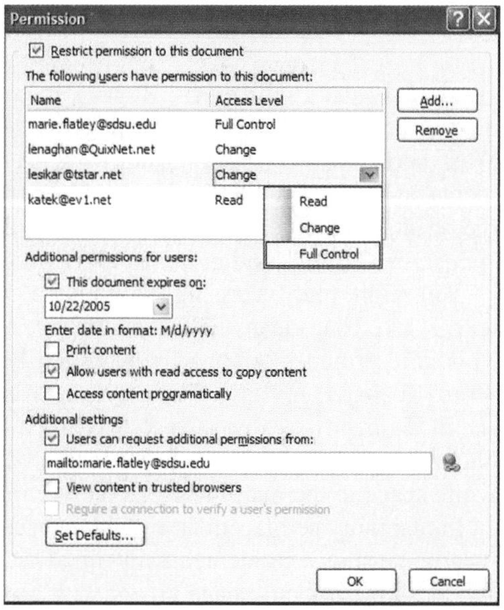

FIGURE 18–9

Illustration of Information Rights Management for Writing

TOOLS FOR PRESENTING MESSAGES

After you have completed the document, you need to consider how to present it. This decision involves both software and hardware choices.

Software

- Today's software gives the writer many options for presenting messages.

Today you can publish your document in print or electronic form. For print publication, you can use desktop publishing software or word processing software. Desktop publishing software is particularly good for layout of long documents that combine text, graphics, and design elements such as long reports, newsletters, manuals, and proposals. This software enables you to present professional-looking documents. Word processors are also capable of combining these elements. Most are capable of doing nearly 80 percent of the tasks full-featured desktop publishing software can do if you take advantage of their features.

For electronic publication, you also can use these programs to generate files in hypertext markup language (html) or portable document file (pdf) format. In addition to the text, graphics, and design elements, electronic documents can contain links, audio, and video elements. At the moment, authoring software is more fully featured for creating html documents (web documents). Web documents allow the writer to have some control over the presentation of the document, but today's browsers allow the reader to override the web documents and present them in a format the reader prefers. Also, browsers often display these html documents differently; therefore, it is the writer's responsibility to test the documents (at least in the default mode) on the most commonly used browsers to assure that the visual look of their documents does not distract from or interfere with the message content. Some writers prefer to keep this control and create electronic documents in pdf, a format that gives the writer control over both the content and look.

Coincidentally, professionals engaged in designing documents for publication have the same major objective as writers—to communicate effectively. Professionals aim for designs that attract the reader but do not distract. Also, they understand that the most successful publications are those in which the design enhances or complements the meaning of the writer.

With publishing programs, you can break out of the traditional-looking page with its roots in the typewriter era to give the reader the best looking, most readable document possible. However, to do this, you need to know about some basic design principles. Attention to the importance of the effect of design on communication was clearly pointed out with the butterfly ballot discussion in the Bush/Gore presidential election. These principles cover three areas: layout, typography, and art.

- Writers can control the look of their messages through effective layout.

Basic Layout Principles. Roger Parker, a nationally recognized expert on design, defines layout as simply "the arrangement of text and graphics on a page." Suzanne West, another expert, goes further with, "A layout is a composition of interrelated elements on a page." While similar, the latter implies that the writer has some control over the results through careful composition of the elements. These elements include *white space, text, visuals,* and *graphic design elements* such as circles, lines, and bullets.

- White space adds emphasis and affects readability.

You might find surprising that today a commonly accepted ratio of white space to text is 1:1. That means half of your page is devoted to text and half to white space. This ratio provides optimum readability. Readability is also improved by using lines 35 to 40 characters long. Therefore, with these two factors in mind, you can clearly see in Figure 18–10 that instead of using a full page of long, double-spaced lines, it is better to use short lines with less spacing between them. This deliberate shifting of the white space to the margins keeps the 1:1 ratio but improves the readability.

- Use white space consistently.

In planning the placement of white space in documents with facing pages, you will want to be sure your elements line up at the top and at the left. The example in Figure 18–11 shows a facing page layout with consistent use of white space in margins and between the lines.

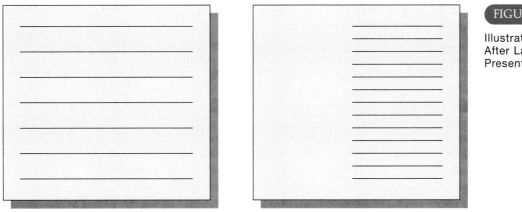

FIGURE 18–10

Illustration of Before and After Layout for Presenting

Before
Double-spaced with long lines

After
Short lines with white space moved to margins

FIGURE 18–11

Illustration of a Facing-Page Layout for Presenting

This facing, double-page spread illustrates copy aligned at top and left, the way our eye has been trained to read pages.

White space also can be used for emphasis. As you already have learned, space denotes importance. When you are writing about a topic, the more space you give it, the more emphasis it gets. The same principle applies to white space. If you leave more white space around certain text or graphics, you will be giving that text or graphic more emphasis.

- Use it to give emphasis.

Another way to get emphasis in the text is through type size and style. Of course, you want headings to stand out, but they should be balanced with the rest of the text. The size of your main heading also will be governed by the number of levels of subheadings you plan to use. And you will want to use a type size smaller than your text type size for captions and footnotes so they do not distract the reader from the text. Type style elements such as bold, italic, or bold italic also can be added to headings, subheadings, text, captions, and footnotes for more emphasis.

- Type size and style also affect readability.

One means of emphasis that should be used sparingly is all uppercase. Using both uppercase and lowercase in headings makes the headings easier to read. However, all uppercase in short phrases will work effectively.

Good layout always includes careful planning of visuals—graphics and drawings. In planning them, give attention to placement and size as well as content. Also, be sure you plan space for the captions in your layout.

A final element of layout is the graphic device. Lines or rules around text or separating text from visuals or white space can be very effective for directing the eye where you want it to go. The thickness of a line can be varied to give differing degrees of emphasis to the material it is highlighting. Tints and shading are other graphic devices that attract attention. Usually these are used to separate related copy in the same text.

- Graphic devices can direct the eye, giving attention to particular parts of the message.

Business Week often uses this device. For example, it may run a story on Hewlett-Packard, including a brief profile of an HP executive in a shaded box accompanying the article. Or it may be reporting on a specific industry in general, detailing explicit facts on specific companies in a table in a shaded box.

- Plan them to enhance the text.

Graphic devices should enhance the text, not distract from it. If your reader just reads the shaded boxes and overlooks the primary content of the report, your layout is not successful. Careful planning for effective use of graphic devices is a prerequisite to effective layout, as discussed in Chapter 13.

When the layout is good, it works well with the typography and art. Now that we have touched on the importance of type size and style in planning the textual component of layout, let us look at some basic principles of typography.

- Understanding type and its terminology helps you communicate with publishing professionals.

Typography Basics. Although you may not be doing much yourself with the technical aspect of type in the majority of documents you produce, knowing the concepts and basic vocabulary is important. Not only will you be able to communicate more effectively with those who work on your documents, but you also will help them to produce better layouts for you.

- A *point* is ¹⁄₇₂ inch; a *pica* is 12 points.

Some word processing terms for measuring, such as pitch and space, are carryovers from the typewriter era. The publishing and typesetting world measures in *points* and *picas*. A point is about ¹⁄₇₂ of an inch, and a pica is 12 points, or about ⅙ of an inch. When you are specifying type size, generally 14-point type and smaller is considered appropriate for text, while type larger than 14 points is usually used for headings. Some programs give you the choice of specifying in inches, centimeters, or picas. If you are working closely with people in the publishing world, you would be wise to work with the terminology they understand.

- *Kerning* is the spacing between characters.

Another term from this area is *kerning*. Kerning refers to the spacing between characters. While standard typewriters, dot matrix printers, and fixed fonts generally use equal spacing for each character, in publishing this space is variable. For example, in the word *The,* a publishing system would allow the *T* to overhang, moving the *h* in for an even-appearing spacing. A fixed-pitch printer, on the other hand, would place the *h* after the overhang, appearing to leave more space between the *T* and *h* than between the *h* and *e*. Also, if copy doesn't quite fit the page, you can squeeze it or stretch it by tightening or loosening the kerning or spacing between characters.

- *Leading* is the spacing between lines.

Leading (pronounced *leding*) is similar to kerning except that it refers to vertical spacing rather than horizontal. When your lines are too close together, you can increase the leading to add more white space between lines. As with kerning, you can adjust the leading to fit copy to the space available.

One other term commonly used in the publishing industry is *typeface*. Typeface refers to the design of the entire uppercase and lowercase set of letters. While there are hundreds of typefaces available today, two common typefaces in use are Times Roman and Arial (see Figure 18–12). Times Roman is a serif type, having feet (cross-lines) at the end of the main strokes. Arial is a sans serif type, having no feet at the ends of its main strokes.

- Computer people use the term *font* for typeface.

When you are talking to computer-oriented people about publishing, you may hear the term *font* used for typeface. However, a font is one typeface in one size and style. Therefore, if you wanted to use an Arial type with standard, bold, and italics in four sizes, you would need 12 fonts—one for each size and one for each style. Today we often use scalable fonts, fonts that can be changed in size within a range. Numerous font libraries are available for purchase, allowing you to prepare a custom document.

FIGURE 18–12

Illustration of Serif and Sans Serif Fonts

Times Roman (Serif)

Arial (Sans Serif)

Since type is a key element in most business documents, you'll want to pay special attention to it. Usually, it will account for more than 90 percent of your document. Your care in selecting and using type will have a big impact on the effectiveness of your design.

Art Fundamentals. *Art* as used here in its broadest sense refers to drawings, graphs, photos, and other illustrations. As a writer you primarily need to remember that art should always serve a message's purpose; it must never serve its own. Whenever you are about to place an art element on a page, ask yourself what purpose it serves. As noted in Chapter 13, need is the sole criterion for including a graphic in a document. Graphics help the reader understand.

- Art should serve the message's purpose.

One purpose of art is to break up large blocks of text. While we often try to conjure up an idea for drawings, graphs, or photos, we also can use the space to emphasize a key idea. By quoting from within the document and setting it off in larger type with ruling lines, we use a technique called a *pull quote.*

- Use it to break up blocks of text.

Whatever the reason we have for our art, we also should strive to use the best art possible. Look for interesting photos, not merely mug shots. Crop or delete photos, eliminating any material that does not work to enhance the text. Choose your art with the reader in mind. In some cases these suggestions might mean using cartoons or illustrations you scan, download, or import from various clip art packages, and in other cases it might mean using high-quality color photos or significant pull quotes. Of course, you need to be sure you do not violate copyrights.

- Choose art for the best communication effect.

Good design expertly integrates layout, typography, and art elements. You will probably want to begin with either some very basic applications or the prepared templates or style sheets bundled with the publishing software. You will get better with practice. Also, you will get better if you read books and magazines on design, pay attention to the designs of others (noting what seems to work), and keep a file of ideas. By always keeping the reader in mind as you design your documents, you will be effective in communicating your message.

- Effective design integrates layout, type, and art.

Hardware

Software is just one component of presenting a message; hardware is another. If the software has features your printer or other output device cannot print, the features are useless. On the other hand, if your hardware has features your software cannot produce, they, too, are useless. Both must work together to produce your message.

- Your choice of output hardware is critical to the appearance of your message.

The most common output device is still the printer. Depending on the formality of your communication, you may find yourself using ink-jet printers for one type of message and laser printers for others. In circumstances where you must have the best-looking documents, you may even use typeset output. Appearance does convey a message, and the hardware you choose to complete the presentation of your document is an important consideration.

- Print and some electronic documents give the writer control of appearance.

Electronic documents have different hardware considerations. The cross-platform formats—portable document format (pdf) and rich text format (rft)—are used to prepare documents that keep their formatting. While they can be printed out, many will be read on the screen. And because writers can use links within a document, reading an electronic document may vary substantially from reading the same document in print form. Keeping the readers appraised of where they are at all times within a document is important. Also, it is important to always give a reader ways to move around the document; including buttons and keystroke alternatives is essential.

TOOLS FOR TRANSMITTING MESSAGES

Transmitting means to send the message. The medium in which you choose to transmit a message communicates to the receiver the importance you attach to the message. Usually a written message gets more attention than an oral message, and a special delivery or urgent message gets more attention than an ordinary message. Even the method of special delivery chosen conveys a message. The client who electronically sends you

- The medium in which you choose to send your message is important.

Adam@Home by Brian Basset

the document you requested is perceived differently from the client who sends it on paper through Federal Express. Knowing what technologies are available to transmit the message will help you decide which is the most appropriate medium to use.

Technologies for sending a variety of oral and visual messages are widely used in business. One booming technology for oral communication is the mobile phone. Once predominantly used in cars, mobile phones can be used in any area of the country equipped for them. With a phone that fits in the palm of the hand, businesspeople can now be reached for important calls as well as conduct business from otherwise inaccessible places. Once like dumb bricks, today's devices are small and smart. Most of today's mobile phones have memories that enable users to reach others with just a few clicks or through voice input, as well as by dialing a complete number. Mobile phones can enable businesspeople to make more productive use of their time. However, the courteous user will be discreet about the time and place of use. Most people do not want to overhear your business calls; therefore, it is best to make them where using your mobile phone will not disturb others. And when in doubt, ask before you make that intrusive call.

As mentioned in Chapter 14, another widely used oral communication technology is the voice messaging system. Not only do these systems answer phones, direct calls, and take messages, but they also act as voice storage systems. For example, you can ask the system to retrieve messages for a particular date or from a particular person. You also can take a message you receive, annotate it with your voice message, and pass it along to another person's voice mailbox. You can even record a message for the system to deliver to several people's voice mailboxes at a specified time. By eliminating telephone tag and interruptions, this technology, too, improves the productivity of those using it.

One technology that combines oral and video communication effectively is videoconferencing. While it has been around for a while, advancements in optical fibers, bandwidth, and software and chip technology will push videoconferencing into even more favor. New developments are making the systems better and lowering the costs. Videoconferencing systems save travel time and expense, and they help eliminate many scheduling problems. Even small and medium-sized companies can afford desktop conferencing systems with inexpensive video cameras. Already available and widely used in Asia, phone systems are being used to send video email as well as to conduct real-time video messaging. Use of this technology is likely to be seen in the United States soon.

Technology also gives us the option of adding audio and video to our written messages. The sounds can be words dictated and attached to a document, or they can be sounds from other sources such as sound clip libraries. Sounds can be used to add interest, emphasis, and clarity to a document. Video also can be added to email. In fact, many current video email systems simply attach video files to email messages. With digital convergence we will see a growth in the use of the compound document.

Written communication, on the other hand, can be transmitted effectively with proven technologies: facsimile, email, text messaging, and instant messaging.

- Mobile technology expands the physical environment of the message sender.

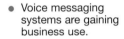

- Voice messaging systems are gaining business use.

- Videoconferencing combines oral and video media.

- Technology enables us to add audio and video to our written documents.

- Facsimile, email, text messaging, and instant messaging are widely used for transmitting written messages.

PART 6   Cross-Cultural, Correctness, Technology, Research

Facsimile transmission (fax) uses telephone lines and Internet connections to send a copy of the document. Faxing is much like photocopying or printing, but the copy is delivered elsewhere. You need to know the telephone number of the receiving fax in order to send the message, and someone on the receiving end usually needs to check for the fax. Currently, you also can use the Internet to send or retrieve a fax. Many companies are setting up these systems on their company portals so users can send and retrieve faxes from their desktops.

Email transmissions work with a variety of sending devices. The desktop computer is probably the widest used at this point, but businesspeople may use other wireless, devices, such as the Palm and PocketPC, more widely in the near future.

Another form of written communication finally catching on in the United States is text messaging. Text messages are typically limited to 160 characters sent through phones or the Internet to the receiver's phone. Text messages are similar to email and fax in that users need to check for them although the phone could alert them to incoming messages.

Finally, written communication can be transmitted with instant messaging (IM) tools. Although widely used by teens in the United States, IM has not been used much as a productivity tool in business. Most businesses worry about security and choose not to use this tool. However, IBM recently introduced new server tools that enable companies to run IM securely. With a large user base already comfortable using the technology and more secure systems, it is likely that businesses will begin to use them internally and perhaps with suppliers and customers when appropriate.

Both fax and email are being effectively used for transmitting written messages. However, while both have the advantage of immediacy, they are both less formal than sending a printed document. You need to evaluate carefully the need for formality in choosing your transmission medium.

Knowing that you have a choice of media for transmitting the message and knowing how to use each one are both important in order to choose the most appropriate

- Although they communicate in writing, fax and email are viewed as informal.

- So use them appropriately.

medium. Because this technology is developing rapidly, you need to make it a priority to keep up-to-date on the latest developments.

TOOLS FOR COLLABORATION

- Computer tools assist groups on a wide variety of tasks.

As discussed in Chapter 10, collaborative writing or group writing tasks occur regularly in business, and they vary widely in the form and nature of the work. However, a wide range of computer tools is available to support various aspects of the process. These tools for computer-supported collaborative work group writing can be divided into two classifications: asynchronous and synchronous. Asynchronous tools are used for different-time/different-place collaboration; synchronous tools, on the other hand, are used for same-time/any-place collaboration.

Asynchronous Computer Tools

- Several computer tools assist the traditional group.

Asynchronous tools include word processing, discussion, and electronic mail. Word processing features useful in group writing include commenting and reviewing. Commenting allows you to insert comments or questions in a document written by someone else but not change it. Reviewing allows others to edit your documents, which can appear as strikeouts (for deletions) or underlining (for insertions). Different colors can be assigned to different kinds of changes, so you can see at a glance the nature and location of the changes. The writer can view the document and decide whether to accept or reject each suggestion. As shown in Figure 18–13, the writer can see the reviewer's suggestions when viewing a document either by moving the cursor over the spot where a comment was made or by viewing comments in the margins.

- Discussion tools are useful when distance or time make getting together difficult.

Another group writing tool is the discussion tool. This tool is useful when groups have a difficult time meeting due to distance and time. To begin, the lead writer enters some text. Others access the system, review the text, and enter their own comments. All members of the group can review all the comments. In some systems, group members have anonymity, but others maintain audit trails so comments can be attributed to specific group members. A variation of the discussion tool is the blog. While discussion tools are usually arranged as threaded discussions with comments on topics grouped together, blogs are arranged chronologically as the origin of their name implies—web

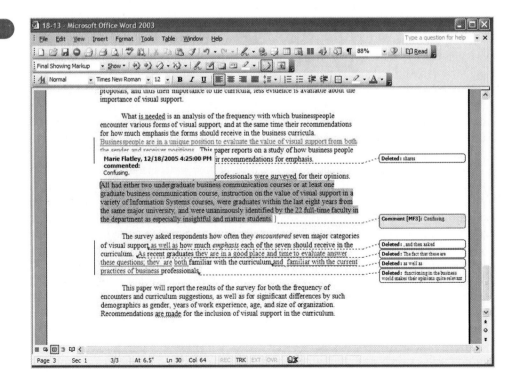

FIGURE 18–13

Illustration of the Reviewing Tool for Collaboration

log. Although blogs are used asynchronously, some become so popular that they can become a form of group chatting when users are connected at the same time.

Electronic mail (email) systems or listservs provide a means for one writer to send a message to others. Unlike conferencing, in these systems access to others' mailboxes is restricted. While you can distribute messages to a whole group, you do not have access to messages one member sends to someone else.

- Electronic mail permits communicating to intended receivers only.

All these tools are designed to work the way groups have traditionally worked. The planning, writing, and revising occur much the way they occur in traditional groups. However, the tools contribute to improvements in both speed and the quality of the final documents.

- Collaborative writing is helped by group authoring tools.

Synchronous Computer Tools

Synchronous computer tools are used by all group members at the same time. However, they can be used either at the same place or at different places. Same-place tools are generally referred to as electronic meeting systems (EMS). Different-place tools are sometimes called whiteboard or collaborative tools.

- Collaborative tools change the group process and improve its output quality.

With the same-place EMS tools, a facilitator conducts the meeting and operates the software that runs on a network. The facilitator may start the group with a question or statement. The group members will comment on the statement through their computers simultaneously and anonymously. For example, members may brainstorm new company policy statements and comment on them. The group under the direction of the facilitator might use other EMS tools to group related comments, rank-order them, and vote for the final policy statement. This kind of EMS collaborative tool has been shown to produce significantly higher quality output than non-computer-supported meetings.

With the different-place collaborative tools, one member of the group initiates the process either on a network or through Internet connections. This tool often provides both a chat box and audio connection where users can talk to each other, a video connection where members can see each other, and a place where a shared document can be viewed and manipulated. The software can be set for different levels and types of control. The use of this technology became more widely accepted after 9/11 when people needed to meet but were hesitant to travel. One web-based provider, WebEx, has become a major player for businesses of all sizes. Businesses are beginning to use this technology to form distributed teams when the need for extensive travel or relocation would otherwise make them impossible.

A LOOK TO THE FUTURE

In addition to the technology discussed this far, you can anticipate further rapid advancements. Joseph Tucci, president and CEO of EMC Corporation, believes innovation will continue forever and that companies will continue to use it to help improve productivity. While some of this innovation is happening in academic institutions such as MIT's Media Lab, much of it is happening at large companies such as IBM and Microsoft. Both companies have some of their brightest, most creative people working on technologies for improving voice recognition and graphics. IBM recently unveiled a young research project called Total Recall, which instantly retrieved documents, whether files, web pages, or email. Another project developed by young researchers is eLumination, which captures real-time transaction data and transforms it into a visual.[2] Microsoft has its scientists conducting research in visual computing and many other areas. You can read about this group's efforts and many others at their website at <http://www.research.microsoft.com/research/topics/>. Among the visual computing group's projects are work on machine learning, statistical learning, and real-time face detection and recognition.

- Computer tools will continue to enhance the communication process . . .

[2] Cade Metz, "A Glimpse of IBM's Future," *PC Magazine,* August 11, 2003, <http://www.pcmag.com/print_article/0,348,a=46143,00.asp>.

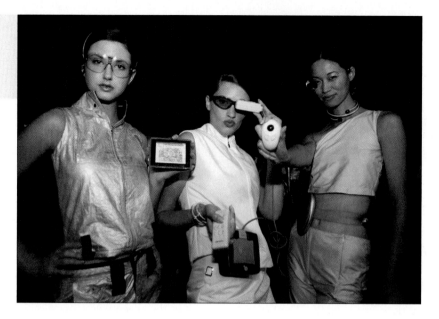

At the moment, the most talked-about future technologies are wireless technologies. One of the most promising developments is in the area of adaptive computing, a development that allows a chip to reconfigure itself on the fly as needed, increasing speed and reducing power consumption considerably.[3] Making phones more energy efficient may lead to Andrew Seybold's prediction that there will be no wired phones left in as few as 10 years. He also believes that the phone will be tied much more closely to the person with the person being the number.[4] Larry Smarr, professor of computer science, believes the idea of carrying around a cell phone as a piece of hardware will vanish. He sees voice communications becoming an Internet feature, and the device we will have will be an interface integrated with the body.[5]

● . . . but humans will continue to form the messages.

However, whatever form these developments take, human minds will continue to control message formulation. In fact, there is no evidence whatsoever that the need for messages communicated in writing and speaking will decrease. Even more important, there is absolutely no evidence that these messages can be handled in a way that does not require basic writing and speaking skills. Business communication is here to stay. In fact, the increasing advancement of the technology of the future is likely to require more—not less—of it.

SUMMARY BY CHAPTER OBJECTIVES

Explain how technology helps in constructing messages.

1. Technology helps a writer construct messages through every step of the writing process including
   • Planning,
   • Gathering and collecting information,
   • Analyzing and organizing information, and
   • Writing and rewriting.

Identify appropriate tools for different stages in the writing process.

2. Each stage of the writing process has a set of tools most appropriate for the tasks in that stage. These include the following:
   • Outlining or brainstorming, project management, and personal information management programs for planning;

---

[3] John Markoff, "Computing's Big Shift: Flexibility in the Chips," *New York Times*, June 16, 2003, <http://www.nytimes.com/2003/06/16/technology/16CHIP.html?ei=5070&en=9a76be2177a.asp>.

[4] Arik Hesseldal (ed.), "Wireless: The Next Quarter Century," *Forbes*, June 6, 2002, <http://www.forbes.com/2002/06/06/0606wireless_print.html>.

[5] Ibid.

- Communications and database programs for gathering and collecting information; and
- Statistical, spreadsheet, graphics, and outlining or brainstorming tools for analyzing and organizing information, and word processing, spelling, thesaurus, grammar and style checking, reference, graphics, drawing, and voice recognition, and information rights management programs for writing.

3. Technology helps in the presentation of documents with both sophisticated hardware and software.
   - Hardware contributes in the printing of documents.
   - Software contributes with publishing features that combine text, graphics, links, audio, and video and that promote good layout and design.

Discuss how technology helps in the presentation of messages.

4. Layout and design refers to the arrangement of text and graphics on a page. Layout involves the careful composition of these basic elements:
   - White space for manipulating emphasis and readability,
   - Text for emphasis and balance as well as for visual clues of organization,
   - Visuals such as graphics and drawings, and
   - Graphic design elements to direct the eye.
   Layout and design also are affected by typography. Aspects writers need to know about include
   - Points and picas, which represent height,
   - Kerning, which determines the spacing between letters,
   - Leading, which determines the spacing between lines, and
   - Typeface, which refers to the design of an entire set of letters.
   Art is a final aspect of layout and design. Its main purpose is always to serve a message's purpose.

Explain basic concepts of document layout and design.

5. Communicators have a variety of choices of media for transmitting their messages.
   - Oral messages can be sent by mobile phone, voice messaging systems, and sound clips.
   - Videoconferencing technology combines oral and visual messages.
   - Written messages can be transmitted by fax, email, text messaging, and instant messaging.

Discuss various ways to transmit messages and the hardware currently used.

6. A range of software tools assists groups of writers in asynchronous and synchronous writing environments.
   - Asynchronous tools such as word processing, discussions, blogs, and email are used for different-time/different-place collaboration.
   - Synchronous tools allow writers to work on a document at the same time. Electronic meeting system tools are used for same-time/same-place writing, and collaboration tools are used for same-time/different-place writing.

Describe how technology assists in collaboration.

7. Business leaders believe technology will continue to advance. Future developments are expected to enhance present technologies, making them better and easier to use. Researchers at large companies are working on a variety of projects, including many in the wireless area. Future developments will likely mean more need for good basic communication skills.

Discuss what impact future developments in technology might have on business communication.

1. Explain how technology can help the writer with both creative and tedious writing tasks.

2. Identify specific software tools that assist with constructing written messages. Explain what each does.

3. Word processing programs are the writer's primary tool. Identify five basic features and two advanced features useful to business writers.

4. Discuss the advantages and disadvantages of spelling checkers and grammar and style checkers.

5. Describe ways graphics software helps writers.

6. Brainstorm some practices or policies businesses might develop for using the Information Rights Management (IRM) tool effectively.

7. Explain what a writer should know about layout and design and why it is important.

8. Identify various ways business writers can transmit oral and written messages.

9. How can technology assist in collaboration?

10. What can we expect to see in future technological developments that will affect business communication?

1. Investigate the school and/or local libraries to determine what current (or future) computer systems will help one find information for business. Report your findings to the class.

2. Compile an annotated list of at least 10 websites with good links to business sources. Three of these links should be for local business information.

3. Locate six examples of digital clip art and sound clips you might use in a business document. Print the examples along with a brief explanation of a good use in a business document.

4. Identify where computers, printers, scanners, and other tools are available at or around your college. Prepare a table with this information, listing times available as well as any costs. Also, be sure to include computer configurations and programs available.

5. Choose a feature from your word processor (such as index, table of contents, templates, or macros) that you have not used much. Learn how to use it and create an example of its use in a business document. Write a brief description of its application.

6. Select a dozen idioms from a reference book (found in your library or bookstore) that seem common to you. Type these into your word processor and run the file through a grammar and style checker. Print a copy of the results and bring it to class for discussion.

7. List a dozen text messaging shortcuts (B4, BTW, B2U) you use or know of along with your meaning. Then ask three different people to tell you what each shortcut means. Write a short report of your results.

8. From a current computer magazine, find an article that relates to communication in business. Write a one-paragraph reaction to it and email your paragraph to someone selected by your instructor.

CHAPTER NINETEEN

Business Research Methods

CHAPTER OBJECTIVES

Upon completing this chapter, you will be able to design and implement a plan for conducting the research needed for a business report. To reach this goal, you should be able to

1 Explain the difference between primary and secondary research.

2 Gather secondary sources using direct and indirect research methods.

3 Evaluate website reliability.

4 Describe the procedures for searching through company records.

5 Conduct an experiment for a business problem.

6 Design an observational study for a business problem.

7 Use sampling to conduct a survey.

8 Construct a questionnaire, develop a working plan, and conduct a pilot test for a survey.

9 Analyze and interpret information clearly and completely for your reader.

Business Research Methods

Introduce yourself to this chapter by assuming the position of administrative assistant to Carmen Bergeron, the vice president for human resources for Pinnacle Industries. Today at a meeting of administrators, someone commented about the low morale among sales representatives since the merger. The marketing vice president immediately came to the defense of her area, claiming that there is no proof of the statement—that in fact the opposite is true. Others joined in with their views, and in time a heated discussion developed. In an effort to ease tensions, Ms. Bergeron suggested that her office conduct a survey of employees "to learn the truth of the matter." The administrators liked the idea.

After the meeting, Ms. Bergeron called you in to tell you that you would be the one to do the research. And she wants the findings in report form in time for next month's meeting. She didn't say much more. No doubt she thinks your college training equipped you to handle the assignment.

Now you must do the research. This means you will have to work out a plan for a survey. Specifically, you will have to select a sample, construct a questionnaire, devise an interview procedure, conduct interviews, record findings—and more. All these activities require much more than a casual understanding of research. There are right ways and wrong ways of going about them. How to do them right is the subject of this chapter.

- The two basic forms of research are secondary research (getting information from published sources) and primary research (getting information firsthand).

You can collect the information you need for your report by using the two basic forms of research: secondary research and primary research. Secondary research is research utilizing material that someone else has published—periodicals, brochures, books, electronic publications, and such. This research, called secondary research, may be the first form of research that you use in some problems (see The Preliminary Investigation in Chapter 10). Primary research is research that uncovers information firsthand. It is research that produces new findings.

To be effective as a report writer, you should be familiar with the techniques of both secondary and primary research. A brief summary of each appears in the following pages.

SECONDARY RESEARCH

- Secondary research can be a rich source of information if you know what to look for and where to look.

Secondary research materials are potentially the least costly, the most accessible, and the most complete source of information. However, to take full advantage of the available materials, you must know what you are looking for and where and how to find it.

The task can be complex and challenging. You can meet the challenge if you become familiar with the general arrangement of a library or other repositories of secondary materials and if you learn the techniques of finding those materials. Also, research must be orderly if it is to be reliable and complete.

- Keep track of the sources you gather in an orderly way.

In the past, researchers used a card system to help them keep track of the sources they identified. This card system could be combined with and adapted to a computer system quite easily. The manual system of organization required that the researcher complete two sets of cards. One set was simply a bibliography card set, containing complete information about sources. A researcher numbered these cards consecutively as the sources were identified. A second set of cards contained the notes from each source. Each of these cards was linked to its source through the number of the source in the bibliography card set.

Since the computer systems in today's libraries often allow users to print, download, email, or transfer directly the citations they find from the indexes and databases, it makes sense to identify each with a unique number rather than recopy the source to a card. Not only is the resulting list more legible than one's handwriting, but it is also complete. Some researchers cut their printouts apart and tape them to a master sheet. Others enter these items in databases they build. And still others export items directly into specialty databases, letting the software organize and number them. With the widespread use of notebook and laptop computers, many researchers are taking notes on computers rather than cards. These notes can be linked to the original source by number as in the manual system.

No matter whether you use a manual, combined, or computer system, using an orderly system is essential.

Finding Publication Collections

The first step in an orderly search for printed information is to determine where to begin. The natural place, of course, is a library. However, since different types of libraries offer different kinds of collections, it is helpful to know what types of libraries are available and to be familiar with their contents.

General libraries are the best known and the most accessible. General libraries, which include college, university, and most public libraries, are called *general* to the extent that they contain all kinds of materials. Many general libraries, however, have substantial collections in certain specialized areas.

Libraries that limit their collections to one type or just a few types of material are considered *special libraries.* Many such libraries are private and do not invite routine public use of their materials. Still, they will frequently cooperate on research projects that they consider relevant and worthwhile.

Among the special libraries are those libraries of private businesses. As a rule, such libraries are designed to serve the sponsoring company and provide excellent information in the specialized areas of its operations. Company libraries are less accessible than other specialized libraries, but a written inquiry explaining the nature and purpose of a project or an introduction from someone known to the company can help you gain access to them.

Special libraries are also maintained by various types of associations—for example, trade organizations, professional and technical groups, chambers of commerce, and labor unions. Like company libraries, association libraries may provide excellent coverage of highly specialized areas. Although such libraries develop collections principally for members or a research staff, they frequently make resources available to others engaged in reputable research.

A number of public and private research organizations also maintain specialized libraries. The research divisions of big-city chambers of commerce and the bureaus of research of major universities, for example, keep extensive collections of material containing statistical and general information on a local area. State agencies collect similar data. Again, though these materials are developed for a limited audience, they are often made available upon request.

Several guides are available in the reference department of most general libraries to help you determine what these research centers and special libraries offer and whom to contact for permission to use their collections. The *American Library Directory* is a geographic listing of libraries in the United States and Canada. It gives detailed information on libraries, including special interests and collections. It covers all public libraries as well as many corporate and association libraries. Also, the Special Libraries Association has chapters in many large cities that publish directories for their chapter areas. Particularly helpful in identifying the information available in research centers is *The Research Centers Directory.* Published by The Gale Group, it lists the research activities, publications, and services of 7,500 university-related and other nonprofit organizations. It is supplemented between editions by a related publication, *New Research Centers.*

The Gale Group also publishes a comprehensive three-volume guide to special library collections, *The Directory of Special Libraries and Information Centers.* Volume one, *Subject Directory of Special Libraries and Information Centers,* describes the contents and services of 23,300 information centers, archives, and special and research libraries, and it contains a detailed subject index. Volume two, *Geographic and Personnel Indexes,* includes the address and telephone number of the facility and the

- A library is the natural place to begin secondary research.

- General libraries offer the public a wide variety of information sources.

- Special libraries have limited collections and circulation, such as . . .

- . . . private business, . . .

- . . . associations, and . . .

- . . . research organizations.

- Consult a directory to determine what special libraries offer.

name and title of the individual in charge. The third volume, *New Special Libraries*, is a periodic supplement of the first. One particularly good source to an organized collection of links to online libraries is at <http://sunsite.berkeley.edu/libweb/>. This site is organized geographically but also allows one to search by library type, name, and other information.

Taking the Direct Approach

- You can begin your research using the direct approach, but you must be familiar with basic references.

When you have found the appropriate library for your research, you are ready for the next challenge. With the volume of material available, how will you find what you need? Many cost-conscious businesses are hiring professionals to find information for them. These professionals' charges range from $60 to $120 per hour in addition to any online charges incurred. Other companies like to keep their information gathering more confidential; some employ company librarians, and others expect their employees to gather the information. If you know little about how material is arranged in a library or online, you will waste valuable time on a probably fruitless search. However, if you are familiar with certain basic reference materials, you may be able to proceed directly to the information you seek. And if the direct approach does not work, there are several effective indirect methods of finding the material you need.

- The direct approach is especially effective with quantitative or factual information.

Taking the direct approach is advisable when you seek quantitative or factual information. The reference section of your library is where you should start. There, either on your own or with the assistance of a research librarian, you can discover any number of timely and comprehensive sources of facts and figures. Although you cannot know all these sources, as a business researcher you should be familiar with certain basic ones. These sources are available in either print or electronic forms. You should be able to use both.

- Encyclopedias offer both general and detailed information.

Encyclopedias. Encyclopedias are the best-known sources of direct information and are particularly valuable when you are just beginning a search. They offer background material and other general information that give you a helpful introduction to the area under study. Individual articles or sections of articles are written by experts in the field and frequently include a short bibliography.

Of the general encyclopedias, two worthy of special mention are *Encyclopedia Americana* and *Encyclopaedia Britannica*. *Britannica* online now requires a subscription at britannica.com. Others gaining wide use and acceptance are *Grolier's Multimedia Encyclopedia* and *Microsoft Encarta*. These are available either online and updated regularly, for sale in software outlets, or even bundled with multimedia computer systems. Also helpful are such specialized encyclopedias as the *Encyclopedia of Banking and Finance*, the *Encyclopedia of Business and Finance*, the *Encyclopedia of Small Business*, the *Encyclopedia of Advertising*, and the *Encyclopedia of Emerging Industries*.

- Biographical directories offer information about influential people.

Biographical Directories. A direct source of biographical information about leading figures of today or of the past is a biographical directory. The best-known biographical directories are *Who's Who in America* and *Who's Who in the World*, annual publications that summarize the lives of living people who have achieved prominence. Similar publications provide coverage by geographic area: *Who's Who in the East* and *Who's Who in the South and Southwest*, for example. For biographical information about prominent Americans of the past, the *Dictionary of American Biography* is useful. You also can find biographical information under the reference section of *Lexis-Nexis Academic Universe*. In addition to links to biographical directories, links to news stories about the person also are provided.

Specialized publications will help you find information on people in particular professions. Among the most important of these are *Who's Who in Finance and Industry; Standard & Poor's Register of Corporations, Directors, and Executives; Who's Who in Insurance;* and *Who's Who in Technology.* Nearly all business and professional areas are covered by some form of directory.

Much secondary research can be done using computers.

Almanacs. Almanacs are handy guides to factual and statistical information. Simple, concise, and selective in their presentation of data, they should not be underestimated as references. *The World Almanac and Book of Facts,* published by Funk & Wagnalls, is an excellent general source of facts and statistics. The *Time Almanac* is another excellent source for a broad range of statistical data. One of its strongest areas is information on the world. The *New York Times Almanac* presents much of its data in tables. It has excellent coverage of business and the economy. *The Job Rated Almanac* by Les Krantz ranks 250 jobs on factors such as salary, dress, benefits, and more.

Almanacs are available online as well. Infoplease.com offers broad coverage of topics, including a business section at <http://www.infoplease.com/almanacs.html>. A more specialized almanac, *The Writer's Almanac,* is a daily extension of Garrison Keillor's radio show sponsored by Minnesota Public Radio.

Trade Directories. For information about individual businesses or the products they make, buy, or sell, directories are the references to consult. Directories compile details in specific areas of interest and are variously referred to as *catalogs, listings, registers,* or *source books.* Some of the more comprehensive directories indispensable in general business research are the following: *The Million Dollar Directory* (a listing of U.S. companies compiled by Dun & Bradstreet), *Thomas Register of American Manufacturers* (free on the web at <http://www.thomasregister.com>), and *The Datapro Directory.* Some directories that will help you determine linkages between parent entities and their subsidiaries include *America's Corporate Families* and *Who Owns Whom* (both compiled by Dun & Bradstreet) as well as the *Directory of Corporate Affiliations.* Thousands of directories exist—so many, in fact, that there is a directory called *Directories in Print.*

- Almanacs provide factual and statistical information.

- Trade directories publish information about individual businesses and products.

- Governments (national, state, provincial, etc.) publish extensive research materials.

Government Publications. Governments (national, state, local, etc.) publish hundreds of thousands of titles each year. In fact, the U.S. government is the world's largest publisher. Surveys, catalogs, pamphlets, periodicals—there seems to be no limit to the information that various bureaus, departments, and agencies collect and make available to the public. The challenge of working with government publications, therefore, is finding your way through this wealth of material to the specifics you need. That task sometimes can be so complex as to require indirect research methods. However, if you are familiar with a few key sources, the direct approach will often produce good results. And at this time, many government publications are moving rapidly to the web.

- The U.S. government publishes guides to its publications.

In the United States, it may be helpful to consult the *Monthly Catalog of U.S. Government Publications.* Issued by the Superintendent of Documents, it includes a comprehensive listing of annual and monthly publications and an alphabetical index of the issuing agencies. It can be searched online at <http://www.gpoaccess.gov/cgp/>. The Superintendent of Documents also issues *Selected United States Government Publications,* a monthly list of general-interest publications that are sold to the public.

- These government publications are invaluable in business research.

Routinely available are a number of specialized publications that are invaluable in business research. These include *Census of Population, Census of Housing, Annual Housing Survey, Consumer Income, Population Characteristics, Census of Governments, Census of Retail Trade, Census of Manufacturers, Census of Agriculture, Census of Construction Industries, Census of Transportation, Census of Service Industries, Census of Wholesale Trade,* and *Census of Mineral Industries.* The *Statistical Abstract of the United States* is another invaluable publication, as are the *Survey of Current Business,* the *Monthly Labor Review,* the *Occupational Outlook Quarterly,* and the *Federal Reserve Bulletin.* To say the least, government sources are extensive.

- Dictionaries provide meanings, spellings, and pronunciations for both general and specialized words and phrases.

Dictionaries. Dictionaries are helpful for looking up meanings, spellings, and pronunciations of words or phrases. Electronic dictionaries add other options; they include pronunciation in audio files and let you find words when you know the meaning only. Dictionaries are available in both general and specialized versions. While it might be nice to own an unabridged dictionary, an abridged collegiate or desk dictionary will answer most of your questions. You should be aware that the name *Webster* can be legally used by any dictionary publisher. Also, dictionaries often include added features such as style manuals, signs, symbols, and weights and measures. Because dictionaries reflect usage, you want to be sure the one you use is current. Not only are new words being added, but spellings and meanings change, too. Several good dictionaries are the *American Heritage Dictionary,* the *Funk & Wagnalls Standard Dictionary,* the *Random House Webster's College Dictionary,* and *Merriam-Webster's Collegiate Dictionary.* To have the most current dictionary available at your fingertips (through toolbars), you may want to subscribe to one such as Merriam-Webster at <http://www.m-w.com/>, which is included with your text.

Specialized dictionaries concentrate on one functional area. Some business dictionaries are the *Dictionary of Business Terms, The Blackwell Encyclopedic Dictionary of Management Information Systems, The Blackwell Encyclopedic Dictionary of Accounting, The Blackwell Encyclopedic Dictionary of Business Ethics, The Blackwell Encyclopedic Dictionary of Finance,* the *Dictionary of Taxation,* the *Dictionary of International Business Terms,* the *Concise Dictionary of Business Management,* and the *Dictionary of Marketing and Advertising.* There are also dictionaries of acronyms, initialisms, and abbreviations. Two of these are the *Acronyms, Initialisms, and Abbreviations Dictionary* and the *Abbreviations Dictionary.*

- Statistical information is available both online and in printed form.

Additional Statistical Sources. Today's businesses rely heavily on statistical information. Not only is this information helpful in the day-to-day business operations, but it also is helpful in planning future products, expansions, and strategies. Some of this information can be found in the publications previously mentioned, especially the government publications. More is available online and can be seen long before it is printed. Even more is available from the various public and private sources described below.

In order to facilitate the collection and retrieval of statistical data for industry, the U.S. government developed a classification system called the Standard Industrial Classification (SIC) code. In the 1930s, this system used a four-digit code for all manufacturing and nonmanufacturing industries.

In 1997, the U.S. government introduced a new industrial classification system—the North American Industry Classification System (NAICS)—to replace the SIC code. The new system is more flexible than the old one and accounts for changes in the global economy by allowing the United States, Mexico, and Canada to compare economic and financial statistics better. It has also been expanded to include new sectors such as the information sector; the health care and social assistance sector; and the professional, scientific, and technical services sector. The United States and Canada began using this system in 1997, and Mexico in 1998. The first NAICS-based statistics were issued in 1999 and are just beginning to be used.

- A new classification system will enable users to compare economic and financial statistics better.

Some of the basic comprehensive publications include the *Statistical Abstract of the United States* and *Standard & Poor's Statistical Service.* These sources are a starting point when you are not familiar with more specialized sources. They include historical data on American industry, commerce, labor, and agriculture; industry data by SIC (and soon NAICS) codes; and numerous indexes such as producer price indexes, housing indexes, and stock price indexes. Additionally, the *Statistical Abstract of the United States* contains an extremely useful guide to sources of statistics.

- Basic publications provide broad coverage and source listings for more detailed statistics.

If you are not certain where to find statistics, you may find various guides useful. The *American Statistics Index* is an index to statistics published by all government agencies. It identifies the agency, describes the statistics, and provides access by category. The *Encyclopedia of Business Information Sources* provides a list of information sources along with names of basic statistical sources. The *Statistical Reference Index* publishes statistics from sources other than the government, such as trade and professional associations. These three directories will help direct you to specialized statistics when you need them.

- Guides help locate sources.

Business Information Services. Business services are private organizations that supply a variety of information to business practitioners, especially investors. Libraries also subscribe to their publications, giving business researchers ready access to yet another source of valuable, timely data.

- Private business services collect and publish data. Many such reports are available in public and university libraries.

Mergent, Inc., one of the best-known of such organizations, publishes a weekly *Manual* in each of five business areas: industrials, over-the-counter (OTC) industrials, international banks and finance, and municipals and governments. These reports primarily summarize financial data and operating facts on all major American companies, providing information that an investor needs to evaluate the investment potential of individual securities or of fields as a whole. *Corporation Records,* published by Standard & Poor's Corporation, presents similar information in loose-leaf form. Both Mergent and Standard & Poor's provide a variety of related services, including *Moody's Investors' Advisory Service* and *Value Line Investment Survey.*

Another organization whose publications are especially helpful to business researchers is The Gale Group, Inc. Gale provides several business services, including publications featuring forecasts and market data by country, product, and company. Its online Business and Company Resource Center is particularly useful. This database provides access to hundreds of thousands of company records, allowing users to search by company name, ticker symbol, SIC and NAICS codes. It provides links to the full text of news and magazine articles, company profiles, investment reports, and even legal actions and suits. Users can print the information as well as email it to others.

International Sources. In today's global business environment, we often need information outside our borders. Many of the sources we have discussed have counterparts with international information. *Principal International Businesses* lists basic information on major companies located around the world. *Major Companies of Europe* and *Japan Company Handbook* are two sources providing facts on companies in their respective areas. The *International Encyclopedia of the Social Sciences* covers all

- Statistical information for the international business environment is available in a wide range of documents.

important areas of social science, including biographies of acclaimed persons in these areas. General and specialized dictionaries are available, too. The *International Business Dictionary and References* includes commonly used business terms in several languages. You will even be able to find trade names in the *International Brands and Their Companies,* published by The Gale Group. For bibliographies and abstracts, one good source is the *Foreign Commerce Handbook.* Even statistical information is available in sources such as the *Index to International Statistics, Statistical Yearbook,* and online at the United Nations Department of Economic and Social Affairs Statistical Division, <http://unstats.un.org/unsd/>. Additionally, the U.S. Bureau of Labor Statistics at <http://www.bls.gov/bls/other.htm> provides links to many countries' statistical portals. With the help of translation tools (see the textbook website for several tools), you can get information you want directly. In addition, libraries usually contain many references for information on international marketing, exporting, tax, and trade.

Using Indirect Methods

If you cannot move directly to the information you need, you must use indirect methods to find it. The first step in this approach is preparing a bibliography or a list of prospective sources. The next two steps are gathering the publications in your bibliography and systematically checking them for the information you need.

- When you cannot find secondary materials directly, try the indirect approach. Start by preparing a bibliography of needed sources.

These two steps are elementary but nonetheless important. Your acquisition of secondary materials must be thorough. You should not depend solely on the material you find on the shelves of your library. Rather, you should use interlibrary loan services and database and Internet searches. And you should gather company or government documents. All checking of the sources must be equally thorough. For each source, review the pages cited in your bibliographic reference. Then take time to learn about the publication by reviewing its table of contents, its index, and the endnotes or footnotes related to the pages you are researching. You should be familiar with both the source and the context of all the information you plan to report; they are as significant as the information itself.

- Gather all available publications. Check each systematically for the information you need.

However, the first step, preparing the bibliography, is still the most demanding and challenging task in indirect research. It is, therefore, helpful to review what this task involves.

- A library's online catalog lists its holdings.

The Online Catalog. Today most libraries use electronic catalogs to list their holdings, giving one numerous ways to locate sources. As you can see from the main menu screen of one system in Figure 19–1, you can locate sources by the standard

The PAC - Library Catalog at San Diego State University - Microsoft Internet Explorer

File   Edit   View   Favorites   Tools   Help

the PAC   InfoDome | IVC

Your Circ Record | Course Reserves | ILL | Help

Quick search by: [Words ▾] **for:** [＿＿＿＿＿＿＿] [Search]

✤ Catalog of materials owned by the SDSU libraries

✤ Articles are NOT included. Use article databases

✤ Telnet / Text version

✤ The PAC en español

✤ Use ILL (Interlibrary Loan) for material NOT found at SDSU (includes links to Circuit and LINK+).

Words
From titles, subjects, authors, and notes

LC Subject
Library of Congress subject headings

Children's Subject
Children's books by juvenile subject headings

Call Numbers
LC, Alternate, Government Document, ISSN, ISBN, etc.

Title
Book, score, report, recording, etc.

Periodical Title
Magazine, journal, newspaper (print or electronic)

Author
Individual, organization, agency, etc.

Author / Title
Combined search

San Diego State University Library & Information Access

Suggest a Book | Comments

Author, Words, Title, and Subject options as well as a few other options. Additionally, this menu gives you tips on how to use it. Becoming familiar with these tips is highly recommended, especially for the systems you access frequently. By using effective and efficient searching techniques, you will reap many rewards.

Two options you need to understand clearly are Words and Subject. When you select the Words option, the system will ask you to enter keywords. It will then search for only those exact words in several of each record's fields, missing all those records using slightly different wording. However, when you select Subject, the system will ask you to enter the Library of Congress subject heading. While you must know the exact heading, sometimes it will cross-reference headings such as suggesting you *See Intercultural Communication* when you enter *cross-cultural communication*. A Subject search will find all those holdings on the subject, including those with different wording such as *intercultural communication, international communication, global communication,* and *diversity.* If you ran multiple searches under the Word option using these terms, you would still miss those titles without the keywords, such as Robert Axtell's book *Dos and Taboos around the World.* With a Subject search, you might even find a management book with a chapter on intercultural communication; however, the book's emphasis might be on something else, such as crisis management, negotiation, or conflict resolution.

The online catalog never gets tired. If you key in the words accurately, it will always produce a complete and accurate list of sources. Let us look at a few results from a subject search on *intercultural communication*. Notice in Figure 19–2 that the system found 464 sources. Assume that is more than you really want; so you decide to select the Modify Search option shown both at the bottom and top of the screen to limit your search. This system then gives you options for limiting your search (see Figure 19–3). You decide to limit the search by material type and year, telling it you want it to find all sources that are Books after 2001 (see Figure 19–4). As you can see in Figure 19–5, 45 entries were found. When you ask the system to display a record, it brings up the screen shown in Figure 19–6. Not only will you find the title and author, but you also will find complete bibliographic information, the call number, and the status, along with subjects this book fits. Furthermore, the system gives you more options, including options helpful in exporting the information, such as MARC Display and Save to List.

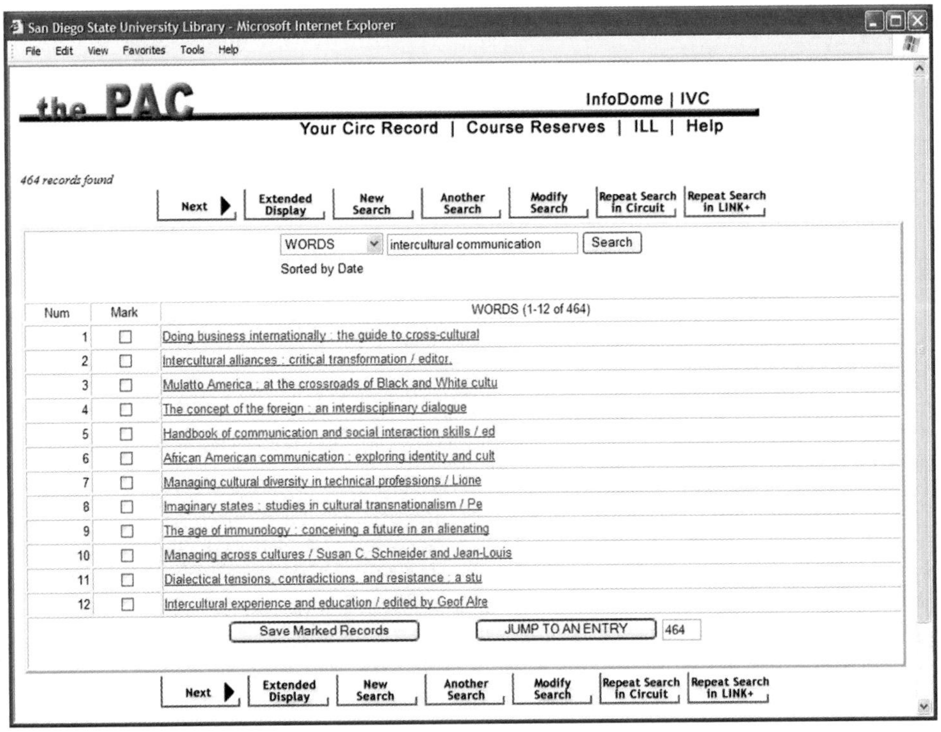

● Electronic catalogs give many search options.

FIGURE 19–2

Illustration of Online Search Results

FIGURE 19–3

Examples of Material-
Type Search Options

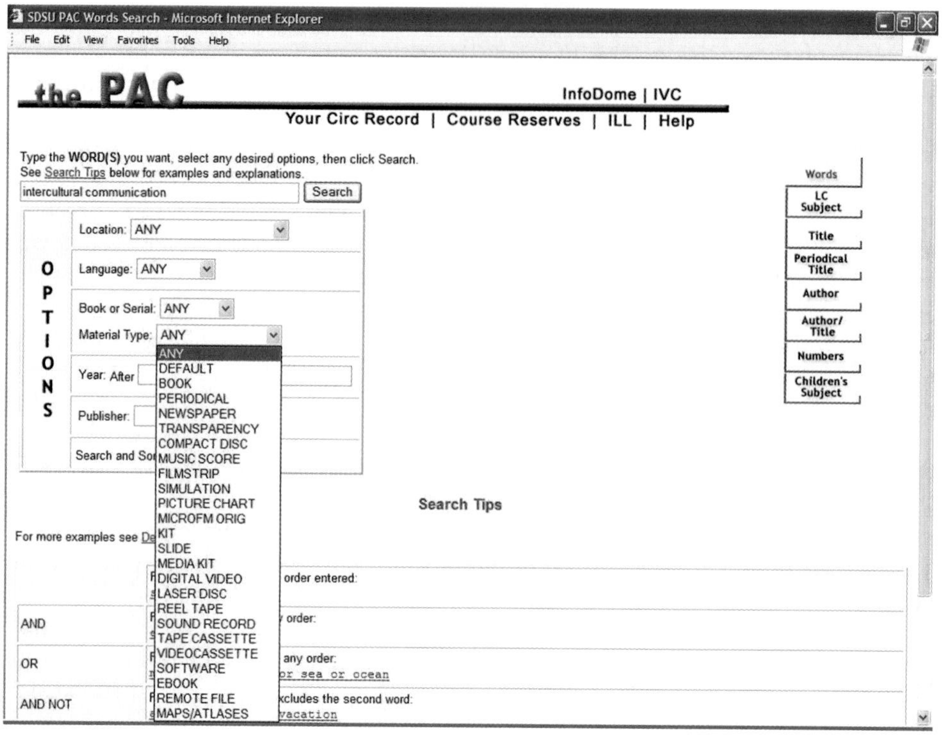

FIGURE 19–4

Search Options
for Books Published
after 2001

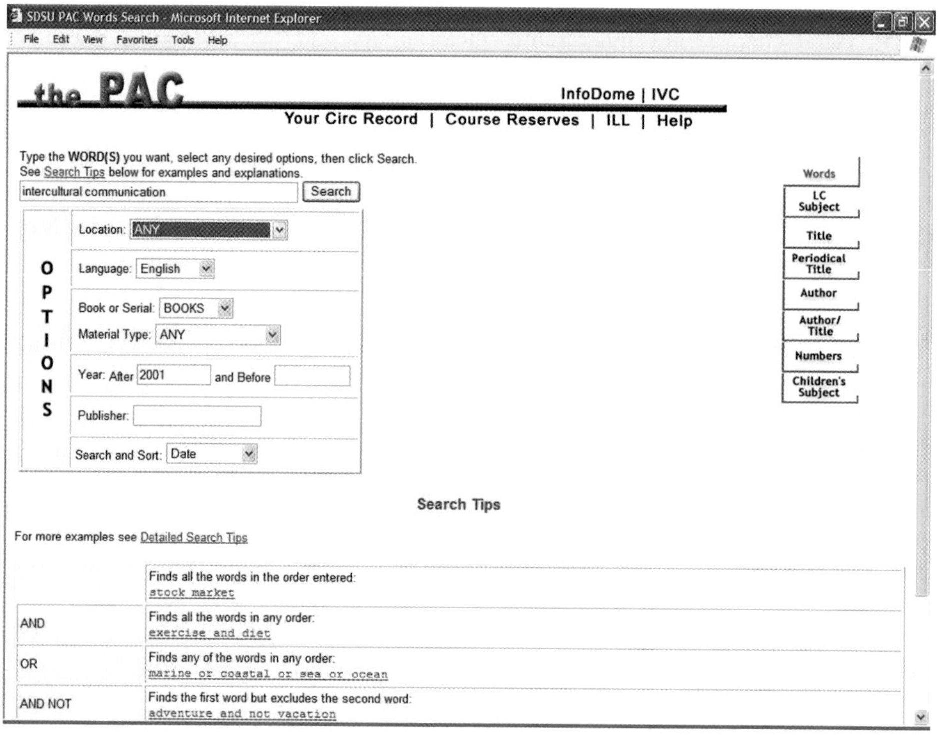

The online catalog is a useful source of information for your library's holdings. Learning how to use it effectively will save you time and will help your searches be fast and accurate.

- To identify articles for your list of prospective sources, consult an index.

Online Databases. The online catalog helps you identify books and other holdings in your library. To identify articles published in newspapers, magazines, or journals, you will need to consult an index, either a general one or one that specializes in the

FIGURE 19–5

Search Results for Books
Published after 2001

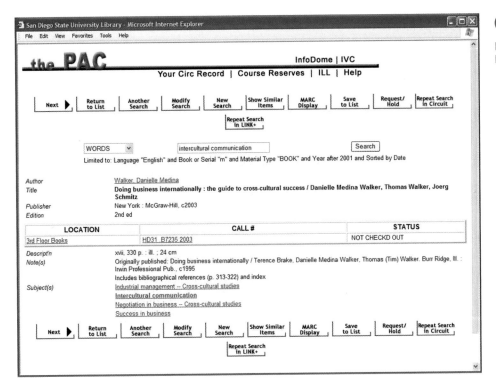

FIGURE 19–6

Illustration of a Retrieved
Record

field you are researching. Regularly updated indexes are available both online and in the reference section of most libraries.

If you are like most business researchers today, you will start your search for periodical literature in an online database. As the sophistication and capacity of computer technology improve, much of the information that was once routinely recorded in print form and accessed through directories, encyclopedias, and indexes is now stored electronically in computer files. These files, known as *databases,* are accessed

● Computer databases
hold much of the
information recorded in
print and accessed
through indexes.

through the use of search strategies. However, one first needs to identify which databases to use.

• Knowing which online databases to use helps business researchers find the kind of information they need.

While there are many databases produced by private and government information services, some of those most useful to business researchers are *ABI/Inform, Factiva, Lexis-Nexis Academic,* and the *Business and Industry Database. ABI/Inform* is one of the most complete databases, providing access to hundreds of business research journals as well as important industry trade publications. Most of the articles are included in full text or with lengthy summaries. It allows basic, guided, and natural language searching. *Factiva,* on the other hand, provides access to current business, general, and international news, including access to various editions of *The Wall Street Journal.* It also includes current information on U.S. public companies and industries. Similarly, *Lexis-Nexis* offers access to the current business and international articles, providing them in full text. Additionally, it includes legal and reference information. Finally, the *Business and Industry Database* covers over 1,000 trade publications, emphasizing facts, figures, and key events. Over 60 percent of its contents are full text, and the remaining include key figures and facts.

• Skilled use of Boolean logic operators—AND, OR, and NOT—helps retrieve the kind of information needed.

Once researchers know where to begin, their search skills become critical. A good command of Boolean logic combined with the knowledge of how to implement it in the databases (or Internet search engines) used will help researchers extract the information they need quickly and accurately. Boolean logic uses three primary operators: AND, OR, and NOT. If search results yield more citations than you need, the results can be limited. Similar to the online catalog, most databases in the guided or advanced mode allow users to limit the search by article or publication type as well as by date. But the use of Boolean logic operators allows users to focus the subject matter more tightly, eliminating citations that are unrelated or tangential to the problem being discussed.

The operator AND is a narrowing term. It instructs the computer to find citations with both terms. The operator NOT is another narrowing term, instructing the computer to eliminate citations with a particular term. It should be used as a last resort because it can eliminate potentially good sources. For example, if one were searching for articles on venture capital, using the NOT term in an attempt to eliminate DotCom companies might eliminate good articles where DotCom was mentioned as an aside or even an article that compared DotCom companies to other funded companies. If a search results in few citations, the OR operator can be used to expand the search by adding variations or synonyms to the basic search term. A search for articles on Dot-Coms AND accountants might add accounting OR comptroller OR controller to expand its results.

If you have difficulty thinking of terms to broaden your search, look at the keywords or descriptors of the items that have already been identified. Often these will give you ideas for additional terms to use. If the search still comes up short, you need to check for spelling errors or variations. Becoming skilled at using Boolean logic will help you get the information you need when you need it.

• A wide variety of business sources are available through the Internet.

The Internet. The Internet is a network of networks. It operates in a structure originally funded by the National Science Foundation. However, no one organization owns or runs this globally connected network. Its users work together to develop standards, which are still emerging. The network provides a wide variety of resources, including many useful to business. Since no one is officially in charge, finding information on the Internet can be difficult. Nevertheless, this network of loosely organized computer systems does provide some search and retrieval tools.

• Using online individual search tools will help find files and text.

These tools can search for files as well as text on various topics. They can search both titles and the documents themselves. Since the Internet is a rapidly growing medium for publishing, the browsers and major portals incorporate links to search tools. Most of the links currently are to individual search engines such as AlltheWeb .com, Google, Hotbot, MSN Search, and Yahoo! Some of these engines compile their indexes using human input, some use software robots, and some use a combination. Google, whose simple, clean screens you see in Figures 19–7 through 19–11, provides users with much more than the ability to search web pages. From the primary search

SOURCE: Copyright © Google, Inc., reprinted with permission.

FIGURE 19–7

Illustration of an
Individual Web Search
Engine—Google

FIGURE 19–8

An Illustration of Results
from a Basic Search

page, users can search images, groups, directories, and news as well as link to advanced
search and translation tools. In Figure 19–7, you may notice that the terms *venture capital women* are entered without the Boolean operator AND. Google automatically
ANDs all terms, freeing the user from having to add the operator each time a search is
conducted. By hitting enter (or clicking on the Google Search button), you execute the
search. Notice the result in Figure 19–8: 416,000 links found in .18 of a second.

FIGURE 19–9

Illustration of the Advanced Search Feature of Google

SOURCE: Copyright © Google, Inc., reprinted with permission.

FIGURE 19–10

An Illustration of Results of an Advanced Search

SOURCE: Copyright © Google, Inc., reprinted with permission.

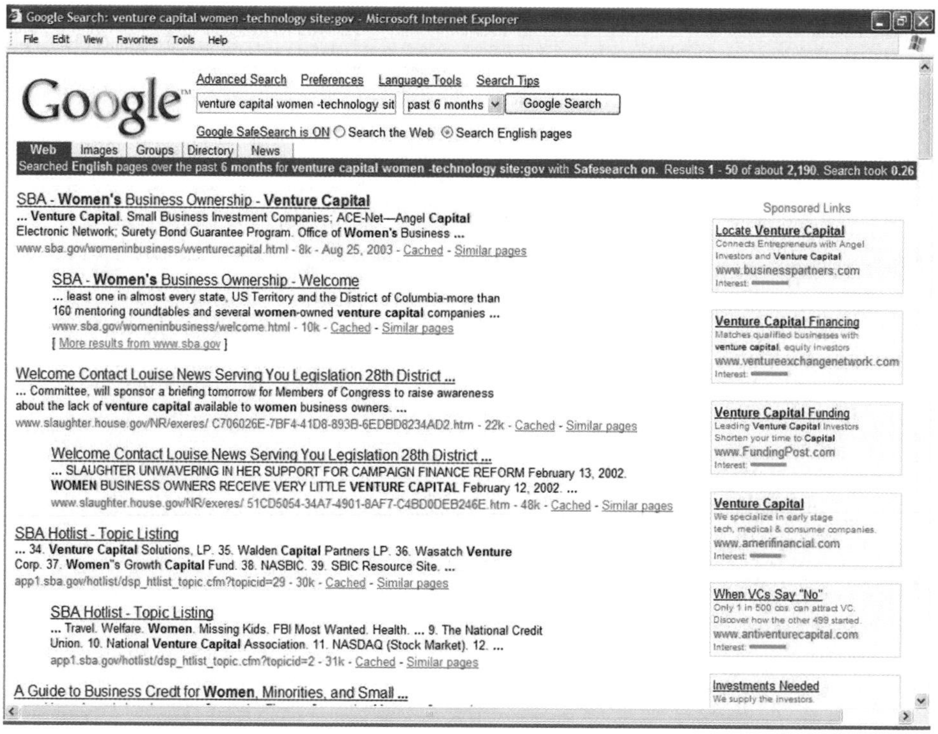

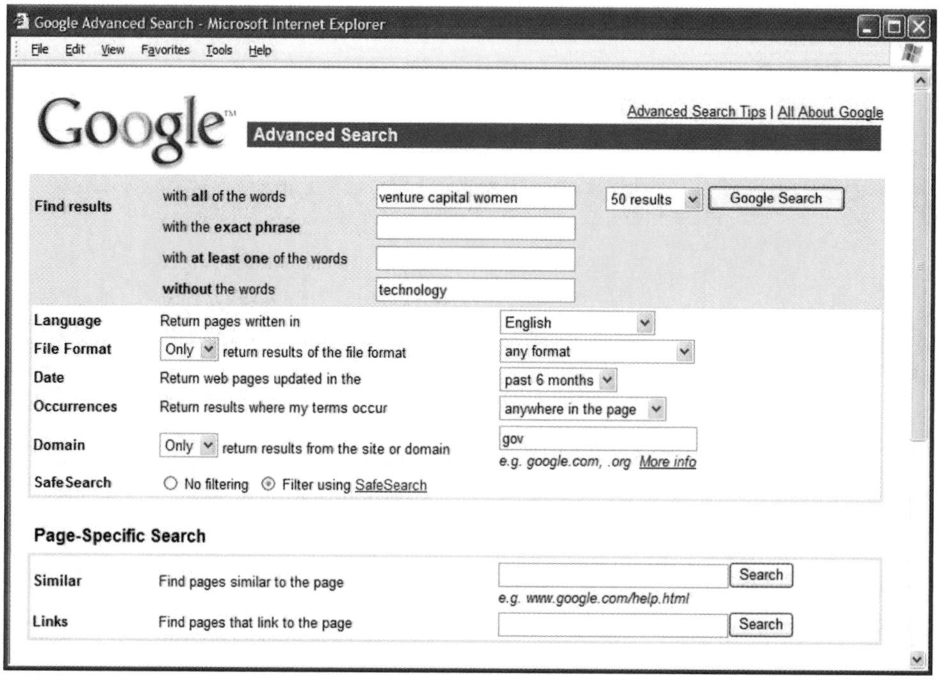

To limit this search, you could use the advanced search tool shown in Figure 19–9. Notice how the first search line **(all)** uses a built-in AND operator, and the third line **(at least one)** uses a built-in OR operator. Additionally, the advanced search allows its user to limit by language, English in this case, and by type of site, .gov here. When this search was run, its results were those shown in Figure 19–10: 2,190 links found in .26 of a second. To further limit the number of links, the user could click on the phrase *Similar pages.* It would return the screen you see in Figure 19–11, showing 31 links.

These are only a few of the features of Google. By thoroughly learning the special techniques and features of the search engines you use most frequently, you will find they can help you immensely in finding the information you need.

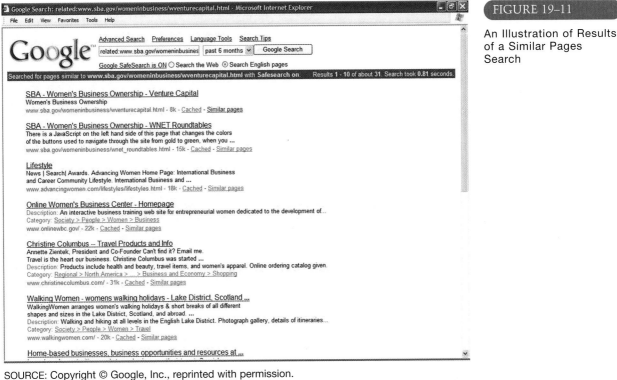

SOURCE: Copyright © Google, Inc., reprinted with permission.

FIGURE 19–11

An Illustration of Results of a Similar Pages Search

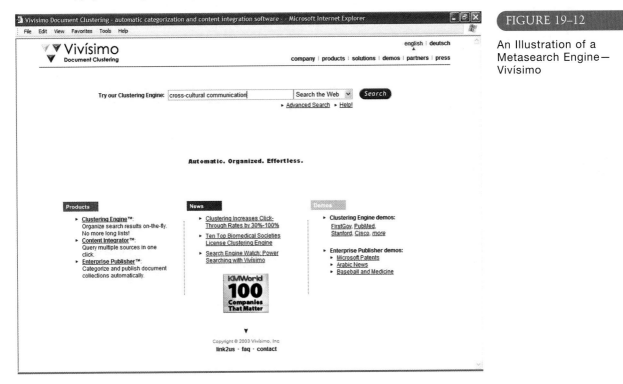

FIGURE 19–12

An Illustration of a Metasearch Engine— Vivísimo

As search engines evolve to meet the changing needs of the Internet's content and its users, new forms of these tools are emerging as well. Metasearch tools allow searchers to enter the search terms once, running the search simultaneously with several individual search engines and compiling a combined results page. Examples of these include Dogpile, EZZwww, Ixquick, Kartoo, Mamma, Metacrawler, and Search .com. You will find links to these and other search tools on the textbook website. Figures 19–12 and 19–13 illustrates how Vivísimo searches once for the phrase *cross-cultural communication,* and then combines the results, organizes them in categories, and presents them in an easy-to-view form.

● Metasearch tools help one use several individual tools more easily.

FIGURE 19-13

An Illustration of Results of a Metasearch

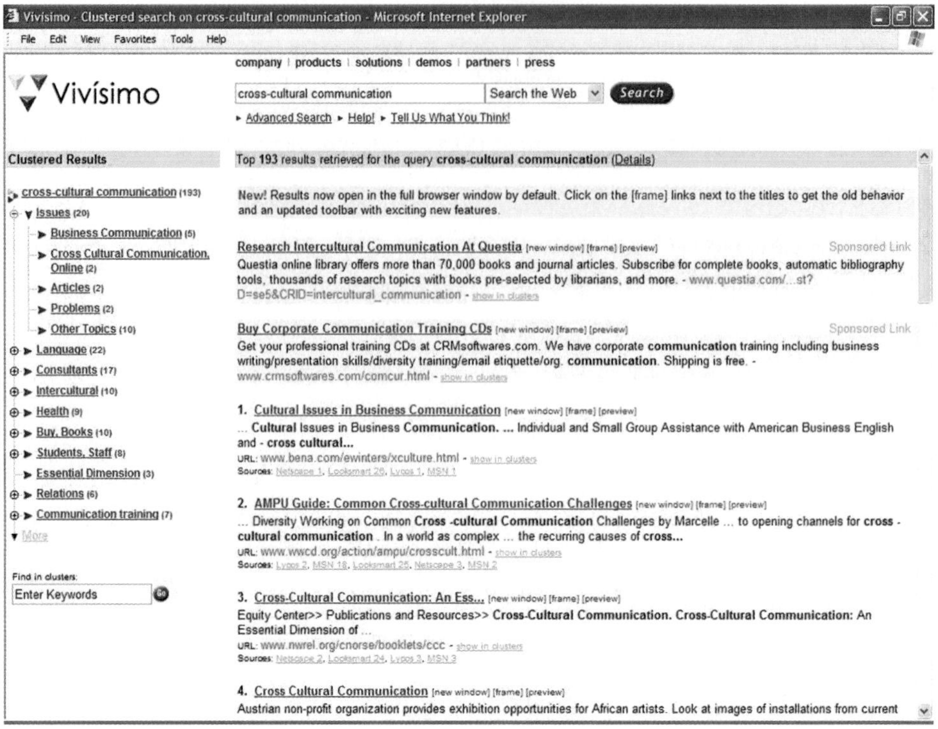

Another type of search tool that is emerging is the specialized search engine. Examples of some of these tools are Yahoo: People Search for finding people, Deja.com for searching newsgroups, Edgar for finding corporate information, FindLaw for gathering legal information, and Mediafinder for finding print items. There are specialty engines for finding information in finance, music, wireless, medicine, and more. These sites are sometimes referred to as the invisible web or deep web.

Another form of gathering information from the web is through use of personal agents. These agents allow users to define the kind of information they want to gather. The information gathered can be ready and waiting when users access their personal website, such as at my.yahoo.com. Or they can be delivered by email or in the form of "push technology," broadcast directly to the connected user's computer screen. You are using push technology if you have news/traffic/weather updates sent to you.

While these tools assist users in finding helpful web documents, it is crucial to remember the tools are limited. You must evaluate the source of the information critically. Also, you must recognize that not all of the documents published on the web are indexed and that no search tool covers the entire web. Skill in using the tools plays a role, but judgment in evaluating the accuracy and completeness of the search plays an even more significant role.

Evaluating Websites

Once you have located information sources, whether print or electronic, you need to evaluate them. Most print sources include items such as author, title of publication, facts of publication, and date in a standard form; however, websites have not yet established a standard form. Additionally, the unmonitored electronic media have introduced a slew of other factors one would want to consider in evaluating the credibility of the source as well as the reliability of the content. For example, most users of search engines do not understand the extent or type of bias introduced in the order search engines present their results; they often rely on one exclusively to find the most relevant sites when even the best of them only index an estimated 16 percent of the Internet content.

One experimental study found that users of website information were particularly susceptible to four types of misinformation: advertising claims, government misinfor-

- Specialized search engines run efficient searches on clearly identified subject-related sites.

- User-defined agents help personalize information needs.

- Users must evaluate the results carefully for both accuracy and completeness.

- All sources need careful evaluation; websites need special attention.

- Research shows many are overconfident in their ability to judge the reliability of websites.

mation, propaganda, and even scam sites. Furthermore, the study found that users' confidence in their ability to gather reliable information was not related to their actual ability to judge the information appropriately. The results also revealed that level of education was not related to one's ability to evaluate website information accurately.[1]

One solution might be to limit one's use of information only to sites accessed through link from a trustworthy site, a site where others have evaluated the links before posting them. However, these sites are clearly not comprehensive and are often late in providing links to new sources. Therefore, developing the skill and habit of evaluating websites critically is probably a better choice. This skill can be honed by getting into the habit of looking at the purpose, qualifications, validity, and structure of websites one uses.

- **Purpose.** Why was the information provided? To explain? To inform? To persuade? To sell? To share? What are the provider's biases? Who is the intended audience? What point of view does the site take? Could it possibly be ironic, a satire, or a parody?

- **Qualifications.** What are the credentials of the information provider? What is the nature of any sponsorship? Is contact information provided accurate? Is it complete—name, email address, street address, and phone? Is it well written, clear, and organized?

- **Validity.** Where else can the information provided be found? Is the information the original source? Has the information been synthesized or abstracted accurately and in correct context? Is the information timely? When was it created? When was it posted? Has the site already been validated? Who links to it? (On Google, enter link:*url* to find links.) How long has the site existed? Is it updated regularly? Do the links work? Do they represent other views? Are they well organized? Are they annotated? Has the site received any ratings or reviews? Is cited information authentic?

- **Structure.** How is it organized, designed, and formatted? Does its structure provide a particular emphasis? Does it appeal to its intended audience?

By critically evaluating websites you use, you will be developing a skill that will help you effectively filter the vast amount of data you encounter.

> • Skills can be honed by habitually asking about the purpose, qualifications, validity, and structure.

PRIMARY RESEARCH

When you cannot find the information you need in secondary sources, you must get it firsthand. That is, you must use primary research, which employs four basic methods:

> • Primary research employs four basic methods.

1. Search through company records.
2. Experimentation.
3. Observation.
4. Survey.

Searching through Company Records

Since many of today's business problems involve various phases of company operations, a company's internal records—production data, sales records, marketing information, accounting records, and the like—are frequently an excellent source of firsthand information.

> • Company records are an excellent source of firsthand information.

There are no set rules on how to find and gather information through company records. Record-keeping systems vary widely from company to company. However, you are well advised to keep the following standards in mind as you conduct your investigation. First, as in any other type of research, you must have a clear idea of the information you need. Undefined, open-ended investigations are not appreciated—nor

> • Make sure you (1) have a clear idea of the information you need, (2) understand the terms of access and confidentiality, and (3) cooperate with company personnel.

---

[1] Leah Graham and Panagiotis Takis Metaxas, " 'Course It's True; I Saw It on the Internet!': Critical Thinking in the Internet Era," *Communications of the ACM* 46, no. 5 (May 2003), 73.

are they particularly productive. Second, you must clearly understand the ground rules under which you are allowed to review materials. Matters of confidentiality and access should be resolved before you start. And third, if you are not intimately familiar with a company's records or how to access them, you must cooperate with someone who is. The complexity and sensitivity of such materials require that they be reviewed in their proper context.

Conducting the Experiment

- Experimentation manipulates one factor and holds others constant.

The experiment is a very useful technique in business research. Originally perfected in the sciences, the experiment is an orderly form of testing. In general, it is a form of research in which you systematically manipulate one variable factor of a problem while holding all the others constant. You measure quantitatively or qualitatively any changes resulting from your manipulations. Then you apply your findings to the problem.

For example, suppose you are conducting research to determine whether a new package design will lead to more sales. You might start by selecting two test cities, taking care that they are as alike as possible on all the characteristics that might affect the problem. Then you would secure information on sales in the two cities for a specified time period before the experiment. Next, for a second specified time period, you would use the new package design in one of the cities and continue to use the old package in the other. During that period, you would keep careful sales records and check to make sure that advertising, economic conditions, competition, and other factors that might have some effect on the experiment remain unchanged. Thus, when the experimentation period is over, you can attribute any differences you found between the sales of the two cities to the change in package design.

- Design each experiment to fit the problem.

Each experiment should be designed to fit the individual requirements of the problem. Nonetheless, a few basic designs underlie most experiments. Becoming familiar with two of the most common designs—the before–after and the controlled before–after—will give you a framework for understanding and applying this primary research technique.

- The before–after design is the simplest. You use just one test group.

The Before–After Design. The simplest experimental design is the before–after design. In this design, illustrated in Figure 19–14, you select a test group of subjects, measure the variable in which you are interested, and then introduce the experimental factor. After a specified time period, during which the experimental factor has presumably had its effect, you again measure the variable in which you are interested. If there are any differences between the first and second measurements, you may assume that the experimental factor, plus any uncontrollable factors, is the cause.

Consider the following application. Assume you are conducting research for a retail store to determine the effect of point-of-sale advertising. Your first step is to select

FIGURE 19–14

The Before–After Experimental Design

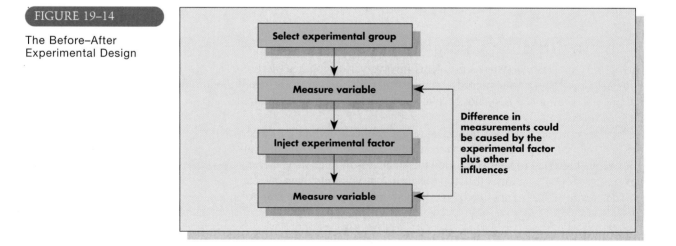

a product for the experiment, Gillette razor blades. Second, you record sales of Gillette blades for one week, using no point-of-sale advertising. Then you introduce the experimental variable: the Gillette point-of-sale display. For the next week you again record sales of Gillette blades; and at the end of that week, you compare the results for the two weeks. Any increase in sales would presumably be explained by the introduction of the display. Thus, if 500 packages of Gillette blades were sold in the first week and 600 were sold in the second week, you would conclude that the 100 additional sales can be attributed to point-of-sale advertising.

You can probably recognize the major shortcoming of the design. It is simply not logical to assume that the experimental factor explains the entire difference in sales between the first week and the second. The sales of Gillette razor blades could have changed for a number of other reasons: changes in the weather, holiday or other seasonal influences on business activity, other advertising, and so on. At best, you have determined only that point-of-sale advertising could influence sales.

- The changes recorded in a before–after experiment may not be attributable to the experimental factor alone.

The Controlled Before–After Design. To account for influences other than the experimental factors, you may use designs more complex than the before–after design. These designs attempt to measure the other influences by including some means of control. The simplest of these designs is the controlled before–after design.

In the controlled before–after design, you select not one group, but two: the experimental group and the control group. Before introducing the experimental factor, you measure in each group the variable to be tested. Then you introduce the experimental factor into the experimental group only.

When the period allotted for the experiment is over, you again measure in each group the variable being tested. Any difference between the first and second measurements in the experimental group can be explained by two causes: the experimental factor and other influences. But the difference between the first and second measurements in the control group can be explained only by other influences, for this group was not subjected to the experimental factor. Thus, comparing the "afters" of the two groups will give you a measure of the influence of the experimental factor, as diagrammed in Figure 19–15.

In a controlled before–after experiment designed to test point-of-sale advertising, you might select Gillette razor blades and Schick razor blades and record the sales of both brands for one week. Next you introduce point-of-sale displays for Gillette only and you record sales for both Gillette and Schick for a second week. At the end of the second week, you compare the results for the two brands. Whatever difference you find in Gillette sales and Schick sales will be a fair measure of the experimental factor, independent of the changes that other influences may have brought about.

- In the controlled before–after experiment, you use two identical test groups. You introduce the experimental factor into one group, then compare the two groups. You can attribute any difference between the two to the experimental factor.

FIGURE 19–15   The Controlled Before–After Experimental Design

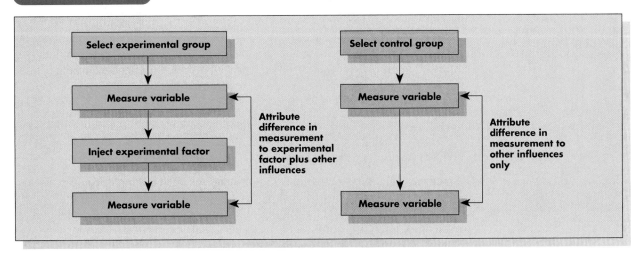

For example, without point-of-sales displays in the control group, if 400 packages of Schick blades are sold the first week and 450 packages are sold the second week, the increase of 50 packages (12.5 percent) can be attributed to influences other than the experimental factor, the point-of-sale display. If 500 packages of Gillette blades are sold the first week and 600 are sold the second week, the increase of 100 can be attributed to both the point-of-sale display and other influences. To distinguish between the two, you note that other influences accounted for the 12.5 percent increase in the sales of Schick blades. Because of the experimental control, you attribute 12.5 percent of the increase in Gillette sales to other influences as well. An increase of 12.5 percent on a base of 500 sales is 63 sales, indicating that 63 of the 100 additional Gillette sales are the result of other influences. However, the sale of 37 additional packages of Gillette blades can be attributed to point-of-sale advertising.

Using the Observation Technique

- Research by observation involves watching phenomena and recording what is seen.

- This form of observation does not involve experimentation.

Like the experiment, observation is a technique perfected in the sciences that is also useful in business research. Simply stated, observation is seeing with a purpose. It consists of watching the events involved in a problem and systematically recording what is seen. In observation, you do not manipulate the details of what you observe; you take note of situations exactly as you find them.

Note that observation as an independent research technique is different from the observation you use in recording the effects of variables introduced into a test situation. In the latter case, observation is a step in the experiment, not an end in itself. The two methods, therefore, should not be confused.

To see how observation works as a business technique, consider this situation. You work for a fast-food chain, such as McDonald's, that wants to check the quality and consistency of some menu items throughout the chain. By hiring observers, sometimes called mystery shoppers, you can gather information on the temperature, freshness, and speed of delivery of various menu items. This method may reveal important information that other data collection methods cannot.

- Observation requires a systematic procedure for observing and recording.

Like all primary research techniques, observation must be designed to fit the requirements of the problem being considered. However, the planning stage generally requires two steps. First, you construct a recording form; second, you design a systematic procedure for observing and recording the information of interest.

- The recording form should enable you to record details quickly and accurately.

The recording form may be any tabular arrangement that permits quick and easy recording of that information. Though observation forms are hardly standardized, one commonly used arrangement (see Figure 19–16) provides a separate line for each observation. Headings at the top of the page mark the columns in which the observer will place the appropriate mark. The recording form identifies the characteristics that are to be observed and requires the recording of such potentially important details as the date, time, and place of the observation and the name of the observer.

- An effective observation procedure ensures the collection of complete and representative information.

The observation procedure may be any system that ensures the collection of complete and representative information. But every effective observation procedure includes a clear focus, well-defined steps, and provisions for ensuring the quality of the information collected. For example, an observation procedure for determining the courtesy of employees toward customers when answering the telephone would include a detailed schedule for making calls, detailed instructions on what to ask, and provisions for dealing with different responses the observer might encounter. In short, the procedure would leave no major question unanswered.

Collecting Information by Survey

- You can best determine certain information by asking questions.

The premise of the survey as a method of primary research is simple: You can best determine certain types of information by asking questions. Such information includes personal data, opinions, evaluations, and other important material. It also includes information necessary to plan for an experiment or an observation or to supplement or interpret the data that result.

FIGURE 19–16

Excerpt of a Common
Type of Observation
Recording Form

Characteristics to be observed

Project 317, Ladies Casual Shoe Preferences

Observer <u>H. C. Hoffman</u>   Date <u>Aug. 17</u>

Place <u>311 Commerce, Dallas.</u>   Tim <u>1:00 – 3:00 pm</u>

COLOR									HEEL H			
BR	BL	W	GR	GY	BR	BL	R	O	0	1/2	1	2
√											√	
					√				√			
		√										
	√											
	√											
√										√		
			√									

Separate line for each observation

Once you have decided to use the survey for your research, you have to make decisions about a number of matters. The first is the matter of format. The questions can range from spontaneous inquiries to carefully structured interrogations. The next is the matter of delivery. The questions can be posed in a personal interview, asked over the telephone, or presented in printed or electronic form.

• Decide which survey format and delivery will be most effective in developing the information you need.

"We sent you on a fact-finding mission and all you found were two facts?"

SOURCE: © Benita Epstein 2000. Reprinted with permission of the artist.

Survey Tools Help Writers Lay Out, Analyze, and Report Results of Questionnaires

Survey tools, both software and web-based tools, help you design professional-looking questionnaires as well as compile and analyze the data collected. Software programs help with construction and layout of questionnaires and allow you to convert the questionnaires to html format for publishing on the web easily. Web-based programs help you create, distribute, and manage data collection for online questionnaires.

Special data entry screens assist you in selecting the types of questions and desired layout. They then arrange the questionnaire automatically while giving you the freedom to move the questions to change the ordering and arrangement if desired. The tools also let you create open-ended questions. All of these questions can be saved in a library for reuse. Some of the tools even include libraries of surveys that can be adapted for one's particular use.

As shown, one program, SurveyMonkey.com, creates a variety of graphics, helping you see the results clearly and accurately as the questionnaires are being submitted.

Businesses can use these tools in a variety of applications, including training program evaluations, employee feedback on policies and procedures, longitudinal studies of ongoing practices such as network advertising revenues, opinion surveys of customers and potential customers, and feedback on customer satisfaction.

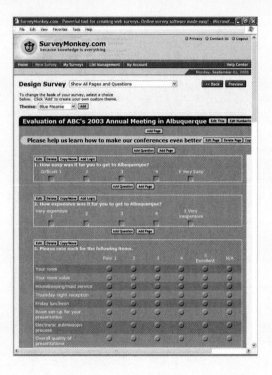
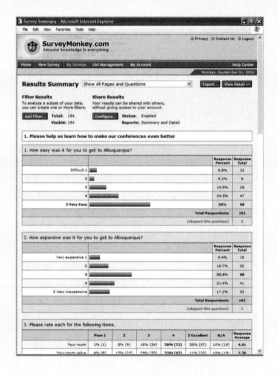

- Also decide whom to interview. If the subject group is large, select a sample.

But the most important is the matter of whom to survey. Except for situations in which a small number of people are involved in the problem under study, you cannot reach all the people involved. Thus, you have to select a sample of respondents who represent the group as a whole as accurately as possible. There are several ways to select that sample, as you will see.

- Survey research is based on sampling.

Sampling as a Basis. Sampling theory forms the basis for most research by survey, though it has any number of other applications as well. Buyers of grain, for example, judge the quality of a multi-ton shipment by examining a few pounds. Quality-control supervisors spot-check a small percentage of products ready for distribution to determine whether production standards are being met. Auditors for large corporations

sample transactions when examining the books. Sampling is generally used for economy and practicality. However, for a sample to be representative of the whole group, it must be designed properly.

Two important aspects to consider in sample design are controlling for sampling error and bias. Sampling error results when the sample is not representative of the whole group. While all samples have some degree of sampling error, you can reduce the error through techniques used to construct representative samples. These techniques fall into two groups: probability and nonprobability sampling.

- Good samples are reliable, valid, and controlled for sampling error.

Probability Sampling Techniques. Probability samples are based on chance selection procedures. Every element in the population has a known nonzero probability of selection.[2] These techniques include simple random sampling, stratified random sampling, systematic sampling, and area or cluster sampling.

Random Sampling. Random sampling is the technique assumed in the general law of sampling. By definition, it is the sampling technique that gives every member of the group under study an equal chance of being included. To assure equal chances, you must first identify every member of the group and then, using a list or some other convenient format, record all the identifications. Next, through some chance method, you select the members of your sample.

- In random sampling, every item in the subject group has an equal chance of being selected.

For example, if you are studying the job attitudes of 200 employees and determine that 25 interviews will give you the information you need, you might put the names of each worker in a container, mix them thoroughly, and draw out 25. Since each of the 200 workers has an equal chance of being selected, your sample will be random and can be presumed to be representative.

Stratified Random Sampling. Stratified random sampling subdivides the group under study and makes random selections within each subgroup. The size of each subgroup is usually proportionate to that subgroup's percentage of the whole. If a subgroup is too small to yield meaningful findings, however, you may have to select a disproportionately large sample. Of course, when the study calls for statistics on the group as a whole, the actual proportion of such a subgroup must be restored.

- In stratified random sampling, the group is divided into subgroups and the sample is randomly selected from each subgroup.

Assume, for example, that you are attempting to determine the curriculum needs of 5,000 undergraduates at a certain college and that you have decided to survey 20 percent of the enrollment, or 1,000 students. To construct a sample for this problem, first divide the enrollment list by academic concentration: business, liberal arts, nursing,

---

[2] William G. Zikmund, *Business Research Methods,* 7th ed. (Mason, OH: South-Western, 2003), 279.

engineering, and so forth. Then draw a random sample from each of these groups, making sure that the number you select is proportionate to that group's percentage of the total undergraduate enrollment. Thus, if 30 percent of the students are majoring in business, you will randomly select 300 business majors for your sample; if 40 percent of the students are liberal arts majors, you will randomly select 400 liberal arts majors for your sample; and so on.

- In systematic sampling, the items are selected from the subject group at constant intervals.

Systematic Sampling. Systematic sampling, though not random in the strictest sense, is random for all practical purposes. It is the technique of taking selections at constant intervals (every *n*th unit) from a list of the items under study. The interval used is based, as you might expect, on the size of the list and the size of the desired sample. For example, if you want a 10 percent sample of a list of 10,000, you might select every 10th item on the list.

- Select the interval randomly or scramble the order of the subject group if you want your systematic sample to be random.

However, your sample would not really be random. By virtue of their designated place on the original list, items do not have an equal chance of being selected. To correct that problem, you might use an equal-chance method to determine what *n* to use. Thus, if you selected the number 7 randomly, you would draw the numbers 7, 17, 27, and so on to 9,997 to make up your sample. Or, if you wanted to draw every 10th item, you might first scramble the list and then select from the revised list numbers 10, 20, 30, and so on up to 10,000 and make up your sample that way.

- For an area or cluster sample, draw items from the subject group in stages. Select randomly at each stage.

Area or Cluster Sampling. In area sampling, the items for a sample are drawn in stages. This sampling technique is appropriate when the area to be studied is large and can be broken down into progressively smaller components. For example, if you want to draw an area sample for a certain city, you may use census data to divide the city into homogeneous districts. Using an equal-chance method, you then select a given number of districts to include in the next stage of your sample. Next you divide each of the selected districts into subdistricts—city blocks, for example. Continuing the process, you randomly select a given number of these blocks and subdivide each of them into households. Finally, using random sampling once more, you select the households that will constitute the sample you will use in your research.

Area or cluster sampling is not limited to geographic division, however. It is adaptable to any number of applications. For example, it is an appropriate technique to use in a survey of the employees in a given industry. An approach that you may take in this situation is to randomly select a given number of companies from a list of all the companies in the industry. Then, using organization units and selecting randomly at each level, you break down each of these companies into divisions, departments, sections, and so on until you finally identify the workers you will survey.

Nonprobability Sampling Techniques. Nonprobability samples are based on an unknown probability of any one of a population being chosen. These techniques include convenience sampling, quota sampling, and referral sampling.[3]

- Convenience samples are chosen for their convenience, their ease and economy of reaching subjects, and their appropriateness.

Convenience Sampling. A convenience sample is one whose members are convenient and economical to reach. When professors use their students as subjects for their research, they are using a convenience sample. Researchers generally use this sample to reach a large number quickly and economically. This kind of sampling is best used for exploratory research.

A form of convenience sampling is *judgment* or *expert* sampling. This technique relies on the judgment of the researcher to identify appropriate members of the sample. Illustrating this technique is the common practice of predicting the outcome of an election, based on the results in a bellwether district.

- Setting quotas assures that the sample reflects the whole. Choose items randomly within each quota.

Quota Sampling. Quota sampling is another nonrandom technique. Also known as *controlled sampling*, it is used whenever the proportionate makeup of the universe under study is available. The technique requires that you refer to the composition of

---

[3] *Ibid.*

FIGURE 19–17

Example of Quota Sample

	Number in Universe	Percent of Total	Number to Be Interviewed
Total student enrollment	4,000	100	400
Sex			
Men students	2,400	60	240
Women students	1,600	40	160
Fraternity, sorority membership			
Members	1,000	25	100
Nonmembers	3,000	75	300
Marital status			
Married students	400	10	40
Single students	3,600	90	360
Class rank			
Freshmen	1,600	40	160
Sophomores	1,000	25	100
Juniors	800	20	80
Seniors	400	10	40
Graduates	200	5	20

the universe in designing your sample, selecting items so that your sample has the same characteristics in the same proportion as that universe. Specifically, it requires that you set quotas for each characteristic that you want to consider in your research problem. Within those quotas, however, you will select individual items randomly.

Let us say that you want to survey a college student body of 4,000 using a 10 percent sample. As Figure 19–17 illustrates, you have a number of alternatives for determining the makeup of your sample, depending on the focus of your research. Keep in mind, though, that no matter what characteristic you select, the quotas the individual segments represent must total 100 percent and the number of items in the sample must total 400. Keep in mind also that within these quotas you will use an equal-chance method to select the individual members of your sample.

Referral Sampling. Referral samples are those whose members are identified by others from a random sample. This technique is used to locate members when the population is small or hard to reach. For example, you might want to survey rolle bolle players. To get a sample large enough to make the study worthwhile, you could ask those from your town to give you the names of other players. Perhaps you are trying to survey the users of project management software. You could survey a user's group and ask those members for names of other users. You might even post your announcement on a newsgroup or listserv; users of the system would send you the names for your sample.

- Referral samples are used for small or hard-to-reach groups.

Constructing the Questionnaire. Most orderly interrogation follows a definite plan of inquiry. This plan is usually worked out in a published (print or electronic) form, called the *questionnaire.* The questionnaire is simply an orderly arrangement of the questions, with appropriate spaces provided for the answers. But simple as the finished questionnaire may appear to be, it is the subject of careful planning. You should plan carefully so that the results are *reliable;* a test of a questionnaire's reliability is its repeatability with similar results. You also want your questionnaire to be *valid,* measuring what it is supposed to measure. It is, in a sense, the outline of the analysis of the problem. In addition, it must observe certain rules. These rules sometimes vary with the problem. The more general and by far the more important ones follow.

- Construct a questionnaire carefully so that the results it provides are both reliable and valid.

Avoid Leading Questions. A leading question is one that in some way influences the answer. For example, the question "Is Dove your favorite bath soap?" leads the

- Avoid leading questions (questions that influence the answer).

respondent to favor Dove. Some people who would say yes would name another brand if they were asked, "What is your favorite brand of bath soap?"

- Word the questions so that all the respondents understand them.

Make the Questions Easy to Understand. Questions not clearly understood by all respondents lead to error. Unfortunately, it is difficult to determine in advance just what respondents will not understand. As will be mentioned later, the best means of detecting such questions in advance is to test the questions before using them. But you can be on the alert for a few general sources of confusion.

- Vagueness of expression, difficult words, and two questions in one cause misunderstanding.

One source of confusion is vagueness of expression, which is illustrated by the ridiculous question "How do you bank?" Who other than its author knows what the question means? Another source is using words respondents do not understand, as in the question "Do you read your house organ regularly?" The words *house organ* have a specialized, not widely known meaning, and *regularly* means different things to different people. Combining two questions in one is yet another source of confusion. For example, "Why did you buy a Ford?" actually asks two questions: "What do you like about Fords?" and "What don't you like about the other automobiles?"

- Avoid questions of a personal nature.

Avoid Questions That Touch on Personal Prejudices or Pride. For reasons of pride or prejudices, people cannot be expected to answer accurately questions about certain areas of information. These areas include age, income status, morals, and personal habits. How many people, for example, would answer no to the question "Do you brush your teeth daily?" How many people would give their ages correctly? How many solid citizens would admit to fudging a bit on their tax returns? The answers are obvious.

- But if personal questions are necessary, use less direct methods.

But one may ask, "What if such information is essential to the solution of the problem?" The answer is to use less direct means of inquiry. To ascertain age, for example, investigators could ask for dates of high school graduation, marriage, or the like. From this information, they could approximate age. Or they could approximate age through observation, although this procedure is acceptable only if broad age approximations would be satisfactory. They could ask for such harmless information as occupation, residential area, and standard of living and then use that information as a basis for approximating income. Another possibility is to ask range questions such as "Are you between 18 and 24, 25 and 40, or over 40?" This technique works well with income questions, too. People are generally more willing to answer questions worded by ranges rather than specifics. Admittedly, such techniques are sometimes awkward and difficult. But they can improve on the biased results that direct questioning would obtain.

- Seek factual information whenever possible.

Seek Facts as Much as Possible. Although some studies require opinions, it is far safer to seek facts whenever possible. Human beings simply are not accurate reporters of their opinions. They are often limited in their ability to express themselves. Frequently, they report their opinions erroneously simply because they have never before been conscious of having them.

When opinions are needed, it is usually safer to record facts and then to judge the thoughts behind them. This technique, however, is only as good as the investigators' judgment. But a logical analysis of fact made by trained investigators is preferable to a spur-of-the-moment opinion.

A frequent violation of this rule results from the use of generalizations. Respondents are sometimes asked to generalize an answer from a large number of experiences over time. The question "Which magazines do you read regularly?" is a good illustration. Aside from the confusion caused by the word *regularly* and the fact that the question may tap the respondent's memory, the question forces the respondent to generalize. Would it not be better to phrase it in this way: "What magazines have you read this month?" The question could then be followed by an article-by-article check of the magazines to determine the extent of readership.

- Ask only for information that can be remembered.

Ask Only for Information That Can Be Remembered. Since the memory of all human beings is limited, the questionnaire should ask only for information that the respondents can be expected to remember. To make sure that this is done, a knowledge of certain fundamentals of memory is necessary.

Recency is the foremost fundamental. People remember insignificant events that occurred within the past few hours. By the next day, they will forget some. A month later they may not remember any. One might well remember, for example, what one ate for lunch on the day of the inquiry, and perhaps one might remember what one ate for lunch a day, or two days, or three days earlier. But one would be unlikely to remember what one ate for lunch a year earlier.

- Memory is determined by three fundamentals: (1) recency,

The second fundamental of memory is that significant events may be remembered over long periods. One may long remember the first day of school, the day of one's wedding, an automobile accident, a Christmas Day, and the like. In each of these examples there was an intense stimulus—a requisite for retention in memory.

- (2) intensity of stimulus, and

A third fundamental of memory is that fairly insignificant facts may be remembered over long time periods through association with something significant. Although one would not normally remember what one ate for lunch a year earlier, for example, one might remember if the date happened to be one's wedding day, Christmas Day, or one's first day at college. Obviously, the memory is stimulated, not by the meal itself, but by the association of the meal with something more significant.

- (3) association.

Plan the Physical Layout with Foresight. The overall design of the questionnaire should be planned to facilitate recording, analyzing, and tabulating the answers. Three major considerations are involved in such planning.

- Design the form for each recording.

First, sufficient space should be allowed for recording answers. When practical, a system for checking answers may be set up. Such a system must always provide for all possible answers, including conditional answers. For example, a direct question may provide for three possible answers: Yes _____, No _____, and Don't know _____.

- Provide sufficient space.

Second, adequate space for identifying and describing the respondent should be provided. In some instances, such information as the age, sex, and income bracket of the respondent is vital to the analysis of the problem and should be recorded. In other instances, little or no identification is necessary.

- Provide adequate identification space.

Third, the best possible sequence of questions should be used. In some instances, starting with a question of high interest value may have psychological advantages. In other instances, it may be best to follow some definite order of progression. Frequently, some questions must precede others because they help explain the others. Whatever the requirements of the individual case may be, however, careful and logical analysis should be used in determining the sequence of questions.

- Arrange the questions in logical order.

Use Scaling When Appropriate. It is sometimes desirable to measure the intensity of the respondents' feelings about something (an idea, a product, a company, and so on). In such cases, some form of scaling is generally useful.

- Provide for scaling when appropriate.

Of the various techniques of scaling, ranking and rating deserve special mention. These are the simpler techniques and, some believe, the more practical. They are less sophisticated than some others,[4] but the more sophisticated techniques are beyond the scope of this book.

The ranking technique consists simply of asking the respondent to rank a number of alternative answers to a question in order of preference (1, 2, 3, and so on). For example, in a survey to determine consumer preferences for toothpaste, the respondent might be asked to rank toothpastes A, B, C, D, and E in order of preference. In this example, the alternatives could be compared on the number of preferences stated for each. This method of ranking and summarizing results is reliable despite its simplicity. More complicated ranking methods (such as the use of paired comparison) and methods of recording results are also available.

- Ranking of responses is one form.

---

[4] Equivalent interval techniques (developed by L. L. Thurstone), scalogram analysis (developed by Louis Guttman), and the semantic differential (developed by C. E. Osgood, G. J. Suci, and P. H. Tannenbaum) are more complex techniques.

FIGURE 19–18

Illustration of a Rating Question

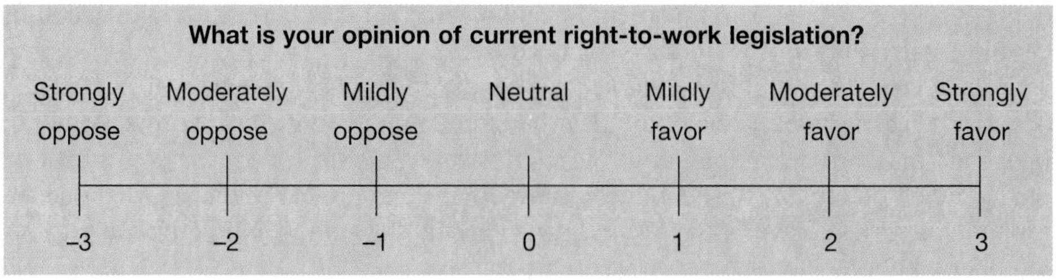

What is your opinion of current right-to-work legislation?

Strongly oppose	Moderately oppose	Mildly oppose	Neutral	Mildly favor	Moderately favor	Strongly favor
−3	−2	−1	0	1	2	3

- Rating is another.

The rating technique graphically sets up a scale showing the complete range of possible attitudes on a matter and assigns number values to the positions on the scale. The respondent must then indicate the position on the scale that indicates his or her attitude on that matter. Typically, the numeral positions are described by words, as the example in Figure 19–18 illustrates.

Because the rating technique deals with the subjective rather than the factual, it is sometimes desirable to use more than one question to cover the attitude being measured. Logically, the average of a person's answers to such questions gives a more reliable answer than does any single answer.

- Select the way of asking the questions (by personal contact, telephone, or mail) that gives the best sample, the lowest cost, and the best results.

Selecting the Manner of Questioning. You can get responses to the questions you need answered in three primary ways: by personal (face-to-face) contact, by telephone, or by mail (print or electronic). You should select the way that in your unique case gives the best sample, the lowest cost, and the best results. By *best sample* we mean respondents who best represent the group concerned. And *results* are the information you need. As you can see in Figure 19–19, other factors will influence your choice.

- Develop a working plan that covers all the steps and all the problems.

Developing a Working Plan. After selecting the manner of questioning, you should carefully develop a working plan for the survey. As well as you can, you should anticipate and determine how to handle every possible problem. If you are conducting a mail or web survey, for example, you need to develop an explanatory message that moves the subjects to respond, tells them what to do, and answers all the questions they are likely to ask (see Figure 19–20). If you are conducting a personal or telephone survey, you need to cover this information in instructions to the interviewers. You should develop your working plan before conducting the pilot study discussed in the following section. You should test that plan in the pilot study and revise it based on the knowledge you gain from the pilot study.

FIGURE 19–19

Comparison of Data Collection Methods

	Personal	Telephone	Online	Mail
Data collection costs	High	Medium	Low	Low
Data collection time required	Medium	Low	Medium	High
Sample size for a given budget	Small	Medium	Large	Large
Data quantity per respondent	High	Medium	Low	Low
Reaches high proportion of public	Yes	Yes	No	Yes
Reaches widely dispersed sample	No	Maybe	Yes	Yes
Reaches special locations	Yes	Maybe	No	No
Interaction with respondents	Yes	Yes	No	No
Degree of interviewer bias	High	Medium	None	None
Severity of nonresponse bias	Low	Low	High	High
Presentation of visual stimuli	Yes	No	Yes	Maybe
Field-worker training required	Yes	Yes	No	No

SOURCE: Pamela L. Alreck and Robert B. Settle, *The Survey Research Handbook*, 3rd ed. (Burr Ridge, IL: McGraw-Hill/Irwin, 2004), 33.

FIGURE 19–20

Illustration of a
Persuasive Request
Cover Message

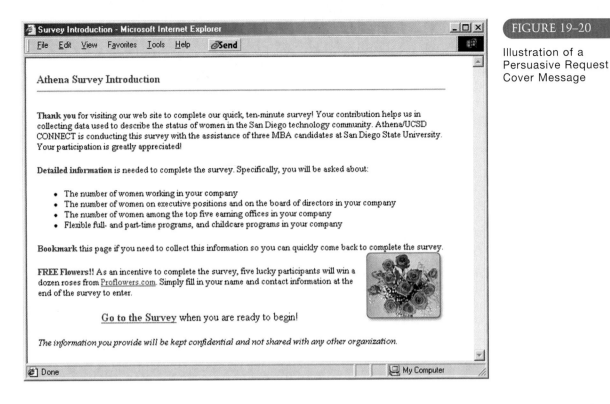

Survey Introduction - Microsoft Internet Explorer

File   Edit   View   Favorites   Tools   Help   ✒Send

Athena Survey Introduction

Thank you for visiting our web site to complete our quick, ten-minute survey! Your contribution helps us in collecting data used to describe the status of women in the San Diego technology community. Athena/UCSD CONNECT is conducting this survey with the assistance of three MBA candidates at San Diego State University. Your participation is greatly appreciated!

Detailed information is needed to complete the survey. Specifically, you will be asked about:

- The number of women working in your company
- The number of women on executive positions and on the board of directors in your company
- The number of women among the top five earning offices in your company
- Flexible full- and part-time programs, and childcare programs in your company

Bookmark this page if you need to collect this information so you can quickly come back to complete the survey.

FREE Flowers!! As an incentive to complete the survey, five lucky participants will win a dozen roses from Proflowers.com. Simply fill in your name and contact information at the end of the survey to enter.

Go to the Survey when you are ready to begin!

The information you provide will be kept confidential and not shared with any other organization.

Done   My Computer

Conducting a Pilot Study. Before doing the survey, it is advisable to conduct a pilot study on your questionnaire and working plan. A pilot study is a small-scale version of the actual survey. Its purpose is to test what you have planned. Based on your experience in the pilot study, you modify your questionnaire and working plan for use in the full-scale survey that follows.

- Test the questionnaire and the working plan. Make any changes needed.

Evaluating and Reporting Data

Gathering information from secondary sources is one step in processing facts for your report. You also need to evaluate it. Ask yourself questions about the writer's credibility, including methods of collecting facts and ability to draw inferences from the facts presented. Does the author draw conclusions that can be supported by the data presented? Are the sources reliable? Are the data or interpretations biased in any way? Are there any gaps or holes in the data or interpretation? You need to be a good judge of the material and feel free to discard it if it does not meet your standard for quality.

- Carefully evaluate the secondary information you find.

In this chapter, you also have learned how to plan and carry out primary data collection properly. Now that you have good data to work with, you must interpret them accurately and clearly for your reader (see Chapter 10 for interpreting procedure). If you are unsure of your reader's level of expertise in understanding descriptive statistics such as measures of central tendency and cross-tabulations, present the statistic and tell the reader what it means. In general, you can expect to explain the statistics from univariate, bivariate, and multivariate analyses. In many cases, graphics help tremendously because they clearly show trends and relationships. Statistical programs such as SPSS and SAS, help you analyze, report, and graph your data. Finally, you have an ethical responsibility to present your data honestly and completely. Omitting an error or limitation of the data collection is often viewed as seriously as hiding errors or variations from accepted practices. Of course, any deliberate distortion of the data is unethical. It is your responsibility to communicate the findings of the report accurately and clearly.

- Report statistics from primary research clearly and completely.

SUMMARY BY CHAPTER OBJECTIVES

1 Explain the difference between primary and secondary research.

1. Primary research is firsthand research. You can conduct primary research in four major ways:
   - Looking through company records.
   - Conducting an experiment.
   - Recording observations.
   - Conducting a survey.

   Secondary research is secondhand research. You conduct secondary research in either a general library (usually public), a special library (usually private), or online.

2 Gather secondary sources using direct and indirect research methods.

2. If you need quantitative or factual information, you may be able to go directly to it, using such sources as the following:
   - Encyclopedias.
   - Biographical directories.
   - Almanacs.
   - Trade directories.
   - Government publications.
   - Dictionaries.
   - Statistical sources.
   - Business information services.

   When you cannot go directly to the source, you use indirect methods. You may begin by searching the following sources:
   - The online catalog.
   - Online databases.
   - The Internet.

3 Evaluate website reliability.

3. Websites must be critically evaluated to ensure that the information is relevant and reliable. The skill can be honed and become habit by looking at the purpose of each site, the qualifications of the information provider, the validity of the content, and the organizational structure and design format.

4 Describe the procedures for searching through company records.

4. Company records are usually confidential. You must either ask the person responsible for the information for it or gather it yourself from company records.

5 Conduct an experiment for a business problem.

5. An experiment is an orderly form of testing. It can be designed using the before–after design or the controlled before–after design.
   - The simplest is the before–after design. It involves selecting a group of subjects, measuring the variable, introducing the experimental factor, and measuring the variable again. The difference between the two measurements is assumed to be the result of the experimental factor.
   - The controlled before–after design involves selecting two groups, measuring the variable in both groups, introducing the experimental factor in one group, and then measuring the variable again in both groups. The second measurement enables you to determine the effect of the experimental factor and of other factors that might have influenced the variable between the two measurements.

6 Design an observational study for a business problem.

6. The observation method may be defined as seeing with a purpose. It consists of watching the events involved in a problem and systematically recording what is seen. The events observed are not manipulated.

7 Use sampling to conduct a survey.

7. A sample is a group representative of the whole group. The procedure for selecting the group is called sampling. A good sample is controlled for sampling error. You may use any of a variety of sample designs. Those discussed in this chapter include probability and nonprobability sampling.

- Probability sampling is based on chance selection procedures. Every element in the population has a known nonzero probability of selection. Some of the techniques are described below.
  — Simple random sampling involves chance selection, giving every member of the group under study an equal chance of being selected.
  — Stratified random sampling involves proportionate and random selection from each major subgroup of the group under study.
  — Systematic sampling involves taking selections at constant intervals (every fifth one, for example) from a complete list of the group under study.
  — Area or cluster sampling involves dividing into parts the area that contains the sample, selecting from these parts randomly, and continuing to subdivide and select until you have your desired sample size.
- Nonprobability sampling is based on an unknown probability of any one of a group being studied. Some of the techniques are described below.
  — Convenience sampling involves selecting members that are convenient, easy to reach, and appropriate as judged by the researcher.
  — Quota sampling requires that you know the proportions of certain characteristics (sex, age, education, etc.) in the group under study. You then select respondents in the same proportions.
  — Referral sampling involves building your sample from other participants' referrals.

8. The questions you ask should follow a definite plan, usually in the form of a questionnaire. You should construct the questionnaire carefully, ensuring that it is valid and reliable, and the questionnaire should follow these general rules.
   - Avoid leading questions.
   - Make the questions easy to understand (avoid vagueness, difficult words, technical words).
   - Avoid questions that touch on personal prejudices or pride.
   - Seek facts as much as possible.
   - Ask only for what can be remembered (consider the laws of memory, recency, intensity, and association).
   - Plan the layout with foresight (enough space for answers and identifying information, proper sequence of questions).
   - Use scaling when appropriate.
   You develop a working plan for conducting the questioning—one that covers all the possible problems and clearly explains what to do. It is usually advisable to test the questionnaire and working plan through a pilot study. This enables you to make changes in the questionnaire and improve the working plan before conducting the survey.

   > Construct a questionnaire, develop a working plan, and conduct a pilot test for a survey.

9. You need to evaluate the facts you gather from secondary research carefully before you include them in your report. Check to make sure they meet the following tests.
   - Can the author draw the conclusions from the data presented?
   - Are the sources reliable?
   - Has the author avoided biased interpretation?
   - Are there any gaps in the facts?
   You must present the primary information you collect clearly and completely. It is your responsibility to explain statistics the reader may not understand.

   > Analyze and interpret information clearly and completely for your reader.

1. Suggest a hypothetical research problem that would make good use of a specialized library. Justify your selection.

2. What specialized libraries are there in your community? What general libraries?

3. Under what general condition are investigators likely to be able to proceed directly to the published source of the information sought?

4. Which database is most likely to contain information on each of the following subjects?
   a. Labor–management relations
   b. Innovation in sales promotion
   c. Accident proneness among employees
   d. Recent advances in computer technology
   e. Trends in responsibility accounting
   f. Viewpoints on the effect of deficit financing by governments
   g. New techniques in interviewing

5. Use your critical skills to evaluate websites, identifying those with problems in advertising claims, government misinformation, propaganda, or scam sites.

6. What advice would you give an investigator who has been assigned a task involving analysis of internal records of several company departments?

7. Define *experimentation*. What does the technique of experimentation involve?

8. Explain the significance of keeping constant all factors other than the experimental variable of an experiment.

9. Give an example of (*a*) a problem that can best be solved through a before–after design and (*b*) a problem that can best be solved through a controlled before–after design. Explain your choices.

10. Define *observation* as a research technique.

11. Select an example of a business problem that can be solved best by observation. Explain your choice.

12. Point out violations of the rules of good questionnaire construction in the following questions. The questions do not come from the same questionnaire.
    a. How many days on the average do you wear a pair of socks before changing?
    b. (The first question in a survey conducted by Coca-Cola.) Have you ever drunk a Diet Coke?
    c. Do you consider the ideal pay plan to be one based on straight commission or straight salary?
    d. What kind of gasoline did you purchase last time?
    e. How much did you pay for clothing in the past 12 months?
    f. Check the word below that best describes how often you eat dessert with your noon meal.
       Always
       Usually
       Sometimes
       Never

13. Explain the difference between random sampling and convenience sampling.

14. Discuss the writer's responsibility in explaining and reporting data.

1. Using your imagination to supply any missing facts you may need, develop a plan for the experiment you would use in the following situations.

   a. The Golden Glow Baking Company has for many years manufactured and sold cookies packaged in attractive boxes. It is considering packaging the cookies in recyclable bags and wants to conduct an experiment to determine consumer response to this change.

   b. The Miller Brush Company, manufacturers of a line of household goods, has for years sold its products through conventional retail outlets. It now wants to conduct an experiment to test the possibility of selling through catalogs (or home shopping networks or the web).

   c. A national chain of drugstores wants to know whether it would profit by doubling the face value of coupons. It is willing to pay the cost of an experiment in its research for an answer.

   d. The True Time Watch Company is considering the use of electronic sales displays ($49.50 each) instead of print displays ($24.50 each) in the 2,500 retail outlets that sell True Time watches. The company will conduct an experiment to determine the relative effects on sales of the two displays.

   e. The Marvel Soap Company has developed a new cleaning agent that is unlike current soaps and detergents. The product is well protected by patent. The company wants to determine the optimum price for the new product through experimentation.

   f. National Cereals, Inc., wants to determine the effectiveness of advertising to children. Until now, it has been aiming its appeal at parents. The company will support an experiment to learn the answer.

2. Using your imagination to supply any missing facts you may need, develop a plan for research by observation for these problems.

   a. A chain of department stores wants to know what causes differences in sales by departments within stores and by stores. Some of this information it hopes to get through research by observation.

   b. Your university wants to know the nature and extent of its parking problem.

   c. The management of an insurance company wants to determine the efficiency and productivity of its data-entry department.

   d. Owners of a shopping center want a study to determine shopping patterns of their customers. Specifically they want to know such things as what parts of town the customers come from, how they travel, how many stores they visit, and so on.

   e. The director of your library wants a detailed study of library use (what facilities are used, when, by whom, and so on).

   f. The management of a restaurant wants a study of its workers' efficiency in the kitchen.

3. Using your imagination to supply any missing facts you may need, develop a plan for research by survey for these problems.

   a. The American Restaurant Association wants information that will give its members a picture of its customers. The information will serve as a guide for a promotional campaign designed to increase restaurant eating. Specifically it will seek such information as who eats out, how often, where they go, how much they spend. Likewise, it will seek to determine who does not eat out and why.

   b. The editor of your local daily paper wants a readership study to learn just who reads what in both print and online editions.

   c. The National Beef Producers Association wants to determine the current trends in meat consumption. The association wants such information as the amount of meat people consume, whether people have changed their meat consumption habits, and so on.

   d. The International Association of Publishers wants a survey of the reading habits of adults in the United States and Canada. It wants such information as who reads what, how much, when, where, and so on. It also wants to gauge reader attitude toward ebooks.

   e. Your boss wants to hire an experienced computer webmaster for your company. Because you have not hired anyone in this category in five years, you were asked to survey experienced webmasters using the web or Usenet groups to gather salary figures.

Corrections for the Self-Administered Diagnostic Test of Correctness

Following are the corrected sentences for the diagnostic test at the end of Chapter 17. The corrections are underscored, and the symbols for the standards explaining the correction follow the sentences.

1. An important fact about this keyboard is, that it has the patented "ergonomic design".
   An important fact about this keyboard is that it has the patented "ergonomic design." *Cma 6.1, QM 3*

2. Goods received on Invoice 2741 are as follows: 3 dozen blue denim shirts, size 15–33, 4 men's gortex gloves, brown, size large, and 5 dozen assorted socks.
   Goods received on Invoice 2741 are as follows: three dozen blue denim shirts, size 15–33; four men's gortex gloves, brown, size large; and five dozen assorted socks. *Cln 1, Apos 1, SC 3, No 1*

3. James Silver_President of the new union_had the privildge of introducing the speaker.
   James Silver, president of the new union, had the privilege of introducing the speaker. *Cma 4.2, Cap, SP*

4. We do not expect to act on this matter_however_until we hear from you.
   We do not expect to act on this matter, however, until we hear from you. *Cma 4.3*

5. Shipments through September 20, 2004_totaled 69,485 pounds_an increase of 17 percent over the year_ago total.
   Shipments through September 20, 2004, totaled 69,485 pounds, an increase of 17 percent over the year-ago total. *Cma 4.4, Cma 4.1, Hpn 2*

6. Brick is recommended as the building material_but the board is giving serious consideration to a substitute.
   Brick is recommended as the building material, but the board is giving serious consideration to a substitute. *Cma 1*

7. Markdowns for the sale total $34,000, never before has the company done anything like this.
   Markdowns for the sale total $34,000; never before has the company done anything like this. *SC 1*

8. After long experimentation a wear_resistant_high_grade_and beautiful stocking has been perfected.
   After long experimentation a wear-resistant, high-grade, and beautiful stocking has been perfected. *Hpn 2, Cma 2.2*

9. Available in white_green_and blue_this paint is sold by dealers all over the country.
   Available in white, green, and blue, this paint is sold by dealers all over the country. *Cma 2.1, Cma 3*

10. Julie Jahn_who won the trip_is our most energetic salesperson.
    Julie Jahn, who won the trip, is our most energetic salesperson. *Cma 3*

11. _Good_he replied_sales are sure to increase.
    "Good," he replied. "Sales are sure to increase." *QM 1, Pd 1, Cap*

12. Hogan's article_Retirement? Never!,_printed in the current issue of Management Review, is really a part of his book A Report on Worker Security.
    Hogan's article, "Retirement? Never!," printed in the current issue of *Management Review,* is really a part of his book, *A Report on Worker Security. Cma 4.2, QM 4, Ital 1*

13. Formal announcement of our Labor Day sale will be made in thirty-two days.
    Formal announcement of our Labor Day sale will be made in 32 days. *No 1*

14. Each day we encounter new problems. Although they are solved easily.
    Each day we encounter new problems, although they are solved easily. *Cma 5.1, Frag*

15. A list of models, sizes, and prices of both competing lines are being sent to you.
    A list of models, sizes, and prices of both competing lines is being sent to you. *Agmt SV*

16. The manager could not tolerate any employee's failing to do their best.
    The manager could not tolerate any employee's failing to do his or her best. *Pn 2*

17. A series of tests were completed only yesterday.
    A series of tests was completed only yesterday. *Agmt SV*

18. There should be no misunderstanding between you and I.
    There should be no misunderstanding between you and me. *Pn 3*

19. He run the accounting department for five years.
    He ran the accounting department for five years. *Tns 2*

20. This report is considerable long.
    This report is considerably long. *AA*

21. Who did you interview for the position?
    Whom did you interview for the position? *Pn 3*

22. The report concluded that the natural resources of the Southwest was ideal for the chemical industry.
    The report concluded that the natural resources of the Southwest are ideal for the chemical industry. *Agmt SV, Tns 1*

23. This applicant is six feet in height, _28 years old, weighs 165 pounds, and has had eight years' experience.
    This applicant is six feet in height, is 28 years old, weighs 165 pounds, and has had eight years' experience. *Prl*

24. While _ reading the report, a gust of wind came through the window, blowing papers all over the room.
    While she was reading the report, a gust of wind came through the window, blowing papers all over the room. *Dng*

25. The sprinkler system has been checked on July 1 and September 3.
    The sprinkler system was checked on July 1 and September 3. *Tns 5*

Physical Presentation of Letters, Memos, and Reports

The appearance of a letter, memo, or report plays a significant role in communicating the message. Attractively presented messages reflect favorably on the writer and the writer's company. They give an impression of competence and care; and they build credibility for the writer. Their attractiveness tells the readers that the writer thinks they are important and deserving of a good-looking document. It reflects the good business etiquette of the writer. On the other hand, sloppy work reflects unfavorably on the writer, the company, and the message itself. Thus, you should want your messages to be attractively displayed.

Currently, the writer has better control over the display in print and portable document format (pdf) than in email and hypertext markup language (html). However, as applications migrate to html output and as more browsers and email programs display standardized html similarly, the writer will gain better control over these electronic displays, too. The material presented here will help you present your documents attractively and appropriately in whichever medium you choose.

Advances in word processing have finally relieved us of much of the tedious, repetitive tasks involved in presenting documents. Yesterday's hot feature in word processing programs was a feature called styles. Styles allowed writers to define and apply a set of commands or keystrokes to a single style just once and then reuse the style. Writers could format a level-one heading once and reuse its style each time they needed to format a level-one heading. Also, if a writer decided to change the level-one formatting, only the style needed to be changed, for the software automatically changed all occurrences linked to the styles. While styles let writers create formatting for use anywhere within a document, today's automated formatting with interactive assistants helps you create a variety of documents.

In addition to creating a professional image consistently, companies that use automated formatting usually are more productive. Not only will the company save time formatting documents, but the assistance also can act as a prompt to the writer. This can help ensure that all components are included. Today's full-featured word processors include automated formatting for a full range of documents and formats can be customized to serve the precise needs of a business. The formats can include text, graphics, macros, styles, keyboard assignments, and custom toolbars.

Several word processors help users create custom formats (or templates) from existing documents. The user simply identifies the document and the software will build the format, a process similar to the reverse engineering that's long been part of manufacturing.

Furthermore, automated formatting is easy to use. Both Word and WordPerfect use *wizards* or *experts* to lead one through the creation of most kinds of business documents. This is especially helpful for the first time one creates a document and for those documents that one creates infrequently. Figures B–1 and B–2 illustrate the process of

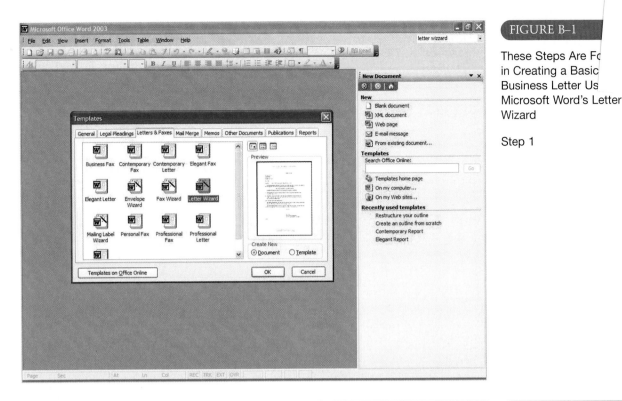

FIGURE B–1

These Steps Are F[...]
in Creating a Basic
Business Letter Us[...]
Microsoft Word's Letter
Wizard

Step 1

FIGURE B–1

(Continued) Step 2

creating a letter using the *wizard* and the *expert* tools. Notice that the writer simply fills in text, clicks buttons, or checks boxes or radio buttons.

BASICS FOR ALL DOCUMENT PREPARATION

To understand formats most effectively, you should know their basic components and how they are used for the documents you create. These basic components are presented here after a discussion of elements that are common to all documents: layout, type, and media.

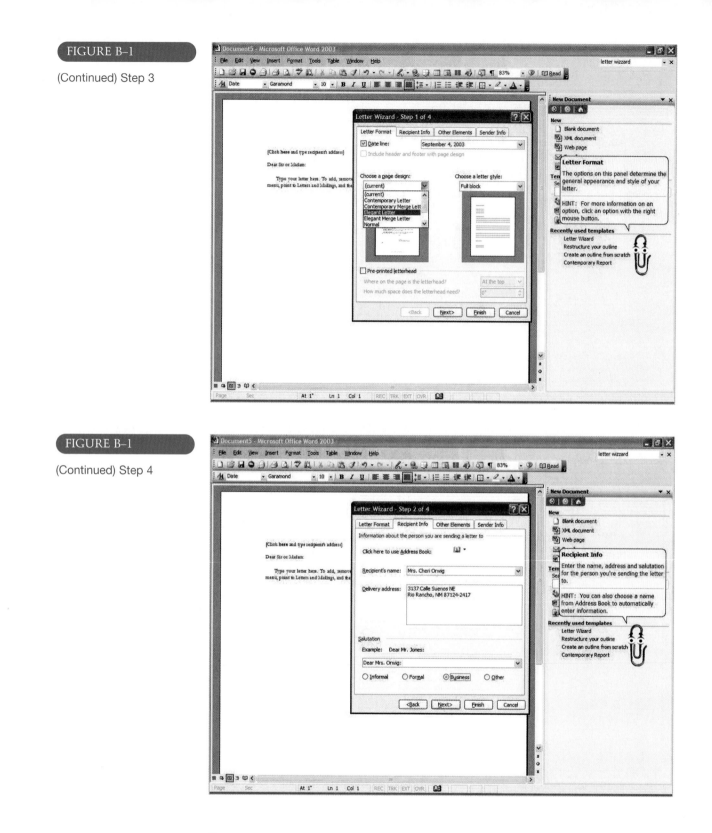

Layout

Common layout decisions involve grids, spacing, and margins. Grids are the non-printed horizontal and vertical lines that determine placement of your document on the page. They allow you to plan the placement of your text and graphics on the page for consistency. The examples shown in Figure B–3 on page 562 illustrate the placement of text on two-, three-, and six-column grids. You can readily see how important it is to plan for this element.

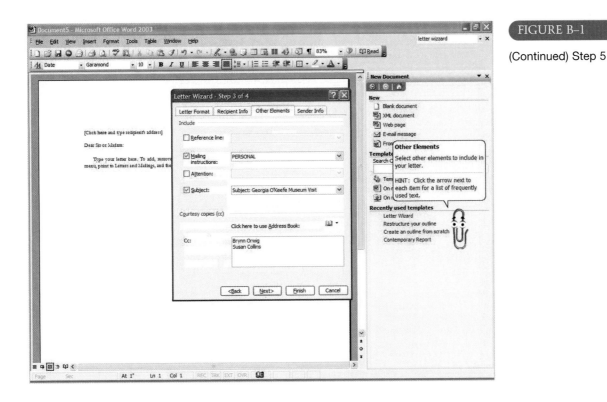

To make your document look its best, you must consider both external and internal spacing. External spacing is the white space—the space some never think about carefully. Just as volume denotes importance in writing, white space denotes importance. Surrounding text or a graphic with white spaces sets it apart, emphasizing it to the reader. Used effectively, white space also has been shown to increase the readability of your documents, giving your readers' eyes a rest. Ideally, white space should be a careful part of the design of your document.

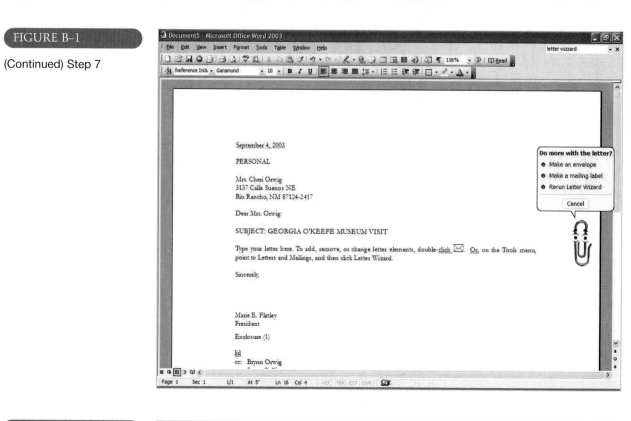

As discussed in Chapter 18, internal spacing refers to both vertical and horizontal spacing. The spacing between letters on a line is called *kerning*. With word processing programs, you can adjust how close the letters are to each other. These programs also allow you to adjust how close the lines are to each other vertically, called *leading*. Currently, many still refer to spacing in business documents as single or double spacing. However, this is a carryover from the typewriter era when a vertical line space was always ⅙ inch or when six lines equaled an inch. Today's software and hardware allow you to control this aspect of your document as well. Deciding on the best spac-

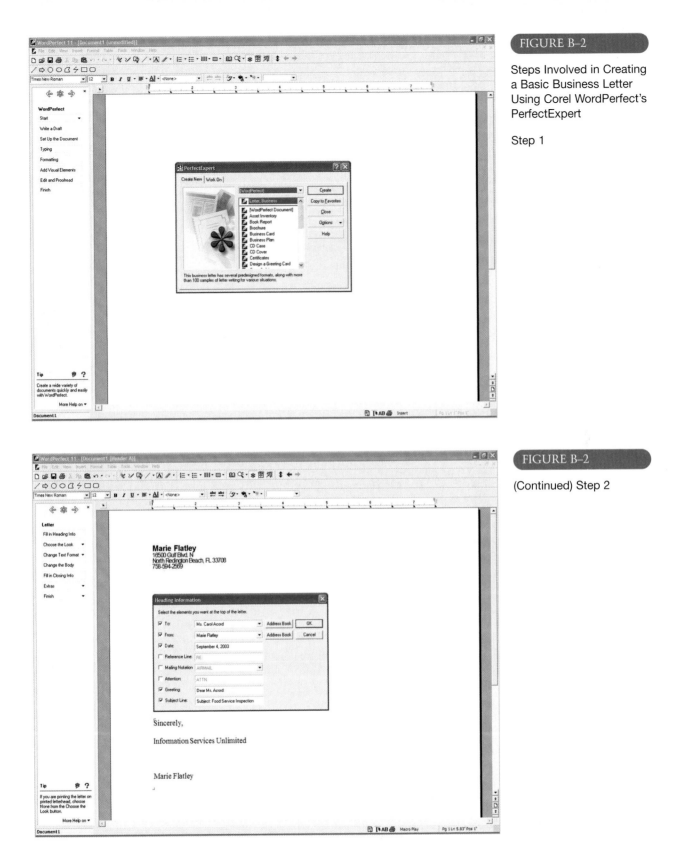

FIGURE B–2

Steps Involved in Creating
a Basic Business Letter
Using Corel WordPerfect's
PerfectExpert

Step 1

ing to use depends on the typeface you decide to use. In any case, you need to make
a conscious decision about the spacing aspect of the layout of your documents.

Another aspect of layout is your margin settings. Ideally, you should want your
document to look like a framed picture. This arrangement calls for all margins to be
equal. However, some businesses use a fixed margin on all documents regardless of

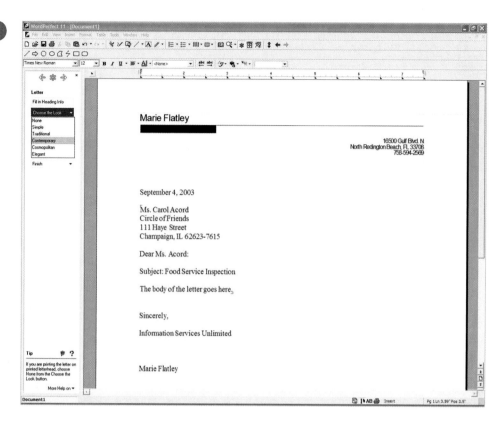

their length. Some do this to line up with design features on their letterhead; others believe it increases productivity. In either case, the side margins will be equal. And with today's software you easily make your top and bottom margins equal by telling the software to center the document vertically on the page. Although all margins will not be exactly equal, the page will still have horizontal and vertical balance. And some word processors are adding "make it fit" experts. With this feature, the writer tells the software the number of pages, allowing the program to select such aspects as margins, font size, and spacing to fit the message to the desired space.

Today's programs also have the capability to align your type at the margins or in the center. This is called *justification*. Left justification aligns every line at the left, right justification aligns every line at the right, and full justification aligns every line at both the left and the right (see Figure B–4 on page 563). Unless you are using a proportional

(Concluded) Step 7

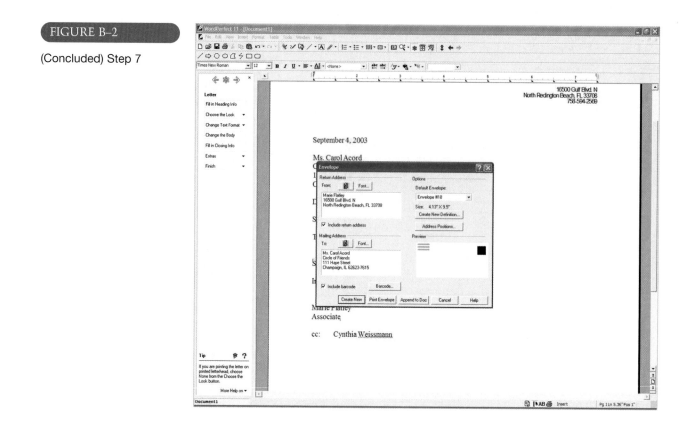

Layout Illustrations on Different Grids

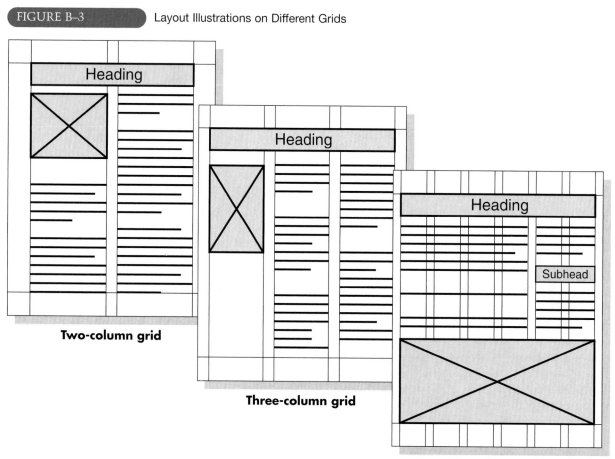

Two-column grid

Three-column grid

Six-column grid

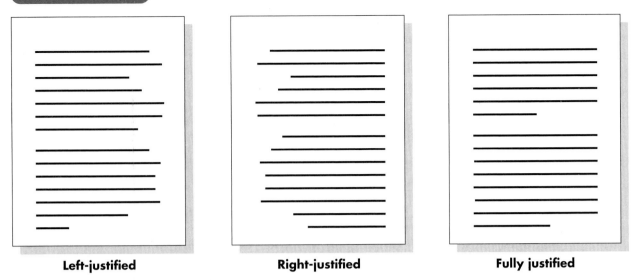

Left-justified   **Right-justified**   **Fully justified**

font, full justification takes the extra spaces between the last word and the right margin and distributes them across the line. This adds extra white spaces across the line, stopping most readers' eyes a bit. Therefore, it is usually best to set a left-justified margin and ignore the resulting ragged right margin. However, if your document's right margin is distracting, you may want to turn on the hyphenation feature. Your software will then hyphenate words at the end of lines, smoothing the raggedness of the right margin.

Type

Type is purported to influence the appearance of your document more than any other aspect. You need to make decisions on the typeface, the type style, and the type size. Typeface refers to the font or shape of the characters. Although thousands of fonts are available, they are generally classified as *serif* or *sans serif.* Serif typefaces have feet; sans serif do not. You can see this clearly in the examples that follow.

New Century Schoolbook and Times Roman are serif typefaces.

Helvetica and Futura are sans serif typefaces.

Since readers use the visual cues they get from the feet to form the words in their minds, they find the text of documents easier to read if a serif typeface is used. Sans serif typefaces are particularly good for headings where clear, distinct letters are important.

Type style refers to the way the typeface can be modified. The most basic styles include normal, **bold,** *italic,* and ***bold italic.*** Depending on your software and printer, you may have other options such as outline or shadow. You usually will decide to use modifications for specific reasons. For example, you may present all actions you want the reader to take in boldface type. Or you may decide to apply different styles to different levels of headings. In any case, use of type styles should be planned.

Finally, you will need to decide on size of type. Type is measured in points. Characters one inch high are 72 points. While this is a standard measure, different typefaces in the same size often appear to be a different size. You need to consider your typeface in choosing size for your documents. Generally, body text is between 9 and 14 points, and headings are 15 points and larger.

Media

The media you choose to transmit your documents also communicate. Text messaging and most email today are perceived as informal media. But choosing these media tells the reader that you are a user of computer technology and may imply that you are also up to date in your business. Choosing to send your message by fax, especially an Internet-based fax, also may imply your currency with the technology. Also, sending a formatted document, an html file, an rtf file, or a pdf document as an attached file both conveys a message and gives you some control over your document's display. However, because you cannot be assured of the quality of the output at the other end, your faxed or attached document may suffer in appearance due to either print quality or paper quality. By choosing paper as your medium, you will have control over appearance while relinquishing control over delivery to company and mail-delivery systems.

Today, paper is still a common choice of medium,[1] in the United States. Standard business paper size is 8½ by 11 inches; in international business its measurements are metric, resulting in paper sized slightly narrower than 8½ inches and slightly longer than 11 inches. Occasionally, half-size (5½ × 8½) or executive size (7¼ × 10½) is used for short messages. Other than these standards, you have a variety of choices to make for color, weight, texture, and such.

The most conservative color choice is white. Of course, you will find that there are numerous variations of white. In addition, there are all the colors of the palette and many tints of these colors. You want your paper to represent you and your business but not to distract your reader from the message. The color you choose for the first page of your document should also be the color you use for the second and continuing pages. This is the color you would usually use for envelopes, too.

Some businesses even match the color of the paper with the color of their printer ink and the color of their postage meter ink. This, of course, communicates to the reader that the writer or company is detail conscious. Such an image would be desirable for accountants or architects where attention to detail is perceived as a positive trait.

The weight and texture of your paper also communicate. While "cheap" paper may denote control of expenses to one reader, it may denote cost cutting to another. Usually businesses use paper with a weight of 16 to 20 pounds and a rag or cotton content of 25 to 100 percent. The higher the numbers, the higher the quality. And, of course, many readers often associate a high-quality paper with a high-quality product or service.

The choice of medium to use for your documents is important because it, too, sends a message. By being aware of these subtle messages, you will be able to choose the most appropriate medium for your situation.

With the basics taken care of, now we can move on to the specifics for the letter, memo, or report.

FORM OF BUSINESS LETTERS

The layout of a letter (its shape on the page) accounts for a major part of the impression made by the appearance of the letter. A layout that is too wide, too narrow, too high, too low, or off-center may impress the reader unfavorably. The ideal letter layout is one that has the same shape as the space in which it is formed. It fits that space much as a picture fits a frame. That is, a rectangle drawn around the processed letter has the same shape as the space under the letterhead. The top border of the rectangle is the dateline, the left border is the line beginnings, the right border is the average line length, and the bottom border is the last line of the notations.

As to the format of the layout, any generally recognized one is acceptable. Some people prefer one format or another, and some people even think the format they prefer is the best. Automated formatting allows you to choose your own format preferences. Generally, the most popular formats are block, modified block, and simplified. These are illustrated in Figure B–5. In all formats, single-spacing is the general rule. The standard formats included with word processors give users a choice of layout. Figure B–6 on page 566 shows the standard choices available in Word.

Agreement has not been reached on all the practices for setting up the parts of the letter. The following suggestions, however, follow the bulk of authoritative opinion.

---

[1] According to a recent study reported in the February 2000 *Wired,* Boston Consulting Group predicts that the consumption of office paper will actually have doubled from 1996 to 2003.

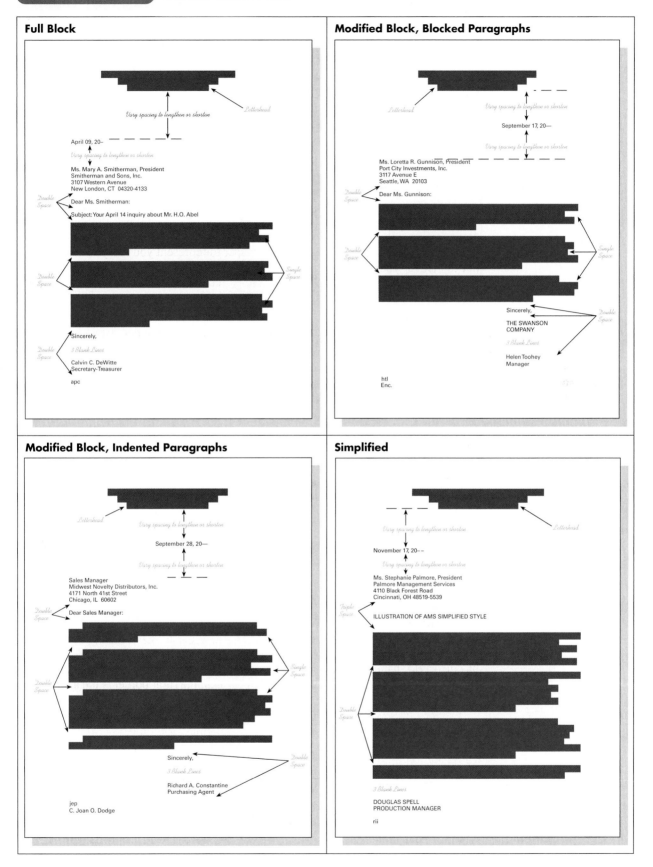

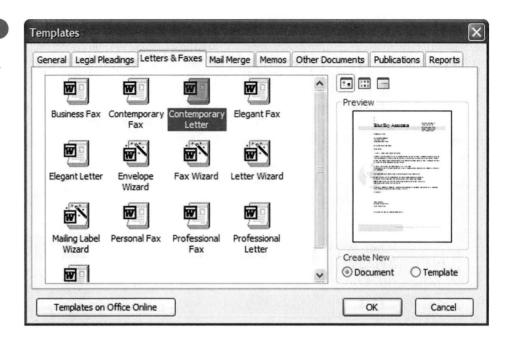

Dateline. You should use the conventional date form, with month, day, and year (September 17, 2004). When you are using a word processor's date feature, be sure to select the appropriate one. If you insert a date code, the date will be updated each time you retrieve the letter. If you use the date text feature, you insert the date the letter was created, and it does not change when you retrieve the letter in the future. Thus, when it is important that you have a record of the date you created the letter, this is the date feature you should use. Abbreviated date forms such as 09-17-03 or Sept. 17, '03 are informal and leave unfavorable impressions on some people. Most word processors allow you to set up your preference and will use that preference when you use the date feature.

Return Address. In most cases, your return address is printed on the letterhead or filled in on it during automated formatting.

Inside Address. The mailing address, complete with the title of the person being addressed, makes up the inside address. Preferably, form it without abbreviations, except for commonly abbreviated words (*Dr., Mr., Mrs., Ms.*). In Word, you can use its smart tag feature to quickly and easily enter addresses stored in Outlook.

Attention Line. Some executives prefer to emphasize the company address rather than the individual offices. Thus, they address the letter to the company in the inside address and then use an attention line to direct the letter to a specific officer or department. The attention line is placed a double space after the inside address and a double space before the salutation. When used, the typical form of attention line is

Attention: Mr. Donovan Price, Vice President

Salutation. The salutation you choose should be based on your familiarity with the reader and on the formality of the situation. As a general rule, remember that if the writer and the reader know each other well, the salutation may be by first name (*Dear Joan*). A salutation by last name (*Dear Mr. Baskin*) is appropriate in most cases.

If you do not know and cannot find out the name of the person to whom you are sending the letter, use a position title. By directing your letter to Director of Human Resources or Public Relations Manager, you are helping your letter reach the appropriate person.

Women's preferences have sharply reduced the use of *Mrs.* and *Miss.* The question many women ask is, Why distinguish between married and single women, when we make no such distinction between married and single men? The logical solution is to use *Ms.* for all women, just as *Mr.* is used for all men. If you know that the woman you are writing has another preference, however, you should adhere to that preference.

Mixed or Open Punctuation. The punctuation following the salutation and the closing is either mixed or open. Mixed punctuation employs a colon after the salutation and a comma after the complimentary close. Open punctuation, on the other hand, uses no punctuation after the salutation and none after the complimentary close. These two forms are used in domestic communication. In international communication, you may see letters with closed punctuation—punctuation distinguished by commas after the lines in the return and inside addresses and a period at the end of the complimentary close.

Subject Line. So that both the sender and the receiver may quickly identify the subject of the correspondence, many offices use the subject line in their letters. The subject line tells what the letter is about. In addition, it contains any specific identifying material that may be helpful: date of previous correspondence, invoice number, order number, and the like. It is usually placed a double space below the salutation. The block may be headed in a number of ways, of which the following are representative:

Subject: Your July 2nd inquiry about . . .

RE: Please refer to Invoice H-320.

Second Page Heading. When the length of a letter must exceed one page, you should set up the following page or pages for quick identification. Always print such pages on plain paper (no letterhead). These two forms are the most common:

Ms. Helen E. Mann   2   May 7, 2005

Ms. Helen E. Mann
May 7, 2005
Page 2

Most standard templates automatically insert this information—name of addressee, date, and page number—on the second and following pages of your letter.

Closing. By far the most commonly used complimentary close is *Sincerely. Sincerely yours* is also used, but in recent years the *yours* has been fading away. *Truly* (with and without the *yours*) is also used, but it also has lost popularity. Such closes as *Cordially* and *Respectfully* are appropriate when their meanings fit the writer–reader relationship. A long-standing friendship, for example, would justify *Cordially;* the writer's respect for the position, prestige, or accomplishments of the reader would justify *Respectfully.* Word's letter template has an insert feature that allows the writer to select the letter's closing (see Figure B–7).

Signature Block. The printed signature conventionally appears on the fourth line below the closing, beginning directly under the first letter for the block form. Most templates will insert the closing. A short name and title may appear on the same line, separated by a comma. If either the name or title is long, the title appears on the following line, blocked under the name. The writer's signature appears in the space between the closing and the printed signature.

Some people prefer to have the firm name appear in the signature block—especially when the letter continues on a second page without the company letterhead. The conventional form for this arrangement places the firm name in solid capitals and blocked on the second line below the closing phrase. The typed name of the person signing the letter is on the fourth line below the firm name.

An Illustration of the
Choices for
Complimentary Closings
in Word

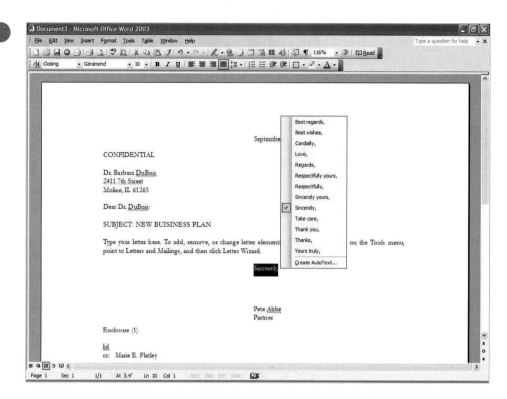

Information Notations. In the lower-left corner of the letter may appear abbreviated notations for enclosures (*Enc., Enc.—3,* and so on) and for the initials of the writer and the typist (*WEH:ga*). However, many businesses are dropping these initials since the reader does not need this information and since most word processors allow businesses to put this information in the document summary. Also, businesses are no longer including filename notations on the letters, since readers do not need them and today's word processors can find files by searching for specific content. Indications of copies prepared for other readers also may be included (*cc: Sharon Garbett, copy to Sharon Garbett*). (See Figure B–2, Step 7, on page 562.)

Postscripts. Postscripts, commonly referred to as the PS, are placed after any notations. While rarely used in most business letters because they look like afterthoughts, they can be very effective as added punch in sales letters.

Folding. The carelessly folded letter is off to a bad start with the reader. Neat folding will complete the planned effect by (1) making the letter fit snugly in its cover, (2) making the letter easy for the reader to remove, and (3) making the letter appear neat when opened.

The two-fold pattern is the easiest. It fits the standard sheet for the long (Number 10) envelope as well as some other envelope sizes. As shown in Figure B–8, the first fold of the two-fold pattern is from the bottom up, taking a little less than a third of the sheet. The second fold goes from the top down, taking exactly the same panel as the bottom segment. (This measurement will leave the recipient a quarter-inch thumbhold for easy unfolding of the letter.) Thus folded, the letter should be slipped into its envelope with the second crease toward the bottom and the center panel at the front of the envelope.

The three-fold pattern is necessary to fit the standard sheet into the commonly used small (Number 6¾) envelope. Its first fold is from the bottom up, with the bottom edge of the sheet riding about a quarter inch under the top edge to allow the thumbhold. (If the edges are exactly even, they are harder to separate.) The second fold is from the right side of the sheet toward the left, taking a little less than a third of the width. The third fold matches the second: from the left side toward the right, with a panel of ex-

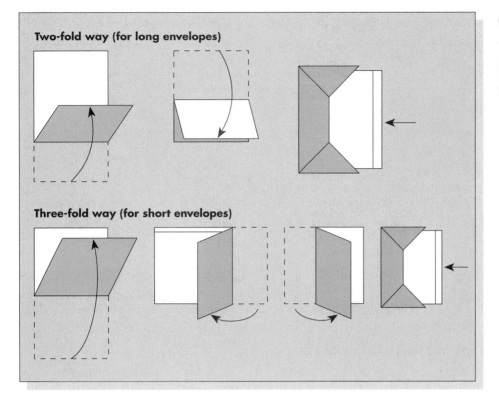

Two-fold way (for long envelopes)

Three-fold way (for short envelopes)

actly the same width. (This fold will leave a quarter-inch thumbhold at the right, for the user's convenience.) So that the letter will appear neat when unfolded, the creases should be neatly parallel with the top and sides, not at angles that produce "dog-ears" and irregular shapes. In the three-fold form, it is especially important for the side panels produced by the second and third folds to be exactly the same width; otherwise, the vertical creases are off-center and tend to throw the whole carefully planned layout off-center.

The three-fold letter is inserted into its cover with the third crease toward the bottom of the envelope and the loose edges toward the stamp end of the envelope. From habit, most recipients of business letters slit envelopes at the top and turn them face-down to extract the letter. The three-fold letter inserted as described thus gives its reader an easy thumbhold at the top of the envelope to pull it out by and a second one at the top of the sheet for easy unfolding of the whole.

Envelope Address. So that optical character recognition (OCR) equipment may be used in sorting mail, the U.S. Postal Service requests that all envelopes be typed as follows (see Figure B–9):

1. Place the address in the scannable area as shown in the white box in Figure B–9. Best to use a sans serif font in 10 to 12 points.

2. Use a block address format.

3. Single-space.

4. Use all uppercase letters (capitals). While today's OCR equipment can read lowercase, the post office prefers uppercase.

5. Do not use punctuation, except for the hyphen in the nine-digit zip code.

6. Use the two-letter abbreviations for the U.S. states and territories and the Canadian provinces.

   Use other address abbreviations as shown in the most recent edition of the Post Office Directory (see www.usps.com). When sending to a foreign country, include only the country name in uppercase on the bottom line.

Form for Addressing Envelopes Recommended by the U.S. Postal Service

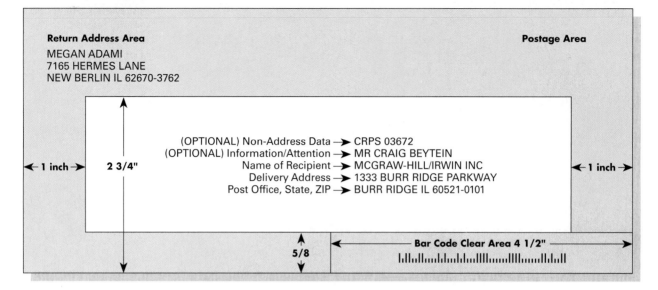

States and Possessions of the United States

Alabama	AL	Kansas	KS	Northern Mariana Islands	MP		
Alaska	AK	Kentucky	KY	Ohio	OH		
American Samoa	AS	Louisiana	LA	Oklahoma	OK		
Arizona	AZ	Maine	ME	Oregon	OR		
Arkansas	AR	Marshall Islands	MH	Palau	PW		
California	CA	Maryland	MD	Pennsylvania	PA		
Colorado	CO	Massachusetts	MA	Puerto Rico	PR		
Connecticut	CT	Michigan	MI	Rhode Island	RI		
Delaware	DE	Minnesota	MN	South Carolina	SC		
District of Columbia	DC	Mississippi	MS	South Dakota	SD		
Federated States of Micronesia	FM	Missouri	MO	Tennessee	TN		
Florida	FL	Montana	MT	Texas	TX		
Georgia	GA	Nebraska	NE	Utah	UT		
Guam	GU	Nevada	NV	Vermont	VT		
Hawaii	HI	New Hampshire	NH	Virginia	VA		
Idaho	ID	New Jersey	NJ	Virgin Islands	VI		
Illinois	IL	New Mexico	NM	Washington	WA		
Indiana	IN	New York	NY	West Virginia	WV		
Iowa	IA	North Carolina	NC	Wyoming	WY		
		North Dakota	ND				

Canadian Provinces and Territories

Alberta	AB	Newfoundland	NF	Prince Edward Island	PE
British Columbia	BC	Northwest Territories	NT	Quebec	PQ
Manitoba	MB	Nova Scotia	NS	Saskatchewan	SK
New Brunswick	NB	Ontario	ON	Yukon Territory	YT

7. The last line of the mailing address should contain no more than 28 characters. The city should be 13 or fewer characters. Also, there should be one space between city

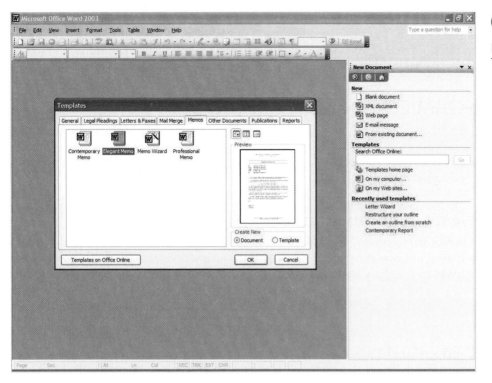

and state; two spaces for the state or province abbreviation; two spaces between the state and zip code; and 10 characters for the zip + 4 code.

8. When the return address must be typed (it is usually printed), block it in the left corner, beginning on the second line from the top of the envelope and three spaces from the left edge of the envelope.

9. Print any on-arrival instructions ("Confidential," "Personal") four lines below the return address.

10. Place all notations for the post office ("Special Delivery") below the stamp and at least three lines above the mailing address.

FORM OF MEMORANDUMS

Memorandums (memos) have basic components in common, but their form varies widely from organization to organization. The basic components are the heading and body. The heading has four elements: *To, From, Date,* and *Subject.* These elements are arranged in various placements, but all are present.

The body of the memo is usually single-spaced with double-spacing between paragraphs. First-level headings are frequently used in long memos. And notations for typist and enclosures are included just as they are in letters. An example of typical template format choices for memos is shown in Figure B–10.

FORM OF LETTER
AND MEMORANDUM REPORTS

Because letter reports are actually letters, the review of letter form presented earlier in this appendix applies to them. Memorandum reports, however, are somewhat different. The conventional memorandum form uses the introductory information: *To, From, Date, Subject.* Many large companies have stationery on which this information is printed or use standard macros, templates, or styles. The report text follows the introductory information.

Both letter and memorandum reports may use headings (captions) to display the topics covered. The headings are usually displayed in the margins, on separate lines, and in a different style. Memorandum and letter reports also may differ from ordinary letters by having illustrations (charts, tables), an appendix, and/or a bibliography.

FORM OF FORMAL REPORTS

Like letters, formal reports should be pleasing to the eye. Well-arranged reports give an impression of competence—of work professionally done. Because such an impression can affect the success of a report, you should make good use of the following review of report form.

General Information on Report Presentation

Your formal reports are likely to be prepared with word processing programs. You will not need to know the general mechanics of manuscript preparation if you use automated formatting, as shown in Figure B–11. However, even if you do not have to format your own reports, you should know enough about report presentation to be sure your work is done right. You cannot be certain that your report is in good form unless you know good form.

Conventional Page Layout. For the typical text page in a report, a conventional layout appears to fit the page as a picture fits a frame (see Figure B–12). This eye-pleasing layout, however, is arranged to fit the page space not covered by the binding of the report. Thus, you must allow an extra half inch or so on the left margins of the pages of a left-bound report and at the top of the pages of a top-bound report.

Special Page Layouts. Certain text pages may have individual layouts. Pages displaying major titles (first pages of chapters, tables of contents, executive summaries, and the like) conventionally have an extra half inch or so of space at the top. Figure B–13 illustrates that some special pages can be created with templates.

FIGURE B–11

Illustration of an APA
Report Format for Word

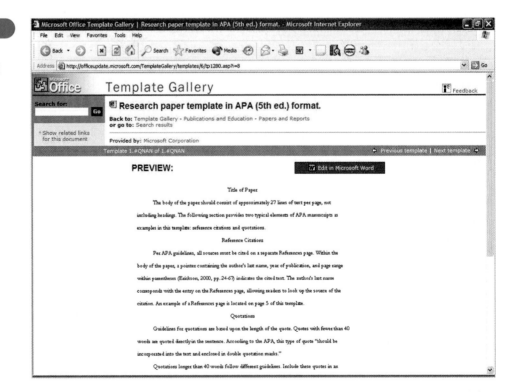

Double-spaced Page

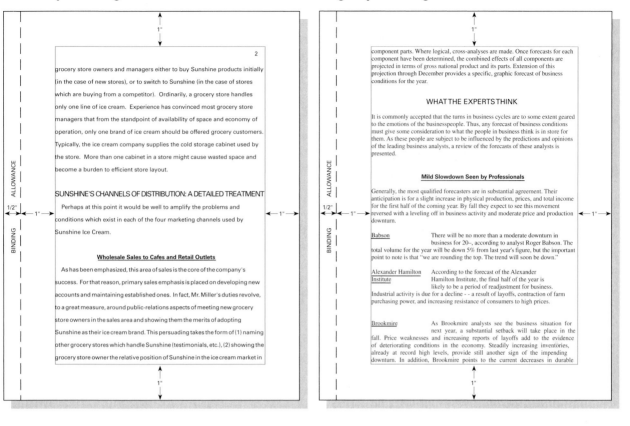

Single-spaced Page

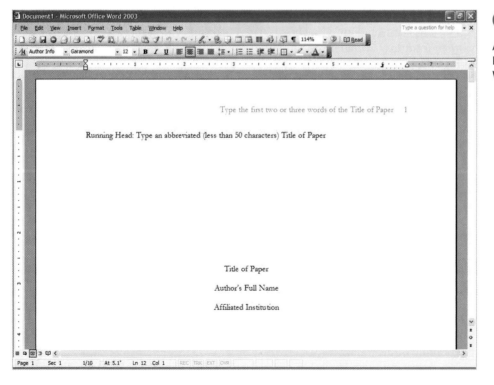

FIGURE B–13

An Illustration of the Report Title Page in WordPerfect

Letters of transmittal and authorization also may have individual layouts. They are arranged in any conventional letter form. In the more formal reports, they may be carefully arranged to have the same general shape as the space in which they appear using the "make-it-fit" feature.

Choice of Form. It is conventional to double-space reports. This procedure stems from the old practice of double-spacing to make typed manuscripts more readable for the proofreader and printer. The practice has been carried over into work that is not to be reproduced. Advocates of double-spacing claim that it is easier to read than single-spacing, as the reader is less likely to lose line place.

In recent years, single-spacing has gained in popularity. The general practice is to single-space within paragraphs, double-space between paragraphs, and triple-space above all centered heads. Supporters of single-spacing contend that it saves space and facilitates reading, as it is like the printing that most people are accustomed to reading.

Patterns of Indentation. You should indent the paragraph beginnings of double-spaced typing. On the other hand, you should block single-spaced typing, because its paragraph headings are clearly marked by extra line spacing.

No generally accepted distance of indentation exists. Some sources suggest ½ inch, and others like 1" and more. Any decision as to the best distance to use is up to you, though you would do well to follow the practice established in the office, group, or school for which you write the report. Whatever your selection, you should be consistent.

Numbering of Pages. Two systems of numbers are used in numbering the pages of the written report. Arabic numerals are conventional for the text portion, normally beginning with the first page of the introduction and continuing through the appendix. Small Roman numerals are standard for the pages preceding the text. Although these prefatory pages are all counted in the numbering sequence, the numbers generally do not appear on the pages before the table of contents. See the text website for specific instructions on how to do this in Word.

Placement of the numbers on the page varies with the binding used for the report. In reports bound at the top of the page, you should center all page numbers at the bottom of the page, a double or triple space below the layout used in the body.

For left-sided binding, you should place the numbers in the upper-right corner, a double or triple space above the top line and in line with the right margin. Exception to this placement is customarily made for special-layout pages that have major titles and an additional amount of space displayed at the top. Such pages may include the first page of the report text; the executive summary; the table of contents; and, in very long and formal works, the first page of each major division or chapter. Numbers for these pages are centered a double or triple space below the imaginary line marking the bottom of the layout.

In documents printed back-to-back, page numbers are usually placed at the top of the page even with the outside margin. Not only are today's word processing programs capable of automatically placing page numbers this way if directed, but many inkjet printers are also capable of two-sided printing.

Display of Headings. Headings (captions) are the titles of the parts of the report. Designed to lead the readers through the report, they must show at a glance the importance of the information they cover.

In showing heading importance by position, you have many choices. If your software and printer make available a variety of typefaces, you can select various progressions of font sizes and styles to fit your needs. Your goal, of course, should be to select forms that show differences in importance at first glance—much as is done in the printing of this book.

You can use any combination of form and position that clearly shows the relative importance of the headings. The one governing rule to follow in considering form and

Type the first two or three words of the Title of Paper   3

Title of Paper

The body of the paper should consist of approximately 27 lines of text per page, not including headings. The following section provides two typical elements of APA manuscripts as examples in this template: reference citations and quotations.

Reference Citations

Per APA guidelines, all sources must be cited on a separate References page. Within the body of the paper, a pointer containing the author's last name, year of publication, and page range within parentheses (Erickson, 2000, pp. 24-67) indicates the cited text. The author's last name corresponds with the entry on the References page, allowing readers to look up the source of the citation. An example of a References page is located on page 5 of this template.

---

positions of headings is that no heading may have a higher-ranking form or position than any of the headings of a higher level. But you can use the same form for two successive levels of headings as long as the positions vary. And you can use the same position for two successive levels as long as the forms vary. You also can skip over any of the steps in the progression of form or position. If you select the format, the headings will be set up for you (see Figure B–14 above).

Mechanics and Format of the Report Parts

The foregoing notes on physical appearance apply generally to all parts of the report. But special notes are needed for the individual construction of the specific report pages. So that you may be able to get and follow these notes, a part-by-part review of the physical construction of the formal report follows.

Title Fly. The title fly contains only the report title. Print the title in the highest-ranking form used in the report, and double-space it if you need more than one line. If your report cover has a window for the title to show through, make sure you place the title in the window.

Title Page. The title page normally contains three main areas of identification, although some forms present this information in four or five spots on the page. In the typical three-spot title page, the first area of identification covers the report title. Preferably, use the highest-ranking form used in the report.

The second area of identification names the individual (or group) for whom the report has been prepared. Precede it with an identifying phrase indicating that individual's role in the report, such as "Prepared for" or "Submitted to." In addition to the recipient's name, include the identification of the recipient by title or role, company, and address, particularly if you and the recipient are from different companies.

The third area of identification names you, the writer of the report. It is also preceded by an identifying phrase—"Prepared by," "Written by," or similar wording describing your role in the report—and it also may identify title or role, company, and address. As a final part of this area of information, you may include the date of publication.

Placement of the three areas of identification on the page should make for an eye-pleasing arrangement. Most word processing software will help you place this page vertically.

Letters of Transmittal and Authorization. As their names imply, the letters of transmittal and authorization are actual letters. You should print them in any acceptable letter form. If the report is important, you should give the letter an ideal layout. An ideal layout is one that fits the letter into a rectangle of the same shape as the space within which it is printed.

Acknowledgments. When you are indebted to the assistance of others, it is fitting that you acknowledge the indebtedness somewhere in the report. If this number is small, you may acknowledge them in the introduction of the report or in the letter of transmittal. In the rare event that you need to make numerous acknowledgments, you may construct a special section for this purpose. This section, bearing the simple title "Acknowledgments," has the same layout as any other text page in which a title is displayed.

Table of Contents. The table of contents is the report outline in its polished, finished form. It lists the major report headings with the page numbers on which those headings appear. Although not all reports require a table of contents, one should be a part of any report long enough to make such a guide helpful to the readers. Most word processors are capable of generating a table of contents—complete with page numbers. See the textbook website for a short tutorial on how to create one in Word.

The table of contents is appropriately titled "Contents" or "Table of Contents." The layout of the table of contents is the same as that used for any other report page with a title display. Below the title, set up two columns. One contains the outline headings, generally beginning with the first report part following the table of contents. You have the option of including or leaving out the outline letters and numbers.

In the table of contents, as in the body of the report, you may vary the form to distinguish different heading levels. But the form variations of the table of contents need not be the same as those used in the text of the report. The highest level of headings is usually distinguished from the other levels, and sometimes typeface differences are used to distinguish second-level headings from lower-level headings. It is acceptable to show no distinction by using plain capitals and lowercase for all levels of headings.

Table of Illustrations. The table (list) of illustrations may be either a continuation of the table of contents or a separate table. Such a table lists the graphics presented in the report in much the same way as the table of contents lists the report parts.

In constructing this table, head it with an appropriately descriptive title, such as "Table of Charts and Illustrations," or "List of Tables and Charts," or "Table of Figures." If you place the table of illustrations on a separate page, layout for this page is the same as that for any other text page with a displayed title. And if you place it as a continued part of the table of contents, you should begin it after the last contents entry.

The table consists of two columns: the first for the graphics titles and the second for the pages on which the graphics appear. The look of the table should match the format and layout of the table of contents. Line spacing in the table of illustrations is optional, again depending on the line lengths of the entries. Preceding the title of each entry, place that entry's number; and should these numbers be Roman or otherwise require more than one digit, align the digits at the right. If your report contains two or more illustration types (tables, charts, maps, and the like) and you have given each type its own numbering sequence, you should list each type separately.

References (or Bibliography). Anytime you use another's idea, you need to give credit to the source. Sometimes business writers interweave this credit into the narrative of their text. But often these sources are listed in a reference or bibliography section at the end of the report. Typically, these sections are organized alphabetically, but they also can be organized by date, subject, or type of source.

The format and content of citations vary by style used as described in Appendix E. Among the widely used formats are *The Chicago Manual of Style, The MLA Style Sheet,* and the *Publication Manual of the American Psychological Association.* The content for most items on the list of references is similar to the footnote. This format can be set up by the report format.

Need to Improvise. The foregoing review covers most of the problems of form you will encounter in preparing reports. But there will be others. When you encounter other problems, you simply improvise an arrangement that appears right to the eye. After all, what appears right to the eye is the basis of conventional report form.

General Grading Checklist: Punctuation, Grammar, Number, Spelling, Proofreading, Technique, Strategy, and Formatting

Listed below are general grading symbols and their descriptions. These symbols give you a general idea of how to improve your writing. You will find more detailed information in your text, particularly in Chapter 17.

Punctuation

Symbol	Explanation	Description
APOS	Apostrophe	1. Use the apostrophe to show the possessive case of nouns and indefinite pronouns. 2. Use an apostrophe to mark the place in a contraction where letters are omitted.
Bkts	Brackets	Set off in brackets words that you wish to insert in a quotation.
Cln	Colon	1. Use the colon to introduce a statement of explanation, an enumeration, or a formal quotation. 2. Do not use the colon when the thought of the sentence should continue without interruption. If introducing a list by a colon, the colon should be preceded by a word that explains or identifies the list.
Cma	Comma	
Dsh	Dash	Use the dash to set off an element for emphasis or to show interrupted thought.
Ex	Exclamation mark	Use the exclamation mark at the end of a sentence or exclamatory fragment to show strong emotion.
Hpn	Hyphen	
Ital	Italics	
Parens	Parentheses	
Pd	Period	
Ques	Question mark	Place a question mark at the end of sentences that are direct questions.
QM	Quotation marks	Use quotation marks to enclose the exact words of a speaker or, if the quotation is short, the exact words of a writer.
SC	Semicolon	

Grammar

Symbol	Explanation	Description
AA	Adjective–adverb Confusion	Do not use adjectives for adverbs or adverbs for adjectives. Adjectives modify only nouns and pronouns; and adverbs modify verbs, adjectives, or other adverbs.
Agmt SV	Subject–verb agreement	Nouns and their verbs must agree in number.
AN	Adverbial noun clause	
Awk	Awkward	Avoid awkward writing where word arrangements are unconventional, uneconomical, or simply not the best for quick understanding.
Dng	Dangling modifier	Avoid the use of modifiers that do not logically modify a word in the sentence.
Frag	Sentence fragment	Avoid words used as a sentence that are not a sentence.
Pn	Pronoun	
Prl	Parallelism	Express equal thoughts in parallel grammatical form.
Tns	Tense	

Number

Symbol	Explanation
No	Number

Spelling

Symbol	Explanation	Description
Sp	Spelling	Spell words correctly. Use the dictionary.
Caps	Capitalization	Capitalize all proper names and the beginning words of sentences.

Proofreading

Symbol				Explanation	Description
Align	═	‖		Align	Line up horizontally or vertically.
Stet	*stet*	. . . .		Let original stand	Don't delete.
Close	⌒⌣			Close up	Close up space.
Del	ᶞ			Delete	Delete.
Ins	∧			Insert	Insert space, punctuation, text, or graphic.
Keep				Keep together	Keep text and/or graphic together.
LC	*lc*	/		Lowercase	Use lowercase.
Caps	*cap*	═		Capitalize	Make all caps.
Mv L	[			Move left	Move left.
Mv R	]			Move right	Move right.
Cntr	] [			Center	Center.
Nl	*nl*			New line	Start new line.
Run	⌒			Run together	Run text together.
Par	⁋			Paragraph	Start new paragraph.
Sp O	*sp*	⬭		Spell out	Spell out.
Trp	*tr*	⌇		Transpose	Transpose.

Symbol	Explanation	Description
Adp	Adaptation	Adapt to the one reader. Here your writing is above or below your reader.
Acc	Accuracy	Check for correct information.
Assign	Assignment	Needs to follow assignment.
AV	Active voice	Use active voice.
Blky	Bulky arrangement	Make your paragraphs more inviting by breaking them into shorter units of thought.
Blame	Blaming	Avoid blaming or accusing the reader.
Chop	Choppy writing	Avoid a succession of short sentences that produce an irritating effect.
COH	Coherence	Needs to be easier to follow with clear, logical development.
Copy	Copying	Avoid copying or following examples too closely. Organize around the unique facts of the case.
CTone	Conversational tone	Be natural or less formal in your word choice.
Dis	Discriminatory	Avoid using words that discriminate unnecessarily against sex, age, race, disability, or sexual orientation.
DL	Dull writing	Bring your writing back to life with vivid, concrete words.
Doc	Documentation	Cite source of information.
Emp–	Emphasis too little	Give appropriate emphasis with placement, volume, words, or mechanical means.
Emp+	Emphasis too much	Give appropriate emphasis with placement, volume, words, or mechanical means.
GW	Goodwill	Needs more goodwill.
Intp	Interpretation	Do more than just present facts. Make the data meaningful in terms of the reader's situation.
Jargon	Jargon	Avoid using jargon.
Los	Loose writing	Use words more economically. Write concisely.
Neg	Negative	Try wording more positively.
Ob	Obvious	Include only necessary information or detail.
Ord	Order of presentation	Needs clear, logical order.
Org	Organization	Needs clearer, tighter organization with setup and follow through.
Pomp	Pompous	Use more humble, sincere words.
Pre	Precise	Be more precise or concrete.
RB	Reader benefit	Needs more reader benefit.
Red	Redundant	Avoid unnecessary repetition.
Resale	Resale	Use more resale here.
RS	Rubber-stamp expression	Avoid overused phrases and time-worn words from the past.
Trans	Transition	Avoid abrupt shift of thought here.
Var	Variety	Vary the words and sentence patterns.
WU	Word use	Use words correctly. Misused words call attention to themselves and detract from the writing.
WW	Wrong word	Wrong words refer to meaning one word and using another.
YVP	You-viewpoint	Revise with the reader in mind.

Message Strategy

Symbol	Explanation	Description
O Dir	Directness needed	The opening is too slow in getting to the goal.
O Ind	Indirectness needed	The opening gets to the goal too fast.
O Qual	Quality	The opening could be improved by making it more on subject, logical, or interesting. It should also set up the rest of the message.
C Ex	Excess information	You have included more information than is needed.
C Exp	Explanation	More or better explanation is needed here.
C Id	Identification	Completely identify the situation.
C Inc	Incomplete	You have not covered all the important facts.
E AC	Action close	A drive for action is appropriate in this situation.
E AC S	Action strong	This action drive is too strong.
E AC W	Action weak	This action drive is too weak.
E IT	Individually tailored	Make your close fit the one case.
E OS	Off subject	An off-subject close is best for this case. These words recall unpleasant things in the reader's mind.

Formatting

Symbol	Explanation	Description
Lay	Layout	Use standard or specified format.
T	Type	Select a readable font for size and style.
Media	Media	Use a medium appropriate for the reader and the context.

Special Grading Checklists: Messages and Reports

MESSAGES

The Opening

O Dir *Directness needed.* This opening is too slow in getting to the goal.

O Ind *Indirectness needed.* This opening gets to the goal too fast.

O Qual *Quality.* This opening could be improved by making it more (1) on subject, (2) logical, or (3) interesting.

Coverage

C Ex *Excess information.* You have included more information than is needed.

C Exp *Explanation.* More or better explanation is needed here.

C Id *Identification.* Completely identify the situation.

C Inc *Incomplete.* You have not covered all the important information.

Ending

E AC *Action close.* A drive for action is appropriate in this situation.

E AC S *Action strong.* This action drive is too strong.

E AC W *Action weak.* This action drive is too weak.

E IT *Individually tailored.* Make your close fit the one case.

E OS *Off subject.* An off-subject close is best for this case. These words recall unpleasant things in the reader's mind.

Technique

Adp *Adaptation.* Your words should be adapted to the one reader. Here yours are (1) above or (2) below your reader.

Awk *Awkward word arrangement.*

Bky *Bulky arrangement.* Make your paragraphs more inviting by breaking them into shorter units of thought.

Chop *Choppy writing.* A succession of short sentences produces an irritating effect.

DL *Dull writing.* Bring your writing back to life with vivid, concrete words.

Emp + *Emphasis, too much.*

Emp – *Emphasis, too little.* Here you have given too much or too little (as marked) emphasis by (1) placement, (2) volume, or (3) words or mechanical means.

Intp *Interpretation.* Do more than just present facts. In this situation, something more is needed. Make the data meaningful in terms of the reader's situation.

Los *Loose writing.* Use words more economically. Write concisely.

Ord *Order of presentation.* This information does not fall into a logical order. The information is mixed up and confusing.

RS *Rubber-stamp expression.* Timeworn words from the past have no place in modern business writing.

Trans *Transition.* Abrupt shift of thought here.

Effect

Conv *Conviction.* This is less convincing than it should be. More fact or a more skillful use of words is needed.

GW *Goodwill.* The message needs more goodwill. Try to make your words convey friendliness. Here you tend to be too dull and matter-of-fact.

Hur *Hurried treatment.* Your coverage of the problem appears to be hurried. Thus, it tends to leave an effect of routine or brusque treatment. Conciseness is wanted, of course, but you must not sacrifice your objectives for it.

Log *Logic.* Is this really logical? Would you do it this way in business?

Neg *Negative effect.* By word or implication, this part is more negative than it should be.

Pers + *Too persuasive.* Your words are too high-pressure for this situation.

Pers – *Not persuasive enough.* More persuasion, by either words or facts, would help your message.

Ton *Tone of the words.* Your words create a bad impression on the reader. Words work against the success of your message if they talk down, lecture, argue, accuse, and the like.

YVP *You-viewpoint.* More you-viewpoint wording and adaptation would help the overall effect of your message.

REPORTS

Title

T 1 Complete? The title should tell what the report contains. Use the five Ws and 1 H as a check for completeness (*who, what, where, when, why*—sometimes *how*).

T 2 Too long. This title is longer than it needs to be. Check it for uneconomical wording or unnecessary information.

Transmittal

LT 1 More directness is needed in the opening. The message should present the report right away.

LT 2 Content of the message needs improvement. Comments that help the readers understand or appreciate the report are appropriate.

LT 3 Do not include findings unless the report has no executive summary.

LT 4 A warm statement of your attitude toward the assignment is appropriate— often expected. You either do not make one, or the one you make is weak.

LT 5 A friendlier, more conversational style would improve the transmittal.

Executive Summary

ES 1 *(If the direct order is assigned)* Begin directly—with a statement of findings, conclusion, or recommendation.

ES 2 *(If the indirect order is assigned)* Begin with a brief review of introductory information.

ES 3 The summary of highlights should be in proportion and should include major findings, analyses, and conclusions. Your coverage here is (*a*) scant or (*b*) too detailed.

ES 4 Work for a more interesting and concise summary.

Organization—Outline

O 1 This organization plan is not the best for this problem. The main sections should form a logical solution to the problem.

O 2 The order of the parts of this outline is not logical. The parts should form a step-by-step route to the goal.

O 3 Do not let one major section account for the entire body of the report.

O 4 One-item subdivisions are illogical. You cannot divide an area without coming up with at least two parts.

O 5 These parts overlap. Each part should be independent of the other parts. Although some repetition and relating of parts may be desirable, outright overlap is a sign of bad organization.

O 6 More subparts are needed here. The subparts should cover all the information in the major part.

O 7 This subpart does not fit logically under this major part.

O 8 These parts are not equal in importance. Do not give them equal status in the outline.

O 9 *(If talking headings are assigned.)* These headings do not talk well.

O 10 Coordinate headings should be parallel in grammatical structure.

O 11 This (these) heading(s) is (are) too long.

O 12 Vary the wording of the headings to avoid monotonous repetition.

Introduction

I 1 This introduction does not cover exactly what the readers need to know. Although the readers' needs vary by problem, these topics are usually important: (*a*) origin of the problem, (*b*) statement of the problem, (*c*) methods used in researching the problem, and (*d*) preview of the presentation.

I 2 Coverage of this part is (*a*) scant or (*b*) too detailed.

I 3 Important information has been left out.

I 4 Findings, conclusions, and other items of information are not a part of the introduction.

Coverage

C 1 The coverage here is (*a*) scant or (*b*) too detailed.

C 2 More analysis is needed here.

C 3 Here you rely too heavily on a graphic. The text should cover the important information.

C 4 Do not lose sight of the goal of the report. Relate the information to the problem.

C 5 Clearly distinguish between fact and opinion. Label opinion as opinion.

C 6 Your analyses and conclusions need the support of more fact and authoritative opinion.

Writing

W 1 This writing should be better adapted to your readers. It appears to be (*a*) too heavy or (*b*) too light for your readers.

W 2 Avoid the overuse of passive voice.

W 3 Work for more conciseness. Try to cut down on words without sacrificing meaning.

W 4 For this report, more formal writing is appropriate. You should write consistently in impersonal (third-person) style.

W 5 A more personal style is appropriate for this report. That is, you should use more personal pronouns (*I*'s, *we*'s, *you*'s).

W 6 The change in thought is abrupt here.

> (*a*) Between major parts, use introductions, summaries, and conclusions to guide the readers' thinking.

> (*b*) Use transitional words, phrases, or sentences to relate minor parts.

W 7 Your paragraphing is questionable. Check the paragraphs for unity. Look for topic sentences.

Graphics

GA 1 You have (*a*) not used enough graphics or (*b*) used too many graphics.

GA 2 For the information presented, this graphic is (*a*) too large or (*b*) too small.

GA 3 This type of graphic is not the best for presenting the information.

GA 4 Place the graphic near the place where its contents are discussed.

GA 5 The text must tell the story, so don't just refer the reader to a figure or table and let it go at that.

GA 6 The appearance of this graphic needs improvement. This may be your best work, but it does not make a good impression on the readers.

GA 7 Refer the readers to the graphics at the times that the readers should look at them.

GA 8 Interpret the patterns in the graphic. Note central tendencies, exceptions, ranges, trends, and such.

GA 9 Refer to the graphics incidentally, in subordinate parts of sentences that comment on their content (for example, ". . . as shown in Figure 5" or "see Figure 5").

Layout and Mechanics

LM 1 The layout of this page is (*a*) too fat, (*b*) too skinny, or (*c*) too low, high, or off-center (as marked).

LM 2 Neat? Smudges and light type detract from the message.

LM 3 Make the margins straighter. The raggedness here offends the eye.

LM 4 The spacing here needs improvement. (*a*) Too much space here. (*b*) Not enough space here.

LM 5 Your page numbering is not the best. See the text for specific instructions.

LM 6 This page appears (*a*) choppy or (*b*) heavy.

LM 7 Your selection of type placement and style for the headings is not the best.

LM 8 This item or form is not generally acceptable.

Documentation and the Bibliography

In writing reports, you will frequently use information from other sources. Because this material is not your own, you may need to acknowledge it. Whether and how you should acknowledge it are the subject of this brief review.

WHEN TO ACKNOWLEDGE

Your decision to acknowledge or not acknowledge a source should be determined mainly on the basis of giving credit where credit is due. If you are quoting verbatim (in the original author's exact words), you must give credit. If you are paraphrasing (using someone else's ideas in your own words), you should give credit unless the material covered is general knowledge.

Today many colleges have academic honesty or academic integrity policies. Businesses, too, have similar ethics policies and codes. Following the policies not only insures that you get full credit for your own work and develop the thinking and writing skills that will be helpful to you the rest of your life, but it also helps you build an ethical character. This character leads others to trust you, serving you well both professionally and personally.

Plagiarism, presenting another's work as your own, and falsifying data are two unethical practices plaguing schools and businesses alike. These practices range from carefully planned, intentional acts to careless, unintentional acts. However, the results are similar. Presenting another's work as your own steals from the creator—often depriving not only the author of the financial rewards honestly earned but also the whole support staff of editors, artists, designers, and production and distribution workers. Plagiarism is also stealing from classmates who write their own papers, but just as important, a cheater loses the opportunity to develop good writing and thinking skills. Additionally, plagiarism affects your reputation as well as the reputation of those in your class, your school, and those who have graduated from your school. It may also affect your family and friends. Falsifying data is equally malicious, especially when others rely on the information you present to make decisions. Worse yet, if you are successful in passing off falsified or plagiarized work as your own, it sets you up to behave unethically in the future. One writer for the *New York Times* recently wrote stories creating facts where he had none. After he did it once and fooled his boss and readers, he continued until he was caught. In addition to being fired and publicly humiliated, his actions brought into question the reporting practices and credibility of the *New York Times*.

In your writing tasks, you can eliminate such problems by following these guidelines.

Write your own papers. Do not buy, beg, or borrow papers from others. Not only are instructors adept at spotting plagiarism, they now have powerful search engines and access to large databases of student papers. These databases even contain papers submitted recently. Tweaking these papers to fit your assignment does not get past these tools, which report percentages of similarity to other works. If you are going to all this work of copying a paper, you might as well do the work yourself and gain the benefits.

Give credit to all ideas that are not your own. Not only do you need to cite exact quotes, but you also need to cite paraphrased material when the ideas come from someplace else. Changing a few words does not make an idea either original or paraphrased. Also be sure to cite charts, tables, photos, and graphics. Give credit to adapted material as well. When in doubt, cite the source.

Use discipline and technological tools to manage the data you gather. Some unintentional problems arise when writers cannot retrieve the information they know they have collected and read, leading them to cite inaccurately or falsely. While making the information-gathering phase of research easier, the Internet has made managing the vast amount of information one finds a major task. By disciplining yourself to follow strict organizational practices, you will find retrieving the information easier when you need it. If you have ever used a money management program to manage your bank accounts, you know that it makes gathering tax information and preparing your tax return much easier. Similarly, tools such as EndNote or RefWorks (presented in Chapter 19) help tremendously, but only if one uses the tools faithfully.

Ask your instructor or school's librarian when you need help. Both these people want to help you learn how to document appropriately. Most will probably be more approachable if you have shown you have tried to find the answer to your question and if you are asking well before the final hour.

HOW TO ACKNOWLEDGE

You can acknowledge sources by citing them in the text, using one of a number of reference systems. Three of the most commonly used systems are the Chicago (*The Chicago Manual of Style*), MLA (Modern Language Association), and APA (American Psychological Association). Although all are similar, they differ somewhat in format, as you will see in the following pages. Because the Chicago system is the most widely used in business books and journals, we will review it first.[1] Then we will illustrate the MLA and APA systems to note primary differences.

After you have selected a system, you must choose a method of acknowledgment. Two methods are commonly used in business: (1) parenthetic author–date references within the text and (2) footnote references. A third method, endnote references, is sometimes used, although it appears to be losing favor. Only the first two are discussed here.

The Parenthetic Author–Date Method

In recent years, the author–date method has become a widely used reference method in business. It involves placing the author's last name and year of publication in parentheses immediately following the material cited. The reference is keyed to a reference list of all publications cited, which appears at the end of the report:

In-text citation: (Robbins 2003)

Reference list citation: Robbins, Stephen P. 2003. *Decide and conquer: Make winning decisions and take control of your life.* New Jersey: Financial Times Prentice Hall.

If specific page numbers are needed, they follow the date:

In-text citation: (Shwom 2003, 3) [a printed source]

---

[1] Examples included here follow the *Chicago Manual of Style*, 15th ed. (Chicago: The University of Chicago Press, 2003).

(Shwom 2003, under "Home Office Organization") [an unpaginated electronic source]

Reference list citation: Shwom, Barbara. 2003. *Best practices of business communication consultants.* New York: Riverhead Books.

Shwom, Barbara. "Best Practices of Business Communication Consultants," *The professional communication consultant,* October 22, 2003, http://www.profconsulting.com/bestpractices.htm.

The authors' last names are listed for works with two or three authors:

In-text citation: (Patel and Reinsch 2003, 9)

Reference list citation: Patel, Ameeta and Lamar Reinsch. 2003. Companies can apologize: Corporate apologies and legal liability. *Business Communication Quarterly* 66, no. 1:9.

For works with more than three authors, *et al.* is used:

In-text citation: (Johnson et al. 2003)

Reference list citation: Johnson, Iris W., C. Glenn Pearce, Tracy L. Tuten, and Lucinda Sinclair. 2003. Self-imposed silence and perceived listening effectiveness. *Business Communication Quarterly* 66 (2):23.

When no author is listed, as in unsigned publications issued by a company, government agency, labor union, or such, the author's name is the organization name:

In-text citation: (Bureau of Labor Statistics 2003)

Reference list citation: U. S. Bureau of Labor Statistics, Department of Labor. *Retirement Expenditures for White, Black, and Persons of Hispanic Origins* 126, no. 5, June 2003. http://www.bls.gov/opub/mlr/ 2003/06/art3full.pdf.

In-text citation: (EPA 2001)

Reference list citation: U. S. Environmental Protection Agency, Office of Air and Radiation. *Healthy Buildings, Healthy People: A Vision for the 21st Century.* October 2001. http://www.epa.gov/iaq/images/ indoor_air_pollution.pdf.

As noted earlier, these references are keyed to a bibliography that appears at the end of the report. To find the details of a reference, the reader turns to the bibliography and traces the reference through the alphabetical listing. For the reference (Lesikar 2005), for example, the reader would find Lesikar in its alphabetical place. If more than one publication by Lesikar is listed, the reader would refer to the one written in 2005.

The Footnote Method

Footnotes are a second means used to acknowledge sources. Two types of footnotes are used in business documents: discussion footnotes and traditional, complete-fact footnotes. The emphasis here is on the traditional footnote, but the uses of the discussion footnote also will be presented.

Traditional Footnote. The traditional method of acknowledging sources (preferred in the humanities) is by footnotes; that is, the references are placed at the bottom of the page and are keyed to the text material by superscripts (raised Arabic numbers). The numbering sequence of the superscripts is consecutive—by page, by chapter, or by the whole work. The footnotes are placed inside the page layout, single-spaced, and indented or blocked just as the text is typed.

Although footnote form varies from one source to another, one generally accepted procedure is the Chicago style (15th edition) presented here. It permits two structures: an abbreviated structure that is used with a bibliography in the report and a structure that is used when the report has no bibliography. This format differs from that of the reference list used with the parenthetic author–date method.

In the abbreviated structure (not accepted by everyone), the footnote reference needs to contain only these parts: (1) author's surname; (2) title of the article, bulletin, or book; and (3) page number.

[3] Godin, *Purple Cow: Transform Your Business by Being Remarkable,* 45. (book reference)

[4] Murphy, "Dispelling Tina's Ghost from the Post-Enron Corporate Governance Debate," 43. (periodical reference)

For the complete reference (usually preferred), the descriptive points are listed in the order mentioned below. Capitals are used only with proper nouns, and abbreviations are acceptable if used consistently.

In the following lists, all the items that could be placed in each type of entry are named in the order of arrangement. Items that are unavailable or unimportant should be passed over. In other words, the following lists give, in order, all the possible items in an entry. The items listed should be used as needed. Each footnote begins with a superscript—an arabic numeral keyed to the text reference and entered (automatically by a word processor).

Book Entry

1. *Name of the author, in normal order.* If a source has two or three authors, all are named. If a source has more than three authors, the name of the first author followed by the Latin et al. or its English equivalent "and others" may be used.

2. *Capacity of the author.* Needed only when the person named is actually not the author of the book but an editor, compiler, or the like.

3. *Chapter name.* Necessary only in the rare instances in which the chapter title helps the reader find the source.

4. *Book title.* Book titles are usually placed in italics. However, if the font used does not allow the reader to easily discriminate between italics and normal style, use underlining to help the reader see the title more clearly. But be sure to avoid underlining if the document will be posted to the web so the reader will not confuse it with an active link.

5. *Edition.*

6. *Location of publisher.* If more than one city is listed on the title page, the one listed first should be used. If the population exceeds half a million, the name of the city is sufficient; otherwise, the city and state (or province) are best given.

7. *Publishing company.*

8. *Date.* Year of publication. If revised, year of latest revision.

9. *Page or pages.* Specific page or inclusive pages on which the cited material is found.

10. *URL for Internet sources or indication of the media (CD, DVD).*

The following are examples of book entries:

A TYPICAL BOOK

[1] Howard Rheingold, *Smart Mobs: The Next Social Revolution* (Cambridge, MA: Perseus Publishing, 2002), 55.

A BOOK WRITTEN BY A STAFF OF WRITERS UNDER THE DIRECTION OF AN EDITOR (chapter title is considered helpful)

[1] Bruce Mitchel Kogut, ed., *The Global Internet Economy* (Cambridge, MA: MIT Press, 2003), 102.

A BOOK WRITTEN BY A NUMBER OF COAUTHORS

[1] Yuling Pan, Suzanne B. K. Scollon, and Ronald Scollon, *Professional Communication in International Settings* (Malden, MA: Blackwell Publishers, 2002), 147.

Periodical Entry

1. *Author's name.* Frequently, no author is given. In such cases, the entry may be skipped, or if it is definitely known to be anonymous, the word *anonymous* may be placed in the entry.

2. *Article title.* Typed within quotation marks.

3. *Periodical title.* Set in italics, which are indicated by underscoring.

4. *Publication identification.* Volume number in Arabic numerals followed by date of publication (month and year or season and year). Volume number is not needed if complete (day, month, year) date is given. See examples below for punctuation differences with and without complete date.

5. *Page or pages* (if applicable).

6. *URL for online periodicals.*

Examples of periodical entries are shown below:

[1] Linda Beamer, "Directness in Chinese Business Correspondence of the Nineteenth Century," *Journal of Business and Technical Communication* 17, no. 2 (2003): 201.

[2] Jeanette Gilsdorf, "Standard Englishers and World Englishes: Living with a Polymorph Business Language," *Journal of Business Communication* 39, no. 3 (2002): 364.

[3] Tommy Peterson, "Coping with Infoglut," *Computerworld* 37, no. 25: 40 (June 23, 2003), http://www.computerworld.com/printthis/2003/0,4814,82314,00.html.

[4] Linda Tischler, "The Art of the Anti-Apology," *Fast Company,* no. 74: 31 (September 2003), http://pf.fastcompany.com/magazine/74/apology.html.

Newspaper Article

1. *Source description.* If article is signed, give author's name. Otherwise, give description of article, such as "Associated Press dispatch" or "Editorial."

2. *Main head of article.* Subheads not needed.

3. *Newspaper title.* City and state (or province) names inserted in brackets if place names do not appear in newspaper title. State (or province) names not needed in case of very large cities, such as New York, Toronto, and Los Angeles.

4. *Date of publication.*

5. *Page* (p.) *and column* (col.). May be used—optional.

6. *URL.* Should be added when available.

The following are typical newspaper article entries:

[1] Nick Wingfield, "WiFi Moochers; Some Wireless Internet Fans, Desperate for a Fix, 'Borrow' Access at Homes, Hotels, Cafes," *The Wall Street Journal,* July 31, 2003, B1.

[2] Claudia H. Deutsch, "It's Not What You Say, but How It Sounds," *New York Times,* September 7, 2003, http://www.nytimes.com/2003/09/07/business/yourmoney/07LUNC.html.

Letters or Documents

1. *Nature of communication.*

2. *Name of writer.*

3. *Name of recipient.*

4. *Date of writing.*

5. *Where filed.*

[With identification by title and organization where helpful.]

An example of an entry citing a letter follows:

[1] Thomas McLaughlin, President, McLaughlin Body Company, Letter to Linda Hittle, December 1, 2004.

Informal Electronic Material

1. *Name of author or owner of site in normal order.*
2. *Type of material.*
3. *Title of document.* Placed in quotes.
4. *Title of complete work.* Presented in italics or underlined as appropriate.
5. *Date of publication.* If revised, last revision.
6. *Complete URL.* If the length exceeds the line length, break after a forward slash.

EMAIL MESSAGE

[1] Jane Adami, email to Bradley mailing list, December 20, 2003.

LISTSERV MESSAGE

[1] Carol Venable, listserv posting, "Communication Skills of Honors Students," February 5, 2004, bizcom@biz.cath.vt.edu.

WEBSITE—WHITE PAPER

[1] Iron Mountain White Papers, "The Ten Biggest Mistakes of E-Mail Records Management—and How to Prevent Them," September 9, 2003, http://ironmountain.ed4.net/enterprise/.

PERSONAL HOME PAGE

[1] Robert Edwards, personal homepage, "Thoughts on Health, Happiness, and Longevity," http://www.thankyoutoo.com/ (accessed September 17, 2003; site now discontinued).

ONLINE RADIO INTERVIEW

[1] John Maxwell, "There's No Such Thing as Business Ethics," CIO Radio, September 9, 2003, http://www2.cio.com/radio/.

WEBCHAT

[1] Dale Atrens, "The Battle of the Bulge," http://sixtyminutes.ninemsn.com.au/sixtyminutes/stories/2003_07_13/story_892.asp, July 13, 2003.

Databases

1. *Name of author(s) or owner in normal order.*
2. *Title.*
3. *Abstract* (if applicable). Placed in brackets if applicable.
4. *Name of published source.*
5. *Volume, number, and date.*
6. *Page numbers* (if any).
7. *Name of database.*
8. *Date of access.* If needed, placed in parentheses.

FULL TEXT

[1] Business Wire, "OutStart Study Reveals Organizations Need to Provide Multiple Learning Channels to Boost Training Effectiveness and ROI," July 14, 2003, http://80-web.lexis-nexis.com.libproxy.sdsu.edu/universe/document?_m=2ca6c35dd878b9a4d8d878fb56cc630f&_docnum=4&wchp=dGLbVzz-zSkVA&_md5=9d6b609cbd04881a837f8f001f0a5898 &taggedDocs=5Z3.

ABSTRACT

[2] Bruce A. Reinig and Bongsik Shin, "The Dynamic Effects of Group Support Systems on Group Meetings,"19, no. 2: 303 http://80-proquest.umi.com.libproxy. sdsu.edu/pqdweb?index=0&did =000000209292681&SrchMode=1&sid=1&Fmt=2& VInst=PROD&VType=PQD&RQT=309&VName=PQD&TS=1063130788&clientId =17862.

The Digital Object Identifier (DOI) citation method, currently being developed, looks promising for providing reliable and permanent electronic source identification.[1] The DOI can be used to identify text, audio, images, software, and such. It was originally developed by a consortium of publishers interested in protecting intellectual content while enabling Internet commerce.[2] The Patricia Seybold Group predicts "that within five years every article, track of music, or other digital asset will be tagged with a unique Digital Object Identifier."[3]

The *Chicago Manual of Style* recommends including the DOI in place of the page number or other locator.[4] Here is how one might use the DOI in a footnote:

[1] Carol Acord and Sharon Garbett, "Learning Entrepreneurship Skills through Successful Ventures in Areas of Personal Interest," *Journal of Business Research* 65, no. 1 (June 2005), doi:10.1965/jbr.2005.1022, http://www.jbr.org/links/doi/10.1965/ jbr.2005.1022.

The types of entries discussed in the preceding paragraphs are those most likely to be used. Yet many unusual types of publications (conference proceedings, computer programs, audiotapes, maps, patents, radio shows, web radio shows, webcasts) are likely to come up. When they do, you should classify the source by the form it most closely resembles: a book or a periodical. Then you should construct the entry that describes the source completely and accurately. Frequently, you will need to improvise—to use your best judgment in determining the source description.

Standard Reference Forms

Certain forms are conventionally used in handling repeated references in footnotes. The more common of these are the following.

Ibid. literally means "in the same place." It is used to refer the reader to the preceding footnote. The entry consists of the superscript, *Ibid.,* and the page number if the page number is different, as shown in these entries:

[1] Patricia T. O'Conner, *Woe is I: The Grammarphobe's Guide to Better English in Plain English* (New York: Riverhead Books, 2003), 37.

[2] *Ibid.,* 141. (refers to O'Conner's book).

Op. cit. ("in the work cited") and *loc. cit.* ("in the place cited") also can refer to references cited earlier in the paper. But they are rarely used today. It is better to use in their place a short reference form (author's last name, title of work, date).

Other abbreviations used in footnote entries are as follows:

Abbreviation	Meaning
cf.	Compare (directs reader's attention to another passage)
ed.	Edition

[1] For updates on the development of this important international standard, check with the International DOI Foundation at http://www.doi.org/.

[2] Bill Rosenblatt, "Solving the Dilemma of Copyright Protection Online," *Journal of Electronic Publishing,* University of Michigan Press, http://www.press.umich.edu/jep/03-02/doi.html.

[3] Patricia B. Seybold, *Protecting Your Digital Assets: Technical Journal Publishers Lead the Way Using Digital Object Identifiers,* Boston, MA: Patricia Seybold Group, February 13, 2003, 3, http://www.doi.org/topics/Protect_Digital_ Asset.pdf.

[4] *The Chicago Manual of Style: The Essential Guide for Writers, Editors, and Publishers,* 15th ed. (Chicago: University of Chicago Press, 2003), 698.

Abbreviation	Meaning
e.g.	For example
et al.	And others
f, ff.	Following page, following pages
i.e.	That is
MS, MSS	Manuscript, manuscripts
n.d.	No date
n.n.	No name
n.p.	No place
p., pp.	Page, pages
vol., vols.	Volume, volumes

Discussion Footnotes. In sharp contrast with traditional footnotes are discussion footnotes. Through discussion footnotes, the writer strives to explain a part of the text, to amplify discussion on a phase of the presentation, to make cross-references to other parts of the report, and the like. The following examples illustrate some possibilities of this footnote type.

CROSS-REFERENCE

[1] See the principle of inflection points on page 72.

AMPLIFICATION OF DISCUSSION AND CROSS-REFERENCE

[2] Lyman Bryson says the same thing: "Every communication is different for every receiver even in the same context. No one can estimate the variation of understanding that there may be among receivers of the same message conveyed in the same vehicle when the receivers are separated in either space or time." See *Communication of Ideas*, 5.

COMPARISON

[3] Compare with the principle of the objective: Before starting any activity, one should make a clear, complete statement of the objective in view.

PRESENTATION OF QUOTED AND PARAPHRASED INFORMATION

You may use data obtained from secondary sources in two ways. You may paraphrase the information (cast it in your own words), or you may use it verbatim (exactly as the original author worded it). In typing paraphrased material, you need not distinguish it from the remainder of the report text. Material you use verbatim, however, must be clearly distinguished.

The procedure for marking this difference is simple. If the quoted passage is short (about 10 lines or less), place it within the text and with quotation marks before and after it. Set off longer quotations from the margins, without quotation marks, as shown in the example below. If the text is double-spaced, further distinguish the quoted passage by single-spacing it.

Of those opposing the issue, Logan Wilson (2003) makes this penetrating observation:

It is a curious paradox that academicians display a scientific attitude toward every universe of inquiry except that which comprises their own profession. . . . Lacking precise qualitative criteria, administrators are prone to fall back upon rather crude quantitative measures as a partial substitute. For example, student evaluations of teachers often lack acceptable reliability and validity statistics. And when they are administered is quite illogical. Moreover, most statements on them relate to contextual factors—office hours, fairness of tests, and such—and not to acquiring knowledge itself. Yet administrators use quantitative scores from these instruments to the minute fraction of a point to assess teaching quality. Multiple measures of teaching performance with an emphasis on student learning would bring a more rational approach to teaching as one dimension of academic responsibility. (201)

These logical, straightforward, and simple arguments of the critics of teacher evaluation appear to be irrefutable.

Frequently, you will find it best to break up or use only fragments of the quoted author's work. Because omissions may distort the meaning of a passage, you must clearly indicate them, using ellipsis points (a series of three periods typed with intervening spaces) where material is left out. If an omission begins after the end of a sentence, you must use four periods—one for final punctuation plus the ellipsis points. A passage with such omissions is the following:

Many companies have undertaken to centralize in the hands of specially trained correspondents the handling of the outgoing email. Usually, centralization has been accomplished by the firm's employment of a correspondence supervisor. . . . The supervisor may guide the work of correspondents . . . , or the company may employ a second technique.

In long quotations it is conventional to show omission of a paragraph or more by a full line of periods, typed with intervening spaces (see example in Pd 3, Chapter 17).

THE BIBLIOGRAPHY

A bibliography is an orderly list of material on a particular subject. In a formal report the list covers references on the subject of the report. The entries in this list closely resemble footnotes, but the two must not be confused. The bibliography normally appears as an appended part of a formal report and is placed after the appendix. It may be preceded by a fly page containing the one word *Bibliography*. The page that begins the list bears the main heading *Bibliography*, usually typed in capital letters. Below this title the references are listed by broad categories and in alphabetical order within the categories. Such listed categories as *Books, Periodicals,* and *Bulletins* may be used. But the determination of categories should be based solely on the types of publications collected in each bibliography. If, for example, a bibliography includes a large number of periodicals and government publications plus a wide assortment of diverse publication types, the bibliography could be divided into these categories: *Periodicals, Government Publications,* and *Miscellaneous Publications.* As with footnotes, variations in bibliographic style are numerous. A simplified form recommended for business use follows the same procedure as described above for footnotes, with four major exceptions:

1. The author's name is listed in reverse order—surname first—for the purpose of alphabetizing. If an entry has more than one author, however, only the name of the first author is reversed.

2. The entry is generally presented in hanging-indention form. That is, the second and subsequent lines of an entry begin some uniform distance (usually about one-half inch) to the right of the beginning point of the first line. The purpose of this indented pattern is to make the alphabetized first line stand out.

3. The entry gives the inclusive pages of articles, but not for books, and does not refer to any one page or passage.

4. Second and subsequent references to publications of the same author are indicated by a uniform line (see bibliography illustration). This line might be formed by striking the underline six consecutive times. But this line may be used only if the entire authorship is the same in the consecutive publications. For example, the line could not be used if consecutive entries have one common author but different coauthors.

Following is an example of a bibliography:

BIBLIOGRAPHY

Books

Godin, Seth. *Purple Cow: Transform Your Business by Being Remarkable.* New York: Upper Saddle River, 2002.

Hayes, Ian S. *Just Enough Wireless Computing.* Upper Saddle River, NJ: Prentice Hall, 2003.

Rheingold, Howard. *Smart Mobs: The Next Social Revolution.* Cambridge, MA: Perseus Publishing, 2002.

Robbins, Stephen P. *Decide and Conquer: Make Winning Decisions and Take Control of Your Life.* Upper Saddle River, NJ: Financial Times Prentice Hall, 2003.

Government Publications

Bahizi, Piere. U. S. Bureau of Labor Statistics, Department of Labor. *Retirement Expenditures for White, Black, and Persons of Hispanic Origins* 126, no. 5, June 2003. http://www.bls.gov/ opub/mlr/ 2003/06/art3full.pdf.

U. S. Environmental Protection Agency, Office of Air and Radiation. *Healthy Buildings, Healthy People: A Vision for the 21st Century.* October 2001. http://www.epa.gov/iaq/images/ indoor_air_pollution.pdf.

Periodicals

Campbell, Kim Sydow, Charles D. White, and Diane E. Johnson. "Leader–Member Relations as a Function of Rapport Management." *The Journal of Business Communication* 40, no. 3 (2003): 170.

Dyrud, Marilyn A. "Focus on Teaching: Preserving Sanity by Simplifying Grading." *Business Communication Quarterly* 66, no. 1 (2003): 78.

Munter, Mary, Priscilla S. Rogers, and Jone Rymer. "Business E-mail: Guidelines for Users." *Business Communication Quarterly* 66, no. 1 (2003): 26.

Reinig, Bruce A. "Toward an Understanding of Satisfaction with the Process and Outcomes of Teamwork." *Journal of Management Information Systems* 19, no. 4: 65.

Miscellaneous

Central Intelligence Agency. *Commonwealth of Independent States—Central European States.* Washington, DC: Central Intelligence Agency, 2003. Map.

Johansen, Jane Thompson, and Paige Ann McFarling. "Computer-Generated Correspondence and Customer Service Policy in Mortgage Loans." Paper presented at the Association for Business Communication Spring Conference, Toronto, Canada, April 4, 2003.

THE ANNOTATED BIBLIOGRAPHY

Frequently, in scholarly writing each bibliography entry is followed by a brief comment on its value and content. That is, the bibliography is annotated. The form and content of annotated bibliographies are illustrated in these entries:

Crystal, David. *English as a Global Language.* 2nd ed.; Great Britain: Cambridge University Press, 2003.

The history of English and its growth are discussed in forecasting its future. Also included is a discussion of the impact of the Internet and the possibility for a family of languages.

Keller, Edward B., and Jonathan L. Berry. *The Influentials: One American in Ten Tells the Other Nine How to Vote, Where to Eat, and What to Buy.* New York: Free Press, 2003.

Based on extensive data from Roper Polls, the authors assert that 10 percent of Americans set the consumption behaviors of the rest by talking about their likes and dislikes. They present a strategy for targeting and serving this influential group.

DIFFERENCES IN APA, MLA, AND CHICAGO FORMATS

As noted previously, the APA and MLA systems differ somewhat from the Chicago style presented in preceding pages. The primary differences are evident from the following illustrations.

Parenthetic Method

Chicago and MLA

In-text citation: (Badaracco 2002)

Reference List: Badaracco, Joseph. 2002. *Leading Quietly: An Unorthodox Guide to Doing the Right Thing.* Boston, MA: Harvard Business School Press.

Traditional Method

Footnotes—Books

Chicago

[1] Joseph Badaracco, *Leading Quietly: An Unorthodox Guide to Doing the Right Thing* (Boston, MA: Harvard Business School Press, 2002), 55.

MLA

[1] Joseph Badaracco, <u>Leading Quietly : An Unorthodox Guide to Doing the Right Thing</u> (Boston, Mass: Harvard Business School Press, 2002) 55.

APA

(Does not use footnotes)

Footnotes—Periodicals

Chicago

[1] Kathryn C. Rentz, "Reflexive Methodology: New Vistas for Qualitative Research," *Journal of Business Communication* 39, no. 1 (2002): 149.

MLA

[1] Kathryn C. Rentz, "Reflexive Methodology: New Vistas for Qualitative Research," <u>Journal of Business Communication</u> 39.1 (2002): 149.

APA

(Does not use footnotes)

Bibliography—Books

Chicago

Badaracco, Joseph. *Leading Quietly: An Unorthodox Guide to Doing the Right Thing.* Boston, MA: Harvard Business School Press, 2002.

MLA

Works Cited

Badaracco, Joseph. <u>Leading Quietly: An Unorthodox Guide to Doing the Right Thing.</u> Boston, Mass: Harvard Business School Press, 2002.

References

Badaracco, J. (2002). *Leading Quietly: An Unorthodox Guide to Doing the Right*

Thing. Boston, Mass: Harvard Business School Press.

Bibliography—Periodicals

Chicago

Rentz, Kathryn C. "Reflexive Methodology: New Vistas for Qualitative Research."

Journal of Business Communication 39, no. 1 (2002): 149.

MLA

Works Cited

Rentz, Kathryn C. "Reflexive Methodology: New Vistas for Qualitative Research."

Journal of Business Communication 39.1 (2002): 149.

APA

References

Rentz, K. C. (2002). Reflexive Methodology: New Vistas for Qualitative Research.

Journal of Business Communication, 39(1), 149.

In place of the specific date of publication, APA style uses volume and number—in this example 39(1).

Whatever system you decide to use, you need to use only one within a paper and to always be complete, accurate, and consistent.

CREDITS

Part 1 Opener, page 1
Michael Eisner, from his USC commencement speech, 2000.

Part 2 Opener, page 19
Quoted with permission from Carlos Dominguez.

Part 3 Opener, page 83
Michael Dell from "Michael Dell's Company is Serious About Linux" by Robert McMillan in *Linux Magazine,* August 2000.

Part 4 Opener, page 271
"An Interview with the Chief Yahoo" by Steven Ferry in *Government Technology,* February, 1999. Reprinted with permission from *Government Technology.*

Part 5 Opener, page 409
"December Strategy for Success: Advancing the Best Idea Wins" from <www.womenworking2000.com/success/docs/03_03_graham_pamela.html>. Reprinted with permission from Pamela Thomas-Graham.

Part 6 Opener, page 451
Quoted with permission from Dawn Meyerriecks.

PHOTO CREDITS

Page 1 AP/Wide World Photos
Page 6 © Michael Newman/Photo Edit
Page 8 © Jose Luis Pelaez/CORBIS
Page 9 © ROB & SAS/CORBIS
Page 19 Courtesy of Cisco Systems, Inc.

Page 23 Courtesy of Stephanie Crown
Page 35 © Jose Luis Pelaez/CORBIS
Page 48 © LWA-Sharie Kennedy/CORBIS
Page 52 © Digital Vision/Getty Images
Page 67 © Tim Brown/Getty Images
Page 73 © Tony Hopewell/Getty Images
Page 83 © FARINA CHRISTOPHER/CORBIS SYGMA
Page 87 © Royalty-Free Images/IndexStock
Page 95 © PhotoDisc/Getty Images
Page 108 © Jean Louis Batt/Getty Images
Page 116 © Alexander Walter/Getty Images
Page 130 © Superstock
Page 161 Source: Canesta
Page 167 © PhotoDisc/Getty Images
Page 177 © Greg Pease/Getty Images
Page 193 © Jim Whitmer
Page 208 Courtesy of the authors
Page 247 © Mike Greenlar / The Image Works
Page 253 © PhotoDisc/Getty Images
Page 271 © Reuters NewMedia Inc./CORBIS
Page 275 © Royalty-Free/ImageState
Page 278 © John Neubauer/Photo Edit
Page 295 © Ryan McVay/Getty Images

Page 305 © Jon Bradley/Getty Images
Page 308 © Javier Pierini/CORBIS
Page 322 © Walter Hodges/Getty Images
Page 344 © Stock Image/SuperStock
Page 354 Courtesy of the authors
Page 393 © PhotoDisc/Getty Images
Page 402 ClickArt Incredible Image Pak 65,000, #NATOT177
Page 404 © LWA- JDC/CORBIS
Page 409 © Evan Agostini/Image Direct/Getty Images
Page 414 © R. W. Jones/CORBIS
Page 423 © Howard Grey/Getty Images
Page 424 © Lisette Le Bon/SuperStock
Page 436 © Charles Gupton/CORBIS
Page 439 © Masterfile
Page 445 © Creatas/PictureQuest
Page 451 Photo Courtesy of DISA
Page 455 © Oliver Benn/Getty Images
Page 459 © Wolfgang Kaehler/CORBIS
Page 499 © James Stirling/Getty Images
Page 513 © Tipp Howell/Getty Images
Page 516 AP/Wide World Photos
Page 523 © LWA-Dann Tardif/CORBIS
Page 541 © Mark Richards/Photo Edit

INDEX

I

Ibid, 592
IBM, 513, 515
IBM ViaVoice, 420
Icenogle, Marjorie L., 413
Icons, 401
Idiom, 33
Illogical constructions, 54
Illustrations. *See* Examples
IM, 513
IMHO, 94
Imperative statement, 478
Impersonal writing, 289
in addition, 78
Indefinite numbers/amounts, 489
Index builder, 503
Indirect order, 100
Inferential statistics, 280
Infoplease.com, 523
Informal communication network, 8
Informal oral communication, 410–431
  dictating messages, 420–421
  listening, 421–424
  meetings, 415–417
  nonverbal communication, 424–427
  talking, 411–414
  telephone technique, 417–419
  voice mail, 419
  wireless telephones, 419
Informal talking, 411–414
Information reports, 273–274
Information rights management (IRM), 507
Information sources. *See* Primary research;
    Secondary research
Initialisms, 94
Initials (acronyms), 26
Inquiries about people, 112, 115–119
Inspiration, 281
Instant messaging (IM), 513
Interactive virtual interviews, 255
Interest inventory, 225
Internal-operational communication, 5–6
*International Encyclopedia of the Social
    Sciences,* 525
International sources of information,
    525–526
Internet search tools, 530–534
Interoffice communication. *See*
    Memorandum (memo)
Intimate space, 426
Invited proposals, 323
IRM, 507
IRM tools, 507
Italics, 477

J

James, Frank, 85n
Japan Company Handbook, 525
Jhao, Jensen J., 462n
Job acceptance, 262
Job agents, 227
Job boards, 248
Job databanks, 226
Job interview, 257–260
  anticipating questions/preparing answers,
    257–259
  behavioral questions, 259
  brainteaser/critical thinking questions,
    259
  helping control the dialogue, 260
  illegal questions, 259
  investigating the company, 257
  online help, 255

Job interview—*Cont.*
  personal appearance, 257
  put yourself at ease, 259–260
Job Rated Almanac, 523
Job refusal, 262
Job resignation, 262–263
Job search, 222–270
  analyzing outside factors, 225–226
  cover message, 247–257. *See also* Cover
    message
  follow-up message, 261
  identify appropriate jobs, 224–226
  job acceptance, 262
  job interview, 257–260. *See also* Job
    interview
  job refusal, 262
  job resignation, 262–263
  keeping up-to-date, 263
  networking, 223–224
  professional reading, 263
  prospecting, 228
  résumé, 229–247. *See also* Résumé
  self-analysis, 224–225
  sources of information, 226–227
  thank-you message, 261
Jones, Gerald E., 401n
Judgment sampling, 542
Justification, 561, 563

K

Kakkurik, Mark, 93n
Kameda, Naoki, 462n
Kawasaki, Guy, 92n
Kerning, 510, 558
Keywords (résumé), 236, 244
Kienzler, Donna S., 405
Komando, Kim, 91n
Kuiper, Shirley, 403

L

Lamb, Linda, 94n
Lasky, Jane, 457n
Layout, 508–510, 556–563
Leader, 389
Leaderwork, 389
Leading, 510
Leading question, 543–544
learn, teach, 33
Left justification, 561, 563
Legal terms, 27
Lehman, Carol M., 196n
Lenaghan, Rosemary, 4
less, fewer, 32
Letter of transmittal, 346–347
Letter reports, 309, 315–317, 571–572
Letters. *See* Business letters
Lexis-Nexis Academic, 530
Lexis-Nexis Academic Universe, 522
Libraries, 521
likewise, 78
Limiting sentence content, 45–46
Line chart, 396–397
Line spacing, 558, 574
List of illustrations, 347, 576
Listening, 421–424
Listserv, 515
loc. cit, 592
LOL, 94
Long, formal reports, 342–382, 572–576.
    See also Report writing
  appended parts, 352–353
  appendix, 352–353

Long, formal reports—*Cont.*
  authorization message, 345–346, 576
  bibliography, 353, 371, 576–577,
    594–597
  body of report, 351
  conclusions, 352
  definitions/acronyms, 351
  ending of report, 351–352
  example, 357–371
  executive summary, 348
  foreword, 347
  headings, 573–574
  historical background, 350–351
  indentation, 574
  introduction, 348–351
  limitations, 350
  line spacing, 574
  numbering of pages, 573
  origin of report, 349
  page layouts, 572–573
  physical layout, 572–576
  preface, 347
  prefatory parts, 344–348
  problem/purpose, 349
  recommendations, 352
  report preview, 351
  scope, 350
  sources/methods of collecting
    information, 351
  structural coherence helpers, 353–355
  table of contents, 347, 576
  title fly, 344–345, 575
  transmittal message, 345–346, 576
Long-form audit reports, 322
Long sentences, 44, 45
Long words, 25–26
Lund, Roger D., 50
Luthans, Fred, 461n

M

Macros, 504
Maes, Jeanne D., 413
Maher, Kris, 229n
Major Companies of Europe, 525
Maps, 397–400
Margin settings, 559–561
Markoff, John, 516n
Mason, Eric, 260
Matter-of-fact statements, 205
Mausehund, Jean, 11
Meaning, 13
Measures of central tendency, 280
Measures of dispersion, 280
Mechanical means of emphasis, 76
Mediafinder, 534
Meeting minutes, 319–321
Meetings, 415–417
Meishi, 456
Memorandum (memo)
  defined, 95–96
  form, 96–97
  formality, 97
  physical representation, 571
  policy memos, 98–99
  techniques for writing, 97–98
Memorandum reports, 571–572
Memorizing, 436–437
Memory, 544–545
Merge feature, 503–504
Mergent, Inc., 525
Merriam-Webster website, 478, 505
Merriam-Webster's Collegiate Dictionary,
    524
Metasearch tools, 533

EXCITING CONTENTS OF NEW STUDENT CD

Grammar Exercises

Test your knowledge with these interactive exercises to improve your grammar & communication skills!

Videos

View realistic business scenarios in these video clips illustrating communication behavior with related discussion and quiz questions that incorporate concepts from the text.

Basic Business Communication Resource Toolkit

This valuable toolkit features an arsenal of effective business communication tools, including a FREE one year Merriam-Webster Online subscription, Bullfighter, and Endnote software. Exercises employing these tools are included to sharpen writing skills and build familiarity with business writing.

Bullfighter

Resourceful tool scans documents to eradicate business jargon and avoid linguistic mishaps.

Merriam-Webster Online Collegiate Dictionary

Free one-year subscription provides access to 165,000 defined terms with audio pronunciations, as well as an online thesaurus, encyclopedia, word games, and more!

Endnote 7

A 30-day trial of this bibliographic software allows you to search Internet libraries, organize references and create Internet bibliographies.

Resource Toolkit Exercises

Helpful exercises will familiarize you with the Toolkit's valuable resources and enforce effective business writing skills.